Fodor's 92
Great Britain

Y0-CBB-128

Fodor's Travel Publications, Inc.
New York and London

ISBN 0–679–02044–6

Fodor's Great Britain

Editor: Caroline V. Haberfeld
Area Editor: Richard Moore
Contributors: Nicky Adamson, Donna Dailey, Gordon Donaldson, John Elsom, Mark Lewes, Pauline Martin, Julie Mishkin, Christopher Pick, Christine Richards, Theodore Rowland-Entwistle, Ron Sands, Kate Sekules, Celia Skidmore, Caroline B. D. Smith, Colin Speakman, Nicholas Stevenson, Gilbert Summers, Gillian Thomas, Emma Tolkien, Angus Waycott
Art Director: Fabrizio La Rocca
Cartographer: David Lindroth
Illustrator: Karl Tanner
Cover Photograph: Zefa/H. Armstrong Roberts

Design: Vignelli Associates

Special Sales

Contents

Maps

Foreword

While every care has been taken to ensure the accuracy of the information in this guide, the passage of time will always bring change, and consequently, the publisher cannot accept responsibility for errors that may occur.

All prices and opening times quoted here are based on information supplied to us at press time. Hours and admission fees may change, however, and the prudent traveler will avoid inconvenience by calling ahead.

Fodor's wants to hear about your travel experiences, both pleasant and unpleasant. When a hotel or restaurant fails to live up to its billing, let us know and we will investigate the complaint and revise our entries where the facts warrant it.

Send your letters to the editors of Fodor's Travel Publications, 201 East 50th Street, New York, NY 10022.

Highlights'92 and Fodor's Choice

Highlights '92

Attractions   Knowing which are the top attractions among British tourist destinations can be important if you object to crowds. Unfortunately, the available tourist-office statistics take into account only those attractions that charge entrance fees and so do not include some of the most popular places, such as cathedrals.

Visitors to Britain—and the locals themselves when they vacation—are amazingly constant in the sights they flock to. Naturally, since almost all visitors to Britain take in London, the capital registers among the highest annual figures. According to the latest statistics, the commercially minded **Madame Tussaud's** waxworks museum, with almost 2½ million visitors, is the country's top attraction for the fifth year running. It is closely followed by the **Tower of London,** the **National Gallery,** and the **British Museum.** The **Natural History Museum,** the **London Zoo** (now in extreme financial difficulties), and **Kew Gardens** rank, too.

Hundreds of thousands pour through the doors of cathedrals and other free sights, and if the statistics were available, **Westminster Cathedral** and **St. Paul's Cathedral** would both certainly be top contenders.

Outside London, **Edinburgh Castle, Windsor Safari Park, Windsor Castle,** the **Roman Baths** in Bath, and the **Jorvik Centre** in York each attract more than 900,000 visitors.

The **National Gallery** might even see an increase in tourism to the new **Sainsbury Wing.** The controversial new building—some call it bland—by Robert Venturi is the largest single addition to the gallery since its opening in 1838 and represents one of this century's biggest privately funded gifts to the nation. Built to house the Early Renaissance paintings, the Sainsbury Wing also contains a new lecture theater, coffee bar, restaurant, the Micro Gallery (a computerized information center), and temporary exhibits. A major **Rembrandt exhibit** opens here in the spring of 1992. The Sainsburys are well known for their huge chain of food stores and for the Sainsbury Centre at the University of East Anglia in Norwich, which houses their modern, African, and Art Nouveau collections in an enormous high-tech building designed by Sir Norman Foster.

Value Added Tax   Value Added Tax (VAT), Britain's sales tax, had been fixed at 15% from June 1979 until last year. In April 1991, it was increased to 17½%. This tax affects virtually every facet of British life, and visitors will see the change especially in hotel rates and restaurant prices, as well as in the general cost of shopping. Although VAT is almost always included in quoted store prices, it is itemized on the bill.

Entry Charges The British have boasted for many decades that almost alone among European countries, entry to most of their museums and galleries was free. It is a sign of the serious recession in Britain, and the enormous cost of the upkeep of ancient buildings, that more and more institutions are now charging entry fees. Cathedrals and churches have been unobtrusively charging admission to parts of their buildings for some time. Entry to Stratford-upon-Avon parish church is free, for example, but you have to pay to view Shakespeare's tomb. In mid-1991 St. Paul's Cathedral in London, with an annual upkeep cost of more than £400,000, introduced a small entry fee, and it is expected that many more historic places of worship will follow the cathedral's lead. On your 1992 visit to Britain, you may well find that establishments we have quoted as being free have started to charge for admission since we went to press.

Events For the past four years Britain has mounted a massive Garden Festival successively in Liverpool, Stoke-on-Trent, Glasgow, and Gateshead. The festivals bring a rundown area back into productive use. The 1992 festival will be held in Ebbw (pronounced Ebbou) Vale, north of Cardiff. Called **Garden Festival Wales** (Gŵyl Gerddi Cymru in Welsh), it will last from May to October.

Scholarly *Lord of the Ring* aficionados have their own J.R.R. **Tolkein conference** at Keble College, Oxford, August 17–24.

Anniversaries Nineteen hundred ninety-two will be the **500th anniversary** of the sailing of **Columbus** to America; the **40th year** since **Queen Elizabeth II** ascended the throne; and the **200th** since the death of the great architect **Robert Adam.** All these anniversaries will be remembered by various events.

Also marked in 1992 is the **50th anniversary** of the arrival in Britain of the **U.S. 8th Airforce,** which helped win World War II. They were based in East Anglia, and the anniversary will be marked there with air shows, Glenn Miller–style concerts, street parties, and services to commemorate those who lost their lives.

Country Matters There is a growing tendency on the part of the British local tourist boards to name their areas after famous historical or fictional characters, as a way of achieving instant identification with their product. In the brochures, Brontë Country, which immediately conjures up the wild scenery of *Wuthering Heights,* was joined early on by Thomas Hardy Country and Shakespeare Country. More recently, a motley crew of notables have joined the act—King Arthur; Constable, the painter; poet Dylan Thomas; and Catherine Cookson, the popular novelist—each is assigned his or her own "Country." Robin Hood Country received yet another shot in the arm from 1991 movies; it didn't even matter that some of the scenes in Sherwood Forest were shot hundreds of miles away.

Fodor's Choice

Although no two people ever agree on what makes a perfect vacation, it's always fun to find out what others think. Here are a few choice ideas to enhance your visit to Britain. For more details, refer to the appropriate chapter.

Scenery

Aira Force Waterfalls (*see* Lake District)

Bwlch y Groes—Pass of the Cross (*see* Wales)

Ceiriog Valley (*see* Wales)

Countryside seen from the Fort William–Mallaig railroad (*See* Scotland—Southwest and Highlands)

Forest of Dean (*see* Heart of England)

Trossachs (*see* Scotland—Southwest and Highlands)

Stately Homes

Blenheim Palace (*see* Thames Valley)

Castle Howard (*see* Peaks and Yorkshire Moors)

Chatsworth (*see* Peaks and Yorkshire Moors)

Cragside (*see* Northeast)

Holkham Hall (*see* East Anglia)

Ightham Mote (*see* Southeast)

Petworth (*see* Southeast)

Tretower Court (*see* Wales)

Restaurants

Bibendum—London (*Very Expensive*)

The Carved Angel—Dartmouth, *see* Southwest (*Expensive*)

Chewton Glen—New Milton, *see* South (*Expensive*)

Country Friends—Shrewsbury, *see* Welsh Borders (*Moderate*)

The Golden Pheasant—Glyn Ceiriog, *see* Wales (*Moderate*)

Horn of Plenty—Tavistock, *see* Southwest (*Moderate*)

Le Manoir aux Quat' Saisons—Great Milton, *see* Thames Valley (*Very Expensive*)

Lock 16 (Crinan Hotel)—Crinan, *see* Scotland—Southwest and Highlands (*Expensive*)

Longueville Manor—Jersey, *see* Channel Islands
(*Very Expensive*)

L'Ortolan—Shinfield, *see* Thames Valley (*Expensive*)

Martin's Restaurant—Edinburgh, *see* Edinburgh
and the Borders (*Moderate*)

Penrhos Court—Kington, *see* Welsh Borders
(*Moderate–Expensive*)

Roger's—Windermere, *see* Lake District (*Expensive*)

Le Talbooth—Dedham, *see* East Anglia (*Expensive*)

Thornbury Castle—Thornbury, *see* Heart of England
(*Very Expensive*)

The Ivy—London (*Expensive*)

The Yew Tree—Seatoller, *see* Lake District (*Inexpensive*)

Hotels

Basil Street Hotel—London (*Expensive*)

Bodysgallen Hall—Llandudno, *see* Wales (*Expensive*)

Buckland Manor—Buckland, *see* Heart of England
(*Expensive*)

Castle Hotel—Taunton, *see* Southwest (*Expensive*)

Crabwall Manor—Chester, *see* Welsh Borders (*Expensive*)

Ettington Park—Stratford-upon-Avon,
see Heart of England (*Very Expensive*)

Greywalls—Gullane, *see* Edinburgh and the Borders
(*Expensive*)

Horsted Place—Uckfield, *see* Southeast (*Very Expensive*)

Kennel Holt Hotel—Cranbrook, *see* Southeast (*Expensive*)

Langley Castle Hotel—Hexham, *see* Northeast (*Moderate*)

Middlethorpe Hall—York, *see* Peaks and Yorkshire Moors
(*Very Expensive*)

The Gore—London (*Expensive*)

Portledge Hotel—Fairy Cross, *see* Southwest (*Moderate*)

Sunlaws Hotel—Kelso, *see* Edinburgh and the Borders
(*Expensive*)

Cathedrals and Churches

Canterbury Cathedral (*see* Southeast)

Durham Cathedral (*see* Northeast)

Gloucester Cathedral (*see* Heart of England)

King's College Chapel (*see* East Anglia)

Salisbury Cathedral (*see* South)

Westminster Abbey (*see* London)

York Minster (*see* Peaks and Yorkshire Moors)

Castles

Berkeley (*see* Heart of England)

Caernarfon (*see* Wales)

Edinburgh (*see* Scotland—Edinburgh and the Borders)

Stirling (*see* Scotland—Southwest and Highlands)

Tower of London (*see* London)

Warwick (*see* Heart of England)

Windsor (*see* Thames Valley)

Gardens

Bodnant (*see* Wales)

Hidcote Manor (*see* Heart of England)

Kew (*see* London)

Levens Hall (*see* Lake District)

Stourhead (*see* South)

Threave (*see* Scotland—Southwest and Highlands)

Ancient Stones

Avebury (*see* South)

Barrow-in-Furness Abbey (*see* Lake District)

Fountains Abbey (*see* Peaks and Yorkshire Moors)

Jedburgh Abbey (*see* Scotland—Edinburgh and the Borders)

Rievaulx Abbey (*see* Peaks and Yorkshire Moors)

Stanton Drew Circles (*see* Heart of England)

Towns and Villages

Bath (*see* Heart of England)

Cambridge (*see* East Anglia)

Ewelme (*see* Thames Valley)

Knutsford (*see* Welsh Borders)

Lavenham (*see* East Anglia)

Portmeirion (*see* Wales)

Rye (*see* Southeast)

York (*see* Peaks and Yorkshire Moors)

Museums and Galleries

Bodelwyddan Castle (*see* Wales)

British Museum (*see* London)

Burrell Collection, Glasgow
(*see* Scotland—Southwest and Highlands)

Corinium Museum, Cirencester (*see* Heart of England)

Fitzwilliam Museum, Cambridge (*see* East Anglia)

Ironbridge Gorge Museum, Ironbridge (*see* Welsh
Borders)

Museum of the Moving Image (*see* London)

National Gallery of Scotland
(*see* Scotland—Edinburgh and the Borders)

Times to Treasure

Sunset from the Mull of Kintyre

A boat ride on Lake Windermere

Champagne at the Henley Regatta

The Edinburgh Tattoo on a fine night

Picnicking on the lawn during a Glyndebourne
performance

The view of Stonehenge on a stormy evening

Searching for a bargain in London's Portobello
market—and finding one!

Going to a Prom Concert at the Royal Albert Hall
on a very popular night

A summer trip on the Fort William–Mallaig railroad

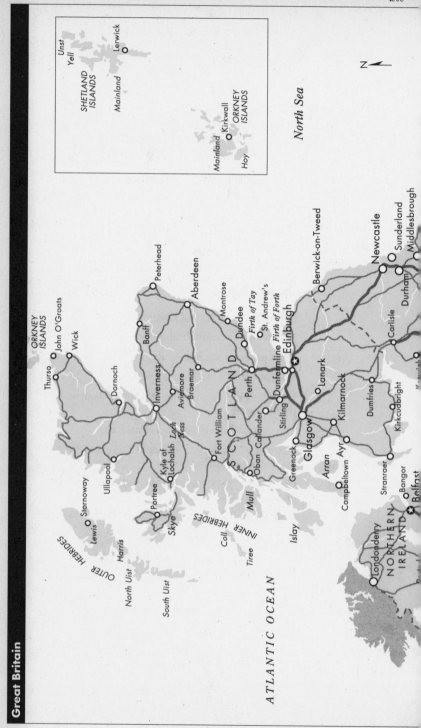

Great Britain

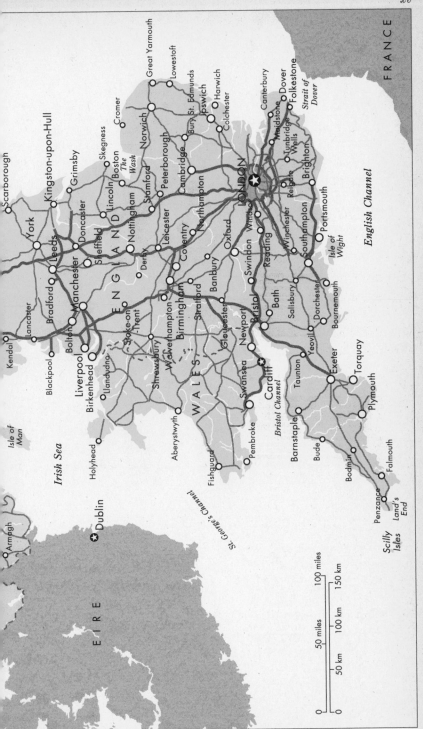

World Time Zones

MONDAY
SUNDAY

+12 +13   -9

-10

International Date Line

-11   -10

+11

+12

+11   +12 -   -11   -10   -9   -8   -7   -6   -5   -4   -3   -2

Numbers below vertical bands relate each zone to Greenwich Mean Time (0 hrs.).
Local times frequently differ from these general indications,
as indicated by light-face numbers on map.

Algiers, **29**	Berlin, **34**	Delhi, **48**	Istanbul, **40**
Anchorage, **3**	Bogotá, **19**	Denver, **8**	Jerusalem, **42**
Athens, **41**	Budapest, **37**	Djakarta, **53**	Johannesburg, **44**
Auckland, **1**	Buenos Aires, **24**	Dublin, **26**	Lima, **20**
Baghdad, **46**	Caracas, **22**	Edmonton, **7**	Lisbon, **28**
Bangkok, **50**	Chicago, **9**	Hong Kong, **56**	London (Greenwich), **27**
Beijing, **54**	Copenhagen, **33**	Honolulu, **2**	Los Angeles, **6**
	Dallas, **10**		Madrid, **38**
			Manila, **57**

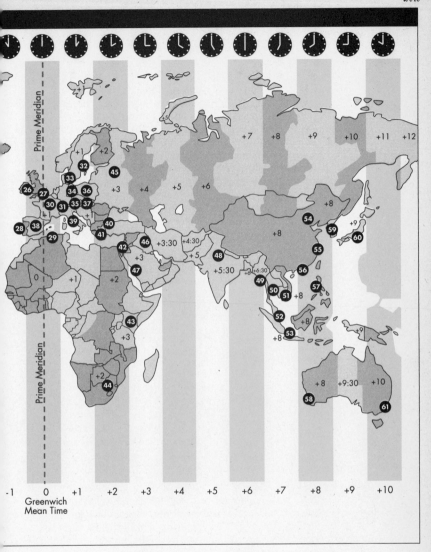

Mecca, **47**

Mexico City, **12**

Miami, **18**

Montreal, **15**

Moscow, **45**

Nairobi, **43**

New Orleans, **11**

New York City, **16**

Ottawa, **14**

Paris, **30**

Perth, **58**

Reykjavík, **25**

Rio de Janeiro, **23**

Rome, **39**

Saigon, **51**

San Francisco, **5**

Santiago, **21**

Seoul, **59**

Shanghai, **55**

Singapore, **52**

Stockholm, **32**

Sydney, **61**

Tokyo, **60**

Toronto, **13**

Vancouver, **4**

Vienna, **35**

Warsaw, **36**

Washington, D C, **17**

Yangon, **49**

Zürich, **31**

Introduction

The British are different, and proud of it. They still have odd customs, like driving on the left and playing cricket. Only reluctantly have they decimalized, turning their cherished pints into liters (except when ordering beer), and inches into centimeters. Until 1971 they still had a bizarre three-tier non-decimal coinage, whereby a meal check might add up, say, to four pounds six shillings and sevenpence halfpenny (today that would translate as £4.33). And although the rest of Europe counts distances in kilometers, the British still cling to their miles—though they now buy material for their drapes in meters, not yards. Logic is not a prominent feature of the British character!

These are symptoms of a certain psychological gulf still existing between Britain and the rest of Europe, a gulf not greatly narrowed by her membership in the European Community since 1973. The English Channel, a mere 22 miles of water between Dover and Calais, has played a crucial role in British history, acting as a kind of moat to protect the "island fortress" from invaders (witness 1940), and preserving a separate mentality. Many Britons want to keep that moat, hence their wariness—more emotional than economic—of the Channel Tunnel, which is slowly nearing completion. Even today, that oft-quoted old newspaper headline, "Fog in Channel, Continent isolated," retains some validity. Yet this proud and insular nation is not unwelcoming to visitors. On its own terms, it is glad to show them the delights and virtues of one of the most genuinely civilized societies in the world.

There is still some truth in the popular foreign perception that the British are reserved. They are given to understatement—"It's not bad," is the nearest a Briton may get to showing enthusiasm—and may look a little solemn and stiff-upper-lipped, for they don't easily show their emotions. Yet they are not on the whole unhappy, even in today's anxious times. (In fact, an international Gallup survey showed that far more people in Britain than in neighboring countries thought of themselves as leading happy lives.) The British are easygoing, accepting of nonconformity and eccentricity; and their strong sense of humor and love of the absurd keeps them on an even keel. They have a strange habit of poking good-humored fun at what they love without meaning disrespect, not least at royalty and religion. This kind of humor often disconcerts foreigners. It helps to understand that British institutions such as the monarchy are so strong and stable that the British can afford to light-heartedly ridicule them without endangering them.

It is a densely populated land. Scotland and Wales have wide open spaces but in England people are crammed 940 to the square mile, more thickly than in any European country save Holland. Yet it is also a green and fertile land, and because the countryside is a limited commodity, the English tend it with special loving care. Everywhere are trim hedgerows, tidy flower beds, and lawns mown smooth as billiard tables—one Oxford don, asked by an American visitor how the college lawn came to be so perfect, said casually, "Oh, it's been mown every Tuesday for the past 500 years." The English love gardens, but are also at ease in untamed surroundings. They relish hiking over moors where the westerly gales blow, or splashing rubber-booted through streams, or birdwatching in a quiet copse. A few people, in their black or scarlet coats and riding caps, still go fox hunting with hounds—"the unspeakable in full pursuit of the uneatable" as Oscar Wilde put it. Others are violent in their condemnation of this blood sport.

This smallish island contains great scenic variety. The Midlands and much of eastern England tend to be flat and dull. But in the watery fenlands, between Cambridge and the sea, the low horizons, broken by rows of poplars or by a distant windmill or tall church spire, have a misty poetic quality, and the sunsets and swirling clouds evoke the subtlety of a Turner skyscape. Kent, southeast of London, with its cherry and apple orchards, is known as "the garden of England"; west of here are the wooded hills of Surrey, and to the southwest the bold, bare ridge of the South Downs, beloved of Kipling. While the east coast of Britain is mainly smooth, with long sandy beaches and an occasional chalky cliff, the west coast is far more rugged: Here the Atlantic gales set the seas lashing against the rocky headlands of Cornwall and south Wales.

The spine of northern England is a line of high hills, the Pennines, where sheep graze on lonely moors, and just to the west is the beautiful mountainous Lake District, where Wordsworth lived. Scotland is even more lovely and mountainous. Beyond the urban belt of the lowlands around Glasgow and Edinburgh, you enter the romantic realm of the Highlands, a thinly populated region where heather and gorse cover the hillsides above silent fjord-like lochs and verdant glens. Roads here are few, but they all seem to lead westward to the Isles, blue-gray jewels in a silver Atlantic sea, with their strange Celtic names: Barra, Eigg, Benbecula, Skye. . . .

Western Britain is washed by the warm waters of the Gulf Stream, and therefore its climate is mild and damp. Indeed, Britain's weather is something of a stock joke, and some foreigners imagine the whole country permanently shrouded in fog. This has not been true for years, since the use of smokeless fuel has cleared polluted mists from urban skies. Yet the weather *is* very changeable, by south European standards, with shower and shine often following each other in swift succession. At least it provides the thrill of the unexpected.

The people are as varied as the landscape, coming as they do from a variety of origins: Celtic, Viking, Saxon, Norman, not to mention later immigrations. Modern mobility and the drift toward cities and to the warmer and wealthier South has tended to mix them up, so that today the London area teems, for instance, with Scots and Tynesiders. Yet regional differences remain distinct, and local loyalties are fierce, even parochial. A London politician newly settled in north Yorkshire was warned by his constituents, "Take no notice o' folk t'oother side o' water!" He feared, as well he might, that this was some anti-EC or anti-American hostility—but discovered they were referring to the people just 10 miles away across the river Tees, in County Durham.

The millions of foreigners who have come to live in Britain during the last few decades have had a generally positive influence. They have widened the horizons of an insular—in every sense of the word—people, even in such matters as cuisine. Until the '50s almost all restaurants served dull British fare, but today in even the smallest provincial town you will find Indians, Chinese, Greeks, Italians, French and others, all serving their national dishes—and they are very popular indeed.

The same can't always be said of the immigrants themselves, especially those from what is euphemistically dubbed the "New Commonwealth"—meaning the Asians and Afro-Caribbeans brought into Britain in the '50s and '60s to provide essential services and fill a chronic labor shortage. Most middle-class British people will profess themselves broadminded, of course, but their day-to-day attitudes still suggest (in contrast to post-civil rights America) that their commitment to a truly racially egalitarian society is only skindeep (if that). The debate over assimilation—to what extent the immigrant communities should be asked to surrender their own identities—still rages. Should schools in Bradford, where a majority of pupils are Moslems, base their moral precepts on the Koran rather than the Bible? Should the history of the Caribbean islands or of Africa be taught to young blacks in south London as part of their culture?

The British are clearly torn between their traditions of tolerance on one hand and their belief on the other hand that even a somewhat anachronistic law must be upheld. Never has this situation been more clearcut than in the confrontation over Rushdie's *Satanic Verses*, when British Moslems saw themselves discriminated against under Britain's ancient blasphemy laws, which applied only to the God of the Christians. Until a clear line is drawn—either rigorous assimilation, or multiculturalism that implies a new respect for alien cultures taking root in their towns and cities—

the British will be constantly wrongfooted, embarrassed, and occasionally very frightened by the newcomers erupting in their midst.

Britain is a land where the arts flourish. It is true that the artist, writer or philosopher is not held in the same public esteem as, say, in France. The average Briton affects a certain philistinism, and "intellectual" and "arty" are common terms of reproach. And yet sales of books and of theater and concert tickets are amazingly high. Helped by the world-wide spread of the English language, the British publishing industry produces around 50,000 new titles a year—too many for profitability. A passion for classical music developed during the last war and has continued ever since, so that even the smallest town has its choral society performing Bach or Handel, and its season of concerts by visiting artists. London theater is regarded by many as the best in the world, both for its standards of production and acting and for its new writing. This richness is reflected in the provinces, where hundreds of theaters, some of them small fringe groups in makeshift premises, attract ready audiences.

Culture thrives also in a classical mode—for example, through the Royal Shakespeare Company with its base in the bard's home town of Stratford-upon-Avon. Like Shakespeare, many leading British writers and other creative artists are closely associated with some particular place, in a land where literature and the other arts have always been nourished by strong local roots, by some *genius loci*. A tour around Britain can thus become a series of cultural pilgrimages: to the Dorset that inspired the novels of Thomas Hardy, to the wild Yorkshire moors where the Brontë sisters lived and wrote, to Wordsworth's beloved Lake District, to the Scottish Border landscapes that pervade the novels of Walter Scott, to Laugharne on the south Wales coast that Dylan Thomas's *Under Milk Wood* has immortalized, to Dickensian London, to the Constable country on the Suffolk/Essex border, or to nearby Aldeburgh where composer Benjamin Britten lived.

These personalities are significant parts of a long national history that lies buried deep in the British psyche. The history began centuries before Christ, when huge stone circles were raised at Stonehenge and Avebury, on the Wiltshire downs. Then came the Romans, who left their imprint across the land up to Hadrian's Wall in the north. Great feudal castles survive as reminders of the dark days when barons and kings were in constant conflict, and peaceful fields the length and breadth of the land became nightmarish landscapes of blood and death. Stately redbrick Elizabethan manors bear witness to the more settled and civilized age of Good Queen Bess.

Britain is rich in old towns and villages, whose streets are lined with buildings dating back for centuries, with old half-timbered houses where black beams criss-cross the white plaster-work, or with carefully proportioned facades that bring a measured classical elegance to the townscape. In many areas, buildings are of local stone—most strikingly in the mellow golden-brown Cotswold villages—and often a simple cottage is topped with a neat thatched roof. Above all, British architecture is famed for its cathedrals dating mostly from the Middle Ages, with Wells, Ely, and Durham among the finest. Local churches, too, are often of great beauty, especially in East Anglia where the wealth of the 15th-century wool trade led to the building of majestic churches on the edge of quite modest villages. Church builders of the past were profligate in their service to God, and modern Britain is deeply in their debt. Unfortunately, the Church is just as deeply in debt, because it has these mammoth edifices to maintain with dwindling congregations to help with its finances.

Despite constant social upheavals, the British maintain many of their special traditions. On a village green in summer, you may see a cricket match in progress between two white-clad teams. It is a slow and stately game that will seem boring to the uninitiated, yet is full of its own skills and subtleties. In village pubs people frequently play darts, or perhaps backgammon, checkers, or chess. The English pub is a venerable institution, as popular as ever and endlessly diverse. With some exceptions, pubs in towns tend to be dull, and many have been modernized in dubious taste, with too much chrome, plush and plastic. But the country pub can be a real joy. It will often be called by the name of the local landed family—*The Bath Arms*, or *Lord Crewe's Arms*—and very possibly it will have old beams and inglenooks, and a blazing log fire in winter. If you sit at a table in the corner, you can have privacy of a sort; but between those who prop up the bar, conversation is general, no introductions are needed, and new acquaintances are quickly made.

British society, while troubled by doubts and uncertainties, and constantly challenged to resolve key social problems, is certainly not in terminal decline, or even slowly fading away. As an American observer remarked during the Falklands War, "The British can be relied upon to fall at every hurdle—except the last." When the chips are down, the British come up trumps. This can't be explained rationally. What was it that sank the Spanish Armada or defeated Goering's Luftwaffe? It certainly wasn't superior economic resources or disciplined social organization. Maybe there is more in the souls of a free people united in a common purpose than generations of economists and sociologists could ever hope to understand. The British are such a people; and their quirkiness, their social "distance," and their habit of driving on the left are inseparable parts of a greater whole. Without Britain, the world would be a poorer place.

1 Essential Information

Before You Go

Government Tourist Offices

Contact the British Tourist Authority (BTA).

In the U.S. 40 W. 57th St., New York, NY 10019–4001, tel. 212/581–4700; 625 N. Michigan Ave., Chicago, IL 60611, tel. 312/787–0490; World Trade Center, 350 S. Figueroa St., Suite 450, Los Angeles, CA 90017, tel. 213/628–3525; 2305 Cedar Springs Rd., Suite 210, Dallas, TX 75201, tel. 214/720–4040.

In Canada 94 Cumberland St., Suite 600, Toronto, Ontario M5R 3N3, tel. 416/925–6326.

In Britain Thames Tower, Black's Rd., London W6 9EL; written inquiries only.

Tour Groups

Package tours with creative itineraries abound, offering access to places you might not be able to get to on your own as well as to the more traditional spots. They also tend to save you some money on airfare and hotels. If group travel is not your cup of tea, look into independent tours—they're more numerous and innovative here than in some other parts of the world, thanks partly to the absence of a language barrier.

When considering a tour, be sure to find out exactly what expenses are included (particularly tips, taxes, side-trips, additional meals, and entertainment); cancellation policies for both you and for the tour operator; and, if you are traveling alone, what the single supplement is. Most tour operators request that bookings be made through a travel agent; there is no additional charge for doing so. Listed below is a sampling of operators and packages; contact your travel agent or the British Tourist Authority for further details.

General Interest Tours From the United States: **American Express Vacations** (Box 5014, Atlanta, GA 30302, tel. 800/241–1700 or in GA, 800/637–6200), is a veritable supermarket of tours—you name it, they've either got it packaged or will customize a package for you. **Maupintour** (Box 807, Lawrence, KS 66044, tel. 913/843–1211 or 800/255–4266) offers Britain by rail, the English countryside, and Yorkshire and the Lake District among other packages. **Globus-Gateway/Cosmos** (150 S. Los Robles Ave., Suite 860, Pasadena, CA 91101, tel. 818/449–0919 or 800/556–5454) together offer nearly two dozen different ways to see Britain. Cosmos is the more budget-minded of the affiliated companies. **Trafalgar Tours** (21 E. 26th St., New York, NY 10010, tel. 212/ 689–8977 or 800/854–0103), has a dozen offerings, including "The London Week," which may be taken on its own or in combination with another tour. Trafalgar, which typically serves a clientele aged 45+, also offers "Cost Saver" vacations that use tourist-class rather than first-class hotels to knock a sizeable amount off the trip's tab. **Olson-Travelworld** (100 N. Sepulveda Blvd., Suite 1010, El Segundo, CA 90245, tel. 800/421–2255, 800/421–5785 in Calif. or 213/615–0711) has "five-star" and "three-star" tours that traverse the city and countryside. **TWA Getaway Vacations** (tel. 800/GETAWAY) offers a wide selection of both escorted and locally hosted tours. "London Theater

Week" includes tickets to two West End shows. **Delta Dream Vacations** (tel. 800/338–2010) touts an 11-day "Accent on Britain" motorcoach tour.

Special Interest Tours *Barge Cruising*	Drift in leisure and luxury down the Avon or the Thames with **Floating Through Europe** (271 Madison Ave., New York, NY 10016), tel. 212/685–5600).
Culture	**Polly Stewart Fritch** (1 Scott La., Greenwich, CT 06831, tel. 203/661–7742) offers "cultural-culinary" tours with cooking demonstrations and behind-the-scenes visits to unique markets. Thanks to some well-placed friends, Fritch's tour occasionally features such extras as an insider's tour of Parliament with time to sip sherry in a private room in the House of Lords.
Music	**Dailey-Thorp Travel** (315 W. 57th St., New York, NY 10019, tel. 212/307–1555) offers deluxe opera and music tours such as "English Festivals Revisited," including concerts and operas in Brighton, Bath, and London. Itineraries vary according to available performances. **Keith Prowse & Co.** (234 W. 44th St., New York, NY 10036, tel. 212/398–1430 or 800/669–8687) arranges packages combining hotels with bookings at the theater, opera, rock concerts, or Stratford.
Singles and Young Couples	**Trafalgar Tours** offers "Club 21-35," faster-paced tours for travelers unafraid of a little physical activity—whether it's bike riding or discoing.
Sports	**Travel Concepts** (62 Commonwealth Ave., Suite 3, Boston, MA 02116, tel. 617/266–8450) has packages that include trips to the British Open golf tournament and the Royal Regatta at Henley-on-Thames. **Keith Prowse & Co.** (*see* above) designs tours starting at two nights to anything from Ascot to the British Open golf tournament to Wimbledon.
English Homes and Country Tours	**Rolfes Travel Inc.** (1126 N. Charles St., Baltimore, MD 21201, tel. 301/244–0077) and **Travel Etcetera Inc.** (1730 Huntington Dr., South Pasadena, CA 91030, tel. 818/441–3184) provide personalized tours of Britain: "Canterbury and the Gardens of Southern England," "Great Libraries," golfing trips, and tours to stately homes not open to the general public.
Walking Tours	**British Coastal Trails** (150 Carob Way, Coronado, CA 92118, tel. 619/437-1211) offers several excellent 8-, 11-, and 12-day scenic walking tours of Great Britain that explore uncrowded parts of beautiful countryside and historic sights. Itineraries include the Cotswolds Villages, the Coasts of Cornwall and Devon, the Yorkshire Dales and the English Lake District, Wales, and the Historic Border Country of Scotland. Tour costs includes hotels (often country inns), dinners, breakfasts, private coach, tour leader, local guides, ferries, and admissions to sights.

Package Deals for Independent Travelers

British Airways (tel. 800/AIR-WAYS) has packages designed for the traveler who doesn't like group travel: You choose the length of stay, and pick from hotel and car rental options. Theater packages are also available. **Pan Am Holidays** (tel. 800/THE–TOUR) offers a theater tour of London entitled "London Center Stage." Fly/drive and London city packages are also available. **Abercrombie & Kent International** (1420 Kensington Rd. Oak Brook, IL 60521, tel. 708/954–2944 or 800/323–7308) offers deluxe self-drive or chauffeur-driven tours. Travelers receive a detailed routing map covering a personally tailored itinerary; stays are at top country hotels. **CIE Tours** (108 Ridgedale Ave., Morristown, NJ 07960, tel. 201/292–3438 or 800/CIE–TOUR) has similar packages on a more moderate scale. Independent packages are also available from **American Airlines FlyAAway Vacations** (tel. 800/321–2121 or 817/355–1234), and **TWA Getaway Vacations, Delta Dream Vacations, American Express** and **Globus-Gateway** (*see* Tour Groups, above).

When to Go

The main tourist season in Britain runs from mid-April to mid-October. Spring is the time to see the countryside at its freshest and greenest, while in September and October the northern moorlands and Scottish highlands are at their most colorful. June is a good month to visit Wales and the Lake District. During July and August, when most of the British take their vacations, accommodations in the most popular resorts and areas are in high demand and at their most expensive. The winter season in London is lively with the Covent Garden Opera, Royal Ballet, and West End theater among the prime attractions.

In the main, the climate is mild, though the weather has been extremely volatile in recent years. Summer temperatures can reach the 90s and the atmosphere can be humid, while in winter there can be heavy frost, snow, and thick fog.

Climate What follows are the average daily maximum and minimum temperatures for major cities in Britain—but note that they are based on long-term averages, and do not necessarily reflect the climatic swings of the last few years:

Aberystwyth (*Wales*)								
Jan.	44F	7C	May	58F	15C	Sept.	62F	16C
	36	2		45	7		51	11
Feb.	44F	7C	June	62F	16C	Oct.	56F	13C
	35	2		50	10		46	8
Mar.	49F	9C	July	64F	18C	Nov.	50F	10C
	38	4		54	12		41	5
Apr.	52F	11C	Aug.	65F	18C	Dec.	47F	8C
	41	5		54	12		38	4

Edinburgh (*Scotland*)								
Jan.	42F	5C	May	56F	14C	Sept.	60F	18C
	34	1		43	6		49	9
Feb.	43F	6C	June	62F	17C	Oct.	54F	12C
	34	1		49	9		44	7
Mar.	46F	8C	July	65F	18C	Nov.	48F	9C
	36	2		52	11		39	4
Apr.	51F	11C	Aug.	64F	18C	Dec.	44F	7C
	39	4		52	11		36	2

London	Jan.	43F 36	6C 2	May	62F 47	17C 8	Sept.	65F 52	19C 11
	Feb.	44F 36	7C 2	June	69F 53	20C 12	Oct.	58F 46	14C 8
	Mar.	50F 38	10C 3	July	71F 56	22C 14	Nov.	50F 42	10C 5
	Apr.	56F 42	13C 6	Aug.	71F 56	21C 13	Dec.	45F 38	7C 4

Plymouth	Jan.	43F 39	6C 4	May	62F 47	17C 8	Sept.	65F 53	19C 12
	Feb.	47F 38	8C 4	June	64F 52	18C 11	Oct.	58F 49	15C 9
	Mar.	50F 40	10C 5	July	66F 55	19C 13	Nov.	52F 44	11C 7
	Apr.	54F 43	12C 6	Aug.	67F 55	19C 13	Dec.	49F 41	9C 5

York	Jan.	43F 33	6C 1	May	61F 44	16C 7	Sept.	64F 50	18C 10
	Feb.	44F 34	7C 1	June	67F 50	19C 10	Oct.	57F 44	14C 7
	Mar.	49F 36	10C 2	July	70F 54	21C 12	Nov.	49F 39	10C 4
	Apr.	55F 40	13C 4	Aug.	69F 53	21C 12	Dec.	45F 36	7C 2

Current weather information for more than 750 cities around the world can be obtained by calling WeatherTrak information service at 900/370–8728 (cost: 95¢ per minute). A taped message will tell you to dial the three-digit access code for the destination in which you're interested. The code is either the area code (in the United States) or the first three letters of the foreign city. For a list of all access codes, send a stamped, self-addressed envelope to Cities, 9B Terrace Way, Greensboro, NC 27403. For more information, call 800/247–3282.

A similar service operated by American Express can be accessed by dialing 900/WEATHER (900/932–8437). As well as supplying a three-day weather forecast for 600 cities worldwide, this service provides international travel information and time and day. Cost is 75¢ per minute.

Festivals and Seasonal Events

Tickets for prestigious sporting events must be obtained months in advance—check first to see if your travel agent can get them. There is a complete list of ticket agencies in *Britain Events*, free from the British Tourist Authority.

Jan. (first two weeks). London International Boat Show is the largest boat show in Europe. *Earls Court Exhibition Centre, Warwick Rd., London SW5 9TA, tel. 0932/854511.*
Jan. Crufts Dog Show sees more than 100 breeds compete. *National Exhibition Centre, Birmingham, West Midlands. Crufts Dog Show Office, tel. 071/493–6651.*
Feb. Jorvik Viking Festival is the occasion for a month-long celebration of Viking history. *York, North Yorkshire, tel. 0904/611944.*

Mar. Daily Mail Ideal Home Exhibition is a consumer show of new products and ideas for the home. *Earls Court Exhibition Centre, Warwick Rd., London SW5 9TA, tel. 071/222–9341.*

Mar. and Sept. Chelsea Antiques Fair is a twice-yearly fair with a wide range of pre-1830 pieces for sale. *Chelsea Old Town Hall, King's Rd., Chelsea, London SW3, tel. 0895/677677.*

Apr. through Dec. Shakespeare Season is held by the world-renowned Royal Shakespeare Company. *Stratford-upon-Avon, Warwickshire CV37 6BB, box office, tel. 0789/295623.*

Apr. Grand National Meeting is considered Britain's premier steeplechase over a 4-mile course. *Aintree Racecourse, Aintree, Liverpool, Merseyside, tel. 051/523–2600.*

Apr. Devizes to Westminster International Canoe Race is a 125-mile race along the Kennet and Avon Canal and the Thames, with no tickets required. *Tel. 0344/483232, ext. 3804.*

Mid-Apr. London Marathon. *Information from Box 262, Richmond, Surrey TW10 5JB, tel. 081/948–7935.*

May. Glasgow Mayfest. City-wide international festival of theater, dance, music, and street events. Glasgow's answer to the Edinburgh Festival. *Festival Dir., 18 Albion St., Glasgow G1 1LH, tel. 041/552–8000.*

May–Sept. Chichester Festival Theatre Season offers classical and contemporary plays. *Chichester Festival Theatre Box Office, Oaklands Park, Chichester, West Sussex PO19 4AP, tel. 0243/781312.*

May–Aug. Glyndebourne Festival Opera Season is an acclaimed festival founded in 1934, with its own private opera house. *Glyndebourne, Lewes, East Sussex BN8 5UU, tel. 0273/812321.*

Mid-May. Royal Windsor Horse Show is a major show-jumping event. *Home Park, Windsor, Berkshire, tel. 0298/72272.*

Mid–late May. Perth Festival of the Arts offers orchestral and choral concerts, drama, opera, recitals and ballet throughout Perth, Tayside. *Tel. 0738/21672.*

Mid–May. Chelsea Flower Show is Britain's major flower show, covering 22 acres. *Royal Hospital, Chelsea, London SW3, tel. 071/834–4333.*

Late May–early June. Bath International Festival is an international celebration of music and the arts throughout Bath, Avon. *Box office, tel. 0225/462231.*

Early June. Beating Retreat by the Guards' Massed Bands has more than 500 musicians on parade at Horse Guards Parade, Whitehall, London SW1. *Premier Box Office, The Ticket Centre, 1B Bridge St., London SW1 2JR, tel. 071/839–6815.*

Late May–early June. Nottingham Festival is a celebration of arts and music throughout Nottingham. *City of Nottingham Arts Dept., 51 Castle Gate, Nottingham NG1 6AF, tel. 062/483504.*

Early June. Derby Day is the world-renowned horse racing event, at Epsom Racecourse, Epsom, Surrey. *Information from United Racecourses Ltd., Racecourse Paddock, Epsom, Surrey KT18 5NJ, tel. 03727/26311.*

Mid-June. Grosvenor House Antiques Fair is one of the most prestigious antiques fairs in Britain. *Grosvenor House, Park La., London W1A 3AA, tel. 0799/26699.*

Mid–late June. Aldeburgh Festival of Music and the Arts was founded in 1948 by composer Benjamin Britten. *Aldeburgh Foundation, High St., Aldeburgh, Suffolk IP15 5AX, tel. 0728/452935.*

Mid-June. Trooping the Colour is Queen Elizabeth's colorful official birthday parade at Horse Guards Parade, Whitehall, London. (Her actual birthdate is in April.) *Write for tickets early in the year to The Brigade Major, H.Q. Household Division, Horse Guards, Whitehall, London SW1 2AX.*

Mid-June. Royal Ascot is a horse race and major social event attended by members of the royal family. *Information from The Secretary, Grand Stand Office, Ascot Racecourse, Ascot, Berkshire SL5 7JN, tel. 0990/22211.*

Late June–early July. Wimbledon Lawn Tennis Championship is always popular, so write early for Center and Number One court tickets to *All-England Lawn Tennis and Croquet Club, Church Rd., Wimbledon, London SW19 5AE, tel. 081/946–2244.*

July. City of London Festival is an arts festival throughout the City. *Tel. 071/377–0540.*

Early July. Henley Royal Regatta is an international rowing event and top social occasion. *Henley-on-Thames, Oxfordshire, tel. 0491/572153.*

Early–mid-July. Llangolen International Musical Eisteddfod sees the little Welsh town of Llangollen overflow with music, costumes, and color. *Musical Office, Llangollen, Clwyd LL20 8NG, tel. 0978/860236.*

Mid-July. Royal Tournament features military displays and pageantry by the Royal Navy, Royal Marines, Army, and Royal Air Force. *Earls Court Exhibition Centre, Warwick Rd., London SW5 9TA, tel. 071/370–8209.*

Mid–July. British Open Championship is played at a different course each year. *Royal and Ancient Golf Club, St. Andrews, Fife KY16 9JD, tel. 0334/72112.*

Mid-July–Mid-Sept. Henry Wood Promenade Concerts is a celebrated series of concerts, founded in 1895. *Royal Albert Hall, Kensington Gore, London SW7 2AP, tel. 071/927–4296.*

Early Aug. Cowes Week is a yachting festival on and off the Isle of Wight, Hampshire. *Tel. 0983/295744.*

Mid-Aug. Three Choirs Festival is an ancient choral and orchestral music festival, to be held in Gloucester in 1992. *The Gloucester Three Choirs Festival, Community House, College Green, Gloucester GL1 2LX, tel. 0452/29819.*

Mid-Aug.–early Sept. Edinburgh International Festival is the world's largest festival of the arts. Festivities include the nighttime **Edinburgh Military Tattoo.** *Information from Edinburgh Festival Society, 21 Market St., Edinburgh EH1 1BW, tel. 031/226–4001.*

Early Sept. Braemar Royal Highland Gathering hosts kilted clansman from all over Scotland. *Princess Royal and Duke of Fife Memorial Park, Braemar, Grampian, tel. 03397/55377.*

Early Sept. Burghley Horse Trials are held on the grounds of England's largest Elizabethan house. *Burghley Horse Trials Office, Stamford, Lincolnshire PE9 2LH, tel. 0780/52982.*

Sept. 11–22. Chelsea Antiques Fair *(see Mar., above).*

Early Oct. Horse of the Year Show features the world's top show jumpers at Wembley Arena, in Greater London. *Information from Wembley Box Office, Wembley Stadium Ltd., Wembley, Middlesex HA9 ODW, tel 081/900–1234.*

Early–mid-Oct. Cheltenham Festival of Literature includes plays, readings and book exhibits. *Cheltenham, Gloucestershire, tel. 0242/521621.*

Nov. 5. Guy Fawkes Day is celebrated in Lewes, with processions and bonfires, to commemorate the attempt to blow up James I and parliament.

Early Nov. London to Brighton Veteran Car Run starts in London's Hyde Park and ends in Brighton in East Sussex; no tickets are required. *Tel. 0753/681736.*

Early Nov. Lord Mayor's Procession and Show coincides with the Lord Mayor's inauguration, with a procession from the Guildhall to the Royal Courts of Justice. No tickets are required. *The City of London. Tel. 071/606–3030.*

Mid to Late Dec. Olympia International Show Jumping Championships is an international equestrian competition. *Olympia, Hammersmith Rd., London W14 8XT, tel. 071/373–8141.*

What to Pack

Pack light because porters and baggage carts are scarce and luggage restrictions on international flights are tight.

Clothing Britain can be cool, damp, and overcast, even in summer. You'll want a heavy coat for winter and a lightweight coat or warm jacket for summer. There's no time of year when a raincoat or umbrella won't come in handy. For the cities, pack as you would for an American city: coats and ties for expensive restaurants and nightspots, casual clothes elsewhere. Jeans are popular in Britain and are perfectably acceptable for sightseeing and informal dining. Tweeds and sports jackets are popular here with men. For women, ordinary street dress is acceptable everywhere.

Miscellaneous You'll need an electrical adapter for your hairdryer and small appliances. The voltage is 220, with 50 cycles. If you plan to stay in budget hotels, take your own soap. Many do not provide soap and some give guests only one tiny bar per room.

Luggage Airlines allow two pieces of check-in luggage and one carry-on piece per passenger. Each piece of check-in luggage cannot exceed 62 inches (length + width + height) or weigh more than 70 pounds. The carry-on luggage cannot exceed 45 inches (length + width + height) and must fit under the seat or in the overhead luggage compartment. Within Europe, airlines allow two pieces of check-in luggage totaling 44 pounds. The restrictions for carry-on luggage are the same as for international flights.

Taking Money Abroad

Traveler's checks and major U.S. credit cards, particularly Visa, are accepted in larger cities and resorts. In smaller towns and rural areas, you'll need cash. Small restaurants and shops in the cities also tend to operate on a cash basis. You won't get as good an exchange rate at home as abroad, but it's wise to change a small amount of money into sterling before you go, to avoid long lines at airport currency exchange booths. Most U.S. banks can exchange dollars for sterling. If your local bank can't provide this service, you can exchange money through Thomas Cook Currency Services. To find the office nearest you, contact them at 29 Broadway, New York, NY 10006, tel. 212/757–6915.

For safety and convenience, it's always best to take traveler's checks. The most recognized traveler's checks are American Express, Barclays, Thomas Cook, and those issued through major commercial banks such as Citibank and Bank of America. Some banks will issue the checks free to established customers, but most charge a 1% commission fee. Buy part of the traveler's checks in small denominations to cash toward the end of your trip. This will save having to cash a large check and ending up with more foreign money than you need. You can also buy traveler's checks in pound sterling, a good idea if the dollar is falling and you want to lock in the current rate. Remember to take the addresses of offices where you can get refunds for lost or stolen traveler's checks.

Banks and bank-operated currency exchange booths in airports and rail stations are the best places to change money. Hotels and privately-run exchange firms will give you a significantly lower rate of exchange.

Getting Money from Home

There are at least three ways to get money from home:

(1) Have it sent through a large commercial bank with a branch in the town where you're staying. The only drawback is that you must have an account with the bank; if not, you'll have to go through your own bank and the process will be slower and more expensive.

(2) Have it sent through American Express. If you are a cardholder, you can cash a personal check or a counter check at an American Express office for up to $1,000; $200 will be in cash and $800 in traveler's checks. There is a 1% commission on the traveler's checks. American Express has a new service called American Express MoneyGram, available in most major cities worldwide. Through this service, you can receive an unlimited amount of cash. It works this way: You call home and ask someone to go to an American Express office or an American Express MoneyGram agent located in a retail outlet, and fill out a MoneyGram. It can be paid for with cash or any major credit card. The person making the payment is given a reference number and telephones you with that number. The MoneyGram agent calls an 800 number and authorizes the transfer of funds to an American Express office or participating agency in the town where you're staying. In most cases, the money is available immediately on a 24-hour basis. You pick it up by showing identification and giving the reference number. Fees vary according to the amount of money sent. For sending $300 the fee is $35; for $5,000, $175. For the American Express MoneyGram location nearest your home and to find out where the service is available overseas, call 800/543–4080. You do not have to be a cardholder to use this service.

(3) Have it sent through Western Union (tel. 800/325–6000). If you have a MasterCard or Visa, you can have money sent for any amount up to $2,000. If not, have someone take cash or a certified cashier's check to a Western Union office. The money will be delivered in two business days to a bank in the city where you're staying. Fees vary with the amount of money sent. For $1,000 the fee is $50, for $500, $40.

British Currency

The unit of currency in Britain is the pound sterling, divided into 100 pence (p). The bills are 50, 20, 10, and 5 pounds (Scotland has £1 bills). Newly designed, smaller bills are being issued over the next three years. The new £5 note is already in circulation. Coins are £1, 50, 20, 10, 5, 2, and 1p. At press time (mid-May) the exchange rate was about US $1.95 and Canadian $2.25 to the pound sterling.

What It Will Cost

This is about the hardest travel question to answer in advance. A trip to Britain can cost as little (above a basic minimum) or as much (with virtually no limit) as you choose. Budgeting is much simplified if you take a package tour. As an indication: a packaged five-day stay in London, including hotel, meals except lunches (but with lunch included on two-full-day sightseeing trips), visits in London and to Windsor and Hampton Court and theater, costs anywhere from £33 to £700, depending upon the hotel category. A good-quality package six-day bus tour of Britain can be had for about £300–£500 (depending on the quality of hotel).

Sample Costs   For dining and lodging costs, see each chapter under that heading.

A man's haircut will cost £5 and up (around £10 at a central London barber); a woman's anywhere from £10 to £25. It costs about £1.50 to have a shirt laundered, from £4 to dry clean a dress, or £4.50 a man's suit. A local paper will cost you about 30p and a national daily 45p. A pint of beer is around £1.30, and a gin and tonic the same—remember that British measures for spirits are on the mean side. A cup of coffee will run from 60p to £1, depending on where you drink it; a ham sandwich £1.50; lunch in a pub, £2 and up (plus your drink).

A theater seat will cost from £5 to £30 in London, less elsewhere; while an evening at Covent Garden could set you back £75 each for the best seats. Nightclubs will take all they can get from you—even the membership fees are variable.

Sales Tax   The British sales tax (VAT, Value Added Tax) was increased in March 1991 from 15% to 17½%. At press time, this increase, the first in many years, had not been fully reflected in prices, so those we quote may be low by a small amount. The tax is almost always included in quoted prices in shops, hotels, and restaurants. Where it is quoted separately, the idea—as in the states—is to make the quoted price look more attractive. *See* Shopping, later in this section, for the ways to recover VAT when you leave the country. There is no VAT in the Channel Islands.

Passports and Visas

American   All U.S. citizens must have a passport to enter Great Britain. Applications for a new passport must be made in person; renewals can be obtained in person or by mail (*see* below). First-time applicants should apply well in advance of their departure date to one of the 13 U.S. Passport Agency offices. In addition, local county courthouses, many state and probate courts, and some post offices accept passport applications. Necessary documents include: (1) a completed passport application (Form DSP–11); (2) proof of citizenship (birth certificate with raised seal or naturalization papers); (3) proof of identity (unexpired driver's license, employee ID card or any other document with your photograph and signature); (4) two recent, identical, two-inch square photographs (black and white or color); (5) $42 application fee for a 10-year passport (those under 18 pay $27 for a five-year passport). If you pay in cash, you must have the exact amount. No change is given. Passports are mailed to you in about 10 working days.

To renew your passport by mail, you'll need completed Form DSP–82, two recent, identical passport photographs, a recent passport less than 12 years old from the issue date, and a check or money order for $35.

A visa is not required for a U.S. citizen to enter Britain for stays of up to six months. For longer stays, contact the British Embassy, 3100 Massachusetts Ave. NW, Washington, DC 20008, tel. 202/462–1340.

Canadian All Canadians must have a valid passport to enter Great Britain. Send your completed application (available from any post office or passport office) to the Bureau of Passports, Suite 215, West Tower, Guy Favreau Complex, 200 René Lévesque Blvd. W, Montreal, Quebec H27 1X4. Include $25, two photographs, a guarantor, and proof of Canadian citizenship. Applications can be made in person at several regional passport offices, including Edmonton, Halifax, Montreal, Toronto, Vancouver, or Winnipeg. Passports are valid for five years and are non-renewable.

Visas are not required for Canadian citizens traveling to Great Britain.

Customs and Duties

On Arrival There are two levels of duty-free allowance for travelers entering Great Britain: one for goods bought outside the EC (European Community of 12 nations) or in a duty-free shop in the EC; and the other, for goods bought in the EC.

In the first category, you may import duty-free: (1) 200 cigarettes or 100 cigarillos or 50 cigars or 250 grams of tobacco (these allowances are doubled if you live outside Europe); (2) two liters of table wine and, in addition, a) one liter of alcohol over 22% by volume (most spirits), b) two liters of alcohol under 22% by volume (fortified or sparkling wine), or c) two more liters of table wine; (3) 50 grams of perfume and 1/4 liter of toilet water; and (4) other goods up to a value of £32.

In the second category, you may import duty-free: (1) 300 cigarettes or 150 cigarillos or 75 cigars or 400 grams of tobacco; (2) five liters of table wine and, in addition, a) 1.5 liters of alcohol over 22% volume (most spirits), b) three liters of alcohol under 22% volume (fortified or sparkling wine), or c) three more liters of table wine; (3) 75 grams of perfume and 375ml of toilet water; and (4) other goods to the value of £265.

No animals or pets of any kind can be brought into the United Kingdom without a 6-month quarantine. The penalties are severe and strictly enforced. Similarly, fresh meats, plants and vegetables, controlled drugs, and firearms and ammunition may not be brought into Britain. There are no restrictions on the import or export of British and foreign currencies. You will face no customs formalities if you enter Scotland or Wales from any other part of the United Kingdom, though anyone coming from Northern Ireland should expect a security check.

On Departure If you are bringing any foreign-made equipment from home, such as cameras, it's wise to carry the original receipt with you or register it with U.S. Customs before you leave (Form 4457). Otherwise you may end up paying duty on your return. **U.S. residents** may bring home up to $400 worth of foreign goods duty-free, as long as they have been out of the country for at least 48 hours and they have not made an international trip in 30 days. Each member of the family is entitled to the same exemption, regardless of age, and exemptions can be pooled. For the next $1,000 worth of goods, a flat 10% rate is assessed; above $1,400 duties vary with the merchandise. Included for travelers 21 or older are one liter of alcohol, 100 cigars (non-Cuban) and 200 cigarettes. Only one bottle of perfume trademarked in the United States may be brought in. However, there is no duty on antiques or art over 100 years old. Anything exceeding these limits will be taxed at the port of entry, and may be taxed additionally in the traveler's home state. Gifts valued at under $50 may be mailed to friends or relatives at home duty-free, but not more than one package per day to any one addressee and not to include perfumes costing more than $5, tobacco, or liquor.

Canadian residents have an exemption ranging from $20 to $300, depending on the length of stay out of the country. For the $300 exemption, you must have been out of the country for one week. You are allowed one $300 exemption for any given year. You may also bring in duty-free up to 50 cigars, 200 cigarettes, two pounds of tobacco, and 40 ounces of liquor, provided these are declared in writing to customs on arrival and accompany the traveler in carry-on or check-in baggage. Personal gifts should be mailed as "Unsolicited Gift—Value under $40." Ask for the Canadian Customs brochure, *I Declare*, for further details.

Traveling with Film

If your camera is new, shoot and develop a few rolls before leaving home. Pack some lens tissue and an extra battery for your built-in light meter. Invest about $10 in a skylight filter: It will protect the lens and reduce haze.

Film doesn't like hot weather so if you're driving in summer, don't store film in the glove compartment or on the shelf under the rear window. Put it behind the front seat on the floor, on the side opposite the exhaust pipe.

On a plane trip, never pack unprocessed film in check-in luggage; if your bags get x-rayed, your pictures could be ruined. Always carry undeveloped film with you through security and ask to have it inspected by hand. (It helps to keep your film in a plastic bag, ready for quick inspection.)

The old airport scanning machines, still in use in some countries, use heavy doses of radiation that can turn a family portrait into an early morning fog. The newer models used in all U.S. airports are safe for anything from five to 500 scans, depending on the speed of your film. The effects are cumulative; you can put the same roll of film through several scans without worry. After five scans, though, you're asking for trouble.

If your film gets fogged and you want an explanation, send it to the **National Association of Photographic Manufacturers** (550 Mamaroneck Ave., Harrison, NY 10528). They will try to determine what went wrong. This service is free.

Staying Healthy

There are no serious health risks associated with travel to Britain. If you have a health problem that might require purchasing prescription drugs while in the country, have your doctor at home write a prescription using the drug's generic name. Brand names vary widely from country to country. To avoid problems clearing customs, diabetics carrying needles and syringes should have a letter from their physician confirming their need for insulin injections.

The **International Association for Medical Assistance to Travelers** (IAMAT) is a worldwide association offering a list of approved doctors whose training meets very high standards. For a list of British physicians and clinics that are part of this network, contact IAMAT, 417 Center St., Lewiston, NY 14092, tel. 716/754–4883. **In Canada:** 40 Regal Rd., Guelph, Ontario N1K 1B5, tel. 519/836–0102. **In Europe:** 57 Voirets, 1212 Grand-Lancy, Geneva, Switzerland. Membership is free.

Inoculations are not needed for visitors coming to Britain.

Insurance

Review your existing health and homeowner policies; some health insurance plans cover health expenses incurred while traveling, some major medical plans cover emergency transportation, and some homeowner policies cover theft of luggage.

Health and Accident
Several companies offer coverage designed to supplement existing health insurance for travelers:

Carefree Travel Insurance (Box 310, 120 Mineola Blvd., Mineola, NY 11501, tel. 516/294–0220 or 800/323–3149) provides coverage for emergency medical evacuation and accidental death and dismemberment. It also offers 24-hour medical phone advice.
International SOS Assistance (Box 11568, Philadelphia, PA 19116, tel. 215/244–1500 or 800/523–8930), a medical assistance company, provides emergency evaluation services, worldwide medical referrals, and optional medical insurance.
Travel Guard International, underwritten by Transamerica Occidental Life Companies (1145 Clark St., Stevens Point, WI 54481, tel. 715/345–0505 or 800/782–5151), offers reimbursement for medical expenses with no deductibles or daily limits, as well as emergency evacuation services.
Wallach and Company, Inc. (243 Church St. NW, Suite 100D, Vienna, VA 22180, tel. 703/281–9500 or 800/237–6615) offers comprehensive medical coverage, including emergency evacuation services worldwide.

Luggage and Trip Cancellation
Luggage loss is usually covered as part of a comprehensive travel insurance package that includes personal accident, trip cancellation, and sometimes default and bankruptcy insurance. Several companies offer comprehensive policies:

Access America, Inc., a subsidiary of Blue Cross-Blue Shield (Box 11188, Richmond, VA 23230, tel. 800/334–7525 or 800/284–8300).
Travel Guard International *(see* Health and Accident, above).

Flight Insurance Flight insurance is often included in the price of a ticket when paid for with American Express, Visa, and other major credit and charge cards. It is usually included in combination travel insurance packages available from most tour operators, travel agents, and insurance agents.

Renting and Leasing Cars

Renting If you're flying into Britain and plan to spend some time first in London, save money by arranging to pick up your car in the city the day you depart; otherwise, arrange to pick up and return your car at the airport. Weigh the added expense of renting a car from a major company with an airport office against the savings on a car from a budget company with offices in town. If you're arriving and departing from different airports, look for a one-way car rental with no return fees. If you're traveling to more than one country, make sure your rental contract permits you to take the car across borders and that the insurance policy covers you in every country you visit. Remember, however, that Britain drives on the left, and the rest of Europe on the right. Therefore, you may want to leave your hire car in Britain and pick up a left-side drive when you cross the Channel.

Be prepared to pay more for a car with automatic transmission. Since they are not as readily available as those with manual transmissions, reserve them in advance. Rental rates vary widely, depending on size and model, number of days you use the car, insurance coverage, and whether special drop-off fees are imposed. In most cases, rates quoted include unlimited free mileage and standard liability protection. Not included are Collision Damage Waiver (CDW), which eliminates your deductible payment should you have an accident; personal accident insurance; gasoline; and European Value Added Tax (VAT). The VAT in Great Britain is 15%.

Driver's licenses issued in the United States and Canada are valid in Great Britain. You might also take out an International Driving Permit before you leave to smooth out difficulties if you have an accident, or as an additional piece of identification. Permits are available for a small fee through local offices of the **American Automobile Association** (AAA) and the **Canadian Automobile Association** (CAA), or from their main offices: **AAA** (1000 AAA Dr., Heathrow, FL 32746, tel. 800/336–4357); **CAA** (2 Carlton St., Toronto, Ontario M5B 1K4, tel. 416/964–3170).

It's best to arrange car rental before you leave. You won't save money by waiting until you arrive in Britain, and you may find that the type of car you want is not available at the last minute. Rental companies usually charge according to the exchange rate of the dollar at the time the car is returned or when the credit card payment is processed. To help you hedge against the falling dollar, these companies guarantee advertised rates if you pay in advance: **Budget Rent a Car** (3350 Boyington St., Carrollton, TX 75006, tel. 800/527–0700) and **Connex Travel International** (23 N. Division St., Peekskill, NY 10566, tel. 800/333–3949).

Other budget rental companies serving Britain include **Europe by Car** (One Rockefeller Plaza, New York, NY 10020, tel. 212/245–1713; 800/223–1516; in CA, 800/252–9401); **Auto Europe** (Box 1097, Sharps Wharf, Camden, ME 04843, tel. 800/223–5555; in ME, 800/342–5202; in Canada, 800/237–2465); **Fore-**

most **Euro-Car** (5430 Van Nuys Blvd., Van Nuys, CA 91404, tel. 800/272–3299); and **Kemwel** (106 Calvert St., Harrison, NY 10528, tel. 800/678–0678). Other companies include **Avis,** (tel. 800/331–1212); **Hertz** (tel. 800/223–6472 or in NY, 800/522–3001); and **National** or **Europcar** (800/CAR–RENT).

Leasing For trips of 21 days or more, you may save money by leasing a car. With the leasing arrangement, you are technically buying a car and then selling it back to the manufacturer after you've used it. You receive a factory-new car, tax free, with international registration and extensive insurance coverage. Rates vary with the make and model of car and length of time used. Before you go, compare long-term rental rates with leasing rates. Remember to add taxes and insurance costs to the car rentals, something you don't have to worry about with leasing. Companies that offer leasing arrangements include **Kemwel, Europe by Car,** and **Auto Europe,** all listed above.

Rail Passes

If you plan on doing a lot of traveling while in Britain, consider purchasing a **BritRail Pass,** which gives unlimited travel over the entire British Rail Network. A variety of passes are offered. The adult first-class pass costs $319 for eight days, $479 for 15 days, $499 for 22 days, and $689 for one month. The adult second-class pass costs $209 for eight days, $319 for 15 days, $399 for 22 days, and $465 for one month. Senior citizens (over 60) can obtain a **Senior Citizen Pass** which entitles the bearer to unlimited first-class travel. It costs $289 for eight days, $429 for 15 days, $539 for 22 days, and $619 for one month. There is also a second-class pass available. Young travelers (aged 16–25) can buy the **BritRail Youthpass,** which allows unlimited second-class travel. It costs $169 for eight days, $255 for 15 days, $319 for 22 days, and $375 for one month.

You *must* purchase the BritRail Pass before you leave home. They are available from most travel agents or from one of these BritRail Travel International offices: 630 Third Ave., New York, NY 10036, tel. 212/575–2667; 94 Cumberland St., Toronto, Ontario M5R 1A3, tel. 416/929–3333; 409 Granville St., Vancouver, B.C., V6C 1T2, tel. 604/683–6896.

If you want the flexibility of a car combined with the speed and comfort of the train, with **BritRail/Drive** (from around $275 per person, based on two adults sharing a car, more for automatic transmission) you can have an eight-day BritRail Pass and four vouchers valid for Hertz car hire from over 80 BritRail stations and a further 40 "downtown" garage locations in other towns. This makes it possible to take the train to a major town, then use the car to get deep into the countryside to visit a stately home or other attraction. If you call your travel agency or Hertz's international desk at 800/654–3001, the car of your choice will be waiting for you at the station as you alight from your train. **BritRail/Drive** must be booked with your travel agent before leaving for Great Britain.

BritRail Pass holders also get useful discounts on **Britain Shrinkers,** escorted rail and coach tours of one to three days out of London to various heritage attractions.

Student and Youth Travel

The **International Student Identity Card (ISIC)** entitles students to youth rail passes, special fares on local transportation, Intra-European student charter flights, and discounts at museums, theaters, sports events, and many other attractions. If purchased in the United States, the $14 card also entitles the holder to $3,000 in emergency medical insurance, plus $100 a day for up to 60 days of hospital coverage. Apply to the **Council on International Educational Exchange (CIEE)**, (205 E. 42nd St., 16th Floor, New York, NY 10017, tel. 212/661–1414). In Canada, the ISIC is available for $CN12 from **Travel Cuts** (187 College St., Toronto, Ont. H5T 1P7, tel. 416/979–2406).

The **Youth International Educational Exchange Card** (YIEE), issued by the **Federation of International Youth Travel Organizations** (FIYTO), (81 Islands Brugge, DK–2300 Copenhagen S, Denmark), provides similar services to nonstudents under 26 years of age. In the United States, the card is available from CIEE (address above). In Canada, the YIEE card is available from the **Canadian Hostelling Association** (CHA), (1600 James Naismith Dr., Suite 608, Gloucester, Ont. K1B 5N4, tel. 613/748–5638).

An **International Youth Hostel Federation** (IYHF) membership card is the key to inexpensive dormitory-style accommodations at thousands of youth hostels around the world. Hostels are situated in a variety of locations, including converted farmhouses, villas, restored castles, and specially constructed modern buildings. There are more than 5,000 hostels in 68 countries around the world. IYHF memberships, which are valid for 12 months from the time of purchase, are available in the United States through American Youth Hostels (AYH, Box 37613, Washington, DC 20013, tel. 202/783–6161), and in Canada through the Canadian Hostelling Association (address above). The cost for a first-year membership is $25 for adults 18–54. Renewal thereafter is $15. For youths (17 and under) the rate is $10 and for senior citizens (55 and older) the rate is $15. Family membership is available for $35. Every national hostel association arranges special reductions for members visiting their countries, such as discounted rail fare or free bus travel, so be sure to ask for an international concessions list when you buy your membership. AYH also publishes an extensive directory of youth hostels around the world. Economical bicycle tours for small groups of adventurous, energetic students are another popular AYH student travel service.

Council Travel, a CIEE subsidiary, is the foremost U.S. student travel agency. It specializes in low-cost charters and serves as the exclusive U.S. agent for many student airfare bargains and student tours. The 80-page *Student Travel Catalog* and *Council Charter* brochure are available free from any Council Travel office in the United States (enclose $1 postage if ordering by mail). Contact CIEE headquarters at the address above, or Council Travel offices in Berkeley, La Jolla, Long Beach, Los Angeles, San Diego, San Francisco, and Sherman Oaks, CA; Boulder, CO; New Haven, CT; Washington, DC; Atlanta, GA; Chicago and Evanston, IL; New Orleans, LA; Amherst, Boston, and Cambridge, MA; Minneapolis, MN; Durham, NC; Portland, OR; Providence, RI; Austin and Dallas, TX; Seattle, WA; and Milwaukee, WI.

The **Educational Travel Center,** another student travel specialist worth contacting for information on student tours, bargain fares, and bookings, may be reached at 438 N. Frances St., Madison, WI 55703, tel. 608/256–5551.

Students who would like to work abroad should contact CIEE's **Work Abroad Department,** at the address given above. The council arranges various types of paid and voluntary work experiences overseas for up to six months. CIEE also sponsors study programs in Europe, Latin America, and Asia, and publishes many books of interest to the student traveler, including *Work, Study, Travel Abroad: The Whole World Handbook* ($10.95 plus $1 postage) and *Volunteer! The Comprehensive Guide to Voluntary Service in the U.S. and Abroad* ($6.95 plus $2.50 per book for first-class postage).

The Information Center at the **Institute of International Education** (IIE) (809 U.N. Plaza, New York, NY 10017, tel. 212/984–5413) has reference books, foreign university catalogues, study-abroad brochures, and other materials that may be consulted by students and nonstudents alike, free of charge. The Information Center is open weekdays 10 to 4.

IIE administers a variety of grant and study programs offered by U.S. and foreign organizations, and publishes a well-known annual series of study-abroad guides, including *Academic Year Abroad, Vacation Study Abroad,* and *Study in the United Kingdom and Ireland.* The institute also publishes *Teaching Abroad,* a book of employment and study opportunities overseas for U.S. teachers. For a current list of IIE publications, along with prices and ordering information, write to the IIE Publications Service at the address given above. Books must be purchased by mail or in person; telephone orders are not accepted. General information on IIE programs and services is available from its regional offices in Atlanta, Chicago, Denver, Houston, San Francisco, and Washington, D.C.

For information on the BritRail Youthpass, *see* **Rail Passes,** above.

Traveling with Children

Publications   *Capital Radio's London for Kids*, magazine format, available from newsstands, £2.

Children's London, a free booklet from the London Visitor and Convention Bureau (Tourist Information Centre, Victoria Station Forecourt, London SW1V 1JT, tel. 071/730–3488).

Family Travel Times is an 8 to 12-page newsletter published 10 times a year by TWYCH (Travel with Your Children, 80 Eighth Ave., New York, NY 10011, tel. 212/206–0688). Subscription includes access to back issues and twice-weekly opportunities to call in for specific advice.

Kids' London by Elizabeth Holt and Molly Perham (St. Martin's Press, 175 Fifth Ave., New York, NY 10010; $5.95).

Family Travel Organizations   **American Institute for Foreign Study** (AIFS) (102 Greenwich Ave., Greenwich, CT 06830, tel. 203/869–9090), offers a family vacation program in Britain specifically designed for parents and children.

Familes Welcome! (Box 16398, Chapel Hill, NC 27516, tel. 800/326–0724) is a travel agency that arranges family-oriented tours to Britain as well as to Europe.

Hotels **Novotel** (International reservations: 800/221–4542) hotels allow up to two children to stay free in their parents' room. **Trusthouse Forte Hotels** in Britain have special Babycare Kits and children's menus; children under five are free and ages six to 13 in parents' room enjoy reduced rates. (Keep in mind that in Britain, hotels will often only allow three people in a room.)

Villa Rentals **At Home Abroad, Inc.** (405 E. 56th St., Suite 6H, New York, NY 10022, tel. 212/421–9165).
Villas International (71 W. 23rd St., New York, NY 10010, tel. 212/929–7585 or 800/221–2260).
Hideaways, Inc. (Box 1464, Littleton, MA 01460, tel. 617/486–8955).
Heritage of England (Box 297, Falls Village, CT 06031, tel. 203/824–5155 or 800/533–5405).

Home Exchange Exchanging homes is a surprisingly low-cost way to enjoy a vacation abroad, especially a long one. The largest home-exchange service, **International Home Exchange Service** (Box 190070, San Francisco, CA 94119, tel. 415/435-3497) publishes three directories a year. Membership, which costs $45, entitles you to one listing and all three directories. **Loan-a-Home** (2 Park Lane, 6E Mount Vernon, NY 10552, tel. 914/664–7640) is popular with the academic community on sabbatical and businesspeople on temporary assignment. There's no annual membership fee or charge for listing your home; however, one directory and a supplement costs $35. Loan-a-Home publishes two directories and two supplements each year. All four books cost $45 per year.

Getting There On international flights, children under two not occupying a seat pay 10% of adult fare. Various discounts apply to children two to 12 years of age. Regulations about infant travel on airplanes are in the process of changing. Until they do, however, if you want to be sure your infant is secure and traveling in his or her own safety seat, you must buy a separate ticket and bring your own infant car seat. Check with the airline in advance; certain seats aren't allowed. Or write for the booklet *Child/Infant Safety Seats Acceptable for Use in Aircraft*, from the Federal Aviation Administration (APA-200, 800 Independence Ave., SW, Washington, DC 20591, tel. 202/267–3479). Some airlines allow babies to travel in their own car seats at no charge if there's a spare seat available; otherwise safety seats will be stored and the child will have to be held by a parent. (If you opt to hold your baby on your lap, do so with the infant outside the seatbelt so he or she won't be crushed in case of a sudden stop.)

Also inquire about special children's meals or snacks. The February 1990 and 1992 issues of **Family Travel Times** includes *TWYCH's Airline Guide*, which contains a rundown of the children's services offered by 46 airlines.

Baby-sitting Services First check with the hotel desk for recommended local childcare arrangements. **Nanny Service** (9 Paddington St., London WIM 3LA, tel. 071/935–3515); **Childminders** (9 Paddington St., London WIM 3LA, tel. 071/935–9763); **Universal Aunts** (Box 304, London SW4 ONN, tel. 071/738–8937).

Miscellaneous For information and advice when in London, call **Kidsline,** tel. 071/222–8070.

Hints for Disabled Travelers

The Information Center for Individuals with Disabilities (Fort Point Pl., 1st floor, 27–43, Wormwood St., Boston, MA 02210, tel. 617/727–5540; TDD 617/727–5236) offers useful problem-solving assistance, including lists of travel agents that specialize in tours for the disabled.

Moss Rehabilitation Hospital Travel Information Service (1200 W. Tabor Rd., Philadelphia, PA 19141, tel. 215/456–9600; TDD 215/456–9602) for a small fee provides information on tourist sights, transportation, and accommodations in destinations around the world.

Mobility International USA (Box 3551, Eugene, OR 97403, tel. 503/343–1284) has information on accommodations, organized study, etc. around the world.

The Society for the Advancement of Travel for the Handicapped (26 Court St., Brooklyn, NY 11242, tel. 718/858–5483) offers access information. Annual membership costs $45, or $25 for senior travelers and students. Send a stamped, self-addressed envelope.

The Itinerary (Box 2012, Bayonne, NJ 07002, tel. 201/858–3400) is a bimonthly travel magazine for the disabled.

Hints for Older Travelers

The American Association of Retired Persons (AARP, 1909 K St. NW, Washington, DC 20049, tel. 202/662–4850) has two programs for independent travelers: (1) the **Purchase Privilege Program,** which offers discounts on hotels, airfare, car rentals, and sightseeing; and (2) the **AARP Motoring Plan,** provided by Amoco, which offers emergency aid and trip routing information for an annual fee of $33.95 per couple. The AARP also arranges group tours through **American Express Vacations** (*see* Tour Groups, above). AARP members must be 50 or older. Annual dues are $5 per person or per couple.

Elderhostel (75 Federal St., 3rd floor, Boston, MA 02110, tel. 617/426–7788) is an innovative educational program for people 60 and older. Participants stay in dorms on some 1,200 campuses around the world. Mornings are devoted to lectures and seminars; afternoons, to sightseeing and field trips. The all-inclusive fee for two-to-three-week trips, including room, board, tuition, and round-trip transportation, is $1,800 to $4,500.

Saga International Holidays (120 Bolyston St., Boston, MA 02116, tel. 800/343–0273) specializes in group travel for people over 60. A selection of variously priced tours allows you to choose the package that meets your needs.

Travel Industry and Disabled Exchange (TIDE, 5435 Donna Ave., Tarzana, CA 91356, tel. 818/368–5648) is an industry-based organization with a $15 annual membership fee. Members receive a quarterly newsletter and information on travel agencies and tours.

National Council of Senior Citizens (925 15th St. NW, Washington, DC 20005, tel. 202/347–8800) is a nonprofit advocacy group with 5,000 local clubs across the country. Annual membership is $12 per person or per couple. Members receive a monthly newsletter with travel information, and an ID card for reduced-rate hotels and car rentals.

Mature Outlook (6001 N. Clark St., Chicago, IL 60660, tel. 800/336–6330), a subsidiary of Sears, Roebuck & Co., is a travel club for people over 50, with hotel and motel discounts and a bimonthly newsletter. Annual membership is $9.95 per couple. Instant membership is available at participating Holiday Inns.

Further Reading

Two good background books on England are *The English World*, edited by Robert Blake, and Godfrey Smith's *The English Companion*, while *The London Encyclopaedia* by Ben Weinreb and Christopher Hibbert is invaluable as a source of information on the capital.

The Buildings of England, by Nikolaus Pevsner, is a multi-volume series that includes a tremendous number of buildings throughout the country.

Mysteries are almost a way of life in Britain, partly because many of the best English mystery writers set their plots in their home territory. Modern whodunits by P. D. James and Ruth Rendell can be relied on to convey a fine sense of place, while Ellis Peters's Brother Cadfael stories recreate life in medieval Shrewsbury with a wealth of telling detail. There are always, of course, the villages, vicarages, and scandals of Agatha Christie's "Miss Marple" books.

For the many fans of the Arthurian legends, there are some excellent, imaginative novels, which not only tell the stories, but give fine descriptions of British countryside. Among them are *Sword at Sunset* by Rosemary Sutcliffe, *The Once and Future King* by T. H. White, and the four Merlin novels by Mary Stewart, *The Crystal Cave*, *The Hollow Hills*, *The Last Enchantment*, and *The Wicked Day*.

Anyone interested in writers and the surroundings which may have influenced their works should get *The Oxford Literary Guide to the British Isles*, edited by Dorothy Eagle and Hilary Carnell, and *Literary Britain*, by Frank Morley.

A highly irreverent—and very funny—version of academic life, *Porterhouse Blue*, by Tom Sharpe, will guarantee that you look at Oxford and Cambridge with a totally different eye. John Fowles's *The French Lieutenant's Woman*, largely set in Lyme Regis, is full of local color for visitors to Dorset.

James Herriot's successfully televised veterinary surgeon books, among them *All Creatures Great and Small*, give evocative accounts of life in the Yorkshire dales.

Two modern poets well worth reading for their handling of the world around them are John Betjeman, who not only celebrated English suburbia but championed the cause of threatened Victorian architecture, and Philip Larkin, a very English poet with a keen eye and a searching sense of local life.

An animal's close-to-the-earth viewpoint can reveal all kinds of countryside insights about Britain. *Watership Down*, by Richard Adam, was a runaway best seller about rabbits in the early 70s, and *Wind in the Willows*, by Kenneth Grahame, gives a vivid impression of the Thames Valley 80 years ago which still holds largely true today.

Suggested British classics include D. H. Lawrence's *Sons and Lovers; Great Expectations* or *David Copperfield* by Charles Dickens. *Tess of the D'Urbervilles* and *The Mayor of Casterbridge,* both by Thomas Hardy; Jane Austen's novels *Pride and Prejudice* and *Northanger Abbey;* and the Barchester novels of Anthony Trollope.

Arriving and Departing

From North America by Plane

As the air routes between North America and Great Britain are heavily traveled, you'll have many airlines and fares to choose from. But fares change with stunning rapidity, so consult your travel agent on which bargains are currently available.

The Airlines Airlines serving London and other major cities in Britain include: **American Airlines** (tel. 800/433–7300); **British Airways** (tel. 800/247–9297); **Delta** (tel. 800/241–4141); **Northwest Airlines** (tel. 800/447–4747); **Pan Am** (tel. 800/221–1111); and **TWA** (tel. 800/892–4141); **United** (tel. 800/538–2929).

Flying Time The flight time to London from New York is about 6½ hours, from Chicago 7½ hours, and from Los Angeles 10 hours.

Luggage Regulations
Carry-on Luggage New rules have been in effect since January 1, 1988 on U.S. airlines in regards to carry-on luggage. The model for these new rules was agreed to by the airlines and then circulated by the Air Transport Association with the understanding that each airline would present its own version.

Under the model, passengers are limited to two carry-on bags. For a bag you wish to store under the seat, the maximum dimensions are 9″ × 14″ × 22″, a total of 45″. For bags that can be hung in a closet or on a luggage rack, the maximum dimensions are 4″ × 23″ × 45″, a total of 72″. For bags you wish to store in an overhead bin, the maximum dimensions are 10″ × 14″ × 36″, a total of 60″. Your two carry-ons must each fit one of these sets of dimensions, and any item that exceeds the specified dimensions will generally be rejected as a carry-on and handled as checked baggage. Keep in mind that an airline can adapt these rules to circumstances, so on an especially crowded flight don't be surprised if you are only allowed one carry-on bag.

In addition to the two carry-ons, the rules list eight items that may also be brought aboard: a handbag (pocketbook or purse); an overcoat or wrap; an umbrella; a camera; a reasonable amount of reading material; an infant bag; and crutches, a cane, braces, or other prosthetic device upon which the passenger is dependent. Infant/child safety seats can also be brought aboard if parents have purchased a ticket for the child or if there is space in the cabin. Note that these regulations are for U.S. airlines only. Foreign airlines generally allow one piece of carry-on luggage in tourist class, in addition to handbags and bags filled with duty-free goods. Passengers in first and business class are also allowed to carry on one garment bag. It is best to check with your airline ahead of time to find out what its exact rules are regarding carry-on luggage.

Checked Luggage   U.S. airlines allow passengers to check in two suitcases whose total dimensions (length + width + height) do not exceed 62″ and whose weight does not exceed 70 pounds.

Rules governing foreign airlines vary from airline to airline, so check with your travel agent or the airline itself before you go. All the airlines allow passengers to check in two bags. In general, expect the weight restriction on the two bags to be not more than 70 lbs. each, and the size restriction on each bag to be 62″ for its total dimensions.

Labeling Luggage   Before you go, itemize the contents of each bag in case you need to file an insurance claim. Put your home address on each piece of luggage, including carry-on bags. If your luggage is lost or stolen and later recovered, the airline will deliver the luggage to your home free of charge.

Lost Luggage and   Airlines are responsible for lost or damaged property only up
Luggage Insurance   to $1,250 per passenger on domestic flights, and $9.07 per pound (or $20 per kilo) for checked baggage on international flights, and up to $400 per passenger for unchecked baggage on international flights. If you're carrying valuables, either take them with you on the airplane or purchase additional insurance for lost luggage. Some airlines will issue additional luggage insurance when you check in, but many do not. Insurance for lost, damaged, or stolen luggage is available through travel agents or directly through various insurance companies *(see* Insurance, above). Two that issue luggage insurance are **Tele-Trip** (tel. 800/228–9792), a subsidiary of Mutual of Omaha, and **The Travelers Corporation.** Tele-Trip operates sales booths at airports, and also issues insurance through travel agents. Tele-Trip will insure checked luggage for up to 180 days; rates vary according to the length of the trip. The Travelers Corporation will insure checked or hand luggage for $500 to $2,000 valuation per person, and also for a maximum of 180 days. Rates for one to five days for $500 valuation are $10; for 180 days, $85. For more information, write **The Travelers Corporation** (Ticket and Travel Dept., 1 Tower Square, Hartford, CT 06183, tel. 203/277–0111 or 800/243–3174). Each company offers the same rates on domestic and international flights. Check the travel pages of your Sunday newspaper for the names of other companies that insure luggage.

Discount Flights   The major airlines offer a range of tickets that can increase the price of any given seat by more than 300%, depending on the day of purchase. As a rule, the further in advance you buy the ticket, the less expensive it is, but the greater the penalty (up to 100%) for canceling. Check with airlines for details.

The best buy is not necessarily an APEX (advance purchase) ticket on one of the major airlines. APEX tickets carry certain restrictions: They must be bought in advance (usually 21 days), they restrict your travel (usually with a minimum stay of seven days and a maximum of 90), and they also penalize you for changes—voluntary or not—in your travel plans. But if you can work around these drawbacks (and most travelers can), they are among the best-value fares available.

Charter flights offer the lowest fares but often depart only on certain days, and rarely on time. Though you may be able to arrive at one city and return from another, you may lose all or most of your money if you cancel your trip. Don't sign up for a charter flight unless you've checked with a travel agency about the reputation of the packager. It's particularly important to know the packager's policy concerning refunds should a flight be canceled. One of the most popular charter operators to Europe is **Council Charter** (tel. 800/223–7402), a division of CIEE (Council on International Educational Exchange). Other companies advertise in Sunday travel sections of daily newspapers.

Somewhat more expensive than a charter, but up to 50% below the cost of APEX fares, are tickets purchased through companies known as consolidators which buy blocks of tickets on scheduled airlines and sell them at wholesale prices. Here again, you may lose all or most of your money if you change plans, but at least you will be on a regularly scheduled flight with less risk of cancellation than a charter. Once you've made your reservation, call the airline to make sure you're confirmed. Among the best-known consolidators are **UniTravel** (tel. 314/569–2501 or 800/325–2222) and **Access International** (101 W. 31st St., Suite 1104, New York, NY 10001, tel. 212/465–0707). Others advertise in the Sunday travel section of the daily newspapers as well.

A third option is to join a travel club that offers special discounts to its members. Three such organizations are **Moment's Notice** (425 Madison Ave., New York, NY 10017, tel. 212/486–0503); **Discount Travel International** (114 Forrest Ave., Narberth, PA 19072, tel. 215/668–7184); and **Worldwide Discount Travel Club** (1674 Meridian Ave., Suite 300, Miami Beach, FL 33139, tel. 305/534–2082). These cut-rate tickets should be compared with APEX tickets on the major airlines.

Travelers willing to put up with some restrictions and inconveniences in exchange for a substantially reduced airfare may be interested in flying as an air courier. A person who agrees to be a courier must accompany shipments between designated points. There are two sources of information on courier deals:

There is a telephone directory that lists courier companies by the cities to which they fly. Send $5 and a self-addressed, stamped, business-size envelope to Pacific Data Sales Publishing (2554 Lincoln Blvd., Suite 275-I, Marina Del Rey, CA 90291).

"A Simple Guide to Courier Travel." Send $14.95 (includes postage and handling) to Box 2394, Lake Oswego, OR 97035. For more information, call 800/344–9375.

Enjoying the Flight If you're lucky enough to be able to sleep on a plane, it makes sense to fly at night. Many experienced travelers, however, prefer to take a morning flight to Great Britain and arrive in the evening, just in time for a good night's sleep. Since the air on a plane is dry, it helps to drink a lot of non-alcoholic liquids while flying; drinking alcohol only contributes to jet lag. Feet swell at high altitudes, so it's a good idea to remove your shoes in flight. Sleepers usually prefer window seats to curl up against; those who like to move about the cabin ask for aisle seats. Bulkhead seats (located in the front row of each cabin) have more legroom, but seat trays are attached to the arms of your seat rather than to the back of the seat in front. Generally bulkhead seats are reserved for the disabled, the elderly, or parents traveling with babies.

Smoking If smoking bothers you, ask for a seat far away from the smoking section. If the airline tells you there are no non-smoking seats left, insist on one: Department of Transportation regulations require all American airlines to find seats for all nonsmokers on the day of the flight, provided they meet check-in time restrictions.

From North America by Ship

The **Queen Elizabeth 2** (QE 2) is the only cruise ship that makes regular transatlantic crossings. Other cruise ships that sail from European ports in the summer and North American ports in the winter make transatlantic repositioning crossings as one season ends and another begins. Some sail straight across, often at reduced rates to passengers. Others have several ports of call before heading for the open sea. Arrangements can be made to cruise one way and fly the other. Since itineraries can change at the last minute, contact the cruise line for the latest information.

Cunard Line (555 Fifth Ave., New York, NY 10017, tel. 800/221–4770) operates four ships that make transatlantic crossings. The *QE2* makes regular crossings April through December, between Southampton, England, and Baltimore, Boston, and New York City. Arrangements for the *QE2* can include one-way airfare. Cunard Line also offers fly/cruise packages and pre- and post-land packages. Check the travel pages of your Sunday newspaper for other cruise ships that sail to Britain.

Staying in Britain

Getting Around

By Plane Because Britain is such a small country, internal air travel is much less important there than in the United States. Broadly speaking, for trips of less than 200 miles, the train is quicker given the time required to get to city centers and from airports, compared with the centrally based rail stations. Flying tends to cost more and many internal U.K. flights exist primarily as feeders from provincial airports into Heathrow and Gatwick for international flights.

For trips over 200 miles—for example, between London and Glasgow or Edinburgh—or where a sea crossing is involved, to places such as the Isle of Man, Belfast, the Channel Islands, or the Scottish islands, air travel has a considerable time advantage.

British airlines have suffered as much from the Gulf crisis as have American ones. It is possible that some of the smaller ones may fold.

British Airways/British Caledonian operates shuttle services between London Heathrow and Edinburgh, Glasgow, Belfast, and Manchester. Passengers can simply turn up and get a flight (usually hourly) without booking, back-up services being available. There are also shuttle services from Gatwick. **British Midlands** operates from Heathrow to Teesside, Belfast, Glasgow, Liverpool, and the Isle of Man; while **Dan Air** flies from Gatwick to Newcastle and Aberdeen and from Heathrow to Inverness.

The Scottish islands are served by **Highland Express** or **Loganair** from Glasgow and Edinburgh, while in the Southwest of England **Brymon Airways** flies from Plymouth and Exeter to the Scilly Isles. For services to the Channel Islands, see Chapter 7.

For reservations or information about all flights within the United Kingdom, contact **British Airways,** Bulova Center, 75–20 Astoria Blvd., Jackson Heights, New York, NY 11370, tel. 800/AIR–WAYS. Local travel agents in Britain can also make reservations.

By Train **British Rail,** Britain's state-owned rail system, offers an excellent way of exploring Britain without the stress and hassle of driving yourself around. There's been a revival of British Rail services in recent years, with new trains being introduced on quiet rural lines, stations being reopened, and even in some cases the re-introduction of vintage steam locomotives on scenic tourist routes. Some of these lines are as splendid as anything in Europe, and worth traveling on just for the mountain or coastal landscapes.

The basic British Rail network is still one of the densest in the world, with most of the main lines between the major cities having frequent service. If you want to travel on a mainline route, especially the InterCity network (*see* below), you can expect to find a train departing within the hour. But this is not true on Sundays or in remote rural areas of northern and western England, Scotland, and Wales, so plan your trip carefully. The *British Rail Passenger Timetable,* issued each year in May and October, and costing around £5.50, contains details of all BR services, as well as information on private, narrow-gauge, and steam lines, and details of special services and rail-based tourist facilities.

You can also find detailed timetables of most rail services in Britain and some ferry services in the *Thomas Cook European Timetable,* issued bi-monthly and on sale in the United States at **Forsyth Travel Library** (9154 W. 57th St., Box 2975, Dept. TCT, Shawnee Mission, KS, 66201). You can order a timetable with Visa or MasterCard Mon.–Sat., 9:30–4:30 (Central Time), tel. 800/FOR–SYTH or in KS or Canada, tel. 913/384–0496. In London, information on rail, coach, and air travel can be obtained (in person only) at the **British Travel Centre** (12 Regent St., London SW1 4PQ, tel. 071/730–3400), Mon.–Sat. 9–6, Sun. 10–4.

British Rail's main passenger network between larger cities is known as **InterCity.** It offers high-speed modern service, either on streamlined InterCity 125 diesel trains (named for their highest speed of 125mph) or electrified routes, including the new 140mph one between London and Yorkshire, which is being extended to Newcastle and Edinburgh.

Traffic can be heavy on the major express routes out of London, and if you're going on a long trip, seat reservations are strongly advised. You can reserve a seat on any InterCity train from any main line station or BR travel agent, at £1 for standard class, £2 for first class. Specify if you want a smoking or non-smoking compartment.

London's suburban and regional services, known as **Network SouthEast,** are largely electrified commuter services that extend to much of the south coast, including Brighton; northwest to Oxford; and northeast to Cambridge. Given the traffic and car parking problems in the London area, Network SouthEast is often a much faster and more convenient way of getting about than by car.

There are two classes of travel on British Rail's InterCity and Network SouthEast services. Standard class is, as its name implies, the regular quality of service and facility; first class offers luxury comfort: more space to move and stretch your legs, deeper cushions. On a long trip, first class is worth the extra cost—particularly if you can enjoy it at a discount with a BritRail Pass. (Discount rates will only be given to passengers who purchase tickets in the United States.) Remember, though, that away from the InterCity network, especially on the rural provincial lines and on suburban services outside London, first-class travel is not usually available.

The London area has fifteen major terminal stations, all serving both main and suburban lines, so be sure you know which station you're arriving at or leaving from. All stations are linked by London's Underground network.

If you'd rather explore a specific part of Britain in greater detail, the series of **Regional Rail Rover** unlimited travel tickets offer excellent value. They cost between £27.50 and £56 (depending on area covered) for a standard class, seven-day pass, and can be bought at main stations and BR travel agents. Tickets are available for each of these areas: Scotland, Wales, Northwest England, the Northeast, Coast and Peaks (the Peak District and part of Snowdonia), Heart of England, East Anglia, East Midlands, and the Southwest. A separate series of tickets covers the Southeast and the London area.

Details of these and other BR facilities in Britain can be obtained from the **British Rail Travel Centre** (Euston Station, London NW1 1DF, tel. 071/388–0519).

By Bus   Britain has a comprehensive bus (short haul) and coach (long distance) network, which offers an inexpensive way of seeing the country. Coaches are much cheaper than trains, usually about half the price or even less, but are generally slower, although some motorway services with the modern **Rapide** coaches reduce the margin considerably. Seats are comfortable, with meal and comfort stops usually arranged on longer trips. (Some coaches have toilet facilities on board). Information about coach services throughout Britain can be obtained from **Victoria Coach Station** (Buckingham Palace Rd., London SW1W 9TP, tel. 071/730–0202).

The British equivalent to Greyhound coaches is **National Express,** with its Scottish associate, **Caledonian Express,** it is by far the largest British operator. Victoria Coach Station in London is the hub of the National Express network, serving around 1,500 destinations. Information is available from any of the company's 2,500 agents nationwide. In London, the main information point is the **Coach Travel Centre** (13 Lower Regent St., London SW1Y 4LR), near the British Travel Centre. There are also National Express sales offices at London's Heathrow and Gatwick airport coach stations.

National Express has two principal ticket offers for tourists. The **BritExpress Card** costs £12 and gives a 30% discount on all adult fares on National Express and Caledonian Express services over a 30-day period. There is also the **Tourist Trail Pass** costing £56 for 5 days, £78 for 8 days, £116 for 15 days, and £160 for 30 days (discounts are available for children, students, and senior citizens). The pass allows unlimited travel on the company's services. The BritExpress Card and the Tourist Trail Pass can be bought in US dollars from the **General Sales Agent, WMA Tours Ltd.,** 909 West Vista Way, Vista, CA 92083.

Britain has an extensive network of local bus services both within the towns and into the countryside. Many routes, even in country areas, still operate those classic British vehicles, double-decker buses. It's difficult to plan a journey by country bus, because recent changes and privatization of bus routes have led to the development of many small companies and up-to-date timetable information isn't always easy to obtain. But the local bus station in whichever region you're staying, and perhaps the local tourist information center, will have precise information about routes and times. Many companies offer day or week "Explorer" or "Rover" unlimited-travel tickets, and those in popular tourist areas invariably operate special scenic services in the summer.

By Car With well over 55 million inhabitants in a country about the size of California, Britain's roads are among the most crowded in the world. And yet, away from the towns and cities, you can find miles of little-used roads and lanes where driving can be a real pleasure—and adventure.

If you are already a member of a motoring organization, there may be reciprocal membership benefits available between your auto club and the Automobile Association (AA) in Britain, including breakdown assistance. Check with your club; they will also be able to advise you about procedures, insurance, and necessary documentation. If your auto club doesn't have such arrangements, both the **AA** (Fanum House, Basingstoke, Hants, RQ21 2EA, tel. 0256/20123) and the **Royal Automobile Club** (RAC) (RAC House, Bartlett St., Box 10, Croydon, Surrey CR2 6XW, tel. 081/686–2525) offer associate membership for overseas visitors with all the benefits of membership. The AA and the RAC have large touring departments offering a wealth of detailed information about motoring in Britain.

Types of Roads There's now a very good network of superhighways (motorways) and divided highways (dual carriageways) throughout most of Britain, though in remoter areas such as Scotland and Wales, where the motorway network has not penetrated, travel is noticeably slower. Motorways shown in blue on most maps and road signs and with the prefix "M" are mainly two or three lanes in each direction, without any right-hand turns. If you'll be covering longer distances, these are the roads to use, though inevitably you'll see less of the countryside. Service areas are situated about an hour's travel time apart (or less). Dual carriageways, usually shown on a map as a thick red line (often with a black line in the center) and the prefix "A" followed by a number perhaps with a bracket "T" (i.e., A304 [T]), are similar to motorways, except that right turns are sometimes permitted and you'll find both traffic lights and traffic circles on them.

The vast network of other main roads, which the map shows as either single red "A" roads, or narrower brown "B" roads, also numbered, are for the most part the old coach and turnpike roads built for horses and carriages in the last century or earlier. Travel along these roads is much slower because passing is more difficult, and your trip might take twice the time it would take along a motorway. On the other hand, you'll see much more of Britain.

Minor roads (shown as yellow or white on maps, unlettered and unnumbered) are the ancient lanes and byways of Britain, roads which are not only living history but a superb way of discovering the real Britain. You have to drive along them slowly and carefully—sometimes there isn't even room for two vehicles to pass and you must reverse into a passing place if you meet an oncoming car or tractor.

Rules of the Road   The most noticeable difference for the visitor is that when in Britain you drive on the left. This takes a bit of getting used to, but it doesn't take very long, particularly if you're driving a British car where the steering and mirrors will be adjusted for U.K. conditions. You should be particularly careful, if you have picked up your cat at the airport, to give yourself time to adjust to driving on the left—especially if you have jet lag.

One of the most complicated questions facing visitors to Britain is that of speed limits. In urban areas, except for certain freeways, it is generally 30mph, but 40mph on some main roads, as indicated by circular red signs. In rural areas the official limit is 60mph on ordinary roads and 70mph on motorways—and traffic police can be hard on speeders, especially in urban areas. In other respects procedures are broadly similar to the United States.

Gasoline   Expect to pay a good deal more for gasoline than in the United States, though costs have been remarkably stable in recent years at about £2 a gallon (45p a liter) for four star—though it can be up to 10p a gallon higher in remote rural locations. Remember, too, that the British Imperial gallon is about 20% more in volume than the U.S. gallon. What you may find confusing is that although service stations advertise prices by the gallon (mainly for the benefit of the conservative British who continue to resist metrification), pumps actually measure in liters. A British gallon is approximately 4.5 liters. Most British people solve the conundrum by buying gas by the tankful or several pounds' worth.

Most gas stations stock 2, 3, and 4 star (91, 94, and 97 octane ratings) plus diesel, and lead-free gas is increasingly common and cheaper than leaded. Service stations are located at regular intervals on motorways and are usually open 24 hours a day, though stations elsewhere usually close from 9 PM to 7AM, and in country areas many close at 6 PM and all day on Sundays.

Car Rental   (*See also* Renting and Leasing Cars in Before You Go, above.) Providing you have a current driving license, you can rent a car with ease at most towns and cities. Costs will, of course, vary according to the size of the vehicle and the type of company you hire from, but on average, a medium-size sedan is around £500 per week (unlimited mileage) or around £50 per day plus mileage charge. These costs include insurance and temporary AA membership. If you use one of the major credit cards as security, a cash deposit isn't required and full payment for the rental (cash or credit) can be made at the end of the trip.

These are just a sample of the car rental agencies operating in Britain: **Avis Rent-a-Car,** (International Reservations, Trident House, Station Rd., Hayes, Middlesex UB3 4DJ, tel. 081/848-8733); **Europcar** (Bushey House, High St., Bushey, Watford, Herts WD2 1RE, tel. 081/950–4080). **Hertz Rent-a-Car** (Radnor House, 1272 London Rd., London SW16 4XW, tel. 081/679-1777). Reservations can also be made in conjunction with the BritRail Pass from the United States *(see* Rail Passes, above). **Kenning Car Hire** (Manor House, Old Rd., Chesterfield, Derbyshire S40 3QT, tel. 0246/208888). Reservations can also be made within the United States, tel. 800/227–8990.

Motorail   One way to combine the convenience of the car with the speed of the train is by **Motorail.** The car is put on a specially designed rail car while passengers relax in comfortable coaches or, in some cases, overnight sleeping compartments. Services exist between London (Euston) and Carlisle, Edinburgh, Fort William, Aberdeen, and Inverness; and between Bristol and Edinburgh. It costs around £380 for a round trip for a car with three passengers between London and Scotland, slightly more in the peak season. Book in advance through British Rail agencies.

By Boat   Most of the islands lying off the coast of Britain are served by regular car ferries, usually linked to train and coach services on the mainland. For shorter crossings, reservations are not needed, but you should reserve for the longer crossings to Ireland, the Isle of Man, and the Channel Islands. Details of most crossings will be found in either the *Thomas Cook European Timetable*, or in the British Rail timetables. For details of crossings to the Channel Islands, see Chapter 7.

Rivers and lakes in Britain are not big enough to maintain regular boat or waterbus systems, with one or two notable exceptions. The Scottish Highlands offer tourist services on Loch Lomond, Loch Etive, and Loch Katrine; details of rail tours using ferries and boat services can be obtained from **Chiltern Trains** (Box 10, Chinnor, Oxford OX9 4UJ, tel. 0844/52198). The Lake District also has regularly scheduled boat services from April until October on the larger lakes—Windermere, Coniston, Ullswater, and Dertwentwater. These services allow passengers to alight and return on foot along the shore or by a later boat.

Telephones

For years, both foreign visitors and the British themselves have cursed the country's inefficient and antiquated phone system. The recent privatization of British Telecom has brought little improvement. Making a phone call in Britain—especially from a public booth—can be a frustrating experience. However, changes are being slowly introduced and central equipment modernized.

Local Calls   Public telephones are plentiful in British cities, particularly London, although you may find many of them vandalized and broken. Other than on the street, the best place to find a bank of pay phones is in a rail station, hotel, or large post office. As part of BT's modernization efforts, the distinctive red boxes are gradually being replaced by generic glass and steel cubicles, but the red boxes remain in more remote areas of the country. The workings of coin-operated telephones vary, but there are usually instructions in each unit. The oldest kind takes only 10p coins; the new ones take 10p, 20p, 50p, and £1 coins. But the newest innovation is the Phonecard, which comes in denominations of 10, 20, 40, and 100 units of 10p each, and can be bought at a number of post offices and newsstands. Cardphones are clearly marked with a special green insignia, and they will not accept coins.

A short local call during the peak period (9 AM–1 PM) costs about 20p, or 2 units. Each large city or region in Britain has its own numerical prefix, which is used only when you are dialing from outside the city. In provincial areas, the dialing codes for nearby towns are often posted in the booth, and some even list international codes.

International Calls The cheapest way to make an overseas call is to dial it yourself, but be sure to have plenty of coins or Phonecards close at hand. After you have inserted the coins or card, dial 010 (the international code), then the country code—for the USA this is 1—followed by the area code and local number. To make a collect or other operator-assisted call, dial 155. *Be wary of making a call home from your hotel—the surcharge can be as much as 300%.*

Operators and Information For information anywhere in Britain, dial either 142 or 192. For the operator, dial 100.

Mail

Postal Rates Airmail letters to the United States and Canada cost 37p; postcards 31p; aerogrammes 32p. Letters and postcards to Europe not over 20 grams, 26p (20p to EC member countries). Letters within the UK, first class 22p, second class and postcards 19p. These rates will have increased by early 1992.

Receiving Mail If you're uncertain where you'll be staying, you can arrange to have your mail sent to American Express, 6 Haymarket, London SW1Y 4BS. The service is free to cardholders; all others pay a small fee. You can also collect letters at London's main post office. Ask to have them sent to Poste Restante, Main Post Office, London. The point of collection is King Edward Building, King Edward Street, London EC1A 1AA. Hours are Monday, Tuesday, Thursday, and Friday 8 AM–7 PM, Wednesday 8:30 AM–7 PM, and Saturday 9 AM–12:30 PM. You'll need your passport or other official form of identification.

Tipping

Some restaurants and most hotels add a service charge of 10%–15% to the bill. In this case you are not expected to tip. If no service charge is indicated, add 10% to your total bill, but always check first. Taxi drivers should also get 10%. You are not expected to tip theater or cinema ushers, elevator operators, or bartenders in pubs. Hairdressers and barbers should receive 10%–15%.

Opening and Closing Times

Banks Banks are open weekdays 9:30–3:30. Some have extended hours on Thursday evenings, and a few are open on Saturday mornings.

Shops Usual business hours are Monday–Saturday 9–5:30. Outside the main centers, most shops observe an early closing day once a week, often Wednesday or Thursday. They close at 1 PM and do not reopen until the following morning. In small villages, many also close for lunch. In large cities—especially London—department stores stay open for late-night shopping (usually until 7:30 or 8) one day a week. Apart from some newsstands and small food stores, almost all shops are closed on Sunday.

National Holidays **England and Wales:** January 1; April 17 (Good Friday); April 20 (Easter Monday); May 4 (May Day); May 25 (Spring Bank Holiday); August 31 (Summer Bank Holiday); December 25, 26. **Scotland:** January 1, 2; April 17; May 4; May 25; August 3; December 25, 26.

Museums, Stately Homes, and Castles

Opening Times Museum and gallery hours vary considerably from one part of the country to another. In large cities, most open weekdays 10–5; many are also open on Sunday afternoons. The majority close one day a week. Holiday closings vary, so be sure to check if you want to visit on a national holiday.

Most stately homes change their opening times at Easter and in October—or alternatively, when Britain changes its clocks for summer time. Many of them close down completely through the winter, usually from October to Easter, or to April 1, whichever is earlier. As they are dependent on local people for staff, opening and closing times can change at a moment's notice. If you are making a special trip to visit an isolated house, always phone first. Many stately homes close their doors half an hour before the stated time, to allow the last parties time to go 'round.

Admission fees Admission to museums is often free, though current economic pressures mean that some of them have started to charge. Stately homes are a different kettle of fish. If they are still in private hands, then their owners can survive only by charging entry fees. These have rocketed over the last few years together with the owner's expenses. Luckily, the great majority of stately homes and nearly all castles belong to either the **National Trust** or to **English Heritage.** If you are thinking of touring the country and visiting lots of castles or stately homes, you should seriously consider buying an annual membership in both organizations before you start out. It would represent a huge saving.

The National Trust **Royal Oak Membership** is available in the U.S. at $40 for individuals, $60 for families. Besides entry to all National Trust properties, this also covers thrice-yearly literature and admission to lectures and other events. Contact: Damaris Horan, Executive Director, Royal Oak Foundation (285 West Broadway, Suite 400, New York, NY 10013, tel. 212/966–6565). English Heritage annual membership has no U.S. version, but its U.K. one is £15 for an adult, £25 for two adults at the same address. Contact: English Heritage Membership Dept., Box 1BB, London W1A 1BB.

Many attractions now offer family tickets that cover two parents and two or three children. Though they look expensive, they represent a considerable reduction on the total cost of individual admissions.

Shopping

Throughout Britain, souvenir and gift shops abound. And don't be surprised if you see many of the same items in very different corners of the country. Certain regions do offer particular specialties, however. Both Wales and Scotland are famous for woolen products. Many towns offer retail outlets selling sweaters, tartans, tweeds, scarves, skirts, and hats at reasonable prices. Traditional Celtic jewelry is also popular. The Midlands offers world-renowned china and pottery, including Wedgwood, Royal Doulton, and Royal Worcester. The factory outlet shops are well worth a detour. The Southwest, especially Devon and Cornwall, is known for its scrumptious edibles—"scrumpy" (strong local cider), homemade toffees, rich fudge, and heavenly clotted cream. Museum and gallery shops all over the country offer high-quality posters, books, art prints, and crafts.

Little-known even to most Brits are the factory shops that sell directly to the public. They are especally popular in northern England, but exist all over the country. The saving can be as much as 50% on the normal store price. *Factory Shop Guides* are published by the authors, Gillian Cutress and Rolf Stricker (34 Park Hill, London SW4 9PB), and cost around £3.

VAT Refunds Foreign visitors need not pay Britain's 17.5% Value Added Tax (VAT) if they take advantage of the Personal Export Scheme. (Note that VAT is almost always included in market prices.) Of the various ways to get a VAT refund, the most common are Over the Counter and Direct Export. Most larger stores operate these services, but you must specifically request them. Their export departments deal with the paperwork.

The easiest and most usual way of getting your refund is the **Over the Counter** method, but to get it you must spend over £75 in one store. You must have identification—passports are best. Ask the store for Form VAT 407, to be given to Customs when you leave the country. Lines at major airports are usually long, so allow plenty of time. The refund will eventually be forwarded to you, minus a small service charge. You can have the refund credited to your charge card or in the form of a British check (American banks will tag on a conversion fee for cashing the check, however). Refunds take up to eight weeks to arrive.

The **Direct Export** method, where the goods go directly to your home, is more cumbersome. VAT Form 407 must be certified by Customs, police, or a notary public when you get home and then sent back to the store, which will refund your money.

In other EC countries the same rules apply, except in France, where refunds can be claimed on departure.

Sports and Outdoor Activities

Biking Avoid main roads. Bikes are banned from motorways and on most dual carriageways or main trunk roads. However, on side roads and the rich network of country lanes, the bike is supreme as a way of exploring Britain. You will find the Ordnance Survey 1:50,000 *Landranger* maps sold throughout Britain invaluable for planning routes along lightly used lanes and country roads.

Some parts of Britain have bicycle routes in towns and through parts of the countryside; for example, in the Peak District National Parks, bikes can be hired by the day for use on special traffic-free trails. Cyclists can legally use public bridleways—green, unsurfaced tracks reserved for horses, walkers, and cyclists.

If you're considering a cycling holiday in Britain, it is well worth joining the **Cyclists' Touring Club,** the national body in Britain that promotes the interests of cycle tourists (69 Meadrow, Godalming, Surrey GU7 3HS, tel. 0483/417217). Membership in the CTC is £20 a year (£10 for students and those under 21). Members receive free advice and information, including a detailed route planning service for any region of Britain, as well as a handbook of recommended bed-and-breakfast accommodations for cyclists, and a regular magazine, *Cycle Touring and Campaigning.* American and Canadian members are welcome.

Boating and Sailing If you feel like taking a boat yourself on the several hundred miles of historic canals and waterways through the British Isles, the **Association of Pleasure Craft Operators** (35a High St., Newport, Shropshire TF10 8JW, tel. 0952/813572) provides a complete list of all their boat-rental operators in Britain.

One of the best areas for boating in Britain is the Broads, in Norfolk, where the local tourist office can help you with up-to-date information on availability of boats and the state of local water pollution, which is a serious problem in those parts. You'll also find regular short river and canal cruises in the major tourist centers such as York, Bristol, Bath, and Stratford-on-Avon during the season.

Camping Britain offers an abundance of campsites. Some are large and well-equipped; others are merely farmers' fields, offering primitive facilities. For information, contact the British Tourist Authority in the United States, or the **Camping and Caravan Club, Ltd.** (11 Lower Grosvenor Pl., London SW1W OEY, tel. 071/828–1012).

Golf There are hundreds of fine courses all over the country, especially in Scotland, the birthplace of the sport. If you plan to play a great deal, a book you'll find useful is *The Golf Course Guide to Great Britain and Ireland* by Donald Steel, published by Collins at £7.95 and available from bookshops in Britain.

Hiking The British have a much gentler name for it—"rambling." The whole country is criss-crossed by meandering trails—there are over 100,000 miles of footpaths in England and Wales—some tiny and local, some very long and of historical importance, such as Peddar's Way in East Anglia, or the Pennine Way in Yorkshire. For £13 (£16.25 joint membership) you can join **The Ramblers Association** (1–5 Wandsworth Rd., London SW8 2XX, tel. 071/582–6878), which issues a magazine every two months and an annual yearbook with articles and over 2,000 bed-and-breakfast accommodations near rambling trails.

Tennis Tennis is a favorite recreation in Britain, and most towns have municipal courts where you can play for a small fee. Country hotels, too, are well-equipped to offer their guests a chance for a game. The hotel service information in each chapter lists tennis availability.

Water Sports Britain is brimming with rivers and lakes, and it is possible to swim and fish on many of them. The only drawback is that pollution is a major problem here, as elsewhere in the world, so check carefully before venturing into any river or stream. The other problem is that the water can often be icy cold!

Most local authorities operate indoor pools, and a few have outdoor ones; entrance fees are minimal. Nearly all large hotels now have pools, as indicated in the hotel entries.

Britain's beaches are variable. In some areas, like Cornwall and the coast of Wales, there are excellent sandy beaches with good swimming. Much of the coast is fringed with pebbled beaches; while no bar to swimming in itself, they don't make for the most pleasant sunbathing or walking. Apart from Cornwall and the southwest generally, the sea around Britain can be very cold most of the year. Pollution, too, is a problem, just as it is on inland waterways. Check the status of any beach before swimming. Many seaside towns have windsurfing boards available.

Dining

Until relatively recently, British food had been condemned the world over for its plainness and mediocrity, but an influx of foreign restaurants and the birth of the New British Cuisine have had a noticeable effect on the quality of the nation's food. It is now possible to eat interesting food all over the country, if you don't mind paying dearly for it.

Mealtimes These vary somewhat depending on the region of the country you are visiting, but in general, breakfast is served between 7:30 and 9, and lunch between 12 and 2. Tea—an essential and respected part of British tradition, and often a meal in itself—is generally served between 4:30 and 5:30. Dinner or supper is served between 7:30 and 9:30, sometimes earlier. You are likely to find dinner served later than 9:30 only in restaurants in the larger cities that cater to after-theater diners. High tea, at about 6, replaces dinner in some areas.

Lodging

Britain offers a wide range of accommodations, from enormous, top-quality, top-price hotels to simple, intimate farm and guest houses.

Hotels British hotels vary greatly, and while the Tourist Board has a system of grading—by "crowns" instead of stars—it is not yet either widely used or particularly helpful. Most hotels have rooms with private bathrooms, although there are still some—usually older hotels—that offer rooms with only washbasins; in this case, showers and bathtubs (and toilets) are usually just down the hall. Many also have "good" and "bad" wings. Be sure to check before you take the room. Generally, British hotel prices include breakfast, but beware: many offer only a Continental breakfast—often little more than tea or coffee and toast. A hotel that includes a traditional English breakfast in its rates is usually a good bet. Hotel prices in London are significantly higher than in the rest of the country, and often the quality and service are not as good. Tourist information centers all over the country will reserve rooms for you, usually for a small fee. A great many hotels offer special weekend and off-season bargain packages.

Bed-and-Breakfasts These small, simple establishments are a special British tradition, and the backbone of budget travel. They offer modest, inexpensive accommodations, usually in a family home. Few have private bathrooms, and most offer only breakfast. Guest houses are a slightly larger, somewhat more luxurious, version. Both provide the visitor with an excellent glimpse of everyday British life that's seldom seen in large city hotels.

Farmhouses Such accommodations have become increasingly popular in recent years. Farmhouses do not offer top hotel standards, but have a special appeal: the rustic, rural experience. Only consider this option if you are touring by car. Prices are generally very reasonable. Ask for the British Tourist Authority booklet *Farmhouse Vacations*.

Holiday Cottages Furnished apartments, houses, cottages, and trailers are available for weekly rental in all areas of the country. These vary from quaint, cleverly converted farmhouses to brand-new buildings set in scenic surroundings. For families and large groups, they offer the best value-for-money accommodations, but as they are often in isolated locations, a car is vital. Lists of rental properties are available free of charge from the **British Tourist Authority.** Discounts of up to 50% apply during the off-season (October to March).

Stately Homes It is possible to stay as a paying guest in a number of the famous stately homes scattered throughout the countryside. Styles range from Jacobean castles and manors to Regency houses. The equally stately prices usually include both meals and lodging. Reservations are essential. For details, contact the **British Travel Centre** (tel. 071/730–3400) or write to the **British Tourist Authority** (Thames Tower, Blacks Rd., London W6 9EL).

University Housing In larger cities and in some towns, certain universities offer their residence halls to paying vacationers out of term time. The facilities available are usually compact single sleeping units, and they can be rented on a nightly basis. For information, contact the **British Universities Accommodation Consortium,** Box 486, University Park, Nottingham NG7 2RD, tel. 0602/504571.

Youth Hostels There are more than 350 youth hostels throughout England, Wales, and Scotland. They range from very basic to almost luxurious. Many are located in remote and beautiful areas; others can be found on the outskirts of large cities. Despite the name, there is no age restriction. The accommodations are inexpensive and generally reliable, and usually include cooking facilities. For further information, contact the **YHA Headquarters,** Trevelyan House, 8 St. Stephens's Hill, St. Albans, Hertfordshire AL1 2DY, tel. 0727/55215.

Great Itineraries

Writers at Home: Southwest England

All of Britain contains a wealth of fictional and real literary figures and places; there are several literary walking tours of London alone. For those who like to venture out on their own and explore more than just isolated plaques commemorating who slept (or was born or died) where, the following excursion takes in some lovely settings as well as enough artistic associations to keep any literature buff happy.

Length of Trip   4 days

Getting Around   By Car. 220 miles round-trip from London (southwest).

By Public Transportation. Trains and buses depart regularly from London to Dorchester and Bath. Local bus and train services are available once you are within the region, but plan carefully to avoid time-consuming waits for the right service.

Two days: Hardy's Wessex

The environs of Dorchester are the place to begin any exploration of Hardy country. The early years of his life were spent in **Higher Brockhampton** (2 mi west of Dorchester on A31), part of the parish of Stinsford, which appears in his writings as "Mellstock." It is best to leave at least a day to visit Sherborne, Cranborne, and Bridport, and to travel to Lullworth Cove, to get a true sense of the countryside that inspired so much of his work. All of these are within 25 miles of Dorchester.

This excursion can also include Salisbury and Stonehenge, which figure prominently in *Jude the Obscure* and *Tess of the D'Urbervilles*, respectively. They can be reached by traveling northwest for 30 miles on A31/A350/A30.

Two days: The Homes of Jane Austen

From rural delights we head for the civilized society of Jane Austen's world and novels. *Persuasion* and *Northanger Abbey* are especially associated with the city of **Bath** (105 mi west of London on A4). She visited Bath frequently in her youth, and lived here between the ages of 26 and 31 (1801–1806).

In 1809 Austen moved with her mother and sister Cassandra to **Chawton,** 50 miles south and 30 miles east of Bath on A36/A31, back through Salisbury and across Wiltshire. You will also pass through Southampton, where she lived for three years, although all records of precisely where have been lost. She lived in Chawton until 1817, and her home there is now a museum. In the last year of her life she moved to lodgings in **Winchester,** 10 miles south on A31. She lived here at 8 College Street, and she is buried at Winchester Cathedral.

Further Information   *See* South; Heart of England.

Aristocratic Houses of West Yorkshire and Derbyshire

Set between the industrial cities of England's east Midlands and Yorkshire are some of the finest mansions (and their accompanying grounds) in the country. Many are within easy reach of one another, making a few days' manor-house spotting simple as well as enjoyable. These two outings are based from York and Nottingham, but you can just as easily start out from a base in Derby, Leeds, or Sheffield.

Length of Trip   4 to 5 days

Getting Around   By Car. 60 miles round-trip from York; 80 miles round-trip from Nottingham.

Two days: Stately Houses in West Yorkshire

There are three houses to visit on this itinerary, which covers an ellipse-shaped area southeast of York. The first stop is **Harewood House,** home of the earl and countess of Harewood and designed in 1759 with grounds landscaped by Capability Brown. It is located on A64/A659 25 miles west of York. **Oakwell Hall,** 12 miles south through Leeds, is an Elizabethan manor house complete with moat. **Lotherton Hall,** east on M62 and north on A642, is a country house museum, with an Edwardian garden, bird garden, and deer park.

Two to three days: Stately Houses in Derbyshire

From Nottingham, follow A453/B587 to Melbourne, and **Melbourne Hall.** Ten miles northwest via the road to Derby and A52 brings you to **Kedleston Hall,** a magnificent mansion designed by the Adam brothers. Heading due north for 20 miles you will reach **Haddon Hall,** and 3 miles farther, to **Chatsworth.** The first is medieval; the second dates from the 17th century. Finally, turning back toward Nottingham for 10 miles on A617, you will come to **Hardwick Hall,** built in 1597.

Further Information *See* chapter 13, Peaks and Yorkshire Moors, for more details about this area.

The Whisky Distilleries of Scotland

Most of Scotland's whisky distilleries are located in the Grampian region, east and south of Inverness along the banks of the Rivers Spey, Fiddich, Isla, and Livet. This excursion begins in Rothes, 50 miles southeast of Inverness on A96/A941, and covers all the major distilleries along the Scottish Tourist Board's "Whisky Trail", which is signposted along the way. This itinerary also includes two distilleries, The Glenlivet and Glen Grant, which are not part of the official trail. Even if you are a teetotaler, the region offers much natural beauty, with rolling green hills and sparkling streams.

Length of Trip 1 to 2 days

Getting Around **By Car.** 65 miles round-trip from Rothes.

By Public Transportation. British Rail goes from Keith to Dufftown, but for most of the journey you must rely on local buses. Call ahead or try to get the appropriate bus schedules at the Inverness tourist office.

Day one: Rothes to Dufftown via Keith

Rothes itself, located on an estuary of the River Spey, is the home of the **Glen Grant** distillery. From here a 10-mile trip east on B9105/B9103/A95 takes you to Keith and the 18th-century **Strathisla** distillery (so named because it is set on the river Isla). Eight miles southwest on B9104 is the **Glenfiddich** distillery, located in Dufftown.

Day two: Tomintoul and back north to Rothes

Setting out from Dufftown southwest on B9009/B9008, after 15 miles you reach **Tomintoul,** near Milton. Tomintoul is also the name of the distillery and the whisky. Now head back north 8 miles on A939/B9136 to **Smith's** distillery, founded in 1823 and the home of Scotland's most famous malt whisky, **Glenlivet.** If you have time to visit only one distillery, make it the Glenlivet. Continuing north on B9008/A95 and B/9012 brings you to Knockando, 8 miles from Glenlivet along the River Spey, and where you will find the **Tamdhu** distillery. From here it is an easy journey back to Rothes east on B9102 and north on A941, and so back to Inverness.

Further Information *See* chapter 16, Scotland—Southwest and Highlands, for more details about this area.

The Best of Roman Britain

The Romans occupied much of Britain from the Cornish coast up into Scotland. Ruins dot the landscape, and a few of Britain's major highways (as well as many minor ones) overlay original Roman roads. The following two journeys present some highlights, but we also urge that if archaeology or a study of Roman times is your passion you can find impressive evidence of the Roman occupation almost anywhere in the country. The first excursion covers parts of western Britain not far north of London, an area that seems to have been particularly prosperous in Roman times; the second takes us north to explore that feat of engineering, Hadrian's Wall.

Length of Trip 4 to 5 days

Getting Around **By Car.** 150 miles round-trip from London (St. Albans and westward); 150 miles round-trip from Newcastle (Hadrian's Wall).

By Public Transportation. This might prove a bit difficult, although there is train and bus service to the major cities covered, as well as to the smaller sites if you are willing to put up with possible delays. The British Tourist Association may be able to help, as they sometimes offer organized tours covering these regions.

Two to three days: St. Albans and Westward

This excursion begins in **St. Albans** (known in Roman times as Verulamium), 20 miles northwest of London on A1, and continues due west to the Roman "villas" of **North Leigh, Chedworth,** and **Gloucester** before heading back south through **Cirencester** to **Bath.** Along the way you will see some fantastic artifacts, tombs, forts, and amphitheaters, as well as the world-famous baths in, naturally, Bath. You may want to do some research beforehand (or even afterwards) in London's **British Museum,** where you will discover a wealth of archaeological finds.

One to two days: Hadrian's Wall

Following the 72-mile long wall, built AD 122–126, from east to west, this journey offers several museum stopping points along the way, the first in **Newcastle-upon-Tyne** and continuing through **Corbridge, Chester, Chesterholm,** and on to **Carlisle** (a city which celebrated its 1,000th anniversary this year).

Further Information *See* London; South; Heart of England; and Peaks and Yorkshire Moors.

Castles and Strongholds

This itinerary, based in northeastern Kent, offers a quick history of castle architecture, and the opportunity to visit some of the best examples Britain has to offer.

Length of Trip 2 to 3 days

Getting Around   **By Car.** 150 miles round-trip from London.

By Public Transportation. Check with British Rail information centers and National Express or other bus companies for full information.

Heading southeast from London on A2/A257 for Sandwich brings you to **Richborough Castle,** an original Saxon fort built in the 4th century. From here take A258 to Deal, where you will find both **Deal Castle,** dating from 1540, and **Walmer Castle,** another Renaissance fortification, converted in the 18th century. Next comes **Dover Castle,** one of England's most impressive, which was still in military use as late as World War II. South down the coast is the town of Hythe and **Lympne Castle,** a 14th-to 15th-century building with a 13th-century Norman east tower. Leaving the best for last, M20 northwest will take you to **Leeds Castle,** a magnificent Norman fortress with 19th-century additions, set on two islands in a lake and surrounded by lovely landscaped park (*see* Tour 4 in Chapter 4 for further information).

2 Portraits of Great Britain

Great Britain at a Glance: A Chronology

2800 BC First building of Stonehenge (later building 2100–1900)

54 BC Julius Caesar's exploratory invasion of England

AD 43 Romans conquer England, led by Emperor Claudius

60 Boudicca, a native British queen, razes the first Roman London (Londinium) to the ground

122–27 Emperor Hadrian completes the Roman conquest and builds a wall across the north to keep back the Scottish Picts

145 The Antonine Wall built, north of Hadrian's, running from the Firth of Forth to the Firth of Clyde

300–50 Height of Roman colonization, administered from such towns as Verulamium (St. Albans), Colchester, Lincoln, and York

383–410 Romans begin to withdraw from Britain; waves of Germanic invaders—Jutes, Angles, and Saxons

c.490 Possible period for the legendary King Arthur, who may have led resistance to Anglo-Saxon invaders; 500 Battle of Badon

563 St. Columba, an Irish monk, founds monastery on the Scottish island of Iona; begins to convert Picts and Scots to Christianity

597 St. Augustine arrives in Canterbury to Christianize Britain

550–700 Seven Anglo-Saxon kingdoms emerge—Essex, Wessex, Sussex, Kent, Anglia, Mercia, and Northumbria—to become the core of English social and political organization for centuries

731 Bede completes the *Ecclesiastical History*

800s Danish Viking raids solidify into widespread colonization

871–99 Alfred the Great, king of Wessex, unifies the English against Viking invaders, who are then confined to the northeast

919–54 Shortlived Norse kingdom of York

1040 Edward the Confessor moves his court to Westminster and founds Westminster Abbey

1066 William, duke of Normandy, invades; defeats Harold at the Battle of Hastings; is crowned at Westminster in December

1086 Domesday Book completed, a survey of all taxpayers in England, drawn up to assist administration of the new realm

1167 Oxford University founded

1170 Thomas à Becket murdered in Canterbury; his shrine becomes center for international pilgrimage

1189 Richard the Lionheart embarks on the Third Crusade

1209 Cambridge University founded

1215 King John forced to sign Magna Carta at Runnymede; it promulgates basic principles of English law: no taxation except through Parliament, trial by jury, and property guarantees

1272–1307	Edward I, a great legislator; 1282–83 conquers Wales and reinforces his rule with a chain of massive castles
1295	The Model Parliament sets future parliamentary pattern, with membership of knights from the shires, lower clergy, and civic representatives
1296	Edward I invades Scotland

1314	Robert the Bruce routs the English at Bannockburn
1337–1453	Edward III claims the French throne, starting the Hundred Years War. In spite of dramatic English victories—1346 Crecy, 1356 Poitiers, 1415 Agincourt—the long war of attrition ends with the French driving the English out from all but Calais, which finally fell in 1558
1348–49	The Black Death (bubonic plague) reduces the population of Britain to around 2½ million; decades of social unrest follow
1381	The Peasants Revolt is defused by the 14-year-old Richard II
1399	Henry Bolingbroke (Henry IV) deposes and murders his cousin Richard II; beginning of the rivalry between houses of York and Lancaster

1402–10	The Welsh, led by Owen Glendower, rebel against English rule
1455–85	The Wars of the Roses—the York/Lancaster struggle erupts in civil war
1477	William Caxton prints first book in England
1485	Henry Tudor (Henry VII) defeats Richard III at the Battle of Bosworth, and founds the Tudor dynasty; he suppresses private armies, develops administrative efficiency and royal absolutism

1530s	Under Henry VIII the Reformation takes hold; he dissolves the monasteries, finally demolishes medieval England and replaces it with a new society Henry's marital history—1534 he divorces Katherine of Aragon after 25 years of marriage; 1536 Anne Boleyn (mother of Elizabeth I) executed in the Tower of London; 1537 Jane Seymour dies giving birth to Edward VI; 1540 Henry marries Anne of Cleves (divorced same year); 1542 Katherine Howard executed in the Tower; 1542 he marries Katherine Parr, who outlives him
1554	Mary I marries Philip II of Spain; tries to restore Catholicism to England
1555	Protestant Bishops Ridley and Latimer burned in Oxford; 1556 Archbishop Cranmer burned
1558–1603	Reign of Elizabeth I—Protestantism re-established; Drake, Raleigh, and other freebooters establish English claims in the West Indies and North America
1568	Mary, Queen of Scots, flees to England; 1587 executed
1588	Spanish Armada fails to invade England

1603	James VI of Scotland becomes James I of England

1605	Guy Fawkes and friends in Catholic plot to blow up Parliament
1611	King James Authorized Version of the Bible published
1620	Pilgrims sail from Plymouth on the *Mayflower* and settle in New England
1629	Charles I dissolves Parliament, decides to rule alone
1642–49	Civil War between the Royalists and Parliamentarians (Cavaliers and Roundheads); the Parliamentarians win
1649	Charles I executed; England is a republic
1653	Cromwell becomes Lord Protector, England's only dictatorship
1660	Charles II restored to the throne; accepts limits to royal power
1665	The Great Fire of London, accession of William III (of Orange) and his wife Mary II as joint monarchs; royal power limited still further
1694	Bank of England founded
1706–09	Marlborough's victories over the French under Louis XIV
1707	The Act of Union: England, Scotland, and Wales join in the United Kingdom of Great Britain (as against the countries being united in the person of the king)
1714	The German Hanoverians succeed to the throne; George I's lack of English leads to a council of ministers, the beginning of the Cabinet system of government
1700s	Under the first four Georges, the Industrial Revolution develops and with it Britain's domination of world trade
1715/1745	Two Jacobite rebellions fail to restore the House of Stuart to the throne; 1746 final defeat takes place at Culloden Moor
1756–63	Seven Years War; Britain wins colonial supremacy from the French in Canada and India
1775–83	Britain loses her American colonies
1795–1815	Britain and her allies defeat French in the Napoleonic Wars; 1805 Nelson killed at Trafalgar; 1815 Battle of Waterloo
1801	Union with Ireland
1811–20	Prince Regent rules during his father's (George III) madness—the Regency period
1825	The Stockton to Darlington railway, the world's first passenger line with regular service
1832	The Reform Bill extends the franchise, limiting the power of the great landowners
1834	Parliament outlaws slavery
1837–1901	The long reign of Victoria—Britain becomes the world's richest country, and the British Empire reaches its height; railways, canals, and telegraph lines draw Britain into one vast manufacturing net
1851	The Great Exhibition, Prince Albert's brainchild, is held in Crystal Palace, Hyde Park

1861 Prince Albert dies

1887 Victoria celebrates her Golden Jubilee; 1901 she dies, marking the end of an era

---

1911–12 Rail, mining, and coal strikes

1914–18 World War I: Fighting against Germany, Britain loses a whole generation, with 750,000 men killed in trench warfare alone; enormous debts and inept diplomacy in the postwar years undermine Britain's position as a world power

1919 Ireland declares independence from England; bloody Black-and-Tan struggle results

1926 General Strike in sympathy with striking coal miners

1936 Edward VIII abdicates to marry American divorcee, Mrs. Wallis Simpson

1939–45 World War II—Britain faces Hitler alone until Pearl Harbor; London badly damaged during the Blitz, September '40–May '41; Britain's economy shattered by the war

1945 Labour wins a landslide victory; stays in power for six years, transforming Britain into a welfare state

1952 Queen Elizabeth accedes to the throne

1969 Serious violence breaks out in Northern Ireland

1972 National miners' strike

1973 Britain joins the European Economic Community after referendum

1975 Britain begins to pump North Sea oil

1981 Marriage of Prince Charles and Lady Diana Spencer

1982 Falklands regained

1987 Conservatives under Margaret Thatcher win a third term in office

1990 Glasgow is European Cultural Capital for the year

1990 John Major takes over as primes minister, ending Margaret Thatcher's illustrious, if controversial, career in office

1991 The Persian Gulf War

1992 Great Britain and the European countries join to form one European Community (EC)

Kings and Queens

To help you sort out Britain's monarchs, we give here a list of
those who have sat on the throne (before 1603 the throne of England, after that the joint throne of England, Scotland, and
Wales). The dates are those of the reign, not of the monarch's
life.

	1042–66	Edward the Confessor
	1066	Harold
House of Normandy	1066–87	William I—The Conqueror
	1087–1100	William II—Rufus (murdered)
	1100–35	Henry I
	1135–54	Stephen
House of Plantagenet	1154–89	Henry II
	1189–99	Richard I—Lionheart (killed in battle)
	1199–1216	John
	1216–72	Henry III
	1272–1307	Edward I
	1307–27	Edward II (murdered)
	1327–77	Edward III
	1377–99	Richard II (deposed, then murdered)
	1399–1413	Henry IV
	1413–22	Henry V
	1422–61	Henry VI (deposed)
House of York	1461–83	Edward IV
	1483	Edward V (probably murdered)
	1483–85	Richard III (killed in battle)
House of Tudor	1485–1509	Henry VII
	1509–47	Henry VIII
	1547–53	Edward VI
	1553	Jane (beheaded)
	1553–58	Mary I
	1558–1603	Elizabeth I
House of Stuart	1603–25	James I (VI of Scotland)
	1625–49	Charles I (beheaded)
Commonwealth	1653–58	Oliver Cromwell (Protector)
	1658–59	Richard Cromwell
House of Stuart (Restored)	1660–85	Charles II
	1685–88	James II (deposed and exiled)
	1689–95	William III and Mary II (joint monarchs)
	1695–1702	William III (reigned alone)
	1702–14	Anne
House of Hanover	1714–27	George I
	1727–60	George II
	1760–1820	George III
	1820–30	George IV (Regent from 1811)
	1830–37	William IV
House of Saxe-Coburg	1837–1901	Victoria
	1901–10	Edward VII
House of Windsor	1910–36	George V

1936	Edward VIII (abdicated)
1936–52	George VI
1952–	Elizabeth II

The Basics of British Architecture

In Britain, you can see structures that go back to the dawn of history, in the hauntingly mysterious circles of monoliths at Stonehenge or Avebury, for example; or the resurrected remains of Roman empire builders preserved in towns such as St. Albans or Cirencester. On the other hand, you can startle your eyes with the very current, very controversial designs of contemporary architects in new developments, including London's Docklands area. Appreciating the wealth of Britain's architectural heritage does not require a degree in art history, but knowing a few hallmarks of various styles can enhance your enjoyment of what you see. Here, then, is a primer of nearly a millennium of various architectural styles.

Norman The solid Norman style, ideal for castle building, arrived in England slightly before the Conquest, with the building of Westminster Abbey in 1040. From 1066 to around 1200, it was clearly the style of choice for buildings of any importance. Norman towers tended to be hefty and square, arches always round-topped, and the vaulting barrel-shaped. Decoration was mostly geometrical, but within those limits, ornate. *Best seen in the Tower of London, St. Bartholomew's and Temple Churches, London; and in the cathedrals of St. Albans, Ely, Gloucester, Durham, and Norwich, and at Tewkesbury Abbey.*

Gothic Early English From 1130–1300, pointed arches began to supplant the rounded ones, buttresses became heavier than the Norman variety, and the windows lost their rounded tops to become "lancet" shaped. Buildings climbed skyward, less squat and heavy, with the soaring effect accentuated by steep roofs and spires. *Best seen in the cathedrals of York, Salisbury, Ely, Worcester, Canterbury (east end), and Westminster Abbey's chapter house.*

Decorated From the late 1100s until around 1400, elegance and ornament became fully integrated into architectural design, rather than applied on to the surface of a solid basic form. Windows filled more of the walls and were divided into sections by carved mullions. Vaulting grew increasingly complex, with ribs and ornamented bosses proliferating; spires became even pointier; arches took on the "ogee" shape, with its unique double curve. This style was one of England's greatest gifts to world architecture. *Best seen at the cathedrals of Wells, Lincoln, Durham (east transept), and Ely (Lady Chapel and Octagon).*

Perpendicular In later Gothic architecture, the emphasis on the vertical grew even more pronounced, featuring slender pillars, huge expanses of glass, and superb fan vaulting resembling frozen winter trees. Walls were divided by panels. One of the chief areas in which to see Perpendicular architecture is East Anglia, where the rich wool towns built magnificent churches in the new style. Houses, too, began to reflect prevailing taste. Perpendicular Gothic lasted for well over two centuries from its advent in around 1330. *Best seen at St. George's Chapel, Windsor; the cathedrals of Gloucester (cloister), and Hereford (chapter house); Henry VII's Chapel, Westminster Abbey; and King's College Chapel, Cambridge.*

Tudor With the great period of cathedral building over, from 1500 to 1560 the nation's attention turned to the construction of spacious homes, characterized by this new architectural style. The rapidly expanding *nouveau riche* class—created by the first two Tudor Henrys (VII and VIII) to challenge the power of the aristocracy—built spacious manor houses, often on the foundations of pillaged monasteries, thus beginning the era of the great stately homes. Brick replaced stone as the most popular medium, with plasterwork and carved wood to carry the elaborate motifs of the age. *Best seen at Hampton Court and St. James's Palace (London).*

Renaissance Elizabethan For a short period under Elizabeth I, 1560–1600, this development of Tudor flourished as Italian influences began to seep into England, seen especially in symmetrical facades. The most notable example was Hardwick Hall in Derbyshire, built in the 1590s by Bess of Hardwick—the jingle that describes it goes "Hardwick Hall, more glass than wall." *Other great Elizabethan houses are Montacute, Somerset; Longleat, Wiltshire; and Burghley House, Cambridgeshire.*

Jacobean The first great modern British architect, Inigo Jones, (1573–1652), synthesized the past of England with the current Italian theories. Two of his finest remaining buildings—the Banqueting Hall, Whitehall, and the Queen's House at Greenwich—epitomize his genius, which was to introduce the Palladian style that dominated British architecture for centuries. It uses the classical Greek orders—Doric, Ionic, and Corinthian. The general run of Jacobean architecture, however, was Elizabethan writ large, with more elaborate decoration and magnificently spacious buildings. There were, in fact, two styles running together for a couple of decades: the classical severity of Inigo Jones, and the ornate but comfortable everyday style. *Jacobean is best seen at the Bodleian Library, Oxford; Hatfield House, Herefordshire; Audley End, Essex; and Clare College, Cambridge.*

Wren Sir Christopher Wren's work constituted an era all by itself. Not only was he naturally one of the world's greatest architects, but he was given an unparalleled opportunity when the disastrous Great Fire of London in 1666 wiped out the center of the capital, destroying no less than 89 churches and 13,200 houses. Although Wren's great scheme for a totally new city center was rejected, he did build 51 churches, the greatest of which was St. Paul's, completed in just 35 years. The range of Wren's designs is extremely wide, from simple classical shapes to the extravagantly dramatic baroque. He was also at home with domestic architecture, where his combinations of brick and stone produced a warm, homey effect. *Wren's ecclesiastical architecture is best seen at St. Paul's Cathedral and the other remaining city churches, his domestic style at Hampton Court Palace, Kensington Palace, and the Royal Hospital in Chelsea.*

Palladian This style is often referred to as Georgian, so-called from the Hanoverian kings George I through IV, although it was introduced as early as Inigo Jones. Its designs were classically inspired, by way of the Italian architectural theorist Palladio, with pillared porticoes, triangular pediments, and strictly balanced windows. In domestic architecture, this large-scale classicism was usually modified to quiet simplicity, preserving mathematical proportions of windows, doors, and the exactly calculated volume of room space, to create a feeling of balance and harmony. There were some outrageous departures from the classical manner at this time, most notably with the Brighton Pavilion, built for the Prince Regent (later George IV). The Regency style comes under the Palladian heading, though strictly speaking it lasted only for the few years of the actual Regency. In Britain, the Palladian style was handled with more freedom than elsewhere in Europe, and America took its cue from the British architects. *Among the best Palladian examples are Regent's Park Terraces (London); the library at Kenwood (London); Royal Crescent and other streets in Bath; Holkham Hall, Blenheim Palace, and Castle Howard.*

Victorian Elements of imaginative fantasy, already seen in the Palladian era, came to the fore during the long reign of Victoria. The country's vast profits made from the Industrial Revolution were spent lavishly. Civic building accelerated in all the major cities with town halls modeled after medieval castles or French châteaus. The Victorians plundered the past for styles, with Gothic—about which the scholarly Victorians were very knowledgeable—leading the field. The supreme example here is the Houses of Parliament in London. (To distinguish between the Victorian variety and an earlier version, which flourished in the late 1700s, the earlier one is commonly spelled "Gothick.") But there were many other styles in the running, including the attractively named—and self-explanatory—"Wrenaissance." *Among the most striking examples are Truro Cathedral, the Albert Memorial (London), Manchester Town Hall, the Foreign Office (London), Ironbridge, and Cragside (Northumberland).*

Edwardian Toward the end of the Victorian era, in the late 1800s, architecture calmed down considerably, with a return to a solid sort of classicism, and to even a muted baroque. The Arts and Crafts movement, especially the work and inspiration of William Morris, produced simpler designs, returning often to medieval models. *Best seen in Buckingham Palace and the Admiralty Arch in London.*

Modern Britain is a strongly traditionalist country when it comes to building. Public opinion is often loud in its resentment of the work of many modern architects, which have been denounced as ephemeral, willful, and ugly; Prince Charles won fans by remarking that a design for a new addition to the National Gallery in Trafalgar Square was like a carbuncle on a much-loved face. One reason for this strength of feeling is that Britain suffered some grossly ill-conceived development after World War II, when there was a pressing need for housing and large areas of cities had to be rebuilt after destruction by German bombs. Matters seem to be improving in the 1980s, however; Britain may be a long way from the United States in architectural achievement—but it does have some interesting things to offer. *Among the new buildings to see are the Lloyd's Tower, some of the Docklands development, Richmond House (79 Whitehall), and the Clore Building at the Tate Gallery (all in London); the campus of Sussex University (outside Brighton), the Royal Regatta Building (Henley), the Sainsbury Centre (Norwich), the Burrell Collection (Glasgow).*

The Performing Arts

by John Elsom

John Elsom is President of the International Association of Theater Critics, and a professor at the City University, London.

Britain may be a comparatively small country, but its arts are as varied as its scenery. Although London's West End theater is justly admired, it only tells the beginning of the performing arts tale.

During the 1960s and early 1970s, for example, British regional repertory theaters grabbed a great deal of the attention. Some of them had already been in existence for fifty years and more—those in Birmingham, Sheffield, Liverpool, and Stratford-upon-Avon—without seriously rivaling London's West End or the commercial touring theaters offering musicals "direct from Drury Lane." Partly as the result of public subsidies through the government-funded Arts Council, partly because of a new involvement by local authorities, but mainly because of a determination among artists to break what they regarded as London's "tyranny of taste," the British repertory movement suddenly began to thrive. Splendid new theaters were built around the country, many with experimental studios attached, and with repertoires which ranged from impressive classical productions to the avant-garde.

This transformation of British theatrical life took place within about five years, from 1965 to 1970. At that time, I was a talent scout for Paramount Pictures, and I can vividly remember the change which it brought about in my working habits. In 1965, my reviewing was confined, with the exception of the Edinburgh Festival, to London, but in 1966, I started regularly to visit the repertory theaters in Nottingham, Bristol, Windsor, and Chichester; and in the following year, other theaters were added to the list, until by the end of the 1960s, I had to drive hundreds of miles a week to see productions all over Britain, for it was no longer safe for a critic who wanted to know what was happening to linger in London.

The oil crisis of 1973, with other factors, slowed down the boom in building repertory theaters, and caused problems for those less well established. Others, however, continued to flourish. In Scotland, for example, the Glasgow Citizens Theatre, once an Edwardian music hall (vaudeville) in the heart of the slums of the Gorbals, now has one of the most exciting companies in Europe, renowned for its spectacular sets (designed by Philip Prowse), its adventurous repertoire which includes European classics freely and sometimes outrageously adapted, and its flashing acting style. In the highlands, the Pitlochry summer theater offers "seven plays in seven days"; while in Perth, Joan Knight has built up a charming local theater in the shell of a Victorian touring theater.

In England, the new repertory theaters are often impressive pieces of civic architecture. The Birmingham Rep's modern building dominates the city center with its great glass wall—a feature which, like the new theaters in Sheffield, Derby, Nottingham, and Leicester, dramatically expresses the role that the arts were intended to play in their redeveloped cities. Coventry, badly damaged by bombing during the war, was rebuilt during the 1950s with a new cathedral, a new shopping center, and a new theater as the three priorities in its plans. In contrast, the Festival Theatre in Chichester, built by private subscription in 1960–61, is set in a charming park just outside the town. The Bristol Old Vic has a modern theatrical development which surrounds a delightful Georgian auditorium, lovingly preserved; while in Manchester, there is an even more startling blend of old and new. Within the magnificent early Victorian stock exchange, built in 1845–49, a space-capsule theater-in-the-round was constructed, like a giant metallic spider trapped in an ornate teapot, and called the Royal Exchange Theatre. Many smaller country towns, such as Colchester, Guildford, Salisbury, and Ipswich, built modern theaters during the 1960s, restoring a Regency pride-of-place to the arts and reversing the century-long drift toward metropolitan centers.

Many of these new theaters have developed their own national, and international, reputations. The Haymarket in Leicester is renowned for its musicals, many of which have transferred to London. Toby Robertson, currently the artistic director at Mold in North Wales, assembles brilliant casts for stately classical revivals, some of which travel down south to London's Haymarket and Shaftesbury Avenue theaters. In Scarborough, a seaside town in Yorkshire, the dramatist-director Alan Ayckbourn has for many years run the Stephen Joseph Theatre, where he tries out his new plays which afterwards travel to London. The Chichester productions regularly transfer, as do those from Birmingham and Sheffield.

But the true strength of these repertory theaters is to be measured not by the hits that go to London and New York, but by the almost tangible enthusiasm that they manage to generate in their home towns. The reverse, unhappily, is also the case, and some repertory theaters, famous in the 1960s, have been reduced to providing mediocre productions to dwindling audiences, and in some cases have closed altogether. There was, however, a different kind of "revival" in the late 1970s, due to an economic crunch that came about, perhaps, as a kind of by-product of Thatcherism.

During the 1960s, it was assumed that theaters could never be run commercially, except in London, and particularly that the old Victorian and Edwardian touring theaters in the regions were useless white elephants. But, by the '70s, it was realized that these old commercial theaters had, in fact, been very carefully designed to provide marvelous settings for plays and musicals with the capacity to entertain large audiences. They were, quite simply, more cost-effective than most modern theaters, with the result that local entrepreneurs took them over, renovated them and started tentative experiments to make regional show business profitable once more. The results in Nottingham, Manchester, and Bath were very impressive: one pantomime at the Palace, Manchester, raised £750,000 in box office receipts alone during a 6-week season. At the Theatre Royal, Norwich, the manager and artistic director, Richard Condon, boasted that he had never received a penny in subsidies, a claim which can be challenged, but the point is that the strength of British regional theater does not derive from public funding alone.

The *British Theatre Directory*, an indispensable guide, lists no less than 378 theaters and 203 performing arts centers outside London, of which only about 60 receive direct Arts Council subsidies. Not all these theaters, it is true, offer continuous programs. Many are seasonal theaters; some seem to change managements every six months; while others are used for weddings and receptions as well, and dubious amateur performances of *Iolanthe*.

But the delight of British regional theaters lies in their great variety and local panache. In the little town of Richmond in Yorkshire, there is a charming Georgian theater which seats about 200 people, in rows and balconies which still reflect 18th-century class divisions—farmers and peasants in the orchestra, gentry, doctors, and errant priests upstairs. In Bagnor, near Newbury, Berkshire, a watermill has been converted into a lovely little theater overlooking a lake, where its artistic director once solemnly told me that he wanted to stage Wagner's *The Ring*, presumably to make good use of the swans. In Porthcurno, near Penzance in Cornwall, an open-air theater has been built on the cliffs overlooking a spectacular bay. There are woodland theaters, theaters in old cowsheds and barns, mountain theaters, and theaters constructed from converted trucks and seagoing barges; and several country-house theaters.

There are, of course, half a dozen artistic meccas in Britain to which all the faithful are drawn. The Glyndebourne Festival Opera House was built by the millionaire, the late John Christie, for his wife, a singer; and in the intentionally long intermissions of its superb productions you can picnic or wander around the glorious gardens, set in the Sussex countryside. A visit to Glyndebourne is expensive. It involves taking the trouble of dressing up in tuxedos and evening gowns, and although it is not far from London, the traveling can be curiously inconvenient, too close for a safari, too far for a jaunt. But all the minor efforts are repaid many times over by the sheer pleasure of the experience—wonderful operas in a magical setting.

Another mecca would be Stratford-upon-Avon, where the Royal Shakespeare Company has its headquarters. Those who have seen RSC productions in London, at the Barbican theater, sometimes form the impression that it is not necessary to visit Stratford. They are much mistaken. The best theater in the world for seeing Elizabethan and Jacobean productions is the recently opened Swan Theatre in Stratford, created inside a Victorian building behind the main Memorial Theatre and built in the style of Shakespeare's own theater, the Globe. Unlike many other historical reconstructions, the Swan Theatre captures the intimacy, flow, and dramatic intensity that the plays of Shakespeare and his contemporaries require. Despite a lack of stage resources, the Swan imposes an acting and directing style upon the RSC which helps rather than hinders the company, and shows it to advantage. More spectacular, but occasionally more wayward productions can be seen in the larger and better equipped Memorial Theatre.

The RSC has led the way in British Shakespearian productions since World War II, and despite the lapses in taste and concentration which unfortunately seem to be becoming more frequent, it remains the best single company in Britain, developing its own style over the years which others attempt to imitate. Its sheer volume of work is impressive: two theaters in London, two in Stratford, an annual season in Newcastle-upon-Tyne, touring productions, educational programs and many transfers to the West End, including hit musicals—though all the work of the RSC is under a threat caused by its extremely precarious financial position.

The tally of artistic meccas in Britain must also include the Edinburgh International Festival of Music and Drama, which has attracted hundreds of thousands of visitors every August since it began in 1947. Edinburgh has many competitors in such exotic places as Dubrovnik, Avignon, and Leningrad, but no real rivals. In terms of tourist attraction, it is the biggest annual arts festival in Europe, and it has drawn other separately organized festivals to its side—a television festival, a film festival, the military tattoo, and an exploding fringe festival.

What is its secret? Edinburgh is a beautiful city, with its Georgian terraces and circuses, its 16th-century Grassmarket, and its Royal Mile which leads to Holyrood Palace from its castle, dramatically placed on a mound dominating the city center. But there are other spectacular and ancient cities in Britain, including Bath, Brighton, Chester, and York, each of which has a festival, albeit much smaller than Edinburgh's. In international terms, the Edinburgh Festival is under-financed, and the city lacks those basic requirements which any festival should have, notably a major opera house. It has some fine hotels, but not enough of them, and the weather in August is unpredictable. Under normal circumstances I would not want to spend part of my summer holiday in Edinburgh.

But the festival is always abnormal. It is a phenomenon, not so much for the official events but for its fringe. More than a thousand small companies from Britain and all over the world come to Edinburgh at their own expense to play in small halls, art galleries, and little studios, which rarely seat more than a hundred people. It is the best shop window for new talent anywhere in the world; and in scouting through the fringe for such talent, you are left with a vivid impression of the general trends in the British performing arts, and the latest fashions in drama, jazz, dance, and revue.

You can also sense the levels of commitment. In some years, the companies on the fringe seem cheerfully sloppy, as careless in their techniques as in their choices of what to perform. In other years, there is a fanatic dedication, the kind of determination which brought the little Traverse Theatre in the Grassmarket into being, or which accounts for Richard DiMarco's successes in promoting events at his art gallery in the Royal Mile. But generalizations about the fringe as a whole are rarely easy to make, for there are sloppy companies and dedicated ones in every festival, and it is easier instead to talk of patches of commitment, the feminist companies one year, the West Indian groups in another.

I do not think that many would dispute my claim that Glyndebourne, Stratford, and the Edinburgh festival are all artistic meccas, but my other candidates are more challengeable, ones which over the years have given me much pleasure, but whose status cannot be proved in terms of tourist statistics.

One, with a continuing record of high artistic excellence, is the Malvern Festival, which has a historical background, with Bernard Shaw as its founder and Edward Elgar as its house composer. It takes place in a delightful spa town, but its theater is unimpressive and its resources are small. Buxton has an enchanting opera house and the town is pretty, set in the Derbyshire peak district, and its short festival season can contain gems, but—like the Ludlow Festival, where productions are staged within the walls of a ruined castle—it has lacked a consistency of artistic management, which also reflects the absence of tradition. No major director wants to go to Buxton.

For the Welsh, there is Royal Eisteddfodd. The Three Choirs Festival, which is mounted in Worcester, Hereford, and Gloucester Cathedrals in alternate years, is a mecca for those who delight in choral music, as is Kings College Chapel in Cambridge, particularly at Christmas, with the Service of Nine Lessons and Carols. Bath as a town is a mecca for all architects, but its festival does not live up to its setting.

There are splendid brass band competitions which attract entries from all over the world, and there are special events for activities that I, in my Sassenach way, can only regard as ethnic oddities, such as highland dancing and bagpipe music.

There are two small festivals which must be mentioned: The Aldeburgh Festival in Suffolk and the Cheltenham Festival of Literature. Aldeburgh is a windswept Victorian seaside town, with a beach of pebbles and arctic conditions for bathing. A more unprepossessing town for a festival is hard to imagine, although the Suffolk coast has an austere beauty of its own. In 1948, the composer Benjamin Britten and the singer Peter Pears started what was intended to be a community festival for the town's inhabitants, converting the nearby Maltings at Snape into a concert hall. Britten was, in fact, the first British composer since Purcell to write operas successfully. Almost singlehandedly, he revived a tradition which had been dormant for two centuries. The struggle of man against the elements, the beating of the waves against a desolate coast, the lives of the Aldeburgh fishermen, all helped to inspire three of Britten's major works, the operas *Peter Grimes*, *Billy Budd*, and *Albert Herring*.

Britten's music, of course, can be heard almost anywhere, but it has a particular significance in Aldeburgh, where it seems to comment on the landscape, the seascape, and the way of life. Over the years, the Aldeburgh Festival has attracted major composers and performers to write and take part in the events, not for any great financial rewards, which were always meager, but out of sheer musical fraternity and gratitude to Britten. Although Britten and Pears are dead, and the Aldeburgh Festival has lost its inspiring leaders, nonetheless it remains an event of unique quality and interest in British musical life.

The Cheltenham Festival of Literature is a civilized, usually undramatic, gathering of authors, poets and publishers, with recitals, readings and theater performances thrown in for good measure. Cheltenham is a Regency spa town in the Cotswolds, with neat parks, elegant terraces, a Pump Room in Pittville Park, and an imposing Victorian town hall. There is very little show business, even less commercial aggression; and it is quite possible to visit Cheltenham at the time of the festival and fail to realize that it is going on at all. A discreet festival has a panache of its own.

The discussions and the talks can be, however, wonderfully stimulating. Every subject under the sun is aired, every topic seems to have its specialist; and the audiences are sometimes as breathtakingly well-informed as the speakers on the platform. The conversations flow over from the halls into the restaurants, cafés and the hotel lounges, as if the 18th-century coffee shops and tearooms had come back to life. If the wit becomes too malicious and in-bred, you can escape to the hills, where among the sheep and the Cotswold hamlets a sense of peace and equilibrium returns.

As examples of the health of the performing arts around the country, the regional opera companies would be obvious candidates—Opera North, the Welsh National Opera, and Scottish Opera. The revival of British opera since the war, led by Britten, but notably followed by Michael Tippett and Harrison Birtwhistle, has been much helped by public subsidies, although these are still low when compared with Continental opera houses. British regional orchestras provide their own unique success stories, with the Hallé Orchestra in Manchester, the Liverpool Philharmonic and, most recently, the Birmingham Symphony Orchestra under its inspirational young conductor, Simon Rattle.

During the 1960s, Liverpool attracted another kind of music lover, specifically to the Cavern Club where four young men with pudding-basin haircuts sang, "She loves you, yeah, yeah, yeah," and went on to make one hit record after another. The Beatles were the first group to write and sing their own songs, and to launch the Mersey sound, and to transform the British pop music industry. It was a sad and aging day for me when a teenage student in Los Angeles asked me, "Paul McCartney? Wasn't he in some other group before Wings?" Now, Liverpool University has established a department in rock music; and throughout Britain, there are small rock and heavy metal groups, with their synthesizers and amplifiers deafening the ears of a generation for whom the Beatles belong not just to the past but to those ancient days when you could actually hear the words.

Fortunately, the Edinburgh Fringe Festival is still the place where old fogies can gawp and shake their heads at what the young turks are doing. When the groups stop coming to Edinburgh in August, then we will know that we are truly growing old. In the meantime, the festival illustrates the continuing strength of the performing arts in Britain, which neither time nor television has so far managed to weaken.

3   London

Introduction

London is an ancient city and its history greets you at every street corner. To gain a sense of the continuity of history in London, stand on Waterloo Bridge at sunset. To the east, the great globe of 17th-century St. Paul's Cathedral glows golden in the dying sunlight, still majestic, despite the towers of glass and steel that hem it in. To the west stand the mock-medieval ramparts of Westminster, home to the "Mother of Parliaments" that has met here, or hereabouts, since the 1250s. And past them both snake the swift, dark waters of the Thames, flowing as they did past the first Roman settlement here nearly 2,000 years ago.

Unlike most European capitals, London has almost no grand boulevards, planned for display. The exception is the Mall, running from Admiralty Arch on Trafalgar Square to Buckingham Palace. It was specifically designed for heraldic processions and stately occasions and, in a typically British way, is surrounded by gardens and lined with spreading trees. Apart from this one extravagance, present-day London still largely reflects its medieval layout, a bewildering tangle of streets. Even when the City was devastated in the Great Fire of 1666, and again in the Blitz of the 1940s, it was rebuilt on its old street plan. Sir Christopher Wren's 17th-century master concept for a classical site, with vistas and crossing avenues, was turned down; and the plans for rebuilding in the 1950s again harked back to the ancient disposition of streets, and so lost a wonderful opportunity for imaginative replanning. (Visitors to London have a problem at first with the fact the City, spelled with a capital "C" refers to just the square mile beside the Tower, where London originated, while Greater London as a whole is the city, without a capital letter.)

In fact, this is all gain for the visitor, who can experience that indefinable historic London atmosphere by wandering the thoroughfares of stately houses which lie next to a muddle of mean streets, and by seeking out the winding lanes and narrow courts that suddenly give onto the grass, trees, and flowerbeds of well-kept squares. These contrasts can best be savored as you walk from one neighborhood to another. London is a walking city, and will repay every moment you spend exploring on foot.

Close-up exploration, however, will also reveal that London, like all great cities, has its darker side: the squalor and crowds that are as much a part of every modern city as they were of medieval ones. Squalor will be near at hand as you stand on Waterloo Bridge.

On an icy winter's evening, when you are coming out of the warm Queen Elizabeth Hall at the southern end of the bridge after a concert, you will pass down-and-outs sheltering in cardboard lean-tos in the open spaces underneath the building, grateful for the mobile soup kitchen that rolls up every night at 10:30. Both Shakespeare and Dickens would have recognized the scene. And where crowds are concerned, London definitely has the edge on any city in western Europe. It starts with the largest population—nearly seven million live here—and has well over the same number of visitors every year. Indeed, in one busy year the tourists numbered 12 million!

But in the midst of all those millions, life goes on as it has for centuries: At the Inns of Court, lawyers follow time-honored precedents as they have for six hundred years; financiers at computers manipulate figures in skyscrapers that rise above the guildhalls of their medieval counterparts, guildhalls that in turn were built over the remains of Roman Londinium; the prime minister and his cabinet deliberate in a sober 18th-century town house off Whitehall; and visitors from all over the world still pass by the tombs in Westminster Abbey as pilgrims did after the Norman Conquest in 1066.

Whether your interests center on the past or the present, on the arts, on shopping, theater or architecture, London has it all. The city fully justifies Dr. Johnson's famous dictum that begins, "When a man is tired of London he is tired of life" and fittingly concludes, "For there is in London all that life can afford."

Essential Information

Arriving and Departing by Plane

Airports and Airlines
London is admirably served by airports. There are two major ones—Gatwick, 28 miles to the south, and Heathrow, 15 miles to the west—and three smaller ones, Luton, 35 miles northwest, Stanstead, 34 miles northeast, and London City, in the Docklands.

Heathrow is the world's busiest airport, with international flights from all over. Among the North American airlines that use it are Air Canada, PanAmerican, TWA, and United. Many other major airlines with transatlantic service from the States and Canada to Europe use Heathrow as a stopping-off point—especially British Airways, with its own terminal, 4.

Gatwick, which has the lion's share of charter flights, has scheduled North American flights too, among them American Airlines, Continental, Delta, Northwest, and Wardair Canada, with several major British airlines on the transatlantic route, including British Airways and Virgin.

Stansted airport just opened a new passenger terminal designed by English architect Norman Foster, making it the third major international airport in the London area.

Luton has no scheduled transatlantic flights. The **London City** airport has only short-haul flights to Paris and Brussels.

From the Airports to Downtown
Heathrow
The Underground's Piccadilly line from all terminals takes you swiftly into central London. Trains run every four to eight minutes and the 40-minute trip costs £2.30 each way.

London Regional Transport runs two bus services from the airport; each costs £4 one way and travel time is about an hour. The A1 leaves for Victoria Station, with intermediate stops along Cromwell Road and Sloane Street, every 30 minutes from 6:40 AM–9:30 PM. The journey time is about an hour, depending on traffic. The A2 bus leaves for Euston Station, with stops at Marble Arch and Russell Square, every 20 minutes from 6AM–9:30 PM.

The **Flightline Coach 767,** operated by Greenline, departs from Heathrow for Victoria Coach Station every hour from 5 AM to

5:15 PM. The journey takes about 65 minutes, and the cost is £5 one way.

By car, the most direct route from the airport is via M4. By taxi, the fare to central London should be about £25, but will depend on the route the driver takes and on the traffic. Be sure you take a regular metered cab, and are not suckered by one of the pirate freelancers.

Gatwick The **Gatwick Express** trains leave for Victoria Station every 15 minutes from 5:30 AM to 10 PM; five times an hour from 10 to midnight; and hourly from midnight to 5 AM. The 30 minute trip costs £6.30 each way. An hourly local train runs throughout the night.

Green Line's **Flightline 777** bus leaves for Victoria Coach Station every 30 minutes; journey time is about 70 minutes and the cost is £5 one way.

By car, take A23 and then M23. The distance is too great for a taxi to be affordable to any except tycoons.

Arriving and Departing

By Car The major approach roads to London are motorways (six-lane highways; look for an "M" followed by a number) or "A" roads (the letter "A" followed by a number); the latter may be "dual carriageways" (divided highways), or two-lane highways. Motorways are usually the faster option for getting in and out of town, although rush-hour traffic is horrendous.

Stay tuned to local radio stations for regular traffic updates.

By Train London has 15 major train stations, each serving a different area of the country, all accessible by Underground or bus. **British Rail** controls all train services. The principal routes that connect London to other major towns and cities are on an Inter-City network *(see* Staying in Britain in Chapter 1); unlike its European counterparts, British Rail has no extra charge for the use of this express service network.

By Bus **National Express** buses operate from Victoria Coach Station (Buckingham Palace Rd., tel. 071/730–0202) to over 1,000 major towns and cities. It's less expensive than the train but trips usually take longer. **Greenline** operates buses within a 30- to 40-mile radius of London, ideal for excursions. Their **Golden Rover** ticket allows unlimited travel for either a day or a week. For information on services and schedules tel. 081/668–7261.

Getting Around

By Underground London's Underground, colloquially known as the tube (a "subway" is an under-the-street pedestrian crossing), is the most widely used form of transportation. Trains run beneath and above ground, out into the suburbs. Stations are clearly marked by London Transport's circular symbol. Trains are all one class and smoking is *not* allowed on board trains or in any part of any station.

There are nine basic lines, plus the East London line and the new Docklands Light Railway; several lines have branches so be sure you know which you want. Electronic platform signs being introduced in many stations tell you the destination, route, and the time you'll have to wait for the next train.

London Underground

63

Diary 20 9/90

Travel Information 071-222-1234
Travelcheck 071-222-1200

UNDERGROUND

Key to lines

Bakerloo
Central
Circle
District
East London
Jubilee
Metropolitan
Northern
Piccadilly
Victoria
Docklands Light Railway†
Network SouthEast

○ Interchange stations
⊖ Connections with British Rail
✤ Connections within walking distance
● Closed Sundays
▲ Closed Saturdays and Sundays
■ Served by Piccadilly line early mornings and late evenings Monday to Friday and all day Sundays
† For opening times see poster journey planners
‡ Certain stations are closed during public holidays

© Copyright London Regional Transport

LRT Registered User No. 92/1365

From Monday to Saturday, trains start just after 5 AM and run until midnight or 12:30. On Sunday trains start two hours later and finish about an hour earlier. Frequency of trains varies but a maximum wait should be no more than about 10 minutes in central areas.

The powers-that-be, in the wake of the terrible King's Cross fire in 1987, have started an overdue program of equipment upgrading which includes replacing wooden escalators with modern metal ones. Escalators all over the Tube system are likely to be put out of commission for long periods of time. If you are unable to walk up very long flights of stairs, check before you start your journey that the escalators are working, though, as they can be stopped at a moment's notice, this advice may not be entirely useful!

By Bus In central London, buses are mainly the traditional bright red double- and single-deckers, though there are increasing quantities of privately owned companies with different colored buses. Not all buses run the full length of their route at all times; check with the driver or conductor. On some buses you pay the conductor after finding a seat, on others you pay the driver upon boarding.

Buses pick up and drop off only at clearly indicated stops. Main stops have a red LRT symbol on a plain white background. When the word "Request" is written across the sign, you must flag the bus down. Buses are a good way of seeing the town, but don't take one if you are in a hurry. Fares start at 50p for short distances.

Fares London is divided into six concentric zones for both bus and tube fares: the more zones you cross, the higher the fare. There's a wide variety of ticket categories; the London Regional Transport booklet *Tickets*, available from Underground ticket counters, gives all the details. **One Day Off-Peak Travelcards** are the handiest. They allow unrestricted travel on bus and tube after 9:30 AM and all day on weekends and national holidays. **One Day Capitalcards** work the same way, but include use of British Rail services in London, too. Travelcards and Capitalcards, for weekly or monthly use, require a photograph. For more information, stop at an LRT Travel Information Centre at the following tube stations: Heathrow, Oxford Circus, Piccadilly Circus, St. James's Park, and Victoria, or call 071/222–1234.

By Taxi Hotels and main tourist areas have taxi ranks; you can also flag them down on the street. If the yellow "for hire" sign is lit on top, the taxi is available. But drivers often cruise at night with their signs unlit to avoid unsavory characters, so if you see an unlit cab, keep your hand up and you might be lucky.

Fares start at £1 and increase by units of 20p per 340 yards or 60 seconds, less after 6 miles. Surcharges are added after 8 PM and on weekends and public holidays. Fares increase annually.

By Car The simple advice about driving in London is: don't. Because the city grew as a series of villages, there was never a central street plan, and the result is a chaotic winding mass, made no easier by the one-way street systems. If you must drive in London, remember the speed limit: 30 mph in the Royal parks as well as (theoretically) on all streets unless you see the large 40 mph signs (and small repeater signs attached to lamp posts) found in the suburbs. Other traffic regulations are as in the rest of the country, except that it is illegal to park on the sidewalk in London. During the day—and probably at all times—it is safest to park only at a meter or in a garage. Otherwise you run the risk of a towaway cost of £62, or "the Boot," which clamps a wheel immovably and costs £57 to have removed, more if the clamped car is towed away.

Important Addresses and Numbers

Tourist Information

The main **London Tourist Information Centre** (tel. 071/730–3488) at Victoria Station provides details about London including information on tube and bus tickets, theater, concert and tour bookings, and accommodations. It also provides information on the rest of Britain. Open daily 9–8:30.

Other information centers located in **Harrods** (Brompton Rd.) and **Selfridges** (Oxford St.) are open store hours only; also at **Heathrow Airport** (Terminals 1, 2, and 3).

The **British Travel Centre** (12 Regent St., tel. 071/730–3400) provides details about travel, accommodations, and entertainment for the whole of Britain. Open weekdays 9–6:30 and weekends 10–4.

Embassies and Consulates

American Embassy (24 Grosvenor Sq., W1A 1AE, tel. 071/499–9000). Located inside the embassy is the American Aid Society, a charity that helps Americans in distress. Dial the embassy number and ask for extension 570 or 571.
Canadian High Commission (Canada House, Trafalgar Sq., SW1Y 5BJ, tel. 071/629–9492).

Emergencies

For police, fire brigade, or ambulance, dial 999.

The following hospitals have 24-hour emergency sections: **Guys,** St. Thomas St., tel. 071/407–7600; **Royal Free,** Pond St., Hampstead, tel. 071/794–0500; **St. Bartholomew's,** West Smithfield, tel. 071/600–9000; **St. Thomas's,** Lambeth Palace Rd., tel. 071/928–9292; **University College,** Gower St., tel. 071/387–9300; **Westminster,** Horseferry Rd. at Dean Ryle St., tel. 071/828–9811.

Pharmacies

Chemists (drug stores) with late hours include **Bliss Chemist,** 5 Marble Arch, tel. 071/723–6116, open daily 9 AM–midnight; and **Underwoods,** 114 Queensway, tel. 071/229–4819, open Mon.–Sat. 9–10, Sun. 10–10.

Travel Agencies

American Express, 6 Haymarket, tel. 071/930–4411, and at 89 Mount St., tel. 071/499–4436; **Hogg Robinson Travel/Diners Club,** 176 Tottenham Court Rd., tel. 071/580–0437; **Thomas Cook,** 45 Berkeley St., Piccadilly, tel. 071/499–4000.

Opening and Closing Times

Banks

Normally open Monday–Friday 9:30–3:30, but some branches do provide services on Saturday. Banks at major airports and train stations also have extended hours.

Museums

Most museums are open Monday–Saturday 10–5 or 10–6, and Sunday 2–5 or 2–6, including most bank holidays, but are closed on public holidays such as Good Friday. Check individual listings for definite opening hours.

Pubs   Since mid-1988 most pubs are open Monday–Saturday 11 AM–
11 PM; Sunday noon–3, and 7–10 or 10:30, but hours are at the
discretion of the landlord.

Shops   Usual business hours are Monday–Saturday 9–5:30 or 9–6.
Some shops have late opening hours on Wednesday or Thurs-
day until 7 or 7:30 PM, and in spite of the laws, many are open on
Sunday.

Guided Tours

Orientation Tours
By Bus   **London Regional Transport's** official guided sightseeing tours
(tel. 071/222–1234) offer a good introduction to the city from
double-decker buses. Tours run daily every half hour from 10 to
5, from Marble Arch, Victoria Station, and Piccadilly Circus.
Tours last about one and a half hours. Tickets are available
from the driver, or in advance from the London Tourist Information Centre at Victoria. Other agencies offering half- and
full-day bus tours include **Evan Evans** (tel. 071/930–2377),
Frames Rickards (tel. 071/837–3111), and **Travellers Check-In**
(tel. 071/580–8284). These tours stop at places of special interest. Prices and pick-up points (many of which are at major hotels) vary.

By River   From April to October boats cruise up and down the Thames.
Most leave from **Westminster Pier** (tel. 071/930–4097), **Charing
Cross Pier** (Victoria Embankment, tel. 071/839–3312), and
Tower Pier (tel. 071/488–0344). Downstream services go to the
Tower of London, Greenwich, and the Thames Barrier; up-
stream destinations include Kew, Richmond, and Hampton
Court. Trips last one to four hours depending on destination;
the shorter runs provide a running commentary on passing
points of interest.

Walking Tours   There are many from which to choose. **London Walks** (tel. 081/
441–8906), **Cockney Walks** (tel. 081/504–9159), **Streets of London** (tel. 081/882–3414), and **Historical Tours** (tel. 081/668–
4019) are just a few of the better-known firms. **Citisights** (tel.
081/806–4325) offers an entertaining program of unusual walks
and day tours led by professional archaeologists and historians. The best bet is to peruse leaflets at the London Tourist Information Centre at Victoria Station—you may find one to suit
your particular interest. The length of walks varies, but is generally around two hours and costs around £3 per person.

Excursions   London Regional Transport, **Evan Evans, Frames Rickards,**
and **Travellers Check-In** all offer day excursions by bus to places
within easy reach of London, such as Hampton Court, Oxford,
Stratford, and Bath.

Personal Guides   **Tour Guides Ltd.** (2 Bridge St., SW1A 2JR, tel. 071/839–2498)
provides customized tours for any size group. The firm uses
only Tourist Board–registered guides, and covers the whole of
Britain as well as London.

Exploring London

Orientation

Traditionally, central London has been divided between the
City to the east, where its banking and commercial interests

lie; Westminster to the west, the seat of the royal court and the government; and the mainly residential areas that surround them both. That distinction still holds, as our itineraries show.

The City route covers London's equivalent of New York's Wall Street, while the **Westminster and Royal London** exploration roves past royal palaces and surveys the government area in and around Parliament Square. Part of another walk, **Legal London, Covent Garden, and Bloomsbury,** explores the capital's legal center, a lively, rejuvenated shopping district, and its university and literary quarter.

London expanded from Westminster during the 17th and 18th centuries. Elegant town houses sprang up in St. James's and Mayfair, and later in Bloomsbury, Chelsea, Knightsbridge, and Kensington. These are today pleasant residential districts, and elegant, if pricey, shopping areas. London also enjoys unique "lungs"—its stupendous parks—thanks to past royalty who reserved these great tracts of land for their own hunting and relaxation. The two largest of them, now administered by the government, feature in the **Two Royal Parks—Knightsbridge and Kensington** walk.

The area along the Thames, once London's most important highway, is currently enjoying a renaissance. The **South Bank** takes you along the river's traditionally less fashionable south side, while the last exploring section, **Up and Down the Thames,** covers out-of-town riverside attractions, old and new.

Highlights for First-time Visitors

British Museum: Tour 2
Covent Garden: Tour 2
Hampton Court Palace: Tour 6
Museum of London: Tour 4
National Gallery: Tour 1
St. James's Park: Tour 1
South Kensington Museums: Tour 3
Tate Gallery: Tour 1
Tower of London: Tour 4
Westminster Abbey: Tour 1

Tour 1: Westminster and Royal London

Numbers in the margin correspond to points of interest on the London map.

Westminster could be called the royal backyard. Generations of monarchs have lived here since King Edward the Confessor moved his court from the City in the 11th century. All the medieval sovereigns occupied the Palace of Westminster until 1512, when Henry VIII vacated it for nearby Whitehall Palace. Except for one building, Whitehall Palace no longer exists; it was destroyed by a series of fires culminating in the most disastrous one in 1698. The court then moved to St. James's Palace, across the park. Buckingham Palace, the residence and administrative headquarters of the present royal family, was first occupied by Queen Victoria after her coronation in 1837.

❶ Start in **Trafalgar Square,** the point from which all distances from London are officially measured. It is also the focal point of New Year's Eve and election night celebrations, and political

London

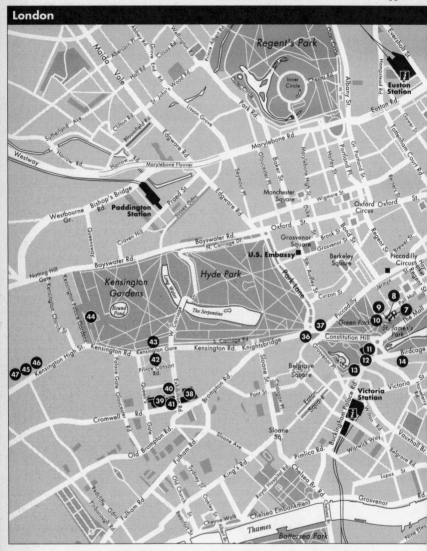

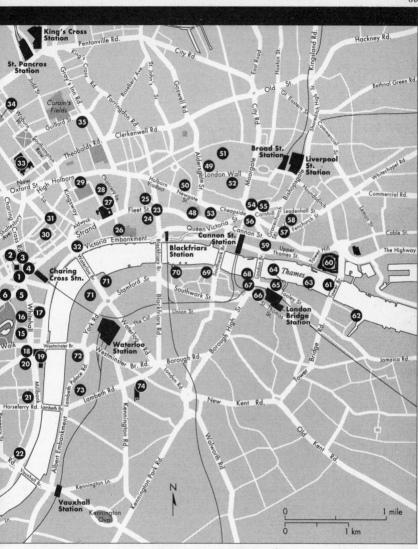

National Postal
Museum, **50**

Natural History
Museum, **39**

Old St. Thomas's
Hospital, **66**

Palace of Westminster,
(Houses of
Parliament), **19**

Parliament Square, **18**

Percival David
Foundation of Chinese
Art, **34**

Queen's Gallery, **12**

Royal Albert Hall, **42**

Royal Courts of
Justice, **27**

Royal Exchange, **55**

Royal Mews, **13**

Royal Opera House, **31**

Science Museum, **40**

Shakespeare Globe
Museum, **69**

Sir John Soane's
Museum, **29**

South Bank Arts
Complex, **71**

Southwark
Cathedral, **67**

St. Bride's Church, **24**

St. James's Palace, **7**

St. John's, **21**

St. Mary-le-Bow, **53**

St. Martin-in-the-
Fields, **4**

St. Paul's
Cathedral, **48**

St. Thomas's
Hospital, **72**

Tate Gallery, **22**

Tower of London, **60**

Tower Bridge, **61**

Trafalgar Square, **1**

Victoria and Albert
Museum, **38**

Wellington Museum
(Apsley House), **37**

Wellington
Barracks, **14**

Westminster
Abbey, **20**

York House, **8**

rallies. Trafalgar Square's present shape and name date only from 1830, when the central portion was leveled to accommodate **Nelson's Column** (185 feet high). Admiral Horatio Nelson is remembered for his victory over Napoleon's navy in 1805 at Trafalgar in Spain, where he lost his life. Lions guard the column's base, and four huge bronze panels depict naval battles against the French. The equestrian statue to the south is of **Charles I,** looking down Whitehall toward the spot where he was executed in 1649.

② The **National Gallery** occupies the classical building which fills the square's north side. It houses one of the world's great European art collections, with works representing most schools from the 14th to the 19th century. Its strengths are Flemish and Dutch masters such as Rubens and Rembrandt, Italian Renaissance works, English 18th- and 19th-century paintings, and French Impressionists. The recently completed Sainsbury Wing now houses the early Renaissance collection. Like most major galleries, the layout can be confusing, so pick up a free floor plan on your way in. *Trafalgar Sq., tel. 071/839–3321 or 071/839–3526 (recorded information). Admission free; admission charge for special exhibitions. Open Mon.–Sat. 10–6, Sun. 2–6.*

Around the corner, at the foot of Charing Cross Road, is the **③** **National Portrait Gallery,** which contains portraits of celebrated (and not so well known) Britons, including monarchs, statesmen, and writers. The gallery is a lot more interesting than you might expect: The collection extends beyond painted portraits to busts, photographs, and even cartoons. You can supplement your knowledge of British history with material from the gallery's shop. *2 St. Martin's Pl., tel. 071/930–1552. Admission free. Open Mon.–Fri. 10–5, Sat. 10–6, Sun. 2–6.*

Across from the entrance to the portrait gallery is the church of **④** **St. Martin-in-the-Fields,** built in 1724, set off by its elegant spire. The church still carries on its traditional role of caring for the destitute. The celebrated Academy of St. Martin-in-the-Fields, which performed the music for the movie *Amadeus,* was founded here. At the **London Brass Rubbing Centre** in the crypt you can take impressions from replica brass tombs; wax, paper, and instructions are provided. There is a craft market spread around the back courtyard. *Trafalgar Sq., tel. 071/437–6023. Fee from 50p according to size of rubbing. Open Mon.–Sat. 10–6, Sun. noon–6.*

Time Out Both the **National Gallery Restaurant** and **Field's** in St. Martin's crypt serve excellent lunches, salads, sandwiches, and pastries, although both can get very crowded.

⑤ **Admiralty Arch,** near the Royal Navy headquarters in the Admiralty Building, marks the entrance to **The Mall,** the great promenade leading from one corner of Trafalgar Square past St. James's Park to Buckingham Palace. The present Mall was laid out in 1904 to provide a stately approach to Buckingham Palace, replacing a more modest avenue dating from 1660. The name Mall (pronounced to rhyme with "pal") comes from a version of croquet called "pell mell" that Charles II and his courtiers used to play here in the late 1600s.

St. James's Park is small but handsome, and like most of London's parks, has royal origins. In ancient times the Thames spread far and wide, and the marshes here were drained by Henry VIII to be used as a playground for his deer. Charles II employed the famous French landscape gardener, Le Nôtre, to reshape it and in 1829 it was given its present look by John Nash, the prolific architect and friend of George IV. Meticulously maintained flowerbeds and many varieties of waterfowl make the park a beautiful place for a stroll, especially on a summer's evening, when illuminated fountains cascade and, beyond the trees, Westminster Abbey and the Houses of Parliament are floodlit.

6 On the other side of the Mall, you'll pass the imposing **Carlton House Terrace,** built in 1827–32 (also by Nash), with a gleaming white stucco facade and massive Corinthian columns. The column at the head of the steps is topped by a statue of the Duke of York, George III's second son and commander-in-chief of the British forces during the French Revolution.

7 To the right up Marlborough Road is **St. James's Palace,** the earliest parts of which date from the 1530s. The palace has declined in importance since 1837, when Queen Victoria moved to Buckingham Palace, but some royal officials still work here, and court functions are occasionally held in the state rooms. All foreign ambassadors to Britain are officially accredited to the Court of St. James's.

Inside the palace is the **Chapel Royal,** said to have been designed for Henry VIII by the painter Holbein. Although redecorated in the mid-19th century, the ceiling still displays the intertwined initials H and A, for Henry VIII and his second wife, Anne Boleyn, the mother of Elizabeth I and the first of Henry's wives to lose her head. *The chapel is only open for Sunday morning services from early October to Good Friday.*

Across from Friary Court on Marlborough Road is the exquisite **Queen's Chapel.** It was built by Inigo Jones in the 1620s for Henrietta Maria, wife of Charles I, and was one of the first purely classical buildings in the country. *The Chapel is only open for services on Sunday mornings at 8:30 and 11:15 from Easter to the end of July.*

8 Turn left at the end of Marlborough Road along Cleveland Row, past **York House,** the London home of the duke and duchess of Kent. Another left turn onto Stable Yard Road brings you to
9 **Lancaster House,** built for the duke of York by Nash in the 1820s and now used for government receptions and confer-
10 ences. On the other side of Stable Yard is **Clarence House,** built by Nash in 1825 for the duke of Clarence, who later became King William IV. Restored in 1949, it is now the home of the Queen Mother (i.e., Queen Elizabeth's mother).

11 **Buckingham Palace** stands at the end of the Mall, behind a huge traffic circle edged with flowerbeds. When the queen is in residence (generally on weekdays except in January, August, September, and part of June), the royal standard flies over the east front. Inside, there are dozens of splendid state rooms used on formal occasions; offices for the royal staff; and, in the north wing, the private apartments of the queen and Prince Philip. Behind the palace lie 40 acres of secluded garden. Neither the palace nor the grounds are open to the public.

That most celebrated of all London ceremonies, the **Changing of the Guard,** takes place in front of the palace daily from April through July, and on alternate days the rest of the year. The guard marches from Wellington Barracks (*see* below) at 11 AM to the palace. The ceremony itself begins promptly at 11:30, but arrive early for a good view; the Queen Victoria Memorial in the traffic circle provides a convenient grandstand.

The palace was originally Buckingham House, built in the early 18th century for the duke of Buckingham. George III bought it in 1762. In 1824, Nash remodeled it for George IV, at which time it acquired palace status. The east end, which faces the public, does not, though, represent Nash's work. The 1913 remodeling of the wing rendered it dull and heavy.

⑫ The former palace chapel, bombed during World War II and rebuilt in 1961, has been converted into the **Queen's Gallery,** where exhibitions from the royal art collections are held. *Buckingham Palace Rd., tel. 071/799–2331. Admission: £1.50 adults, 80p children and senior citizens. Open Tues.–Sat. 10:30–5, Sun. 2–5.*

⑬ **The Royal Mews,** farther along the road, house the queen's horses and the gilded state coaches. *Buckingham Palace Rd. Admission: £1 adults, 50p children. Open Wed.–Thurs. 2–4; closed before state occasions, and Ascot week (mid-June).*

Birdcage Walk, once the site of the royal aviaries, runs along
⑭ the south side of St. James's Park past **Wellington Barracks,** the regimental headquarters of the Guards Division. The elite troops that guard the sovereign and mount the guard at Buckingham Palace live here. The **Guards Museum** relates their history; many conflicts, including the Falklands campaign, are represented. Battle paintings, uniforms, and a cat o' nine tails are among the displays. *Wellington Barracks, Birdcage Walk, tel. 071/930–4466, extensions 3271 and 3253. Admission: £2 adults, £1 children under 16 and senior citizens. Open Sat.– Thurs. 10–4.*

Next to the museum stands the **Guards Chapel,** rebuilt in the early '60s after it was bombed in 1944.

Off Birdcage Walk to the right is **Queen Anne's Gate,** lined with handsome 18th-century town houses, now mostly used as offices. A very formal statue of Queen Anne is hidden among them.

Back on Birdcage Walk and still following the perimeter of St. James's Park, turn left on to Horse Guards Road. Between the massive bulks of the Home Office and the Foreign Office nestles
⑮ the **Cabinet War Rooms,** a labyrinth of underground offices used by the British high command during World War II. Many strategic decisions were made here. You can see the Prime Minister's Room, where Winston Churchill made some of his inspiring war-time broadcasts, and the Transatlantic Telephone Room, used when he spoke directly to President Roosevelt. *Clive Steps, King Charles St., tel. 071/930–6961 or 071/735–8922. Admission: £3.50 adults, £1.75 children under 16, £2.30 senior citizens. Open daily 10–5:15.*

Continue along Horse Guards Road to the mid-18th-century
⑯ Horse Guards Building, overlooking **Horse Guards Parade.** Originally the tilt yard (a place for jousting contests) of Whitehall Palace, the square is now the site of the **Trooping the Colour** each June, the great military parade marking the queen's official birthday. (Her real birthday is April 21.) The "Colour"

(or flag) displayed identifies the battalion selected to provide the monarch's escort for that year. Cross the parade ground and walk through the arch.

The queen's Life Guards—cavalrymen in magnificent uniforms—stand duty on the facade overlooking Whitehall. The guard changes here at 11 AM Monday through Saturday, and at 10 AM on Sunday.

17 The **Banqueting House,** across Whitehall, survived the Whitehall Palace fire; Charles I was beheaded here in 1649. The Banqueting House was built by Inigo Jones in 1625; the main hall's magnificent ceiling frescoes, painted by Rubens for Charles I in 1630, honor the house of Stuart. Charles and his father, James I, assume a god-like stance—typical of the attitude that led to Charles's downfall at the hands of Cromwell and the Parliamentarians. *Whitehall, tel. 071/930–4179. Admission: £1.90 adults, £1.25 children under 15, £1.45 senior citizens. Open Tues.–Sat. 10–5, Sun. 2–5.*

Walking toward Parliament Square, you pass on the right the entrance to **Downing Street,** a terrace of three unassuming 18th-century houses. No. 10 has been the official residence of the prime minister since 1732. The cabinet office, the hub of the British system of government, is on the ground floor; the prime minister's private apartment is on the top floor. The chancellor of the exchequer, the chief finance minister, occupies no. 11. Downing Street is cordoned off, but you should be able to catch a glimpse of it from Whitehall.

The **Cenotaph,** in the center of Whitehall, commemorates the dead of both world wars. On Remembrance Day in November the sovereign lays a tribute of silken Flanders poppies here, symbolic of the blood-red flowers that grew on the killing fields of World War I. A statue of Winston Churchill dominates traf-
18 fic-beleaguered **Parliament Square,** at the foot of Whitehall. Other statues in the square are mostly of 19th-century prime ministers, but Abraham Lincoln is here, too, and outside the Houses of Parliament are Richard I (Richard the Lionheart) and Oliver Cromwell, Lord Protector of England during the country's sole, brief republican period in the 1650s.

19 The only remains of the original **Palace of Westminster** (still the official name of the complex) is the 240-foot long **Westminster Hall,** built at the end of the 11th century; the fine hammer-beam roof was added by Richard II in 1397. The hall, where the country's early parliaments met and which once housed the law courts, is now used only on ceremonial occasions. The rest of the palace, extended and altered over the centuries, was destroyed by fire in 1834. It was rebuilt in mock-medieval Gothic style with an ornate interior by architect Augustus Pugin, whose many delightful touches include Gothic umbrella stands. Parts of this building, notably the Chamber of the House of Commons, were badly damaged by bombing in 1941, but were reconstructed on virtually identical lines, though with modern amenities incorporated.

The palace contains the debating chambers and committee rooms of the two Houses of Parliament, the Commons (whose members are elected) and the Lords (which contains a mixture of appointed and hereditary members), plus offices and libraries. The public is admitted only to the public gallery of each House; note that the line for the Lords is generally much shorter than for the Commons, but the debates to be heard there are a lot less dramatic.

The most famous features of the palace are the towers at each end. At the south end is the 336-foot **Victoria Tower**. At the other end is **St. Stephen's Tower**, better known as **Big Ben**, after the 13-ton bell in the tower which strikes the hours. It is thought to have been named after Sir Benjamin Hall, Commissioner of Works when the bells were installed in the 1850s. A light shines from the top of the tower when Parliament meets at night.

② Westminster Abbey is the most ancient of London's great churches. Britain's monarchs have been crowned here since the coronation of William the Conqueror on Christmas Day 1066. There has almost certainly been a church here since the 6th century, and some historians believe the site was a place of pagan worship long before Christianity reached Britain. The present abbey is a largely 13th- and 14th-century rebuilding of the 11th-century church founded by Edward the Confessor. Two notable later additions are the Henry VII Chapel, built in the early 1500s, and the 18th-century twin towers over the west entrance. Early morning is a good time to catch something of the abbey's sacred atmosphere and to avoid the hordes of visitors; better still, attend a service.

There is space here to mention only a few of the abbey's many memorials. **Winston Churchill's** is just inside the west door (he is buried near Blenheim Palace, where he was born). The **Tomb of the Unknown Warrior** contains the body of a nameless World War I soldier buried in earth brought from France with his corpse; nearby hangs the **U.S. Congressional Medal** awarded to him symbolically. Among the many other non-royal people commemorated in the abbey are Robert Baden-Powell, founder of the Boy Scout movement, and the Wesleys, pioneers of Methodism. **Poets' Corner** memorializes an idiosyncratic collection of British writers.

Behind the high altar, the **Chapel of Edward the Confessor** contains Edward I's primitive oak Coronation Chair, and just beyond lies the **Henry VII Chapel,** an exquisite example of the rich Late Gothic style—the last riot of medieval design in England. Binoculars will help you spot the statues high up on the walls and the details of the abbey's stained glass. Striking effigies adorn the royal tombs of Elizabeth I and her sister "Bloody" Mary; Mary, Queen of Scots; Henry V; Richard II and his wife Anne of Bohemia; and many more. *Broad Sanctuary, tel. 071/ 222-5752. Admission to nave free; to Poets' Corner and Royal Chapels: £2.20 adults, 50p children (Royal Chapels free Wed. 6–8 PM). Open Mon., Tues., Thurs., Fri. 9–4:45; Wed. 9–7:45; Sat. 9–2, 3:45–5:45; Sun. for services only; closed to visitors during weekday services.*

Medieval monks strolled in the **Cloisters,** discussing the state of government and of their souls. There is also a **Brass Rubbing Centre,** where you can take impressions from facsimiles of old tombs. *Tel. 071/222-2085. Admission free. Fee charged for each brass rubbed, approx. £2.50–£6.50. Open late Mar.–late Oct., Mon.–Sat. 9–5.*

The Norman **Undercroft,** just off the cloisters, houses a museum on the abbey's history; among its exhibits are lifelike royal effigies that used to be carried in funeral processions. The **Pyx**

Chamber next door displays silver vessels and other treasures. The **Chapter House,** where Parliament first met, was built in the 1240s and is remarkable for its feeling of space and its daring design. A single column, like a frozen fountain, supports the roof. *Tel. 071/222–5152. Joint admission: £1.60 adults, 80p children under 16 and senior citizens. Open daily 10:30–1:45.*

Outside the abbey's west front an archway leads to **Dean's Yard,** a quiet, green courtyard. This side of the abbey was once the monks' living quarters; it's now used by **Westminster School,** a prestigious private ("public") school on the abbey grounds.

Continue through the courtyard, turn immediately left, then first right into Barton Street which leads via Cowley Street and Lord North Street to Smith Square, one of London's most attractive Georgian residential areas. The splendidly classical **㉑** church of **St. John's** (1729) has been deconsecrated and now functions as one of London's favorite small concert halls. Turn left back onto Millbank then right to follow the river to the Tate.

㉒ The **Tate Gallery** is Britain's most important museum of British and modern art. Its new director has instituted an innovative policy of rehanging the whole gallery every nine months. While a rotation like this does put all of the extensive collection on exhibit at one time or another, it also means that favorite pieces may not be on view when you are visiting. Another new development is the emphasis put on the British holdings. The Clore Gallery, with the magnificent (J.M.W.) Turner Bequest, including one hundred of his finished oil paintings, has escaped the changes. *Millbank, tel. 071/821–1313 or 071/821–7128 (recorded information). Admission free; fee for special exhibitions. Open Mon.–Sat. 10–5:50, Sun. 2–5:50; closed Good Friday, May Day holiday, Dec. 24–26, Jan. 1.*

Tour 2: Legal London, Covent Garden, and Bloomsbury

This walk explores three diverse areas that exemplify London's rich history: the Inns of Court, where the country's top lawyers have had their chambers or offices for centuries; Covent Garden, the former monastery garden turned market place; and literary Bloomsbury.

㉓ Start at **Ludgate Circus,** a drab traffic circle west of St. Paul's Cathedral, where **Fleet Street,** once traditional home of Britain's newspaper industry, begins. High operating costs have driven the newspapers to other parts of London, and none is now left here.

㉔ Walk west along Fleet Street. On the left stands **St. Bride's Church,** rebuilt by Christopher Wren following the Great Fire of 1666 and restored again after it was bombed in 1940. The spire was added in 1703, and became the model for multi-tiered wedding cakes. The crypt's small museum contains Roman and later antiquities found in the area. *Tel. 071/353–1301. Admission free. Open daily 9–5.*

Time Out Try a pint of real ale and a slab of cheese at **Ye Olde Cheshire Cheese** on Wine Office Court. This 17th-century inn was a favorite watering hole of Dr. Samuel Johnson, the 18th-century lexicographer and pundit, and his biographer James Boswell.

㉕ Around the corner, on Gough Square, is **Dr. Johnson's House,** where he compiled his dictionary. *17 Gough Sq., tel. 071/353–3745. Admission: £1.50 adults, £1 children under 16 and senior citizens. Open May–Sept., Mon.–Sat. 11–5:30, Oct.–Apr., Mon.–Sat. 11–5.*

The Inns of Court—there are four in all, and this walk visits three—were founded at different times during the Middle Ages to provide food and lodging for lawyers; as the centuries passed, they became more or less permanent residences and offices combined. Their atmosphere is reminiscent of Oxford or Cambridge colleges, hardly surprising, since they were founded in the same era as places for serious study. The Inns of Court retain an important educational role: Aspiring lawyers, or barristers, must pass a series of examinations held here. More quirkily, they must establish their attendance by eating a certain number of dinners in the Hall of the Inn to which they are attached.

㉖ The **Inner** and **Middle Temples** (there never was an Outer Temple) lie immediately south of Fleet Street. Enter through the **Old Mitre Court** passageway to see one of the finest groupings of unspoiled historic buildings in London. The two Temples derive their names from the land on which they stand, once owned by the Knights Templar, the chivalric order founded during the first Crusade in the 11th century. The following century, the Knights built the **Temple Church** here, one of only three round churches in Britain. The worn tombs of the Knights can still be seen on the floor. About 1250, the choir was extended in Early English style, a particularly pure form of Gothic; this is probably the country's finest example. *The Temple, tel. 071/353–8462. Admission free. Open daily 10–4.*

The **Inner Temple Hall** is not open to the public, but the superb Elizabethan **Middle Temple Hall** may be freely visited (unless in use by the Inn). *Tel. 071/353–4355. Admission free. Open weekdays 10–noon, 3–4.*

Return to Fleet Street through the **Inner Temple Gateway.** At the entrance is an early Jacobean half-timbered building inside which is **Prince Henry's Room,** with oak paneling and an elaborate plaster-work ceiling. It is named after the eldest son of James I, who became Prince of Wales in 1610, but died before he could succeed his father. *17 Fleet St., tel. 071/353–7323. Admission: 10p. Open weekdays 1:45–5, Sat. 1:45–4.*

㉗ Across the way, on the left, stand the **Royal Courts of Justice,** where important civil cases are heard. Though it looks medieval, the building dates from the 1870s. The magnificent main hall—238 feet long and 80 feet high—dwarfs the bewigged and gowned figures that scurry through it. *Strand, tel. 071/936–6000. Admission free. Open weekdays 9–4:30; closed national holidays.*

Now walk up **Chancery Lane,** past the **Public Record Office** on the right, where a small museum displays historic documents such as the Domesday Book of 1085. *Tel. 071/876–3444. Admission free. Open weekdays 9:30–4:45.*

28 **Lincoln's Inn,** probably the most beautiful of the Inns and the one least damaged during World War II, lies left of Chancery Lane. The buildings date from various periods beginning with the late 15th-century **Old Hall** and **Old Buildings. Stone Buildings, New Square,** is the only intact 17th-century square in London. The chapel was remodeled by Inigo Jones in 1619–23. *Chancery La., tel. 071/405–1393. Gardens open daily 8–7, chapel open weekdays 12:30–2:30; the public may also attend 11:30 Sunday service in the Chapel during legal terms. Guided tours are available in summer; for information, tel. 071/405–1393.*

The adjoining **Lincoln's Inn Fields** is the capital's largest and oldest square—more like a small park—surrounded by handsome buildings. The magnificent 1806 portico on the south side fronts the Royal College of Surgeons. The square's great attraction, however, is **Sir John Soane's Museum,** one of the most **29** idiosyncratic and fascinating museums in London. Sir John Soane, who lived here from 1790 to 1831, was a gifted architect and an avid collector. The exhibits include Hogarth's series of paintings, *The Rake's Progress,* and the sarcophagus of the Egyptian Emperor Seti I, which Soane bought for £2,000 after the British Museum refused it. *13 Lincoln's Inn Fields, tel. 071/405–2107. Admission free. Open Tues.–Sat. 10–5.*

Southwest of Lincoln's Inn Fields on Portsmouth Street is the 16th-century antique shop that Dickens reputedly used as the model for his *Old Curiosity Shop.*

30 **Covent Garden** lies about half a mile to the west. The original "Covent Garden" produced fruit and vegetables for the 13th-century Abbey of St. Peter at Westminster. Later, it passed into the hands of the earls (later the dukes) of Bedford. In 1630, the fourth earl commissioned Inigo Jones to lay out a square, with St. Paul's Church at one end and colonnaded houses on two sides. Only the church now remains. The fruit, flower, and vegetable market established in the later 1700s flourished until 1974, when its traffic grew to be too much for the narrow surrounding streets and it was moved south of the Thames.

Since then, the area has been transformed through small-scale projects rather than massive redevelopment, making Covent Garden one of the most appealing areas of London for adults and children alike. The 19th-century **Market Building** is now an elegant shopping arcade. On the south side is the lively **Jubilee open-air market** where crafts and flea-market goods are sold from open stalls. Open-air entertainers perform under the portico of **St. Paul's Church,** where George Bernard Shaw set the first scene of *Pygmalion* (reshaped as the musical *My Fair Lady*). The church, entered from Bedford Street, is known as the actors' church; inside are numerous memorials to theater people.

On the east side of the market area are two of London's newer museums. The **London Transport Museum** houses a steam locomotive, a tram, and a modern underground car among other relics of London's transport. This really is a "hands-on" museum: Visitors are positively encouraged to operate many of the exhibits. *39 Wellington St., tel. 071/379–6344. Admission: £2.60 adults, £1.20 children 5–16 and senior citizens, children under 5 free. Open daily 10–6.*

On the same block, the **Theatre Museum** holds a comprehensive collection on the history of English theater—not just drama, but also opera, music hall (vaudeville), pantomime, and musical comedy. Scripts, playbills, costumes, props, and memorabilia of stars are displayed. *Russell St., tel. 071/836–7891. Admission: £2.50 adults, £1.50 children aged 5–14 and senior citizens. Open Tues.–Sat. 11–8, Sun. 11–7.*

Time Out There's a good selection of eating places in and around the market building. **Crank's** (11 The Market) serves quiches, salads, and cakes. The **Theatre Museum Café** does cream teas plus muffins, open sandwiches, salads, and pastries; it's open to passers-by, too.

The streets around the central market are packed with history. Garrick Street is home to the **Garrick Club,** London's equivalent of New York's Players Club. Actors and publishers are among today's members; in the 19th century, Dickens, Thackeray, and Trollope were on the club's roster. Opposite, at the end of tiny Rose Street, is the **Lamb and Flag,** a highly atmospheric pub that Dickens used to visit when he worked in nearby Catherine Street. Shops on Long Acre specialize in maps and art books; at the **Glasshouse** you can watch the glassblowers practicing their craft.

31 Bow Street is famous for the **Royal Opera House,** home of both the Royal Ballet and the Royal Opera Company. The theater is the third on this site, its interior all rich Victorian gilt and plush seats, with excellent acoustics. The **Magistrates Court,** opposite the theater, was established in 1749 by Henry Fielding, magistrate, journalist, and novelist. He employed a band of private detectives, the "Bow Street Runners," and paid them out of the fines imposed in the court. They were the forefathers of the modern police force.

To the north, Neal Street and the surrounding lanes make for out-of-the-ordinary shopping: Eastern goods, clothes, pottery, and jewelry.

Bloomsbury is a semiresidential district north of Covent Garden that contains a number of elegant 17th- and 18th-century squares; it is home to the British Museum and the University of London. The Bloomsbury Group, once based here, was a coterie of writers and painters that included the novelists E. M. Forster and Virginia Woolf; her husband, Leonard; the poet Rupert Brooke; Bertrand Russell, the philosopher; and J. M. Keynes, the economist.

32 South of Bow Street, by the end of Waterloo Bridge and on the Strand, is the new home of the **Courtauld Institute Galleries.** This collection of paintings has moved into the majestic rooms of Somerset House from its former hidden galleries in Woburn Square. Here you can see some of the best French Impressionist work anywhere, with Manets, Van Goghs, and Gauguins supported by dozens of Old Masters. But the more convenient location means that there are always long lines. *Somerset House, The Strand, tel. 071/873–2526. Admission: £2.50. Open Mon., Wed–Sat. 10–6; Tues. 10–8; Sun. 2–6.*

33 Museum Street, lined with print and secondhand book shops, leads to the **British Museum** on Great Russell Street, a monumental, severely Greek edifice built in the first half of the 19th century. The vast collection of treasures here includes Egyptian, Greek, and Roman antiquities; Renaissance jewelry, pottery, coins, glass; and drawings from virtually every European school since the 15th century. It's best to concentrate on one area that particularly interests you or, alternatively, take one of the Museum's guided tours, which cost £5 per person and last one and a half hours (tel. 071/636–1555, ext. 8299). Some of the highlights are the Elgin Marbles, sculptures from the Parthenon in Athens; the Rosetta Stone, which helped archaeologists decipher Egyptian hieroglyphics; and the Mildenhall Treasure, a cache of Roman silver found in East Anglia in 1842. The King's Library, part of the **British Library,** contains illuminated and printed books, including many from the earliest days of printing. In 1993, the British Library will move to its controversial new home on Euston Road, Kings Cross. *Great Russell St., tel. 071/636–1555 or 071/580–1788 (recorded information). Admission free. Open Mon.–Sat. 10–5, Sun. 2:30–6.*

The university area lies to the north of the British Museum. Inside the **Senate House** skyscraper (1932) are administrative offices and the university library. **University College,** at the north end of Gower Street, founded in 1826, was the first college in Britain to admit Jews and Roman Catholics. Behind University College, Gordon Square contains restored 19th-century townhouses and, at no. 53, the **Percival David Foundation of Chinese Art,** a collection of Chinese ceramics from the 10th to the 19th century. *53 Gordon Sq., tel. 071/387–3909. Admission free. Open weekdays 10:30–5 (sometimes closed 1–2 for lunch).*

Turn right onto Tavistock Place, second right into Woburn Place and continue until you see Guildford Street on your left. Go past Coram Fields (on your left) and continue until you come to the fourth road on the right, Doughty Street. A little way down is the **Dickens Museum** at no. 48, the house where Charles Dickens lived from 1837 to 1839. During this fertile period he finished *Pickwick Papers*, wrote all of *Oliver Twist* and started *Nicholas Nickleby*. The house now boasts a fascinating collection of Dickens memorabilia relating in particular to his early life and novels. *Tel. 071/405–2127. Admission: £1.50 adults, 50p children under 16. Open Mon.–Sat. 10–5; closed Sun.*

Tour 3: Around Two Royal Parks— Knightsbridge and Kensington

Hyde Park and Kensington Gardens together form a great swath of green that cuts across the heart of London. They are bordered on one side by opulent Knightsbridge and Kensington and their glamorous shopping and restaurant districts. This walk includes fewer "must-see" landmarks of British history than the others, although there are some excellent museums en route.

Start at traffic-clogged **Hyde Park Corner.** On the central island is the triumphal **Wellington Arch,** originally intended to adorn the back gate of Buckingham Palace. The original statue of the Duke of Wellington, victorious at the Battle of Waterloo against the French in 1815 and later prime minister, was moved to Aldershot and replaced by *Peace in Her Chariot* in 1912. The mansion standing by the park entrance is **Apsley House,** built in the 1770s by celebrated Scottish architect Robert Adam. The London home of the first Duke of Wellington for some 30 years,

37 it is now the **Wellington Museum.** The interior is much as it was in the Iron Duke's day, full of heavy, ornate pieces; there's also a fine equestrian portrait of Wellington by Goya. *149 Piccadilly, tel. 071/499–5676. Admission: £2 adults, £1 children under 16 and senior citizens. Open Tues.–Sun. 11–5.*

Hyde Park (361 acres) was originally a royal hunting ground, while **Kensington Gardens** (273 acres), which adjoins it to the west, was once the park of Kensington Palace. Both contain fine trees—though many were lost during the 1987 windstorm—and a surprisingly large variety of wildlife; almost 100 species have been recorded, including cormorant, heron, and little grebe.

Enter the park through the **Decimus Burton Gateway** beside Apsley House. Almost immediately you reach **Rotten Row,** the long sandy avenue used for horseback riding that runs along the bottom of the park. The odd name derives from *route du roi* ("the King's Way"), a route William III and Queen Mary took from their home at Kensington Palace to the court at St. James's.

To the north is an artificial, crescent-shaped lake called the **Serpentine** in Hyde Park and **Long Water** in Kensington Gardens, formed in 1730 by damming a river that used to flow here. The Serpentine has its own atmosphere: festive in the summer, with its deckchairs, rowboats, and swimmers; melancholy on windy winter days.

Leave the park on the south side via **Park Close** for **Knightsbridge.** The high rise to the right is the Hyde Park Barracks, headquarters of the Household Cavalry; the soldiers often exercise their horses in the park. At precisely 10:28 every morning (9:28 on Sundays) you should be able to see the mounted Guards leaving for the Changing of the Guard ceremony at the Horseguards (*see* Tour 1, above).

Brompton Road takes you to **Harrods** and the museums of South Kensington. A main point of interest at Harrods is the ground-floor **Food Hall** with its fine tiled ceiling and artful arrays of edibles. Despite its fame as a deluxe department store, Harrods doesn't have the flair of the best in the United States; it's also phenomenally crowded, especially during sales.

Time Out Richoux (86 Brompton Rd.) offers a substantial all-day menu, or try the side attractions such as scones with jam and cream.

Off Brompton Road, Beauchamp (pronounced "Beecham") Place and Walton Street are good places to shop away from Harrod's crowds.

38 Beyond **Brompton Oratory,** an Italianate, late 19th-century church, stands the massive **Victoria and Albert Museum,** crowned with cupolas. The V&A, as it is known, originated in the 19th century as a museum of ornamental art, and has extensive collections of costumes, paintings, jewelry, musical instruments, and crafts from every part of the globe. The collections from India, China, Japan, and the Islamic world are especially dazzling. *Cromwell Rd., tel. 071/938–8500 or 071/938–8349 (recorded information). Admission: £2 donation requested. Open Mon.–Sat. 10–5:50, Sun. 2:30–5:50.*

Time Out The V&A café-restaurant is just the place to recharge after visiting the collections. You can enjoy fresh salads, sandwiches, hot lunches, or just coffee or tea.

Next to the V&A are three museums devoted to science. The **39 Natural History Museum** occupies an ornate late-Victorian building with modern additions; note the little animals carved into the cathedral-like entrance. The collections are excellent (and don't miss the full-size model of a blue whale), especially in the areas of human biology and evolution. *Cromwell Rd., tel. 071/938–9388 or 071/725–7866 (recorded information). Admission: £2.50 adults, £1.25 children under 15 and senior citizens. Open Mon.–Sat. 10–6, Sun. 1–6.*

40 The **Science Museum** concerns itself with everything from locomotives to space technology, the history of medicine to computers. Working models and "hands-on" exhibits are informative and fun (great for children). *Cromwell Rd., tel. 071/938–8000 or 071/938–8123 (recorded information). Admission: £2.50 adults, £1 children 6–14, £1.50 senior citizens. Open Mon.–Sat. 10–6, Sun. 11–6.*

41 The **Geological Museum** is primarily for the rock enthusiast, although children enjoy the earthquake simulator. The main themes are the earth's history and geology; there is also a large gemstone collection. *Exhibition Rd., tel. 071/938–9123. Admission: £1 adults, 50p children under 15 and senior citizens. Open Mon.–Sat. 10–6, Sun. 1–6.*

Exhibition Road runs back toward the parks past the Imperial College of Science (part of the University of London). At the center of the campus is the **Queen's Tower**—the only survivor of the original 1890s Imperial Institute demolished in the 1960s. There's an uninterrupted view of London from the upper gallery; displays tell the history of the Tower. *Admission: 60p. Open July–Sept., daily 10–5:30.*

On the left off Exhibition Road stands the grandiose bulk of the **42 Royal Albert Hall,** named after Queen Victoria's consort. It is the venue of the summer Promenade Concerts, and choral and symphony concerts throughout the year. Note the pseudo-Greek frieze called "The Triumph of Arts and Letters" that runs round its exterior below the dome.

43 Across the road in **Kensington Gardens** is the **Albert Memorial,** the expression of Queen Victoria's obsessive devotion to her husband's memory. The monument, epitomizing high Victorian taste, commemorates Albert's many interests. For instance, the statue holds the catalogue of the Great Exhibition of 1851, which took place in the Crystal Palace (destroyed in a 1936 fire) in Hyde Park. The memorial is in a bad way physically, and is frequently shrouded in scaffolding and fencing while work is carried out.

From the **Flower Walk,** strike across Kensington Gardens to the **Round Pond,** a favorite place for children and adults to sail **44** toy boats; and then head for **Kensington Palace,** a royal home since the late 17th century. The Prince and Princess of Wales and Princess Margaret now have apartments here. It was a simple country house until William III bought it in 1689. The interior was remodeled by leading architects Wren, Hawksmoor, Vanbrugh, and William Kent during the 18th century. Eighteen-year-old Princess Victoria was living here when, on

June 20, 1837, she learned that her uncle William IV had died, which meant her accession to the throne. Some of the state apartments (a few are open to the public) have remained unchanged since the 1830s when young Victoria lived here with her dominating mother and governess. The **Court Dress Collection** is open to visitors; it consists of court dress and uniforms from 1750 to the 1950s. Court dress and behavior were governed by strict rules, and the exhibition reveals this curious world of rigid etiquette. *Kensington Gardens, tel. 071/937–9561. Admission: £3.50 adults, £2.30 children under 16, £2.60 senior citizens. Open Mon.–Sat. 9–5, Sun. 1–5.*

Immediately behind the palace is **Kensington Palace Gardens** (called Palace Green at the south end), a wide, leafy avenue of mid-19th century mansions. This is one of the few private roads in London with uniformed guards at each end; there are several foreign embassies here, including that of the Soviet Union.

Just west, past the towering modern Royal Garden Hotel, **Kensington Church Street** runs up to the right. **St. Mary Abbotts Church** on the corner looks medieval but was built in the 1870s. This is rich territory for antiques enthusiasts: The street's shops (all the way up to Notting Hill) carry everything from Japanese armor to Victorian commemorative china. Tucked away behind the church is **Kensington Church Walk,** a pretty lane lined with tiny shops (go down Holland Street, take the second left).

Time Out **Muffin Man** (12 Wright's La., off Kensington High St.) provides a refuge from the crowds of shoppers; salads and sandwiches, and scones and cakes at teatime, are the specialties. They serve breakfast all day!

If you follow **Kensington High Street** (another flourishing shopping street) westward, you'll come to the **Commonwealth Institute,** recognizable by its huge, tentlike copper roof. The Institute focuses on the cultures of Commonwealth countries with frequent exhibitions, concerts, and film shows. *230 Kensington High St., tel. 071/603–4535. Admission free. Open Mon.–Sat. 10–5, Sun. 2–5.*

On the eastern side of the Commonwealth Institute is **Linley Sambourne House,** built and furnished in the 1870s by Mr. Sambourne, for over 30 years the political cartoonist for the satirical magazine *Punch*. Full of pictures, furniture, and ornaments, it provides a marvelous insight into the day-to-day life of a prosperous, cultured family in late Victorian times. Some of the scenes from the movie *A Room with a View* were shot here. *18 Stafford Terr., tel. 071/994–1019. Admission: £2. Open Mar.–Oct., Wed. 10–4, Sun. 2–5.*

Time Out The pretty pub on the corner of Edwardes Square (two blocks beyond the Commonwealth Institute, across the High Street), the **Scarsdale Arms,** is an ideal spot for a drink and a filling bar snack.

A little way past the Commonwealth Institute, on the right, is **Melbury Road** which leads to **Holland Park Road.** Lord Leighton, the Victorian painter par excellence, lived at no. 12. The exotic richness of late 19th-century aesthetic tastes is captured in **Leighton House,** especially the Arab hall, which is lavishly lined with Persian tiles and pierced woodwork. The rest of the property has been somewhat neglected, but thanks to the generosity of John Paul Getty III, the house is now being set to rights. This neighborhood was one of the principal artists' colonies of Victorian London. If you are interested in domestic architecture of the 19th century, wander through the surrounding streets. *12 Holland Park Rd., tel. 071/602-3316. Admission free. Open Mon.–Sat. 11–5 (Mon.–Fri. 11–6 during exhibitions).*

Tour 4: The City

The City, the traditional commercial center of London, is the capital's oldest quarter, having been the site of the great Roman city of Londinium. Over the past 2,000 years the City has been continually renewed. The wooden buildings of the medieval City were destroyed in the Great Fire of 1666, and rebuilt in brick and stone. There were waves of reconstruction in the 19th century, and again after World War II to repair the devastation wrought by air attacks. Since the '60s, modern office towers have completely changed the City's skyline, as the great financial institutions indulged in conspicuous construction.

Throughout these changes, the City has preserved its unique identity. It is governed by the Lord Mayor and the Corporation (city council) of London, as it has been for centuries. Commerce remains the City's lifeblood, but with banking now ascendant over trade. Until the first half of the 19th century, merchants and traders who worked in the City also lived there. Now, despite a huge work force, scarcely 8,000 people actually live within the City's 677 acres. Try, therefore, to explore on a weekday. On weekends, the streets are empty, and most of the shops—even some of the churches—are closed.

48 **St. Paul's Cathedral** was rebuilt after the Great Fire of 1666 by Sir Christopher Wren, the architect who designed 50 other City churches to replace those lost in the Fire. St. Paul's is Wren's greatest work and fittingly, he is buried in the crypt, his epitaph composed by his son: *Lector, si monumentum requiris, circumspice*—Reader, if you seek his monument, look around you. The cathedral has been the scene of many state pageants, including Winston Churchill's funeral in 1965 and the wedding of the Prince and Princess of Wales in 1981. Fine painting and craftsmanship abound—the choir stalls are by the great 17th-century wood carver Grinling Gibbons—but overall the atmosphere is somewhat austere and remote. Perhaps this is because Wren's design was based on Italian Renaissance style rather than the English medieval tradition. The fact that the church was built in just 35 years also helps to account for its unusually unified quality.

The cathedral contains dozens of monuments and tombs. Among those commemorated are two national heroes: Nelson, victor over the French at Trafalgar in 1805; and Wellington, who defeated the French on land at Waterloo ten years later. The essayist and lexicographer Dr. Johnson (another notable here) and even George Washington have their places. In the ambulatory (the area behind the high altar) is the **American Chapel,** a memorial to the 28,000 Americans stationed in Britain during World War II who lost their lives in active service.

Henry Moore's sculpture *Mother and Child*, donated by the artist in 1984, stands near the entrance to the ambulatory.

The cathedral's crowning glory is its dome. It consists of three distinct shells: an outer timber-framed dome covered with lead; the interior dome, built of brick and decorated with frescoes of the life of St. Paul by the 18th-century artist Sir James Thornhill; and, in between, a brick cone that supports and strengthens both. There is a stunning view down to the body of the church from the **Whispering Gallery,** high up in the inner dome. The gallery's name comes from its remarkable acoustics: Words whispered at one point can be heard clearly on the opposite point 112 feet away.

Above the Whispering Gallery are the **Stone Gallery** and the **Golden Gallery,** both commanding fine views across London from the cathedral's exterior. These galleries also afford close views of the flying buttresses and western tower. The steps to the Golden Gallery just below the lantern, ball and cross, though safe, are very steep; from them you can see the brick cone that divides the inner and outer domes. *Tel. 071/248–2705. Cathedral open Mon.–Sat. 7:30–6, Sun. 8–6. Admission to ambulatory (American Chapel): 70p adults; to Crypt and Treasury: £1.20 adults, 60p children; to galleries: £2 adults, £1 children. Ambulatory, Crypt, and galleries open Mon.–Fri. 10–4:15. Sat. 11–4:15. Guided tours of the cathedral weekdays at 11, 11:30, 2, and 2:30. Cost: £4 adults, £1.80 children.*

Time Out At **Balls Brothers Wine Bar** (2 Old Chance Ct., St. Paul's Churchyard), freshly made soup and grilled steak in French bread are two specialties. Arrive early at lunchtime.

A short walk north of the cathedral to **London Wall,** so called because it follows the line of the wall that surrounded the Roman settlement, brings you to the **Museum of London.** Its imaginative displays bring London to life from Roman times to the present. Among the highlights are the Lord Mayor's Ceremonial Coach, a reenactment of the Great Fire, and the Cheapside Hoard—jewelry hidden during an outbreak of plague in the 17th century and never recovered by its owner. The 20th-century exhibits include a Woolworth's counter and elevators from Selfridge's; both stores (founded by Americans) had considerable impact on the lives of Londoners. *London Wall, tel. 071/600–3699. Admission free. Open Tues.–Sat. 10–6, Sun. 2–6; closed national holidays.*

Time Out **Millburn's,** the museum's restaurant, provides basic refreshments in an area short on family eating places.

50 The **National Postal Museum** is housed in the General Post Office and contains one of the world's most important collections of postage stamps, philatelic archives, and an extensive reference library. *King Edward Bldg., King Edward St., tel. 071/239–5420. Admission free. Open Mon.–Thurs. 9:30–4:30, Fri. 9:30–4; closed weekends, national holidays.*

51 The **Barbican** is a vast residential complex and arts center built by the City of London that takes its name from the watch tower that stood here in the Middle Ages, just outside the City walls. The arts center contains a concert hall, where the London Symphony Orchestra is based, two theaters, an art gallery for major exhibitions, cinema, library, café, and restaurant. The Royal Shakespeare Company, which stages the plays of Shakespeare, other classics, and more modern works, has its London base here. *Silk St., tel. 071/638-4141. Admission free. Open Mon.-Sat. 9 AM-11 PM, Sun. noon-11 PM. Barbican art gallery: admission varies according to exhibition, open Mon.-Sat. 10-6:45, Sun. noon-5:45.*

Almost the only building in this area to even partially survive the German bombings of 1940 and 1941 is **St. Giles without Cripplegate,** St. Giles being the patron saint of cripples. Today it is the parish church of the Barbican, and stands just south of the main complex, forlornly swamped by its towering modern neighbors. Only the church tower and walls are original; the remainder was rebuilt in the 1950s.

52 On the south side of London Wall stands the **Guildhall,** the home of the Corporation of London, which elects the Lord Mayor of London here each year with great ceremony. The building dates from 1410, with much reconstruction over the centuries. *King St., tel. 071/606-3030. Admission free. Great Hall open weekdays 9:30-5 unless a function is being held. Library open weekdays 9:30-4:45.*

Now walk south to **Cheapside.** This was the chief market place of medieval London (the Old English word *ceap* meant market), as the area's street names indicate: Milk Street, Ironmonger Lane, Bread Street, etc. Many of them still follow the medieval **53** layout. The church of **St. Mary-le-Bow** on Cheapside was rebuilt by Wren after the Great Fire, and again after it was bombed in World War II; it is said that to be a true Cockney you must be born within the sound of Bow bells.

A short walk east along Cheapside brings you to a seven-way **54** intersection. The **Bank of England,** Britain's treasury, is the huge building on the left. A new museum here highlights the history of the Bank and its role in the world economy. *Bartholomew La., tel. 071/601-4444. Admission free. Open Good Friday-Sept., Mon.-Sat. 10-6, Sun. 2-6; Oct.-Good Friday, weekdays 10-6.*

55 At right angles to the Bank is the **Royal Exchange,** originally built in the 1560s for merchants and traders to conduct business. The present building, opened in 1844 (the third on the site), is now occupied by the **London International Financial Futures Exchange.** You can watch the hectic trading from the Visitors' Gallery. *Cornhill, tel. 071/623-0444. Admission free. Open weekdays 11:30-1:45.*

56 The third major building at this intersection is the **Mansion House,** the official residence of the Lord Mayor (not open to the general public).

Continue east along Cornhill, site of a Roman basilica and a medieval grain market. Turn right onto Gracechurch Street **57** and left onto **Leadenhall Market.** There's been a market here since the 14th century; the glass and cast-iron building here dates from 1881.

Time Out **The Bull's Head** wine bar (80 Leadenhall St.) also has a restaurant and the **Leadenhall Wine Bar** (26 Leadenhall Market) offers a fixed-price buffet plus a daily special. **Hamiltons Res-**

taurant (28 Leadenhall Market) serves fish, meat, pasta, and pizzas.

---

58 Just behind the market is one of the most striking examples of contemporary City architecture: the headquarters of **Lloyd's of London,** designed by Richard Rogers and completed in 1986. Its main feature is a 200-foot-high barrel vault of sparkling glass that looks "alive" in all weathers; it encloses a great atrium ringed with twelve tiers of galleries used largely as offices. Since its founding in the 19th century, Lloyd's has earned its fame by underwriting every kind of risk imaginable: ships, aircraft, oil rigs, even Betty Grable's and Madonna's legs! An exhibition details the history of Lloyd's; there is also an open trading area. *1 Lime St., tel. 071/623–7100, ext. 6210, 5786. Admission free. Open weekdays 10–2:30.*

Time Out Lloyd's was founded in a coffee house, so **Lloyd's Coffee House** at the foot of the modern building is an apt place for a coffee break.

59 The **Monument,** to the south, is a massive column of white stone designed by Wren and erected in 1667 to commemorate the Great Fire. It stands 202 feet high, with its base exactly 202 feet from the site of the small bakery shop in Pudding Lane where the fire started. At the summit is a gilt urn with flames leaping from it, 311 steps up from the street. *Monument St., tel. 071/626–2717. Admission: £1 adults, 25p children. Open Mon.–Sat. 9–2.*

60 The **Tower of London** is one of London's most popular (hence, crowded) sights. Visit as early in the day as possible, and see the Crown Jewels first, as they draw the most visitors. Then join one of the excellent free one-hour tours given by the Yeoman Warders of the Tower (the "Beefeaters"), who wear a picturesque Tudor-style uniform. Tours start from the Middle Tower (near the entrance) about every 30 minutes.

The Tower served as both fortress and palace in medieval times; every British sovereign from William the Conqueror (11th century) to Henry VIII (16th century) lived here, and it is still officially a royal palace. The Tower has such a long history and its buildings have known so many uses that it can be difficult to grasp the overall story. The **History Gallery** is a useful walk-through display which answers most questions about the Tower and its inhabitants.

The **White Tower** is the oldest and most conspicuous building in the entire complex. When it was completed in about 1097, it dominated the whole settlement, forcing home the power of England's new Norman overlords. Inside, the austere **Chapel of St. John** is one of the Tower's few unaltered structures, a Norman chapel of great simplicity, almost entirely lacking in ornamentation.

The **Royal Armouries,** England's national collection of arms and armor, occupies the rest of the White Tower. 16th- and 17th-century armor dominate the displays, including pieces belonging to Henry VIII and Charles I. Armor from Asia and the Islamic world is on show in the **Oriental Armoury** in the **Waterloo Barracks,** including 18th-century elephant armor, brought to England by Lord Clive. Gruesome instruments of torture and punishment lie mercifully still in the **Bowyer Tower,** while the

New Armouries house examples of almost every weapon made in the Tower for British forces between the 17th and 19th century.

Surrounding the White Tower are structures dating from the 11th to the 19th century. Sir Walter Raleigh was held prisoner in the **Bloody Tower** (originally the Garden Tower) in relative comfort between 1603 and 1616; he passed the time writing his *History of the World.* The young princes, sons of Edward IV, supposedly murdered on the orders of their uncle Richard III, lived and probably died in the Bloody Tower. Next door stands the **Wakefield Tower,** where Henry VI was allegedly murdered in 1471 during the Wars of the Roses, England's medieval civil war.

Tower Green was the site of the executioner's block. It was a rare honor to be beheaded inside the Tower in relative privacy; most people were executed outside on Tower Hill, where the crowds could get a better view. Important prisoners were held in the **Beauchamp Tower** to the west of Tower Green; its walls are covered with graffiti and inscriptions carved by prisoners.

The **Crown Jewels,** in the high-security **Jewel House,** are a breathtakingly impressive collection of regalia, precious stones, gold, and silver. The Royal Sceptre contains the largest cut diamond in the world. The Imperial State Crown, made for Queen Victoria's coronation in 1838, is studded with 3,000 precious stones, mainly diamonds and pearls. *Tower Hill, tel. 071/ 709–0765. Admission: £5.50 adults, £3 children under 5, £4 senior citizens; reduced admission during Feb. when the Jewel House is closed. Open Mar.–Oct., Mon.–Sat. 9:30–5, Sun. 2–5; Nov.–Feb., Mon.–Sat. 9:30–4.*

At press time, work was in progress on the **Tower Hill Pageant,** London's first "dark ride" museum, in which visitors board automated vehicles to be transported past various tableaux depicting London's history from Roman times to WWII. The Museum of London had a big hand in the design and conception of what promises to be quite an experience. Also on display will be Roman, Saxon, and Medieval archaeological finds, and a brand new complex of shops and restaurants will be on hand for visitors to the museum and the neighboring Tower. *Tower Hill Vaults, Tower Hill, tel. 071/924–2465. Admission charge not available at press time. Open daily 9:30–5:30.*

61 **Tower Bridge** may look medieval, but it was built in 1885–94. It is the only Thames bridge that can be raised to allow ships to pass, although with the virtual extinction of London's shipping trade and the movement of big ships on the Thames, the complex lifting mechanism is used only four or five times a week. A tour of the bridge starts from the North Tower, where an elevator takes you most of the way to the top. Awaiting are displays on the history and design of the bridge; a dramatic trek along the high walkways that connect either side of the structure; and superb views up- and downriver. Another elevator in the south Tower descends to ground level. The last stop is the machine room, where the original boilers, steam and hydraulic engines, pumps, and accumulators are all in gleaming working order. *Tel. 071/407–0922. Admission: £2.50 adults, £1 children under 16 and senior citizens. Open Apr.–Oct., daily 10–6:30; Nov.–Mar., daily 10–4:45.*

Tour 5: The South Bank

Southwark, on the south bank of the Thames, has long been neglected. Full of derelict 19th-century warehouses, it seemed a perfect location for Jack the Ripper movies. Now ambitious new building complexes with stylish museums and stores are turning it into a riverside center of activity again.

The first settlement here was Roman. Across the river from the City proper, and thus outside its jurisdiction, by the Middle Ages Southwark had acquired a reputation for easy living. Londoners used to go there to enjoy a night in one of the many inns—Southwark was famous for good, strong beer—or to sample the pleasures of the Southwark "stews" (brothels, not casseroles!). Bear-baiting and the theater were other forms of entertainment here. At the Elizabethan Globe Theatre, Shakespeare was both actor and shareholder, and his plays were staged regularly.

62 Start at **Butler's Wharf,** a short distance downstream (east) of the south end of Tower Bridge. This was originally a large warehouse, and has been converted into a residential and commercial complex. Until 1982 there was a brewery here; its tower is all that remains. A new **Design Museum** opened here in July 1989, focusing on the history and evolution of mass-produced goods and services. Films, sound recordings, posters, and other advertising material help place the exhibits in their contemporary social and cultural context. Permanent displays of "classic" design are combined with temporary theme exhibitions which emphasize how mass-produced consumer goods are developed. There is also a riverside café. *Butlers Wharf, tel. 071/403–6933, 071/407–6265. Admission: £2.50 adults, £1.50 children and senior citizens. Open Tues.–Sun. 11:30–6:30.*

63 Upstream of Tower Bridge lies **H.M.S. *Belfast,*** the largest and one of the most powerful cruisers ever built for the Royal Navy (a ferry runs between it and the Tower of London). The *Belfast* stood off Normandy on D-Day in 1944, protecting the landing beaches, and after the war served in the Far East. When her service career ended in 1963, she was saved from the scrapyard by the Imperial War Museum. Naval and World War II enthusiasts will want to tour the *Belfast;* the armaments, mess decks, punishment cells, operations room, and engine room are open to view. Others can admire it from the riverside. *Symon's Wharf, Vine Lane, Tooley St., tel. 071/407–6434. Admission: £3.50 adults, £1.75 children under 16 and senior citizens. Open mid-Mar.–Oct., daily 11–5:30; Nov.–early Mar., daily 11–4:30.*

64 **Hay's Galleria** is a shopping mall housed beneath a dramatic 100-foot-high, 300-foot-long glass barrel-vault roof. In the center is a massive kinetic sculpture, *Navigators,* by David Kemp. Shaped like a huge comic boat, parts of which move under the water jets, it recalls the history of Hay's Wharf, one of London's oldest, dating from 1651. Planners hope that the Galleria will develop into a Covent Garden on the Thames.

Time Out Reasonably priced lunch spots are rare here, but **The Horniman at Hay's** has acceptable pub food. Alternatively, eat a take-out snack on a bench overlooking the river and Custom House across the way.

Walking westward from the Galleria, follow the riverside path past the Cottons building, with its offices overlooking a 100-foot-high atrium and water garden, to **London Bridge.**

65 On **Tooley Street,** below Hay's Galleria, is **the London Dungeon,** which recreates scenes of medieval torture, execution, disease, persecution, and—on a different level—the Great Fire of 1666. The Dungeon's appeal may be lost on the squeamish, but teenagers will probably love it! *28–34 Tooley St., tel. 071/387–1405. Admission: £5 adults, £3 children under 14 and senior citizens. Open daily 10–4:30.*

66 **Old St. Thomas's Hospital,** on St. Thomas Street (over the railway viaduct from Tooley Street), provides an insight into hospital life of only a few generations ago. This operating theater dates from 1821 and has been restored to its original state. Surgeons at the time worked in aprons stained with blood from previous operations, washing facilities scarcely existed, and a sawdust box underneath the table caught patients' blood; when it was full, the surgeon called for more sawdust. The herb garret next door, where medicinal herbs were dried and stored, has also been restored. *St. Thomas St., tel. 071/806–4325. Admission: £1 adults, 60p children and senior citizens. Open Mon., Wed., Fri. 12:30–4, other times by appointment.*

67 **Southwark Cathedral** is the largest Gothic church in London after Westminster Abbey—building began on it in 1220. The chief feature of interest for American visitors is the Harvard Chapel. It commemorates John Harvard, founder of the great American university, baptized here in 1608. Shakespeare's younger brother Edmund is buried here.

Around the corner, **St. Mary Overie Dock** is an office development built on the site of the London palace of the Bishops of Winchester; the massive west wall of the great hall has been preserved, and you can see the outline of a rose window. The
68 *Kathleen & May,* one of the last surviving wooden three-masted schooners, is permanently moored here. She was one of hundreds of schooners that plied the coasts of Britain in the early 20th century. On board is a maritime exhibition including a rare film of the *Kathleen & May* under sail. *St. Mary Overie Dock, tel. 071/403–3965. Admission £1 adults, 50p children under 14 and senior citizens. Open Apr.–Oct, daily 10–5; Nov.–Mar., weekdays 10–5.*

Time Out **The Old Thameside Inn** serves morning coffee, pastries, lunches, and old-fashioned high tea.

Now walk west along Clink Street, where one of Southwark's several prisons stood, past the Bankside pub and under Cannon Street Railway Bridge and Southwark Bridge. On the left, a
69 narrow street called Bear Gardens leads to the **Shakespeare Globe Museum,** site of a massive project by American actor/director Sam Wanamaker to rebuild Shakespeare's Globe Playhouse to its original open-roof design of 1599, using authentic Elizabethan materials and techniques wherever possible. It is expected to open in the summer of 1993 (along with shops and a piazza), but for the moment there is little to see. The museum, though, fills in the background of this 300-year-old theater district. *Bear Gardens, tel. 071/620–0202. Admission: £1 adults, 50p children and senior citizens. Open Mon.–Sat. 10–5, Sun. 1:30–5.*

The riverside path passes Cardinal's Wharf and then continues along Bankside toward **Blackfriars Bridge.**

On the far side of the bridge, beyond the **Oxo Tower,** is **Coin Street,** a residential enclave that has been preserved from development. At **Gabriel's Wharf** there are craft shops, studios, and a craft market.

⑩

A short walk along the new embankment promenade—look for the display panels which identify the buildings across the river—brings you to the **National Theatre,** the first of the concrete buildings looking like giant bunkers that make up the **South Bank Arts Complex.** The foyers, open to the public six days a week, are full of activity, with bookshops, bars, cafés, exhibitions, and free performances. The National Theatre Company plays here regularly in three auditoria, each with its distinct character. Although performances can be uneven, its best work is electrifying. *South Bank, tel. 071/928–2252 (box office); 071/928–8126 (recorded information). Open Mon.–Sat. 10 AM–11 PM. 1½-hour tours of the theater 5 times daily, between 10:15 and 6; cost: £2.50 adults, £1.75 children and senior citizens.*

⑪

Time Out The National Theatre's bars and snack counters are ideal places to relax any time of day.

Underneath Waterloo Bridge nearby are the **National Film Theatre** (N.F.T.) and the new **Museum of the Moving Image** (M.O.M.I.). The N.F.T. screens art and historic films drawn mainly from its huge archives. M.O.M.I. celebrates every aspect of the moving image from Chinese shadow plays of 2,500 BC to the latest fiber optics and satellite images; cinema and television take center stage, however. This is very much a hands-on museum, with the emphasis on participatory displays, especially of film and television-making processes. *South Bank, tel. 071/928–3535 or 071/401–2636 (recorded information). Admission: £3.95 adults, £2.75 children, students, and senior citizens. Open Tues.–Sat. 10–8, Sun. 10–6; last admission 1½ hours before closing.*

Time Out Open to all, the **N.F.T. cafeteria** serves lunch and dinner.

The rest of the arts complex, on the far side of Waterloo Bridge, consists of three concert halls and the **Hayward Gallery,** which hosts large-scale art exhibitions. The gallery is surmounted by a tall, skeletal sculpture made of neon tubing. At night hectic colors run up and down it, their speed and intensity governed by the velocity of the wind playing through an anemometer at the top. *Belvedere Rd., tel. 071/928–3144 or 071/261–0127 (recorded information). Admission: varies according to exhibition. Open Mon.–Wed. 10–8, Thurs.–Sat. 10–6, Sun. 12–6.*

The three concert halls, the **Royal Festival Hall,** the **Queen Elizabeth Hall,** and the **Purcell Room,** are used for every kind of musical event, from major symphony and choral concerts to recitals of the latest electronic compositions. The Festival Hall has a well-stocked bookstore, a record shop, and exhibition space.

Time Out The Festival Hall's eateries include a salt-beef bar, pasta counter, salad bar, coffee shop, and spacious cafeteria.

The next stretch of the embankment affords photogenic views across the river to Big Ben and the Houses of Parliament. The path runs in front of **County Hall,** formerly the seat of local government for Greater London (The Greater London Council, or G.L.C.). After considerable controversy the G.L.C. was disbanded in 1986. The huge building's future remains undecided; its chill, classical facade dates from 1932.

72 The river frontage on the far side of **Westminster Bridge** is occupied by **St. Thomas's Hospital.** In early 1989 St. Thomas's became the site of the **Florence Nightingale Museum,** dedicated to the famous nurse's life and work and also featuring the evolution of modern nursing techniques. *Gassiot House, 2 Lambeth Palace Rd., tel. 071/620–0374. Admission: £2 adults, £1 children and senior citizens. Open Tues.–Sun. 10–4.*

73 Beyond St. Thomas's stands **Lambeth Palace,** the London residence of the Archbishop of Canterbury—the senior archbishop of the Church of England—since the early 13th century. It's rarely open to the public, but you can admire the fine Tudor gatehouse.

Beside the palace, in the yard of the now-deconsecrated **St. Mary's Church,** are buried the two John Tradescants, father and son, who were royal gardeners in the 17th century. They traveled widely in Europe and America, bringing back plant specimens not previously known in this country; their garden in Lambeth became a pioneer nursery. St. Mary's Church now houses the Tradescant Trust's **Museum of Garden History.** This unique collection includes a duplication of a 17th-century knot garden (the name describes its shape) containing only plants grown in the 17th century, especially those grown by the Tradescants. *St. Mary-at-Lambeth, Lambeth Palace Rd., tel. 071/261–1891. Admission free; donations welcome. Open early Mar.–early Dec., weekdays 11–3, Sun. 10:30–5; closed Sat.*

74 The **Imperial War Museum** lies a short walk inland from Lambeth Palace, down Lambeth Road. Its holdings constitute the country's principal collection of 20th-century war artifacts. Among the hardware on display are a Battle of Britain Spitfire, a World War I tank, and a German V1 pilotless flying bomb, a type dropped on London in 1944–5. The "Blitz Experience" gives you the sights, sounds, and smells of London during the World War II bombing. *Lambeth Rd., tel. 081/755–8922. Admission: £3 adults, £1.50 children and senior citizens. Blitz Experience: £1 adults, 50p children. Open daily 10–6.*

Tour 6: Up and Down the Thames

The River Thames unites the oldest and the newest areas of London. It's spanned by bridges of different design. The earliest, Richmond, dates from 1774, and the most recent, London Bridge, from 1973—the former London Bridge having been sold and rebuilt in Arizona. The river has played an important role in the history of London and from it the familiar historic buildings and sites take on a new and dramatic perspective. Points of interest such as Greenwich, the Thames Barrier, Hampton Court Palace, and Kew are serviced by BritRail (*see* Arriving and Departing by Train, above). Also, boat excursions can be taken in either direction from piers at Westminster, Charing Cross, and Tower Bridge. *Tel. 071/730–4812 for the recorded Riverboat Information Service.*

Greenwich   Downstream, a few miles past the imposing bulk of the Tower of
London, lies **Greenwich.** At its heart are the late-17th-century
buildings of the **Royal Naval College,** once an old sailors' home;
the college has been here since 1873. The buildings are the
work of Sir Christopher Wren and his two assistants,
Hawksmoor and Vanbrugh, later celebrated architects in their
own right. You can visit the grand **Painted Hall,** the college dining hall, dramatically decorated with huge frescoes by Sir
James Thornhill, who also painted the dome in St. Paul's Cathedral. It was here that Nelson's body lay in state at Christmas of 1805, after the Battle of Trafalgar. Across from the
Painted Hall is the **College Chapel.** The airy 18th-century interior is a delight of pastel shades and intricate, delicate detail.
The pulpit maintains the naval theme; it's made from the top
deck of a three-decker sailing ship. *King William Walk, tel.
071/858-2154. Admission free. Open Fri.–Wed. 2:30–4:45.*

Two dry-docked boats alongside the river are the *Cutty Sark,*
the last of the 19th-century clipper ships, and the tiny *Gipsy
Moth IV,* which Sir Francis Chichester sailed singlehandedly
around the world in 1966. *Cutty Sark: King William Walk, tel.
081/858-3445. Admission: £1.80 adults, 80p children under 16
and senior citizens. Open Mon.–Sat. 10–5, Sun. 12–5. Gipsy
Moth IV: King William Walk, tel. 081/853-3589. Admission:
20p adults, 10p children and senior citizens. Open Apr.–Oct.,
Mon.–Sat. 10–6, Sun. noon–6.*

The **National Maritime Museum** charts Britain's illustrious
maritime heritage through maps, paintings, and models.
Among the highlights are the original royal barges, displayed
in the **Barge House.** *Romney Rd., tel. 081/858-4422. Joint admission with Old Royal Observatory: £3 adults, £1.50 children
and senior citizens. Open late Mar.–Oct., Mon.–Sat. 9–6,
Sun. noon–6; Nov.–mid-Mar., Mon.–Sat. 9–5, Sun. noon–5.*

On the hill behind the museum and the Naval College, in **Greenwich Park,** is the **Old Royal Observatory,** founded in 1675 by
Charles II, who was a great patron of the sciences. Many original telescopes and astronomical instruments are on display
here. The world's prime meridian (zero degrees longitude)
runs through the courtyard: Straddle the line and you'll have a
foot in each hemisphere. *Greenwich Park, tel. 081/858-1167.
Admission and times as National Maritime Museum.*

A craft market takes place on weekends in the Victorian covered market, and there's also an antiques market at the foot of
Crooms Hill most weekend mornings.

Time Out   Try the **Trafalgar Tavern,** a historic pub on the river just beyond the Naval College, or the **Dolphin Coffee Shop** on the Maritime museum grounds, which is also open to the public.

Thames Barrier   A major attraction just a few miles downriver is the Thames
Barrier. Constructed between 1975–1982, it is the world's largest moveable flood barrier, designed to prevent the Thames
from overflowing its banks into extensive parts of central and
south London. Boats depart frequently from Greenwich Pier
to visit this awesome piece of civil engineering. An additional
attraction at the barrier is Hallett's *Panorama* (an oil painting
and sculpture) of the city of Bath. *Unity Way, off Woolwich
Rd., tel. 081/854-1373. Admission (including the Panorama):*

£2 adults, £1.20 children and senior citizens. Open daily 10:30–5:30.

Hampton Court Palace A series of royal palaces and grand houses line the Thames west of central London, built as aristocratic country residences close to the capital when the river was the primary means of travel. The most celebrated is **Hampton Court Palace,** surrounded by rolling parkland, some 20 miles upstream. It was begun in 1514 by Cardinal Wolsey, taken from him by Henry VIII, and expanded 150 years later by Sir Christopher Wren for William and Mary. Steeped in history and hung with priceless paintings and tapestries, Hampton Court provides a magical trip out of town, especially if you are able to go on a sunny day from spring through to the fall, to see the gardens at their colorful best. *East Molesey, tel. 081/977–8441. Admission: state apartments, and maze £3.40 adults, £1.70 children and senior citizens; maze only £1 adults, 50p children and senior citizens; grounds free. State apartments open daily 10–6 Apr.–Sept.; daily 10–4:30 Oct.–Mar. Tudor tennis court open Apr.–Sept. only; Grounds open daily 8–dusk.*

Nearer London, **Ham House** is an exquisite late-17th-century riverside mansion. Rich, heavy furnishings; period portraits; and powerfully carved furniture lend a sense of opulence and luxury. *Ham St., Richmond, tel. 081/940–1950. Admission: £2 adults, £1 children under 16 and senior citizens. Open Tues.–Sun. and national holidays 11–5.*

Richmond **Richmond** is an old, wealthy suburb of London with elegant 18th-century houses fronting its green; **Richmond Hill** has many good antiques shops. **Richmond Park** is one of the last vestiges of the vast medieval forests and hunting grounds that once pressed in on London; deer still roam here.

Time Out **The Cricketers,** Richmond Green, does good pub lunches: coffee and afternoon teas are served from the Stumps. **Mrs. Beetons,** on Hill Rise, serves filling traditional dishes.

Kew **The Royal Botanic Gardens** at **Kew** are the headquarters of the country's leading botanical institute as well as a public garden of 300 acres and over 60,000 species of plants. Two 18th-century royal ladies, Queen Caroline (wife of George II) and Princess Augusta (widow of Frederick, Prince of Wales), both avid gardeners, were responsible for its founding.

Kew Palace, on the grounds, was home to George III for much of his life. Its formal garden has been redeveloped on a 17th-century pattern. The 19th-century greenhouses, notably the **Palm House** and the **Temperate House,** are among the highlights here. In the ultramodern Princess of Wales Conservatory opened in 1987, there are ten climatic zones, their temperatures all precisely controlled by computer. *Royal Botanic Gardens, tel. 081/940–1171. Admission: £3 adults, £1 children, £1.50 senior citizens and students. Gardens open daily 9:30–6:30, greenhouses 10–6:30 (both open Sun. and national holidays until 8); in winter closing times depend on the light, usually 4 or 5. Kew Palace, tel. 081/940–3321. Admission: £1 adults, 50p children under 16 and senior citizens. Open Apr.–Sept., daily 11–5:30.*

London for Free

London is a gift to the freeloader. But in order to enjoy the free delights of the city, you should make a very small investment in a wander-at-will Underground ticket. Once you have that, the city's your oyster.

Galleries Most of the museums still have no admission fees, though there is a growing movement toward charging for entry. Among the most important ones that open their doors without charge are: The British Museum, the National Gallery, the National Portrait Gallery, the Museum of London, and the Tate Gallery. Most churches are all, or partly, free. You may have to pay to visit parts of St. Paul's and Westminster Abbey, but the main areas are still without charge. All of Wren's lovely City churches are free.

The commercial art galleries in and around Bond Street allow visitors to browse for free, and some will even lend you their expensive catalogues without charge. This is also true of the great auction houses, Christie's and Sotheby's, whose offerings often rival all but the topmost museums.

Parks The great parks are a summer vacation in themselves. To lie on the grass in Hyde Park or by the Serpentine, or to wander among the deer in the park of Hampton Court Palace, is to enjoy the best of country life in the middle of the city. Spend a few dollars on a picnic, and you can relax for hours.

To the north lies Hampstead Heath, a spreading parkland with views over the city. It also boasts Kenwood House, a lovely mansion with art treasures that's free to all (*see* Off the Beaten Track, below). In the summer, there are free open-air concerts.

Speakers' Corner, in Hyde Park, close to Marble Arch, has been a source of free fun for decades. But though the entertainment there on a Sunday morning is nothing like as freewheeling and bizarre as it used to be, it can still provide the occasional thought-provoking or laughable performance.

Concerts In fact, there is music all over the place that the freeloader can enjoy. Bands play in the parks, many churches have magnificent choirs, the foyers of the National Theatre, the Royal Festival Hall, and the Barbican host free musical events during the day and particularly in the early evening.

Above all, London herself is a free show. You can wander the streets, explore the tiny alleys and lanes, search out historic houses where famous people have lived—all without spending a cent.

What to See and Do with Children

On London's traditional sightseeing circuit, make for the **Royal Mews** (*see* Tour 1) where some of the Queen's horses can be seen close up; the **Whispering Gallery** in **St. Paul's Cathedral** (*see* Tour 4), where it is fun to try the echo; and the many attractions of the **Tower of London** (*see* Tour 4); or take the elevator to the high walkways of **Tower Bridge** (*see* Tour 4).

Museums with hands-on activities include the **London Transport Museum** in Covent Garden (*see* Tour 2), the **Science Museum,** and the **Natural History Museum** (*see* Tour 3).

The **Gardens of the Zoological Society of London,** known simply as the Zoo, were founded over 150 years ago, absorbing over the years other collections, such as the royal menagerie, which used to be housed in the Tower of London. The zoo itself is one of the busiest mazes in the world, and you can wander around for hours. Major attractions include: (1) the Mappin Terraces, which were built some 70 years ago as a natural habitat for animals such as goats, pigs, and bears; (2) the Children's Zoo, where children can play with the smaller animals; (3) the Snowdon Aviary, designed by Lord Snowdon in 1965 when he was married to Princess Margaret; (4) the Lion Terraces; (5) the Elephant and Rhino Pavilion, an oddly delicate name for such a massive, castle-like structure; (6) the Small Bird House; and (7) the Tropical House, with its darting hummingbirds. One fascinating and unique exhibit is the Moonlight World, on the lower floor of the Charles Clore Pavilion. Here night conditions are simulated so that visitors can watch nocturnal animals during the day. The process is reversed at night, when the cages are lit, and the animals take up their daytime activities. A visit to the zoo could last hours and, for an interested child, even a whole day. Although it is one of London's major tourist attractions, the zoo remains the private gardens of the Royal Zoological Society, which has increasing difficulty in finding the necessary funds—a fact reflected in the cost of admission. *Regent's Park, tel. 071/722–3333. Admission £4.80 adults, £2.90 children under 16, £3.90 senior citizens. Open daily 9–6.*

Four museums specifically designed with children in mind are the **London Toy and Model Museum** north of Kensington Gardens, where there is a train in the garden and a mass of manufactured toys and models on display; the **Bethnal Green Museum of Children** in east London which has traditional toys, dolls, dollhouses, and puppets; and the **Horniman Museum,** an educational museum in south London with ethnographic and natural history collections. **Pollock's Toy Museum,** set in two tiny adjoining 18th-century houses, is one of London's most charming collections. Narrow, winding staircases lead to a treasure trove of dolls, toys, and teddy bears. **London Toy and Model Museum,** *21–23 Craven Hill, tel. 071/262–9450. Admission: £2.20 adults, £1.20 children under 15 and senior citizens. Open Tues.–Sat. 10–5:30, Sun. 11–5:30; closed Mon. except national holidays.* **Bethnal Green Museum,** *Cambridge Heath Rd., tel. 081/981–1711 or 081/980–3204. Admission free. Open Mon.–Thurs. and Sat. 10–6, Sun. 2:30–6.* **Horniman Museum,** *100 London Rd., tel. 081/699–1872. Admission free. Open Mon.–Sat. 10:30–6, Sun. 2–6.* **Pollock's Toy Museum,** *1 Scala St., tel. 071/636–3452. Admission: 80p adults, 40p children. Open Mon.–Sat. 10–5.*

Other child-pleasers include **Guinness World of Records** in the Trocadero at Piccadilly Circus, **Light Fantastic** in Covent Garden, and the **London Dungeon,** on Tooley Street (*see* Tour 5)—but note that it is not suitable for young or sensitive children. *Guinness World of Records, tel. 071/439–7331. Admission: £4 adults, £2.60 children, £3.25 senior citizens. Open daily 10–10. Light Fantastic, 48 South Row, The Market, Covent Garden, tel. 071/836–6423. Admission: £1.25 adults, 75p children. Open Mon.–Wed. 10–6, Thurs., Fri. 10–10, Sat. 10–7, Sun. 11–8.*

If it's raining, a novel idea might be to try brass-rubbing at the **Brass Rubbing Centre** in Westminster Abbey or at **The London Brass Rubbing Centre** at St. Martin-in-the-Fields Church in Trafalgar Square (*see* Tour 1).

A fun outdoor activity is boating on the **Serpentine,** the lake in **Hyde Park** (*see* Tour 3).

Places where children might actually enjoy shopping are around the **Covent Garden** area and in **Hamley s,** the huge toy shop on Regent's Street. At Christmas, Santa is at **Selfridges** on Oxford Street and is generally thought to be the best in town—be prepared for lines, though.

Off the Beaten Track

Beyond Regent's Park, the northern reach of central London, the city changes dramatically. You'll notice a marked "neighborhood" feel here and larger open spaces to explore.

Regent's Canal, a narrow-boat canal built in the 19th century, runs through the park to the zoo (*see* What to See and Do with Children, above). Just east of the zoo on the towpath is **Camden Lock** with its weekend market (*see* Shopping, below) and the starting point for barge trips—details from the Regent's Canal Information Centre at the junction of the canal and Camden High Street. Or you can follow the canal on foot. Go east and you'll traverse urban badlands that culminate at the Thames; westbound is more refined. The houses along the canal share their backyards with the houseboats that serve as permanent residences for Londoners who can't afford (or don't want) life on dry land. Over the next two miles, both houses and boats get fancier until you reach London's **"Little Venice,"** a watery millionaire's row of elegant homes. (Pick up public transportation again at Warwick Avenue tube, Bakerloo line.)

Due north of Camden is **Hampstead** and **Hampstead Heath.** A village until the late 1800s, it still has a rural feel despite its very 20th-century High Street. Keats and Dr. Johnson are among the many who left their literary legacy here. Wander through the network of lanes and squares that spreads outwards from the Hampstead tube station. The **Heath** is a semiwild open space where you can walk—and see—for miles. **Kenwood House,** on its northern edge, contains the **Iveagh Bequest,** a grand collection of paintings. The spacious house is set in a large park, where summer concerts are held in the open air. *Hampstead Lane, tel. 081/348–1286. Admission free. Open Easter–Sept. daily 10–6, Oct.–Easter daily 10–4.*

East of the Tower are the **Docklands.** The area became derelict after London's main port moved downstream, but is now said to be Europe's largest building site. Offices and residences are going up at a terrific rate—thus far it looks like an inhospitable planet that's been invaded by overzealous aliens. The only vestige of the old docklands are the pubs, looking somewhat ill at ease among their new neighbors.

The **Docklands Light Railway,** a new overhead rapid transit railway, serves the area. Its westernmost terminus, Tower Gateway, is a few minutes' walk from the Tower of London and Tower Hill tube. Island Gardens Station, at the other end of the line, will deposit you directly opposite the old seaport of Greenwich, which you can reach via a foot tunnel under the Thames.

Another way of visiting Docklands is to join one of **Citisights** walking tours. These explore the whole area, accompanied by a knowledgeable guide who can direct you to the newest developments and historic points of interest. *Citisights of London, 145 Goldsmiths Row, tel. 071/739–2372. Fee: £3.*

Dulwich Village in southeast London has handsome 18th-century houses lining its main street. Most of the land here belongs to the Dulwich College Estate, founded in the 17th century by actor Edward Alleyn. Well-kept **Dulwich Park** is set ablaze each May when the rhododendrons burst into bloom. **Dulwich College Picture Gallery,** across from the park entrance, is a fine small gallery designed by Sir John Soane, with works by Rembrandt, Van Dyck, Rubens, Poussin, and Gainsborough among others. *College Rd., tel. 081/693–5254. Admission: £1.50 adults, children under 16 free, 50p senior citizens. Open Tues.–Fri. 10–1 and 2–5, Sat. 11–5, Sun. 2–5.*

The **Royal Air Force Museum** in Hendon, north London, is a must for flying and military enthusiasts. The story of the R.A.F. is told in great detail. There are uniforms, guns, and radar equipment on display as well as informative sections on World War I and II and the exploits of Bomber Command. **The Battle of Britain Museum** in the same complex (no extra charge) explains how the R.A.F. fought off the German threat in 1940. The nearest Underground station is Colindale on the Northern line. *Grahame Park Way, tel. 081/205–2266. Admission: £3.60 adults, £1.80 children under 16 and senior citizens. Open daily 10–6.*

St. Albans, 24 miles northwest of London, can be reached by train from either Kings Cross or St. Pancras stations. Called "Verulamium" by the Romans, St. Albans is now a residential suburb for commuters, but it retains its ancient market-town character. It takes its present name from Alban, Britain's first Christian martyr, who was executed by the Romans in AD 209 for sheltering a Christian priest. The shrine erected where he died became an abbey and, later, St. Albans Cathedral.

Begin a visit to St. Albans on St. Peter's Street, where the open-air market established by the Saxons is still held each Wednesday and Saturday. Walk north to **St. Peter's Church** on the right-hand side, or south to the medieval and now pedestrianized **French Row,** which takes its name from the French soldiers quartered here after being recruited by the barons to fight King John in 1215, the year of the Magna Carta. The **Clock Tower** at the south end of French Row was built in 1411 as a tower from which curfew was rung. It is one of only two remaining in the country. *Admission free. Open Good Friday–mid-Sept., weekends and national holidays 10:30–5.*

At the end of French Row opposite the junction with High Street, the arch of **Waxhouse Gate** is all that remains of a 15th-century gateway to the abbey. The path through the gate is the shortest pedestrian route to **St. Albans Cathedral,** founded in the 8th century by Offa II, king of Mercia (one of the seven original Anglo-Saxon kingdoms). Built mainly with bricks taken from a nearby Roman site, it was expanded in the 11th century and became the principal Benedictine abbey in England. Later, part of the Magna Carta was prepared here. Inside is an 1872 reconstruction of St. Alban's shrine, made from 2,000 pieces of marble, and beside it, a 15th-century decorated timber "watching-loft" for the monk who guarded the shrine. The Saxon pillars in the transepts were probably looted from an earlier church. The nave is one of the longest medieval ones in existence. *Tel. 0727/60780. Admission free. Open 10–5:45 winter, 10–6:45 summer (depending on the changing of the clocks for summertime).*

Leave the cathedral by the west door and cross to the **Abbey Gatehouse,** once part of the abbey and then the city jail. Today it is part of **St. Albans School** (for boys), one of the oldest schools in Britain, possibly of Saxon origin. Nicholas Breakspear, the only English pope (he reigned as Adrian IV, 1154–59), was a pupil here.

Down Abbey Mill Lane, right beside the river Ver, **Ye Olde Fighting Cocks** is an octagonal, timber-framed inn that claims to be the oldest inhabited pub in England. St. Albans **City Museum and Art Gallery** offers an interesting collection of natural-history and folk-life exhibits, as well as an assortment of craftsmen's tools. *Hatfield Rd., tel. 0727/56679. Admission free. Open Mon.–Sat. 10–5, Sun. 2–5.*

The **Verulamium Museum,** just opposite St. Michael's Church, offers an extensive collection of Roman artifacts, including well-preserved mosaic tiles, jewelry, pottery, glassware, and a large selection of tools. Your ticket also allows you to visit the **hypocaust,** an under-floor Roman heating system housed in its own modern annex. Very close to the museum, you can see an excavated Roman theater, unique in Britain. *Museum—St. Michael's St., tel. 0727/66100, weekends 54659. Admission: £1.10 adults, 55p children. Open Apr.–Oct., Mon.–Sat. 10–5:30, Sun. 2–5:30; Nov.–Mar., Mon.–Sat. 10–4, Sun. 2–4. Theater—tel. 0727/35035. Admission: 80p adults, 30p children. Open daily 10–5 (10–4 in winter).*

Sightseeing Checklist

Historic Buildings	**Banqueting House:** Tour 1
	Buckingham Palace: Tour 1
	Clarence House: Tour 1
	Houses of Parliament: Tour 1
	Inns of Court: Tour 2
	Lambeth Palace: Tour 5
	Lancaster House: Tour 1
	Lloyd's of London: Tour 4
	Royal Albert Hall: Tour 3
	Royal Courts of Justice: Tour 2
	St. James's Palace: Tour 1
	York House: Tour 1
Museums and Galleries	**Bank of England Museum:** Tour 4
	Barbican Gallery: Tour 4
	H.M.S. *Belfast:* Tour 5
	British Museum: Tour 2
	Cabinet War Rooms: Tour 1
	Commonwealth Institute: Tour 3
	Courtauld Institute: Tour 2
	Cutty Sark: Tour 6
	The Design Museum: Tour 5
	Dickens Museum: Tour 2
	Dulwich College Picture Gallery: Off the Beaten Track
	Florence Nightingale Museum: Tour 5

Geffrye Museum of Furniture and Decorative Arts. Sequence of rooms furnished with pieces dating from the 16th century to the 1930s, plus staircases, paneling, and portraits from old London houses; the museum is located in a row of 18th-century almshouses. *Kingsland Rd., E2, tel. 071/739–9893. Admission free. Open Tues.–Sat., bank holiday Mon. 10–5, Sun. 2–5.*

Geological Museum: Tour 3

Guards Museum: Tour 1

Ham House: Tour 6

Hampton Court Palace: Tour 6

Hayward Gallery (South Bank): Tour 5

Imperial War Museum: Tour 5

Institute of Contemporary Arts: Tour 1

Iveagh Bequest: Off the Beaten Track

The Jewish Museum. Founded over 50 years ago, the Jewish Museum illustrates the long history of Jewry in Britain, dating back to the 13th century. There are manuscripts, embroidery, and silver—many items of great intrinsic worth, and all of them of interest. *Woburn House, Tavistock Sq., tel. 071/388–4525. Admission free. Open Sun., Tues.–Thurs. (and Fri. in summer) 10–4; Fri. in winter 10–12:45. Closed national and Jewish holidays.*

Dr. Johnson's House: Tour 2

Kathleen & May: Tour 5

Kensington Palace and Court Collection: Tour 3

Kenwood House (*see* Iveagh Bequest, above)

Leighton House: Tour 3

Linley Sambourne House: Tour 3

London Toy and Model Museum: What to See and Do with Children

London Transport Museum: Tour 2

The Monument: Tour 4

Museum of Garden History: Tour 5

Museum of London: Tour 4

Museum of the Moving Image (South Bank): Tour 5

National Gallery: Tour 1

National Maritime Museum: Tour 6

National Portrait Gallery: Tour 1

National Postal Museum: Tour 4

Natural History Museum: Tour 3

Old Royal Observatory: Tour 6

Old St. Thomas's Hospital: Tour 5

Percival David Foundation of Chinese Art: Tour 2

Pollock's Toy Museum: What to See and Do with Children

Queen's Gallery: Tour 1

Royal Academy of Arts. The academy mounts major exhibitions, often ones that are on an international tour, as well as its own Summer Exhibition of mixed amateur and professional work. *Burlington House, Piccadilly, tel. 071/439–7438. Admission: varies according to the exhibition. Open daily 10–6.*

Royal Mews: Tour 1

Royal Naval College: Tour 6

Science Museum: Tour 3

Shakespeare Globe Museum: Tour 5

Sir John Soane's Museum: Tour 2

Tate Gallery: Tour 1

Theatre Museum: Tour 2

Tower Bridge: Tour 4

Tower Hill Pageant: Tour 4

Tower of London: Tour 4
Victoria and Albert Museum: Tour 3
Wallace Collection. London's answer to the Frick, peaceful Hertford House contains a wealth of 18th-century French paintings and furniture, mostly purchased immediately after the French Revolution, as well as arms and armor, porcelain, Majolica, and pictures by such masters as Rembrandt, Canaletto, and Rubens. *Hertford House, Manchester Sq., tel. 071/935–0687. Admission free. Open Mon.–Sat. 10–5, Sun. 2–5.*
Wellington Museum: Tour 3

Churches

Brompton Oratory: Tour 3
Chapel Royal, St. James's Palace: Tour 1
Guards Chapel: Tour 1
Queen's Chapel: Tour 1
St. Bride's: Tour 2
St. Giles without Cripplegate: Tour 4
St. Martin-in-the-Fields: Tour 1
St. Mary Abbotts: Tour 3
St. Mary-le-Bow: Tour 4
St. Paul's Cathedral: Tour 4
Southwark Cathedral: Tour 5
Temple Church: Tour 2
Westminster Abbey: Tour 1

Parks and Gardens

Hyde Park: Tour 3
Kensington Gardens: Tour 3
Kew Gardens: Tour 6
Hampstead Heath: Off the Beaten Track
Regent's Park: Off the Beaten Track
St. James's Park: Tour 1
Richmond Park: Tour 6

Other Places of Interest

Barbican Arts Centre: Tour 4
Gardens of the Zoological Society of London (the Zoo): What to See and Do with Children
Guinness World of Records: What to See and Do with Children
Hay's Galleria: Tour 5
Light Fantastic: What to See and Do with Children
London Dungeon: Tour 5
London Planetarium. The Planetarium, beside Madame Tussaud's, brings the night sky to life. In the evening there are laser light shows set to rock music. *Marylebone Rd., tel. 071/486–1121, Admission £3.15 adults, £2.10 children, £2.50 senior citizens. Joint ticket with Madame Tussaud's, see below. Planetarium open daily 11–4:20 (shows every 40 min.); Laserium Admission: £4.65 adults, £3.65 children. Open Tues.–Sun., one-hour shows from 6 PM.*
Madame Tussaud's. Still maintains its position as one of London's most sought-after attractions, with an ever changing parade of wax celebrities. Get there early to avoid the long lines. *Marylebone Rd., tel. 071/935–6861. Admission: £5.60 adults, £3.85 children, £4.15 senior citizens. Joint ticket with Planetarium (see above), £7.25 adults. £4.85 children, £5.65 senior citizens. Open Easter–Sept., daily 9:30–5:30; Oct.–Easter, daily 10–5:30.*
Thames Barrier Visitor Centre: Tour 6

Shopping

Shopping is just as much a priority in London as sightseeing, and you'll soon discover that London is conveniently divided into areas specializing in particular goods. Below we list districts and what you can expect to find there.

Chelsea A fashion mecca in the Swinging Sixties, and again in the punked-out seventies, King's Road today is a reminder that even the most outrageous look eventually looks obsolete. Although once-trendy punks still gather here to pose, buy clothes, or get their hair cut and colored these days you're more likely to rub shoulders with Australian punk anachronisms. Other parts of Chelsea are good for antiques and furniture shoppers.

Covent Garden Crafts stalls and boutiques cluster around this lively restored 19th-century market and in the network of surrounding streets. Strolling is as pleasant a pastime as shopping (*see* Tour 2).

Kensington Antiques abound here, especially on Kensington Church Street. Kensington High Street, while not as upscale as Knightsbridge, still has a number of good clothing stores (*see* Tour 3).

Knightsbridge This is the area for the committed shopper. Harrods's gaudy Edwardian bulk dominates Brompton Road, but there are delights all around, on Sloane Street (for fashions and fabrics), Beauchamp Place, and Walton Street (*see* Tour 3).

Mayfair Bond Street (Old and New), Savile Row, and the Burlington Arcade are where you'll find traditional British goods for men and women, with South Molton Street adding a raffish modern accent. Prices and quality are tip-top.

Oxford Street Despite its renown as Britain's premier shopping street, Oxford Street is to be endured rather than enjoyed. Selfridges, Marks and Spencer, and John Lewis are all good department stores; hidden St. Christopher's Place, across from the Bond Street tube, adds a chic touch. Otherwise Oxford Street is shoddy and the crowds incredibly dense.

Piccadilly Though its stores are few, Piccadilly boasts some classy ones, such as Simpson department store, Hatchards bookstore, and Fortnum and Mason, with its elegant gourmet foods and accessories. There are also fine shopping arcades, Burlington Arcade the most splendid.

Regent Street Quality stores and broad sidewalks make Regent Street an appealing alternative to Oxford Street. Liberty, for textiles and accessories, is a perennial favorite.

St. James's Though his suits may be custom-tailored on Savile Row, the English gent comes here, especially along Jermyn Street, for the rest of his classic wardrobe, where a purchase is seen as an investment.

Specialty Stores There is space to include only a few London specialist stores, but note their locations: Stores selling the same wares are often grouped together.

London Shopping

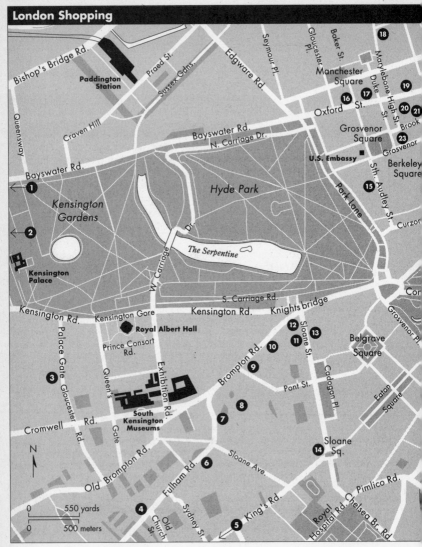

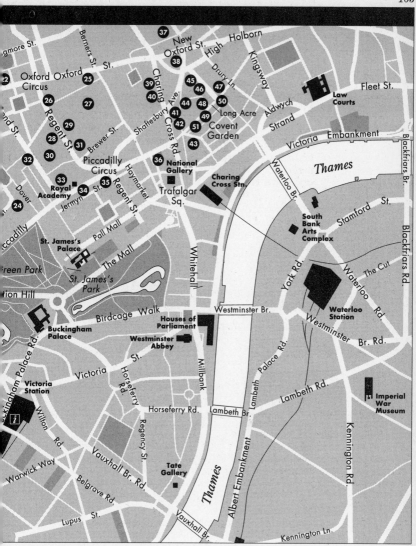

Antiques   Two prime areas are the Camden Passage Market (*see* Street
Markets, below) and Kensington Church Street, with antiques
of every description and price. Also worth a visit are:

Gray's Antique Market (58 Davies St., and around the corner
Gray's Mews, at 1–7 Davies Mews, tel. 071/629–7034) is a gag-
gle of smaller places all selling curios and collectibles; allow
yourself plenty of time here.
Lunn Antiques (86 New King's Rd., tel. 071/736–4638), at the
Parson's Green end of New King's Road (way off the map's
edge), is a treasure chest of antique linen, lace, and period
clothing. Many are of near-museum quality.

Books   Charing Cross Road is London's book country, with a couple of
dozen stores there or thereabout. Especially large and interesting are: **Foyles** (no. 119, tel. 071/437–5660) and **Waterstones**
(no. 121–125, tel. 071/434–4291) next door. **Hatchards** (187–188
Piccadilly, (tel. 071/437–3924) not only has a huge stock, but a
well-informed staff to help you choose.

Travel books and maps are the specialty of **Stanford** (12 Long
Acre, tel. 071/836–1321); art books of **Zwemmer** (24 Lichfield
St., tel. 071/379–7886), just off Charing Cross Rd.; and sci-fi,
fantasy, horror, and comic books of **Forbidden Planet** (71 New
Oxford St., tel. 071/836–4179). **Books for Cooks** (4 Blenheim
Cres., tel. 071/221–1992), in Notting Hill Gate, is packed with
useful volumes for the voracious.

Among the secondhand meccas are: **Quinto** (83 Marylebone
High St., tel. 071/935–9303) with a fascinating galleried section at the back; **Skoob Books** (15 Sicilian Ave. and branches,
tel. 071/404–3063), which is not only for those who can read titles backward; and **Bertram Rota** (9–11 Langley Court, tel.
071/836–0723), a very upmarket, first-editions spot in Covent
Garden.

China and Glass   All of London's department stores carry classic Wedgwood or
Minton and their less expensive competitors.

Thomas Goode (19 South Audley St., tel. 071/499–2823) carries
enormous lines of crystal and china. Their very best is very expensive, but their range is fairly wide.

Clothing   Many leading international houses have major branches in London. Most department stores have fashion floors, for example,
Harvey Nichols, Harrods, and Selfridges. John Lewis, Simpson, and Liberty provide more traditional, though still stylish,
clothes. What is true for women's wear is even more so for
men's. London is still renowned for men's clothing, especially
in the more sober, traditional categories. Two stores stocking
largely traditional clothes for both men and women are:

Burberrys (165 Regent St., tel. 071/734–4060 and 18–22 The
Haymarket, tel. 071/930–3343), famous for its trademark tartan, is laid out like a country house filled with classic clothing
and magnificent raincoats.
Lord's (66–70 Burlington Arcade, tel. 071/439–5808) has a supply of luxuriant cashmere, plus shirts, ties, and scarves in
abundance. Paisley is popular here.

Women's Wear   **Browns** (23–27 South Molton St., tel. 071/491–7833 and 6C
Sloane St., tel. 071/493–4232) put the South Molton Street mall
on the map for trendy shoppers. Here you'll find styles by

Azzedine Alaïa and Sonia Rykiel, plus the latest from France, Italy, Germany . . . and Britain.

Droopy & Browns (99 St. Martin's Lane, tel. 071/379–4514). Sumptuous, theatrical clothing for every occasion—weddings, balls, cocktails, or everyday—can be found here.

English Eccentrics (155 Fulham Rd., tel. 071/589–7154) focuses on unusual prints and historical patterns. It specializes in sweaters, separates, and scarves, mainly for women; but with increased attention being paid to male fashion.

Janet Reger (2 Beauchamp Pl., tel. 071/584–9360). Janet Reger's lingerie is legendary; this is its home base.

Nicole Farhi (25–26 St. Christopher's Pl., tel. 071/486–3416) is a store for the career woman; styles are practical but some prices are on the high side. The less expensive clothing tends to be sporty casual wear in different weights of cotton.

Rebecca (66 Neal St., tel. 071/379–4958). These secondhand clothes have been selected with care, hence their higher prices. The styles go back to the '30s, with lingerie and cashmere among the best buys.

Men's Wear **Sam Walker** (41 Neal St., tel. 071/240–7800), provides a refined way to buy secondhand clothing. Most of the stock is pre–World War II, with nostalgia in every fold and pocket.

Tommy Nutter (19 Savile Row, tel. 071/734–0831). This is the store of one of London's contemporary tailoring legends. It's ideal for the modern, well-dressed yuppie.

Crafts A revived interest in traditional crafts has meant a new wave of stores devoted to selling fine craftwork. Here are a few:

Combined Harvest (128 Talbot Rd., just off Portobello Rd., tel. 071/221–4870) markets the work of some 50 craftsworkers at reasonable prices. Commissions are accepted.

Craftsmen Potters Shop (7 Marshall St., tel. 071/437–7605) is a cooperative carrying a wide spectrum of the potter's art.

Naturally British (13 New Row, tel. 071/240–0551) offers British crafts, from pottery to rocking horses.

Nina Campbell (9 Walton St., tel. 071/225–1011) is for those passionate about Italian marbled paper and looking for unusual small gifts made from it.

Gifts Gifts can be fun or serious; London offers everything from Big Ben saltshakers to a $5,000 antique print of St. Paul's Cathedral. Department stores are a good choice for gift hunting, as are the major museum shops, most of which sell books, posters, and reproductions of items in their collections. Below are some other places you might look:

Frog Hollow (15 Victoria Grove, tel. 071/581–5493). Their specialty is superbly made cuddly toys (supposedly favorites of Princess Diana), with the accent on frogs—even one that transforms into a prince!

General Trading Co. (144 Sloane St., tel. 071/730–0411). This is an Aladdin's cave of exotic wares. Rumor has it that the Prince and Princess of Wales had their wedding gift list here. General Trading Company offers gifts from the world over with an emphasis on the Far East: Indian crafts, Italian lighting fixtures, and Chinese toys.

Hamleys (188–196 Regent St., tel. 071/734–3161) has six floors of toys and games for both children and adults, ranging from teddy bears to computer games and all the latest space-age gimmickry.

Neal Street East (5 Neal St., tel. 071/240–0135). The "East" in the name refers to the Orient. This is a colorful labyrinth of Far Eastern goods.

The Tea House (15A Neal St., tel. 071/240–7539). Devoted to everything concerning the British national drink. The variety of teapots here is astounding, with classical 17th-century reproductions, and even a caricature of the British bobby.

Gizmos **Authentics** (42 Shelton St., tel. 071/240–9845), an ultramodern store, all black and steel, with a proliferation of high-tech items.

Oggetti (133 Fulham Rd., tel. 071/581–8088 or 101 Jermyn St., tel. 071/930–4694) sells gifts and gadgets with an Italian flair and a high price tag.

Jewelry Jewelry—precious, semiprecious, and totally fake—sells furiously all over London's West End. Here are a few suggestion on where to buy it:

Asprey (165–169 New Bond St., tel. 071/493–6767). If you're in the market for a six-branched Georgian candelabrum, or an emerald and diamond brooch, you won't be disappointed here.

Butler and Wilson (20 South Molton St., tel. 071/409–2955 or 189 Fulham Rd., tel. 071/352–3045). All that glitters here isn't gold—costume jewelry (and their window displays) is their forte.

Garrard (112 Regent St., tel. 071/734–7020). Its connections with the royal family go back to 1722; this is the firm that keeps the Crown Jewels glittering. But they are also a family jeweler of enormous scope, from antique to modern. (Charles bought Diana's engagement ring here.)

Sheer Decadence (44 Monmouth St., tel. 071/379–4161) is full of wild, Baroque jewelry and accessories—dazzling yet affordable.

Linen London is a good place to find fine linens. Many department stores carry a wide range of linen goods, including Liberty and Harrods; but below are two specialists you might want to try:

The Irish Linen Co. (35–36 Burlington Arcade, tel. 071/493–8949) is a tiny store packed with crisp, embroidered linen for the table, the bed, and the nose.

The Monogrammed Linen Shop (168 Walton St., tel. 071/589–4033). This is the place for Italian bed linen—with matching robes and pajamas—plus christening gowns and table linens. As their name indicates, they also monogram.

Prints Prints are another London specialty. Below are two of many print stores in Central London:

CCA Galleries (8 Dover St., tel. 071/499–6701) offers an interesting range of work by contemporary printmakers. Their prices are reasonable and their knowledgeable staff helpful.

Grosvenor Prints (28–32 Shelton St., tel. 071/836–1979). Located in the tangle of streets northwest of Covent Garden, Grosvenor Prints sells antiquarian prints—especially of London buildings and dogs! Its eccentricity and wide selection virtually guarantee a find.

Department Stores London's department stores range from Harrods—the English Bloomingdale's—to middle-range stores to the bargain houses. Most of the best department stores are around Regent Street and Oxford Street, with two notable exceptions in Knightsbridge.

Liberty (200 Regent St., tel. 071/734–1234). Full of nooks and crannies, Liberty is like a dream of an eastern bazaar realized as a western store. Famous principally for its fabrics, it also carries Oriental goods, menswear, womenswear, fragrances, soaps, and accessories.

John Lewis (278 Oxford St., tel. 071/629–7711) claims as its motto, "Never knowingly undersold." This is perhaps the most traditional of English department stores, with a wonderful selection of dress fabrics and drapes.

Selfridges (400 Oxford St., tel. 071/629–1234). London's mammoth upmarket version of Macy's, Selfridges' extras include a food hall, a branch of the London Tourist Board, a theater ticket counter, and a Thomas Cook travel agency. **Miss Selfridge** is their outpost for trendy, affordable young women's clothes (also on Oxford Street, east of Oxford Circus).

Harrods (87 Brompton Rd., tel. 071/730–1234), one of the world's most famous department stores, is currently owned by an Egyptian family. You'll either love it or wonder what the big deal is. Although it's now less elegant than its former self, it is still a British institution. The food halls are stunning—so are the crowds!

Harvey Nichols (109 Knightsbridge, tel. 071/235–5000). Renowned for its household furnishings, jewelry, and above all, fashion, Nichols has a pleasantly glitzy atmosphere for browsing, with a fun, young "Zone" in the basement.

Simpson (203 Piccadilly, tel. 071/734–2002) is a traditional department store and home of Daks, the classic British design brand. A barber shop, restaurant, and wine bar add to the store's appeal.

Street Markets   Street markets are mainly a weekend happening and, as many of them are open Sunday morning, provide diversion during an otherwise quiet time in London. A morning in the markets, followed by a hearty lunch and an afternoon in a park or museum, is as much a Londoner's kind of Sunday as it is a tourist's.

Bermondsey (Tower Bridge Rd., SE1), Fri. 4:30 AM–noon. Known also as New Caledonian Market, this is one of London's largest markets, selling both junk and treasures from British attics. Note that it's on Fridays only, starting at 4:30 AM. The real bargains start going then, but there'll be a few left if you arrive later. Take the 15 or 25 bus to Aldgate, then a number 42 bus over Tower Bridge to Bermondsey Square; or take the tube to London Bridge and walk.

Camden Lock (Dingwalls) Market (NW1). Stores: Tues.–Sun. 9:30–5:30, stalls on weekends 8–6 (approximately). This sprawling market in one of London's most "happening" quarters—trendy types abound—has recently undergone a major reshuffle, and much of it is now indoors. Still, it remains a good place for cheap and secondhand clothing, records, books, crafts, and jewelry. Canal trips begin here, too; check at the Regent's Canal (Camden Lock) Information Centre.

Camden Passage (Islington, N1). Wed. and Sat. 8:30 AM–3 PM. Hugged by curio stores, the passage drips with jewelry, silverware, and myriad other items for sale. Saturday is when the stalls go up; the rest of the week, only the stores are open. Bus 19 or 38 or the tube to the Angel stop will get you there.

Petticoat Lane (Middlesex St., E1). Sun. 9–2. Petticoat Lane is the familiar name of this famous market on Middlesex Street. You'll find bargain leather goods, clothes, cameras, videos, and stereos. Liverpool Street, Aldgate, or Aldgate East tubes are closest.

Portobello Market (Portobello Rd., W11). Fruit and vegetables Mon.–Wed., Fri.–Sat. 8–5, Thurs. 8–1; antiques Sat. 8 AM–5 PM. The Notting Hill Gate end is far and away the most expensive, but the further you walk, the more realistic the prices become and the more basic the goods on sale are. It's a fun place to explore, but don't expect to find any bargains here. Take bus 52 or the tube to Ladbroke Grove or Notting Hill Gate.

Sports and Fitness

London is not a particularly sports-oriented place—however, there are a few events that sports fans may want to try to see. For a recorded update on London's sports clubs and facilities, call **Sportsline**, weekdays 10–6, tel. 071/222–8000.

Spectator Sports Tickets for the **Wimbledon tennis championships** are costly, hard to obtain, and sell out months in advance. But you can gain entrance by arriving early in the day and standing on line; this is especially recommended during the first week of the two-week championship, when it is not so difficult to get in and there are plenty of top stars to be seen playing on the outer courts, where there are no reserved seats and the atmosphere is pleasantly informal. Take the tube to Southfield. To obtain tickets in advance, write to the All England Lawn Tennis and Croquet Club, Church Rd., Wimbledon, London SW19 5AE.

Two annual events that are fun for spectators are the Boat Race (the rowing race between Oxford and Cambridge Universities) and the London Marathon. The **Boat Race,** held on a Saturday in late March or early April, starts at Putney and finishes at Mortlake, which is a good place to stand and watch. The crowd is good-humored and there's generally lots of space to see what's happening. The **Marathon,** held on a Sunday in late April and modeled on the New York version, is a similarly pleasant occasion, with families and friends turning out in force to cheer on thousands of participants. The race starts on Blackheath, at the top end of Greenwich Park, and finishes at the south end of Westminster Bridge.

Wembley Stadium is the scene of the **Cup Final,** played each May at the end of the soccer season, and it is also the venue of other major soccer and rugby matches. Soccer league club matches are often the scene of, at best, exuberant partisanship; at worst, shocking violence. If you want to go to a match, telephone the club in advance to find out how to reach the stand (in England, spectators sit in a stand, and if you want to stand up to watch the match you go to the unroofed tiers called "terraces")—or better still, go with people who know their way around locally.

Golf There are many fine golf courses in the outer suburbs of London where the built-up area gradually merges into the countryside. Although almost all clubs in London are private, visitors are often able to play on them by paying a greens fee, which varies widely from club to club. It is best, especially with private courses, to telephone in advance to find out what the fee is and the restrictions (if any) for visitors. A letter of introduction from your home course is always useful. For a complete rundown of the area courses, as well as those throughout England, pick up the *Golf Course Guide* for £5.95 at larger London bookstores.

Hotel Fitness Centers These clubs are only suitable for someone staying in the hotel, as membership for outsiders is astronomically expensive—in one case £1,200 a year.

The Peak Health Club at the Hyatt Carlton Tower (2 Cadogan Pl., tel. 071/235–5411) offers the most complete hotel fitness facilities in central London, with Nautilus-type stations, Lifecycles, rowing machines, treadmills, aerobics classes, even a sauna equipped with TV. Tennis is available across the street in Cadogan Gardens.

Le Meridien Piccadilly (Piccadilly, tel. 071/734–8000) houses the elegant, turn-of-the-century Champney's Club with free weights, Universal stations, treadmills, exercycles, simulated golf, squash, and a pool. Aerobics, yoga, and body-shaping classes round out the program.

The Olympian Health Club in the St. James Court Hotel (Buckingham Gate, tel. 071/834–6655) offers treadmills, a rowing machine, electronically monitored cycles, 14 Universal stations, plus yoga and aerobics.

Jogging Centrally located **Green Park** and **St. James's Park** are adequate for short runs, except on summer afternoons when the many deck chairs make the going too crowded. Far better is bucolic **Hyde Park** which, with adjoining **Kensington Gardens,** measures four miles around. Here you can run on asphalt trails among formal rose gardens and ballfields. A two-and-a-half-mile loop can be made by starting either at Hyde Park Corner or at Marble Arch, and turning at the Serpentine. **Regent's Park** is near much of north London and its perimeter measures about two and a half miles. For longer runs, try **Hampstead Heath** (Hampstead tube) or the wilder **Richmond Park** (Richmond tube), home to deer and other animals (stick to the lightly traveled roads).

Dining

Although London can offer cuisine from nearly all over the world, rents and local taxes have forced the cost of eating out higher and higher, so the breadth of choice has a price tag attached. Reasonably priced restaurants with courteous service are worth their weight in saffron. But there is an escape hatch. Many establishments offer set menus—especially at lunchtime—that are half the price of their à la carte meals, making even the fanciest spots viable to a visitor on a restricted budget.

A serious dining problem in London is the number of places that are closed on Sunday or late at night: It's wise to check first.

The law obliges all British restaurants to display their prices, including V.A.T. (sales tax) outside. Read them carefully, looking for hidden extras like service, cover, and minimum charges, usually at the bottom in fine print!

Highly recommended restaurants are indicated by a star ★.

Category	Cost*
Very Expensive	over £40
Expensive	£25–£40
Moderate	£12–£25
Inexpensive	under £12

per person, including first course, main course, dessert, and VAT; excluding drinks and service

St. James's

Very Expensive **Duke's Restaurant.** Traditional English fare is served in this small dining room graced with antiques, inside the Edwardian Duke's Hotel. *Feuilleté* of salmon in a mild Stilton sauce and bread-and-butter pudding are typical specialties, though imaginative French dishes are also offered. The set lunch is a good value. *35 St. James's Pl., tel. 071/491–4840. Reservations advised. Jacket and tie required. AE, DC, MC, V.*

The Ritz. The marble-and-gold Louis XVI dining room here has perhaps one of the prettiest views in London, overlooking Green Park. In the evening there's a live cabaret. You can be sure to find good English cooking with a French accent—roast meat and game, smoked and poached fish, as well as more experimental cuisine. Stick to house wines and set-price menus to escape with change. *Piccadilly, tel. 071/493–8181. Reservations required. Jacket and tie required. AE, DC, MC, V.*

Expensive **Le Caprice.** The cool and elegant decor here matches the (often well-known) clientele exactly. The menu caters to all tastes with crudités, hamburgers, or main courses like salmon fishcakes with sorrel sauce. Dark and white chocolate mousse follows. The brunches are excellent. *Arlington House, Arlington St., tel. 071/629–2239. Reservations required. Jacket and tie required. AE, DC, MC, V. Closed Sat. lunch.*

Green's. The focus is on seafood, with grills and steaks for the evening meal. Green's has the air of a gentleman's club, and the food is very much in keeping: oysters, crab, pigeon pie, and desserts such as toffee pudding. *36 Duke St., St. James's, tel. 071/930–4566. Reservations advised 2 days in advance. Jacket and tie required. AE, DC, MC, V. Closed Sun. dinner, national holidays.*

Inexpensive **The Fountain.** Pastel shades set the cool tone at this elegant
★ restaurant at the back of Fortnum and Mason's, which offers light meals, toasted snacks, sandwiches, and ice cream sodas. Go for Welsh rarebit or cold game pie by day, fillet steak by night; great for pre-theater meals (full meals are available in the St. James's Room restaurant in the store). *181 Piccadilly, tel. 071/734–4938. Reservations accepted for dinner only. Dress: informal. AE, DC, MC, V. Closed Sun., national holidays.*

Mayfair

Very Expensive **Chez Nico.** Those with refined palates and very deep pockets
★ should not miss Nico Ladenis's exquisite gastronomy. He is one of the world's Great Chefs, and is famous for knowing it. Nowhere is food taken more seriously; the menu is in untranslated French; vegetarians and children are not welcome. *35 Great*

Portland St., W1, tel. 071/436–8846. Jacket and tie required. Reservations required at least ten days in advance. MC, V. Closed weekends, public holidays, 3 weeks in Aug.

Le Gavroche. Billed as one of London's finest restaurants, Le Gavroche (near the U.S. Embassy) is sumptuous in both decor and cuisine—for example, duck with foie gras, or lobster and champagne mousse. The classy dining room is a restful dark green, hung with oil paintings. *43 Upper Brook St., tel. 071/ 408–0881. Reservations advised at least 1 week in advance. Jacket and tie required. AE, DC, MC, V. Closed weekends, 10 days at Christmas, national holidays.*

★ **Le Meridien Oak Room.** Grand Venetian chandeliers and bleached oak paneling adorn the restaurant of Le Meridien Piccadilly Hotel. The food is haute cuisine: langoustine (crayfish) gazpacho and the fig tart are especially good. *Piccadilly, tel. 071/734–8000. Reservations advised. AE, DC, MC, V. Jacket and tie required. Closed Sat. lunch, Sun.*

Expensive **The Veeraswamy.** Founded in 1927, London's oldest Indian restaurant has been redecorated and slightly Anglicized since then—you can even get cocktails before your meal. Give the king prawn *masala* (medium hot shrimp curry) or the lamb *kadai ghosht* (curried lamb with peppers) a try. *99 Regent St., tel. 071/734–1401. Reservations advised. Dress: informal. AE, DC, MC, V. Closed Dec. 25–26.*

Moderate **Pizzeria Condotti.** This pizzeria, run by cartoonist Enzo Apicella, is lined with the original modern paintings and, naturally, cartoons. Choose a salad, like the *insalata Condotti* (mixed salad with mozzarella and avocado) or a first-class pizza. *4 Mill St., tel. 071/499–1308. No reservations. Dress: informal. AE, DC, MC, V. Closed Sun., Dec. 25–26.*

Inexpensive **The Chicago Pizza Pie Factory.** A bright basement locale serving huge pizzas with salad and garlic bread at reasonable prices. This is one of American entrepreneur Bob Payton's places, and good gimmicks—like heart-shaped pizzas on Valentine's day—make it a popular spot. *17 Hanover Sq., tel. 071/ 629–2669. Reservations advised for lunch. Dress: casual. No credit cards. Closed for Christmas.*

Knightsbridge

Very Expensive **Bibendum.** If you want to be in the social swim when you get
★ back home, be sure to eat here. It's not easy to get in, but if you plan in advance, or luck out on short notice, then you can discover for yourself what everyone is talking about. Bibendum is in the latest part of the Conran empire, the reconditioned Michelin House, with its art deco motif and tiled murals featuring the roly-poly tire man himself. The restaurant decor boasts glorious stained glass windows and integrates maps from the Michelin guidebooks. Chef Simon Hopkinson produces exemplary classic French dishes—this is where to find the perfect *boeuf bourgignon* or to order adventurously, having the tripe or brains. The set price menu at lunchtime is money well spent. *Michelin House, 81 Fulham Rd., tel. 071/581–5817. Reservations required. Dress: informal but chic. MC, V. Closed Sun.*

Turner's. Here's a restaurant dedicated to serious eating. The decor is gentle—pale blue prints on linen and upholstery, etched glass, and fresh flowers. The light French food is handled imaginatively. Try the pike mousse in a shallot and saffron

London Dining

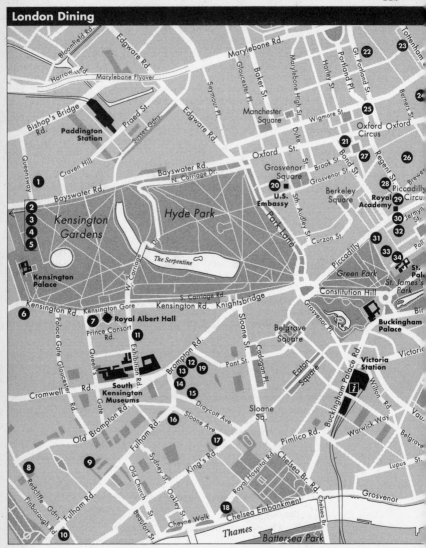

The Agra, **23**
Auntie's, **22**
Belvedere, **2**
Bertorelli's, **43**
Bibendum, **16**
Blakes Hotel
Restaurant, **9**

Café Pacifico, **42**
Chez Nico, **25**
Chiang Mai, **35**
Chicago Pizza Pie
Factory, **35**
Corney and
Barrow, **52**
Crank's, **26**

Duke's Restaurant, **34**
English Garden, **17**
The Fountain, **30**
Frére Jacques, **44**
Gallipoli, **53**
Green's, **32**
Hollands, **5**
The Ivy, **41**

Joe Allen's, **47**
Joe's Café, **15**
Julie's, **4**
Kalamaras, **1**
Kensington Place, **3**
La Bastide, **36**
La Tante Claire, **18**
Le Boulestin, **45**

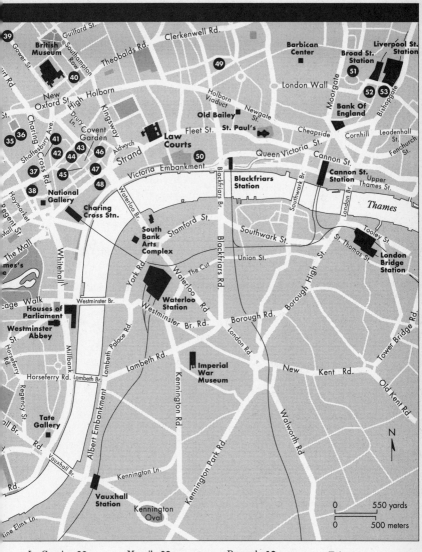

Le Caprice, **33**	Manzi's, **38**	Parson's, **10**	Tui, **11**
Le Gavroche, **20**	New World, **37**	Pizzeria Condotti, **27**	Turner's, **13**
Le Meridien Oak Room, **29**	The North Sea Fish Restaurant, **39**	The Ritz, **31**	The Veeraswamy, **28**
Le Suquet, **14**	O Fado, **19**	Rouxl Britannia, **51**	White Tower, **24**
Lou Pescadou, **8**	One Ninety Queen's Grate, **7**	Rudland and Stubbs, **49**	
Luba's Bistro, **12**	Orso, **46**	Savoy Grill, **48**	
Maggie Jones, **6**	Oscar's Brasserie, **50**	Truckles of Pied Bull Yard, **40**	

sauce, or the fillet of beef with Madeira and wild mushrooms. *87–89 Walton St., tel. 071/584–6711. Reservations advisable 2–3 days in advance. Dress: neat but casual. AE, DC, MC, V. Closed Sat. lunch, national holidays, 1 week at Christmas.*

Moderate **O Fado.** This is one of London's few Portuguese restaurants, set in a basement with live fado music in the evenings Wednesday through Saturday. Seafood is the specialty—pork with clams is one of their more unusual dishes. *50 Beauchamp Place, tel. 071/589–3002. Reservations essential for dinner Fri. and Sat. Dress: informal. AE, MC, V. Closed one week at Christmas.*

Inexpensive **Luba's Bistro.** Russian cuisine such as chicken Kiev and beef
★ strogonoff are served at long wooden tables; bring your own wine. *6 Yeoman's Row, tel. 071/589–2950. Reservations advised. Dress: informal. MC, V. Closed Sun., Christmas, national holidays.*

South Kensington

Very Expensive **Blakes Hotel Restaurant.** Black lacquer furniture, fresh flowers, and displays of Thai tribal costumes give Blakes an intimate, oriental air. Though wine list prices are high, the cuisine is good and extraordinarily varied. Try the sashimi, eaten with black lacquer chopsticks; chicken *falaise* with lobster, garlic, and ginger sauce; or Szechuan duck, with roasted salt and pepper. *33 Roland Gdns., tel. 071/370–6701. Reservations advised. Jacket and tie required. AE, DC, MC, V. Closed Dec. 25–26.*

Expensive **One Ninety Queen's Gate.** A fabulous upholstered and flower-bedecked restaurant offering peasant-influenced, profoundly satisfying food such as stuffed venison with haggis followed by a tropical fruit *gratin. 190 Queen's Gate, SW7, tel. 071/581–5666. Jacket and tie advised. Reservations advised. AE, DC, MC, V. Closed Sat. lunch, Sun. dinner, Christmas.*

Moderate **Lou Pescadou.** In this Provençal-style restaurant boats are the
★ theme and fish the specialty. Typical dishes are *petite bouillabaisse* (fish soup), or red mullet poached in tarragon sauce; the oysters and sea urchins are excellent. *241 Old Brompton Rd., tel. 071/370–1057. No reservations. Dress: informal. AE, DC, MC, V. Closed Sun., Aug., Christmas.*
Tui. Wake up your taste buds with a crab-claw and shrimp hot pot, or a green beef curry. *19 Exhibition Rd., tel. 071/584–8359. Reservations advised. Dress: informal. AE, DC, MC, V. Closed national holidays.*

Kensington and Notting Hill

Very Expensive **Belevedere.** This spacious country-style restaurant in Holland Park, surrounded by flowerbeds, is at its best for summer dining. The cuisine is "French creative": Begin with salmon parfait with dill and watercress sauce, and go on to either Dover sole or monkfish. You could finish your meal with a smooth malt whisky from the 92 varieties always in stock. *Holland House, Holland Park, tel. 071/602–1238. Reservations required. Jacket and tie required. AE, DC, MC, V. Closed Sat. lunch, Sun., Christmas, national holidays.*

Expensive **Kensington Place.** The local glitterati make this high-tech palace a noisy and chic setting for some of London's most fashionable food—grilled foie gras with sweet corn pancake, for instance. *201 Kensington Church St., W8, tel. 071/727–3184. Dress: casual stylish. Reservations advised. MC, V. Closed Aug. bank holiday, Christmas.*

Julie's. Upstairs is the champagne bar and downstairs is a basement restaurant, both decorated in Victorian ecclesiastical style. The dishes are Anglo-French: salmon-and-halibut terrine, roast pheasant with chestnut stuffing and rowan jelly. Sunday lunch is popular, and there's a garden for outside eating. *135 Portland Rd., tel. 071/229–8331. Reservations advised for dinner, required on weekends. Jacket and tie required. AE, DC, MC, V. Closed Dec. 25 and 31, Easter.*

Moderate **Kalamaras.** This is actually two Greek restaurants, one "micro" and one "mega"—next door to each other. The smaller "micro" is unlicensed, cheaper, and more cramped. Try a *mezze* (sampler) for the first course, and go on to kebabs and salads. *76–78 Inverness Mews, tel. 071/727–9122. Reservations advised. Dress: informal. AE, DC, MC, V. Closed for lunch. Closed Sun., national holidays.*

Maggie Jones. This country cottage-style restaurant—which is supposed to take its name from its proximity to Princess Margaret, who lives next door in Kensington Palace—serves hearty fare such as steak and kidney pie and mackerel baked in gooseberries, to the accompaniment of popular English songs of the 1930s. The fixed price lunch is an especially good value. *Old Court Pl., Kensington Church St., tel. 071/937–6462. Reservations required for dinner and Sun. lunch. Dress: informal. AE, DC, MC, V. Closed Dec. 25–26, Jan. 1, national holidays.*

Inexpensive **Hollands.** London's only Filipino wine bar, this is a relaxed and friendly place with a bar downstairs, a restaurant area and rooftop conservatory (lovely in summer) upstairs. The food is Filipino (stir-fried squid with ginger) or wine bar staples (steak, taramosalata). *6 Portland Rd., W11, tel. 071/229–3130. Dress: casual. Reservations advised for restaurant. AE, MC, V. Closed Christmas.*

Chelsea

Very Expensive **★** **La Tante Claire.** The *haute cuisine* in this small chic restaurant is famous—hot pâté de foie gras on shredded potatoes with sweet wine and shallot sauce, or pig's feet stuffed with sweetbreads and wild mushrooms. The nearby Thames embankment invites after-dinner strolls. *68 Royal Hospital Rd., tel. 071/352–6045. Reservations required 3–4 weeks in advance for dinner, 2–3 days for lunch. Jacket and tie required. AE, DC, MC, V. Closed weekends, Jan. 1, 10 days at Easter, 3 weeks Aug.–Sept., 2 weeks at Christmas.*

Expensive **English Garden.** This summery restaurant, like an airy conservatory just off King's Road, serves traditional English specialties of fresh salmon fishcakes with watercress mayonnaise, and saddle of hare with juniper berries. *10 Lincoln St., tel. 071/584–7272. Reservations required. Jacket and tie required. AE, DC, MC, V. Closed national holidays.*

Le Suquet. This is a tiny, noisy fish restaurant with a French seaport atmosphere. The hefty seafood platter offers great value, or try oysters or grilled sea bass. *104 Draycott Ave., tel. 071/581–1785. Reservations required at least 2 days in advance. Dress: informal. AE, DC, MC, V.*

Moderate **Joe's Café.** A stylish brasserie just across the road from Bibendum. Light dishes at lunchtime, more choice—and expense—in the evening. *126 Draycott Ave., SW3, tel. 071/225–2217. Reservations advised. AE, DC, MC, V. Closed Sun. dinner, Christmas.*

Inexpensive **Parson's.** Its Edwardian interior bursts with swan-neck lamps and other colonial furnishings, set off by large windows. Try their avocadoburgers or enchiladas with Australian wine or Japanese beer while classical, folk, or African music plays. *311 Fulham Rd., tel. 071/352–0651. No reservations. Dress: informal. AE, DC, MC, V. Closed Dec. 25–26.*

Soho

Expensive **La Bastide.** An elegant, grown-up restaurant where heavy velvet drapes and linen napery set off generous and hearty regional French cuisine—whether the region is Burgundy (*coq au vin*, frogs' legs) or Brittany (*crêpes*, seafood). Wines and cheeses are always excellent. *50 Greek St., W1, tel. 071/734–3300. Jacket and tie advised. Reservations advised. AE, DC, MC, V. Closed Sat., Sun. lunch, Sun. dinner, national holidays.*

Moderate **Chiang Mai.** Modeled on a traditional Thai stilt house, this res-
★ taurant's freshly cooked food is deliciously spicy and an excellent value. Risk a *tom yum* (hot and sour soup) or a *tad tra prou* (beef, pork or chicken with fresh Thai basil and chili). *48 Frith St., tel. 071/437–7444. Reservations advised for dinner. Dress: informal. AE, MC, V. Closed Sun., national holidays.*

Manzi's. One of London's oldest and most traditional restaurants has dining rooms on two floors. Downstairs is more lively and atmospheric. The speed and dexterity with which the waiters weave their way between the tables carrying trays of Dover sole or alligator in butter sauce is truly remarkable. The decor features kitsch Moulin Rouge murals and monstrous plastic lobsters. *1–2 Leicester St., tel. 071/734–0224. Reservations advised. Dress: informal. AE, DC, MC, V. Closed Dec. 25–26.*

Inexpensive **Cranks.** This is a popular vegetarian chain (other branches at Covent Garden, Great Newport St., Adelaide St., Tottenham St., and Barrett St.), with a consciously nutritious but still tasty menu. Lunch is self-service; dinner is candlelit waiter-service. The Marshall Street branch is open until 11 PM, but the other branches seem to work on the assumption that vegetarians go to bed earlier than carnivores, and close at 8. *8 Marshall St., tel. 071/437–9431. Reservations advised for dinner. Dress: informal. AE, DC, MC, V. Closed Sun., national holidays.*

New World. A large (700-seat), cheerfully decorated Cantonese restaurant in London's tiny Chinatown, New World serves *dim sum* at lunchtime; other good choices are shrimp with a hot curry sauce, and a sampling of Pekinese and Szechuan dishes. *1 Gerrard Pl. tel. 071/734–0677. Reservations not required. Dress: informal. AE, DC, MC, V. Closed Dec. 25.*

Covent Garden

Very Expensive **Le Boulestin.** The hautest of French haute cuisine is served in this grand basement restaurant. Specialties include roast guinea fowl with shallots, and fillet of smoked pork; menus change regularly. The cheese and wine selections are magnificent. *1a Henrietta St., tel. 071/836–7061. Reservations advised 1 week in advance for dinner. Jacket and tie required. AE, DC, MC, V. Closed Sat. lunch, Sun., national holidays, last 3 weeks in Aug., 10 days at Christmas.*

★ **The Savoy Grill.** This classic Grill-in-the-Grand-Manner continues to attract literary and artistic names, as well as its share of tycoons. The cooking is top notch. Order a seafood omelet—named after the novelist, Arnold Bennett—or fillet of pork with fresh cranberries. The yew-paneled interior and low lights make for quiet, intimate dining. *Strand, tel. 071/836–4343. Reservations advised for lunch, and for dinner Thurs.–Sat. Jacket and tie required. AE, DC, MC, V. Closed Sat. lunch, Sun., Aug.*

Expensive **The Ivy.** An unpretentious, stylish hangout with generous portions of updated classic dishes from practically everywhere. Eat anything, from one of the only real Caesar salads in London (apart from Joe Allen's) to roast grouse, shrimp gumbo, or braised oxtail. *1 West St., W1, tel. 071/836–4751. Dress: casual smart. Reservations advised. AE, DC, MC, V. Closed national holidays.*

★ **Orso.** An Italian Joe Allen's (*see* below), this basement restaurant has the same efficient staff and a glitzy showbiz clientele. The menu changes seasonally, but past specialties have included a warm scallop-and-asparagus salad starter followed by grilled fillet of lamb with artichokes and balsamic vinegar. *27 Wellington St., tel. 071/240–5269. Reservations required. Jacket and tie required. No credit cards. Closed Dec. 25–26.*

Moderate **Bertorelli's.** Right across from the stage door of the Royal
★ Opera House, Bertorelli's draws many opera buffs and singers, so reserve well in advance for pre- and post-opera meals. The decor is modern trattoria style, but the food is traditional Italian. Recommended are the hot mushroom-and-garlic salad and whatever is the fresh fish of the day. *44a Floral St., tel. 071/836–3969. Reservations required. Dress: informal. AE, DC, MC, V. Closed Christmas.*

Frère Jacques. This airy, light place—a combination wine bar and brasserie—has the best seafood in the area. The oysters are excellent and the shellfish platter is a joy. *38 Long Acre, tel. 071/836–7823. Reservations advised. Dress: casual. AE, DC, MC, V. Open daily.*

★ **Joe Allen's.** This well-known basement café, located behind the Strand Palace Hotel, is a great place to spot stage and screen personalities. The Caesar salad and barbecued ribs are a real treat. After 9 PM there's a pianist—not always audible through the diners' din. *13 Exeter St., tel. 071/836–0651. Reservations required. Dress: informal. No credit cards. Closed Dec. 25–26.*

Inexpensive **Café Pacifico.** A lively atmosphere pervades this converted warehouse where reasonably priced Mexican food is served. The bar boasts a range of tequilas, and try their frozen margarita. On Sunday night, enjoy live music as you devour *ceviche* (marinated spiced fish, cold-cooked in lime juice) or *fajitas* (marinated beef or chicken with onions, peppers, tortillas, cheese, and guacamole). *5 Langley St., tel. 071/379–7728. No reservations. Dress: informal. MC, V. Closed for lunch. Closed national holidays.*

Bloomsbury

Expensive **The White Tower.** Barely changed since its founding in 1938, the White Tower is an elegant Greek restaurant (something of a contradiction of terms in London), though its menu isn't exclusively Greek. There are portraits on the walls, glass partitions between the tables, and a rhapsodic menu. Dishes range from the traditional—*taramasalata*—to the unique—roast duckling stuffed with crushed wheat. *1 Percy St., tel. 071/634–8141. Reservations required. Jacket and tie required. AE, DC, MC, V. Closed weekends, national holidays, 3 weeks in Aug., 1 week at Christmas.*

Moderate **Auntie's.** If you want unashamedly English food ("the Colonel's curried egg mayonnaise," Barnsley lamb chop with plum-and-mint sauce, tipsy fruit trifle) in an Edwardian atmosphere, this is where to get it. The walls are hung with theater bills. An intimate atmosphere prevails; Auntie's is small. *126 Cleveland St., tel. 071/387–1548. Reservations advised. Dress: informal. AE, DC, MC, V. Closed Sat. lunch, Sun., 2 weeks mid-Aug., Christmas.*

Inexpensive **The Agra.** Media professionals flock here for its great value in curried dishes ranging from a mild chicken *korma* (cream-and-coconut sauce) to hot fish curry. Overhead fans, low lighting, and attentive waiters add a touch of class. *135–137 Whitfield St., tel. 071/387–8833. Reservations advised for dinner. Dress: informal. AE, DC, MC, V. Closed Christmas.*

The North Sea Fish Restaurant. This popular cabbies' haunt is also known to locals and tourists for its fresh fish. The seafood platter is recommended; the Dover sole (their most expensive dish) is superb. It's a bit tricky to find—head south down Judd Street three blocks from St. Pancras station. *7–8 Leigh St., tel. 071/387–5892. Reservations advised. Dress: informal. AE, DC, MC, V. Closed Sun., Christmas, national holidays.*

Truckles of Pied Bull Yard. A winebar, but with a difference. There's plenty of outdoor seating, ideal for summer visitors to the British Museum nearby who want to have their lunch in the sun. *Pied Bull Yard, off Bury Pl., tel. 071/404–5334. Dress: informal. AE, DC, MC, V. No dinner Sat. Closed Sun.*

City

Very Expensive **Corney and Barrow.** This lunch-only restaurant serves unusual dishes—quail and blackberry soup!—in daringly modern surroundings while Baroque music plays. It's convenient to the Barbican Arts Centre. *109 Old Broad St., tel. 071/638–9308. Reservations advised. Jacket and tie required. AE, DC, MC, V. Closed for dinner. Closed weekends, national holidays.*

Expensive **Gallipoli.** This is some setting: a 200-year-old Turkish bath-house, mosaics gleaming, with belly dancers and strains of live music (9 PM to 2:30 AM) wafting through. The clientele is mixed, but the food has a definite Turkish slant. Try a kebab with yogurt, or fillet of duck with honey, lime, and orange. *8 Bishopsgate Churchyard, tel. 071/588–1922. Reservations advised. Jacket and tie required. AE, DC, MC, V. Closed Sun., national holidays, Dec. 25–26.*

Oscar's Brasserie. Because it's within Temple Chambers, Oscar's is usually full of lawyers who enjoy its Provençal cooking. Fish is the chef's specialty, and you should try the monkfish marinated with fresh herbs and limes. Menus change daily. *5 Temple Ave., Temple Chambers, tel. 071/353–6272. Reservations required for lunch. Jacket and tie required. AE, DC, MC, V. Closed weekends, national holidays, Aug., 10 days at Christmas.*

Moderate   **Rouxl Britannia.** The name is a pun on "Roux," the last name of the brothers who own this lunch brasserie. Its decor is black and white with French café chairs. Try roast wing of skate, or tongue with horseradish sauce. *Triton Court, 14 Finsbury Sq., tel. 071/256–6997. Reservations advised. Dress: informal. AE, DC, MC, V. Closed for dinner. Closed weekends, national holidays.*

Rudland & Stubbs. This informal oyster bar/fresh fish restaurant adjoins Smithfield meat market. Try the *goujons* of salmon with zucchini and salmon sauce, or the John Dory in dill sauce. *35–37 Greenhill Rents, tel. 071/253–0148. Reservations advised. Dress: informal. MC, V. Closed Sat. lunch, Sun., national holidays.*

Pubs

Admiral Codrington. This friendly, fashionable Chelsea pub has a Victorian atmosphere complete with gaslight, antique mirrors, and Toby jugs. There's a vine-covered patio for summer drinking and barbecues. On Sunday, there's a traditional roast; on other days, shepherd's pie, sandwiches, or salads. Their malt whisky selection is impressive. *17 Mossop St., tel. 071/589–4603.*

Black Friar. You can't miss it—it's the wedge-shaped ornate building sporting a statue of a friar outside Blackfriars tube station. It was built in 1875 and is a triumph of Victorian extravagance, with red marble pillars, a magnificent mosaic ceiling, with friars, devils, and fairies everywhere—all very art nouveau. There are six kinds of beer on tap. *174 Queen Victoria St., tel. 071/236–5650.*

The George Inn. Edging a courtyard where Shakespeare's plays were once performed, the present building dates from the late 17th century and is London's last remaining galleried inn. Dickens was a regular here. Entertainments include Shakespeare performances, jousting, and morris dancing; drinks are served at both a real ale bar and a wine bar, and there's a full restaurant. *77 Borough High St., tel. 071/407–2056.*

The Lamb. Dickens lived close by and was a regular here. This jolly, cozy pub has original cut-glass Victorian screens and home-cooked food. You can eat or drink outside on the patio (very crowded in the summer). *94 Lamb's Conduit St., tel. 071/405–0713.*

Lamb and Flag. This 17th-century pub was once known as "The Bucket of Blood" because the upstairs room was used as a ring for fist-fighting. Now it's a trendy, friendly pub, serving food (lunchtime only) and real ale near Covent Garden, off Garrick Street. *33 Rose St., tel. 071/836–4108.*

Prospect of Whitby. This historic riverside tavern dates from 1520, and is named after a ship. It was once called "The Devil's Tavern" because of the thieves and smugglers who congregated here. It's ornamented with nautical memorabilia and pewter. The à la carte menu and pub food are both recommended. *57 Wapping Wall, tel. 071/481–1095.*

Sherlock Holmes. This pub was known as the Northumberland

Arms in the days when Arthur Conan Doyle frequented it. It figures in *The Hound of the Baskervilles*, and you'll see the hound's head and monstrous paws among other Holmes memorabilia in the bar. Upstairs there's a reconstruction of Holmes's study. Try the "Sherlock Holmes Chicken" or fish. *10 Northumberland St., tel. 071/930–2644.*

Wine Bars

★ **Archduke.** This is one of the few congenial South Bank nightspots, and convenient for post-theater or concert dinners. It's built into the railway arches under Hungerford Bridge beside the Festival Hall. The jazz begins at 8:30. The food is standard (quiche, apple pie), but the upstairs restaurant serves more substantial dishes; sausages from many countries are a specialty. *153 Concert Hall Approach, tel. 071/928–9370.*

Bentley's. Seafood, oysters in particular, is the specialty here. Upstairs there's a restaurant, but the marble-countered wine bar is warmer and slightly cheaper. Recommended are the clam bisque and baked fish pie. It's a two-minute walk from Piccadilly Circus. *11 Swallow St., tel. 071/734–0401.*

Carriages. Close to Buckingham Palace, so it's no coincidence that the downstairs bar is called Charlie's Bar and is decorated in a polo theme. There's live jazz every night, food, and an emphasis on champagne. This is a good spot to relax in after traipsing around the royal properties. *43 Buckingham Palace Rd., tel. 071/834–8871.*

Ebury Wine Bar. This was one of England's original 1960s wine bars, and it's still popular. The food is commendable; try spring chicken and lemon tarragon cream, with plum cheesecake to finish. Port and sherry from the "wood" (barrel) is available, as are 60 kinds of wine. There's a £5 minimum charge. *139 Ebury St., tel. 071/730–5447.*

Sloane's Wine Bar. This outfit serves coffee and snacks all day, plus lunch and dinner. Next to the Royal Court Theater, it's a magnet for Sloane Rangers (British yuppies with old money). *51 Sloane Sq., tel. 071/730–4275.*

Solange's. You'll find Solange's in a little lane next to the Leicester Square tube, close to the theaters. There are tables outside in summer, and it's always crowded. The brasserie food is excellent, though service is eccentric at best. *11 St. Martin's Ct., tel. 071/240–0245.*

Whittington's Wine Bar. This vaulted cellar in the City is named for its reputed owner of yore, Dick Whittington, "Thrice Mayor of London." Deep fried artichoke with hollandaise sauce is among his unusual dishes. The wine list is long, but the hours short: It closes at 7 PM. *21 College Hill, tel. 071/248–5855.*

Lodging

London hotels are among Europe's—indeed the world's!—most expensive. We are aware that readers feel some London hotels do not merit their inflated prices, especially when compared with their courteous Continental counterparts. Therefore, although our grading system is based on price (which does not always indicate quality) we have tried to select the ones whose caliber is tried and proven. We quote the average room cost; in some establishments, especially those in the Very Expensive category, you could pay considerably more—well past the £200 mark in some cases. Regardless of price, you should confirm *exactly* what your room costs before checking in. As in most other European countries, British hotels are obliged by law to display a price chart at the reception desk; study it carefully.

The custom these days in all but the cheaper hotels is for quoted prices to cover room alone; breakfast, whether continental or "Full English," comes as an extra. VAT (Value Added Tax—sales tax) is usually included, and service, too, in nearly all cases. The hotels listed here are graded by their spring 1991 rates, so check current figures, and remember to take into account seasonal fluctuations. Be sure to reserve, as seasonal events, trade shows, or royal occasions can fill hotel rooms for sudden, brief periods. If you arrive in London without a room, the following organizations can help: **Room Centre (UK) Ltd.,** Kingsgate House, Kingsgate Pl., NW6 4HG, tel. 071/328–1790; **The British Travel Centre,** 12 Regent St., Piccadilly Circus, SW1Y 4PQ, tel. 071/730–3400; **Hotel Reservation Centre,** by Platform 8 at Victoria Station, tel. 071/828–1849; and **The London Tourist Board Information Centres** at Heathrow and Victoria Station forecourt (no telephone reservations).

Visitors to London should be aware that certain accommodations agencies charge outrageous booking fees, so contact hotels directly wherever possible.

Highly recommended lodgings are indicated by a star ★ .

Category	Cost*
Very Expensive	over £130—and way, way up
Expensive	£95–£130
Moderate	£50–£95
Inexpensive	under £50

*All prices are for two people sharing a double room and include service, breakfast, and VAT.

Mayfair and St. James's

Very Expensive **Brown's.** A country hotel atmosphere pervades, with wood paneling, grandfather clocks, and large fireplaces. The rooms vary in size; some are quite small, but all are comfortably furnished with armchairs, sweeping drapes, and brass chandeliers. Founded by Lord Byron's butler in 1837, this "discreet" hotel is close to Bond Street's fashion stores and art galleries. *34 Albemarle St., W1A 4SW, tel. 071/493–6020. 133 rooms with bath. Facilities: restaurant, lounge, writing room, cocktail bar. AE, DC, MC, V.*

★ **Claridges.** This legendary hotel has one of the world's classiest guest lists. The liveried staff are friendly, not at all condescending, and the rooms luxurious. It was founded in 1812, but present decor is either 1930s Art Deco or country-house style. Have a drink in the lounge (24 hours a day) and hear the orchestra, or retreat to the peaceful reading room. The rooms are spacious, the staircase and elevator are grand. *Brook St., W1A 2JQ, tel. 071/629–8860. 200 rooms with bath. Facilities: 2 restaurants, lounge (with orchestra), hairdresser, valet. AE, DC, MC, V.*

London Lodging

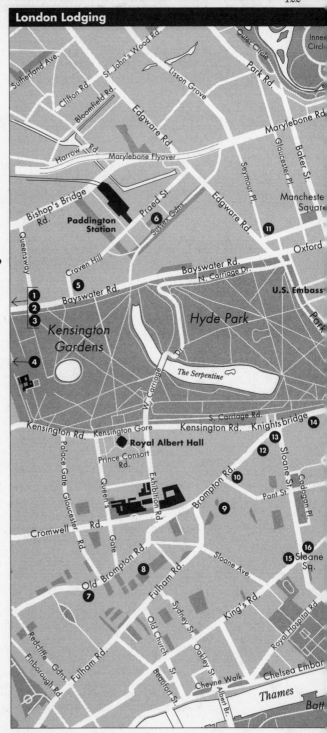

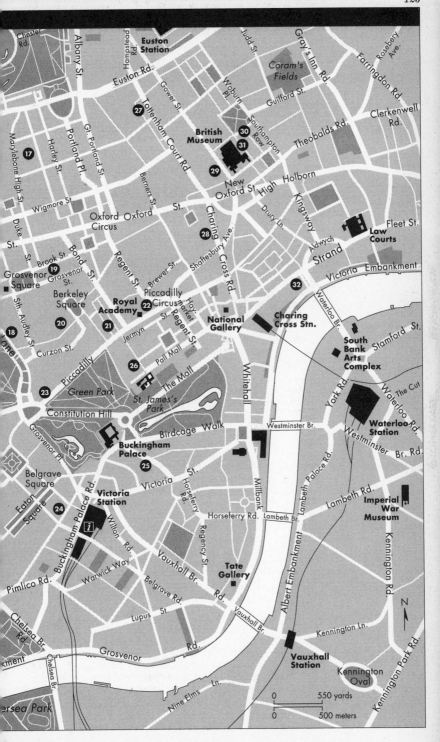

The Dorchester. Its massive refurbishment complete, this London landmark resumes its place among the great hotels. Everyone rich and famous has stayed here, and are now returning in droves to experience the enlarged rooms, climate control, marble bathrooms, new facilities, and cleaned-up, sumptuous decor. *Park La., W1A 2HJ, tel. 071/629-8888. 197 rooms, 55 suites, all with bath. Facilities: 3 restaurants, bar, lounge, night club, health club (no pool), business center, banqueting suites, ballroom, shopping arcade, free in-house movies, CNN, air-conditioning, valet, theater ticket desk. AE, DC, MC, V.*

Duke's. Exclusive, small, and Edwardian, with a gaslit entrance, Duke's is situated in a quiet cul-de-sac in the heart of St. James's. Portraits of dukes hang on the walls, one indication among many of its old-world character. The rooms aim at country-style comfort. Top-floor rooms are the biggest. *35 St. James's Pl., SW1A 1NY, tel. 071/491-4840. 62 rooms with bath. Facilities: restaurant, valet. AE, DC, MC, V.*

Inn on the Park. An eminent situation near Hyde Park and an opulent interior are the hallmarks. It was once one of Howard Hughes's hideaways. The rooms are exquisitely furnished and comfortable: The beds are gigantic, the bathrooms straight from Hollywood, with plenty of extras, such as bathrobes. The entrance hall is a wonder of marble and mahogany. *Hamilton Pl., Park La., W1A 1AZ, tel. 071/499-0988. 228 rooms with bath. Facilities: restaurant, air conditioning, shopping arcade, in-house movies, valet, garden. AE, DC, MC, V.*

Le Meridien. This massive turn-of-the-century building, reopened as a hotel in 1986 after a major renovation, could hardly be more central. It boasts one of London's best hotel dining rooms (the Oak Room) and the most opulent, best equipped health club. Decor is unremarkable, but comfortable. *Piccadilly, W1V OBH, tel. 071/734-8000. 284 rooms, all with bath. Facilities: 3 restaurants, bar, health club, library, business center, shops. AE, DC, MC, V.*

Expensive　**Chesterfield.** This townhouse, former home of the Earl of Chesterfield, is very popular with visitors from the United States. It is deep in the heart of Mayfair, and has welcoming paneled public rooms, a good restaurant, spacious bedrooms, and an outstandingly helpful staff. *35 Charles St., W1X 8LX, tel. 071/491-2622. 113 rooms with bath. Facilities: restaurant, in-house movies. AE, DC, MC, V.*

Clifton-Ford. This is one of London's most peaceful hotels, located on a quiet Georgian street just a short walk from Regent's Park. It dates from 1965, but has since been updated. Rooms are standard/international with the latest accessories. In the evening, a pianist plays in the lounge-foyer. *47 Welbeck St., W1M 8DN. tel. 071/486-6600. 240 rooms with bath. Facilities: restaurant, lounge, bar, laundry, valet, in-house movies. AE, DC, MC, V.*

Moderate　**Edward Lear.** Once the house of Edward Lear (most famous for his nonsense verse), this good-value hotel has an attractive entranceway. Rooms, refurbished in 1990, vary enormously in size, and ones at the back are quieter. The breakfast room has huge French windows, and the management proudly uses the same butcher as the queen. *28-30 Seymour St., W1H 5WD, tel. 071/402-5401. 30 rooms, 15 with bath. V.*

Kensington

Very Expensive ★ **Blakes.** This is one of the most exotically designed hotels in town. The Victorian exterior belies the interior, an arty mix of Biedermeyer, bamboo furniture, rich fabrics, leather, four-poster beds, and oriental screens. There's a startlingly realistic model of Marlene Dietrich in the bar. The rooms are decorated in anything from black moiré silk to a more severe gray. Guests tend to be in the music or movie business. *33 Roland Gdns., SW7 3PF, tel. 071/370–6701. 52 rooms with bath. Facilities: restaurant, satellite TV. AE, DC, MC, V.*

Expensive ★ **Number Sixteen.** Luxury bed-and-breakfasts are rare; this one's in a porticoed series of linked Victorian houses. It lies between leafy Onslow Square and busy Old Brompton Road, not far from the South Kensington tube. Inside is a fascinating mix of antiques. The hotel has an informal yet civilized atmosphere, and a charming garden. *16 Sumner Pl., SW7 3EG, tel. 071/589–5232. 32 rooms with bath. Facilities: bar, garden. AE, DC, MC, V.*

Inexpensive ★ **Vicarage.** A family concern for nearly 30 years, the Vicarage feels like a real home. It's beautifully decorated, and quiet, overlooking a garden square near Kensington's shopping streets. *10 Vicarage Gate, W8 4AG, tel. 071/229–4030. 19 rooms, none with bath. No credit cards.*

Knightsbridge, Chelsea, and Belgravia

Very Expensive ★ **Berkeley.** A remarkable mixture of the old and the new, the Berkeley is a luxurious modern-style hotel. Its splendid penthouse swimming pool is open to the sky when the weather's good. The rooms are decorated in an array of styles (such as a powder-blue theme with Wedgwood moldings), each with an anteroom and palatial bathroom. Some of the antique furniture comes from the old Berkeley in Mayfair. French cuisine is served in the restaurant, while the Buttery's fare is Mediterranean. *Wilton Pl., SW1X 7RL, tel. 071/235–6000. 160 rooms with bath. Facilities: rooftop heated indoor and outdoor pool, gymnasium, masseur, sauna, hairdresser, movie theater, florist. AE, DC, MC, V.*

Capital. Reserve way ahead if you want a room here—the same goes for their superb restaurant. Small and elegant, on a quiet street near Harrods, it's recommended for the excellent, welcoming service it gives. Try for one of the 10 individually designed rooms in the Edwardian wing, formerly part of the Squires Hotel (fashionable in the 1920s). The whole hotel is beautifully decorated. *22–24 Basil St., SW3 1AT, tel. 071/589–5171. 48 rooms with bath. Facilities: air conditioning, bar. AE, DC, MC, V.*

St. James' Court. This elegant turn-of-the-century apartment house was converted into a stylish hotel at vast expense. Fine marble adorns the grand reception area and your bathroom will be truly glamorous. Other features include a stately courtyard with fountain and a frieze portraying scenes from Shakespeare. One restaurant serves Mediterranean cuisine; the other, Chinese. *Buckingham Gate, SW1E 6AF, tel. 071/834–6655. 400 rooms with bath. Facilities: 2 restaurants, coffee shop, fitness center with sauna, spa pools. AE, DC, MC, V.*

Expensive **Basil Street.** Female guests automatically become members of
★ the ladies' club here, the **Parrot Club.** This gracious Edwardian
hotel has been family-run for nearly eight decades. Coffee, tea,
and cocktails are available in the upstairs lounge. Each room is
different—antique-filled, and amazingly quiet. You can write
letters home in the peaceful Gallery, which has polished wood-
en floors and fine Turkish carpets. This is a true "period" hotel.
*Basil St., SW3 1AH, tel. 071/581–3311. 92 rooms, 72 with bath.
Facilities: restaurant, winebar. AE, DC, MC, V.*

Beaufort. The Beaufort, a stone's throw from Harrods, is the
dream hotel of owner/designer Diana Wallis. It's got all the
comforts of home—if your home happens to be a masterpiece of
quiet sophistication. The bedrooms are extremely comfortable,
with pale marbled wallpapers, lots of bird and flower designs,
and squashy armchairs. *33 Beaufort Gdns., SW3 1PP, tel. 071/
584–5252. 29 rooms with bath. AE, DC, MC, V.*

★ **Eleven Cadogan Gardens.** This gabled late-Victorian town
house is the perfect spot for a pampered honeymoon, though
very difficult to get into. Fine period furniture and art, and the
books and magazines help to create the ambience of a Victorian
family house; the 1990s have barely touched it. Rooms have mahogany furniture and fine bedspreads and drapes. The best
rooms are at the back. There's also a private garden. *11
Cadogan Gdns., Sloane Sq., SW3 3RJ, tel. 071/730–3426. 60
rooms with bath. Facilities: garden, chauffeur-driven car. No
credit cards.*

The Royal Court. A striking reception hall with chandeliers,
one from the Vatican, welcomes you. The light, elegant interior
has original Victorian cornices. The rooms and bathrooms,
however, fulfill modern needs. **Court's** coffee bar is a popular
rendezvous (open 10:30 AM to 11 PM), and the **Old Poodle Dog**
restaurant, with its wicker chairs and hanging baskets of
ferns, provides relaxed surroundings for a meal. *Sloane Sq.,
SW1W 8EG, tel. 071/730–9191. 102 rooms with bath. Facilities:
pub, cafe/bar, in-house movies. AE, DC, MC, V.*

Moderate **Claverley.** Sited on a quiet, tree-lined street, the Claverley offers friendly, attractive surroundings with the wealthy world
of Knightsbridge shopping just around the corner. Some rooms
have four-poster beds. *13–14 Beaufort Gdns., SW3 1PS, tel.
071/589–8541. 36 rooms with bath. AE, V.*

Ebury Court. Five 19th-century converted houses make up this
Old-World-style family-run hotel near Victoria Station. The
rooms are smallish and chintzy, but the antique furniture lends
character—including one with a grandfather clock and Hep-
plewhite four-poster bed. You must buy temporary membership for use of the bar and lounge. The restaurant offers
intimacy and excellent value. *26 Ebury St., SW1W 0LU, tel.
071/730–8147. 38 rooms, 12 with bath. Facilities: restaurant,
club (with bar and lounge). MC, V.*

Bayswater and Notting Hill Gate

Very Expensive **Halcyon.** This extremely expensive spot, one of London's best
small hotels, is worth every penny. Its address on a quiet street
lends an intimate atmosphere in spite of its luxurious trappings—four poster beds, marble baths, a patio garden, a superb lounge with a magnificent grandfather clock, and an
attentive, uniformed staff. The Kingfisher restaurant serves
imaginative cuisine in a French provincial setting. *81 Holland*

Park, W11 3RZ, tel. 071/727–7288. 44 rooms with bath. Facilities: restaurant, patio, some Jacuzzis. AE, DC, MC, V.

Whites. The cream facade of this Victorian "country mansion" looks out at Kensington Gardens. Thick carpets, gilded glass, marble balustrades, silk drapes, and Louis XV-style furniture make this the most luxurious hotel in the area. Some rooms have balconies (one room has a four-poster bed) and the muted colors (powder blue, old rose, lemon yellow) are set off by crystal wall-lights. *Lancaster Gate, W2 3NR, tel. 071/262–2711. 55 rooms with bath. Facilities: restaurant, lounge, air conditioning, laundry, in-house movies. AE, DC, MC, V.*

Expensive **Abbey Court.** You enter this 1850 building through a stately, double-fronted portico to find yourself in a luxury bed-and-breakfast filled with Empire furniture and oil portraits. Ask for a four-poster bed. Kensington Gardens is close by. The owner is the Director of Historic House Hotels. *20 Pembridge Gdns., W2 4DU, tel. 071/221–7518. 22 rooms with bath. Facilities: Jacuzzis, patio. AE, DC, MC, V.*

Moderate **Portobello.** Within walking distance of the Portobello antiques
★ market, this tiny Victorian hotel (with some very tiny rooms!) overlooks a delightful private garden. Repeat guests cherish its relaxed informality. The suites have adjoining sitting rooms, and there's a bright congenial basement bar. *22 Stanley Gdns., W11 2NG, tel. 071/727–2777. 25 rooms with bath. Facilities: restaurant, bar. AE, DC, MC, V. Closed 10 days over Christmas.*

Inexpensive **Norfolk Court.** This little Regency hotel is less than a minute from Paddington tube. Some second-floor rooms have French windows and balconies overlooking the square. There are art deco touches in the landing windows and the breakfast room. *20 Norfolk Sq., W2 1RS, tel. 071/723–4963. 28 rooms, 9 with private bath. No credit cards.*

Bloomsbury, Soho, and Covent Garden

Very Expensive **The Savoy.** This historic, grand, late Victorian hotel has recently celebrated a century of stylish luxury. It has always been a favorite address for stars visiting London; some even take up semipermanent residence. The best suites overlook the river and can cost over £500 a night; other rooms in 1920s style still have the original bathrooms with their enormous shower nozzles. Service is generally excellent, and the Savoy Grill is famous for classic food. The world's first martini is supposed to have been mixed in the American bar here. *Strand, WC2R OEU, tel. 071/836–4343. 202 rooms with bath. Facilities: hairdresser, florist, theater ticket desk, 3 restaurants, 2 bars, valet, in-house movies. AE, DC, MC, V.*

Marlborough Crest. Houseplants, gleaming brass, and elegant furnishings set the tone in this Edwardian hotel close to the British Museum. The rooms are of a reasonable size, with floral fabrics and reproduction furniture. Dine in its chic **Brasserie Saint Martin,** or have a drink at the **Duke's Head** pub. *Bloomsbury St., WC1B 3QD, tel. 071/636–5601. 169 rooms with bath. Facilities: brasserie, air conditioning, in-house movies. AE, DC, MC, V.*

Expensive **Grafton Hotel.** The drawing room here retains an Edwardian air with red-plush armchairs, Ionic columns, and open fireplaces. There are stained-glass windows on every landing. The rooms are fairly modern, especially in the executive wing, completed in 1990. This is a good choice if you're planning to travel on to the north of England or to Scotland: trains leave from nearby Euston or King's Cross station. *130 Tottenham Court Rd., W1P 9HP, tel. 071/388–4131. 236 rooms with bath. Facilities: restaurant, bar, in-house movies. AE, DC, MC, V.*

Moderate   **Hazlitt's.** This hotel, deep in the heart of Soho, was once home to William Hazlitt, the Regency essayist (1778–1830). The reasonably-priced rooms are all different, furnished with polished mahogany, oak, and pine, with hundreds of framed prints throughout, and a claw-foot Victorian tub in every bathroom. This is a one-of-a-kind. *6 Frith St., W1V 5TZ, tel. 071/439–1524. 23 rooms with bath. AE, DC, MC, V.*

Inexpensive   **Ruskin.** Immediately opposite the British Museum, the family-owned hotel is both pleasant and quiet—thanks to its double-glazed windows. Rooms are clean, though somewhat lacking in character; back rooms overlook a pretty garden. Notice the country-scene mural (c. 1808) in the lounge. *23–24 Montague St., WC1B 5BN, tel. 071/636–7388. 35 rooms, 7 with shower. AE, DC, MC, V.*

St. Margaret's. Set in a tree-lined Georgian street, this hotel has been run by a friendly Italian family for many years. Its spacious rooms, towering ceilings, and prime location by Russell Square are highlights. The back rooms have a garden view. *24 Bedford Pl., WC1B 5JL, tel. 071/636–4277. 64 rooms, 45 with bath. No credit cards.*

The Arts and Nightlife

The Arts

For a schedule of London arts events, consult the weekly magazine *Time Out*, good for both mainstream and fringe—London's equivalent to Off-Broadway—events. The *Evening Standard* carries listings, as do the major Sunday papers, the daily *Independent* and *Guardian*, and Friday's *Times*.

Further information on any aspect of the arts in London is available from **Greater London Arts**, 9 White Lion St., N1 5PD, tel. 071/837–8808. Open weekdays 9:30–5:30.

Theater   Most theaters have a matinee twice a week (Wednesday or Thursday and Saturday) and nightly performances at 7:30 or 8, except Sundays. Prices vary; expect to pay from £6 for an upper balcony seat to at least £20 for the stalls (orchestra) or dress circle. Reserve tickets at the box office, over the phone by credit card (numbers in the phone book or newspaper marked "cc" are for credit card reservations), or through ticket agents such as **Keith Prowse** (tel. 071/741–9999; locations listed under **Keith** in the phone book). To reserve before your trip use **Keith Prowse's New York office** (234 W. 44th St., Suite 902, New York, NY, 10036, tel. 212/398–1430 or 800/223–4446).

Half-price, same-day tickets are sold (subject to availability) from a booth in Leicester Square, facing the Swiss Center. Open Mon.–Sat. 12–2 for matinees, 2:30–6:30 for evening shows. There is always a long line. Larger hotels have reservation services, but add hefty service charges.

Beware the scalpers! They not only charge outrageous prices and corrupt ticket availability; they sometimes sell forged tickets. Even box-office employees have been caught selling tickets at way above official price, so know the prices ahead of time. The only extra you should ever pay is a nominal booking charge.

Concerts Ticket prices for symphony orchestra concerts are relatively moderate, ranging from £5–£15. International guest appearances usually mean higher prices; you should reserve well in advance for such performances. Those without reservations might go to the hall half an hour before the performance for a chance at returns: tickets that people return to the box office when they can't use them.

The London Symphony Orchestra is in residence at the **Barbican Arts Centre,** although the Philharmonia and the Royal Philharmonic also perform here. The **South Bank Arts Complex,** which includes the **Royal Festival Hall, Queen Elizabeth Hall,** and the small **Purcell Room,** forms another major venue. Between the Barbican and South Bank, there are concert performances every night of the year. The Barbican also features chamber music concerts with such smaller orchestras as the City of London Sinfonia.

For a chance to experience a great British institution, try the **Royal Albert Hall** during the Promenade Concert season lasting eight weeks from July to September. Special "promenade" (standing) tickets are usually around £3 and are available at the hall on the night. Other summer pleasures are the outdoor concerts by the lake at **Kenwood** (Hampstead Heath) or **Holland Park.** Check the listings or call the **English Heritage Concert Line** (tel. 071/734–6010) for details.

Numerous lunchtime concerts take place across London in smaller concert halls and churches. They feature string quartets, vocalists, jazz ensembles, or gospel choirs. **St. John's,** Smith Square, and **St. Martin-in-the-Fields** are two of the more popular locations. Performances usually begin about 1 PM and last an hour.

Opera The classiest venue for opera in London is the **Royal Opera House** (Covent Garden) where international casts appear. Tickets range from £1.50 in the upper balcony (where visibility will be almost nil) to £101 for the best seat. Performances are divided into booking periods and sell out early. (English "surtitles" now appear on a screen over the stage for some operas.)

English-language operas are staged at the **Coliseum,** St. Martin's Lane, home of the English National Opera Company. Prices here are generally lower than at the Royal Opera House, ranging from £6 to £7.50, and productions are unconventional and often a lot more exciting.

Ballet The Royal Opera House is also the home of the world famous **Royal Ballet.** Prices are slightly lower for the ballet than opera, but tickets go faster; reserve ahead. The **English National Ballet** (formerly the Festival) and visiting international companies perform at the Coliseum from time to time. **Sadler's Wells Theatre** hosts various ballet companies—including the Royal and the Rambert—as well as regional ballet and international modern dance troups. Again, prices here are much lower than at Covent Garden.

Opera and Ballet **Coliseum,** St. Martin's La., WC2N 4ES, tel. 071/836–3161.
Box Office **Royal Opera House,** Covent Garden, WC2E 9DD, tel. 071/240–
Information 1066. **Sadler's Wells,** Rosebery Ave., EC1R 4TN, tel. 071/278–
8916.

Movies Despite the video invasion, West End movies still thrive. Most
of the major houses (**Odeon, Cannon,** etc.) are found in the
Leicester Square/Piccadilly Circus area, where tickets average £4 to £7. Monday and matinees are sometimes better buys
at £2 to £4; lines are also shorter.

Cinema clubs and repertory houses screen a wider range of
movies: classics, Continental, and underground, as well as rare
or underrated masterpieces. Most charge a membership fee of
around £1; sometimes the membership card must be bought
half an hour before the screening. The best is the **National Film
Theatre** (in the South Bank Arts Complex), associated with the
British Film Institute. The main events of the annual London
Film Festival take place here in the fall; there are also lectures
and presentations by visiting celebrities. Temporary daily
membership costs 40p.

The **Institute of Contemporary Art** (ICA) presents films on various aspects of the arts, and the **Commonwealth Institute** (Holland Park) shows Commonwealth-produced films. The national
museums and galleries also have occasional screenings.

Nightlife

Cabaret **Comedy Store.** The best comedy in town is at the crowded
Comedy Store. Many comics got their start at this "Alternative" comedy showcase, and it's popularity is reflected in
the sometimes long lines. *28a Leicester Sq., tel. 071/839–
6665. Admission: £5–£6. Shows Tues.–Thurs. and Sun.
at 8:30 PM, Fri.–Sat. at 8 PM and midnight. Dress: informal.*
Madame Jo Jo's. Possibly the most fun of any London cabaret.
There are two outrageous drag shows nightly, with food and
drink at reasonable prices. The place is luxurious, and civilized—what more could anyone ask? *8 Brewer St., tel. 071/734–
2473. Admission: Mon.–Thurs. £6, Fri. and Sat. £8. Shows at
12:15 AM and 1:15. Stylish dress.*

Nightclubs **Camden Palace.** Perennially popular with both London and visiting youth, this multi-tiered dance hall features different
themed nights, three bars, and a colorful light show. Ameri-
can-style food is served. *1A Camden High St., NW1, tel. 071/
387–0428. Admission: £3–£7. Open Tues.–Sat. 9 PM–3 AM.
Dress: casual stylish.*
Legends. A large choice of cocktails is served at the upstairs
bar, while downstairs is the extensive, cool dance floor and
main bar. *Old Burlington St., tel. 071/437–9933. Admission:
Mon.–Thurs. £6 after 10 PM, Fri.–Sat. £8 after 10 PM. Open
Mon.–Thurs. 5:30 PM–2 AM, Fri. 5:30 PM–3 AM, Sat. 9 PM–3 AM.
Stylish dress. AE, DC, MC, V.*
Stringfellows. The art deco restaurant along with the show on
the downstairs dance floor attracts a celebrity crowd most
nights. *16 Upper St. Martin's Lane, tel. 071/240–5534. Admission: £6–£12.50. Open Mon.–Sat. 8 PM–3:30 AM. High-fashion,
stylish dress. AE, DC, MC, V.*

Jazz   **Bass Clef.** Situated, along with its annex, **Tenor Clef,** in an out-of-the-way warehouse on the northern edge of the City, this restaurant/jazz club offers some of the best live jazz in town and a gourmet Anglo-French menu. *85 Coronet St., tel. 071/729–2440. Admission: £3.50–£7 depending on the band. Open Tues.–Sat., 7:30 PM–2AM. AE, DC, MC, V.*

Ronnie Scott's. The legendary Soho jazz club has always drawn a host of international talent—and audiences. *Frith St., tel. 071/439–0747. Admission: £10–£12 non-members. Open Mon.–Sat. 8:30 PM–3 AM, Sun. 8PM–11:30 PM. Reservations advised; essential some nights. AE, DC, MC, V.*

Rock   **The Rock Garden.** Talking Head, U2, and The Smiths all made appearances here when they were still relatively unknown. Bands perform in the standing-room-only basement, so eat first in the American restaurant upstairs. *The Piazza, Covent Garden, tel. 071/240–3961. Admission: £4–£7 depending on the band. Open Mon.–Sat. 7:30 PM–3 AM, Sun. 8 PM–midnight. AE, DC, MC, V.*

Marquee. Soho's original rock club, now relocated to a bigger sauna, features two live bands every night. *105 Charing Cross Rd., tel. 071/437–6601. Admission: £4–£6, depending on the band. Open daily 7:30 PM–11 PM.*

Discos   **Hippodrome.** An enormous cavern of a high-tech disco that always attracts a line to the Charing Cross Road. The light show with lasers is extreme; the six bars and balcony restaurant usually packed. *Cranbourne St., W1, tel. 071/437–4311. Admission: £6 Wed., £8 Mon., Tue., Thur., £10 Fri., £12 Sat.; half price for diners. Dress: smart casual.*

Casinos   By law, you must apply for casino membership in person; applications usually take about two days, and in many cases clubs prefer an endorsement from an existing member.

Crockford's. Civilized and far removed from Las Vegas glitz, this 150-year-old club hosts an international clientele who come to play American roulette, punto banco, and blackjack. *30 Curzon St., tel. 071/493–7771. Membership £150 a year. Open daily 2 PM–4 AM. Jacket and tie required.*

Sportsman Club. This is one of the few casinos in London with both a dice table and punto banco, American roulette, and blackjack. *Tottenham Court Rd., tel. 071/637–5464. Membership £3.45 a year. Open daily 2 PM–4 AM. Jacket and tie required.*

For Singles   **The Limelight.** Owned by New York's Limelight proprietor Peter Gatien, this club has earned its popularity through special one-night shows and events. *136 Shaftesbury Ave., tel. 071/434–1761. Admission: Mon.–Fri. £7, Sat. £10. Mon.–Sat. 9:30 PM–3 AM. Casual chic dress.*

4 The Southeast

Introduction

Though it is one of the most densely populated areas of Britain—the inevitable result of its close proximity to London—the Southeast still has some of England's loveliest countryside. Its landscape is punctuated with hundreds of small farms, their tiny fields ringed by neat green hedges, with picturesque villages and gentle, rolling hills and woodlands. It is prime commuter country.

Four counties, Surrey, Kent, and Sussex, East and West, make up the Southeast. The northern parts of Surrey and Kent have been overrun by the suburban sprawl of London, and now mainly consist of bedroom communities. Yet Kent's abundant apple orchards have earned it the title of "Garden of England." Kent is also known for its undulating chalk hills and distinctive oast houses: tall, cylindrical brick buildings with conical tops, where hops are dried for English beer.

Sussex abounds with deep, narrow lanes leading to small, quiet villages, each with its ancient church and public house. The coasts of Sussex and Kent are one long chain of seaside resorts, a natural magnet for thousands of city-weary vacationers; and the busy ports of Newhaven, Folkestone, Dover, and Ramsgate serve as gateways to continental Europe. It is from near Folkestone that the Channel Tunnel is being dug, which will change forever Britain's isolation from the Continent.

Much of England's history is rooted in the Southeast, not least because here the dividing English Channel is at its narrowest. The Romans landed in this area, and stayed to rule Britain for four centuries. So did the Saxons, who gave England her principal language. (Sussex means the land of the South Saxons.) William of Normandy defeated the Saxons at a battle near Hastings in 1066, thereby acquiring his title "the Conqueror." Canterbury has been the seat of the Primate of All England—the archbishop of Canterbury—since Pope Gregory the Great dispatched St. Augustine to convert the heathen hordes of Britain in 597. And long before any of these invaders, the ancient Britons blazed trails across the land which formed the routes for today's modern highways.

Essential Information

Important Addresses and Numbers

Tourist Information The **Southeast England Tourist Board** will send you a free illustrated booklet on the region. They also arrange tours and excursions for the Southeast area. *1 Warwick Park, Tunbridge Wells, Kent TN2 5TA, tel. 0892/540766. Open Mon.–Thurs. 9–5:30, Fri. 9–5.*

Local tourist information centers, normally open Mon.–Sat. 9:30–5:30, but varying according to the season, include:

Arundel: 61 High St., tel. 0903/882268.
Brighton: Marlborough House, 54 Old Steine, tel. 0273/23755.
Canterbury: 34 St. Margaret's St., tel. 0227/766567.
Chichester: St. Peter's Market, West St., tel. 0243/775888.
Dover: Townwall St., tel. 0304/205108.
Eastbourne: 3 Cornfield Rd., tel. 0323/411400.

Gatwick Airport: International Arrivals Concourse, South Terminal, tel. 0293/560108.
Guildford: 155 High St., tel. 0483/444007.
Hastings: 4 Robertson Terr., tel. 0424/718888.
Lewes: 32 High St., tel. 0273/471600.
Maidstone: The Gatehouse, Old Palace Gdns., Mill St., tel. 0622/673581.
Rye: 48 Cinque Ports St., tel. 0797/222293.
Tunbridge Wells: Monson House, Monson Way, tel. 0892/515675.

Travel Agencies **American Express:** 66 Churchill Sq., Brighton, tel. 0273/21242. **Thomas Cook:** 58 North St., Brighton, tel. 0273/25711; 109 Mount Pleasant Rd., Tunbridge Wells, tel. 0892/32372. There are other offices in Dover, Eastbourne, and Hove.

Car Rental Agencies **Brighton: Avis,** the Brighton Marina, tel. 0273/773233 or 673738; **Hertz,** 47 Trafalgar St., tel. 0273/738227.
Canterbury: Europcar, Sturry Rd. Service Station, 118 Sturry Rd., tel. 0227/470864.
Dover: Avis, Eastern Docks, tel. 0304/206265; **Hertz,** 173–177 Snargate St., tel. 0304/207303.

Arriving and Departing by Plane

Gatwick Airport (tel. 0293/31299) has direct flights from many U.S. cities and is more convenient than Heathrow if you are heading straight for this region. Gatwick is in the heart of the Southeast, on the Surrey side of the Sussex border, 28 miles south of London. The terminal spans the British Rail main line, which fans out from there to feed all the major coastal towns. The airport is also close to major highways A23 and M23, handy if you plan to travel onward by either bus or car.

Getting Around

By Car Major road routes radiating outward from London to the Southeast are, from west to east: A23/M23 to Brighton (52 miles); A21, passing by Tunbridge Wells to Hastings (65 miles); and A2/M2 via Canterbury (56 miles) to Dover (71 miles). To get to Worthing, take A24; to Eastbourne, A22; and to Folkestone, take A20/M20. All these roads link up with London's orbital route, M25, which runs through the top of the region. M25 also runs northeast, under the Thames through the Dartford Tunnel (toll 70p).

A good link route for traveling through the region, from Hampshire across the border into Sussex and Kent, is A272 (which becomes A265). It runs through the weald (uplands), which separates the north downs from the more inviting south downs. Though smaller, less busy roads forge deeper into the downs, even the main roads take you through lovely countryside and villages. The main route south from the downs to the Channel ports and resorts of Kent is A27. To get to Romney Marsh (just across the Sussex border in Kent), take A259 from Rye. The principal roads in the Southeast are constantly being enlarged and upgraded to handle the ever-increasing flow of traffic to the Channel ports. As 1993, the scheduled opening date for the Channel Tunnel, draws closer, visitors can expect even more lane closings and other delays.

By Train British Rail's Network Southeast serves the area from the following London stations: Victoria and Charing Cross (for eastern areas) and Waterloo (for the west). Travel time to Victoria from Gatwick Airport is about 30 minutes, with departures every 20 minutes all day long. From London, the trip to Brighton takes about 1 hour by the fast train; and to Dover, 1½ hours. A coastal line runs west from Dover to Hastings, with connections in Eastbourne for Lewes, and in Brighton for Chichester.

By Bus **National Express** (tel. 071/730–0202) serves the region from London's Victoria Coach Station. The journey to Brighton and Canterbury takes about two hours; to Chichester, about three hours. Private companies operating within the region are linked by county coordinating offices: **East Sussex,** tel. 0273/481000; **West Sussex,** tel. 0243/777556; **Surrey,** tel. 081/541-9365; and **Kent,** tel. 0622/671411. Maps and timetables are available at train stations, local libraries, and tourist information centers. Tourist centers can also provide you with information about special excursions run by local bus companies.

Guided Tours

The Southeast England Tourist Board (tel. 0892/540766) can arrange private tours, tailored to your personal interests, hosted by qualified Blue Badge guides. These tours last from one hour to a full day.
The Guild of Guides (tel. 0227/459779, 462017) provides individual guides who have a specialized knowledge of Canterbury.

Exploring the Southeast

Orientation

We begin our southeastern tour in the heart of Kent, in the cathedral town of Canterbury. Then we work our way south to Dover, England's "continental gateway." From Dover we head west along the Sussex coast to Brighton, taking in the historic seaside towns along the way. Leaving Brighton, we continue west to Chichester, then swing north into Surrey, stopping in Guildford, Farnham, and Tunbridge Wells before beginning our final circuit through eastern Kent, with its abundance of historic buildings.

Most of the towns described can easily be reached by public transportation. Local buses, trains, and sometimes even steam trains provide a regular service to most major tourist sites. But if you're especially interested in stately homes or quiet villages, it might be wiser to rent a car and strike out on your own.

Highlights for First-time Visitors

Brighton Pavilion: Tour 3
Canterbury Cathedral: Tour 1
Dover Castle and the White Cliffs: Tour 1
Hever Castle: Tour 4
Ightham Mote: Tour 4
Leeds Castle: Tour 4
Lewes: Tour 2
Petworth House: Tour 3
Rye: Tour 2

Winchelsea: Tour 2

Tour 1: Canterbury to Dover

Numbers in the margin correspond to points of interest on the Southeast and Canterbury maps.

❶ The city of **Canterbury,** cradled in the rolling Kent countryside on the banks of the River Stour, is just 56 miles from London and is the undisputed star of the southeast region. Iron Age capital of the kingdom of Kent, headquarters of the Anglican church, and center of international pilgrimage, Canterbury offers a wealth of historic treasures. It also maintains a lively day-to-day atmosphere, a fact that has impressed visitors since 1388, when poet Geoffrey Chaucer wrote *The Canterbury Tales*, chronicling the journey from London to the shrine of St. Thomas à Becket. Canterbury was one of the first cities in Britain to "pedestrianize" its center, bringing a measure of tranquillity to its streets. To see it at its best, walk around in the morning before the tourist buses arrive, or in the evening after they depart.

Canterbury is bisected by a road running northwest, beside which lie all the major tourist sites. This road begins as St. George's Street, then becomes High Street, and finally turns into St. Peter's Street. Begin your tour of the city center at the St. George's Street end. Here you will see a lone church tower

❷ marking the site of **St. George's Church**—the rest of the building was destroyed in World War II—where playwright Christopher Marlowe was baptized in 1564. Continuing up St.

❸ George's Street, just before you reach the modern **Longmarket** shopping center, you come to Butchery Lane and the colorful **Roman Pavement.** This ancient mosaic floor and hypocaust, the Roman version of central heating, were excavated in the 1940s, just one of the many long-hidden relics that were laid bare by German bombs. *Butchery Ln., tel. 0227/452747. Closed for redevelopment, possibly until 1993. Check locally.*

Mercery Lane, with its medieval-style cottages and massive, overhanging timber roofs, runs right off the High Street and

❹ ❺ ends in the tiny **Buttermarket.** Here the immense **Christchurch Gate,** built in 1517, leads into the cathedral close.

❻ **Christchurch Cathedral** is the focal point of the city of Canterbury and the first of England's great Norman cathedrals. It is a living textbook of medieval architecture. The building was begun in 1070, demolished, and begun anew in 1096, and then systematically expanded over the next three centuries. When the original choir burned to the ground in 1174, it was replaced by a new one, designed in the Gothic style, with tall, pointed arches. Don't be surprised to find a play or concert taking place in the nave; in recent years the dean and Chapter (the cathedral's ruling body) have revived the medieval tradition of using the cathedral for occasional secular performances. In the Middle Ages, only the presbytery (the area around the high altar) was considered sacred, and the nave was often used as a meeting place, sometimes even as a market.

The cathedral was only a century old, and still relatively small in size, when Thomas à Becket, the archbishop of Canterbury, was murdered here on December 29, 1170. Becket, an uncompromising defender of ecclesiastical interests, had angered his friend Henry II, who was heard to exclaim, "Who will rid me of this troublesome priest?" Thinking they were carrying out the king's wishes, four knights burst in on Becket in one of the side chapels and killed him. Two years later Becket was canonized, and Henry II's subsequent submission to the authority of the Church and his penitence helped establish the cathedral as the undisputed center of English Christianity.

Becket's tomb—destroyed by Henry VIII in 1538 as part of his campaign to reduce the power of the church and confiscate its treasures—was one of the most extravagant shrines in Christendom. It was placed in **Trinity Chapel,** where you can still see a series of 13th-century stained glass windows illustrating Becket's miracles. So hallowed was this spot that in 1376, Edward the Black Prince, warrior son of Edward II and a national hero, was buried near it. Over Edward's copper-gilt effigy hang replicas of his colorful surcoat, helmet, gauntlets, and a variety of other accouterments. The faded originals are displayed in a glass case on the left.

The actual site of Becket's murder is down a flight of steps just to the left of the nave. Here you will see a modern commemorative altar, jagged and dramatic in design. A nearby plaque tells of the meeting between Pope John Paul II and Archbishop Robert Runcie, who knelt here together in prayer on May 19, 1982. In the corner, a second flight of steps leads down to the enormous Norman undercroft, or vaulted cellarage, built in the early 12th century. The room has remained virtually unchanged since then. Its roof is supported by a row of squat pillars whose capitals dance with fantastic animals and strange monsters.

If time permits, be sure to explore the **Cloisters** and other small monastic buildings to the north of the cathedral. The 12th-century octagonal water tower is still part of the cathedral's water supply. As you pass through the great gatehouse back into the city, look up at the sculpted heads of two young figures: Prince Arthur, elder brother of Henry VIII; and the young Catherine of Aragon, to whom he was betrothed. After Arthur's death, Catherine married Henry. Her failure to produce a male heir led to Henry's decision to divorce her after 25 years of marriage, creating an irrevocable breach with the Catholic church that altered the course of English history.

As you leave the cathedral, cross the High Street and turn onto St. Margaret's Street. Here, in a disused church, you will find a **❼** unique and vivid exhibition called **The Pilgrims' Way.** This is a dramatization not only of Chaucer's *Canterbury Tales,* but also of 14th-century English life. First you will encounter Chaucer's pilgrims at the Tabard Inn near London, the starting point of their travels. Next you will come to a series of tableaux illustrating five of the tales. Then, passing through a reconstruction of the city gate, you may enter the marketplace. Don't be surprised if one of the figures comes to life: an actor dressed in period costume often forms part of the scene. The visit ends at a replica of Becket's shrine. *St. Margaret's St., tel. 0227/454888. Admission: £3.75 adults, £1.50 children, £2.50 senior citizens, £11 family ticket. Open weekdays 10–4:30, weekends 9:30–5:30.*

Return to the High Street and turn left. Just past where the High Street crosses the little River Stour, you will see a

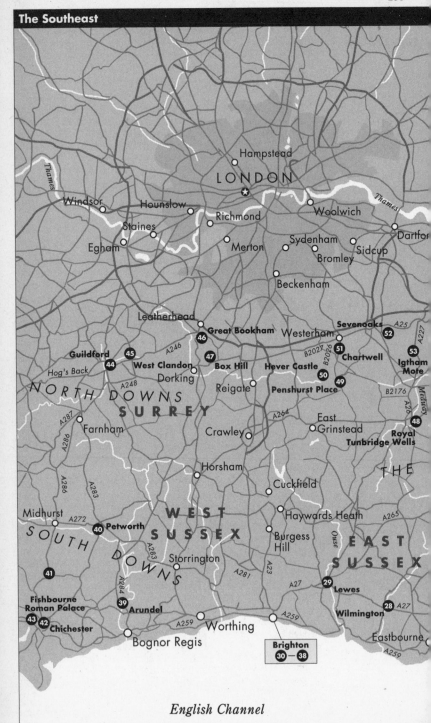

English Channel

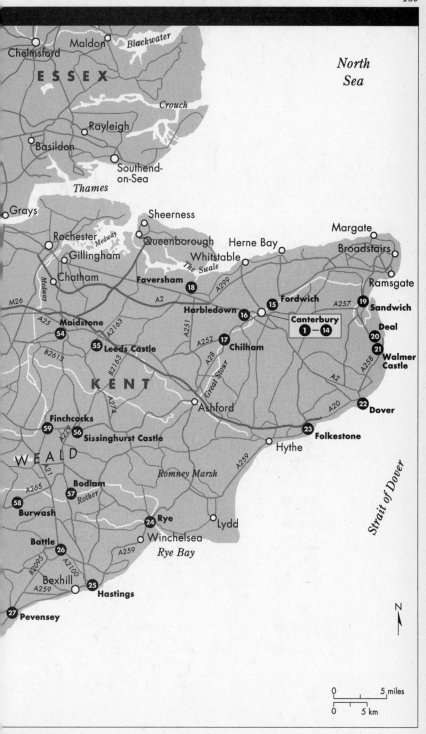

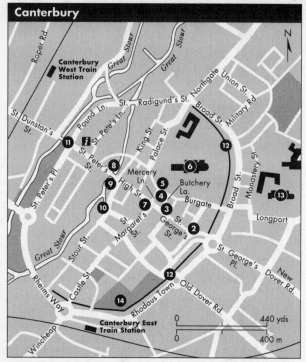

8 distinctive group of half-timbered cottages known as the **Weavers' Houses,** built in the 16th century. These were occupied by Huguenot weavers who settled in Canterbury after escaping religious persecution in France. Before you cross the bridge **9** over the river, stop in at the 12th-century **Eastbridge Hospital.** The hospital (which we would now call a hostel) lodged poor pilgrims who came to pray at the tomb of Thomas à Becket. The infirmary hall, the chapel, and the crypt are open to the public. *25 High St. Admission free. Open Mon.–Sat. 10–6, Sun. 11–6.*

Just before the High Street becomes St. Peter's Street, you will see Stour Street running off to the left. Follow this a few **10** blocks west until you arrive at the medieval **Poor Priests' Hospital,** now the site of the comprehensive **Canterbury Heritage Museum.** This is one of Canterbury's most popular museums. Its exhibits provide an excellent overview of the city's history and architecture. It can get crowded, so it's a good idea to visit it early in the day. *20 Stour St., tel. 0227/452747. Admission: £1.20 adults, 60p children, 90p senior citizens, £3 family ticket. Open Mon.–Sat. 10:30–4.*

St. Peter's Street runs to Westgate, Canterbury's only **11** surviving city gate house. It now contains the **Westgate Museum of Militaria.** Climb to the roof to catch a panoramic view of the city spires before following the landscaped, riverside gardens back to the center of town. *Tel. 0227/452747. Admission: 50p adults, 25p children. Open Oct.–Mar., Mon.–Sat. 2–4; Apr.–Sept., Mon.–Sat. 2–5.*

Time Out If you are hungry on your pilgrimage, try **Il Vaticano** (35 St. Margaret's St.), for fresh pasta with a wide selection of delicious sauces.

---

⑫ For a panoramic view of the town, follow the circuit of the **medieval city walls,** built on the line of the original Roman walls. Those to the south survive intact, towering some 20 feet high. A broad walkway runs along the top. Follow the walkway **⑬** clockwise, along Broad Street, passing the ruins of **St. Augustine's Abbey.** This is the burial place of Augustine, England's first Christian missionary, sent here from Rome in AD 597. The abbey was later seized by Henry VIII, who destroyed some of the buildings and converted others into a royal manor for his fourth wife, Anne of Cleves. Farther on, just opposite the **⑭** Canterbury East train station, you will see the **Dane John Mound,** originally part of the city defenses.

Before beginning your wide, counterclockwise tour of the region around Canterbury, drive about 1½ miles east to the village of **Fordwich.** This was originally the port of Canterbury, where the Caen stone quarried in Normandy and shipped across the Channel to be used in the construction of the cathedral was brought ashore.

A mile to the west of Canterbury, along the Roman road (now **⑯** A2), lies the village of **Harbledown** with its cluster of almshouses. Built in the 11th century to house the poor, they provide a scenic backdrop for this peaceful hamlet. Harbledown was customarily the spot from which pilgrims caught their first glimpse of Canterbury.

From Harbledown, take the minor roads south through Chartham Hatch to join A28, stopping off in the hilltop village **⑰** of **Chilham** on the way to Wye. Energetic visitors will find this a good place from which to walk the last few miles of the Pilgrim's Way, following the traditional pilgrims' route back to Canterbury.

The Chilham village square is filled with textbook examples of English rural architecture. The 14th-century **church** contains an old school desk covered with the carved initials of bored schoolchildren from the early 18th century onwards. On public holidays in the summer, the **Chilham Castle Gardens** are the setting for medieval jousting displays. *Tel. 0227/730319. Admission: £2.50 adults, £1.25 children. Open Apr.–mid-Oct., daily 11–5.*

Time Out The **White Horse,** a 16th-century inn nestled in the shadow of the church, offers a pleasant beer garden and wholesome evening and afternoon meals; there's a log fire in winter.

---

⑱ A252 and A251 (11 miles) will take you northwest to **Faversham.** In Roman times, Faversham was a thriving seaport; today the port is hidden from sight, and you could pass through the town without knowing it was there. The town center with its beautifully preserved Tudor houses grouped around the market hall looks like a stage set.

Time Out The **Sun Inn** on West Street is the flagship of the Shepherde Neame Brewery chain, established in Faversham in the 17th century. The pub dates even earlier, to the 16th century. Lunches are available every day. The inn follows the local tradition of hanging up hops in September; they are not only decorative, but add fragrance.

From Faversham you have a choice of taking A299 north to the seaside towns of **Whitstable, Herne Bay, Margate, Broadstairs,** and **Ramsgate**—long the playground of vacationing Londoners—or doubling back through Canterbury on A2 to pick up A257 for the ancient **Cinque Ports** (pronounced "sink") lining the eastern and southern coast. The latter offer much more in the way of history and atmosphere, and are generally much less crowded. The ports, originally five in number (hence *cinque*, from the Norman French), were Sandwich, Dover, Hythe, Romney, and Hastings. They were granted considerable privileges and powers of self-government in the Middle Ages in return for providing armed patrols of the English Channel against the ever-present threat of French and Spanish invasion.

19 **Sandwich,** the first of the original five ports you come to, still preserves its Tudor air. The 16th-century barbican (gate house) beside the toll bridge is one of the town's oldest surviving buildings. Another interesting building is the **Guildhall,** also 16th-century, with its small museum of local history, open to visitors when the court is not in session.

About 6 miles south of Sandwich is the larger seaside town of **20** **Deal**. It was here that Caesar's legions landed in 55 BC during the invasion of Britain, and from here that William Penn set sail in 1682 on his first journey to America. **Deal Castle,** erected in 1540 and built in an intricate design of concentric circles, is the largest of the coastal defenses built by Henry VIII. Cannons perched on the battlements overlook the gaping moat. The castle museum offers a range of exhibits of prehistoric, Roman, and Saxon Britain. *Victoria Rd., tel. 0304/372762. Admission: £1.60 adults, 80p children, £1.20 senior citizens. Open Apr.– Sept., daily 10–6; Oct.–Mar., daily 10–4.*

21 About a mile south of Deal stands **Walmer Castle,** another of Henry VIII's fortifications. Converted in 1730 into the official residence of the Lord Warden of the Cinque Ports, it now has the atmosphere of a cozy country house. Among the famous Lord Wardens once in residence were the Duke of Wellington, hero of the Battle of Waterloo, who lived here from 1829 until his death here in 1852 (there's a small museum of Wellington memorabilia); and Sir Winston Churchill. The present Lord Warden is the Queen Mother, though she rarely stays here. After you have seen the castle chambers, take a stroll in the gardens. The moat has been converted to a grassy walk flanked by flower beds. *Tel. 0304/364288. Admission: £2.20 adults, £1.10 children, £1.60 senior citizens. Open Apr.–end Sept., daily 10–6; Oct.–Mar., daily 10–4.*

22 Following A258 7 miles south from Walmer, you arrive at the city of **Dover,** Britain's historic gateway to continental Europe. Many visitors find Dover disappointing. Both the savage bombardments of World War II and the shortsightedness of postwar developers have left their scars on the city center. But **Dover Castle,** towering high above the chalk ramparts of the famous White Cliffs, is a spectacular sight and well worth a visit. It was one of the mightiest medieval castles in western Europe. The first building on the site was the Roman Pharos, or lighthouse, which still remains, casting its long shadow over the encircling walls. Most of the castle itself dates back to Norman times. It was begun by Henry II in 1181, but incorporates additions from almost every succeeding century, a testament to the skill of the ancient builders. It was still in use as a defense during World War II. The massive keep (central structure), with its dense walls 17 to 22 feet thick in places, is the most imposing area of the castle. A museum here offers an interesting range of exhibits, with objects dating back to the 12th century. One of the most intriguing is a large-scale model of the Battle of Waterloo. *Castle Rd., tel. 0304/201628. Admission: £3 adults, £1.50 children, £2 senior citizens. Open Apr.–Sept. daily 10–6, Oct.–Mar. daily 10–4.*

Time Out To rest your feet, stop in at the efficient, modern restaurant within the castle grounds. It offers tasty meals at reasonable prices.

Before you leave Dover, visit the 14th-century **Maison Dieu Hall,** located in the town hall. It was founded in 1221 as a hostel for pilgrims traveling from the Continent to Canterbury. A museum houses a varied collection of flags and armor, while the stained-glass windows tell the story of Dover through the ages. *Biggin St., tel. 0304/201200. Admission free. Open weekdays 10–4:30, Sat. 10–noon.*

Tour 2: Along the South Coast to Brighton

From Dover, the coast road (A20, then A259) winds through **❷❸ Folkestone** (another popular seaside resort) across **Romney Marsh**—reclaimed from the sea and famous for its sheep and, **❷❹** at one time, its ruthless smugglers—to the town of **Rye.** Over the years the sea has receded, and this once-port is now nearly 2 miles inland. Its steep hill provides dramatic views of the surrounding countryside. The medieval **Landgate,** one of three city gates, and the 13th-century **Ypres Tower**—part of the original 13th-century fortifications—remain intact. Follow Mermaid Street down to the site of the ancient port. While you are in the area, be sure to visit the **Rye Town Model,** a huge scale model of the town incorporating an imaginative and historic *son et lumière* (sound and light) show. *Strand Quay, tel. 0797/223902. Admission £2 adults, £1.50 children and senior citizens. Open Easter–Oct., daily 10:30–5 (shows on the half-hour).*

Another interesting museum is **Lamb House,** an early Georgian structure that has been home to several well-known writers. The most famous was the American Henry James, who lived here from 1898 to 1916. The ground-floor rooms contain some of his furniture and personal belongings. There is also a pretty walled garden. *West St., tel. 0797/223763. Admission: £1.40 adults, 70p children. Open Apr.–Oct., Wed. and Sat. 2–6.*

Leaving Rye, continue along the coast road (A259) through farmland and tiny villages to the city of **Hastings,** about 12 miles away.

Time Out The 18th-century **New Inn** in **Winchelsea,** about 3 miles outside Rye, is an excellent place to stop for a traditional pub lunch.

Perched, like Rye, atop its own small hill, Winchelsea is one of the prettiest villages in the region. The town was built on a grid system devised in 1283, after the sea destroyed an earlier settlement at the foot of the hill. Some of the original town gates still stand.

㉕ Hastings, headquarters of the Norman invasion of 1066, is now a large, slightly run-down seaside resort. A visit to the old town provides an interesting overview of 900 years of English maritime history. Along the beach, the tall wooden **Net Shops,** unique to the town, are used for drying local fishermen's nets. And in the town hall you'll find the famous **Hastings Embroidery.** Nearly 250 feet long, the piece was made in 1966 by members of the Royal School of Needlework to mark the 900th anniversary of the Battle of Hastings. It depicts legends and great moments from British history. *Queen's Rd., tel. 0424/ 718888. Admission: £1 adults, 50p children and senior citizens. Open Oct.–Apr., weekdays 11:30–3:30; June–Sept., Mon.–Sat. 10–5.*

All that remains of **Hastings Castle,** built by William the Conqueror in 1069, are fragments of the fortifications, some ancient walls, and a number of gloomy dungeons. Nevertheless, it is worth a visit—especially for the excellent aerial view it provides of the chalky cliffs, the coast, and the town below. *West Hill, tel. 0424/718888. Admission: £2 adults, £1.25 children and senior citizens. Open mid-Mar.–Oct., daily 10–5.*

From Hastings you can either follow the coast road directly to Brighton or take a detour, first north along A2100 about 7 **㉖** miles to the town of **Battle.** Battle takes its name, not surprisingly, from the crucial Battle of Hastings that took place here in 1066, giving William the Conqueror and his Norman warriors control of England. The ruins of **Battle Abbey,** the great Benedictine abbey William erected after his victory, are worth the trip. The high altar stood on the spot where the last Saxon king, Harold II, was killed. Though the abbey was destroyed in 1539 during Henry VIII's destructive binge, you can wander across the battlefield and see the remains of many of the domestic buildings. The **Abbot's House** (closed to the public) is now a girls' school. *High St., tel. 04246/3792. Admission: £1.90 adults, 95p children, £1.50 senior citizens. Open Easter–Sept., daily 10–6; Oct.–Easter, daily 10–4.*

㉗ Leaving Battle, take B2095 and A259 to **Pevensey.** This was an important Roman settlement (called Anderida), and was the place where William the Conqueror landed. The town is dominated by the extensive remains of **Pevensey Castle,** once an important Norman stronghold. Its massive outer walls were originally Roman structures and enclose a smaller castle built in the early 1100s by Count Robert de Mortain, half-brother of William the Conqueror. Inside, you will notice 20th-century machine-gun emplacements. These were added in 1940 to help ward off a possible German invasion. *Tel. 0323/762604. Admission: £1.30 adults, 65p children, 95p senior citizens. Open Apr.–Sept., daily 10–6; Oct.–Mar., Tues.–Sun. 10–4.*

Seven miles west of Pevensey on A27 lies the village of **㉘ Wilmington,** which grew up around the walls of **Wilmington Priory.** The remains of this 13th-century Benedictine monastery now house an agricultural museum. *The Street, tel. 0323/ 870537. Admission: £1 adults, 50p children. Open mid-Mar.– Oct., Mon.–Sat. 11–5:30, Sun. 2–5:30. Closed Tues.*

While you are visiting the priory, notice the chalky downs above it. There, cut into the turf, is the vivid figure of the **Long Man of Wilmington.** He stands about 226 feet high and holds a staff in each hand. Historians estimate he could have been carved 2,000 years ago.

㉙ Stay on A27 and head for **Lewes,** a town so rich in architectural history that the Council for British Archaeology has named it one of the 50 most important English cities. The **High Street** is lined with old buildings of all descriptions, dating from the late Middle Ages onward, including a timber-frame house once occupied by Thomas Paine, author of *The Rights of Man.*

Towering over the town, high above the valley of the River Ouse, stand the majestic ruins of Lewes Castle, an early Norman edifice, begun in 1100. For a panoramic view of the surrounding region, climb the keep and look out from the top. You can also stop in at the Barbican House museum of local history, just opposite the 14th-century Barbican Gate, to see the **Town Model and Living History Center.** This interesting museum contains an interpretative display of the town's history, including a 25-minute *son et lumière* program. *169 High St., tel. 0273/ 474379. Admission: £2.50 adults, £1.25 children. Open Apr.– mid-Sept., weekdays 11–5, Sun. 1–5.*

As you leave Lewes, continue west on A27 for 8 miles until you reach Brighton, one of the Southeast's liveliest seaside resorts.

Tour 3: Brighton to Royal Tunbridge Wells

㉚ An article in Britain's *Independent* newspaper summed up the attractions of **Brighton** this way: "Pleasing decay is a very English taste. It is best indulged in at the seaside, especially off-season, when wind and rain enhance the melancholy romance of cracked stucco, rusting ironwork, and boarded-up shops. Brighton is a supreme example, with its faded glamour combined with raucous vulgarity."

Numbers in the margin correspond to points of interest on the Brighton map.

Brighton was mentioned in the *Domesday Book* as Brighthelmstone in 1086, when it paid the annual rent of 4,000 herrings to the Lord of the Manor; it changed its name in the 18th century. The town owes its modern fame and fortune to the supposed medicinal virtues of seawater. In 1750, physician Richard Russell published a book recommending seawater treatment for glandular diseases. The patient was directed not only to swim in seawater, but to drink it—warm, and laced with such ingredients as vipers' eyes! The fashionable world flocked to Brighton to take Dr. Russell's "cure," and sea bathing became a popular pastime. Russell became known as "Dr. Brighton." When you visit the promenade across from the Palace Pier, you will notice a comfortable old pub called Dr. Brighton's Tavern, where his patients used to stay.

The next windfall for the town was the arrival of the Prince of Wales (later George IV), who acted as Prince Regent during the madness of his father, George III. "Prinny," as he was called, created the Royal Pavilion, an extraordinary pleasure palace (*see* below) that attracted London society. The influx of visitors triggered a wave of villa building. Fortunately this was one of the greatest periods in English architecture. The elegant terraces of Regency houses, most of them built to the east of the Pavilion, on the seafront and on the streets and squares leading off it, are today among the town's greatest attractions.

The coming of the railroad set the seal on Brighton's popularity: One of the most luxurious trains in the country, the Pullman "Brighton Belle," brought Londoners to the coast within an hour. They expected to find the same comforts and recreations they had in London and, as they were prepared to pay for them, Brighton obliged. This helps to explain the town's remarkable range of restaurants, hotels, and pubs. Horse racing was—and still is—another strong attraction.

Although fast rail service to London has made Brighton an important base for commuters, the town has unashamedly set itself out to be a pleasure resort. In the 1840s it featured the very first example of that peculiarly British institution, the amusement pier. Although that first pier has gone, the recently restored **Palace Pier** follows the great tradition. The original mechanical amusements, including the celebrated flipcard device, "What the Butler Saw," are now museum exhibits, but you can still admire the handsome ironwork in its original setting.

The heart of Brighton is the **Steine** (pronounced "steen"), the large open area close to the seafront. This was a river mouth until the Prince of Wales had it drained in 1793. One of the houses here was the home of Mrs. Maria Fitzherbert, later the Prince's wife. But the most remarkable building on the Steine, perhaps in all Britain, is unquestionably the **Royal Pavilion,** the Prince of Wales's extravagant fairy-tale palace. First planned as a simple seaside villa and built in the fashionable classical style of 1787, the pavilion was rebuilt between 1815 and 1822 for the Prince Regent, who favored an exotic, eastern design with Chinese interiors. When Queen Victoria came to the throne in 1837, she so disapproved of the palace that she stripped it of its furniture and planned to demolish it. Fortunately, the Brighton city council bought it from her, and it is now lovingly preserved and recognized as unique in Europe. After a lengthy process of restoration, the pavilion looks much as it did in its magnificent heyday. The interior is once more filled with quantities of period furniture and ornaments, some given or lent by the present royal family. The two great set pieces are the **Music Room,** styled in the form of an oriental pavilion, and the **Banqueting Room,** with its enormous flying-dragon "gasolier," or gaslight chandelier, a revolutionary new invention in the early 19th century. The upstairs rooms (once used as bedrooms) contain a selection of cruel caricatures of the Prince Regent, most produced during his lifetime, and illustrations of the pavilion at various stages of its construction. *Old Steine, tel. 0273/603005. Admission: £3 adults, £1.50 children, £2 senior citizens, £4.50 and £7.50 family tickets. Open Oct.– May, daily 10–5; June–Sept., daily 10–6.*

The grounds of the pavilion contain the **Brighton Museum and Art Gallery.** The buildings are almost as interesting as the collection they house, for they were originally designed as a stable block for the prince's horses. The museum has especially interesting Art Nouveau and Art Deco collections. *Church St., tel. 0273/603005. Admission free. Open Tues.–Sat. 10–5:45, Sun. 2–5.*

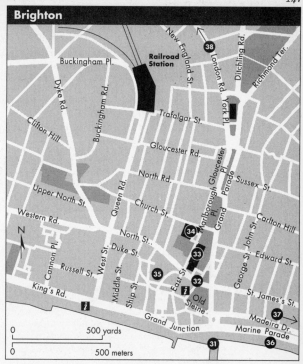

Brighton

Time Out One of the elegant upstairs bedrooms in the pavilion is now a tearoom, offering a variety of snacks and light meals.

---

35 Just west of the Old Steine lies **The Lanes,** Brighton's oldest section. This maze of alleys and passageways was once the poorest part of town, home to legions of fishermen and their families. It is said that the name "Lanes" actually refers to their fishing lines. Today The Lanes section is filled with restaurants, boutiques, and, especially, antiques shops. Vehicular traffic is barred from the area, and visitors may wander at will.

The heart of The Lanes is Market Street and Square, lined with fish and seafood restaurants. The large **Pump House** pub was once an actual pumping station, bringing seawater up from the beach and distributing it to Brighton's many bathing establishments. The **Bath House Arms,** nearby, was one of these. You can spend hours wandering through The Lanes, for the architecture is as varied as the merchandise on sale.

36 37 If you feel an urge to escape Brighton's summer crowds, take **Volk's Electric Railway** along the **Marine Parade** to the **Marina.** Built by inventor Magnus Volk in 1883, this was the first public electric railroad in Britain. For nearly 200 years the city of Brighton has struggled to build a sophisticated harbor and marina. What they have achieved is well short of a dream.

Time Out While you're visiting the revitalized Palace Pier, stop in at the **Palm Court Café** for coffee (the beans are freshly ground) or a light meal. The café has a pleasant Victorian ambience.

North of the Brighton town center, on the main London road, is
❸❽ Preston Manor. This beautifully preserved gentleman's residence, with its collection of paintings, silver, porcelain, and
furniture, evokes the opulence of Edwardian times. The present house was built in 1738, with additions in 1903. You can also
wander through the extensive grounds. *Preston Park, tel.
0273/603005, ext. 59. Admission: £2.20 adults, £1.10 children,
£1.75 senior citizens, £3.20 and £5 family ticket. Open Tues.–
Sun. and national holidays 10–5.*

*Numbers in the margin correspond to points of interest on the
Southeast map.*

❸❾ Leaving Brighton, follow the coast road (A27) west to **Arundel,**
about 23 miles away. This tiny hilltop town is dominated by an
11th-century castle, home of the dukes of Norfolk for more than
700 years, and an imposing **Roman Catholic cathedral**—the
duke is Britain's leading Catholic peer.

The ceremonial entrance to **Arundel Castle** is at the top of the
High Street, but visitors can enter at the bottom, close to the
parking lot. The keep, rising from its conical mound, is as old as
the original castle, while the barbican (gate house) and the Barons' Hall date from the 13th century. The interior of the castle
was reconstructed in the then-fashionable Gothic style of the
19th century. Among the treasures on view are the rosary
beads and prayer book used by Mary, Queen of Scots, at her execution. The spacious grounds are open to the public. *Tel. 0903/
883136. Admission: £3.50 adults, £2.50 children, £3 senior citizens. Open Apr.–Oct., Sun.–Fri. 1–5 (Jun.–Aug. from 12).*

Twelve miles north of Arundel by A284, and just off A283 in the
❹⓿ village of **Petworth,** stands **Petworth House,** built between 1688
and 1696. An extensive deer park was added later by the celebrated landscape architect Lancelot "Capability" Brown. The
house holds a fine collection of English paintings, including
works by Thomas Gainsborough, Sir Joshua Reynolds, J.M.W.
Turner, and Sir Antony Van Dyck. Other treasures include
Greek and Roman sculpture and Grinling Gibbons wood carvings. *Tel. 0798/42207. Admission: £3.30 adults, £1.75 children.
Open Apr.–Oct., Tues.–Thurs. and weekends 1–5; closed Mon.
and Fri.*

Time Out   You can have either a light lunch or tea in the **Servants' Block** at
Petworth House.

Leaving Petworth, follow A272 about 7 miles west to **Midhurst.**
Then turn off onto A286, running south over the downs into the
❹❶ village of **Singleton.** Here, stop in at the **Weald and Downland
Open Air Museum,** a sanctuary for endangered historical buildings. Among the "rescued" structures are a cluster of medieval
houses, a working water mill, a Tudor market hall, and an ancient blacksmith's shop. The architectural styles on display
span more than 400 years. *Tel. 0243/63348. Admission: £2.80
adults, £1.25 children, £2 senior citizens, £7.50 family ticket.
Open Apr.–Oct., daily 11–5; Nov.–Mar., Wed. and Sun. 11–4.*

From Singleton, head south on A286 for about 8 miles until you
❹❷ come to **Chichester,** capital city of West Sussex. The city itself,
founded by the Romans, sits on the low-lying plains between
the wooded south downs and the sea. Though it boasts its own
giant cathedral and has all the trappings of a large, commercial

city, Chichester is not much bigger than many of the provincial towns around it. The city walls and major streets follow the original Roman plan; the intersection of the four principal streets is marked by a 15th-century cross. The Norman **cathedral,** near the corner of West and South streets, also stands on Roman foundations. Inside, a glass panel reveals a group of Roman mosaics uncovered during recent restoration efforts. Other treasures include two of the most important Norman sculptures in Britain: *The Raising of Lazarus* and *Christ Arriving in Bethany,* both in the choir aisle. You will also see some outstanding modern works by artists John Piper, Marc Chagall, and Graham Sutherland.

43 As you drive west from Chichester on A259, stop at **Fishbourne Roman Palace,** about half a mile away. This is the largest Roman villa in Britain. Probably built as a residence for Roman emperor Tiberius Claudius Cogidubnus, the villa contains a remarkable range of mosaics. Sophisticated bathing and heating systems remain, and the gardens have been laid out much as they were in the 1st century AD. *Salthill Rd., Fishbourne, tel. 0243/785859. Admission: £2.50 adults, £1 children, £1.80 senior citizens. Open Mar.–Apr. and Oct., daily 10–5; May–Sept., daily 10–6; Nov., daily 10–4; Dec.–Feb., Sun. 10–4.*

To continue on the northward circuit into Surrey, return to Chichester and join A286, then take A287 to Guildford.

44 **Guildford,** the largest town in Surrey and the county's capital, lies only 28 miles from London on the main railroad line between the capital and the naval port of Portsmouth. Its proximity to both cities has made it an important commuter town—and it is growing at an alarming rate—but Guildford has managed to retain a faint 18th-century air. The steep **High Street** is lined with gabled merchants' houses and preserves a pleasant, provincial appearance. **Guildford Grammar School,** at the top end, contains one of Britain's three surviving medieval chained libraries (books were so precious during the Middle Ages, they were literally chained to prevent theft). The school was founded in 1507. *Tel. 0483/502424. Open by appointment only.*

Farther along the High Street is the **Hospital of the Blessed Trinity,** with its massive Tudor facade. It was founded in 1619 as an almshouse by George Abbot, archbishop of Canterbury. Abbot, one of the translators of the King James Bible, was born in Guildford. The hospital is now an old people's home; the male residents wear Tudor hats and coats bearing Abbot's emblem. *High St., tel. 0483/62670. Chapel and common room open Sat. (call for admission times).*

Time Out   **Rats Castle** (80 Sydenham Rd.) is close by the center of town, and presents a wide range of food, in a pub decorated with Edwardian tiles. There's a summer garden.

Next you come to the **Guildhall,** its exquisite 16th-century structure concealed behind a 17th-century facade. For years this building served as the center of the town's government. Be sure to visit the **courtroom,** with its original paneling and stained glass windows. The impressive **Guildhall Clock,** glittering with gold, reaches out over the street like a giant outstretched arm. *High St., tel. 0483/505050. Admission free. Open May–Sept., Tues. and Thurs. 2–5.*

Across from the Guildhall is what appears to be a triumphal arch. This was the facade of the **Corn Exchange,** built in 1810. Turn left off the High Street onto **Quarry Street. St. Mary's Church** has a Saxon tower, while most of the building dates from the 1100s. Farther along is **Castle Arch,** complete with a slot for a portcullis, and beyond that, the remains of the castle itself. **The Guildford Museum,** in Castle Arch, contains interesting exhibits on local history, along with memorabilia of Charles Dodgson (better known by his pen name, Lewis Carroll), author of *Alice in Wonderland.* Dodgson spent the last years of his life in a house on nearby Castle Hill. *Quarry St., tel. 0483/444750. Admission free. Open Mon.–Sat. 11–5.*

The ruined shell of a Norman keep (70 feet high, with walls up to 14 feet thick) is all that survives of **Guildford Castle.** For many years the castle served as the main jail for Surrey and Sussex. Notice the giant chessboard in the grounds. *Castle St., tel. 0483/505050. Admission: 65p adults, 35p children. Open Apr.–Sept., daily 10:30–6.*

Guildford Cathedral, looming on its hilltop across the River Wey, is only the second Anglican cathedral to be built on a new site since Henry VIII's Reformation of the 1500s. It was consecrated in 1961. The red brick exterior is severely simple, while the interior, with its quantities of stone and plaster, has a bright, cool appearance. *Stag Hill, tel. 0483/65287. Donation requested.*

45 Just outside Guildford, east on A246, is **West Clandon.** Here you'll want to visit **Clandon Park,** which started out as an Elizabethan manor but was transformed in the 1730s by Venetian architect Giacomo Leoni into the gracious Palladian-style residence you see today. The real glory of the house, now a National Trust property, is its interior, especially the two-story Marble Hall, one of the most imposing rooms created in the 18th century. There's a fine collection of furniture, needlework, and porcelain, and in the basement an interesting regimental museum, full of weapons and medals. The extensive parkland (privately owned and not open to the public) was another of Capability Brown's landscaping achievements. *Tel. 0483/222482. Admission: £3 adults, £1.50 children. Open Mar. 31–Oct., Sat.–Wed. 1:30–5:30.*

46 Leaving Clandon Park, follow A246 east 8 miles to **Great Bookham,** and visit **Polesden Lacey.** This handsome Regency house, built on the site of one owned by 18th-century playwright Richard Brinsley Sheridan, was from 1906 to 1942 the home of society hostess Mrs. Ronald Greville. Her many famous guests included Edward VII. Elizabeth, now the Queen Mother, and her husband, the Duke of York (later George VI), stayed here on their honeymoon. Today owned and maintained by the National Trust, Polesden Lacey contains beautiful collections of furniture, paintings, porcelain, and tapestries. In the summer, open-air theatrical performances are given on the grounds. *Tel. 0372/58203. Admission varies according to time of year—£5–£4.20 adults, £2.50–£2.10 children. House open Apr.–Oct., Wed.–Sun. 1:30–5:30; Mar. and Nov., weekends 1:30–4:30; grounds open daily all year 11–sunset.*

47 As you start making your way southeast to Royal Tunbridge Wells via Dorking, you'll pass under the shadow of **Box Hill,** named for the box trees that grow in such profusion here. It is a favorite spot for walking excursions. When you reach Dorking itself, take any of the major roads running east through Reigate or Crawley (both uninspiring London commuter towns) and follow the signs for Royal Tunbridge Wells, about 28 miles away.

Tour 4: Tunbridge Wells, Stately Homes, and Castles

(48) Although the city is officially known as **Royal Tunbridge Wells,** locals ignore the prefix "royal" (it was only added in 1909, during the reign of Edward VII). The town was named after the neighboring city of Tonbridge, a few miles up the road towards London, but the spelling was changed to distinguish it. Tunbridge Wells owes its prosperity to the 17th and 18th centuries' passion for spas and mineral baths, initially as medicinal treatments, and later as social gathering places. In 1606, a spring of chalybeate (mineral) water was discovered here, drawing legions of royal visitors from the court of King James I. It is still possible to drink the waters when a "dipper" (the traditional water dispenser) is in attendance at the spring from Easter to September each year. Tunbridge Wells reached its zenith in the mid-18th century, when Richard "Beau" Nash presided over its social life. Today it is a pleasant town and home to many London commuters.

The Pantiles, a promenade near the spring, derives its odd name from the Dutch "pan tiles" that originally paved the area. Now bordered on two sides by busy main roads, The Pantiles remains a tranquil oasis.

Across the road from The Pantiles is the **Church of King Charles the Martyr,** built in 1678 and dedicated to Charles I, who was executed by Parliament in 1649 following the English Civil War. Its plain exterior belies its splendid interior; take special note of the beautifully plastered ceiling. The people of the fashionable world came to the church to enhance their spiritual health after ministering to their bodies with mineral treatments in the 1700s. A network of alleyways behind the church leads back to the High Street.

Time Out **The Compasses,** a spacious, well-kept pub decorated in Victorian style and located on a tiny, steep lane (Little Mount Sion) off the High Street, offers tasty homemade food, and, in the winter, cozy open fires.

The buildings at the lower end of the High Street are mostly 18th–century, but as the street climbs the hill, changing its name to Mount Pleasant Road, the buildings become more modern. Here you'll find the **Tunbridge Wells Museum and Art Gallery,** which houses a permanent exhibition of interesting Tunbridge Ware pieces: small, wood-carved items inlaid with different-colored wooden fragments. *Mount Pleasant, tel. 0892/26121. Admission free. Open Mon.–Sat. 9:30–5.*

Within a 15-mile radius of Tunbridge Wells lies a remarkable array of historic homes, castles, and other monuments. Moving clockwise to the west, following A26 and B2176, you first arrive **(49)** at **Penshurst Place,** one of England's finest medieval manor houses. The **Baron's Hall,** built in 1341, retains its original timber roof. Elizabethan poet and soldier Sir Philip Sidney was

born here in 1554, and it is still the home of the Sidney family.
Items on view include an impressive collection of tapestries and
family portraits. There is a convenient coffee shop. *Tel. 0892/
870307. Admission: £3.50 adults, £1.75 children, £3 senior citizens. Open Apr.–Sept., Tues.–Sun. and national holidays
1–5; grounds open 12:30–5.*

Time Out   **The Spotted Dog,** which first opened its doors in 1520, today
tempts visitors with an inglenook fireplace, heavy beams, imaginative lunchtime and evening meals, and a splendid view of
Penshurst Place.

Next, follow a series of sign-posted minor roads about 3 miles
50   west to 13th-century **Hever Castle,** the family home of Anne
Boleyn. It was here that she was courted and won by Henry
VIII. He later gave Hever to his fourth wife, Anne of Cleves,
after he divorced her. The castle was acquired in 1903 by
American millionaire William Waldorf Astor, who built an entire Tudor village to house his staff and had the gardens laid out
in Italianate style, with a large topiary maze. *Tel. 0732/865224.
Admission: castle and grounds £4.40 adults, £2.20 children, £4
senior citizens, £11 family ticket; grounds only £3 adults, £1.80
children, £2.60 senior citizens, £7.80 family ticket. Open Apr.–
mid-Nov., Tues.–Sun. 1–5:30; grounds: 11–6.*

From Hever, more minor roads, B2027 and B2026, lead you
51   north to Sir Winston Churchill's home, **Chartwell.** He lived in
this Victorian house from 1922 until his death in 1965. It was
acquired by the National Trust and has been decorated to appear as it did in Churchill's lifetime—even down to a half-
smoked cigar in an ash tray. In the garden you can see a wall he
built himself. *Near Westerham, tel. 0732/866368. Admission:
£3.70 adults, £1.90 children; garden only: £1.50 adults, 80p
children. Open Easter–Oct., Tues.–Thurs. noon–5, weekends
and national holidays 11–5; Mar. and Nov., weekends and
Wed. 11–4.*

From Chartwell, drive north to Westerham, then pick up A25
52   and head east for 8 miles until you arrive in **Sevenoaks.** In the
center of town you will find the entrance to **Knole,** the home of
the Sackville family since 1603. Begun in the 15th century,
Knole, with its vast complex of courtyards and buildings, resembles a small town. You'll need most of an afternoon to explore it thoroughly. The house is famous for its collection of
tapestries and embroidered furnishings. Paintings on display
include a series of portraits by 18th-century artists Thomas
Gainsborough and Sir Joshua Reynolds. The decorated staircase was a novelty in its day. The house is set in a 1,000-acre
deer park. *Tel. 0732/450608. Admission: £3 adults, £1.50 children; grounds only: 75p. Open Apr.–Oct., Wed.–Sat. and national holidays 11–5, Sun. 2–5.*

Leaving Sevenoaks, follow A25 westward to A227 (8 miles) un-
53   til you see signs for **Ightham** (pronounced "Item") **Mote.** Finding the house itself requires careful navigation through the
narrow, winding lanes of rural Kent, but it is worth the effort.
This is an outstanding example of a small, medieval manor
house, complete with moat. (The "mote" in the name, however,
refers not to the fortifications, but to the role of the house as a
meeting place, or "moot".) The exterior of Ightham Mote has
changed little since it was built, in the 14th century, but on

close inspection you'll find it does encompass styles of several different periods: The Tudor chapel, the medieval Great Hall, the hand-painted Chinese wallpaper, and the 18th-century Palladian window are just some of its fascinating and incongruous features. *Ightham, tel. 0732/810378. Admission: weekdays £3, Sundays £3.50 adults, £1.80 children. Open Easter–Oct., Mon. and Wed.–Fri. noon–5:30, Sun. 11–5:30.*

After your visit to Ightham, return to A25 and drive east 10
54 miles to **Maidstone,** Kent's county town, with its backdrop of chalky downs. The bubbling River Medway runs right through
55 town. Only 5 miles outside the town center on A20 stands **Leeds Castle,** a fairy-tale stronghold commanding two small islands on a peaceful lake. Since the 10th century this site has held a castle, and some of the present structure is 13th century Tudor. Leeds (not to be confused with Leeds in the North) was a favorite home of many English queens, and Henry VIII liked the place so much he had it converted from a fortress into a grand palace. The house offers a fine collection of paintings and furniture, plus an unusual **dog-collar museum.** The castle's singular setting makes it a popular spot for important scientific and political conferences. *Tel. 0622/765400. Admission: castle and grounds, £5.60 adults, £3.90 children, £4.60 senior citizens; grounds only, £4.10 adults, £2.40 children, £3.10 senior citizens. Open Nov.–Mar., weekends noon–4; Apr.–Oct., daily 11–5.*

From Leeds Castle, make your way south on B2163 and A274 through Headcorn until you come to another lovely fortress—
56 or what's left of it—**Sissinghurst Castle,** nestled deep in the Kentish countryside. The gardens, laid out in the 1930s around the remains of this moated Tudor castle, were the creation of the writer Vita Sackville-West (one of the Sackvilles of Knole) and her husband, the diplomat Harold Nicolson. The grounds are at their best in June and July, when the roses are in bloom. *Cranbrook, tel. 0580/712850. Admission: Tues.–Sat. £4 adults, £2 children; Sun. £4.50 adults, £2.30 children. Open Apr.–mid-Oct., Tues.–Fri. 1–6:30, weekends and Good Friday 10–6:30.*

Time Out   **Claris's Tea Shop** (3 High St., Biddenden), near Sissinghurst Castle, serves traditional English teas in a 15th-century setting, and displays attractive English craft items. There's a pretty garden for summer teas. Closed on Mondays.

As you leave Sissinghurst, continue south along A229 through **Hawkhurst,** a little village that was once the headquarters of a notorious and ruthless gang of smugglers. Turn right at the
57 Curlew pub to arrive in the tiny Sussex village of **Bodiam.** Here, surrounded by a wide moat, stands **Bodiam Castle.** Built in 1385 to withstand a threatened French invasion, it was "slighted" (partly demolished) during the English Civil War of 1642–45 and has been uninhabited ever since. You can climb some of the towers and enjoy the illusion of manning the battlements against an invisible enemy. *Tel. 058083/436. Admission: £1.70 adults, 90p children. Open Nov.–Mar., Mon.–Sat. 10–sunset; Apr.–Oct., daily 10–6 (or sunset); closed Dec. 25–28.*

Follow the minor road back past the Curlew to rejoin A21, then turn northward onto A265. A few miles west along this road lies
58 **Burwash,** where **Batemans,** a beautiful 17th-century house just

off the main road, was the home of the writer Rudyard Kipling from 1902 to 1936. It was built for a prominent ironmaster in the 17th century, when Sussex was the center of England's iron industry. Kipling's study looks exactly as it did when he lived here. The garden contains a water mill that still grinds flour; it is thought to be one of the oldest working water turbines. Close by, between Burwash Common and the river, is the setting for *Puck of Pook's Hill*. *Tel. 0435/882302. Admission: weekdays, £3 adults, £1.50 children, weekends £3.50 adults, £1.80 children. Open Apr.–Oct., Sat.–Wed. and Good Friday 11–5:30.*

Returning to A21, continue north to the town of **Lamberhurst** and England's largest vineyard. Thirty years ago, grape-growing in England was a rich man's hobby. Today it is an important rural industry, and the wines produced at **Lamberhurst Vineyard** are world-renowned. *Ridge Farm, tel. 0892/890844. Admission: Guided tours May–Oct. £2.50 adults, £1.50 children, £2.25 senior citizens. Phone for times of tours.*

59 A visit to **Finchcocks,** an elegant Georgian mansion located between Lamberhurst and Goudhurst, is a must for music lovers. It contains a magnificent collection of historical keyboard instruments (**Finchcocks Living Museum of Music**), which are played whenever the house is open. Formal concerts and other musical events are held here during the spring and fall. *Goudhurst, tel. 0580/211702. Admission: £3.75 adults, £2 children. Open Apr.–Sept., Sun. and national holidays 2–6; in Aug., Wed.–Sun. also.*

What to See and Do with Children

The seaside towns of the Southeast provide traditional entertainment for children of all ages. **Howlett's Zoo Park** includes a large group of tigers and gorillas, as well as many other animals. *Bekesbourne, near Canterbury, tel. 0227/721286. Admission: £5 adults, £3 children and senior citizens, £14 family ticket. Open Mar. 31–Dec.; summer, daily 10–5; winter, daily 10–4.*

Drusilla's Zoo Park is known as "the best small zoo in the south," and includes a miniature railroad and adventure playground. *Alfriston, East Sussex, tel. 0323/870234. Admission: £3.95 adults, £3.75 children, £2.75 senior citizens. Zoo open all year daily; 10:30–dusk.*

The Children's Farm offers a trail through a 600-acre working farm with a variety of small tame wild animals as well as ordinary farm animals. The Farm has a package deal with the Kent and Sussex steam railway to visit the farm and take a trip on the train. *Great Knell, Beckley, near Rye, tel. 079726/250. Admission: £3 adults, £2.50 children and senior citizens. Open Apr.–Oct., Sun.–Fri. 10:30–5:30, daily in Aug.*

The **Eurotunnel Exhibition Centre** has lots of working models and hands-on exhibits to interest mechanically minded children (*see* Off the Beaten Track).

The **Sea Life Centre** in Brighton boasts the largest collection of sharks in Britain. Entrance is close to the shore end of the Palace Pier. *Marine Parade, tel. 0273/604233/4. Admission: £3.75 adults, children, and senior citizens, £10 families. Open Oct.–Mar., daily 10–5; Apr.–Oct., daily 10–6.*

Off the Beaten Track

Consider a visit to the Medway towns of **Rochester** and **Chatham** in north Kent. **Rochester** is closely associated with Charles Dickens; he lived at Gad's Hill Place, just outside of town, for many years. Dickens fans will enjoy a tour of the ambitious **Charles Dickens Centre,** where exhibits include life-size models of many of his characters. *Eastgate House, High St., tel. 0634/844176. Admission: £1.90 adults, £1.20 children and senior citizens, £5.10 family ticket. Open daily 10–5.*

Visitors to Rochester should also stop in at **Rochester Castle,** one of the finest surviving examples of Norman military architecture. The keep, built in the 1100s, partly based on the Roman city wall, is the tallest in England. *Tel. 0634/402276. Admission: £1.30 adults, 65p children, 95p senior citizens. Open Apr.–Sept. daily 10–6, Oct.–Mar. daily 10–4; closed Mon.*

Nearby is **Rochester Cathedral,** built in the 11th, 12th, and 14th centuries on a site consecrated in AD 604. *Tel. 0634/843366. Donation requested.*

Chatham, just next door to Rochester, is the home of the **Chatham Historic Dockyard.** Royal Navy ships sailed to battle from here for hundreds of years. You can see the ancient Ropery in action, where great ship's hawsers are twisted, plus many other relics of Britain's naval heritage. *Alexandra Gate, Dock Rd., tel. 0634/812551. Admission: £4.50 adults, £2.50 children, £4 senior citizens; guided tours £5 and £2.50. Open summer, Wed.–Sun. and national holidays 10–6; winter, Wed. and weekends 10–4:30.*

Between Dover and Folkestone, near Junction 12 of the M20 motorway, is the **Eurotunnel Exhibition Centre,** which tells the story of the building of the Cross Channel Tunnel with all the best modern visual aids—including a full-size drilling rig. The tunnel itself is expected to open in 1993. *Tel. 0303/270111. Admission: £2.50 adults, £1.50 children and senior citizens. Open Tues.–Sun. 10–5.*

The Southeast also boasts three steam railroads. The **Romney, Hythe, and Dymchurch Railway** is just across Romney Marsh and is a main line service in miniature with locomotives one-third normal size. Some lucky children use it regularly to travel to school. (New Romney Station, tel. 0679/62353.) Another interesting stop for train enthusiasts is the **Bluebell Railway,** a full-size working railroad "museum" manned by enthusiastic volunteers. The station shed houses a collection of historic locomotives. Steam trains run daily June to September, with reduced service at other times. (Sheffield Park Station, near Uckfield, East Sussex, tel. 082572/3777; or for timetable information 082572/2370). The **Kent and East Sussex Railway** is similar to the Bluebell line. Trains run daily July 16–Sept. 4, with service reduced at other times. (Town Station, Tenterden, Kent, tel. 05806/2943.)

The **Leonardslee Gardens** at Lower Beeding, about 15 miles north of Brighton (by A23 and A281), boast an impressive and colorful assortment of rhododendrons, azaleas, and camellias in the spring and an attractive display of autumn tints in the fall. The gardens celebrated their centenary in 1989. *Tel. 0403/891212. Admission: £2.50 Apr., Jun., and Oct.; £2 Jul.–Sept.;*

£3 May (£4 on Sun.). Open mid-Apr.–mid-June, daily 10–6; July–Sept., weekends noon–6; Oct., weekends 10–5.

For a pleasant excursion near Arundel, try the **Arun Riverside Walk,** starting from the Arundel town bridge. In about half an hour it brings you to the **Wildfowl Trust,** a preserve sheltering an assortment of England's wild birds. *Mill Rd., Arundel, West Sussex, tel. 0903/883355. Admission: £3 adults, £1.50 children, £2 senior citizens. Open Apr.–Oct., daily 9:30–6:30; Nov.–Mar., daily 9:30–5.*

Shopping

The Southeast has a wide range of sophisticated shops with London prices. The region is also particularly rich in crafts shops, which have sprung up in recent years as a reaction against mass production. The shops below have been chosen for their outstanding quality. All those listed are open between March and October, and some are open all year. They all sell their own products and are sources for unusual, one-of-a-kind gifts. The Southeast England Tourist Board provides a full list of crafts shops.

Aylesford   A visit to the **Aylesford Friary Pottery** will kill two birds with one stone. The buildings themselves are interesting—it's a restored 13th-century Carmelite friary—and the pottery pieces made there are very collectible, solid, creamy items that look good and feel reassuring to the hand. There's a tea room, and the potting friars give demonstrations of their work. (Located on the north edge of Maidstone, just off the M26 at junction 6.)

Arundel   The **Arundel Fine Glass and Engraving Studio** (7 Castle Mews, Tarrant St.) is the workshop of Jacques Ruijterman. Here you can buy engraved glass from stock or have a design of your own choice interpreted in glass.

Baynton-Williams (49 Maltravers St.) are specialists in prints and maps, and may well be able to find you an old print of Arundel for your wall.

Brighton   The main shopping area to head for is **The Lanes,** especially if you are interested in antiques or jewelry. This cluster of alleys and tiny squares also has clothing boutiques, coffee shops, and pubs. Across North Street from the Lanes lie the **North Lanes,** a network of narrow streets full of interesting little stores, less glossy than those in the Lanes, but sometimes more interesting—there are even street stalls on weekends.

The Pavilion Shop (4–5 Pavilion Buildings) makes a fitting port of call following a visit to the pavilion next door. This elegant and imaginative shop not only carries well-designed souvenirs of Regency Brighton, but has high-quality fabrics, wallpapers, and ceramics based on material in the pavilion itself. If you are interested in interior design with a historical slant, this is the store to visit.

Holleyman and Treacher (21A Duke St., at the western edge of The Lanes) is a book collector's dream, with a wealth of books on all subjects, and especially interesting for those it carries on Brighton and Sussex. It also has a large stock of antique prints at all prices.

Pecksniff's Bespoke Perfumery (45/46 Meeting House Lane) has an original approach to the art of fragrance. In a room full of wooden drawers and brown glass bottles, Frank O'Brien will mix and match his ingredients to suit your needs. The results are very attractive and far from expensive.

Henfield Woodcrafts (Harwoods Farm, West End La., Henfield, Sussex), 10 miles northwest of Brighton on A23/A281, is a workshop specializing in an ancient English country craft, treenware—dishes, cups, plates, and bowls made of turned wood, often English hardwood. Among their most popular products are thin-walled goblets.

Canterbury **Spindles** (15A The Burgate), housed in the building reputed to figure in *David Copperfield*, is a treasure house for anyone interested in spinning and weaving. It holds workshops, has hands-on exhibits to teach children about fibers and spinning wheels, and sells yarn and fleeces.

National Trust Shop (24 The Burgate), is next door to Spindles, and stocks the National Trust line of household items, which make ideal gifts.

Compton **The Pottery** (Brickfields, Compton, Surrey) lies on the southwest edge of Guildford, and specializes in yet another old English type of craftsmanship: *scraffito* and *slip-tailed* ware, with the decoration either incised in the pottery or trailed on with colored glazes. Mary Wondrausch, the owner, is a noted potter who creates commemorative pieces for birthdays and anniversaries and offers customized designs as well.

Lewes **The Old Needle Makers** (12 Flitcroft St.) is inside the shell of an early 19th-century candle and needle factory, just off the High St., in a setting of huge beams and cobbled floors. Twenty small craft-based shops sell kitchenware, flowers and baskets, cosmetics, tops, and fire grates and fire accessories.

Sports and Fitness

Activity Center **Bewl Water Activity Centre** takes advantage of its location at one of England's largest reservoirs (just east of Wadhurst, which is 6 miles southeast of Tunbridge Wells by A267 and B2099), providing a wide range of aquatic sports in and on the water. There's also an adventure playground. *Lamberhurst, tel. 0892/890661. Open all year.*

Golf The Southeast is particularly well served with golf courses. Local tourist offices can supply you with a list of those in the area; here's just a few of those that welcome visitors. **Brighton and Hove,** Dyke Rd., Brighton, tel. 0273/556482. **Guildford,** High Path Rd., Merrow, Guildford, tel. 0483/63941. **Hastings,** Battle Rd., St. Leonard's-on-Sea, tel. 0424/852981. **Leeds Castle,** Maidstone, tel. 0627/80467 (a scenically beautiful and challenging course). **Royal Cinque Ports,** Deal, tel. 0304/374007. **Tunbridge Wells,** Langton Rd., Tunbridge Wells, tel. 0892/23034.

Horseback Riding Horseback riding is popular, especially on the downs of East Sussex. The County Planning Department provides a leaflet of addresses throughout Sussex and the weald of Kent. Call 0273/475400 for your copy. You might also try: **Haslemere Riding Stables,** Beech Farm, Grayswood Rd., Haslemere, tel.-0428/644779. **Mitchbourne Riding Stables,** Malthouse Lane, Chichester, tel. 0903/892230.

Hiking Ardent walkers will want to explore both the **North Downs Way** and the **South Downs Way.** These paths follow ancient trackways along the tops of the scenic chalk downs. Section-by-section guides are available from the Southeast England Tourist Board (1 Warwick Park, Tunbridge Wells, Kent, tel. 0892/40766).

Dining and Lodging

Dining Around the coast, seafood—much of it locally caught—is a specialty. You'll find not just the ubiquitous fish and chips (though they are often at their best in the southeast), but also local dishes such as Sussex smokies, as well as good international fish cuisine. In the larger towns, trendy restaurants tend to spring up for a time and then disappear. This is an area in which to experiment.

Highly recommended restaurants are indicated by a star ★.

Category	Cost*
Very Expensive	over £35
Expensive	£25–£35
Moderate	£12–£25
Inexpensive	under £12

per person, including first course, main course, dessert, and VAT; excluding drinks

Lodging There is a wide choice of accommodations in the Southeast, from simple guest houses to luxury hotels (with prices to match). The seaside resorts have plenty of lodgings, but these can get booked up at the height of the season, especially in towns such as Brighton and Eastbourne, which are also popular as conference centers.

Highly recommended lodgings are indicated by a star ★.

Category	Cost*
Very Expensive	over £130
Expensive	£80–£130
Moderate	£45–£80
Inexpensive	under £45

All prices are for two people sharing a double room, including service, breakfast, and VAT.

Arundel **Avisford Park Hotel.** This converted Georgian house is just 3
Lodging miles west of Arundel on B2132. It began as the home of an admiral and was a private school before its conversion into a hotel in 1974. The rooms have been carefully refurbished, with close attention to detail. It's an excellent place to stay if you're looking for a hotel with plenty of sports facilities. *Yapton La., Walberton BN18 OLS, tel. 0243/551215. 100 rooms with bath. Facilities: restaurant, indoor and outdoor swimming pools, snooker room, squash court, tennis courts, sauna, solarium,*

fitness rooms, croquet, 9-hole golf course, horseback riding. AE, MC, V. Expensive.

Norfolk Arms Hotel. Like the cathedral and the castle in Arundel, this 18th-century coaching inn was also built by the dukes of Norfolk. The main body of the hotel is traditional in appearance, with lots of narrow passages and cozy little rooms. There is an annex with modern rooms in the courtyard block. All guest rooms are furnished to a pleasing standard of comfort. *22 High St., BN18 9AD, tel. 0903/882101. 34 rooms with bath. Facilities: restaurant, in-house movies, games room. AE, DC, MC, V. Moderate.*

Brighton   **English's Oyster Bar.** Buried in the heart of The Lanes, this is
Dining   one of the few genuinely old-fashioned seafood havens left in
★   England. It's been a family business for over 200 years. You can either eat succulent oysters and other seafood dishes at the counter, or have a table in the restaurant section. Ideal for lunch after a morning of antiques hunting. *29–31 East St., tel. 0273/27980. Reservations advised. Dress: informal. AE, DC, MC, V. Expensive.*

Donatello. This is a new Italian restaurant in the heart of The Lanes shopping quarter. It has a brick wall and pine decor, bright with plants and checked cloths. The food is standard Italian, with an emphasis on pizzas. Donatello is a brother eatery to Pinnochio's, close to the Theatre Royal, and looks like it will be just as popular. *3 Brighton Pl., tel. 0273/774577. Reservations advised in summer. Dress: informal. AE, DC, MC, V. Moderate.*

La Scala. Three doors from the Theater Royal, La Scala is just the place for pre- and post-theater dining—the actors often eat here. Every dish on the long menu is named after an opera, and you'll eat to the sound of arias. There's an attentive maitre d' and a good-value wine list. *15 New Rd., tel. 0273/25648. Reservations advised. Dress: informal. Cash preferred. Evenings only, Mon.–Sat. Moderate.*

Lodging   **The Grand Hotel.** This classic old hotel on the seafront has been completely repaired and redecorated after a bomb attempt on Prime Minister Margaret Thatcher's life blew down one corner. The decor, especially in the public rooms, is of the spectacular chandelier-and-marble variety, but the bedrooms are traditionally comfortable. The restaurant has a good reputation. *King's Rd., BN1 2FW, tel. 0273/21188. 163 rooms with bath. Facilities: restaurant, indoor pool, solarium, sauna. AE, DC, MC, V. Very Expensive.*

Hospitality Inn. This is the newest hotel in Brighton, a little east of the Grand, along the seafront. It is built around a huge atrium, with sea views, and is very popular with conference delegates. It's smoothly designed, with an excellent color sense and ultramodern bedrooms, but on the pricey side for what it offers. The restaurant, **La Noblesse,** has delicious food, with not-too-expensive fixed menus. *King's Rd., BN1 1JA, tel. 0273/206700. Facilities: restaurant, indoor pool, sauna, gym, in-house movies. AE, DC, MC, V. Very Expensive.*

Granville Hotel. Located on hotel row, to the west of the Grand, the hotel has been converted from three former grand residences facing the sea. It is moderate in size, so service can be attentive. The bedrooms are all very comfortable; several are quite large, seven have four poster beds, and two include Jacuzzis. *123 King's Rd., BN1 2FA, tel. 0273/26302. 25 rooms* *with bath. Facilities: restaurant, bar, coffee shop, solarium. AE, DC, MC, V. Expensive.*

★ **Topps.** Two Regency houses have been turned into this attractive hotel, run by the owners, Paul and Pauline Collins. All the rooms are attractive and well-equipped, with lush bathrooms. The atmosphere is relaxed, friendly, and highly recommendable. The basement restaurant, called, appropriately, **Bottoms,** is worth a visit even if you're not staying at the hotel. The interesting English menu is prepared by Pauline Collins, and, as the place is small, reservations are a must. *17 Regency Sq., BN1 2FG, tel. 0273/729334. 12 rooms with bath. AE, DC, MC, V. Moderate.*

Lodging **The Dove.** An alternative if Topps (*see* above) is full, The Dove, next door, is another well-converted Regency house where you will receive a warm welcome from its husband-and-wife owners. Four of the rooms have a sideways sea view from their bow windows. There is no restaurant, but there is an à la carte breakfast. *18 Regency Sq., BN1 2FG, tel. 0273/779222. 8 rooms with bath. Moderate.*

Canterbury **Restaurant Seventy-Four.** An elegant paneled room in a 16th-
Dining century wine merchant's house complements the very best of modern British cooking. Some of the unusual specialties are highly recommended—try the veal with crab sauce and mousse, or duck liver with port sauce. All the fresh ingredients are combined with great skill and sensitivity; the flavors are subtle and mouth-watering. This is one of the best restaurants in the area. *74 Wincheap, tel. 0227/67411. Reservations required. Dress: informal. AE, DC, MC, V. Moderate.*

George's Brasserie. This stylish bistro in a long, narrow upstairs room, has predominantly French cuisine chalked on a blackboard menu. Specialties include fresh salmon, served hot and marinated with fresh herbs. There's an interesting choice of cheeses, including sheep and goat cheese; the desserts are filling and old-fashioned. *71 Castle St., tel. 0227/65658. Reservations advised. Dress: informal. AE, DC, MC, V. Inexpensive.*

Dining and Lodging **Slatters.** The site on which this hotel is built has been occupied since Roman times, and a tiny section of Roman foundations can be seen in the cellar under the restaurant. Elsewhere there are Tudor beams and a medieval wall, but the main attraction of the hotel is its strictly 20th-century comfort, well-furnished guest rooms, restaurant, and bars. Rebuilding is pending. *St. Margaret's St., CT1 2TR, tel. 0227/463271. 32 rooms, 28 with bath. Jacket and tie required in restaurant. AE, DC, MC, V. Expensive.*

County. This traditional English hotel was first licensed in the year of the Spanish Armada, 1588, and it still maintains certain links with the past—ask for a room with a four-poster bed. The bar is pleasantly traditional, and **Sully's Restaurant** has a reputation as a gourmet's choice. *High St., CT1 2RX, tel. 0227/766266. 74 rooms with bath. Jacket and tie required in restaurant. AE, DC, MC, V. Moderate.*

Lodging **Pointers.** A friendly hotel in a Georgian building, within easy walking distance of the cathedral and city center (straight out beyond Westgate). *1 London Rd., CT2 8LR, tel. 0227/456846. 14 rooms; 10 with bath or shower. Facilities: restaurant. AE, DC, MC, V. Moderate.*

Chichester
Dining

Micawbers. You're sure to find something tasty here. Despite its Dickensian name, this is a provincial French restaurant, especially good for local seafood. *13 South St., tel. 0243/786989. Dress: informal. Reservations advised. AE, DC, MC, V. Closed Sun. Moderate.*

Lodging

Dolphin and Anchor Hotel. Immediately across from the cathedral, this hotel originally consisted of two separate inns, the Dolphin and the Anchor, both considerably older than the present 18th-century facade would suggest. Locals and visitors naturally gravitate to the hotel, for it hosts a wide range of functions, from conferences to family occasions. The modern guest rooms are colorful and attractively decorated. *West St., PO19 1QE, tel. 0243/785121. 54 rooms with bath. Facilities: restaurant. AE, DC, MC, V. Expensive.*

Ship Hotel. Staying in this hotel is something of an architectural experience. Built in 1790, it was originally the private home of Admiral Sir George Murray (one of Admiral Nelson's right-hand men). Outstanding features are the classic Adam staircase and colonnade. The hotel is gradually being restored to its 18th-century appearance throughout, with all the elegance of that age. *North St., PO19 1LB, tel. 0243/782028. 36 rooms with bath. Facilities: restaurant. AE, DC, MC, V. Moderate.*

Cranbrook
Dining and Lodging
★

Kennel Holt Hotel. This is a quiet hotel in a red brick Elizabethan manor house, surrounded by beautiful, well-kept gardens. The owners take pains to see that visitors are treated like guests in a private house. The library, for example, is well-stocked with books for that rainy day. Ruth Cliff, who taught for 16 years at a Cordon Bleu college, supervises the delicious menu; try the sole accompanied by asparagus and Mornay sauce, or lamb with red currants and port. Antiques and flowers grace the restaurant as well as the rest of the hotel. There's a separate restaurant for non-residents. *Goudhurst Rd., TN17 2PT, tel. 0580/712032. 10 rooms, 8 with bath or shower. Jacket and tie, and reservations required in restaurant. Facilities: croquet, in-house movies. AE, DC, MC, V. Expensive.*

Dorking
Lodging

The White Horse. For a taste of both ancient and modern, stay at this inn. The foundations of the hotel probably go back to the 13th century, while the interior is mostly 18th-century and has been attractively—but carefully—brought up to date. All the rooms are cheerfully furnished and offer high standards of comfort. There is an adequate if unremarkable restaurant. *High St., RH4 1BE, tel. 0306/881138. 68 rooms with bath. Facilities: pool. AE, DC, MC, V. Expensive.*

Faversham
Dining

Read's. Read's, just outside Faversham, is quite a find. The food, French-oriented, is magnificent, the work of chef/proprietor David Pitchford. In elegant surroundings he presents cuisine to challenge the serious eater—a comparison of wild and farmed salmon, for example, in the same dish. Try breast of Gressingham duck dressed with foie gras and Sauternes, or veal normande. The wine list contains some unusual bottles. This is an excellent spot for lunch, at which there's a set menu for £12. *Painters Forstal, ME13 OEE (2¼ miles southwest of Faversham on A2), tel. 0795/535344. Dress: neat but casual. Reservations required. AE, DC, MC, V. Closed Sun., Mon. Expensive.*

Dining and Lodging
★

The White Horse Inn. Just outside Faversham on the old London to Dover road (now A2), this 15th-century coaching inn retains much of its traditional character, although it has been fully and comfortably modernized. There's a friendly bar and an excellent restaurant specializing in steak and lobster dishes. *The Street, Boughton ME13 9AX, tel. 0227/751343. 13 rooms with bath or shower. Dress in restaurant: informal. Moderate.*

Guildford **Café de Paris.** The proprietor, Jean Clemaron, is also the chef of
Dining this restaurant, which could be nothing else but French, with its fresh, clean decor and interesting menu. The place is in two sections: a bistro where you can have a glass of wine and a single dish, and a more formal restaurant. For à la carte specialties try the lobster thermidor or *côtes de boeuf* (ribs of beef in sauce). *35 Castle St., tel. 0483/34896. Dress: informal. Weekend reservations required. AE, DC, MC, V. Moderate.*

★ **Rumwong.** The elegant waitresses at this Thai restaurant wear their traditional long-skirted costumes, so at busy times the dining room looks like a swirling flower garden. On the incredibly long menu, the Thai name of each dish is given with a clear English description. Try the fisherman's soup, a mass of delicious salt water fish in a clear broth, or *yam pla muek*, a hot salad with squid. *16–18 London Rd., tel. 0483/36092. Reservations required Fri. and Sat. Dress: informal. MC, V. Closed Mon. Moderate.*

Lodging **The Angel.** The Angel was the last of the old coaching inns for
★ which Guildford was famous. The courtyard, into which coaches and horses rattled, is still open to the sky, and light lunches are served here in summer. The hotel is at least 400 years old and is even said to have a ghost. Guest rooms are unfussily decorated and comfortable. There's an excellent restaurant in the medieval stone cellar and an informal coffee shop for light refreshments. *High St., GU1 3DR, tel. 0483/64555. 27 rooms with bath. AE, DC, MC, V. Expensive.*

Carlton Hotel. This old-fashioned Victorian house has been converted into a central modern hotel with pleasant rooms. There's a restaurant and bar, and adequate parking. *36–40 London Rd., GU1 2AF, tel. 0483/576539. 38 rooms, 13 with bath. Inexpensive.*

Haslemere **Morels.** Chef Jean-Yves Morel is also the proprietor of this
Dining prize-winning restaurant, one of the best in the country. Sever-
★ al cottages were taken in over the years to make an interesting, varied dining space, cool—white and blue—and intimate. Specialties, which change regularly, include slices of guinea-fowl, quail, and rabbit in an orange and Dubonnet sauce, and venison with a game sauce and chestnut mousse. *25–27 Lower St., tel. 0428/51462. Reservations required. Jacket and tie required. AE, DC, MC, V. Closed Sat. lunch, Sun and Mon. Expensive.*

Herstmonceux **The Sundial.** An old Sussex farmhouse, skillfully enlarged, pro-
Dining vides the setting for this popular restaurant, which chef Gius-
★ eppe Bartoli and his French wife, Laurette, have run since 1966. The menu is extensive, with some imaginative combinations. The fish dishes are particularly successful and the vegetables fresh and expertly cooked. The Dover sole flavored with thyme is recommended. *Gardner St., tel. 0323/832217. Reservations advised. Dress: informal. AE, DC, MC, V. Closed Sun. evening and Mon. Expensive.*

Lewes **Kenwards.** Hidden in a passage near the tower of St. Michael's
Dining church, Kenwards has a striking interior of bare rafters and different levels. The menu changes weekly, but always outlines

excellent, straightforward cooking with lots of fresh vegetables and herbs. Especially good is the turbot with ginger and chervil. There is a buffet at lunchtime and a very sensible wine list. In the summer, there is garden dining. As a final welcome touch, the menu says "We do not expect tips." *Pipe Passage, 151A High St., tel. 0273/472343. Reservations advised. Dress: informal. MC, V. Closed Sat. lunch, Mon. evening, and Sun. Moderate.*

Rye
Dining and Lodging

The Mermaid. The Mermaid is one of the classic old inns of England, serving this ancient town for nearly six centuries, and was once the headquarters of one of the notorious smuggling gangs that ruled the Romney Marshes. Its age can be seen in every nook and cranny, with sloping, creaky floors, oak beams and low ceilings, a huge open hearth in the bar, and a few four-poster beds. Every detail in this inn will make the seeker of atmosphere very happy. But be warned, the Mermaid is *very* popular with tourists. *Mermaid St., TN31 7EU, tel. 0797/223065. 28 rooms, 25 with bath. AE, DC, MC, V. Facilities: restaurant. Moderate.*

Lodging

Jeake's House. This lovely old house (1689), on the same cobblestoned street as the Mermaid (*see* above), has cozy bedrooms furnished with antiques, and many have views over the town. Breakfast is served in a former chapel. *Mermaid St., TN31 7ET, tel. 0797/222828. 9 rooms, 6 with bath or shower. AE, MC, V. Moderate.*

Tonbridge
Lodging

Rose and Crown. This was originally a 16th-century inn and it features a distinctive, later-added portico. Inside, low-beamed ceilings and Jacobean woodwork make both the bars and the restaurant snug and inviting. Guest rooms in the main building are traditionally furnished, while in the new annex they are more modern in style; all are attractive and cozy. *125 High St., TN9 1DD, tel. 0732/357966. 51 rooms with bath. AE, DC, MC, V. Moderate.*

Tunbridge Wells
Dining

Thackeray's House. This mid-17th-century house, once the home of Victorian novelist William Makepeace Thackeray, is a must for gourmets. Its owner, Bruce Wass, is also the chef, and tolerates none but the freshest ingredients. Everything is cooked with great flair and imagination. Specialties include saddle of veal and chocolate Armagnac loaf. Below the main restaurant, there is a friendly little bistro, **Downstairs at Thackeray's,** with food every bit as good as upstairs, but less expensive. *85 London Rd., tel. 0892/511921. Reservations required. Jacket and tie required. MC, V. Closed Sun., Mon., and Christmas week. Expensive.*

Lodging

Spa Hotel. This hotel, run by the Goring family, who also have the Goring hotel in London, has carefully chosen furnishings and details that help retain the atmosphere of a country house for this Georgian mansion, though guest rooms are equipped with many thoughtful modern extras. The extensive grounds give superb views across the town and into the weald of Kent. The **Chandelier Restaurant** is very popular with locals. *Mt. Ephraim, TN4 8XJ, tel. 0892/20331. 75 rooms with bath. Facilities: indoor pool, sauna, tennis, croquet, jogging track, beauty parlor, Jacuzzi. AE, DC, MC, V. Expensive.*

Periquito. This Regency building, which dates from the early 19th century, overlooks the common and has gardens in the front and rear. There's a pleasant, restful atmosphere, enhanced by homey guest rooms and courteous, helpful staff. *84 Mt. Ephraim, TN4 8BU, tel. 0892/542911. 66 rooms, 45 with bath. Facilities: sauna, solarium, gymnasium. AE, DC, MC, V. Moderate.*

Uckfield
Dining and Lodging

Horsted Place. This very special hotel was once a house belonging to Prince Philip's Treasurer, and it frequently accommodated the Queen and other members of the royal family. It is still beautifully furnished, with many interesting features, such as a magnificent Victorian staircase and the Gothic library with a secret door that leads to a hidden courtyard. The dining room—Gothic like the library—offers superb haute cuisine (try the pot roast quail). *Little Horsted, (2½ mi from Uckfield), TN22 5TS, tel. 082575/581. 17 rooms with bath. Facilities: restaurant, indoor pool, gardens, tennis. AE, DC, MC, V. Very Expensive.*

Wadhurst
Dining and Lodging

Spindlewood Hotel. This 19th-century country-house hotel, set on extensive grounds well off the main road, (6 miles from Tunbridge Wells via A267 and B2099), has built its reputation around its restaurant. The proprietor, Robert Fitzsimmons, is so confident that you'll come back that he mails out copies of the menu when it is changed every six weeks. Specialties include medallions of venison marinated with juniper berries. *Wallcrouch, Wadhurst, TN5 7JG, tel. 0580/200430. 9 rooms with bath. Reservations required for restaurant. Dress: informal. AE, DC, MC, V. Moderate.*

West Clandon
Dining
★

The Onslow Arms. The bar here is a favorite with locals. There's a fast-food area but the main emphasis of this old inn is an extremely sophisticated restaurant to which customers make a special journey from London. (Take A246/247 4 miles northeast of Guildford.) The outstanding cellar (you could pay up to £100 for a bottle of wine) is matched by superb French cuisine; among the notable dishes are *tournedos Charles le Téméraire* (thick beef fillets with a special sauce), *tournedos la Barbuie aux huitres et saffron* (thick beef fillets with oysters and saffron), and spit-roast suckling pig. *The Street, West Clandon, tel. 0483/222447. Reservations required. Jacket and tie required. AE, DC, MC, V. Closed Sun. evening and Mon. Expensive.*

The Arts

Festivals

The Southeast is a region of festivals, particularly for music and drama. In Kent, **Canterbury** has a three-week-long arts festival every September–October (tel. 0227/472820).

There are **Dickens Festivals** in June in two towns associated with the writer: **Rochester** (tel. 0634/43666), and **Broadstairs** (tel. 0843/63453).

The **Brighton Festival** (tel. 0273/29801), an international event held every May, covers drama, music from classical to rock, dance, visual arts, and literature.

Opera

Glyndebourne Opera House (Glyndebourne, near Lewes, East Sussex, tel. 0273/812321) is one of the world's leading opera houses. Nestled beneath the Downs and surrounded by superb gardens, Glyndebourne combines excellent productions, a lovely setting, and a sense of timelessness. But you must book far in advance to get seats, and the whole visit will be *very* expensive

—worth every cent to the aficionado. The season runs from May to August.

Theater   Canterbury has two main theaters. The **Gulbenkian Theatre** (Giles La., tel. 0227/769075), named after the oil magnate who provided a generous donation, is part of the University of Kent and mounts a full range of plays, particularly experimental works. The **Marlowe** (St. Margaret's St., tel. 0227/767246) is named after the Elizabethan playwright, atheist, and spy, who was born in Canterbury.

The Festival Theatre, Chichester (tel. 0243/781312), presents middle-of-the-road productions of classics and modern plays for the undemanding theatergoer for the five months May to September. Like Glyndebourne (*see* above), it has an international reputation and can provide the evening focus for a relaxed day out of London.

Brighton has several theaters. **The Dome** (tel. 0273/674357), beside the Pavilion, was converted into an auditorium from the Prince Regent's stables in the 1930s. It stages classical and pop concerts. The **Theatre Royal** (New Rd., tel. 0273/28488), close to the Pavilion, is a very attractive Regency building with a period gem of an auditorium. It is a favorite venue for shows either on their way to London's West End or just having left it. The **Gardner Centre for the Arts** (tel. 0273/685861), on the campus of Sussex University, a few miles northeast of town at Falmer, presents a mixed program of plays, concerts, and cabaret just east of Brighton at Falmer.

In Guildford, Surrey, the **Yvonne Arnaud Theatre** (Milbrook, tel. 0483/60191) is an unusual horseshoe-shaped building on an island in the Wey River. It frequently previews West End productions, and there is also a restaurant.

5 The South

Introduction

The South, made up of Hampshire (Hants), Dorset, and Wiltshire, offers a wide range of attractions, and not a few quiet pleasures. Two of England's most important cathedrals, Winchester and Salisbury (pronounced Sawlsberry), are here; they vie for the visitor's attention with stately homes, attractive market towns, and literally hundreds of prehistoric remains, two of which, Avebury and Stonehenge, are among Europe's most impressive.

The landscape of the South incorporates the gentle, gardenlike features of London's Home Counties, and the bleaker, harsher terrain of Salisbury Plain surrounding Stonehenge, and the Dorset heathlands. The region is spanned by rolling grass-covered chalk hills—the Downs—wooded valleys, and fertile meadows through which flow deep, clear rivers. The dairy herds of Dorset's meadows are famous for their delicious, rich cream.

The southern coast owes much of its prosperity through the centuries to its protected harbors and sandy beaches, but it has perilous stretches, too, such as the Fossil Coast of Lyme Regis, or Chesil Bank, where the tides and currents play strange and sinister games, striking fear into the hearts of sailors.

This area has been quietly central to England's history for well over 4,000 years, occupied successively by prehistoric man, the Celts, the Romans, and the Saxons—Winchester was Alfred the Great's capital in the late 9th century, and the seat of Wessex, one of the original seven Anglo-Saxon kingdoms. History has continued to be made here, right up to the modern era. Forces sailed from ports along this coast for Normandy on D-Day, and to recover the Falklands nearly 40 years later.

Essential Information

Important Addresses and Numbers

Tourist Information **The Southern Tourist Board,** 40 Chamberlayne Rd., Eastleigh, Hants S05 5JH, tel 0703/620006. Open Mon.–Thurs. 8:30–5, Fri. 8:30–4:30.
Tourist information centers are normally open Mon.–Sat. 9:30–5:30, but vary according to season. They include:
Bournemouth: Westover Road (overlooking the bandstand), tel. 0202/291715.
Dorchester: 7 Acland Rd., tel. 0305/67992.
Portsmouth: The Hard, tel. 0705/826722.
Ryde: Western Esplanade (near hovercraft terminal), tel. 0983/62905.
Salisbury: Fish Row (just off Market Sq.), tel. 0722/334956.
Winchester: The Guildhall, The Broadway, tel. 0962/840500.

Travel Agencies **American Express:** 99 Above Bar, Southampton, Hants SO9 1FY, tel. 0703/634828.
Thomas Cook: 7 Richmond Hill, Bournemouth, Dorset BH2 6HF, tel. 0202/299766; 19 High St., Ryde, Isle of Wight PO33 2HW, tel. 0983/67314; 18 Queen St., Salisbury, Wilts SP1 1EY, tel. 0722/412787; and 107A High St., Winchester, Hants SO23 9AG, tel. 0962/841661.

Car Rental **Bournmouth: Avis,** Hendy Lennox Ltd., 17A Christchurch
Agencies Rd., Lansdowne, tel. 0202/293218; **Budget Rent a Car,** Dovefar
Ltd., Wessex Hotel, West Cliff Rd., tel. 0202/296163; **Hertz,**
Palace Parking, Hinton Rd., tel. 0202/291231.

Salisbury: Europcar Ltd., Fisherton Yard, Fisherton St., tel.
0722/335625; **EuroDollar Rent-a-Car,** Bemerton Service Station, Wilton Rd., tel. 0722/335117.

Arriving and Departing

By Car The South is linked to London and other major cities by a well-
developed road network, which includes M3 to Winchester (59
miles); M3 and A33 to Southampton (77 miles); A3 to Portsmouth (70 miles); and M27 along the coast, from Southampton
to Portsmouth. A30 (off M3) is the main route to Salisbury. A31
connects Bournemouth to Dorchester and the rest of Dorset.

By Train **British Rail** serves the South from London's Waterloo Station
(tel. 071/928–5100). Travel times average an hour to Winchester; an hour and a quarter to Southampton; two hours to
Bournemouth; and 2½ hours to Weymouth. Portsmouth takes
an hour and 40 minutes, and Salisbury about the same. There is
at least one fast train every hour on all these routes.

By Bus **National Express** (tel. 071/730–0202) serves the region from
London's Victoria Coach Station. There are hourly departures
throughout the day for Southampton (2½ hours), and Portsmouth (also 2½ hours). Buses leave every two hours for Winchester (two hours); Bournemouth (2½ hours); and Salisbury
(2¾ hours).

Getting Around

By Plane There is a small airport at Southampton, useful for flights to
the Channel Islands (*see* Chapter 7). *Information tel. 0703/
629600.*

By Car The area covered in this chapter involves very easy driving. In
northeast Hampshire and in many parts of neighboring Wiltshire there are any number of lanes, overhung by trees and
lined with thatched cottages and Georgian houses. Often the
network of such lanes starts immediately as you leave a main
highway. Salisbury Plain has long straight roads surrounded
by endless vistas, and the problem here is to keep to the speed
limit!

By Train A "Hants (Hampshire) and Dorset Rover" ticket is valid
throughout the region for seven days, or you can get a "Network SouthEast" card, valid for a year, which entitles you to
one-third off particular fares—this may not apply to all parts of
the region, though. For local information call British Rail
Bournemouth, tel. 0202/292474; Salisbury, tel. 0722/27591; or
Southampton, tel. 0703/229293.

Guided Tours

Orientation Tours **Alder Valley** (tel. 0252/27181) offers area tours aboard all sorts
of tourist buses—single or double-decker, mini, and open-top.

Special-Interest The **Southern Tourist Board** (tel. 0703/620006) and **Wessexplore**
Tours (tel. 0722/26304) can reserve qualified Blue Badge guides for
private tours of different lengths and themes, ranging from an

hour in Salisbury Cathedral to a full-day exploration of prehistoric sites or maritime history. The guides can arrange to meet you anywhere in the region.

Bookmark Tours (150 Carob Way, Coronado, CA 92118, tel. 619/437–1211) organize tours of **Jane Austen's England,** starting in London, and taking in all the main locations associated with her life and work.

Exploring the South

Orientation

We begin our tour of the scenic southern region in the lovely cathedral city of Winchester, just 64 miles southwest of London. From there we meander southward to the coast, stopping at the bustling ports of Southampton and Portsmouth before striking out for the restful shores of the Isle of Wight, vacation home to Queen Victoria.

Returning to the mainland, the second tour swings northwest to Salisbury, renowned for its glorious cathedral, then heads west across Salisbury Plain to Avebury and Stonehenge, in Wiltshire, skirting the top of Dorset on our way. From Stonehenge we dip south to the wild, scenic expanse of the New Forest, ancient hunting preserve of William the Conqueror. Our final tour follows the Dorset coastline, immortalized by the literary works of Thomas Hardy and John Fowles, taking in the cities of Bournemouth, Dorchester, Weymouth, and a host of picturesque and historic villages.

By Bus **Hampshire Bus** (tel. 0962/52352) has a comprehensive service in the Southampton, Eastleigh, Winchester, Andover, and Basingstoke areas.

Southern Vectis (tel. 0983/62264) provides bus service throughout the Isle of Wight. "Rover" tickets for unlimited travel are available by the day or the week, and include a discount at many restaurants and places of interest.

Wilts (Wiltshire) & Dorset Bus Co. (tel. 0202/673555) offers both one-day "Explorer" and seven-day "Busabout" tickets; they also conduct "Explorer Special" tours around Bournemouth.

By Ferry **Sealink British Ferries** (tel. 0304/203203) operates a car ferry service between the mainland and the Isle of Wight. The crossing takes about 35 minutes from Lymington to Yarmouth; 40 minutes from Portsmouth to Fishbourne. Fares vary according to departure days and size of vehicle.

Red Funnel Ferries (tel. 0703/330333) runs a car ferry and hydrofoil service between Southampton and Cowes.

Hovertravel (tel. 0705/829988 and 0983/811000) has a hovercraft shuttle between Southsea and Ryde.

Highlights for First-time Visitors

Avebury: Tour 2
Carisbrooke Castle: Tour 1
HMS *Victory* and *Mary Rose*: Tour 1
Longleat: Tour 2
Maiden Castle: Tour 3

Salisbury Cathedral: Tour 2
Stonehenge: Tour 2
Stourhead Gardens: Tour 2
Wilton House: Tour 2
Winchester Cathedral: Tour 1

Tour 1: From Winchester to the Isle of Wight

Numbers in the margin correspond to points of interest on the South and Winchester maps.

1 **Winchester** is among the most historic of English cities, and as you walk its graceful, unspoiled streets, a sense of the past envelops you. Though it is now merely the county seat of Hampshire, for more than four centuries Winchester served as England's capital. Here, in AD 827, Egbert was crowned first king of England, and his successor Alfred the Great held court until his death in 899. After the Norman Conquest in 1066, William I ("the Conqueror") had himself crowned in London, but took the precaution of repeating the ceremony in Winchester. The city remained the center of commercial and political power until the 13th century. Medieval Winchester was also the ecclesiastical center of England, renowned throughout Europe for its illuminated manuscripts, some of which you can still see in the cathedral library.

2 Start your tour at the **Cathedral,** the city's greatest monument. It was begun in 1079 and consecrated in 1093, though its original Norman structure was altered several times during the Middle Ages. In the cathedral's tower, transepts, and crypt, as in the core of the great nave, you can see some of the world's best surviving examples of Norman architecture. Other features, such as the arcades, the clerestory (the wall dividing the aisles from the nave), and the windows, are Gothic alterations carried out during the 12th and 13th centuries. The remodeling of the nave in the Perpendicular style (*see* The Basics of British Architecture in Chapter 2) was not completed until the 15th century. Little of the original stained glass has survived, thanks to Cromwell's Puritan troops, who ransacked the cathedral in the 17th century, during the English Civil War.

Among the many important people buried in the cathedral are William the Conqueror's son, William II (Rufus), mysteriously murdered in the New Forest in 1100; Izaak Walton, author of *The Compleat Angler,* whose memorial window in Silkestede's Chapel was paid for by "the fishermen of England and America"; and Jane Austen, whose memorial window can be seen in the north aisle of the nave. In the retro-choir, look for the statuette of William Walker, the diver, "who saved this cathedral with his two hands." This curious inscription refers to Walker's heroic underpinning of the building's flooded foundations (1906–12), when the medieval ones had proved too shallow.

3 Behind the cathedral is the **Close,** an area containing the Deanery, Dome Alley, and Cheyney Court. On the right, as you enter Cheyney Court, you will see the **King's Gate,** built in the 13th century, one of two gates remaining from the original city wall. **St. Swithin's** church is built over the King's Gate. Turn left onto College Street and proceed to number 8, the house where Jane Austen died on July 18, 1817, three days after writing a comic poem (copies are usually available in the cathedral) about the legend of St. Swithin's Day—a remarkable testimony to her unfailing cheerfulness.

⑤ Continue along College Street to **Winchester College,** founded in 1382. It is probably England's oldest "public" (i.e., private) school. Among the original buildings still in use is Chamber Court, center of college life for six centuries. Look out for "scholars"—students holding academic scholarships—clad in their traditional gowns. *College St., tel. 0962/868778. Admission: £2 adults, £1.50 children and senior citizens. Guided tours Apr.–Sept., Mon.–Sat. 11:15, 2:15, and 3:30, Sun. 2:15 and 3:30.*

Time Out Try a half-pint of draft bitter or dry cider at **The Royal Oak** (Royal Oak Passage, off High St.), a traditional pub which claims to have Britain's oldest bar. Unusually, it has a non-smoking cellar bar.

---

⑥ A few blocks west of the cathedral is another of Winchester's important historical sites, the medieval **Great Hall,** which is all that remains of the city's castle. It has witnessed many historic events: The English Parliament met here for the first time in 1246; Sir Walter Raleigh was tried for conspiracy against King James I and condemned to death here in 1603 (though he wasn't beheaded until 1618); and Dame Alice Lisle was sentenced here by the infamous Judge Jeffreys (*see* Dorchester in Tour 3) to be burned at the stake for sheltering a fugitive, following Monmouth's Rebellion in 1685. (King James II, in a rare act of mercy, commuted her sentence to beheading.) On the west wall of the hall hangs what is said to be King Arthur's Round Table, with places for 24 knights and a portrait of Arthur which bears a remarkable resemblance to King Henry VII. In fact, the table is a Tudor forgery; the real Arthur was probably a Celtic cavalry general who held off the invading Saxons following the fall of the Roman Empire. Henry VII revived the Arthurian legend for political purposes. He named his eldest son Arthur, though the boy did not live to inherit the throne. *Castle Hill, tel. 0962/ 84676. Admission free. Open Mar.–Oct., daily 10–5; Nov.– Feb., weekdays 10–5, weekends 10–4.*

⑦ Retrace your steps along High Street to **The Square,** across from the cathedral, and have a look at Winchester's past through the exhibits in the **City Museum.** Objects on display include Celtic pottery, Roman mosaics, and Saxon coins. *The Square, tel. 0962/848269. Admission free. Open Apr.–Sept., Mon.–Sat. 10–5, Sun. 2–5; Oct.–Mar., Tues.–Sat. 10–5, Sun. 2–4.*

⑧
⑨ For a change of scenery and era, visit the **City Mill,** an 18th-century water mill situated at the foot of **St. Giles's Hill,** just east of High Street. Then climb the hill for a panoramic view of the city. *1 Water Lane, tel. 0962/53723 (also for Youth Centre). Admission: 50p. Open Apr.–Sept., Tues.–Thurs. and Sat. 1:45– 4:45.*

Numbers in the margin correspond to points of interest on the South map.

⑩ Eight miles northeast of Winchester, by A31 and B3046, lies the town of **Old Alresford** (pronounced "Awlsford"), now the starting point of the **Watercress Line,** a 10-mile railroad reserved for steam locomotives. Originally named for its special

The South

Mouth of the Severn

AVON

Avon

Bristol

Bath

Melksham

Devizes

Weston-super-Mare

Trowbridge

WILTSHIRE

B3098

SOMERSET

Westbury

Wells

Frome

A361

A3098

Warminster

Shepton Mallet

34 **Longleat House**

B3092

SALISBURY PLAIN

33 **Stourhead House**

A303

Wylye

B3092

Tisbury

Nadder

DEVON

B3081

Swallowcliffe

A30

32 **Shaftesbury**

Yeovil

Sherborne

A352

Illminster

Blandford Forum

48 **Cerne Abbas**

Wimbourne Minster

43

DORSET

A3349

Godmanstone

A35

Tolpuddle

A351

54

Bridport

A35

47 **Dorchester**

Poole

44

Lyme Regis

49 **Maiden Castle**

Wareham

Brownsea Island

45

53 **Abbotsbury**

A352

PURBECK HILLS

Chesil Beach **52**

A354

B3070

Corfe Castle

46

50 **Weymouth**

Lulworth Cove

N

Isle of Portland **51**

0   10 miles

0   15 km

A4

A360

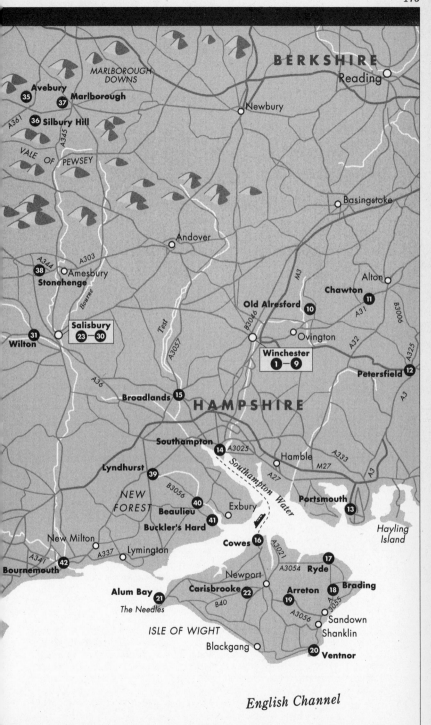

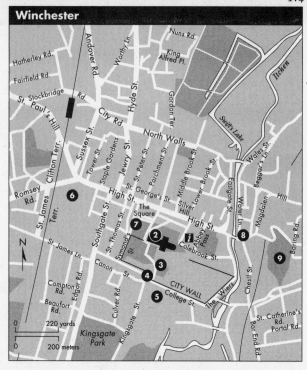

deliveries of local watercress, the line takes visitors on a nostalgic tour through 19th-century England. *Tel. 0962/733810. Operates Mar.–Oct., variable hours.*

Time Out   About halfway between Winchester and Old Alresford, turn north off A31 for **Ovington.** Here you will find **The Bush Inn,** an unspoilt, friendly country pub and restaurant with open log fires and a quiet riverside garden.

Leaving Old Alresford, continue east about 8 miles along A31 to **Chawton,** the village where Jane Austen lived for the last eight years of her life (she moved to Winchester only during her final illness). Here she wrote *Emma, Persuasion,* and *Mansfield Park.* The rooms of the unassuming, red-brick house retain the atmosphere of restricted gentility in which the unmarried daughter of a clergyman was expected to live her life two hundred years ago. *Jane Austen's House, Chawton, tel. 0420/83262. Admission: £1.50 adults, 50p children. Open Apr.–Oct., daily 11–4:30; Nov.–Dec. and Mar., Wed.–Sun. 11–4:30; Jan. and Feb. weekends only.*

From Chawton, follow B3006 southeast, then A325 southwest for 10 miles to the Georgian market town of **Petersfield,** set in a wide valley between wooded hills and open downs. Two miles south on A3 you will see signs for **Queen Elizabeth Country Park.** Here, amid 1,400 acres of chalk hills and shady beechwood, you can navigate scenic hiking trails and climb to the top of Butser Hill (888 feet) to take in a splendid view of the coast. *Tel. 0705/595040. Admission free. Open without restriction.*

Fifteen miles south of Petersfield along A3 is the city of **Portsmouth,** England's naval capital and principal port of departure for British forces. Fleets have left from here for centuries, from ancient times right up to D-Day and the 1982 Falklands War. The harbor covers about 7 square miles and incorporates the world's first dry dock (built in 1495) and extensive defenses. These include **Porchester Castle,** founded more than 1,600 years ago. It has the most complete set of Roman walls (constructed in the 3rd century) still existing in northern Europe. The keep's central tower affords a sweeping view of the harbor and coastline. *Near Fareham, tel. 0705/378291. Admission: £1.15 adults, 60p children under 16, children under 5 free, 85p senior citizens. Open Easter–Sept., Tues.–Sun. 10–6; Oct.–Easter, Tues.–Sun. 10–1 and 2–4.*

Portsmouth Naval Base has an unrivaled collection of ships on display, of which the most outstanding is Nelson's flagship, H.M.S. *Victory.* She has been painstakingly restored to appear as she did at the time of her last and most famous battle at Trafalgar (1805). You can inspect the cramped gun-decks, visit the cabin where Nelson entertained his officers, and stand on the spot where he was mortally wounded by a French sniper. *The four main sights in the Portsmouth Naval Base, H.M.S.* Victory, *the* Mary Rose, *H.M.S.* Warrior, *and the Royal Naval Museum, are all run by the Portsmouth Heritage Trust (tel. 0705/839766). Admission: to each of the three ships when visited separately—£3.50 adults (the* Warrior's *fee also includes the museum);* Victory *£2 children and senior citizens,* Mary Rose *£2.25 children, £2.50 senior citizens;* Warrior *and museum £2 children, £3 senior citizens. All-inclusive and family tickets are also available. Open Mar–Oct., daily 10–6; Nov.–Feb., daily 10:30–5.*

In 1982, a much-publicized exercise in marine archaeology succeeded in raising the *Mary Rose,* flagship of the Tudor navy, which capsized and sank in the harbor in 1545 while heading out to attack French warships. Described at the time as "the flower of all the ships that ever sailed," the *Mary Rose* is now housed in a specially constructed enclosure, where her timbers are continuously sprayed with water to prevent them from drying out and breaking up. Thousands of remarkably well-preserved objects—including tools, weapons, pots, and surgical instruments—were found on board during the excavation, and a selection can be seen in the museum located in the same complex. The exhibition is one of the most dramatic and fascinating archaeological displays in the world.

Time Out After you've visited the *Victory* and the *Mary Rose,* stop in at **Sally Port** (High St.) for a tasty pub lunch.

H.M.S. *Warrior,* another of Portsmouth's great ships, is now berthed near H.M.S. *Victory* and the *Mary Rose.* The *Warrior* was built in 1860 as Britain's first armored battleship—the fastest, longest (over 400 feet), and most powerful warship of her day. She spent her active life guarding the Channel against foreign attack. Close by is the **Royal Navy Museum,** with its fine collection of painted figureheads, relics of Nelson's family, and galleries of paintings and mementos recalling different periods of naval history.

The even more popular **D-Day Museum,** near the corner of Southsea Common, tells the complex story of D-Day. A variety of exhibits vividly reconstructs the many stages of planning, the communications and logistics involved in the maneuver, as well as the actual invasion. The centerpiece of the museum is the **Overlord Embroidery,** a 272-foot tapestry with 34 panels illustrating the history of World War II, from the Battle of Britain in 1940 to D-Day itself (June 6, 1944) and the first days of the liberation. It is modeled on the Bayeux Tapestry. *Clarence Esplanade, Southsea, tel. 0705/827261. Admission: £3 adults, £1.80 children, £2.25 senior citizens, £7.80 family ticket. Open daily 10:30–4:30.*

⑭ The maritime history of **Southampton,** 21 miles west of Portsmouth on A27 and A3025, is mainly commercial, rather than military. It boasts the best natural deep-water harbor in the country. Though the city was badly damaged during World War II, considerable parts of its castellated walls remain. They incorporate a variety of old buildings, including **God's House Tower,** originally erected for the manufacture of gunpowder, and now a comprehensive museum of Southampton's archaeological history. *Town Quay, tel. 0703/220007. Admission free. Open Tues.–Fri. 10–noon and 1–5, Sat. 10–noon and 1–4, Sun. 2–5.*

Mayflower Park and the **Pilgrim Fathers' Memorial** on Western Esplanade commemorate the sailing of the *Mayflower* from Southampton on August 15, 1620. (The ship was forced to stop in Plymouth for repairs before continuing on its historic journey to the New World.) John Alden, the hero of Longfellow's poem, *The Courtship of Miles Standish,* was a native of Southampton.

Other city attractions include an impressive art gallery, extensive parks, and the superb **Tudor House Museum** and garden, one of the best surviving examples of a large Tudor manor. *St. Michael's Sq., tel. 0703/24216. Admission free. Open Tues.–Fri. 10–5, Sat. 10–4, Sun. 2–5.*

Time Out A good place to stop for lunch is **The Red Lion** (55 High St.), the city's oldest pub. While modern on the outside, its ancient inside, with a half-timbered bar and original minstrels' gallery, create an intriguing Tudor ambience.

Eight miles north of Southampton, just off A3057, is **⑮ Broadlands,** home of the late Lord Mountbatten, uncle of Queen Elizabeth II. This beautiful 18th-century Palladian mansion, with gardens laid out by Capability Brown, and wide lawns sweeping down to the banks of the river Test, is undoubtedly the grandest house in Hampshire. It abounds with ornate plaster moldings and paintings of British and Continental royalty, as well as personal mementos of Lord Mountbatten's distinguished career in the navy and in India. In 1947, the Queen and the Duke of Edinburgh spent their honeymoon here, and the Prince and Princess of Wales spent a few days of theirs here in 1981. *Romsey, tel. 0794/516878. Admission: £4.50 adults, £3 children, £3.60 senior citizens. Open Apr.–Sept., daily 10–5. Closed Fri. except in Aug., Sept., and national holidays.*

Leaving Broadlands, rejoin A3057 and follow it back to Southampton. From here you can catch a ferry to the Isle of Wight.

Since the 19th century, when Queen Victoria chose the **Isle of Wight** for her vacation home, the small, diamond-shape island has been an important tourist resort. Nonetheless, many foreign visitors, eager to cover a varied itinerary of "must-see" spots, neglect the island, unintentionally helping to preserve its quiet, traditional character.

Although the island is within easy reach of the mainland (car ferries leave from Southampton, Portsmouth, and Lymington), it offers a striking contrast. It has no highways or large housing complexes, and is only 23 miles long. It presents a peaceful picture of steep chalk cliffs, curving bays, and quiet villages, with the occasional elegant country house rising amid manicured lawns and gardens. Its sandy beaches are a haven for vacationers.

16 If you embark from Southampton, your ferry will cross the Solent and dock at **Cowes,** internationally known for "Cowes Week," its annual yachting festival, held in July or August. At the north end of High Street, on the **Parade,** a tablet commemorates the sailing from Cowes in 1633 of two ships carrying the founders of the state of Maryland. Just to the east of the town, Queen Victoria built **Osborne House,** styled after an Italian villa by Prince Albert. The Queen spent much time here during her last years, until her death in 1901. The staterooms have scarcely been altered since her time. *Tel. 0983/200022. Admission: £4.30 adults, £2.20 children, £3.20 senior citizens. Open Apr.–Sept., daily 10–6, Oct. 10–5.*

17 Leave Cowes by A3021 and follow the signs on A3054 to the town of **Ryde,** a summer resort offering a variety of family attractions. Following the construction of **Ryde Pier** in 1814, elegant (and occasionally ostentatious) town houses sprang up along the seafront and on the slopes behind, commanding fine views of the harbor. In addition to its long, sandy beach, Ryde has a large boating lake (rowboats and pedalboats can be rented) and children's playgrounds.

Time Out A 10-minute walk along the seafront brings you to **The Solent Inn,** a small, traditional pub which serves lunches (weather permitting) in its pleasant garden. If you're looking for a coffee or a quiet lunch in the heart of town, stop in at **De Luce,** on Union Street.

At **Flamingo Park,** a water fowl reserve 2½ miles east of Ryde, many of the birds will eat from your hand. *Springvale, Seaview, tel. 0983/612153. Admission: £2.50 adults, £1.50 children, £2.25 senior citizens. Open Apr., daily 2–5:30; May–Sept., daily 10–5:30; Oct., daily 2–5.*

18 Three miles south of Ryde on A3055 is the village of **Brading,** whose church stands opposite what is said to be the oldest house (dating from the 16th century) on the island. A mile or so south, however, lie the much older remains of the substantial, 3rd-century **Brading Roman Villa,** whose splendid mosaic floors and heating system have been carefully preserved, along with other relics. *Tel. 0983/406223. Admission: £1.50 adults, 75p children. Open Apr.–Sept., Mon.–Sat. 10–5:30, Sun. 10:30–5:30.*

Following B3055 south from Brading brings you to the twin resorts of **Sandown** and **Shanklin,** which share the same bay. Shanklin is the quieter of the two. More interesting than the beach, however, is the medieval village of **Arreton,** about 3 miles inland on A3056. Here a group of old farm buildings which were once part of the local manor have been restored as a **Country Crafts Village.** More than a dozen local craftspeople have established their studios in the village, working in wood, wool, leather, clay, metal, and other materials. You can browse and buy items direct from the makers. *Tel. 0983/528353. Admission free. Open daily 9:30–5.*

Leaving Arreton, rejoin the coast road, A3055, outside Sandown and follow it south toward **Ventnor.** The south coast resorts are the sunniest and most sheltered on the island. Ventnor itself rises from such a steep slope that the ground floors of some of its houses are level with the roofs of those across the road. The **Botanic Gardens** here are among the best in Britain, laid out over 22 acres and containing more than 3,500 species of trees, plants, and shrubs. They are open all year, with no restrictions in hours and no admission charge. There's an excellent restaurant, the **Garden Tavern,** in the Gardens.

The southwestern coast of the Isle of Wight is the least developed part of the shoreline, although families will find a welcome exception at **Blackgang,** where the deep chine (cleft in the cliffs) contains a **fantasy theme park** (*see* What to See and Do with Children, below). Farther west, at the tip of the island, stand the **Needles,** a long line of jagged chalk stacks jutting out of the sea like monstrous teeth. Take the chairlift to the beach at **Alum Bay,** where you can catch a good view of the multicolored sands in the cliff strata. The **Alum Bay Glass Company** welcomes visitors interested in buying souvenirs or just watching glassblowing and jewelry crafting. *Tel. 0983/753473. Admission: 40p adults, 30p senior citizens, 20p children. Open daily 10:30–5; no glassmaking on Sat.*

From Alum Bay, head inland about 14 miles to **Carisbrooke,** former capital of the island (the modern-day capital is **Newport,** one mile east). Above the village of Carisbrooke stands **Carisbrooke Castle,** originally built by the Normans but enlarged with a new ring of defenses in Elizabethan times. King Charles I was imprisoned here during the English Civil War. You can see the small window in the north curtain wall through which he tried to escape; and stroll along the battlements to watch the donkey-wheel, where a team of donkeys draws water from a deep well. *Tel. 0983/522107. Admission: £2.60 adults, £1.30 children, £1.90 senior citizens. Open Apr.–Sept., Tues.–Sun. 10–6; Oct.–Mar., Tues.–Sun. 10–4.*

Time Out For lunch, bar snacks, and local ale, visit **The Castle** (High St.), an attractive old pub in nearby Newport.

Leaving Newport, follow A3020 north about 5 miles to Cowes. From here you can catch a ferry back to Southampton. There, pick up A36 and head north to the ancient city of Salisbury, about 23 miles away.

Tour 2: Salisbury, Stonehenge, and the New Forest

Numbers in the margin correspond to points of interest on the Salisbury map.

㉓ Like Winchester, **Salisbury** is a historic cathedral city, and its old stone buildings—shops and houses—grew up in the shadow of the great church. But unlike Winchester, Salisbury did not become important until the 13th century, when the diocese of Old Sarum (the original settlement 2 miles to the north) was transferred here. The cathedral at Old Sarum was razed (today **㉔** only ruins remain), and **Salisbury Cathedral** was built. The local people relocated along with the ecclesiastical center, and the city of Salisbury was born. In the 19th century, novelist Anthony Trollope based his tales of ecclesiastical life, notably *Barchester Towers*, on life in Salisbury, although his fictional city of Barchester is really an amalgam of Winchester and Salisbury.

Salisbury continues to be dominated by its towering cathedral, a soaring hymn in stone. It is unique among medieval British cathedrals in that it was conceived and built as a whole, in the amazingly short span of only 38 years (1220–58). The spire, which commands the surrounding countryside, was added in 1320 and is a miraculous feat of medieval engineering—even though the point, 404 feet above the ground, is 2½ feet off vertical. For a fictional, keenly imaginative reconstruction of the human drama underlying such an achievement, read William Golding's novel, *The Spire*.

The interior of the cathedral is remarkable for its lancet windows and sculpted tombs of crusaders and other medieval heroes. The clock in the north aisle—probably the oldest working mechanism in Europe, if not the world—was made in 1386. The spacious **cloisters** are the largest in England, and don't overlook the octagonal **Chapter House,** which contains a marvelous 13th-century frieze showing scenes from the Old Testament. Here you can also see one of the four original copies of the **Magna Carta,** the charter of rights which the English barons forced King John to accept in 1215; it was sent here for safekeeping in the 13th century.

The **Cathedral Close** (grounds) appears much as it did when it was first laid out. Its wide lawns are flanked by historic houses, some of which are open to the public. One of these is the impres-**㉕** sive **Mompesson House** on the north side, which boasts some fine original paneling and plasterwork, as well as a fascinating collection of 18th-century drinking glasses, and an attractive walled garden. *Tel. 0722/335659. Admission: £2.30 adults, £1.20 children. Open Apr.–Oct., Sat.–Wed. noon–5:30.*

㉖ Leaving the close on the north side will take you through **High Street Gate,** one of the four castellated stone gateways built to separate the close from the rest of the city, and into the heart of the modern town. Turn right into Silver Street and you will **㉗** find one of Salisbury's best-known landmarks, the **Poultry Cross.** This little hexagonal structure is the last remaining of the four original market crosses, and market dealers still set up **㉘** their stalls beside it. A narrow side street links it to **Market Square,** site of one of southern England's most popular markets, held on Tuesdays and Saturdays. Permission to hold an

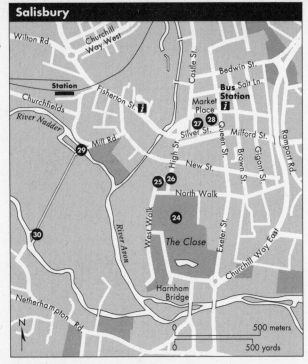

annual fair here was granted in 1221, and that right is exercised for three days every October.

Many medieval cities in England boast handsome half-timbered houses, but Salisbury has more than most. A particularly fine example can be found close to Market Square, at no. 8 Queen Street. This house, originally the home of a successful wool merchant, is now a store selling fine china and glassware. You can browse here and see the old staircase, the fireplaces of local Chilmark stone, and the Jacobean oak paneling.

29 Just west of High Street lies Mill Road, which leads you across Queen Elizabeth Gardens to **Long Bridge.** Cross the bridge and continue on the town path; the view from here inspired a classic 19th-century painting, John Constable's *Salisbury Cathedral,* now hung in the Constable Room of London's National Gallery.
30 Continue farther along the town path in the same direction until you come to the **Old Mill,** dating from the 12th century. It is now a restaurant and coffee shop under the same management as the Old Mill Hotel next door.

Numbers in the margin correspond to points of interest on the South map.

Salisbury stands close to the confluence of five rivers (the Avon, the Bourne, the Nadder, the Wylye, and the Ebble), each of which winds slowly through its own wooded valley into the heart of Wiltshire.

31 Following the valley of the Nadder west about 5 miles along A30 will lead you to the ancient town of **Wilton,** from which the county takes its name. A traditional market is held here every Thursday. But the main attraction is **Wilton House and Gardens,** home of the Earl of Pembroke. The original Tudor house burned down in 1647, but the present mansion replacing it was designed by Inigo Jones, Ben Jonson's stage designer and the architect of London's Banqueting House. It contains a superb collection of paintings by Rubens, Breughel, and Rembrandt, among others, as well as family treasures such as Napoleon's pearl-inlaid dispatch box and a lock of Queen Elizabeth I's hair. The main focus of interest, however, is the house itself. Among the staterooms are a "single cube room" (designed as an exact 30-foot cube) and a "double cube room" (twice the dimensions), both elaborately decorated with moldings of fruit and flowers, gilded in different shades of gold, and sumptuously furnished with 18th-century sofas and chairs upholstered in red velvet. It was in this double cube room that Eisenhower planned the Normandy invasion. The gardens have a number of magnificent old cedars and an imposing Palladian bridge built in 1737. *Tel. 0722/743115. Admission: Inclusive ticket, £4.20 adults, £3 children, £3.50 senior citizens. Open Easter–Oct., Tues.–Sat. and national holidays 11–6, Sun. 1–6. Restaurant opens at 12:30.*

32 Continuing west on A30 for about 13 miles will bring you into Dorset and the charming village of **Shaftesbury.** When you reach the village, head for **Gold Hill,** a steep, cobbled street lined with cottages. From the top you can catch a sweeping view of the surrounding countryside. Though Gold Hill itself is something of a tourist cliché (it has even appeared in TV commercials), it is still well worth visiting.

33 Nine miles northwest of Shaftesbury (follow B3081 to B3092), close to the village of **Stourton,** lies another of Wiltshire's many country-house-and-garden combinations. Most of **Stourhead House** was built between 1721 and 1725 by a wealthy banker named Henry Hoare. The pavilions (containing the library and picture gallery) were added by his grandson about 70 years later. The library (which escaped the fire that gutted the central block in 1902) has a stepladder, a writing desk, and book tables made by Thomas Chippendale, as well as a beautiful carved wood chimneypiece. Many of the rooms contain Chinese and French porcelain and other objets d'art. The most famous piece of furniture is a 17th-century Italian cabinet inlaid with marble and semiprecious stones, which was brought from Rome in 1742.

The house is set in extensive grounds, and just over the hill is a celebrated landscaped garden, in which temples, grottoes, and bridges have been skillfully placed among colorful shrubs, trees, and flowers. A walk around the lake (1 mile) reveals a series of ever-changing vistas. The best time to visit is early summer, when the massive banks of rhododendrons are in full bloom, but it is beautiful at any time of year. *Stourton, near Mere, tel. 0747/840348. House admission: £3.50 adults, £1.70 children. Open Apr. and Oct., Sat.–Wed. 2–6; May–end Sept., Sat.–Thurs. 2–6. Gardens open all year, daily 8AM–7 PM or sunset. Gardens admission: Mar.–Oct. £3.50 adults, £1.70 children, Nov.–Feb. £2.30 adults, £1.20 children. Open daily 8 AM–dusk.*

34 Follow B3092 about 6 miles north from Stourhead House to yet another famous private estate—**Longleat House,** home of the Marquess of Bath. The glorious Italian Renaissance–style building was completed in 1580 (for just over £8,000, an astronomical sum at the time), and contains outstanding tapestries, paintings, porcelain, and furniture, as well as notable period features of its own, such as the Victorian kitchens, the Elizabethan minstrels' gallery, and the great hall, with its massive wooden beams. Giant antlers of the extinct Irish elk decorate the walls. In 1966, the grounds of Longleat became Britain's first safari park. Giraffes, zebras, camels, rhinos, and lions are all on view.

Apart from the house and safari park, Longleat offers an impressive collection of dollhouses, a butterfly garden, a private railroad, the world's largest hedge maze, and an adventure castle. All of these make it an extremely popular and sometimes uncomfortably crowded place to visit, particularly in summer and during school vacations, so don't expect to have the place to yourself! *Near Warminster, tel. 09853/551. Admission: inclusive ticket for all attractions, £9.50 adults, £7.50 children and senior citizens. House only, £3.50 adults, £1.50 children under 14, £2.80 senior citizens. Open Easter–Sept., 10–6; Oct.–Easter, 10–4. Closed Christmas. Longleat Safari Park, tel. 09853/328. Admission: £4.50 adults, £3.50 children and senior citizens. Open Easter–Oct., daily 10–6.*

35 From Longleat, go north on B3092 to Frome, then take A361 to Trowbridge. Follow it through Devizes to **Avebury** (a total of 25 miles or so). As you approach Avebury, on your left you will pass **Cherhill Down,** with a vivid white horse carved into its slope. This is the first in a series of hillside carvings in Wiltshire; you will encounter others along the route. But unlike the others, this one isn't an ancient symbol—it was put there in 1780 to indicate the highest point of the Downs between London and Bath. (The best view of the horse is from A4, on the approach from Calne.)

Time Out **The Waggon and Horses** (Beckhampton), just beside the traffic circle linking A4 and A301, is an excellent place to enjoy a tasty sandwich lunch (they've won prizes for them) beside a blazing fire. The thatch-roofed pub is built of stones taken from the Avebury site.

36 Turning right at the traffic circle onto A4, **Silbury Hill** rises up on your right. This man-made mound, 130 feet high, dates from about 2,500 BC. Excavations over 200 years have provided no clue as to its original purpose, but the generally accepted notion is that it was a massive burial chamber.

Next, turn left onto B4003 and follow the **Kennett Stone Avenue,** a sort of prehistoric processional way leading to Avebury. The stones of the avenue were spaced 80 feet apart, but only the last half mile survives intact. The lost ones are marked with concrete. The **Avebury monument** at the end consists of a wide, circular ditch and bank, about 1,400 feet across and well over half a mile around. The perimeter is broken by entrances at roughly the four points of the compass, and inside stand the remains of three stone circles. The largest one originally had 98 stones, though only 27 remain. Many of the stones on the site were destroyed centuries ago, especially in the 17th century, when they were the target of religious fanaticism.

The first stones at Avebury predate those at Stonehenge by at least 200 years, but here they are much more domesticated—

literally so, for many were pillaged to build the thatched cottages you see flanking the fields. Recently a furor has arisen over the lord of the manor's plans to build a jazzy visitors' center, though at press time, no decision had been reached. Finds from the Avebury area are displayed in the **Alexander Kieller Museum,** run by English Heritage. *Tel. 06723/250. Phone for admission fees. Open Good Friday–late Sept., daily 10–6; Oct.–Easter, daily 10–4.*

The entire area is crowded with relics of the prehistoric age, so be sure to stop off at the **West Kennett Long Barrow,** a chambered tomb dating from around 3,250 BC, a mile east of Avebury on A4. About 7 miles east of Avebury on A4 is the attractive **⓷7** town of **Marlborough,** which developed as an important staging post on the old London–Bath stagecoach route. Today it is better known for its unusually wide main street, its elegant Georgian houses—these replace the medieval town center, which was destroyed in a great fire in 1653—and its celebrated public school. The grounds of the school, on the west side of town, enclose a small, manmade hill called Castle Mound, or Maerl's Barrow, which gave the town its name. This was said to be the grave of Merlin, King Arthur's court wizard, but it is clearly much older than the period when the historical Arthur may have lived. A tourist information center open in summer is housed in the 15th-century deconsecrated church of St. Peter and St. Paul.

Time Out | If you need a restorative after exploring Marlborough, relax under the traditional oak beams of **Sun** on High Street, a handsome 16th-century inn.

Leaving Marlborough, join A345 to continue the southward journey (about 17 miles) toward Stonehenge. At Amesbury, turn west onto A344. Here, near the junction with A303, stands one of England's most visited and most puzzling monuments.

⓷8 Most days, **Stonehenge** is dwarfed by its lonely isolation on the wide sweep of Salisbury Plain, the great circle of stones enclosed by barriers to keep back the relentless throngs of tourists. During the summer solstice, Stonehenge becomes the target of the feeble remnants of the Alternate Society, who embark on an annual struggle with the police to celebrate, in the monument's imposing shadow, a barely understood pagan festival. But if you visit in the early morning, when the crowds have not yet arrived, or in the evening, when the sky is heavy with scudding clouds, you can experience Stonehenge as it once was: a magical, mystical, awe-inspiring place.

Stonehenge was begun around 2,800 BC, enlarged between 2,100 and 1,900 BC, and altered yet again by 150 BC. It has been excavated and rearranged several times over the centuries. The medieval phrase "Stonehenge" means "hanging stones." (Interestingly enough, the use of "henge" to denote a circular arrangement of stone or wooden elements seems to have come from Stonehenge itself—an example of what wordsmiths call back-formation.) The monument, however, did not start out with great stones at all, but with the ditch and bank that still encircle the site. The first stone to be added was probably the Heel Stone, which stands outside the circle, near the main road.

Many of the huge stones that ringed the center were brought here from great distances. The original 80 bluestones (dolerite), which made up the two internal circles, were transported from the Preseli Mountains, near Fishguard on the Atlantic coast of Wales, presumably by raft on sea and river. Next they were dragged on rollers across country—a total journey of 130 miles as the crow flies, but closer to 240 by the easiest route. Later, great blocks of sarsen stone were quarried in north Wiltshire, dressed, and fitted together with primitive joints. The labor involved in quarrying, transporting, and carving these stones was astonishing, all the more so when you remember that it was accomplished before the major pyramids of Egypt were built.

We still do not know why the great project at Stonehenge was undertaken in the first place. It is fairly certain that it was a religious site, and that worship here involved the cycles of the sun; the alignment of the stones to point to sunrise at midsummer and sunset in midwinter makes this clear. One thing is certain: The Druids had nothing to do with the construction. The monument had already been in existence for nearly 2,000 years by the time they appeared.

There has been speculation that Stonehenge may have been a kind of neolithic computer, with a sophisticated astronomical purpose. Such theories are, of course, pure guesses, but fascinating nonetheless. *Stonehenge Decoded* by Gerald S. Hawkins is but one of many intriguing books on the subject.

As you can't get very close to the monoliths, and then only along one section of the site, it's a good idea to take a pair of binoculars along to make out the details more clearly. *Near Amesbury. Admission: £1.90 adults, 95p children, £1.50 senior citizens. Open Apr.–Sept., daily 10–6; Oct.–Mar., daily 10–4.*

Leaving Stonehenge, head south along A36 to Salisbury, then **39** follow A36 and local roads another 15 miles or so to **Lyndhurst,** known as the "capital of the New Forest." Alice Hargreaves (*née* Liddell), Lewis Carroll's Alice, is buried in the churchyard here. The town provides an excellent base for travelers wishing to explore this beautiful wooded region. This is also a good, easy area for hiking. Ask the **Tourist Information Center** in the main parking lot for details of local walks (tel. 0703/282269).

You have a choice of routes now. To explore the depths of the New Forest, continue southwest out of Lyndhurst along A35 (the road continues southwest to Bournemouth). **The New Forest** consists of 145 square miles of mainly open, unfenced countryside interspersed with dense woodland. It is the largest area of open countryside in southern Britain and a natural haven for herds of free-roaming deer, cattle, and hardy New Forest ponies.

The forest was "new" in 1079, when William the Conqueror cleared the area of farms and villages and turned it into his private hunting forest. He left it unfenced so as not to hinder the free run of deer, the main quarry of the royal hunting parties. Three centuries ago, large numbers of oaks were cut down to build houses and ships, but otherwise the landscape has not changed much over the last 1,000 years. Although some favorite spots can get crowded in summer, there is ample room to accommodate the many visitors who use the parking lots, picnic grounds, and campgrounds as hiking bases. Miles of walking trails criss-cross the region. Although minor roads pass through the forest, the best way to explore the area is to get out of your car and walk.

If you decide to explore more of the southern coastline, leave Lyndhurst by B3056 and travel the 6 miles or so to the town of **Beaulieu** (pronounced "Bewley"). It offers three major attractions (and one ticket gets you into all of them). These are the ruins of **Beaulieu Abbey; Palace House,** one of Britain's most popular stately homes; and the **National Motor Museum,** offering an unrivaled collection of vintage cars.

Beaulieu Abbey was established by King John in 1204 for the Cistercian order of monks, who gave their new home its name, which means "beautiful place." It was badly damaged three centuries later during the reign of Henry VIII, leaving only the cloister, the doorway, the gatehouse, and two buildings, one of which today contains a well-planned exhibition recreating daily life in the monastery. The gatehouse has been incorporated into Palace House, home of the Montagu family since 1538. In this stately home you can see drawing rooms, dining halls, and a number of very fine family portraits. The present Lord Montagu is noted for his work in establishing the **National Motor Museum,** which traces the development of motor transport from 1895 to the present with over 200 classic cars, buses, and motorcycles. Museum attractions include a monorail, audio-visual presentations, and a trip in a 1912 London bus. *Beaulieu, near Southampton, tel. 0590/612345. Admission to Palace House, Abbey, and Motor Museum: £6 adults, £4 children, £4.60 senior citizens. Open Easter–Sept., 10–6; Oct.–Easter, 10–5.*

Among local places of interest is **Buckler's Hard,** an almost perfectly restored 18th-century hamlet of 24 brick cottages, leading down to an old shipyard on the river Beaulieu. Nelson's favorite ship, H.M.S. *Agamemnon,* was built here of New Forest oak, as recalled in the fascinating **Maritime Museum.** *Beaulieu, tel. 0590/616203. Admission: £2.20 adults, £1.30 children, £1.70 senior citizens. Open Easter–May, daily 10–6; Jun.–Sept., daily 10–9; Oct.–Easter, daily 10–4:30.*

From Beaulieu, take any of the minor roads leading west through Lymington and pick up A337 for the popular seaside resort of Bournemouth, a journey of about 18 miles.

Tour 3: Southern Literary Landscapes: Bournemouth to Lyme Regis

Unlike most other large towns in the south of England, **Bournemouth** has a relatively short and uneventful history. It was founded in 1810 by Lewis Tregonwell, an ex-Army officer who had taken a liking to the area when stationed there some years before. He settled near what is now **The Square** and planted the first pine trees in the steep little valleys—or chines—cutting through the cliffs to the famous Bournemouth sands. The scent of fir trees was said to be good for "consumption" sufferers (tuberculosis), and the town grew steadily as more and more people came for prolonged rest cures. Today Bournemouth is one of the south coast's most popular vacation destinations.

The Square and the beach are linked by gardens laid out with flowering trees and lawns. This is an excellent spot to relax and listen to stirring music wafting from the **Pine Walk bandstand.** Regular musical programs take place at the **Pavilion** and at the **Winter Gardens** (home of the Bournemouth Symphony Orchestra) nearby. There are also regular shows at the **Bournemouth International Centre** in Exeter Road (tel. 0202/297297), which includes a selection of restaurants, bars, and a swimming pool.

Time Out Stop at **The Coriander** (14 Richmond Hill), just up the road from the Pine Walk bandstand, for an inexpensive lunch with a Mexican flavor.

On the corner of Hilton Road stands **St. Peter's** parish church, easily recognizable by its 200-foot-high tower and spire. Lewis Tregonwell is buried in the churchyard. Here, too, you will notice the elaborate tombstone of Mary Shelley, author of *Frankenstein* and wife of the great Romantic poet, whose heart is buried with her. Admirers of Shelley will want to visit the **Casa Magni Shelley Museum** in **Boscombe** (on the west side of Bournemouth), with its touching collection of Shelley memorabilia. *Boscombe Manor, Beechwood Ave., tel. 0202/551009. Small admission fee. Open June–Sept., Mon.–Sat. 10:30–5; Oct.–May, Thurs.–Sat. 10:30–5.*

In Bournemouth itself you will find the interesting **Russell-Coates Art Gallery and Museum.** This late-Victorian mansion, perched on top of East Cliff, overflows with Victorian paintings and miniatures, cases of butterflies, and treasures from the Far East, including an exquisite suit of Japanese armor. *Tel. 0202/551009. Admission: £1 adults, 50p children, free on Sat. Open Mon.–Sat. 10–5.*

Time Out If you are looking for an old-fashioned tea, try the lounge of the **Cumberland Hotel** (East Overcliffe Drive), which shifts out of doors in summer.

Leaving Bournemouth, follow the signs northwest (A341) to
43 the quiet market town of **Wimbourne Minster,** 10 miles away. Its impressive twin-towered **Minster** (or church) makes it seem like a miniature cathedral city. A Tudor building in High Street is now the **Priest's House Museum** and garden. The museum features Roman and Iron-Age exhibits, including a cryptic, three-faced Celtic stone head. *23 High St., tel. 0202/882533. Admission: 80p adults, 20p children. Open Good Friday–Sept., Mon.–Sat. 10:30–4:30, Sun. 2–4:30.*

Time Out At 26 Westborough you'll find **Quinneys,** a bakery and eating house run by the Skidmore family for nearly 30 years. They sell delicious pastries and cakes, and have a daily-changing blackboard of lunch specialties, such as grilled trout.

Turning south now, follow A349 about 6 miles to the fast-
44 growing modern town of **Poole,** which has one of the largest natural harbors in the world, with more than 90 miles of serrated coastline harboring myriad bays, inlets, and islands.
45 Ferries make regular trips to **Brownsea Island,** which belongs to the National Trust and is open to visitors who enjoy roaming the woods, relaxing on the beach, and observing rare water fowl. *Boats from Poole Quay (tel. 0202/680580 or 0202/666226)*

leave about every 30 minutes. Round trip: £2.75 adults, £1.75 children, £2.50 senior citizens. Landing charge: £1.70 adults, £4.50 family ticket. Operates Apr.–Sept., daily 10–8 (or dusk).

46 From Poole, follow A351 southwest to Wareham, then southeast about 12 miles to **Corfe Castle,** whose spectacular ruins rise majestically on a hill overlooking the pretty village of Corfe. The castle site guards a gap in the surrounding range of hills, and has been fortified from very early times. The present ruins are of the castle built between 1105, when the great central keep was erected, and the 1270s, when the outer walls and towers were built. It owes its ramshackle state to Cromwell's soldiers, who blew it up in 1646 during the Civil War. This is one of the most impressive ruins in Britain, and will stir the imagination of all history buffs. It is looked after by the National Trust, and they run a coffee shop at the entrance. *Tel. 0929/ 480921. Admission: £2 adults, £1 children under 16. Open Mar.–Oct., daily 10–5:30; Nov.–Feb., weekends, noon–3:30.*

47 From Corfe Castle, take A351 and A352 west for 21 miles to **Dorchester.** Dorchester is in many ways a traditional southern country town. To appreciate its character, visit the local Wednesday market in the **Market Square,** where you can find Dorset delicacies such as Blue Vinney cheese (which some connoisseurs prefer to Blue Stilton), and various handcrafted items, which are also available at the **Dorset Crafts Guild Shop** (*see* Shopping, below).

Dorchester owes much of its fame to its connection with Thomas Hardy, whose bronze statue looks westward from a bank on **Colliton Walk.** Born in a cottage (now preserved by the National Trust) in the hamlet of Higher Brockhampton, about 3 miles northeast of Dorchester, Hardy attended school in the town and was apprentice to an architect here. Later he had a house, Max Gate (not open to the public), built to his own design on the edge of Dorchester. Hardy's study there has been reconstructed in the **Dorset County Museum,** which houses a diverse and fascinating collection. Exhibits range from ancient Celtic and Roman remains to a vicious, 19th-century mantrap, used to snare poachers. It was this very trap that Hardy had in mind when writing the mantrap episode in *The Woodlanders. High West St., tel. 0305/262735. Admission: £1.50 adults, 75p children. Open Mon.–Sat. 10–5.*

Time Out Try lunch at **The Royal Oak** (20 High West St.), whose first license to sell liquor was granted in 1697.

Roman history and artifacts abound in Dorchester. The town was laid out by the Romans around AD 70, and if you walk along **Bowling Alley Walk, West Walk,** and **Colliton Walk,** you will have followed the approximate line of the original Roman town walls. On the north side of Colliton Park lies an excavated **Roman villa** with a marvelously preserved mosaic floor. Possibly even more interesting is **Maumbury Rings,** the remains of a Roman amphitheater on the edge of town. The site was later used as a place of execution. (Hardy's *Mayor of Casterbridge* contains a vivid evocation of the Rings.) As late as 1706, a girl was burned at the stake here.

The town is also associated with Monmouth's Rebellion of 1685, when Charles II's illegitimate son, the Duke of Monmouth, led a rising against his unpopular uncle, James II. The rising was ruthlessly put down, and the Chief Justice, Lord Jeffreys, conducted the Bloody Assizes to try rebels and sympathizers, many of whom were from Dorset and Hampshire (*see* Winchester in Tour 1). A swearing, bullying drunkard, Jeffreys was the prototypical hanging judge, and memories of his mass executions lingered for centuries throughout the South. His courtroom in Dorchester was located in what is now the Antelope Hotel on South Street.

Time Out | Sample the homemade cakes and other pastries at the poetically named **Horse with the Red Umbrella** (10 High West St.).

Excursions to the north of Dorchester will quickly bring you onto the Downs, the chalky hills which curve across the northern half of the county, sheltering quiet villages and remote farms linked by narrow, winding roads. Take time to explore one of the last undeveloped areas of southern England; there are no major highways or railroads here, and it still retains much of the rural, strongly agricultural atmosphere of the 19th century.

48 North, 3 miles on A352, is the village of **Cerne Abbas,** worth a short exploration on foot. Some appealing Tudor houses line the road beside the church. Nearby you can also see the original village stocks. If you pass through the graveyard, you will arrive at a shallow pool known as **St. Augustine's Well.** Legend holds that the saint created it by striking the ground with his staff, thereby ensuring a regular supply of baptismal water. Tenth-century **Cerne Abbey** itself is now a ruin, with little left to see except its old gateway, though the nearby Abbey House is still in use.

Cerne Abbas's main claim to fame is the colossal **figure of a giant,** cut in chalk on a hillside overlooking the village. The 180-foot-long giant with a huge club bears a striking resemblance to Hercules, although he probably originated as a tribal fertility symbol long before the Romans. His outlines are formed by two-foot-wide trenches, regularly cleared of overgrowth by local people.

49 Return to the outskirts of Dorchester on A352 or any one of a number of scenic minor roads. Here, stop first at **Maiden Castle** (2 miles southwest, on A354), which is, after Stonehenge, the most extraordinary pre-Roman archaeological site in England. It is not a castle at all, but an enormous, complex hill fort of stone and earth, built, like Stonehenge, by England's mysterious prehistoric inhabitants. Many centuries later it was a Celtic stronghold. In AD 43, the invading Romans, under the general (later emperor) Vespasian, stormed it. One of the grimmest exhibits now on display in the Dorset County Museum in Dorchester was excavated here: the skeleton of a Celtic warrior transfixed by a Roman arrow. To experience an uncanny silence and sense of mystery, climb Maiden Castle early in the day (access to it is unrestricted), when other tourists are unlikely to be stirring.

Any road leading south from Dorchester will bring you to the characteristic quiet bays, shingle beaches, and low chalk cliffs of the Dorset coast. The well-marked **Dorset Coast Path** enables you to walk along some or all of the shoreline, or you can drive the narrow, country lanes hugging the coast (*see* Sports and Fitness, below).

50 About 8 miles south of Dorchester on A354 is **Weymouth,** Dorset's main coastal resort, known both for its wide, safe, sandy beaches and its royal connections. King George III took up sea-bathing here for his health in 1789, setting a trend among the wealthy and fashionable people of his day. Their influence has left Weymouth with many fine period buildings, including the Georgian row houses lining the esplanade. Historical details clamor for your attention. A wall in **Maiden Street,** for example, still holds a cannonball that was embedded in it during the Civil War. Nearby, a **column** commemorates the launching of the American forces from Weymouth on D-Day, June 6, 1944.

Time Out Try the **Cork and Bottle** cellar bar on the Esplanade for a satisfying pub lunch.

51
52 A 5-mile-long peninsula jutting south from Weymouth leads to the Isle of **Portland,** the eastern end of the unique geological curiosity known as **Chesil Beach**—a 200-yard-wide, 30-foot-high bank of pebbles that decrease in size from east to west. The beach extends for 18 miles along the shore. Here a powerful undertow makes swimming dangerous. Tombstones in local churchyards attest to the many shipwrecks the beach has caused.

53 At the western end of Chesil Beach lies the village of **Abbotsbury.** A lagoon here is a famous breeding place for swans, first introduced by Benedictine monks in the 11th century. The swans have remained ever since, building new nests every year in the soft, moist pampas grass. *Abbotsbury Swannery, New Barn Rd., tel. 0305/871684. Admission: £2.30 adults, 80p children under 16, £2 senior citizens. Open Apr.– Nov., daily 9:30–5.*

On the hills above Abbotsbury stands **Hardy's Monument**— dedicated not to the novelist, as many suppose, but to Sir Thomas Masterman Hardy, Nelson's flag captain at Trafalgar, to whom Nelson's dying words, "Kiss me, Hardy" (or was it, "Kismet, Hardy"?) were addressed. The monument itself is without much charm, but the surrounding view more than makes up for it. In clear weather you can scan the whole coastline between the Isle of Wight and Start Point in Devon.

Time Out The thatched **Ilchester Arms,** near to the Swannery, is an ideal spot for lunch, with lots of good hot dishes in a conservatory restaurant.

54 Two more places of interest in southwest Dorset are the so-called **Fossil Coast** and the ancient town of **Lyme Regis.** The cliffs in this area are especially fossil-rich. In 1810, a local child named Mary Anning dug out a complete ichthyosaurus here (it is on display in London's Natural History Museum). You may prefer to browse in the **Fossil Shop** in Lyme Regis. The town itself is famous for its curving stone breakwater, **The Cobb,** built by King Edward I in the 13th century to improve the harbor. It was here that the Duke of Monmouth landed in 1685 in his ill-fated attempt to overthrow his uncle, James II. The Cobb figures prominently in the movie *The French Lieutenant's*

Woman, based on John Fowles's novel. Fowles himself is currently Lyme's most famous resident.

What to See and Do with Children

Apart from beaches and ordinary playgrounds, many tourist attractions in the South now incorporate adventure playgrounds or similar facilities for children. Here are a few additional ideas.

Blackgang Chine is a theme park built on top of a cliff overlooking a former smugglers' landing place. It features Dinosaur-Land, Smugglers-Land, Jungle-Land, and other attractions for ages 3–12. *Ventnor, Isle of Wight, tel. 0983/730330. Admission: £3.50 adults, £2.50 children. Open Apr.–Oct., daily 10–5; late May–late Sept., daily 10–10.*

Paulton's Park is a large theme park for children of all ages, with a Gypsy Museum, Rio Grande Train, Cap'n Blood's Cavern, Magic Forest, and various rides. There's enough to occupy a full day, and refreshments are also available. *Just off exit 2 of M27, near Southampton, tel. 0703/814442. Admission: £5.25 adults, £4 children and senior citizens. Open Apr.–Oct., daily 10–7.*

Dorchester's popular **Dinosaur Museum** has life-size models and various interactive displays. *Icen Way, off High East St., tel. 0305/269880. Admission: £2.50 adults, £1.50 children, £1.80 senior citizens, £6.80 family ticket. Open daily 9:30–5:30.*

A good conventional amusement park, also open daily, is located beside the long, safe beach of **Hayling Island,** a family vacation resort close to Portsmouth and joined to the mainland by a bridge.

Both adults and children will love **Natural World** in Poole, a superb aquarium and "seaquarium" featuring sharks, piranhas, crocodiles, and rarer creatures. *Poole Quay, tel. 0202/686712. Admission: £2.95 adults, £1.50 children, £8 family ticket. Open daily 10–6.*

Off the Beaten Track

Close to Stockbridge (10 miles northwest of Winchester by A272), is **Danebury Hill,** a fascinating Iron Age hill fort, where careful excavations have revealed the structure of complex earthworks surrounding a complete town. Danebury Hill can be visited any time without charge, and it lies in a good area for hiking.

An important slice of English history, not without contemporary significance, can be found in the Dorset village of **Tolpuddle,** about 7 miles east of Dorchester on A35. A small museum here commemorates six 19th-century farm laborers who were transported to hard labor in the Australian convict colony for resisting exploitation by their employer, and who thus won fame as early martyrs in the labor union movement.

From east to west between Salisbury Plain and the Marlborough Downs lies the beautiful **Vale of Pewsey.** It is especially famous for its splendid **White Horse** cut into the hillside. This one is relatively modern, though the custom of inscribing giant horses on Wiltshire hills dates back to prehistoric times.

Shopping

In the South these days, well-known chain stores are being increasingly challenged by newly established, independent specialist stores. These are now so numerous as to constitute a specialty in their own right and a boon to the visitor—not only as outlets for such local crafts as jewelry and ceramics, but also as the first choice of shoppers with discriminating tastes in everything from food to furniture.

Bere Regis **Paws Jewelry,** (Southbrook Workshop, tel. 0929/471808), located 11 miles eastward from Dorchester, on A35, is a diamond dealership specializing in attractive jewelry. It's wise to check by phone before dropping in.

Bournemouth **Alderholt Mill** (Sandleheath Rd., west of Fordingbridge, off B3078) specializes in woodwork and ceramics. Exhibitions by local artists are also held in this attractive converted water mill.

Cerne Abbas **Cerne Valley Forge** (Mill Lane) keeps the traditional craft of wrought iron still very much alive.

Dorchester **Dorset Crafts Guild Shop** (19 Durngate St.). Serious crafts collectors will be interested in a visit. The stock is drawn from over 60 Dorset studios and tends toward upscale pricing.
Aquarius Pottery (Yew Tree Cottage, Uploders, near Bridport, 1 mi off A35, west of Dorchester) is a beautifully situated country workshop whose owner makes domestic and ornamental pottery in various colors, including his own "Aquarius blue."

Poole **Poole Pottery** (The Quay) has a shop where you can buy the creamy ware which has been popular in Britain for many years, as well as watch demonstrations of the pottery being made and decorated.

Ryde The **Royal Victoria Arcade** (Union St.) contains 22 small stores selling books, antiques, jewelry, clothes, and Victoriana.
Don't be misled by the small size of **G & M Jewellery** (123 High St.), where jewelry is made to order, repairs are done, and many delicate items in unusual materials—onyx, crystal, hematite, titanium—are produced.

Salisbury **Watsons** (8-9 Queen St.) is worth visiting for its circa-1306 building, which has some original windows, a carved oak mantelpiece, and other period features. The company specializes in Aynsley and Wedgwood bone china, Waterford and Dartington glass, Royal Doulton crystal, and a wide range of fine ornaments.

Winchester The **Antiques Market** (King's Walk) sells crafts and gift items, as well as antiques. A complete list of local antique stores is available from Winchester Tourist Information Center (tel. 0962/840222, ext. 2361).
H.M. Gilbert, an antiquarian bookseller, is located at 19 The Square, in a network of ancient streets. His shop is housed in five medieval cottages, with the antiquarian section in a 15th-century hall.

Markets Open-air markets are an almost daily event throughout the South (a complete list is available from the Southern Tourist

Board). Among the best are Salisbury's traditional city market (Tues. and Sat.), Kingsland Market in Southampton for bric-à-brac (Thurs.), and a general country market (Wed.) at Ringwood, near Bournemouth. New Forest ponies are rounded up Wild West style and auctioned to dealers at the pony market, held six times a year beside the B3506 (Lyndhurst to Beaulieu road) near the Beaulieu Station Hotel. Check dates with the Lyndhurst Tourist Information Center (tel. 0703/282269).

Sports and Fitness

With miles of coastline and accessible countryside, the South has plenty of facilities for golf, hiking, horseback riding, and the local favorite, fishing. Local tourist information offices are an excellent source of information on the sports opportunities in each area.

Bicycling Bicycling is always a good (and healthy) way to explore an area. Rent a bicycle for a week or even just half a day, in order to discover the delights of this fairly level area of the English countryside.

Bikes can be rented from many centers; try **Peter Hansford, Bridge Rd.**, Park Gate, Southampton, tel. 0489/573249; **Weymouth Cycles,** 6C King St., Weymouth, tel. 0305/787677; or **H. Duck,** 114 High St., Marlborough, tel. 0672/512170.

Golf Golf is a popular pastime in this area. Apart from private clubs, there are municipal courses where you can have an inexpensive game. Here is just a small selection of the local courses you may want to try; non-members are usually welcome, but call first to check. In the New Forest go to **Lyndhurst Golf Course,** tel. 0703/282450; other courses include **Romsey Golf Club,** Nursling, Southampton, tel. 0703/734637; **Shanklin & Sandown,** The Fairway, Shanklin, Isle of Wight, tel. 0983/403217; **Salisbury and South Wiltshire Golf Club,** Netherhampton, Salisbury, tel. 0722/742645; **Marlborough Golf Club,** The Common, Marlborough, tel. 0672/512147; **Lyme Regis Golf Club,** Timber Hill, Lyme Regis, tel. 02974/2963.

Hiking The **Dorset Coast Path** runs from Lyme Regis to Poole, 72 miles in all. You can walk all or only a part of the route. There are some highlights along the way, especially Golden Cap, the highest point on the South Coast, with spectacular views; the swannery at Abbotsbury; Lulworth Cove; and Chesil Bank. *Details from any local tourist office.*

Horseback Riding The New Forest was custom-built for riding and there's no better way to enjoy this huge area of woodland and heathland than on horseback. There are many riding stables in and around the forest, as well as in other parts of the South, and most cater to the novice as well as the more accomplished rider. **The New Park Stables Equestrian Centre,** Lyndhurst Rd., Brockenhurst, tel. 05902/3467, gives full instruction. Try also **Bramble Hill Riding Centre,** Bramble Hill Hotel, Bramshaw, tel. 0703/812420; **Russell Equestrian Centre,** Black Farm, Gaters Hill, West End, Southampton, tel. 0703/473693.

Dining and Lodging

Dining Fertile soil, well-stocked rivers, and a long coastline ensure excellent farm produce and a plentiful stock of fish throughout the South. Try fresh-grilled river trout or sea bass poached in brine, or dine like a king on the New Forest's famous venison.

Highly recommended restaurants are indicated by a star ★.

Category	Cost*
Very Expensive	over £35
Expensive	£25–£35
Moderate	£12–£25
Inexpensive	under £12

per person including first course, main course, dessert, and VAT; excluding drinks

Lodging Modern hotel chains are well represented in all the major centers, while rural areas offer a wide choice of elegant country house hotels, traditional coaching inns, and modest guest houses. Note that some seaside hotels, especially in the Bournemouth area, are unwilling to accept one-night bookings in the busy season.

Highly recommended hotels are indicated by a star ★.

Category	Cost*
Very Expensive	over £130
Expensive	£80–£130
Moderate	£45–£80
Inexpensive	under £45

All prices are for two people sharing a double room, including service, breakfast, and VAT.

Abbotsbury **Manor Hotel.** Ancient features at this comfortable hotel/
Dining restaurant (whose pedigree is over 700 years old) include flagstone floors and beamed ceilings. Among the English and French dishes in which the Manor specializes are scallops and guinea fowl. It also has 10 rooms for lodging. *Beach Rd., West Bexington (3 mi west of Abbotsbury), tel. 0308/897616. Reservations advised. Dress: informal. AE, MC, V. Moderate.*

Bonchurch **Winterbourne Hotel.** This Isle of Wight manor house was one of
Lodging Charles Dickens's many homes. The bedrooms are named after characters in *David Copperfield*, part of which he wrote here. The furnishings are, of course, Victorian, and the gardens beautifully kept. *Near Ventnor, PO38 1RQ, tel. 0983/852535. 19 rooms, 17 with bath. Facilities: restaurant, outdoor pool. AE, DC, MC, V. Closed Nov.–Feb. Moderate.*

Blandford Forum **La Belle Alliance.** There are constantly-changing set menus in
Dining this attractive, small, country restaurant. The relaxed decor (pink and green) and the friendly husband-and-wife owners make for an enjoyable meal. This is one of the increasing num-

ber of British restaurants that bans smoking. There are also five bedrooms. *Portnam Lodge, Whitecliffe Mill St., tel. 0258/ 452842. Reservations advised. Open Tues.–Sat. dinner, Sun. lunch. AE, MC, V. Moderate.*

Bournemouth
Dining

Langtry Manor Hotel. The French cuisine here is served on lacy tablecloths, with real silver cutlery and other details in keeping with the restaurant's Edwardian atmosphere (Lillie Langtry was the mistress of King Edward VII and he built this house for her in 1877). The dishes include Lillie's Special—meringue in the shape of a swan. There's an Edwardian banquet every Saturday. *26 Derby Rd., East Cliff, tel. 0202/23887. Reservations advised. Dress: informal. AE, DC, MC, V. Moderate.*

Sophisticats. As the name suggests, there's a lot of felinity in the decor here. This useful restaurant, hidden in a shopping mall, just outside the center of town, is especially adept with seafood, though there's Javanese fillet steak on the menu, too. It's quite small (seating just 32), so a reservation's a good idea. *43 Charminster Rd., tel. 0202/291019. Dress: informal. Open Tues.–Sat., dinner only. No credit cards. Moderate.*

Lodging
★

Carlton Hotel. Formerly a private mansion, built in 1900, this gracious cliff-top hotel has large rooms, some with balconies overlooking the sea. The hotel's restaurant, **Fredericks,** is very expensive, with a set dinner menu, but the setting is sumptuous and the food excellent. *Meyrick Rd., East Overcliff BH1 3DN, tel. 0202/22011. 65 rooms with bath. Facilities: restaurant, swimming pool, sauna, solarium, gym, games room, hairdresser, spa. AE, DC, MC, V. Expensive.*

Norfolk Royale. This hotel has been delightfully refurbished in full Edwardian style. It's just five minutes' walk from the city center. Some rooms are specially set aside for ladies, non-smokers, or the disabled. *Richmond Hill BH2 6EN, tel. 0202/ 551521. 95 rooms with bath. Facilities: 2 restaurants (1 buffet), coffee shop, swimming pool, Jacuzzi, steam room, in-house movies. AE, DC, MC, V. Expensive.*

Dorchester
Dining and Lodging
★

Yalbury Cottage. A thatched roof and inglenook fireplaces enhance the traditional character of Yalbury Cottage, just 2½ miles east of Dorchester, close to Hardy's cottage. Lamb Fenchurch (with port and red-currant sauce), and beef fillets in puff pastry, are among the English and Continental dishes featured. There are also eight comfortable bedrooms available. *Lower Brockhampton, DT2 8PZ, tel. 0305/262382. Reservations advised. Dress: informal. MC, V. Closed Jan. Moderate.*

Lodging
★

Casterbridge Hotel. This Georgian building (1790) reflects its age with period furniture and old-world elegance—it's small but full of character. *49 High East St., DT1 1HU, tel. 0305/ 264043. 15 rooms with bath. Facilities: bar, conservatory, courtyard garden. AE, DC, MC, V. Closed Dec. 25–26. Moderate.*

Freshwater
Lodging

Farringford Hotel. Although this was once the splendid home of the Victorian poet laureate, Alfred, Lord Tennyson, it is now an unpretentious hotel. The 18th-century house, set in 33 acres of grounds, offers 24 self-catering suites and cottages, as well as normal bedrooms. *Bedbury Lane, PO40 9PE, tel. 0983/ 752500. 68 rooms with bath. Facilities: restaurant, 9-hole golf, outdoor pool, tennis. AE, DC, MC, V. Moderate.*

Hamble
Dining
★

Beth's Restaurant. Just 7 miles southeast of Southampton, French and English dishes are served in this small Queen Anne house (1710) on the quayside. This family-run restaurant has the relaxed atmosphere of a private home. The specialties include braised sea bass and lobster. *The Quay, Hamble, tel. 0703/454314. Reservations advised. Dress: informal. AE, DC, MC, V. Closed Jan. 1–22. Moderate.*

Lynmouth
Lodging
★

Rising Sun. A recent conversion from a 14th-century inn and a row of thatched cottages has created this intriguing hotel. It has great views over Lynmouth, especially from the terraced garden out back. The rooms are furnished either in pine or older pieces, and the whole effect is comfortable and welcoming. The poet Shelley spent his honeymoon in a cottage in the garden. *The Harbour, EX35 6EQ, tel. 0598/53223. 16 rooms with bath. Facilities: restaurant, garden. AE, MC, V. Closed Jan.– mid-Feb. Moderate.*

Marlborough
Lodging

Ivy House. This Georgian house is right on Marlborough's attractive, colonnaded High Street, and makes an excellent touring base. The bedrooms are comfortably furnished, with small modern bathrooms attached. There is a courtyard bistro for relaxed meals. *43 High St., SN8 1HJ, tel. 0672/55333. 38 rooms with bath. Facility: restaurant. AE, DC, MC, V. Moderate.*

New Milton
Dining and Lodging
★

Chewton Glen. Once the home of Captain Frederick Marryat, author of *The Children of the New Forest* and many naval adventure novels, this 18th-century country house is now a deluxe hotel set in extensive grounds. All the rooms are sumptuously furnished with an eye to the minutest detail. Gourmets consider its restaurant, the **Marryat Room,** and the cooking of its chef, Pierre Chevillard, worthy of a pilgrimage. With genuinely helpful and friendly staff, Chewton Glen deserves its fine reputation. *Christchurch Rd., New Milton BH25 6QS, tel. 0425/275341. 46 rooms with bath. Facilities: swimming pool, tennis, golf course, helipad, in-house movies. Restaurant reservations required. Jacket and tie required. AE, DC, MC, V. Expensive.*

Poole
Lodging

Antelope Hotel. This historic coaching inn lies near the quay. It is partly 15th, partly 18th century, and has been well modernized. The bedrooms at the back are the quietest, but those in front have more character. *Old High St., BH15 1BP, tel. 0202/ 672029. 21 rooms with bath. Facilities: restaurant. AE, DC, MC, V. Moderate.*

Portsmouth
Dining

Bistro Montparnasse. Candles, prints, and pink tablecloths help foster the intimate atmosphere of a traditional French restaurant. Among the dishes featured are mussels in saffron sauce, and a refreshingly sharp lemon soufflé. *103 Palmerston Rd., Southsea, tel. 0705/816754. Reservations advised. Dress: informal. AE, DC, MC, V. Closed Sun. and Mon. Moderate.*

Romsey
Dining

Old Manor House. This is one of those restaurants that is inseparable from its owner/chef, in this case Mauro Bregoli. The decor is very typical of the area, with oak beams and huge fireplaces, and the food is rich and flavorsome. Specialties include quenelle of pike, duck breast with apples, hare, and venison. The winelist is exceptionally good. *21 Palmerston St., tel. 0794/517353. Reservations required. Jacket and tie required. MC, V. Closed Sun. evening, Mon., 3 weeks Aug., Christmas. Expensive.*

Lodging
★
Potters Heron Hotel. An ideal place to stay if you're visiting Broadlands, this hotel has been renovated, adding a modern extension to the original thatched building. There's a choice of old or new rooms to suit your taste; many have balconies. Dine in the English restaurant with its table d'hôte and à la carte menus. *Ampfield (3 mi east of Romsey) SO51 9ZF, tel. 0703/ 266611. 60 rooms with bath. Facilities: sauna, game rooms, fitness equipment. AE, DC, MC, V. Closed Christmas. Moderate.*

Ryde
Dining
Dean House. In this comfortable, stylish restaurant on a hill overlooking the seafront, the talented chef specializes in traditional English dishes such as smoked fish and pepper steak. *2 Dover St., The Esplanade, tel. 0983/62535. Reservations required. Dress: informal. AE, DC, MC, V. Moderate.*

Lodging
The Ryde Castle. Ivy-clad walls, battlements, and commanding views of the sea set the scene at this first-class hotel with many period features. It was originally built in the 16th century by Henry VIII to defend the Solent. It is now being tastefully modernized, and standards of service and comfort are high. *The Esplanade, PO33 1JA, tel. 0983/63755. 17 rooms with bath. Facilities: 2 restaurants, 3 bars, lounge, in-house movies. AE, DC, MC, V. Expensive.*

Salisbury
Dining
★
Crustaceans. Here, the serene blue-and-pink decor makes for a stylish, contemporary setting. This restaurant offers traditional fish dishes, including Dover sole, bass, turbot, and John Dory, as well as more exotic items such as bouillabaisse and crayfish. During the winter season you can sample local game, too. *2–4 Ivy St., tel. 0722/333948. Reservations advised. Jacket and tie required. MC, V. Closed Sun. and Mon. lunch. Jan. Moderate.*

Harper's. This is a spacious, airy, second-floor restaurant overlooking the market place. Its cuisine mingles English and French dishes and its specialties include chicken with ginger and fillet of salmon. There is a good-value Shopper's Special lunch. Friendly staff make dining here a pleasure. *7 Ox Row, Market Place, tel. 0722/333118. Reservations advised. Dress: informal. DC, MC, V. Closed Sun. Moderate.*

Dining and Lodging
Red Lion Hotel. A former coaching inn—parts of the building date from 1320—this hotel has been in the same family for 70 years. There's a choice of comfortable rooms in either modern or antique style. It's centrally located and an ideal base for exploring the city. *Milford St., SP1 2AN, tel. 0722/23334. 50 rooms with bath. Facilities: restaurant, bistro. AE, DC, MC, V. Expensive.*

★
Byways House. Friendly service, good value for money, and a quiet location are some of the reasons the century-old hotel is popular with visitors. Ask for a room with a view of the cathedral. *31 Fowlers Rd., SP1 2QP, tel. 0722/28364. 20 rooms, 13 with bath. Facilities: large garden. No credit cards. Moderate.*

Southampton
Dining
La Brasserie. This is a busy spot at lunchtime, popular with the business community, though it quiets down in the evening. The decor is straightforward and ungimmicky, while the atmosphere is as traditionally French as the menu. *33-34 Oxford St., tel. 0703/221046. Reservations advised at lunch. Dress: informal. AE, MC, V. Closed Sat. lunch and Sun. Moderate.*

Lodging **The Dolphin Hotel.** Originally a Georgian coaching inn—though there's been an inn of some sort on this site for seven centuries—the Dolphin offers stylish accommodations in large, comfortable rooms. The service is excellent—discreet but attentive. *35 High St., SO9 2DS, tel. 0703/339955. 74 rooms with bath. Facilities: restaurant, garden. AE, DC, MC, V. Expensive.*

Warminster **Bishopstrow House.** It's not often that you'll find a Georgian
Dining and Lodging house converted into a luxurious hotel that combines modern
★ features, such as Jacuzzis, with antiques and fine carpets. There's an airy conservatory, attractive public areas, and peaceful rooms overlooking the grounds (25 acres) or an interior courtyard. The restaurant offers imaginatively prepared meals, lovely views into the gardens, and a fixed-price menu which is regularly changed. Bishopstrow House is 1½ miles out of town. *Boreham Rd., BA12 9HH, tel. 0985/212312. 32 rooms with bath. Facilities: indoor and outdoor pools, tennis, fishing available, helipad. AE, DC, MC, V. Very Expensive.*

West Lulworth **Castle Inn.** This is a charming thatched hotel just five minutes'
Lodging walk from the sea. It has a flagstone bar and other 15th-century features. There's a good restaurant with an à la carte menu for evening meals and Sunday lunch. There are satisfying walks to take in the immediate vicinity. *Main St., BH20 5RN, tel. 092941/311. 16 rooms, 10 with bath. Facilities: bar, garden. AE, DC, MC, V. Inexpensive.*

Weymouth **Perry's.** A fairly basic restaurant, right by the harbor, with
Dining simple dishes of the best local seafood. Try skate with capers and black butter—a fish not found in many restaurants these days. *The Harbourside, 4 Trinity Rd., tel. 0305/785799. Reservations advised. Dress: informal. MC, V. Closed Sun. lunch. Moderate.*

Dining and Lodging **Streamside Hotel.** Quiet and cozy, this hotel/restaurant on the
★ outskirts of town always graces its tables with fresh flowers and candles. The cuisine is English, with specialties such as smoked salmon with melon and steak in cream and brandy sauce. There are 15 comfortable rooms available, and the hotel, with award-winning gardens, is only 200 yards from the beach. *Preston Rd., DT3 6PX, tel. 0305/833121. Reservations advised. Dress: informal. AE, DC, MC, V. Moderate.*

Winchester **Royal.** This is quite a classy hotel, with an attractive walled
Dining and Lodging garden and some very comfortable bedrooms. It's within easy reach of the cathedral, but lies on a quiet side street. You can have an excellent lunch in the bar, or a fuller meal in the moderately priced restaurant. This is a Best Western hotel, but one of the swankier links in a chain that's better known for its budget prices. *St. Peter St., SO23 8BS, tel. 0962/840840. 59 rooms with bath. Facilities: restaurant, garden. Reservations advised for the restaurant. Jacket and tie required. AE, DC, MC, V. Expensive.*

Wykeham Arms. This old inn is centrally located, close to the cathedral and the college. The four popular bars are happily cluttered with everything from old sports equipment to pewter mugs. The seven bedrooms are comfortably furnished in pine. The restaurant is very popular with the locals, so call ahead. *75 Kingsgate St., SO23 9PE, tel. 0962/61611. 7 rooms with bath. Facilities: restaurant, garden, sauna. Moderate.*

Lodging   **Lainston House.** This is an elegant country-house hotel with wood paneling and other restored 17th-century features. All rooms are attractively decorated and comfortably furnished, but do try for the Garden Suite, which has access to the grounds. *Sparsholt (3½ mi northwest of Winchester) SO21 2LT, tel. 0962/63588. 32 rooms with bath. Facilities: tennis, 63 acres parkland, helipad. AE, DC, MC, V. Expensive.*

Wooton Common   **Lugley's.** A Victorian cottage converted into a restaurant on *Dining*   the edge of Newport, Isle of Wight, is a certainty for a cozy am-★   bience. In its homey atmosphere enjoy such English delicacies as smoked haddock mousseline, and lobster with coconut sauce, or rose petal ice cream. *Staplers Rd., Wootton Common, tel. 0983/882202. Reservations advised. Dress: informal. No credit cards. Open Tues.–Sat. dinner only. Closed 2 weeks Feb. and Nov. Moderate.*

The Arts

Festivals   The **Salisbury Festival** (tel. 0722/23883), held in September, features excellent classical concerts, recitals, and plays.

Bournemouth holds a **Music Festival** June–July, with choirs, brass bands, and orchestras, some often visiting from overseas.

The **Gold Hill Fair,** a traditional street fair held in Shaftesbury in July, features music and crafts. For information, call 0747/51881.

Theaters   The refurbished **Mayflower Theatre** (Commercial Rd., tel. 0703/229771) in Southampton is among the larger theaters outside London and has a full program of popular plays and concerts.

The **Nuffield Theatre,** on Southampton University campus, has its own repertory company and also hosts national touring companies, which perform some of the leading West End productions. Call 0703/671871 for program details.

The **Salisbury Playhouse** (Malthouse Lane, tel. 0722/25173) presents high caliber drama all year 'round, and is the focus for the Salisbury Festival.

6 The Southwest

Introduction

The Southwest of England, known as the West Country, comprises three counties—Somerset, Devon, and Cornwall—each with its own distinct character. Long one of Britain's favorite vacation areas, the region offers an endless variety of natural and historic attractions. Despite a continuous influx of visitors, the Southwest has managed to retain its rugged, magical beauty, and in addition to its pleasant villages and popular beaches, offers vast tracts of moorland and unspoiled wooded stretches, ideal for walking.

Although King Arthur's name is linked with more than 150 places in Britain, no area of the country can claim stronger ties than the West Country. According to tradition, Arthur was born at Tintagel Castle in Cornwall and later lived at Camelot, in the kingdom of Avalon (said to be Glastonbury, in Somerset).

Somerset, the region's tranquil northernmost county, is characterized by miles and miles of rolling green countryside. Along the north coast stand the Quantock and Mendip hills, and at their feet the stark, heather-covered expanse of Exmoor, setting for R. D. Blackmore's historical romance, *Lorna Doone*. Below this lies the county's boggy "Sedgemoor" region, known as the Levels. Central Somerset boasts some of England's richest agricultural land.

Devon, farther south, is famed for its wild moorland (especially Dartmoor, home to wild ponies and an assortment of strange "tors," rock outcrop mounds sometimes eroded into weird shapes, sometimes covered in smooth turf), soft, green hills, quiet villages with thatched cottages, and rocky beaches. Its large coastal towns are as interesting for their cultural and historical appeal—many were smugglers' havens—as for their scenic beauty. The best time to visit Devon is late summer and early fall, during the end-of-summer festivals, especially in the small towns of eastern Dartmoor.

Cornwall, England's southernmost county, offers a mild climate, and nowhere are you more than 20 miles from the sea. This is a land of Celtic legend, where the ancient Cornish language survived until the 18th century. Until relatively recently, the county regarded itself as separate from the rest of Britain. Its northern coast is punctuated with high jagged cliffs that look dangerous and dramatic and are a menace to passing ships, while the south coast relaxes with sunny beaches, delightful coves, and popular resorts.

Essential Information

Important Addresses and Numbers

Tourist Information Major tourist information centers for the Southwest region include the following:

The West Country Tourist Board, Trinity Court, 37 Southernhay E, Exeter, Devon EX1 1QS, tel. 0392/76351. Open weekdays 9:30–5.
The Cornwall Tourist Board, County Hall, Station Rd., Truro, Cornwall TR1 1BR, tel. 0872/74282.

Devon Tourism, County Hall, Exeter EX2 4QQ, tel. 0392/47023.
Somerset Tourism, County Hall, Taunton, Somerset TA1 4DY, tel. 0823/255010.

Local tourist information centers, normally open Mon.–Sat. 9:30–5:30, but varying according to season, include:

Exeter: Civic Centre, Paris St., tel. 0392/72434.
Penzance: Station Rd., tel. 0736/62207.
Plymouth: Civic Centre, Royal Parade, tel. 0752/264849.
St. Ives: The Guildhall, Street-an-Pol, tel. 0736/796297.
Truro: City Hall, Boscawen St., tel. 0872/74555.
Wells: Town Hall, Market Pl., tel. 0749/72552.

Travel Agencies **American Express:** 7 Raleigh St., Plymouth, tel. 0752/228708.
Thomas Cook: 9 Old Town St., Plymouth, tel. 0752/667245.

Car Rental Agencies **Exeter: Avis,** Speedway Garage, Cowie St., tel. 0392/59713; **Plymouth: Avis,** Holiday Inn, Armada Way, tel. 0752/21550; **Europcar Ltd.,** Grevan Cars Ltd., 19 Union St., tel. 0752/669859; **Hertz,** Walkham Business Park, tel. 0752/705819.
Truro: Godfrey Davis Europcar Ltd., Tristan Motors, James Pl., tel. 0872/76825.

Arriving and Departing

By Air Plymouth has a small airport, 3 miles from town which accommodates flights to the Channel Islands (*see* Chapter 7). *Information tel. 0752/705151.*

By Car The fastest way from London to the heart of the Southwest is via the M4 and M5 motorways. The M4 bypasses Bristol (115 miles) to meet the M5, which heads south to Exeter, in Devon (172 miles). There, it joins A30, which leads all the way to Land's End, at the tip of Cornwall.

By Train **British Rail** serves the region from London's Paddington Station (tel. 071/262–6767). Average travel time to Exeter, 2¼ hours; to Plymouth, 3¾ hours; and to Penzance, about 5 hours.

By Bus **National Express** (tel. 071/730–0202) serves the region from London's Victoria Coach Station. Average travel time to Bristol is 2½ hours; to Exeter, 3¾ hours; to Plymouth, 4½ hours; and to Penzance, about 8 hours.

Getting Around

By Car Driving in the region can be tricky, especially in its western parts. Most of the routes between the A roads are twisting country lanes flanked by high stone walls and thick hedges, which severely restrict visibility.

The two main roads heading west once you are in the region are A39 (to the north) and A38 (to the south). A3071, which branches north from Penzance, is also a useful route. If you want to visit Dartmoor, you will have to rely on a handful of narrower "B" roads. However, A30 does cross Bodmin Moor, passing right beside Jamaica Inn (of Daphne du Maurier fame) on its way to Cornwall.

By Train Regional **Rail Rover** tickets are available for seven days' unlimited travel throughout the Southwest, and there are localized **Rovers** covering Devon or Cornwall.

By Bus **Western National Ltd.** (tel. 0752/222555) operates a regular service in Plymouth and throughout Cornwall, and also offers one-day **Explorer** and seven-day **Key West** tickets valid for unlimited travel within its network.

Guided Tours

The **West Country Tourist Board** (tel. 0392/76351) maintains a register of professionally qualified guides, and lists of local guides may be obtained from individual tourist information centers.

Designer Touring (28 Peasland Rd., Torquay TQ2 8PA, tel. 0803/326832) offers a guide service traveling by bus or car.

Exploring the Southwest

Orientation

Our circular tour of the Southwest covers a lot of territory, from the gentle hills of Somerset, two hours outside London, to the remote and rocky headlands of Devon and Cornwall. The first leg starts in the cathedral city of Wells, in the heart of Somerset, and continues via Glastonbury, possibly the Avalon of Arthurian legend, south to Taunton, then west along the Somerset coast into Devon. Tour 1 ends at the clifftop ruins of Tintagel Castle in Cornwall, legendary birthplace of Arthur.

Our second tour travels southwest from Tintagel along the north Cornish coast to Land's End, the westernmost tip of Britain, known for its savage land and seascapes and panoramic views. From Land's End we turn northeast, stopping off in the popular seaside resort of Penzance, the harbor city of Falmouth, and a string of pretty Cornish fishing villages. Next we set off across the boggy, heath-covered expanse of Bodmin Moor, and then turn south to Plymouth, Devon's largest city.

For the final tour from Plymouth back to Wells, you have a choice of heading north to explore the vast, boggy reaches of Dartmoor Forest (setting for the Sherlock Holmes classic *The Hound of the Baskervilles*) or continuing east along Start Bay to Torbay, known as the "English Riviera." Both routes end in the ancient Roman capital of Exeter, Devon's county seat. From Exeter we meander south to Exmouth, then turn northeast to Yeovil in Somerset, re-entering King Arthur country at Cadbury Castle, the legendary Camelot.

Highlights for First-time Visitors

Buckland Abbey: Tour 2
Glastonbury Tor: Tour 1
Land's End: Tour 2
The Lizard Peninsula: Tour 2
Lydford Gorge: Tour 2
Mayflower Steps, Plymouth: Tour 2
Montacute House: Tour 3
St. Michael's Mount: Tour 2
Tintagel: Tour 1
Wells Cathedral: Tour 1
Wookey Hole and the Cheddar Caves: Off the Beaten Track

Tour 1: King Arthur Country— From Wells to Tintagel

Numbers in the margin correspond to points of interest on the Southwest map.

1 **Wells,** England's smallest cathedral city, lies at the foot of the Mendip Hills, about 132 miles southwest of London. While it feels more like a quiet country town than a city, Wells is home to one of the great masterpieces of Gothic architecture. The city's name refers to the underground streams that bubble up into St. Andrew's Well within the grounds of the Bishop's Palace. Spring water has run through the High Street since the 15th century.

The ancient **Market Place** in the city center is surrounded by 17th-century buildings. William Penn was arrested here in 1695 for preaching without a license at the Crown Hotel (*see* Dining and Lodging, below). Though the elaborate fountain at the entrance to the square is only 200 years old, it's on the same spot as the lead conduit that brought fresh, but undrinkable, spring water to the market in medieval times.

The great west towers of the famous **Cathedral Church of St. Andrew** are visible for miles. To appreciate the elaborate west front facade, approach the building on foot from the cathedral green, accessible from Market Place through a great medieval gate called "penniless porch" (named after the beggars who once waited here to collect alms from worshippers). The cathedral's west front is twice as wide as it is high and is adorned with some 300 statues. This is the oldest surviving English Gothic church, begun in the 12th century. Vast inverted arches were added in 1338 to stop the central tower from sinking to one side. Present erosion is causing a great deal of anxiety, and a restoration program is underway. The cathedral also boasts a rare, medieval clock, consisting of the seated figure of a man called Jack Blandiver who strikes a bell on the quarter hour while mounted knights circle in mock battle. Near the clock you will find the entrance to the chapter house—a small, wooden door opening onto a great sweep of stairs worn down on one side by the tread of pilgrims over the centuries. Every capital (column top) and pillar in the church has a carving; look for the one of a man with toothache and another with a thorn in his foot.

Time Out | The **Cathedral Cloisters Café** serves scones, cake, sandwiches, soup, and a hot dish at lunchtime.

The second great gate leading from Market Place, the Bishop's Eye, takes you to the **Bishop's Palace.** Most of its original 12th- and 13th-century residences remain, and you can also see the ruins of a late 13th-century great hall, which lost its roof in the 16th century because Edward VI needed the lead! The palace is surrounded by a moat, fed from wells, which is home to a variety of waterfowl, including swans. *Market Pl., tel. 0749/78691. Admission: £1 adults, 50p children. Open Easter–Oct., Thurs. and Sun. 2–6; Aug. and national holidays, daily 11–6.*

North of the cathedral is **Vicar's Close,** Europe's oldest street, with two terraces of handsome 14th-century houses. A tiny medieval chapel at the end is still in use.

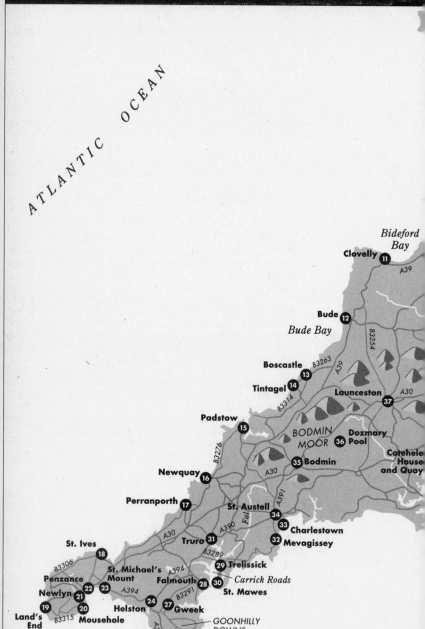

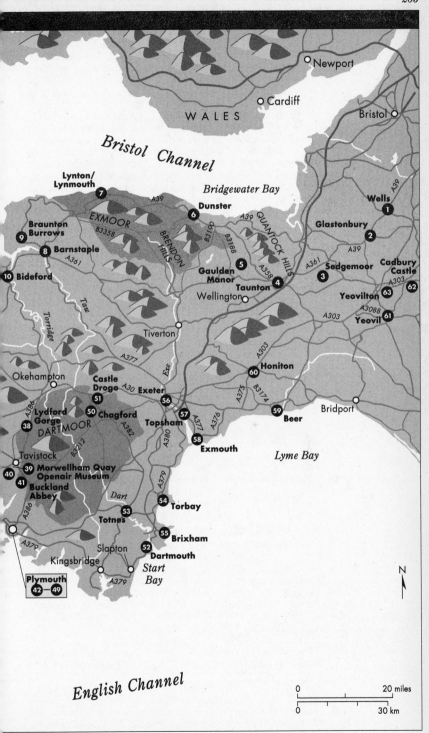

2 Five miles southwest of Wells, just off A39, is **Glastonbury,** steeped in history and an intertwining network of myth and legend, much of it contradictory. The town lies at the foot of **Glastonbury Tor,** a grassy hill rising 520 feet. In legend, Glastonbury is identified with Avalon, the paradise into which King Arthur was born after his death. It is also said to be the burial place of Arthur and Guinevere, his queen. And according to Christian tradition, it was to Glastonbury, the first Christian settlement in England, that Joseph of Arimathea brought the Holy Grail, the chalice used by Christ at the Last Supper. At the foot of the Tor is **Chalice Well,** the legendary burial place of the Grail. It's a stiff climb up the Tor, but you'll be rewarded by the view across the Vale of Avalon. At the top stands a ruined tower, all that's left of **St. Michael's Church,** which collapsed after a landslide in 1271. The tor is now owned by the National Trust, and is open free to the public.

In the town below lie the ruins of the great **Abbey of Glastonbury.** According to legend, this is the site upon which Joseph of Arimathea built a church in the 1st century; a monastery had certainly been erected here by the 9th century. The present ruins are those of the abbey completed in 1524 and destroyed shortly thereafter, during Henry VIII's dissolution of the monasteries in 1539. *Tel. 0458/32267. Admission: £1.50 adults, £1 children, £1.20 senior citizens. Open June–Aug., daily 9–7:30; Sept.–May, daily 9:30–dusk.*

While you are in Glastonbury, visit the Abbey Barn, which now houses the **Somerset Rural Life Museum.** This 14th-century tithe barn stored the portion of the town's produce due the church (one-tenth of the total harvest) and is more than 90 feet long. *Chilkwell St., tel. 0458/31197. Admission: £1 adults, 25p children and senior citizens. Open Easter–Oct., weekdays 10–5, weekends 2–6:30; Nov.–Easter, weekdays 10–5, weekends 2:30–5.*

From Glastonbury take A39 and A361 to Taunton, 22 miles away. The road crosses the Somerset Levels, marshes which have been drained by open ditches (known as "rhines"), where peat is dug. Off on the right, past Westonzoyland, lies
3 **Sedgemoor,** where in 1685 the duke of Monmouth's troops were routed by those of his uncle James II in the last battle fought on English soil. R. D. Blackmore's novel, *Lorna Doone,* is set during Monmouth's Rebellion.

4 **Taunton,** Somerset's principal town, lies in the heart of the southwestern cider-making country. In these parts, cider rather than beer is the traditional beverage. Fermented and alcoholic, it can be a lot more potent than English beer. In the fall, some cider mills open their doors to visitors. If you're interested, visit **Sheppys,** a local farm, shop and cider museum. *Three Bridges, Bradford-on-Tone (on A38 west of Taunton), tel. 0823/461233. Small admission charge. Open Mon.–Sat. 8:30–6; Easter–Christmas, Sun. noon–2.*

Time Out Porters Wine Bar (49 East Reach) in Taunton serves both light lunches and more substantial meals at very reasonable prices.

North of Taunton you will see the outlines of the **Quantock** and **Brendon hills.** The eastern Quantocks are covered with beech trees and are home to herds of handsome red deer. Climb to the top of the hills for a spectacular view of the Vale of Taunton

Deane and to the north the Bristol Channel. Nearby, in a quiet valley between these two lines of hills, is **Gaulden Manor,** a small 12th-century manor house built of red sandstone. Its elegant grounds include an Elizabethan herb garden. Henry Wolcott, who lived here in the 17th century, was an ancestor of Oliver Wolcott, a signer of the U.S. Declaration of Independence. It was also the home of the Turberville family, a name familiar to readers of *Tess of the d'Urbervilles,* by Thomas Hardy. *Tolland (9 mi northwest of Taunton) tel. 09847/213. Admission: £2.50 adults, £1 children; garden only, £1. Open May–June, Sun. and Thurs. 2–5:30; July–mid-Sept., Sun., Wed., and Thurs. 2–5:30.*

From Tolland, follow B3188, B3190, and A39 about 12 miles northwest to the village of **Dunster,** which lies between the Somerset coast and the edge of Exmoor National Park. Dunster is a picture-book village with a broad main street. Look for the eight-sided **yarn market building** dating from 1589. The village is dominated by its 13th-century fortress, **Dunster Castle,** National Trust property boasting fine plaster ceilings and a magnificent 17th-century staircase. Note that there is a steep climb up to the castle from the parking lot. *Tel. 0643/821314. Admission: £4 adults, £2 children; gardens only: £1.90 adults, £80p children. Open Apr.–Sept., Sun.–Thurs. 11–5. Gardens open Apr.–May and Sept., Sun.–Thurs. 11–5; June–Aug., daily 11–5; Oct., Sun.–Thurs. 2–4.*

Heading west, the coast road A39 mounts **Porlock Hill,** an incline so steep that signs are posted to encourage drivers to "Keep Going." The views across Exmoor and north to the Bristol Channel and Wales are worth it. Nineteen miles west of Dunster lie **Lynton** and **Lynmouth,** a pretty pair of Devonshire villages separated by one of the steepest hills in England. Lynmouth, a fishing village, is at the bottom, crouching below 1,000-foot cliffs at the mouths of the rivers East and West Lynne.

Barnstaple, 21 miles southwest on A39, on the banks of the river Taw, is northern Devon's largest city. It's a bustling market town, surrounded by modern developments, though the center retains its traditional look. Try to visit on Friday, market day, to see the colorful scene in Butchers' Row and Pannier Market, which echoes markets that have been held here for many centuries.

West of Barnstaple, along the Taw estuary, lie desolate stretches of sand dunes offering long vistas of marram grass and sea. **Braunton Burrows,** 10 miles west on the north side of the estuary, is a National Nature Reserve, with miles of trails running through the dunes. This is a first-class bird-watching spot, especially in winter.

Broad Bideford Bay is fed by the confluence of the Taw and Torridge rivers. **Bideford** itself lies on the Torridge estuary, about 8 miles west of Barnstable by A39. Cross the river either by the 14th-century, 24-arch bridge or by the more modern structure to reach the scenic hillside sheltering the town's elegant houses. At one time they were all painted white, and Bideford is still sometimes referred to as the "little white town." The area was a mainstay of 16th-century shipbuilding; the trusty vessels of Sir Francis Drake and other Elizabethan adventurers were built here.

Next, continue west about 10 miles along A39 around the bay to
Clovelly, a picturesque seaside town perched precariously
among the cliffs. Its cottages and stores cling to the sides of a
steep, cobbled road leading down to the tiny harbor. This road
isn't open to private cars, but if the thought of walking back up
again is daunting, there is a Land Rover service (during the
summer) to the parking lot at the top.

Fifteen miles south along A39 and B3263, just across the Cornish border, is **Bude,** a popular Victorian seaside town known
for its long sandy beaches. But beware: during the summer
months, the town and beaches are overrun with tourists.
Boscastle, another 15 miles farther on, is a somewhat more
tranquil spot. Some of the stone and slate cottages at the foot of
the steep valley here date from the 1300s.

Five miles southwest along the coast by B3263 is the ruined
clifftop castle of **Tintagel,** said to have been the birthplace of
King Arthur. Archaeological evidence, however, suggests that
the castle dates from much later, about 1150, when it was the
stronghold of the earls of Cornwall. Archaeologists also believe
that the site may have been occupied by the Romans. The earliest identified remains at the castle itself are of Celtic (5th-cen-
tury) origin, and these may have some connection with the
legendary Arthur. But legends aside, nothing can detract from
the stunning castle ruins, dramatically set on the wild, windswept Cornish coast, part on the mainland, part on an island
connected by a narrow isthmus. (There are also traces of a Celtic monastery on the island.) You can still see the ruins of the
Great Hall, some walls, and the outlines of various buildings.
Paths lead down to the pebble beach, to a cavern known as **Merlin's Cave.** Although it is worth the effort, exploring Tintagel
Castle involves some arduous climbing up and down steep
steps, which can become slippery in wet weather, so go carefully. *Tel. 0840/770328. Admission: £1.60 adults, 80p children,
£1.20 senior citizens. Open Apr.–Sept., daily 10–6; Oct.–Mar.,
daily 10–4.*

In the town of Tintagel itself, which has more than its share of
tourist junk—including Excaliburgers!—stop in at the **Old
Post Office,** situated in a 15th-century stone manor house with
smoke-blackened beams. *Admission: £1.60 adults, 80p children. Open Apr.–Sept., daily 11–6; Oct., daily 1–5.*

Tour 2: The Devon and Cornwall Coasts— From Tintagel to Plymouth

Fifteen miles south of Tintagel by A39 and A389, lies the town
of **Padstow,** an important port until a treacherous sand bar
formed here. According to legend, this "Doom Bar" appeared
when a fisherman shot at a mermaid; in retaliation she flung
sand across the estuary mouth. Though modern development
has crowded the town's Tudor and medieval buildings—a few
survive, such as the Elizabethan facade of Prideaux Place—the
sand dunes remain unspoiled and are popular bird-watching
points.

About 14 miles southwest of Padstow by B3276 is **Newquay,** the
largest town on the north Cornwall coast and its principal resort. Established in 1439, the town was once the center of the
trade in pilchards (a small herring-like fish). On the headland
overlooking the town sits a little white Victorian hut, where a

lookout known as a "huer" watched for offshore pilchard schools; when he spotted one, he would direct the boats to the fishing grounds.

17 Eight miles south of Newquay lie the sandy shores of Perran Bay, and **Perranporth.** This 3-mile stretch of beach is one of Cornwall's most popular seaside spots and, hence, extremely crowded in high season. The swell here attracts swarms of surfers, too. The best times to visit are the beginning and end of the summer. There are enchanting coastal walks to be had along the dunes and cliffs.

18 Leaving Perranporth, continue south about 20 miles along A30 to the fishing village of **St. Ives,** named after St. Ia, a 5th-century, female Irish missionary said to have arrived on a floating leaf. The town has attracted artists and tourists for more than 100 years, and is now a well-established artists' colony. Despite this, it has barely been touched by 20th-century development. Dame Barbara Hepworth, who pioneered abstract sculpture in England, lived in St. Ives for 26 years. The garden/studio where she died tragically in a fire in 1975 is now the **Barbara Hepworth Museum and Sculpture Garden** run by London's Tate Gallery (parking outside the village). *Trewyn Studio, Barnoon Hill, tel. 0736/796226. Admission: 50p adults, 25p children and senior citizens. Open summer, Mon.–Sat. 10–5:30, winter, Mon–Sat. 10–4:30.*

Examples of other artists' work can be found at the St. Ives Society of Artists in the **Old Mariner's Church** (tel. 0736/795582) in Norway Square. Admission: 20p.

Pottery has long been a favorite St. Ives's craft, largely due to Bernard Leach, who brought the art here from Japan early this century. His studio, where his family still pots, is on the outskirts of town. *Tel. 0736/796398. Showroom open weekdays 10–5.*

Time Out Built in 1312, the **Sloop Inn** beside St. Ives harbor is one of England's oldest pubs. Pub lunches are available in the handsome, wood-beamed rooms every day except Sunday.

The B3306 coastal road south from St. Ives is a winding route passing through some of Cornwall's most beautiful countryside. Stark hills crisscrossed by low stone walls drop abruptly to rocky cliffs and wide bays. Evidence of the ancient tin-mining industry—the remains of smokestacks and pumping houses—is everywhere. In some places the workings extended beneath the sea, forcing miners to toil away with the noise of waves crashing over their heads. Be careful if you decide to explore: many of the old shafts are open and unprotected.

19 B3306 ends at the western tip of Britain at what is, quite literally, **Land's End.** Although the point draws tourists from all over the world, and a multi-million dollar glitzy theme park has been added, its savage grandeur remains undiminished. The sea crashes against its rocks and lashes ships battling their way around it. Approach it from one of the coastal footpaths for the best panoramic view. Over the years, sightseers have caused some erosion of the paths, but new ones have recently been built, and Cornish "hedges" (granite walls covered with turf) planted to prevent future erosion.

20 Leaving Land's End start your journey northeast along B3315, stopping in at **Mousehole** (pronounced "Mowzel"), an archetypal Cornish fishing village of tiny stone cottages. It was the home of Dolly Pentreath, supposedly the last native Cornish speaker, who died in 1777.

21 A stone's throw north of Mousehole along the coast is **Newlyn,** the most important fishing port in the county and also a popular artists' colony at the end of the 19th century. A few of the appealing fishermen's cottages that first attracted artists here remain. The **Penlee House Museum and Art Gallery** in Penzance exhibits paintings by members of the so-called Newlyn School. *Penlee Park, tel. 0736/63625. Admission free to museum; 50p to gallery. Open weekdays 10:30–4:30 (gallery closed 12:30–2:30), Sat. 10:30–12:30.*

22 From Newlyn, it's only 1½ miles to the popular seaside resort of **Penzance,** with its spectacular views over Mount's Bay. Because of the town's isolated position, it has always been open to attack from the sea. During the 16th century, Spanish raiders destroyed most of the original town, and the majority of old buildings you see date from as late as the 18th century. The main street is called Market Jew Street, a folk mistranslation of the Cornish expression "Marghas Yow," which actually means "Thursday Market." Look for **Market House,** constructed in 1837, an impressive, domed granite building that is now a bank.

One of the prettiest streets in Penzance is **Chapel Street,** formerly the main street. It winds down from Market House to the harbor, where typical Georgian and Regency houses suddenly give way to the extraordinary **Egyptian House,** whose facade is an evocation of ancient Egypt. Built around 1830 as a geological museum, today it houses a National Trust shop. A little farther down the street is the 17th-century **Union Hotel** (*see* Dining and Lodging, below), where in 1805 the death of Lord Nelson and the victory of Trafalgar were first announced from the minstrels' gallery in the assembly rooms. Nearby is one of the few remnants of old Penzance, the **Turk's Head,** an inn said to date from the 13th century.

Time Out Another Penzance inn, the 15th-century **Admiral Benbow** (Chapel St.), was once a smugglers' pub and is full of seafaring memorabilia, a brass cannon, model ships, ropes everywhere, and figureheads. It's a popular pub, serving good, solid food. Try the steak and Guinness pie.

The town's **Nautical Museum,** also on Chapel Street, simulates the lower decks of a four-deck man-of-war, and exhibits items salvaged from shipwrecks off the Cornish coast. *19 Chapel St., tel. 0736/68890. Admission: £1.50 adults, 75p children, £3.50 family ticket. Open Easter–mid-Oct., Mon.–Sat. 10–5.*

23 About 3 miles east of Penzance on A394 is one of Cornwall's greatest natural attractions, **St. Michael's Mount,** a spectacular granite and slate island rising out of Mount's Bay just off the coast. What was originally the site of a Benedictine chapel founded by Edward the Confessor is now a 14th-century castle perched at the highest point, 200 feet above sea level. In its time, the structure on the Mount has been a church, a fortress, and a private home. The buildings around the base of the rock range from medieval to Victorian, but appear harmonious. The mount is surrounded by fascinating gardens, where a great variety of plants flourish in micro-climates—snow can lie briefly on one part while it can be 70° in another. To get there, follow the causeway or, when the tide is in, take the ferry which runs only during the summer months, however. As numbers are restricted on the Mount, expect delays. *Marazion, tel. 0736/ 710507. Admission: £2.80 adults, £1.40 children, £7.50 family ticket. Open Apr.–Oct., weekdays 10:30–4:45; Oct.–Apr., Mon., Wed., Fri. by guided tour only at 11, noon, 2, 3.*

24 Take the coastal road out of Penzance and continue 13 miles east to **Helston.** This attractive Georgian town is most famous for its annual "Furry Dance," which takes place on Floral Day, May 8 (unless the date is a Sunday or Monday, when it takes place on the nearest Saturday). The whole town is decked with flowers for the occasion, while dancers weave their way in and out of the houses following a 3-mile route. To explore more of the coastline, follow A3083 from Helston down the **Lizard**

25 **Peninsula,** the southernmost point in mainland Britain, and officially designated an Area of Outstanding Natural Beauty. In winter this flat heathland can look bleak, but in summer tourists flock here. The huge, eerily rotating dish antennae of the **Goonhilly Satellite Communications Earth Station** are visible from the road as it crosses Goonhilly Downs, the backbone of the peninsula. The National Trust owns much of the Lizard coastline, so this spectacular coastal area is protected from development. One path here, close to the tip, plunges down 200-

26 foot cliffs to tiny **Kynance Cove,** with its handful of pint-sized islands. The sands here are only reachable 2½ hours before and after low tide. The Lizard's cliffs are made of greenish, serpentine rock, interspersed with granite; local souvenirs are carved out of the stone.

27 Head back north to the fishing village of **Gweek,** 2 miles east of Helston. Sitting at the head of the Helford river, Gweek is known for its **Seal Sanctuary,** which shelters sick and injured seals brought in from all over the country. Try to be there for feeding time, 11 AM and 4 PM. *West of Helford, tel. 032622/361. Admission: £3.75 adults, £1.80 children, £3 senior citizens. Open summer, daily 9:30–5:30; winter, 9:30–4:30.*

28 Take B3291 seven miles northeast to **Falmouth,** site of one of the finest natural harbors in the country. It's a combination of busy resort town, fishing harbor, yachting center, and commercial port, yet its bustle adds to rather than detracts from its charm. The oldest section is on the eastern side of the Pendennis peninsula, while the western (seaward) side is lined with modern hotels. In the 18th century, Falmouth was a mailboat port, and in Flushing, a village across the inlet, are the slate-covered houses built by prosperous mailboat captains. A ferry service now links the two towns. On Falmouth's quay, near the early 19th-century **Customs House,** is the **King's Pipe,** an oven in which seized contraband was burned.

At the end of the Pendennis peninsula stands formidable **Pendennis Castle,** built by Henry VIII in the 1540s and later improved by his daughter Elizabeth I. From here there are sweeping views over the English Channel and across the stretch of water known as the Carrick Roads, to St. Mawes Castle on the Roseland peninsula (*see* below) which was designed as a companion fortress to guard the roads. *Pendennis Head, tel. 0326/316594. Admission: £1.60 adults, 80p children,*

£1.20 senior citizens. Open Apr.–Sept., Tues.–Sun. 10–6; Oct.–Mar., Tues.–Sun. 10–4.

㉙ From Falmouth, circle around the Carrick Roads estuary, stopping off at **Trelissick** on B3289, where the **King Harry Ferry,** a chain-drawn car ferry, runs to the Roseland peninsula at regular intervals throughout the day, except Sundays during the winter. From its decks you can see all the way up and down the Fal, a deep, narrow river with steep, wooded banks. The river's great depth provides ideal mooring for old ships waiting to be sold; these mammoth shapes lend a surreal touch to the riverscape.

㉚ If you go over on the ferry, make your way south down the Roseland peninsula to **St. Mawes.** At the tip of the peninsula stands the Tudor-era **St. Mawes Castle.** Its cloverleaf shape makes it seemingly impregnable, yet during the Civil War, its royalist commander surrendered without firing a shot. (In contrast, Pendennis Castle held out at the time for 23 weeks before submitting to the siege.) *St. Mawes, tel. 0326/270526. Admission: 95p adults, 45p children, 75p senior citizens. Open Apr.– Sept., daily 10–6; Oct.–Mar., Tues.–Sun. 10–4.*

The shortest route from St. Mawes to Truro is via the ferry. The longer way swings in a circle on A3078 for 19 miles through attractive countryside, where subtropical shrubs and flowers thrive in the gardens along the way, and you pass the village of **Probus,** with its tall decorated church tower (123 feet) covered with gargoyles and pierced stonework.

㉛ **Truro** is a compact, elegant Georgian city, nestled in a crook at the head of the river Truro. Though Bodmin is the county seat of Cornwall, Truro is Cornwall's only real city. Just over 100 years ago, construction begun on the **Cathedral Church of St. Mary**—the first cathedral built in England since the completion of St. Paul's in London in the early 1700s. The cathedral dominates the city and although comparatively modern (built 1880–1910), it evokes the feeling of a medieval church, with an impressive exterior in early English Gothic style. The inside is not so interesting, apart from a side chapel which is all that remains of the original 16th-century parish church. In front of the west porch there is an open, cobbled area called High Cross, and the city's main shopping streets fan out from here, with shops that range from large, modern stores, to tiny establishments tucked away in narrow lanes and alleyways.

Time Out   The **Globe** (Frances St.) is a thoroughly comfortable pub, with paneling, oak beams, and relaxing chairs. The self-service lunchtime bar food is homemade and great value.

For an overview of Truro's Georgian housefronts, take a stroll down **Lemon Street.** The 18th-century facades along this steep, broad street are of mellow-colored stone, unusual for Cornwall, where granite predominates. Another typical Georgian street is **Walsingham Place,** a curving, flower-lined street which is closed to traffic, making it a tranquil oasis. Near here you will find Truro's **Royal Cornwall Museum,** which offers a sampling of Cornish art, archaeology, and an extensive collection of Cornish minerals. There's a new café and shop. *River St., tel. 0872/ 72205. Admission: 50p adults, 25p children and senior citizens; children accompanied by adults free. Open Mon.–Sat. 9–5.*

Just east of the cathedral, near the Quay, the rivers Allen and Kenwyn merge into the river Truro, which then becomes the River Fal. Truro's days as an important port for tin and copper export were over by the early 18th century, but there is still some commercial traffic here, and pleasure boats ply the river in the summer. However, during the winter months there is not enough water at low tide to reach the city, and then boat trips begin and end at **Malpas,** just south of Truro. *Enterprise Boats, 66 Trefusis Rd., Flushing (north of Falmouth), tel. 0326/ 74241. River Fal trips leave from Truro and Falmouth four times a day during the summer. The one-way trip takes about one hour.*

From Truro, continue eastward on A390, turn right at Sticker, and follow signs on side roads to the busy fishing town of
㉜ **Mevagissey,** around 15 miles due east. (Like most Cornish coastal villages, it is not suitable for cars, so if you stop to visit use the large parking lot on the outskirts.) About 4 miles north
㉝ is **Charlestown,** a harbor town built in 1791. It is still active in china clay export, which explains the strange white dust coating the 18th-century houses along the port. It was also one of the ports from which 19th-century emigrants left for America. Its period look has made it a popular film location. The center of
㉞ the china clay industry is **St. Austell,** just inland of Charlestown. The hinterland here, with its brilliantly white heaps of clay waste visible for miles around (*see* Off the Beaten Track, below), is known as the "White Alps of Cornwall."

㉟ From St. Austell, follow A391 13 miles north to **Bodmin.** This was the only Cornish town recorded in the 11th-century Domesday Book, William the Conqueror's census of English towns and holdings. During World War I, both the Domesday Book and the Crown Jewels were sent to Bodmin Prison for safekeeping. From the **Gilbert Memorial** on the Beacon hill you can see both of Cornwall's coasts.

For another taste of Arthurian legend, follow A30 northeast out of Bodwin across the boggy, heather-clad granite plateau
㊱ of Bodmin Moor to **Dozmary Pool.** A considerable lake rather than a pool, it was here that King Arthur's magic sword Excalibur was supposedly returned to the Lady of the Lake after Arthur's last battle.

Time Out   At Bolventor, in the center of Bodmin Moor, just off A30, look for **Jamaica Inn,** made famous by Daphne du Maurier's novel of the same name. Originally a farmstead, it is now Cornwall's best-known pub and a good spot to try a Cornish pasty for lunch.

After crossing Bodmin Moor, the first large town you come to is
㊲ **Launceston** (pronounced "Lanson"), Cornwall's ancient capital. Parts of its medieval walls survive, including the South Gate. For a full view of the town and surrounding countryside, climb up to the ruins of 14th-century **Launceston Castle.** *Tel. 0566/772365. Admission: 95p adults, 45p children, 75p senior citizens. Open Apr.–Sept., daily 10–6; Oct.–Mar., Tues.–Sun. 10–4.*

Leaving Launceston, continue east along A30, following the
㊳ signs to **Lydford Gorge,** 9 miles away, where the river Lyd has carved a spectacular chasm through the rock. Two long paths, above and below, lead along the gorge, past gurgling whirl-

pools and waterfalls with names such as the Devil's Cauldron and the White Lady. *Lydford, tel. 082282/441/320. Admission: £2.20. Open Apr.–Oct., daily 10:30–6; winter, walk restricted to main waterfall.*

East of Lydford, pick up A386 south via Tavistock, then A390. Before reaching Gunnislake on this road, you'll find **Morwellham Quay Openair Museum.** This was England's main copper exporting port in the 19th century, and it has been restored as a working museum, with quay workers and coachmen in costume, and a copper mine open to visitors. *Tel. 0822/832766 or 0822/833808 (recorded information). Admission: £5.45 adults, £3.95 children, £4.95 senior citizens. Open Mar.–Oct., daily 10–5:30 (last admission at 4); Nov.–Feb., daily 10–4 (last admission 2:30).*

At Albaston, turn left off A390 for **Cotehele House and Quay.** Formerly a busy port, Cotehele now offers a late medieval manor house complete with original furniture, armor, and needlework; gardens; a restored mill; and a quay museum, the whole complex now run by the National Trust. *St. Dominick (north of Saltash), tel. 0579/50434. Admission: £4.40; gardens and mill only £2.20. Open Apr.–Oct., 11–4. Gardens only Nov.–Mar., daily during daylight hours.*

Return via A390 to Tavistock, and take A386 6 miles south to **Buckland Abbey,** a 13th-century Cistercian monastery which became the home of Sir Francis Drake in 1581. Today it is full of mementos of Drake and the Spanish Armada. The abbey has a licensed restaurant. *Yelverton, tel. 0822/853607. Admission: £3.60 adults, £1.80 children; gardens only, £1.60 adults, 80p children. Open Easter–Oct., Fri.–Wed. 10:30–5:30; church only Nov.–Mar., Wed., Sat., and Sun. 2–5.*

Next, follow A386 (or any of a number of attractive minor roads) about 9 miles south from Buckland Abbey to **Plymouth,** Devon's largest city.

Numbers in the margin correspond to points of interest on the Plymouth map.

Plymouth has long been linked with England's commercial and maritime history, but it didn't attain the status of a city until 1914, when the three separate towns of Plymouth, Stonehouse, and Dock (later renamed Davenport) were amalgamated. From the **Hoe,** a wide, grassy esplanade with crisscrossing walkways high above the city—and especially from **Smeaton's Tower**—you can get a magnificent view of the many inlets, bays, and harbors that make up Plymouth Sound. At the end of the Hoe stands the huge **Royal Citadel,** built by Charles II in 1666. A new **visitors center** displays exhibits on both old and new Plymouth.

The **Barbican,** which lies east of the Royal Citadel, is the oldest surviving section of Plymouth (much of the city center was destroyed by air raids in World War II). Here, Tudor houses and warehouses rise from a maze of narrow streets leading down to the fishing docks and harbor. Many of these buildings have become antiques shops, art shops, and bookstores. By the harbor you can visit the **Mayflower Steps,** where the Pilgrims embarked in 1620; the **Mayflower Stone** marks the exact spot. Plymouth was the last port visited by the *Mayflower* before the crossing to North America. Nearby, on St. Andrew's Street,

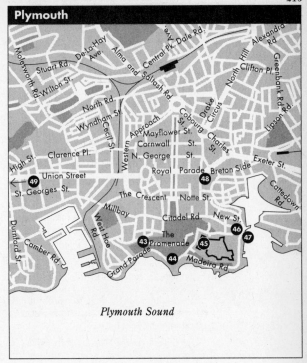

Plymouth Sound

48 the largely 18th-century **Merchant's House** has a museum of local history. *33 St. Andrew's St., tel. 0752/668000, ext. 4383. Admission: 65p adults, 15p children. Open weekdays 10–1 and 2–5:30, Sat. 10–1 and 2–5.*

49 The **Royal Naval Dockyard,** on the west of town, was begun in the late 17th century by William III. It is still a navy base and much is hidden behind the high dock walls but parts of the 2-mile-long frontage can be seen from pleasure boats that travel up the river Tamar. *Plymouth Boat Cruises Ltd., Millpool House Head, Millbrook, Torpoint, Cornwall, tel. 0752/822797; also Tamar Cruising, Penhellis, Maker La., Millbrook, Torpoint, Cornwall, tel. 0752/822105. Both companies run one-hour boat trips around the sound and the dockyard, leaving every 40 minutes from Phoenix Wharf and the Mayflower Steps in the Barbican. Cost: £2.50 adults, £1 children. Service available Easter–Oct., daily 10–4.*

Three and a half miles east of Plymouth city center lies **Saltram House,** a lovely 18th-century house built around the remains of a late-Tudor mansion. It has two fine rooms designed by Robert Adam and paintings by Sir Joshua Reynolds, first president of the Royal Academy of Arts, who was born nearby in 1723. The house is set in a beautiful garden, with rare trees and shrubs. There is a restaurant in the house and a cafeteria in the Coach House. *Plympton, tel. 0752/336546. Admission: £4.40 adults, £2.20 children; garden only, £1.60 adults, 80p children. Open Apr.–Oct., Sun.–Thurs. 12:30–6 (Oct. to 5); garden only Nov.–Mar., daily 11–6 or dusk.*

Tour 3: From Plymouth to Wells

Numbers in the margin correspond to points of interest on the Southwest map.

From Plymouth, you have a choice of routes north to Exeter. If rugged, desolate, moorland scenery appeals to you, take A386 and B3212 northeast across Dartmoor Forest. Even on a summer's day, the scarred and brooding hills of this sprawling national park appear a likely haunt for monsters such as the fearsome Hound of the Baskervilles. Sir Arthur Conan Doyle set his Sherlock Holmes thriller of that title in the landscape here. Sometimes this wet, peaty wasteland vanishes completely in rain and mist, while in very clear weather you can see as far north as Exmoor.

Much of Dartmoor's northern reaches consists of open heath and moorland, uninvaded by roads: wonderful, if often wet, walking territory. But it is also an easy place to lose your bearings. A large area is used as an army range (clearly marked when firing is in progress). Beware, too, of sudden weather changes; Dartmoor mists are notorious. The lusher areas, such as the countryside around Fingle's Bridge near Moretonhampstead, and Becky Falls, on Becks Brook, border its rivers. Dartmoor's earliest inhabitants left behind countless stone monuments, burial mounds, and hut circles, all of which make it startlingly easy to imagine prehistoric man roaming the bogs and hill pastures here.

If you have crossed the moor by B3212, turn left 3 miles before Moretonhampstead, where you see the signs to Chagford. **⑤⓪ Chagford** was once a tin-weighing station and before that, an area of fierce fighting in the 17th century between the Roundheads (who supported Parliament) and the Cavaliers (who supported the king) in the Civil War. A Roundhead was hanged in front of one of the pubs on the village square.

⑤① ** An intriguing house near Chagford is **Castle Drogo, at Drewsteignton across A382. Though designed by the Edwardian architect Sir Edwin Lutyens and built between 1910 and 1930, it is an extraordinary interpretation of a medieval castle, complete with battlements. Situated high above the Teign Valley, it offers extensive views across the river to the moors beyond. *Tel. 06473/3306. Admission: £3.80; adults, £1.60 children; grounds only, £1.60 adult, 80p children. Open Apr.–Sept., daily 11–6; Oct., daily 11–5.*

Another route from Plymouth follows A379 east for 21 miles to **Kingsbridge** and on to Start Bay, where the sea is on one side and **Slapton Ley,** a lake and a haven for wildfowl, on the other. American forces requisitioned much of the land near here before the D-Day landings, and a Sherman tank remains as a memorial to the 700 U.S. soldiers killed during a rehearsal exercise—a disaster kept secret until very recently. A379 continues north along the coast to **Dartmouth,** an important port in **⑤② ** the Middle Ages and now, like so many coastal towns, a favorite haunt of yacht owners. Traces of its past include the old houses in **Bayard's Cove** near Lower Ferry, the 16th-century covered **Butterwalk,** and the two castles guarding the entrance to the river Dart. But the town is dominated by the **Royal Naval College,** built in 1905. Two ferries cross the river here; in summer, to avoid long waiting lines, you may want to try the inland route via Totnes (B3207 and A381).

Time Out The **Cherub** (Higher St.) built around 1380, was originally a wool merchant's house. It is now a popular pub with a wide range of lunchtime food—all of it appetizing and reasonably priced.

53 **Totnes,** about 9 miles north of Dartmouth, is a busy market town which preserves an atmosphere of the past, particularly on summer Tuesdays and Saturdays, when most of the shopkeepers dress in Elizabethan costume. If you climb up to the ruins of Totnes's **Norman castle,** you can get a wonderful view of the town and the river. *Tel. 0803/864406. Admission: 95p adults, 45p children, 75p senior citizens. Open Apr.–Sept., daily 10–6; Oct.–Mar., Tues.–Sun. 10–4.*

54 **Torbay,** 5 miles due east of Totnes, describes itself as the "English Riviera." Since 1968, the towns of Paignton and Torquay have been amalgamated with Torbay to form the Southwest's most important resort. (Torquay was supposed to be the site of **55** the hotel in television's *Fawlty Towers.)* **Brixham,** at the western point of the bay, has kept much of its original charm, partly because it is still a fishing village.

Leaving the Torbay area, follow one of the coast roads (A379 or A380) north to Exeter.

56 Devon's county seat, **Exeter,** is much smaller than Plymouth to the south, but has been the capital of the region since the Romans established a fortress here 2,000 years ago. Little evidence of the Roman occupation exists, apart from the great city walls. Despite being badly bombed in 1942, Exeter retains much of its medieval character, as well as the gracious architecture of the 18th and 19th centuries.

At the heart of Exeter is the great Gothic **Cathedral of St. Peter,** begun in 1275 and taking around a century to complete. The twin towers are even older survivors of an earlier Norman cathedral. The 300-foot stretch of unbroken Gothic vaulting, rising from a forest of ribbed columns, is the longest in the world. Myriad statues, tombs, and memorial plaques adorn the interior. In the minstrels' gallery, high up on the left of the nave, stands a group of carved figures singing and playing musical instruments, including bagpipes. The cathedral is surrounded by a charming **Close,** a pleasant green space for relaxing on a sunny day. The buildings along the east side date from the 15th century, though many facades are of a later date. Don't miss the 400-year-old door to No. 10, the bishop of Crediton's house; this heavy oak door is ornately carved with angels' and lions' heads.

In one corner of the Close is **Mol's Coffee House** (now a store), with its black-and-white, half-timbered facade bearing the coat of arms of Elizabeth I. It is said that Sir Francis Drake met his admirals here to plan strategy against the Spanish Armada in 1588. Mol, incidentally, was an Italian gentleman who arrived here in 1596. Near Mol's stands the **Royal Clarence Hotel** (*see* Dining and Lodging, below). Built in 1769, it was the first inn in England to be described as a "hotel"—a designation applied by an enterprising French manager. It is named for the duchess of Clarence, who stayed here in 1827 on her way to visit her husband, the future William IV.

Time Out While you're exploring the Close, stop in at **Tinley's,** ideal for lunch, coffee, snacks, or one of Devon's famous cream teas (served with jam, scones, and cream). Baking is done on the premises. Remains of the original city wall, which the house was built against, can be seen on the first floor.

On High Street, just behind the Close, stands the **Guildhall,** the oldest municipal building in the country. Town council meetings are still held here. The present hall dates from 1330, although a guildhall has been on this site since at least 1160. Its timber-braced roof is one of the earliest in England, dating from about 1460. *Tel. 0392/72979. Admission free. Open Mon.–Sat. 10–5:30, unless in use for a civic function.*

Behind the Guildhall lie Exeter's main shopping areas, Harlequins Arcade and the Guildhall Shopping Centre. In their midst stands the tiny 11th-century Norman **Church of St. Pancras,** a survivor not only of the 1942 Blitz, but of the dramatic urban renewal efforts of the 1950s and '60s.

On the far end of these two shopping areas is Queen Street, home of the **Royal Albert Memorial Museum,** where natural history displays, a superb collection of Exeter silverware (*see* Shopping, below), and the works of some West Country artists are housed. There is also a fine archaeological section. *Tel. 0392/265858. Admission free. Open Tues.–Sat. 10–5:30.*

Off Queen Street, behind the museum, is **Rougemont Gardens,** which was first laid out at the end of the 18th century. The land was once part of the defensive ditch of **Rougemont Castle,** built in 1068 by decree of William the Conqueror. Here you will find the original Norman gatehouse and the remains of the Roman city wall, the latter forming part of the outer wall of the ancient castle; nothing else is left. The spot offers a panoramic view of the countryside and the Haldon Hills rising up in the west.

Rougemont Gardens belonged originally to John Patch, who became chief surgeon of Exeter when he was only 25. His attractive house, built in the late 1700s, stands at the foot of the castle walls and now houses the **Rougemont House Museum of Costume and Lace.** The permanent collection includes superb displays of the local Honiton lace and costumes in period room settings. *Tel. 0392/265858. Admission: £1 adults, 50p children and senior citizens, £2 family ticket, free on Fri. Open Sept.–June, Mon.–Sat. 10–5:30; July and Aug., Mon.–Sat. 10–5:30, Sun. 2–6.*

Return to the cathedral and make your way down to the river and historic waterfront. This now tranquil spot was once the center of Exeter's medieval wool industry. The **Customs House,** built in 1682, is the earliest surviving brick building in the city; it is flanked by Victorian warehouses. There is also a Heritage Centre in **Quay House** (a stone warehouse contemporary of the Customs House) which documents the maritime history of the city and offers an audiovisual display. *The Quay, tel. 0392/ 265213. Admission free. Open Sept.–June, daily 10–5; July–Aug., daily 10–6.*

Close to the Customs House, in the canal basin, is the **Exeter Maritime Museum,** comprising the largest collection of historic, working ships in the country. The more than 140 vessels on exhibit include a dhow (used for pearl diving in the Persian Gulf), a Chinese junk, a Danish steam tug, and a swan-shaped rowboat. This is a hands-on museum; you can board nearly all the boats, as well as try your hand at winding a winch or turning a capstan. *Haven Banks, tel. 0392/58075. Admission: £3.25 adults, £1.90 children, £9.50 family ticket. Open Sept.–June, daily 10–5; July–Aug., daily 10–6. Closed Dec. 25–26.*

57 Five miles south of Exeter on A376 is the town of **Topsham,** full of narrow streets and hidden courtyards. Once a bustling port, it is rich in 18th-century houses and inns. **Topsham Museum** occupies a 17th-century Dutch-style merchant's house beside the river. *25 the Strand, tel. 039287/3244. Admission: 60p adults, 35p children and senior citizens. Open Feb.–Nov., Mon., Wed., Sat. 2–5; also Aug., Sun. 2–5.*

Time Out Topsham boasts several fine pubs including **The Bridge,** a 16th-century inn by the river, which offers a choice of traditional ales; and the **Steam Packet,** next to the quay. The latter—all flagstones, scrubbed boards, brick, and stripped stonework—is named after the passenger ships that once sailed between Topsham and London.

Leaving Topsham, continue south on A376 toward Exmouth, stopping off at **A la Ronde,** an extraordinary 16-sided circular house built in 1798 and inspired by the Church of San Vitale in Ravenna, Italy. Among the 18th and 19th-century curiosities here is an elaborate display of feathers and shells. The property has recently been acquired by the National Trust. *Summer La., on A376 near Exmouth, tel. 0395/265514. Admission: £2.40 adults, £1.20 children. Open Apr.–Sept., Sun.–Thurs. 11–5:30; Oct., Sun.–Thurs. 11–4:30.*

58 **Exmouth** itself is now a large, sprawling town and a popular seaside resort, but its 19th-century elegance lives on in the houses on the **Beacon,** the swanky part of town. Both Lady Byron and Lady Nelson, the respective widows of the poet and the admiral, ended their days here. The Devon coast from Exmouth to the Dorset border 26 miles to the east has been designated an Area of Outstanding Natural Beauty. The reddish, grass-topped cliffs of the region are punctuated by quiet, seaside resorts such as **Budleigh Salterton, Sidmouth,** and **Seaton.**

59 **Beer,** just outside Seaton, about 15 miles from Exmouth, was once a favorite haunt of smugglers. It was also the source of the white stone used to build Exeter Cathedral. Some of the old quarries can still be visited. *Beer Quarry Caves, Quarry La., tel. 029780/282. Admission: £2.20 adults, £1.55 children and senior citizens, £7 family ticket. Open Apr.–Sept., daily 9–5.*

60 Ten miles inland from Beer on B3174/A375 is the town of **Honiton,** whose long High Street is lined with handsome Georgian houses. Modern storefronts have intruded, but the original facades have been preserved at second-floor level. For three centuries the town was known for lacemaking, and the Honiton lace industry was revived when Queen Victoria selected the fabric for her wedding veil in 1840. The town has a **lace museum,** as well as stores where both old and new lace are sold. *All Hallows Museum, High St., tel. 040487/397. Admission: 50p* *adults, 20p children. Open mid-May–Oct., Mon.–Sat. 10–5; Oct., Mon.–Sat. 10–4.*

Time Out For a satisfying lunch, try **Dominoes** winebar (178 High St.), where you can get everything from crispy Szechuan duck to steak and oyster pie.

61 Leaving Honiton, take A30 and A303 east toward **Yeovil,** about 30 miles away. This part of Somerset is famous for its golden limestone, used in the construction of local villages and mansions. A fine example is **Montacute House** on A3088 (turn right off A303 at Stoke sub Hamdon) built in the late 16th century. This Renaissance house has a 189-foot gallery brimming with Elizabethan and Jacobean portraits, most on loan from the National Portrait Gallery. *Tel. 0935/823289. Admission: £4 adults, £2 children; garden and park only, Mar.–Nov., £2 adults, £1 children, Nov.–Apr. £1 adults, 50p children. Open Apr.–Oct., Wed.–Mon. 12:30–5:30. Garden and park open daily 11:30–5:30 or dusk.*

62 **Cadbury Castle,** 9 miles northwest of Yeovil off A359, provides this chapter's last contact with King Arthur. It is said to be the site of Camelot—one among several contenders for the honor. Glastonbury Tor, rising dramatically in the distance across the plain, adds to the atmosphere of Arthurian romance. There is even a legend that every seven years the hillside opens and Arthur and his followers ride forth to water their horses at close-by Sutton Montis. Cadbury Castle is, in fact, an Iron-Age fort (c. 650 BC), with grass-covered, earthen ramparts forming a green wall 300 feet above the surrounding fields.

63 Seven miles west, in **Yeovilton,** the 20th century reasserts itself with the **Fleet Air Arm Museum.** Here, more than 50 historic aircraft are on show, including the Concorde 002. *Royal Naval Air Station, tel. 0935/840565. Admission: £4 adults, £2 children, £3 senior citizens, £11 family ticket. Open Mar.–Oct., daily 10–5:30; Nov.–Feb., daily 10–4:30.*

From Yeovilton it's about 17 miles along A37 and A361 to Wells, our original starting point. A number of major roads including the M4/M5 route will take you back to London from here.

What to See and Do with Children

Renewed emphasis on nature and conservation, together with the open spaces of the Southwest, make this an area full of entertainment for children.

Buckfast Butterfly Farm and Dartmoor Otter Sanctuary's colorful inhabitants come from around the world. The farm is on A38, halfway between Exeter and Plymouth. *Buckfastleigh, tel. 0364/42916. Admission: £2.95 adult, £2.45 senior citizens, £1.75 children. Open Easter–Nov., daily 10–5:30.*

Cheddar Caves and Wookey Hole *(see* Off the Beaten Track, below).

Dart Valley Steam Railway is one of many steam railroads in the Southwest. It runs through seven wooded miles of the Dart valley down to Kingswear, across from Dartmouth, at the mouth of the river. *Buckfastleigh, tel. 0364/42338. Trains run at Easter and daily in the summer.*

Flambards Theme Park is a three-in-one park with an aircraft collection, a re-creation of a war-time street during the Blitz, and a reconstructed Victorian village. *Near Helston, tel. 0326/ 574549 or 0326/573404. Admission: £6.99 adults, £5.99 children, £3.50 senior citizens. Open Easter–Nov., daily 10–5.*

The National Shire Horse Centre offers three daily parades of shire horses (the largest breed of draft horse, originally bred to carry knights in armor), flying displays at the falconry center, and an adventure playground. *Yealmpton (on A379 east of Plymouth), tel. 0752/880268. Admission: £4.25 adults, £2.95 children, £3.75 senior citizens. Mid-Mar.–Oct. flying displays Sun.–Thurs. 1 and 3:30, parades daily 11:30, 2:30, 4:15; Nov.– mid-March no parades or flying displays; closed Christmas.*

Off the Beaten Track

Signs in Wells town center will direct you 2 miles north to **Wookey Hole,** a fascinating complex of limestone caves reaching deep into the Mendip Hills. In addition to a geological and archaeological museum, there is a large underground lake, and several newly opened chambers to explore, plus a working paper mill and a display of Madame Tussaud's early waxwork collection dating from the 1830s. The caves may have been the home of Iron Age people. *Tel. 0749/72243. Admission: £4.50 adults, £2.95 children, £3.95 senior citizens. Open Mar.–Oct., daily 9:30–5:30; Nov.–Feb., daily 10:30–4:30. Closed one week before Christmas.*

Six miles farther north by A371 lie the **Cheddar Caves.** This beautiful, subterranean world of stalactites, stalagmites, and naturally colored stone is enhanced by holograms and stunning man-made optical effects. Evidence in the caves, discovered in the 19th century, suggests that they were occupied during the Stone Age. *Cheddar, tel. 0934/742343. Admission: £4 adults, £2.50 children and senior citizens. Open summer, daily 10– 5:30; winter, daily 10:30–4:30.*

At **Chewton Cheese Dairy** north of Cheddar Gorge, you can see how Cheddar cheese is made in the traditional truckles, and watch butter being churned by hand. *Priory Farm, Chewton Mendip (north of Wells), tel. 076121/666. Shop and restaurant open Mon.–Sat. 8:30–5, Sun. 10–4:30; cheesemaking Mon.– Wed., Fri., and Sat., best time to view noon–2:30.*

Winegrowers in Somerset are reviving a British tradition which goes back to the 10th century. At **Pilton Manor,** 6 miles southeast of Wells, you can wander in the vineyard, taste English wines, and have lunch in the wine bar; stuffed vine leaves are a specialty. *The Manor House, Pilton, Shepton Mallet, tel. 074989/325. Admission: free. Open for exploration May–Sept. Wed.–Sun. 11–5. Open for bottle sales daily 8:30–5 all year.*

The wool trade was the mainstay of Devon's wealth for centuries, and at Uffculme, 6 miles east of Tiverton by A373, **Coldharbour Mill** has been restored as a working museum where you can see the stages in the transformation of fleece into cloth. *Uffculme, Cullompton, tel. 0884/840960. Admission: £2.75 adults, £1.50 children, £7.50 family ticket. Open Easter–Oct., daily 11–5; Nov.–Easter, weekdays 11–5.*

The 11-mile-long **Grand Union Canal,** opened in 1814, runs past Tiverton, and in the summer you can travel up part of it by horse-drawn barge. *Grand Western Houseboat Co., The Wharf, Canal Hill, Tiverton, tel. 0884/253345. Call for sailing times and ticket prices.*

China clay has been St. Austell's main industry for 200 years. **Wheal Martyn,** an old mine 2 miles north of St. Austell on A391, offers an audiovisual presentation on the history and processes of the china clay industry, a history trail through the mine, and several other exhibits, including two waterwheels. *Carthewm, tel. 0726/850362. Admission: £3.50 adults, £1.75 children. Open Apr.–Oct., daily 10–6.*

Shopping

The Southwest is a rich area to explore if you are interested in crafts, especially pottery. Whole groups of artists and craftsmen have settled down here, in Devon and Cornwall especially, to pursue their calling in the warm air of this attractive region. Ancient crafts, too, are still carried on, such as the making of baskets and shoes.

Barnstaple The **Litchdon Pottery** shop (11 Litchdon St.) sells interesting decorative pieces, such as pots, bowls, and plaques.

Bridgwater At Over Stowey, a few miles west of Bridgwater, are the **Quantock Weavers,** who produce hand-knitted and woven items in hand-spun wool, including ponchos, scarves, shawls, and rugs. (Follow brown Tourist Board signs from A39.)

Dartington Near Dartington Hall (2 miles north of Totnes) is a collection of stores selling world-famous Dartington lead crystal (made at Torrington in north Devon), as well as shoes, woolens, farm foods, kitchenware, pottery, and many other Devon wares. Another outstanding establishment is **Dartington Trading Centre** (Shinners Bridge, 2 miles west of Totnes), a collection of shops and two restaurants, housed inside what was originally the Dartington Cider Press. Handmade crafts from Devon include clothes, glassware, and kitchenware.

The **Dartington Glass** factory (Linden Close, Great Torrington, near Bideford, tel. 0237/471011) has tours of the works weekdays 9:30–10:30 and noon–3:30, every 15 minutes. There are also a "seconds" shop and café on the premises.

Exeter Until 1882 Exeter was the silver assay office for the entire West Country, and it is still possible to find **Exeter silver,** particularly spoons, in some antiques and silverware stores. The earliest example of Exeter silver dates from 1218 (a museum piece), but Victorian pieces are still sold—the Exeter assay mark is three castles. You'll find an excellent silver collection in Exeter's Royal Albert Memorial Museum *(see* Tour 3). Try **William Bruford** (1 Bedford St.) for interesting antique jewelry and silver.

Glastonbury Somerset is sheep country, and sheepskin products abound throughout the region. One of several good outlets is **Morlands Factory Shop** (2 miles out of town on A39 to Street), which sells a range of goods, including coats, slippers, and rugs; there is also a history center.

Plymouth **Dolls and Miniatures** (54 Southside St., The Barbican). This is an attractive store, specializing in antique and reproduction dolls, dolls houses, and kits. They also run an overseas mail order service.

St. Ives — Though St. Ives is full of crafts stores, one of the better ones is the **Sloop Craft Market** by the harbor; here a variety of goods, ranging from watercolor paintings to leather bags and belts and ships in bottles are sold. Since many of the artisans have workshops here, it's often possible to watch them at work.

Stoke St. Gregory — Basket-making from willow is a traditional craft of the Somerset Levels. At the **Willow and Wetland Visitor Centre** (P.H. Coate & Son, Meare Green Court, Stoke St. Gregory, 10 miles east of Taunton), you can see this craft practiced and buy the finished products as well. There is also a museum of basket-making with displays on this unique "wetland" area.

Taunton — **Makers** (7A Bath Pl.) is a shop owned and run by 12 Somerset craftshops and sells jewelry, silver work, painted silk scarves, pots, wood turnery, and designer knitwear.

Markets — Market days in Barnstaple are Tuesday and Friday. In Exeter there is a daily market on Sidwell Street. Glastonbury has a market every Tuesday, and Wells on Wednesday and Saturday.

Sports and Fitness

Hiking — Of the many magnificent walks to be had in the Southwest, one of the very best is a clifftop hike along the coast from Hartland Quay down to Lower Sharpnose Point. Around 10 miles in length, this walk, along some of the highest cliffs in Britain, provides breathtaking views. The coast below Bude is also ideal for walking, especially the section around Tintagel.

Dartmoor, as we have said, is not for the unwary, but with sufficient local advice to follow, hikers may find many walks of great interest. The areas around Widgery Cross, Becky Falls, and the Bovey Valley, and—for the really energetic and adventurous—Highest Dartmoor, south of Okehampton, are all worth considering.

A much shorter walk, but no less spectacular, is along the Lydford Gorge *(see* Tour 2).

Horseback Riding — The open spaces of the Southwest are ideal for cross-country **pony riding,** and it is often possible to ride the Dartmoor and Exmoor breeds of ponies. Centers include **Lydford House Riding Stables** (Lydford House Hotel, Lydford, tel. 082282/347) and **Skaigh Stables Farm** (Skaigh La., near Okehampton, tel. 0837/840429).

Water sports — Looe, on the south coast of Cornwall, is known for shark **fishing,** and boats can be rented for mackerel fishing from most harbors on Devon and Cornwall's south coast.

The south coast of Devon and Cornwall is one of Britain's main **sailing** areas. There are plenty of safe harbors, new marinas, and deep-water channels off the coast. The broad estuaries at Falmouth, Plymouth Sound, and Torbay are the major centers.

Surfing is relatively new in Britain, but world championship competitions have been held at Newquay on Cornwall's north coast, where there is an almost perpetual groundswell. Remember, wetsuits are essential in the chilly British waters.

Its beaches have long made the Southwest one of Britain's main family vacation areas. Be aware of the tides, particularly if you want to explore around an adjoining headland; otherwise you may find yourself cut off by the incoming tide. At many of the major resorts, flags show the limits of safe **swimming,** as there can be strong undertows, especially on the northern coast.

Dining and Lodging

Dining Somerset is the home of Britain's most famous cheese, the ubiquitous Cheddar, from the Mendip Hills village. If you are lucky enough to taste real farmhouse Cheddar, made in the traditional "truckle" (*see* Off the Beaten Track, above), you may find it hard to return to processed cheese. The calorie-conscious should beware of Devon's cream teas, which traditionally consist of a pot of tea, homemade scones, and lots of "clotted" cream and strawberry jam. "Clotted," i.e., specially thickened, cream is a regional specialty; it's sometimes called "Devonshire cream."

Cornwall's specialty is the "pasty," a pastry shell filled with chopped meat, onions, and potatoes. The pasty was originally devised as a handy way for miners to carry their dinner to work. The modern pasty may bear little resemblance to its tasty original, but excellent local pasties can still be found.

"Scrumpy," a homemade dry cider available throughout the Southwest, is refreshing, but deceptively mild. English wine, which is similar to German wine, is available in Somerset (*see* Off the Beaten Track, above), while in Cornwall you can get mead made from local honey.

Highly recommended restaurants are indicated by a star ★.

Category	Cost*
Expensive	£25–£35
Moderate	£12–£25
Inexpensive	under £12

*per person, including first course, main course, dessert, and VAT; excluding drinks

Lodging There is a wide range of accommodations throughout the Southwest, ranging from national hotel chains which extend as far west as Plymouth, to bed-and-breakfast places. With the growth of the tourist industry, many farmhouses in rural areas have begun renting out rooms.

Highly recommended lodgings are indicated by a star ★.

Category	Cost*
Very Expensive	over £130
Expensive	£80–£130
Moderate	£45–£130
Inexpensive	under £45

*All prices are for two people sharing a double room, including service, breakfast, and VAT.

Barnstaple
Dining and Lodging

Lynwood House. The emphasis at this family-run hotel/restaurant is on fresh local fish, including salmon from the river Taw. Be sure to try the fish soup. Lynwood House, located on A377 between Barnstable and Exeter, also has five bedrooms. *Bishops Tawton Rd., tel. 0271/43695. Reservations advised. Dress: informal. MC, V. Moderate.*

The Royal and Fortescue Hotel. Edward VII, who stayed here when he was Prince of Wales, gave this Victorian hotel its royal name. It's conveniently situated in the center of town. All rooms are furnished to a high standard and there's a choice of à la carte or table d'hôte menu in the restaurant. *Boutport St., EX31 1HG, tel. 0271/42289. 62 rooms, 33 with bath. Facilities: live music and dances weekly. AE, DC, V. Moderate.*

Dartmouth
Dining
★

The Carved Angel. Situated on the quay with views of the harbor, its offerings include Provençal cuisine and fresh local products, such as river Dart salmon and samphire, a seashore plant used in fish dishes. The restaurant enjoys a long-standing reputation as one of the Southwest's finest eateries. *2 South Embankment, tel. 0803/832465. Reservations required. Jacket and tie required. No credit cards. Closed Sun. dinner, Mon., and Jan. Expensive.*

Mansion House. The upstairs dining room in this elegant 18th-century mansion is reached by a lovely sweeping staircase, and the food is in keeping with the surroundings. Specialties include turbot with foie gras and mushrooms, with a menu that changes regularly. *Mansion House St., tel. 0803/835474. Reservations required. Jacket and tie required. No credit cards. Closed Sun. and Mon. Expensive.*

Lodging

Royal Castle Hotel. Here's a hotel that really earned the name "Royal"—several monarchs have slept here. Part of Dartmouth's historic waterfront, it was built in the 17th century, reputedly of timber from wrecks of the Spanish Armada. There are traditional fireplaces and beamed ceilings, and six rooms have four-poster beds. *11 The Quay, TQ6 9PS, tel. 0803/833033. 25 rooms with bath or shower. Facilities: live music and dancing Sun., non-smoking library lounge. DC, MC, V. Moderate.*

Stoke Lodge Hotel. Three miles southwest of Dartmouth by A379, it was once a 17th-century family house, and is now a family-run hotel surrounded by four acres of gardens. It is equipped for year-round vacations—and children—with indoor and outdoor swimming pools. *Cinders La., Stoke Fleming TQ6 0RA, tel. 0803/770523. 24 rooms with bath. Facilities: restaurant, sauna, Jacuzzi, indoor and outdoor pools. No credit cards. Moderate.*

Exeter
Dining

Golsworthy's. Part of St. Olaves Court Hotel, set in a Georgian house with a walled garden, this candlelit French restaurant in the heart of the city offers both set and à la carte menus. *Mary Arches St., tel. 0392/217736. Weekend reservations required. Jacket and tie required. AE, DC, MC, V. Closed for lunch Sat. and Sun. Moderate.*

Tudor House. Tapestries, beams, and antique furniture set the mood for the sensible old-fashioned cuisine that is offered here, such as rack of lamb or duck in yellow bean sauce. There's a good wine list, helpfully annotated. *Tudor St., tel. 0392/73764. Reservations advised. Jacket and tie required. AE, DC, MC, V. Closed Sun. and Mon. Moderate.*

Lodging **Rougemont Hotel.** Large, rambling, and Victorian—complete with chandeliers, molded ceilings, and pillars—this hotel is ideal for those who want comfortable accommodations downtown. Most of the rooms have recently been refurbished. *Queen St., EX4 3SP, tel. 0392/54982. 90 rooms with bath. Facilities: restaurant, in-house movies. AE, DC, MC, V. Expensive.*

The Royal Clarence Hotel. This historic hotel (*see* Tour 3) is located within the cathedral Close, in the heart of Exeter. It boasts a good restaurant and has been made a great deal more attractive by recent redecoration. The most expensive rooms are those with a view of the cathedral. *Cathedral Yard, EX1 1HD, tel. 0392/58464. 54 rooms with bath. Facilities: restaurant, carvery, two bars. AE, DC, MC, V. Moderate.*

The White Hart. It is said that Oliver Cromwell stabled his horses here; and in any event, guests have been welcomed since the 15th century. The main building has all the trappings of a period inn—beams, stone walls, a central courtyard, and warm hospitality—but there are also fully modern bedrooms in a new wing. *65 South St., EX1 1EE, tel. 0392/79897. 61 rooms with bath. Facilities: restaurant, bar, garden. AE, DC, MC, V. Moderate.*

Exmouth **River House.** The ambience here is wonderful, with the Exe es-
Dining tuary flowing right under the windows, water birds nearby, and a great view of Powderham Castle. The food ain't bad either! Try the fresh salmon or brill—but the meat is delicious, too. The husband-and-wife team are friendly and welcoming. There are also two bedrooms. *The Strand, Lympstone, tel. 0395/265147. Reservations required. Dress: informal. AE, MC, V. Closed Sun. evening and Mon. Moderate.*

Lodging **Royal Beacon Hotel.** Overlooking the sea with views across the estuary to Torbay in the distance, this gracious, relaxed Georgian hotel was once a posting house where messengers and coaches changed their horses. *The Beacon, EX8 2AF, tel. 0395/ 264886. 30 rooms with bath. Facilities: two restaurants, horseback riding, sauna, sunbed. AE, DC, MC, V. Moderate.*

Fairy Cross **The Portledge Hotel.** More peaceful, rural surroundings than
Lodging these would be hard to imagine. It's set in 60 acres of parkland
★ on the edge of Bideford Bay. The house is a 17th-century mansion, but parts of it date from the 11th century. There are family portraits, lovely paneling, antiques, and attractive fabrics everywhere. *Near Bideford, EX39 5BX, tel. 02375/262. 35 rooms with bath. Facilities: restaurant, coffee shop, garden, tennis, croquet, swimming pool, fishing. AE, DC, MC, V. Moderate.*

Falmouth **Pandora Inn.** This thatched pub, with both a patio and a moored
Dining pontoon for summer dining, is a great discovery. The ambience is a combination of maritime memorabilia and fresh flowers, and you can eat either in the bars or in the candlelit restaurant. The backbone of the menu is fresh seafood—try the seafood stroganoff or crab thermidor. *Restronguet Creek, Mylor, tel. 0326/72678. Reservations advised. Dress: informal. MC, V. Closed Sun. in winter. Moderate.*

★ **The Seafood Bar.** The window of this restaurant is a fish tank, and beyond it is the very best seafood. Try the thick crab soup; the turbot cooked with cider, apples, and cream; or the locally caught lemon sole. *Quay St., tel 0326/315129. Reservations advised. MC, V. Open for dinner only. Moderate.*

Lodging **Falmouth Hotel.** Enormous, award-winning gardens surround
★ this massive Victorian building by the sea. Apart from the
rooms in the main hotel there are cottages on the grounds with
basic cooking facilities. *Castle Beach, TR11 4NZ, tel. 0326/
312671. 73 rooms with bath. Facilities: restaurant, wine bar,
swimming pool, sauna. AE, DC, MC, V. Closed Christmas.
Moderate.*

Greenbank Hotel. Mailboat captains used to stay at this harbor-
side hotel. Although it has been well modernized, it hasn't lost
its maritime atmosphere; watch the yachts sail past the picture
windows of the lounges. *Harbourside, TR11 2SR, tel. 0326/
312440. 42 rooms with bath. Facilities: restaurant, garden, solarium, sea fishing. AE, DC, MC, V. Closed Christmas–early
Jan. Moderate.*

Hotel St. Michaels. This seaside hotel overlooking Falmouth
Bay is in a long, low white building with beautiful gardens
sweeping down to the sea. *Gyllyngvase Beach, Seafront, TR11
4NB, tel. 0326/312707. 75 rooms with bath. Facilities: indoor
pool, sauna, Jacuzzi. AE, DC, MC, V. Moderate.*

Gittisham **Combe House Hotel.** Rolling parkland, 2,000 acres in all, sur-
Lodging rounds this Elizabethan manor house. From the imposing entrance hall with its huge, open fireplace, to the individually
decorated bedrooms—all of them large—the emphasis is on
style and comfort. *Near Honiton, EX14 0AD, tel. 0404/42756.
15 rooms with bath. Facilities: restaurant, 1½-mile river
stretch suitable for dry fly-fishing. AE, DC, MC, V. Closed
Jan.–mid-Feb. Expensive.*

Glastonbury **No. 3.** This French-style restaurant is elegant yet relaxed; it's
Dining in a Georgian house next to the abbey ruins. There are log fires
★ in the winter and a terrace for summer evenings. The fixed,
four-course menu features mainly seafood; try the Cornish lobster in season. There are also six attractive bedrooms available. *3 Magdalene St., 0458/32129. Reservations required.
Jacket and tie required. AE, V. Closed lunch (except Sun.),
Sun. and Mon. dinner. Moderate.*

Lodging **George and Pilgrims Hotel.** Pilgrims en route to Glastonbury
Abbey stayed here in the 15th century. Today, all the modern
comforts are here, but you can enjoy them in rooms with flagstone floors, wooden beams, and antique furniture; ask for a
room with a four-poster bed or, if it appeals to you, the one
room that is supposed to be haunted. *1 High St., BA6 9DP, tel.
0458/31146. 14 rooms, 12 with bath. Facilities: restaurant, Pilgrims Bar. AE, DC, MC, V. Moderate.*

Helston **Nansloe Manor.** Although near Helston's center, this peaceful
Dining and Lodging manor house gives the impression of being deep in the country,
with its rhododendron-lined driveway and five acres of
grounds. The à la carte menu at the restaurant is short but
changes frequently. *Meneage Rd., TR13 0SB, tel. 0326/574691.
7 rooms with bath. MC, V. Moderate.*

Honiton **New Dolphin Hotel.** The age of this former coaching inn shows
Lodging in the sloping floors, but every room has modern comforts. It's
conveniently located in the town center. *High St., EX14 8LS,
tel. 0404/42377. 14 rooms with bath. MC, V. Moderate.*

Montacute **The King's Arms.** Built of the same warm, golden stone as near-
Dining and Lodging by Montacute House *(see Tour 3)*, this 16th-century inn fea-
★ tures charming interior decor; one room has a four-poster bed.

Meals available range from bar snacks to a full à la carte menu in the Abbey Room Restaurant. *Bishopston, TA15 6UU, tel. 0935/822513. 11 rooms with bath. AE, MC, V. Closed Christmas. Moderate.*

Okehampton
Dining and Lodging

Lewtrenchard Manor. This spacious 1620 manor house, on the northern edge of Dartmoor (off A30), once belonged to the clergyman who wrote the hymn *Onward Christian Soldiers*. It is full of paneled rooms, stone fireplaces, and ornate leaded windows. Some bedrooms have antique four posters. The restaurant serves good fresh fish, caught by the fishing fleet an hour away. *Near Okehampton, EX20 4PN, tel. 056683/256. 8 rooms, 7 with bath. Facilities: restaurant, garden, fishing, helipad. AE, DC, MC, V. Closed last 3 weeks in Jan. Expensive.*

Penzance
Dining

Berkeley. Atypical for its after-dinner dancing (until 1 AM) and 1930s decor, Berkeley's serves homemade pasta in such dishes as tortellini with crab or mushrooms, or you can try their fresh scallops or lemon sole. *Abbey St., tel. 0736/62541. Reservations advised. Dress: informal. AE, MC, V. Dinner only. Closed Sun.; also Mon.–Wed. Oct.–mid-June. Moderate.*

Lodging
★

Abbey Hotel. Staying in this small, privately run 17th-century hotel is like visiting someone's home; the drawing room is filled with books and many of the rooms are furnished with antiques. The attractive restaurant has a short but intriguing menu, with seafood gratin, rack of lamb, and homemade ice cream. Dining privileges are normally reserved for residents, but you may be able to get a booking. *Abbey St., TR18 4AR, tel. 0736/66906. 7 rooms with bath. AE, MC, V. Closed 2 weeks in Jan. Moderate.*

Union Hotel. Spanish pirates burned the Union down in 1597; it was also here that the victory at Trafalgar and the death of Nelson in 1805 were first announced. The present building dates from the 17th century, although tasteful refurbishment has taken place since then. *Chapel St., TR18 4AE, tel. 0736/62319. 28 rooms, 18 with bath. AE, DC, MC, V. Moderate.*

Plymouth
Dining
★

Chez Nous. This French—*very* French—restaurant is worth searching for among the rows of stores in the shopping district. Fresh local fish is served, and the atmosphere is pleasant and relaxed. *13 Frankfort Gate, tel. 0752/266793. Reservations advised. Dress: informal. AE, DC, MC, V. Closed Sun., Mon., national holidays, and first 2 weeks in Feb. and Sept. Expensive.*

Piermaster's. Fresh fish landed at nearby piers is served here. Located in the Barbican, the Piermaster has "basic seafront," decor, with a tiled floor and wooden tables. *33 Southside St., Barbican, tel. 0752/229345. Reservations advised. Dress: informal. AE, DC, MC, V. Closed Sun. Moderate.*

Lodging

Copthorne Hotel. Situated downtown, this large, efficient, modern hotel offers the expected comforts. Its Burlington Restaurant has been given an Edwardian look. *Armada Centre, Armada Way, PL1 1AR, tel. 0752/224161. 135 rooms with bath. Facilities: restaurant, bar, swimming pool, sauna, solarium, in-house movies. AE, DC, MC, V. Expensive.*

Bowling Green. This reconditioned Victorian house overlooks Sir Francis Drake's bowling green on Plymouth Hoe. It's in a central location for shopping and sightseeing. *9–10 Osborne Pl., Lockyer St., PL1 2PU, tel. 0752/667485. 12 rooms, 4 with bath. MC, V. Inexpensive.*

Portloe
Lodging
★

The Lugger. This small hotel on the edge of a tiny cove is made up of several 17th-century cottages. Many of the snug cottage bedrooms look out to sea, while in the beamed bar the world of the smugglers doesn't seem so far away. It's definitely worth the drive through the narrow, banked roads 12 miles southeast from Truro to get here. *TR2 5RD, tel. 0872/501322. 20 rooms with bath. Facilities: restaurant, sauna, solarium. AE, DC, MC, V. Closed mid-Nov.–early-Mar. Moderate.*

St. Ives
Lodging

Garrack Hotel. A family-run hotel overlooking the beach and with great coastal views, the Garrack offers a relaxed, undemanding atmosphere. There are traditional rooms in the main house and more modern ones in the annex. *Burthallan Ln., TR26 3AA, tel. 0736/796199. 21 rooms, 16 with bath. Facilities: garden, indoor pool, sauna, restaurant, coffee shop. AE, DC, MC, V. Moderate.*

Taunton
Dining and Lodging
★

The Castle. The ivy-covered battlements and towers of this 300-year-old building will leave you in no doubt as to why this hotel, reputed to be among England's finest, has the name it does. Bedrooms are individually decorated, and garden suites have separate dressing rooms. In the hotel's restaurant, the *haute cuisine* dishes range from classic roasts to elaborate seafood dishes such as poached scallops with mussels, tomatoes, garlic, and ginger. The cheese selection includes many English cheeses and is served with homemade walnut bread. *Castle Green, TA1 1NF, tel. 0823/272671. 35 rooms with bath. Facilities: garden. Jacket and tie required in restaurant. Reservations advised. AE, DC, MC, V. Expensive.*

Lodging

Falcon Hotel. Three and a half miles east of Taunton by A358 is this small family-run hotel, with a friendly, homey feel. As it is located just off M5 at exit 25, it makes a fine first stop in the West Country. *Henlade, TA3 5DH, tel. 0823/442502. 11 rooms with bath. MC, V. Moderate.*

Tavistock
Dining and Lodging
★

The Horn of Plenty. A "restaurant with rooms" is the way this establishment (now under new management) describes itself. From the restaurant in a Victorian house there are magnificent views across the wooded, rhododendron-filled Tamar valley. The menu is rethought every month, but the cooking is mainly classic French with some traditional English recipes. A converted barn next to the house offers seven modern guest rooms. It is located 3 miles west of Tavistock on A390. *Gulworthy, PL19 8JD, tel. 0822/832528. 6 rooms with bath. Reservations required. Dress: informal. Closed lunch Mon. and Christmas. AE, MC, V. Restaurant: Expensive. Hotel: Moderate.*

Topsham
Lodging

Globe Hotel. A modern wing with eight rooms has been added at this cozy, family-run, 16th-century coaching inn. All rooms are comfortable and well-appointed. *34 Fore St., EX3 0HR, tel. 039287/3471. 14 rooms with bath. AE, MC, V. Moderate.*

Torquay
Dining

Remy's. This restaurant offers delightful, straight-forward French country cooking. Lamb with basil and tomato, sweetbreads with a Calvados sauce, and above all fish freshly caught by local boats, are among the specialties. The wine list has a selection of good Alsatian vintages. *3 Croft Rd., tel. 0803/292359. Reservations advised. Dress: informal. Closed Sun., Mon. and lunch. AE, MC, V. Moderate.*

Lodging
★
The Imperial. This is arguably Devon's most luxurious hotel, perched high above the sea, overlooking Torbay. The gardens surrounding the hotel are magnificent, and the interior . . . well, imperial, with chandeliers, marble floors, and the general air of a bygone world. Most bedrooms are large and very comfortable, some with seaward balconies. The staff is attentive. *Parkhill Rd., TQ1 2DG, tel. 0803/294301. 166 rooms with bath. Facilities: restaurant, beauty parlor, health center, tennis, squash, indoor and outdoor pools. AE, DC, MC, V. Very expensive.*

Fairmount House Hotel. This Victorian hotel near the thatched village of Cockington, on the edge of Torquay, has a pretty garden and a restaurant that favors fresh local produce. *Herbert Rd., Chelston, TQ2 6RW, tel. 0803/605446. 7 rooms with bath. Facilities: restaurant. AE, MC, V. Inexpensive.*

Totnes
Lodging
The Cott. The exterior of this inn has remained almost completely unchanged since 1320. It is a long, low, thatched building with flagstone floors, thick ceiling beams, and open fireplaces. Bar snacks and more elaborate meals are available from the restaurant. *Shinner's Bridge, Dartington (2 mi west of Totnes on A385) TQ9 6HE, tel. 0803/863777. 6 rooms. AE, DC, MC, V. Moderate.*

Truro
Dining
Bustapher Jones. Exotic dishes such as Moroccan lamb with apricots, nuts, garlic, and ginger appear on this winebar's menu, as well as steak-and-salad fare. The dining room is decorated with prints and stained-glass windows. *62 Lemon St., tel. 0872/79029. Weekend reservations advised. Dress: informal. MC, V. Closed Sun. lunch and Christmas. Moderate.*

Dining and Lodging
Alverton Manor. This was once a bishop's house, then a convent, and now an up-to-date hotel/restaurant, both efficient and atmospheric. The rooms are large, with French cherrywood furniture. Talented chefs come and go in the Terrace Restaurant, but the standard of cooking stays high with the help of the best local produce. *Tregolis Rd., TR1 1XQ, tel. 0872/76633. 25 rooms. Facilities: garden. Reservations required for restaurant. Jacket and tie required. AE, DC, MC, V. Expensive.*

Wells
Dining
Ancient Gate House. Traditional Italian dishes made largely from local produce are the specialty here. There is also an English menu. *20 Sadler St., tel. 0749/72029. Reservations advised. Dress: informal. AE, DC, MC, V. Moderate.*

Dining and Lodging
The Crown. This hotel has been a landmark in Wells since the Middle Ages; William Penn was arrested here in 1695 for illegal preaching. There is a period atmosphere to the place, enhanced by the fact that four of the rooms have four-poster beds. There's also a particularly helpful staff. The Penn Bar and Eating House serves salads and such traditional hot dishes as steak-and-kidney pie. *Market Pl., BA5 2RP, tel. 0749/73457. 21 rooms with bath. AE, DC, MC, V. Moderate.*

Lodging
Swan Hotel. Built in the 15th century, this former coaching inn faces the cathedral. Several of the rooms have four-poster beds, and on cold days you can relax in front of a log fire in one of the lounges. *11 Sadler St., BA5 2RX, tel. 0749/78877. 32 rooms with bath. Facilities: restaurant. AE, DC, MC, V. Moderate.*

The Arts

Festivals Several towns in the Southwest have arts festivals that run for one or more weeks. Among the best known is the **Exeter Festival** (tel. 0392/265200), a mixture of musical and theatrical events held in late May and early June. The **Three Spires Festival** (tel. 0872/863346), based in Truro Cathedral, takes place in June. At **St. Endellion,** near Wadebridge in Cornwall a music festival is regularly held at Easter. Contact the local tourist information centers for details.

Local **country festivals** abound in late August and early September. Keep an eye out for banners announcing them as you pass through the smaller villages at this time of year, or consult local tourist information centers. The villages of northern and eastern Dartmoor have some particularly colorful celebrations; try Moretonhampstead's.

Theaters At the **Northcott Theatre,** Exeter (tel. 0392/54853), and the **Theatre Royal** in Plymouth (0752/669595), plays are produced throughout the year, often by one of the best London companies in preparation for a London West End run.

A theater peculiar to this area is the open-air **Minack Theatre** (tel. 0736/810694) in Porthcurno near Penzance in Cornwall. It was begun in the early 1930s, using the natural slope of the cliff to form an amphitheater, and terraces and bench seats have since been added. With the sea as a backdrop, plays are performed here throughout the summer, ranging from classical dramas to modern comedies.

7 The Channel Islands

Introduction

The Channel Islands, though part of Britain since 1066, have a self-ruling system, and thus have no allegiance to the Parliament in Westminster, just to the monarch. For governmental purposes, the archipelago is divided into two sections, called bailiwicks. There is the Bailiwick of Jersey, consisting solely of that island, and the Bailiwick of Guernsey, which includes Guernsey and the smaller islands of Alderney, Sark, Herm, and Jethou. Each of the bailiwicks has its own government, called states, headed by a bailiff and a lieutenant-governor, who is the Queen's representative and the states' contact person with Westminster. Alderney, though part of the Bailiwick of Guernsey, also has its own states. Tiny Sark is a feudal island, ruled over by a hereditary Seigneur. Jethou is privately owned and not open to the public.

The most popular of the islands is Jersey (44½ sq mi), because of its winning combination of a mild climate, magnificent beaches, well-run hotels and restaurants, all promoted by a strong department of tourism. Second to Jersey, both in size and as a tourist attraction, is Guernsey (24½ sq mi). Boasting 2,000 hours of sunshine a year, Guernsey runs at a much more relaxed pace.

The Islands, situated 8 miles from France, have had an eventful history; they had been fortified over and over against constant threats of invasion, and today castles and coastal forts remain as the legacy of this past. Also telling of the islands' history are the ubiquitous German fortifications attesting to the German occupation during World War II.

Essential Information

Important Addresses and Numbers

Tourist Information
There is only one information office for the Islands in London, **Jersey Tourism Office,** 35 Albermarle St., London W1X 3FB, tel. 071/493–5278. On the islands the offices are:

Jersey Tourism Department, Weighbridge, St. Helier, 0534/78000; general information tel. 0534/24779; accommodation tel. 0534/31958.
Guernsey Tourist Board, Crown Pier, general information tel. 0481/723552; accommodation tel. 0481/23552. Guernsey also handles information for Alderney, Herm, and Sark.
Alderney States Tourist Office, Queen Elizabeth II St., tel. 048182/2994.
Sark Tourism Committee, Information Centre, tel. 048183/2345.

Travel Agencies
Jersey and Guernsey
The House of Bellingham, 33 Queen St., St. Helier, Jersey, tel. 0534/27575; 41 Commercial Arcade, St. Peter Port, Guernsey, tel. 0481/726333.
Thomas Cook, 14 Charing Cross, St. Helier, Jersey, tel. 0534/77955; 22 Le Pollet, St. Peter Port, Guernsey, tel. 0481/724111.
Keith Prowse Travel Jersey Ltd., 13 Cattle St., St. Helier, Jersey, tel. 0534/77715.
Marshall's Travel, 1 Quennevais Precinct, St. Brelade, Jersey, tel. 0534/41278.

OSL Channel Islands Travel Service Ltd., Guernsey Airport, Forest, Guernsey, tel. 0481/35471.

Alderney   **Raymond Travel Bureau,** Box 12 Victoria St., Alderney, tel. 048182/2881.

Car Rental Agencies *Jersey*   **Avis,** St. Peter's Garage, St. Peter, tel. 0534/83288; **Budget Rent a Car,** Airport Rd., St. Brelade, tel. 0534/46191; **Europcar,** Arrivals Hall, Jersey Airport, St. Peter. tel. 0534/43156; **Hertz,** Arrivals Hall, Jersey Airport, tel. 0534/45621.

Guernsey   **Avis,** South Esplanade, St. Peter Port, tel. 0481/724343; **Budget Rent a Car,** Fort Road Motors, PO Box 180, Fort Rd., St. Peter Port, tel. 0481/735353; **Hertz,** T.L. Car Sales, La Vallaize Airport, Forest, tel. 0481/38008.

Currency   Although the islands use pounds and pence, both of the Bailiwicks have their own version of them, with specially printed bills. This currency is *not* legal tender elsewhere in the UK, though you will be able to use UK currency on the islands. Financial wheeling and dealing is big business here, and you'll find bureaus de change at banks, travel agencies, the main post offices, airports, and the main harbors.

Arriving and Departing

Jersey is well served by flights from both mainland Britain and the Continent. There are direct flights from Heathrow (British Airways), Gatwick (Air Europe, Dan-Air), Plymouth (Brymon), Southampton (Air UK, Jersey European, Channel Island Travel Service), Manchester (Air Europe Express, BA, Channel Island Travel Service, Loganair), and Glasgow (British Midland, Channel Island Travel Service, Loganair). Flying time from London is 1 hour, from Manchester 1 hour 20 minutes, from Plymouth ¾ of an hour. The London/Jersey return fare is £72 (£82 in summer, and £59 with a Jersey Saver (Dan-Air).

Guernsey Airport is served by Air UK, British Midland, Brymon, Jersey European, Loganair, and Guernsey Airlines, which flies from Gatwick.

For further flight information contact: British Airways, tel. 081/897–4000; Brymon (tel. 0752/707023; Dan-Air, tel. 0345/100200; Loganair, tel. 041/889–3141; Jersey European, tel. 0345/078400; Channel Island Travel Service, tel. 0534/46181; Air UK, tel. 0345/666777; Air Europe Express, tel. 061/489–2922; British Midland, tel. 0203/325151; Guernsey Airlines, tel. 0293/546571.

By Boat   You can sail to Jersey or Guernsey from Poole, Weymouth, or Torquay. Most boats call at Guernsey first since it is closer to the British mainland than is Jersey. The average time for the trip from Poole by the night ferry is 8¼ hours to Geurnsey, 2¼ hours more to Jersey. By day, ferry time is 5½ hours and 3½. An average fare runs from £55 for a 5-day Saver return for a foot passenger to £212 and up for a car with two passengers. The lines serving these routes are:

From Weymouth Condor Ltd. (tel. 0305/761551), with daily sailings March–October.

From Torquay Torbay Seaways (tel. 0803/214397), sailing April–December.

From Poole British Channel Island Ferries (tel. 0202/681155), which operates car ferries with night sailings all year and day sailings April–October. This is an associate company of the go-ahead Brittany Ferries, and the biggest of the operators on the route. They also have vacation offers with hotel accommodation on both Jersey and Guernsey, plus trips to France.

Getting Around

By Car You can ship your car through by ferry from mainland Britain at fairly low rates, but the islands are small and can easily be explored by local bus. If you choose to drive, however, another option is to rent a car (*see* above). The traffic, especially on Jersey, can be regularly snarled up, especially in high season. Driving is on the left, and the speed limit is 40 mph on Jersey; 35 or 25 on Guernsey, depending on the area; 35 on what open road there is on Alderney, 25 in town, 12 on the main street; cars are not permitted on Sark.

By Bus Jersey and Guernsey have excellent island-wide bus services. There are buses only in summer on Alderney. There are regular bus services to and from both Jersey and Guernsey airports. Bus services are **Jersey Motor Transport Co.** (Central Bus Station, Weighbridge, St. Helier, tel. 0534/21201) and **Guernsey-bus** (Picquet House, St. Peter Port, tel. 0481/724677).

Between the Islands Island hopping by sea or air will add fun to your archipelago vacation. There are regular daily flights all summer between Jersey, Guernsey, and Alderney, fewer flights in winter. You can also fly from here to France for a quick visit.

Larger ferries do the trip between Jersey and Guernsey; fast hydrofoils skim around all the islands. Sark can be reached from Guernsey in around 45 minutes by **Sark Shipping** (tel. 0481/724059); Herm from Guernsey in 15 minutes by **Herm Seaways** (tel. 0481/724677); **Condor** (tel. 0481/726121) a twice-weekly service from both Jersey and Guernsey to Alderney in summer.

Exploring
the Channel Islands

Orientation

The tours of Jersey and Guernsey begin in the capital cities of St. Helier and St. Peter Port, respectively. Although the two largest of the archipelago, these islands are still relatively small, hence you will find most attractions to be in or close to these cities.

Alderney and Sark—though preserved and scenic—offer little for travelers looking for formal attractions like zoos, museums, or festivals. A visit to these islands is suggested as a jaunt to break up the time in the larger resort areas (*see* Getting Around, above).

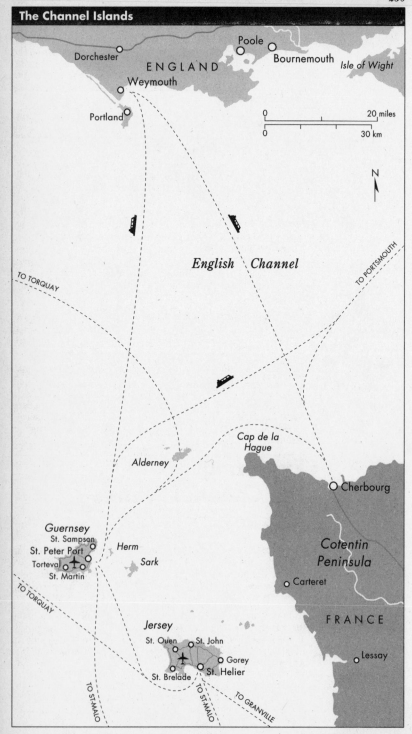

The Channel Islands

Dorchester

ENGLAND

Poole

Bournemouth

Isle of Wight

Weymouth

Portland

| 0 | | 20 miles |
| 0 | | 30 km |

N

English Channel

TO TORQUAY

TO PORTSMOUTH

Cap de la Hague

Alderney

Cherbourg

Guernsey

St. Sampson

St. Peter Port

Herm

Torteval

Sark

St. Martin

Cotentin Peninsula

Carteret

TO TORQUAY

FRANCE

Jersey

St. Ouen

St. John

Gorey

Lessay

St. Brelade

St. Helier

TO ST-MALO

TO ST-MALO

TO GRANVILLE

Jersey

Numbers in the margin correspond to points of interest on the St. Helier map.

❶ A good place to begin your island tour is at **Fort Regent,** in the capital city of St. Helier. The panoramic view you get from the fort will give you an idea of the town's layout.

When the fort was built, between 1806 and 1811, it was constructed high on a rock, as a defense against Napoleon's army (although the measure was never tested). In World War II, German anti-aircraft guns were sited in the fort. In 1958, the British government sold the fortification to the State of Jersey, which in 1967 turned it into a vast leisure complex. Today visitors enjoy the terraced swimming pool, concert hall, squash courts, World of Sea Aquarium, restaurants, bars, and cafés. During peak season there are guided tours that include two audio-visual presentations of the island's history. *Tel. 0534/73000. Admission: £3, £1 for additional attractions; coupon books for attractions, £1.05 and £3.50; wristbands £3.25.*

❷ Leave Fort Regent by cable car and turn left onto Hill Street to reach **Royal Square.** Now shaded by chestnut trees, the square used to be the site of executions and was the location of the town pillory.

Among those put to death were four alleged witches who were hanged and then burned in 1611. Witchcraft and its punishment were constant elements in Jersey life for most of the 16th and 17th centuries, with endless trials all over the island.

❸ Presently, the States offices, the **Royal Court** (the law court), and the **States Chamber** (Jersey's parliament) surround the square. On the west side is the **parish church** of St. Helier, or "Town Church," evidence of the 900-year-old legacy of churches that have stood here. The 12th–14th-century structure currently houses the processional cross and the chair in which the Bailiff sits when he attends service; both treasures were gifts from the diocese of New Jersey.

❹ Exiting the parish church, turn south onto Pier Road to reach the **Jersey Museum.** The museum is run jointly by the Jersey Heritage Trust and the Société Jersiaise, which was founded in 1873 to preserve Jersey's traditions. The museum is in a lovely building, completed in 1817 for the merchant and shipbuilder Philippe Nicolle, and contains some fascinating collections that shed light on Jersey's past. Among the displays are works by local artists; recreations of Victorian rooms; and memorabilia of Lillie Langtry, the beautiful mistress of Edward VII. "The Jersey Lily" was born on the island and is buried in St. Saviour's churchyard. *9 Pier Rd., tel. 0534/75940. Admission: £1.20 adults, 60p children and senior citizens. Open Mon.–Sat. 10–5.*

❺ From the museum, walk west past the bus station to **Weighbridge,** the busy center of St. Helier's harbor life. Follow the Esplanade west again to reach **The Island Fortress–Occupation Museum,** which has an extensive display of World War II propaganda relating to Germany's presence on the island. Videos describing the event are screened. *9 Esplanade, tel. 0534/34306. Admission: £2 adults, £1 children, £1.50 senior citizens. Open Mar.–Nov., daily 9:30 AM–10 PM.*

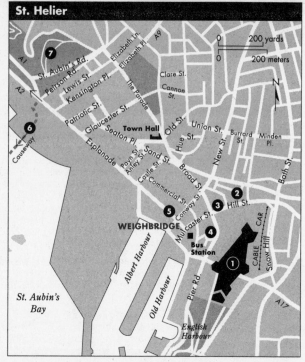

As you follow the Esplanade west, you will pass on the left the
Albert Harbour Marina, where yachts from all over the world
berth. You can take short or long cruises from here, including
an evening cocktail trip down the coast, or a weekend jaunt to
Brittany.

6 On the opposite side of the harbor is **Elizabeth Castle.** The castle juts out into the sea, but is joined to the esplanade by a
7 causeway that is opposite the Grand Hotel, by **Peoples' Park.**
You can cross the causeway between high tides but keep an ear
open for the bell which is rung from the castle's gatehouse half
an hour before the sea covers the stones; the water can get up to
15 feet deep. When the causeway is not useable, an amphibious
craft takes visitors across.

The little island was a holy isle beginning in the 6th century
with the arrival of Helier, the missionary son of a Belgian aris-
tocrat. Legend places his cell on the headland beyond the castle, still called **Hermitage Rock.** Close to the castle's entrance
there's an exhibition telling the building's story, a military museum in what were once the barracks in the Lower Ward. In the
granite-built Governor's House in the heart of the complex
there are waxwork tableaux of events in the castle's long history. Chief among them is the meeting of Sir Philippe de Carteret
and Charles II, who took refuge here in 1646. Carteret had
been born on Jersey, at St. Ouen in 1610, and while he was Bailiff the island was a haven for Royalists on the run from
Cromwell's troops. For his sterling service to the Royal cause,
after the Restoration Carteret was one of the eight men to
whom Charles entrusted the territory of the Carolinas be-

tween the Hudson and the Delaware. The region was called New Jersey in Carteret's honor. *St. Aubin's Bay, tel. 0534/ 23971. Admission: £1.20 adults, 60p children and senior citizens. Open Apr.–Oct., daily 9:30–5:30.*

You can explore other parts of Jersey by taking roads that radiate from St. Helier, or by doing a circular tour. The following highlights are arranged clockwise, starting just west of the capital. About 1½ miles from Elizabeth Castle is St. Matthew's Church, the "**Glass Church.**" This Victorian chapel was restored by Lady Florence Boot in 1934 as a memorial to her husband, Sir Jesse Boot, a millionaire pharmacist known throughout Britain for his drugstores, Boots. Lady Boot employed the fashionable Parisian glass sculptor, René Lalique (1860–1945), to transform the interior with glass. Inside, the church is embellished with fluid glass forms—the front seems to be supported by a cluster of icicles; the glass cross, pillars, and altar rail all glitter with refracted light. *Millbrook, St. Aubin's Rd., St. Lawrence. Admission free. Open weekdays 9–6 (or dusk), Sat. 9–1, Sun. for worship only.*

From Millbrook, A1 and A12 (Grand Route de St. Ouen) will take you to the northwest corner of the island, where you will find the **Battle of Flowers Museum.** The event, for which the museum is named, has been held annually (except during wartime) since 1902. Originally, the decorated floats were torn to pieces for ammunition in the battle, but now they survive longer, some to become exhibits in this museum. For the purpose of longevity, the exhibits on display are made with materials like dyed hare's tail and marram grass instead of flowers. There is a lakeside tearoom beside the museum that's open from May to September. *La Robeline, Mont des Corvées, St. Ouen, tel. 0534/82408. Admission: £1.25 adults, 60p children, £1 senior citizens. Open Easter–Dec., daily 10–5. For information on the Battle of Flowers contact The Executive Secretary, Jersey Battle of Flowers Assoc., Meadow Bank, St. Peter's Valley, St. Lawrence, tel. 0534/30178.*

Half a mile inland from Bouley Bay is the zoo of the **Jersey Wildlife Trust.** The Trust was started in 1963 by wildlife writer Gerald Durrell, who chose the 25 acres of Augres Manor as a center for breeding and conserving endangered species, including gorillas, orangutans, lemurs, snow leopards, and marmosets, together with many kinds of birds and reptiles. The preserve has proved successful, and many birds have been released back into the wild. This is a great place for a family outing, as well as for anyone interested in conservation. There's also a café, the Café Dodo, named after a bird Durrell was too late in saving. *Les Augres Manor, Trinity, tel. 0534/61949. Admission: £3.50 adults, £2 children and senior citizens. Open daily 10–6 (or dusk).*

Just over a mile south of the zoo you will find the **Eric Young Orchid Foundation.** The central viewing area is landscaped with small waterfalls, rocks, and trees, and vivid cascades of showy orchids, their seductive scent heavy in the air. Five big greenhouses radiate outward—each recreates the jungle environment that is needed to breed orchids. Eric Young, like Gerald Durrell, was a leading specialist who found ideal conditions on Jersey for pursuing his life's work. *Victoria Village, Trinity, tel. 0534/61963. Admission £2 adults, £1 children, £1.50 senior citizens. Open Thurs–Sat. 10–4.*

East of Victoria Village for 3½ miles of winding road stands
Gorey Castle, otherwise named **Mont Orgeuil** (Mount Pride).
For centuries Jersey's chief fortress, the castle rises square-
cut on its granite rock above the busy harbor. Built mainly in
the 14th century as a series of concentric defenses, the castle is
pierced by five gateways, each designed to be individually de-
fensible. At the heart of the castle is the great Somerset Tower,
and around it are grouped the Guard House, the Great Hall,
and the Kitchen. To one side of the Great Hall is St. Mary's
Chapel (12th century), probably the oldest part of the castle,
though traces of Iron Age defenses have been found. There are
waxwork tableaux of significant historical events at Mont
Orgeuil's, including Puritan William Prynne who was imprisoned here and branded on both cheeks with the letters SL,
meaning seditious libeller, for defaming Charles I and his
French wife, Henrietta Maria. *Tel. 0534/53292. Admission:
£1.20 adults, 60p children and senior citizens. Open Apr.–
Oct., daily 9:30–5.*

Guernsey

About 16,000 people, just over one third of the population of
Guernsey, live in **St. Peter Port,** the island's capital, which lies
on the east coast, facing France, just 8 miles away. The city has
prospered over the centuries from the harbor around which the
town climbs. Over the years additions have been made to the
harbor, the most recent of which is the city's third marina,
North Beach, with docking facilities for 800 craft.

Guernsey is well placed for trade—legal or illegal—between
France and England. In the 18th and 19th centuries, St. Peter
Port was a haven for privateers who preyed on merchantmen
plying the sea lanes; the operations were licensed by the British who skimmed off part of the considerable profits. Victor
Hugo furnished his house (*see* below) in the 1850s and '60s with
some of the looted pieces flooding onto the Guernsey market. In
a modern version of its privateering past, St. Peter Port is now
home to many tax exiles, who have luxurious houses in the "mil-
lionaires' estates" on the town's outskirts.

*Numbers in the margin correspond to points of interest on the
St. Peter Port map.*

❶ The heart of the old town is around the harbor, and is usually
jammed with traffic. The **parish church** of St. Peter is right beside The Quay. The church dates back at least to the days of
William the Conqueror, though the oldest part of the present
building is from the 12th century. Historical events throughout
the centuries have played havoc with the church, including an
air raid in 1944 that caused much damage.

❷ The southern arm of the harbor, Castle Pier, leads out to **Castle
Cornet,** where you can get a bird's-eye view of St. Peter Port
and across to France. The castle was built early in the 13th century to guard the fledgling town, and was badly damaged in an
explosion in 1672, when the powder magazine was struck by
lightning. Today the castle contains three museums, the **Royal
Guernsey Militia Museum,** the **Armoury,** and the **Main Guard
Museum,** that house a very mixed collection, ranging from model ships to relics from the German occupation to island art.
There's a cafeteria, and every day at midday one of the cannons
is fired. *Castle Emplacement, tel. 0481/721657 or 726518. Ad-*

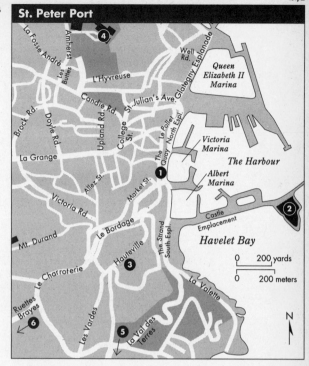

St. Peter Port

mission: £2 adults, 75p children, £1 senior citizens. Open Apr.–Oct., daily 10:30–5:30.

3 You will have to climb up from Castle Pier to Hauteville (High Town) in order to reach **Hauteville House,** once the home of writer Victor Hugo (1802–85). For 18 years he was a voluntary political exile on Guernsey; in 1856 he bought this house. It is now owned by the City of Paris, and is a completely French enclave, filled with the lovely old furniture and tapestries. From the top floor he could see across to his beloved France, and also into the house of his mistress, Juliette Drouet, who lived across the street. *Tel. 0481/21911. Admission: £2 adults, £1 children and senior citizens. Open Apr.–Sept., Mon.–Sat. 10–11:30, 2–4:30. Guided tours only, limited to 15 people.*

4 Just north of the town center, inland from the North Beach Marina, is the **Beau Sejour Centre,** a multi-purpose sports and entertainment complex built 15 years ago. Equipped with an indoor heated pool, squash, badminton, and tennis courts, a "trim trail," a cinema/theater, a cafeteria, and a bar, this is the perfect place to come on a rainy day. *Amherst, tel. 0481/728555. Admission: holiday membership £1.50. Open: 9 AM–11 PM, but check for times of pool and other activities.*

5 **Sausmarez Manor** (not to be confused with Saumarez Manor, northwest of St. Peter Port), about 2 miles to the south of downtown St. Peter Port, is Guernsey's only stately home open to the public. Although there was a Norman house on the site, the present building is a solid, plain structure, dating to the 18th century, and set among lovely gardens. The history inside, however, spans the centuries. Tapestries, family portraits, James II's wedding attire, and the log of the *Centurion*, the ship that circumnavigated the world and captured Spain's richest treasure galleon, are on display. Sir Edmund Andros, whose family lived in the house from 1557 to 1749, was Bailiff of Guernsey, as well as Governor of New York and Massachusetts. *Tel. 0481/35571. Admission: £2 adults, £1 children. Open for guided tours: late May–Sept., Tues.–Thurs. 10:30–12 and 2:30–4:30.*

❻ The **German Military Underground Hospital,** 2½ miles southwest of St. Peter Port, is the main relic attesting to the German occupation here. These grim catacombs were built by slave labor, and many of the workers died on the job and are entombed in the concrete. Intended as a hospital for soldiers fighting in Europe, this place was used for a short while but underground conditions caused further suffering, and the wounded had to be brought back into the daylight. This is not the only underground system on the island to survive from the years of World War II: There is also a network at **La Vallette** (tel. 0481/22300) that has been converted into a military museum; another, also a museum, near the **German Occupation Museum** (tel. 0481/38205); and a third in the **St. Saviour's Tunnel** (tel. 0481/64679). *Underground Hospital, La Vassalerie Rd., St. Andrew's, tel. 0481/39100. Admission: £1.50 adults, £1 children and senior citizens. Open Nov. and Mar., Sun. and Thurs. 2–3; Apr. and Oct., daily 2–4; May–Sept., daily 10–noon and 2–5.*

Alderney and Sark

Alderney (6 sq mi) and **Sark** (3.5 × 1.5 mi) are the "other islands"—much smaller in size and less traveled by tourists. Both are rich in landscapes that can be appreciated by touring the craggy coastlines, where cliffs and rocks teem with seabirds and other wildlife.

Because of its proximity to France, Alderney had been looked upon throughout history as a fortress island. In the 1800s, a chain of 12 forts was built around the coast; today some of those stand as desireable private homes. Also significant in Alderney's past was the German occupation during World War II, when the island's population was evacuated and three concentration camps were set up. The **Alderney Society's Museum** (High St., tel. 048182/3222) attests to this horrible event.

Sark, considered the odd-man-out of the Channel Islands, has turned its back on the 20th century and banned the automobile, allowing only horse- or tractor-drawn carriages as means of transportation. Even planes are prohibited from flying overhead unless special permission has been granted. The tranquil island can be reached by ferry, and is divided into two, with the smaller part, Little Sark, joined to the main island by a narrow neck of land whose vertiginous drop is 260 feet.

Off the Beaten Track

Guernsey   For a departure from castles and fortresses, visit the **Friquet Flower and Butterfly Centre** (Le Friquet, Castel, tel. 0481/54378). Walk among thousands of free-flying butterflies, and, later, partake in an evening barbecue or dinner at the restaurant. The **Tropical Vinery and Gardens** (St. Saviour's, tel. 0481/

63566) has glass houses crowded with hibiscus, lemons, limes, bougainvillea, and bananas. Also, for 100 years of tomato-growing history, see the **Tomato Centre** (King's Mills, Castel, tel. 0481/54389), and taste the tomato wine!

Jersey At **La Hogue Bie,** Grouville, halfway between St. Helier and Mont Orgueil castle, is one of the finest Neolithic tombs in Western Europe. It lies in a mound topped by two medieval chapels, and was excavated in 1924. The museum here has archaeological, farming, and old Jersey Railway exhibits. There is also another German bunker with an extensive occupation display. *Tel. 0534/53823. Admission: £1.20 adults, 60p children and senior citizens. Open mid-Mar.–Oct., daily 10–4:30.*

The **Carnation Nursery and Butterfly Farm** in the north of the island (off B23), has magnificent displays of carnations grown under glass in the grounds of an old farmhouse. Visitors can also wander among hundreds of rare and exotic butterflies, living and breeding in their natural habitat. *Retreat Farm, St. Lawrence, tel. 0543/65665. Admission free. Open summer, daily 9–5; winter, weekdays 9–5:30, Sat. 9–1.*

What to See and Do With Children

The Channel Islands are ideal for family vacations. All of them make special provisions for children, and adventure parks abound. In Jersey, **Fort Regent** (*see* Jersey, above) has year-round attractions and activities, though summer is a particularly festive time. One of its features, Humfrey's Playground, is for kids up to age 14.

The colorful birds and Jambo, the gentle gorilla, make the **Jersey Zoo** at the Jersey Wildlife Trust (*see* Jersey, above), a fascinating spot for all the family. **Guernsey Toys** (25–27 Victoria Rd., St. Peter Port, tel. 0481/723871), makes cuddly soft toys, and children can see the process at work.

Shopping

Unlike the rest of Britain, the Channel Islands don't add 15% VAT to the cost of the merchandise, therefore items tend to be less expensive than on the mainland. **St. Helier** and **St. Peter Port** are full of shops selling everything from cosmetics to liquor, and the towns are well equipped with all the major chains that you find throughout Britain.

Jersey Shopping in St. Helier can be a lot glitzier than in St. Peter Port. Pedestrian malls on **Queen Street** and **King Street** have classic shops selling international brands, while smaller boutiques line roads like **Bath Street, New Street,** and **Halkett Place.** Two major markets are the **Central Market** and **Indoor Market,** also in this area.

For crafts, visit the **Oatlands Craft Centre** (St. Sampson's, tel. 0481/49478), where glassblowers, silversmiths, potters, and quilters demonstrate and sell their works. Also visit the Bee Centre (in the complex), from which come the beeswax candles on sale.

Guernsey The main shopping district in St. Peter Port begins in the **Pollet,** near Queen Elizabeth marina. The area is a network of mostly pedestrian cobbled lanes with specialty shops—particularly jewelers. This is a great place to buy a watch.

For antiques and women's fashions head for the old quarter and **Mill Street, Mansell Square,** and **Trinity Square.** Walking along these quaint streets will provide you with as much fun as will the shopping.

Sports and Fitness

Bicycling The islands are ideal for cycling, and once you get off Jersey's main roads, and into less crowded routes, you'll be able to enjoy the fantastic scenery. On Guernsey, the pace of the bike is in keeping with the rhythm of island life. While in St. Helier, Jersey, rent from **Doubleday Garage** (19 Stopford Rd., tel. 0534/31505); **Lawrence de Gruchy** (46 Don St., tel. 0534/30090); and the **Hire Shop** (St. Albin's Rd., Milbrook, tel. 0534/73699). On Guernsey, you can rent bikes from **The Cycle Shop** (The Bridge, St. Sampson's, tel. 0481/49311); **Moullins Cycle Shop** (St. George's Esplanade, St. Peter Port, tel. 0481/721581); and **West Coast Cycles** (Les Tamaris, Portinfer Lane, Vale, tel. 0481/53654). On Sark, **Jackson's Cycle Hire** (tel. 0481/832161) and **Isle of Sark Carriage and Cycle Hire** (tel. 0481/832262) rent bikes.

Golf Jersey has two 18-hole courses, both of which can be used by any visitor who is affiliated with a golf club back home. These are **La Moye** (St. Brelade, tel. 0534/43401) and **Royal Jersey Golf Club** (Grouville, tel. 0534/54416).

The 18-hole **Royal Guernsey** (L'Ancresse Vale, tel. 0481/47022) has wonderful views of the beach and sea. To play here visitors must produce handicap certificates, and they can't play Sundays, Thursdays, and Saturday afternoons. On Alderney there is a **9-hole course** (Route des Carriers, tel. 048182/2835), which welcomes players anytime but on competition days.

Walking On all the islands the best routes for walking are along the coastlines, where there are well-marked trails almost all the way around. On Jersey's north coast, journey from **Grosnez** in the west to **Rozel** in the east. Part of this route will take you along 300-foot cliffs. On Guernsey, the coastal trail runs for almost 30 miles, with views as sensational as those in Jersey.

Watersports
Diving To dive in Jersey, contact **Watersports** (First Tower, tel. 0534/32813) or the **Underwater Centre** (Bouley Bay, tel. 0534/61817). In Guernsey contact the **Blue Dolphin Sun Aqua Club** (Rue des Cottes, St. Sampson's, tel. 0481/53878).

Sail-Boarding and Surfing At **St. Ouen,** in Jersey, there's great surfing. Windsurfing is popular at **St. Aubin** and **St. Brelade's Bay.** Rent equipment from **Watersplash** (St. Ouen's Bay, tel. 0534/82885) or the **Gorey Watersports Centre** (Grouville Bay, tel. 0534/522033). In Guernsey try the surf at **Vazon Bay.** The island's windsurfing authority is **Windsurfing International** (Cobô, tel. 0481/53313).

Swimming The unpolluted water and magnificent beaches are a major attraction of these islands. Although the tides can be fierce, most popular beaches have guards on duty. Two of many good swimming beaches on Jersey are **St. Clement's Bay** and **Royal Bay** of Grouville, both of which have excellent sand and safe water.

On Guernsey, try **Vazon Bay,** with one section reserved for surfers; **Petit Pot Bay,** especially for sunbathing; and **L'Ancresse Bay,** where the shallow water is appropriate for children.

Dining and Lodging

Dining The specialty of the Channel Islands is the seafood, in all its delectable glory. Crab and lobster dishes are on many menus, but don't overlook the daily catch from the tiny harbors around the coasts. Another specialty is the Jersey Ormer or sea ear—appropriately named for the shell's resemblance to the human ear. When you tire of seafood, the locally bred lamb is superb. Thick cream slathers the desserts, making for a perfect ending to your island meal.

Highly recommended restaurants are indicated by a star ★.

Category	Cost*
Very Expensive	over £35
Expensive	£25–£35
Moderate	£10–£25
Inexpensive	under £10

per person, including first course, main course, dessert, and VAT; excluding drinks

Lodging Jersey is chockablock with hotels, guest houses, and B&Bs, all carefully organized and well-regulated by the **Jersey Hotel and Guest House Assoc.** (60 Stopford Rd., St. Helier, Jersey JE2 4LB, tel. 0534/21421). You can get a comprehensive listing from the Jersey tourist board or from the Guernsey tourist board (*see* Important Addresses and Numbers, above). Lodgings range from luxury hotels to simple guest houses. When booking a room with a hotel, you may want to inquire about half-board offers, which include bed, breakfast, and one main meal, at a savings. Getting around Jersey is simple, and you may feel more comfortable away from the comparative razzmatazz of St. Helier. Guernsey is Jersey writ small, more relaxed, with hotels to match. If you are thinking of staying on Alderney or Sark, plan well ahead.

Highly recommended lodgings are indicated by a star ★.

Category	Cost*
Very Expensive	over £120
Expensive	£75–£120
Moderate	£40–£75
Inexpensive	under £40

All prices are for two people sharing a double room, including service, breakfast, and VAT.

Alderney
Dining **Nellie Gray's.** One of the few places to dine on Alderney, Nellie Gray's is reliable and has a homey atmosphere. Like most of the restaurants on the Islands, the menu here relies on the day's

catch and local produce. You can eat in the garden or indoors. *Victoria St., St. Anne, tel. 048182/3333. Reservations required. Dress: informal. AE, DC, MC, V. Closed Nov.–Apr., and Sun. Moderate.*

Dining and Lodging   **Georgian House.** You get a choice of great bar food—steak and mushroom pie, or fresh fish—in this friendly, whitewashed townhouse, or you can have a full meal in the dining room. During summer enjoy barbecue in the garden, or, on Wednesday and Saturday evenings (year round), there's a carvery buffet. For overnighters, there are four bedrooms. *Victoria St., St. Anne, tel. 048182/2471. Reservations advised for the restaurant. Dress: informal. AE, DC, MC, V. Bar: Inexpensive. Restaurant: Moderate.*

Guernsey   **Da Nello's.** This popular restaurant is one of a chain of four in
Dining   St. Peter Port. The chef here is Tim Vidamour, who brings his French flair to the cooking. Fresh fish is always available, and daily dishes reflect the day's catch. For those who prefer meat there is a charcoal grill. The set lunch menu is excellent value. *46 Le Pollet, St. Peter Port, tel. 0481/21552. Reservations advised. Dress: informal. AE, DC, MC, V. Moderate.*

Dining and Lodging   **La Frégate.** This is a small 17th-century manor house that's been carefully converted into a hotel with an attentive staff. Its position in colorful gardens on a quiet hillside that overlooks the harbor and islands makes it an excellent choice for a restful vacation. The bedrooms are all comfortable and sizeable, and some have balconies. The restaurant, with big windows overlooking the town, serves top-notch cuisine, especially the seafood dishes. Try the *timbale de crustacés*, or the home-marinated salmon with dill. *Les Côtils, St. Peter Port, tel. 0481/24624. 13 rooms with bath. AE, DC, MC, V. Expensive.*

Lodging   **Imperial Hotel.** This is a simple hotel that's very popular for family vacations. The bedrooms, decorated with sturdy furnishings, are uncluttered, and some offer views of the sandy beaches of Rocquaine Bay. There are two bars reserved for residents, and another, the Portlet Bar, is the haunt of locals. *Torteval, tel. 0481/64044. 16 bedrooms, 14 with bath. MC, V. Moderate.*

Jersey   **Victoria's.** This is the restaurant of the Grand Hotel, and is *the*
Dining   place to go for dinner and dancing. The decor is firmly Victorian. There's a long menu, but critic's choice is the lemon sole or the medallions of lamb. *Grand Hotel, Pierson Rd., tel. 0534/22301. Reservations required. Jacket and tie required. AE, DC, MC, V. Closed Sun. Expensive.*

Granite Corner. This is one of the few truly French restaurants on the island and is set in an attractive little cottage, tucked away beside Rozel Bay. The Patron/chef, Jean-Luc Robin, comes from Périgord in southwest France, and his specialties, reflecting his home region, often feature truffles from the area. He is also a whiz with fish caught fresh from Rozel Bay. If you prefer meat, try the classic *tournedos Rossini. Rozel Harbour, St. Martin, tel. 0534/63590. Reservations essential. Dress: Informal chic. AE, DC, MC, V. Closed Sun. evening and Mon. Moderate.*

Jersey Pottery. This restaurant is part of the Jersey Pottery complex and boasts that Queen Elizabeth lunched here when visiting her dukedom. The restaurant is in an attractive conservatory and offers great seafood. As it's very popular and often full, the cafeteria is an alternative. *Gorey Village, Grouville, tel. 0534/51119. Reservations advised. Open for lunch only, Mon.–Fri. Moderate.*

Dining and Lodging   **Hotel l'Horizon.** L'Horizon is one of Jersey's luxury hotels and has wonderful views overlooking St. Brelade's Bay. It is under new management, which has spent a mint to bring the hotel back to its former high standard. Though the hotel is big, it manages to maintain a bright, upbeat feeling throughout, with large, comfortable bedrooms, and plenty of places to relax in comfort. There are two restaurants—the **Crystal Room** and the **Star Grill.** The food is the same in both, but the atmosphere differs; the Crystal Room is traditionally elegant, while the Grill is more relaxed. Both offer marvellous views of the bay. Try the quail salad, roast saddle of lamb, or any of the wonderful seafood dishes, especially the scampi in mouthwatering ginger, honey, and lemon sauce. If you want to drop by for a special tea, try the **Beach Lounge,** where you can have scones and Jersey cream in ritzy surroundings, or the terrace and enjoy the panoramic view. *St. Brelade's Bay, St. Brelade, tel. 0534/43101. 103 rooms with bath. Facilities: 2 restaurants, garden, indoor pool, sauna, solarium, in-house movies. AE, DC, MC, V. Reservations and jacket and tie required for the restaurants. Very expensive.*

Longueville Manor. The Manor is one of Britain's few members of the Relais and Châteaux group. It's set in lovely grounds and has the look of polished age, elegance, and comfort, derived from long-established, caring proprietors. Antiques abound, the bedrooms are supremely comfortable, and the bathrooms are luxurious. The food in the classically panelled dining room is essentially traditional English—venison pâté with onion marmalade, grilled salmon with bearnaise sauce, liver with sausage, and black pudding are all specialties. There's passion-fruit sorbet or the Eton Mess, an unbelievable creation with crushed meringue, strawberries, and Jersey cream topping it off. *Longueville, St. Saviour, tel. 0534/25501. 33 rooms with bath. Facilities: restaurant, gardens, outdoor pool, in-house movies. Reservations and jacket and tie required for the restaurant. AE, DC, MC, V. Very Expensive.*

Château la Chaire, This dignified, mock-French château is hidden on a cul-de-sac just above Rozel Harbour. The building is large but offers only 13 bedrooms, though all are luxurious and sunny; some of the bathrooms have Jacuzzis. The property is opulent, and the restaurant is no exception. This is the place to try Jersey's excellent fresh fish in a variety of elegant preparations. *Rozel Bay, tel. 0534/63354. 13 rooms with bath. Facilities: restaurant, garden, in-house movies. Reservations and jacket and tie required for the restaurant. AE, DC, MC, V. Expensive.*

Moorings Hotel. This seaside hotel is not one of Jersey's fanciest, but it does offer attractively decorated, very cozy bedrooms (13 of them with harbor views), and friendly, helpful service. The restaurant, too, is on the simple side, but the lamb carved from the trolley, and the superbly fresh seafood dishes, are all well above average. *Gorey Pier, tel. 0534/53633. 16 rooms with bath. Facilities: restaurant, patio. Reservations required for the restaurant. Dress: informal. AE, DC, MC, V. Moderate.*

The Old Court House Inn. This is an ancient inn—the core of the building is around 500 years old—with a few rooms, two atmospheric lunchtime bars, and a fine restaurant. It is yet another place to tuck in to local seafood—grilled oysters, crab creole, Jersey plaice, all feature on the big menu. The busy inn overlooks the harbor; the best view, though, is from the penthouse. *The Bulwarks, St. Aubin's Harbour, tel. 0534/46433. 9 rooms with bath. Facilities: restaurant, 2 bars, patio. Reservations advised for the restaurant. Dress: informal. MC, V. Moderate.*

Sark
Dining and Lodging

Stock's Buffet. For a relaxed lunch—and what else would you expect on Sark?—try the restaurant of Stock's Hotel. Lunchtime fare consists of such dishes as quiche, or the local lobster and crab. Their seafood provençal is memorable. If you feel like staying over, there are 24 bedrooms and a thoroughly peaceful atmosphere. The restaurant also serves a more formal dinner. For a light snack, Stocks' cakes and pastries rank high on the menu. *Tel. 048183/2001. Reservations not needed. Dress: informal. AE. Closed Oct.–Easter. Buffet: Inexpensive. Hotel: Moderate.*

The Arts

Festivals
Jersey has a **Jazz Festival** in April, staged at the Pomme d'Or Hotel (tel. 0534/78644) in St. Helier. The **Battle of Flowers** is held in August (*see* Exploring), and a **Folk and Blues Festival** is held in September, in People's Park, St. Helier. Films, theater, and celebrity concerts are put on all year in Fort Regent (*see* Exploring).

Performing Arts
During the summer months there are concerts by visiting bands in the Howard Davis Park, St. Helier. The **Jersey Arts Centre** (Phillips St., St. Helier, tel. 0534/73767), has regular exhibitions of art, as well as drama, films, and music.

Guernsey has an **Eisteddfod** at the end of February, an **International Dance Festival** in June, and a **Battle of Flowers** in August. Contact the tourist board for the latest dates.

8 The Thames Valley

Introduction

Like many another great river, the Thames creates the illusion that it flows not only through its own prosperous countryside, but through long centuries of history, too. The magic of past times seems to rise from its swiftly moving waters like an intangible mist. In London, where it is a broad, oily stream, it speeds almost silently past great buildings, menacingly impressive, as if resenting its confining embankments. Higher upstream it is a busy part of the living landscape, flooding meadows in spring and fall, linking a chain of great houses created by power-brokers who needed to be near the capital, and rippling past places that are of significance not just to England but to the world. Runnymede is one of these. It was here, on a riverside greensward, that his barons forced King John to sign the Magna Carta, and so initiated a crucial step in the western world's progress toward democracy.

Nearby rises the splendid medieval bulk of Windsor Castle, home to eight successive royal houses. Anyone who wants to understand the mystique of the British monarchy should be sure to visit Windsor, where a fraction of the present Queen's vast wealth is on display in surroundings of pomp, power, and solid magnificence.

Further upstream lies Oxford, where generations of the country's ruling elite have been educated at the famous university. Unlike peaceful Cambridge, deep in the fen country, Oxford is a bustling modern city, with major industrial developments on its outskirts, but the colleges maintain their scholarly calm amid the traffic's clamorous rush.

Scattered throughout the spreading landscape of trees, meadows, and rolling hills, are endless small villages and larger towns, some totally spoiled by ill-considered modern building, some still sleepily preserving their ancient charm. Reading is a sad example of the former, Ewelme the epitome of the latter. Apart from the meandering thread of the river, which ties the area together, the Thames Valley is crisscrossed by superhighways carrying the heavy streams of traffic between London, the West Country, and the Midlands. These highways have joined the railroad in converting much of this area into commuter territory for London. But you can easily leave these beaten tracks, and head down leafy lanes to discover timeless villages and scenic vistas, kept green and flourishing by the Thames and its wandering tributaries.

Essential Information

Important Addresses and Numbers

Tourist Information **The Thames and Chilterns Tourist Board** (The Mount House, Church Green, Witney, Oxfordshire OX8 8DZ, tel. 0993/778800) is the main tourist information center for the region. Open weekdays 9–5.

Local tourist offices include:

Henley: Town Hall, tel. 0491/578034.
Oxford: St. Aldate's, tel. 0865/726871.
Windsor: Central Station, tel. 0753/852010.

Travel Agencies **Thomas Cook,** 5 Queen St., Oxford, tel. 0865/240441.
Travel House of America, 1 Bolton Rd., Windsor, tel. 0753/855031.

Car Rental **Oxford: Europcar Ltd.,** Hartwells of Oxford, Oxford Rd., tel.
Agencies 08675/3071; **Hertz,** City Motors Ltd., The Roundabout, Woodstock Rd., tel. 0865/57291.

Arriving and Departing

By Car M4 and M40 radiate westward from London, bringing Oxford (57 miles) and Reading (42 miles) within an hour's drive. In rush hour, however (8–10 AM and 4–6 PM), the journey can take considerably longer, as the roads around London jam up.

By Train **British Rail** serves the region from London's Paddington Station (tel. 071/262–6767). There are fast trains to the main towns, and a reliable commuter service to stations throughout the area, including Henley and Windsor. There are also hourly services to Oxford (travel time is one hour). A "Network Southeast" card, valid for one year, entitles you to one-third off certain fares.

By Bus **City Link** (tel. 0865/711312) runs a regular London–Oxford service, with departures every 20 minutes throughout the day from London's Victoria Coach Station. Travel time is one hour and 40 minutes.
London Link (tel. 0734/581358) offers a regular London–Reading shuttle, and services from Heathrow and Gatwick airports to Oxford. Another service—the Reading-based **Bee Line** (tel. 0734/581358)—serves the smaller towns of Berkshire and the surrounding countryside.

Getting Around

By Car Although the road network within the region is extensive and generally well-maintained, the high level of car ownership in this wealthy section of the commuter belt means that traffic is surprisingly heavy throughout the day, even on the smaller roads.

Parking in towns can be a problem, too, so visiting motorists should be patient and allow plenty of time for journeys.

By Train For local timetables, phone 0865/722333 (Oxford area), 0734/595911 (Reading area), or 0753/38621 (Windsor area).

By Bus The **Oxford Bus Company** (tel. 0865/711312) offers a one-day "Compass" ticket and a seven-day "Freedom" ticket, both providing unlimited bus travel within Oxford.

A local bus service links the towns along the Thames between Oxford and Windsor.

Guided Tours

Orientation **Guide Friday** (Windsor tel. 0753/855755, Oxford tel. 0865/790522) organizes tours of Windsor and Oxford with fully trained guides at moderate rates (£4.50 for an adult, £2 for a child).

River Tours The best way to see the Thames region is from the water. During the summer months, the choice of river trips ranges from 30-minute outings to all-day excursions.

Hobbs and Sons (tel. 0491/572035) offers trips along the Henley Reach, and also rents self-drive motorboats or rowboats from Station Road, Henley on Thames.

Salter Brothers (tel. 0865/243421) runs daily steamer cruises, mid-May to mid-Sept. Boarding points include Windsor (Thameside), Oxford (Folly Bridge), Abingdon, Henley, Marlow (Higginson Park), and Reading.

Thames River Cruises (tel. 0734/481088) conducts outings from Caversham Bridge, Reading, Easter–Sept.

Windsor Boat Company (tel. 0753/862933) operates 35-minute and two-hour river trips from Windsor. Embarkation point, The Promenade.

Exploring the Thames Valley

Orientation

We begin our tour of the Thames Valley in the lively tourist town of Windsor, due west of London, favorite home-away-from-home for Britain's royal family. From there we follow the river north and west to Henley, site of the famous regatta. Using Henley as a base, we then follow a semicircular sweep east to Marlow and west to Wallingford—the countryside immortalized by the children's classic *The Wind in the Willows*—stopping in the busy town of Reading, Berkshire's county seat. Finally we head northwest to the historic city of Oxford, and end our tour with a visit to some of the region's stately homes and palaces.

Highlights for First-time Visitors

Blenheim Palace: Tour 3
Eton College: Tour 1
Ewelme: Tour 2
Magdalen College, Oxford: Tour 3
Runnymede: Tour 1
Stoke Poges: Tour 1
Vale of the White Horse, Uffington: Tour 3
Windsor Castle: Tour 1

Tour 1: Royal Berkshire—Windsor and Environs

Numbers in the margin correspond to points of interest on the Thames Valley map.

① **Windsor,** just 21 miles west of London and easily reached by train, bus, car, or even boat, offers a rewarding day out for capital-based visitors. The town's principal attraction is the castle, rising majestically on its bluff above the Thames, visible for miles around. But the city itself, with its narrow streets brimming with shops and ancient buildings, is well worth a visit on its own account.

The most impressive view of Windsor Castle is from the A332 road, on the southern approach to the town. Begun by William the Conqueror in the 11th century, the castle was transformed and extended by Edward III in the mid-1300s. One of his largest contributions was the enormous and distinctive round tower. Finally, between 1824 and 1837, George IV transformed what was essentially still a medieval castle into the fortified royal palace you see today. In all, work on the castle was spread over more than eight centuries, with most of the kings and queens of England demonstrating their undying attachment to it. In fact, Windsor is the only royal residence that has been in continuous use by the royal family since the Middle Ages.

When the Queen isn't in residence, visitors can view the state apartments. She uses the castle far more often than any of her recent predecessors, and it has become a kind of weekend home—close, but not too close, to London, with plenty of space for peaceful relaxation. Here you get a sense of the immense wealth of the royal family. The rooms overflow with fine pictures, antique furniture, porcelain, armor, and tapestries.

As you enter the castle, **Henry VIII's gateway** leads uphill into the wide castle precincts, where visitors are free to wander. Directly opposite the entrance is **St. George's Chapel,** where the Queen invests new knights at the colorful Order of the Garter ceremonies in June, and where several of her predecessors are buried, including her father, George VI. Built in the 15th- and 16th-century Perpendicular style, and one of England's finest churches, the chapel features elegant stained-glass windows, a high, vaulted ceiling, and intricately carved choir stalls. The heraldic banners of the Knights of the Garter hang in the choir, giving it a richly medieval look (the knights have been installed at Windsor for more than 640 years). Members of the choir live close by in the 15th-century timbered buildings of the Horseshoe Cloister.

The **North Terrace** provides especially good views across the Thames to Eton College (*see* below), perhaps the most famous of Britain's exclusive "public" boys' schools. From the terrace, you enter the **State Apartments,** a sequence of splendid rooms containing priceless furniture, including a magnificent Louis XVI bed; Gobelins tapestries; and paintings by Canaletto, Rubens, Van Dyck, Holbein, Dürer, and del Sarto. The high points of the tour are the **Throne Room** and the **Waterloo Chamber,** where Sir Thomas Lawrence's portraits of Napoleon's victorious foes line the walls. You can also see a collection of arms and armor, much of it exotic.

Queen Mary's Doll's House, on display to the left of the castle entrance, is a perfect palace-within-a-palace, with functioning lights, running water, and even a library of Lilliputian-size books especially written by famous authors of Queen Mary's day (the 1920s). You may also want to see an exhibition of items from the **Queen's Collection of Master Drawings;** she owns a large number of drawings by Leonardo da Vinci, plus 87 Holbein portraits, and many others.

Just outside the bounds of Windsor Castle, on St. Albans Street, you'll find the **Royal Mews,** where the royal horses are kept, with carriages, coaches, and splendid red and gold harness. The highlight is the Scottish State Coach, used by the Prince and Princess of Wales for their 1981 wedding. *Tel. 0753/ 868286. Admission: Precincts, free; State Apartments, £2.80 adults, £1.20 children, £1.80 senior citizens; Dolls' House, £1.40 adults, 60p children, £1.20 senior citizens; Royal Mews, £1.30 adults, 60p children, £1 senior citizens. Open daily, with*

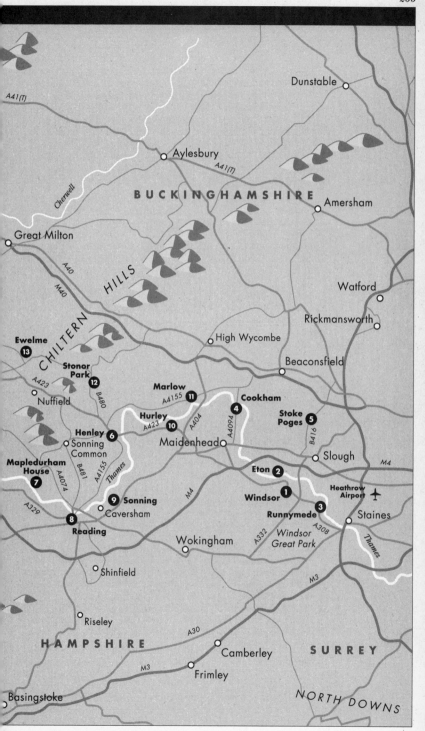

different seasonal hours, except when Queen is in residence; schedule is complicated, so check before visiting.

Opposite Windsor castle, and recently incorporated into the railroad station there, is the **Royalty and Empire Exhibition**, constructed by Madame Tussaud's. It re-creates in wax the arrival of Queen Victoria to celebrate her Diamond Jubilee in 1897, showing models of Victoria's entourage about to board the Ascot landau drawn by four gray Windsor horses. An honor guard of 70 scarlet-uniformed soldiers presents arms, and a military band plays the royal salute. You can also see an audiovisual presentation on Victoria's 64-year reign. *Thames St., tel. 0753/857837. Admission: £3.95 adults, £2.80 children, £2.95 senior citizens. Open Apr.–Oct., daily 9:30–5:30; Nov.–Mar., daily 9:30–4:30.*

Only a small part of old Windsor—the settlement which grew up around the castle in the Middle Ages—has survived. Opposite the castle entrance you can explore tiny Church Lane and Queen Charlotte Street, both narrow and cobbled. The old buildings now house antiques shops or restaurants. Around the corner, on High Street, stands the colonnaded **Guildhall** built in the 1680s by Sir Christopher Wren, who designed London's St. Paul's Cathedral (his father was dean of Windsor). Wren also built himself a fine house overlooking the river in Thames Street, now the Sir Christopher Wren's House Hotel (*see* Dining and Lodging, below).

Time Out The **Dôme** (5 Thames St.) will provide a good lunch with a French accent: pâté, charcuterie, or interesting salads.

A footbridge across the Thames links Windsor with its almost ② equally historic neighbor, **Eton**. With its single main street leading from the river to the famous school, Eton is a much quieter town than Windsor and retains an old-fashioned charm. The splendid redbrick, Tudor-style buildings of **Eton College**, founded in 1440 by King Henry VI, border the north end of High Street; drivers are warned of "Boys Crossing." During the college semesters, the schoolboys are a distinctive sight, dressed in their pinstripe trousers, swallow-tailed coats, top hats, and white collars. The oldest buildings, grouped around a quadrangle called School Yard, include the **Lower School**, which is one of the oldest schoolrooms in use in Britain. The Gothic **Chapel** rivals St. George's at Windsor in both size and magnificence. Beyond the cloisters are the school's famous playing fields where, according to the duke of Wellington, the Battle of Waterloo was won, since so many of his officers had learned discipline in their schooldays there. The **Museum of Eton Life** has displays on the school's history, and there are guided tours of the Lower School and chapel. *Brewhouse Yard, tel. 0753/ 863593. Admission: £2.20 adults, £1.40 children; £2.80 or £5.50 adults, £2.20 or £5.50 children with tour. Open daily during college terms 2–4:30; out-of-term, 10:30–4:30.*

Just south of Windsor Castle, stretching for some 8 miles (about 5,000 acres), is **Windsor Great Park,** the remains of an ancient royal hunting forest. Much of it is open to the public and can be explored by car or on foot. Focal points include the 3-mile **Long Walk,** the **Royal Mausoleum** at Frogmore, where Queen Victoria and her husband Prince Albert are buried (open only two days a year, in May); **Virginia Water,** a 2-mile-long lake; and

Windsor Castle

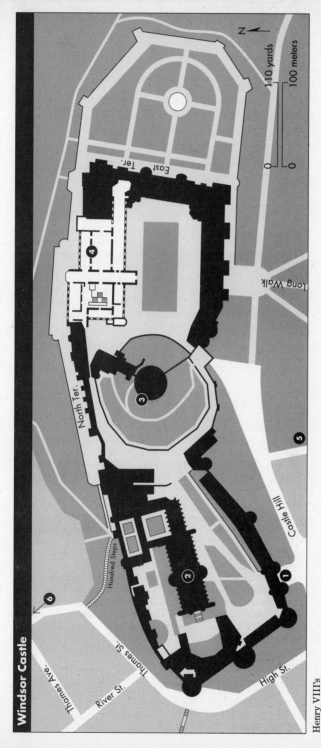

Henry VIII's
Gateway, **1**
Round Tower, **3**
Royal Mews, **5**
Royalty and Empire
Exhibiton, **6**
St. George's Chapel, **2**
State Apartments, **4**

the **Savill Garden,** which offers a huge variety of trees and shrubs. *Wick Lane, Englefield Green, Egham, tel. 0753/ 860222. Admission (garden): £2.20 adults, children under 16 free, £2 senior citizens. Open weekdays 10–6, weekends 10–7 or sunset.*

Windsor Safari park, also close by, offers another interesting diversion (*see* What to See and Do with Children, below).

❸ Directly southeast of Windsor on the A308 is **Runnymede,** a tiny island in the middle of the Thames where King John, under his barons' compulsion, signed the Magna Carta in 1215, affirming the individual's right to justice and liberty. On the wooded hillside, in a meadow given to the United States by Queen Elizabeth in 1965, stands a **memorial to President John F. Kennedy.** Nearby is another memorial, in the style of a classical temple, erected by the American Bar Association to commemorate the 750th anniversary of the signing of the Magna Carta.

North of Windsor, the river winds past the towns of Slough and Maidenhead to arrive in the prettier, more rural surroundings **❹** upstream from the village of **Cookham.** The Cookham area was the subject of the paintings of Sir Stanley Spencer (1891–1959), some of which are on display at the **Stanley Spencer Gallery.** *King's Hall, Cookham, tel. 06285/20890. Admission: 50p. Open Easter–Oct., daily 10:30–5:30; Nov.–Easter, weekends and national holidays, 11–5.*

Near Cookham, in woods high above the river, stands **Cliveden House,** the imposing country mansion made famous by the Astors, who had it rebuilt in the 1860s. The house now belongs to the National Trust, which has leased it for use as a *very* exclusive hotel. The public can visit the lovely grounds and formal gardens with their fine views over the Thames, as well as three rooms in the west wing of the house. Among the attractions in the grounds is a small amphitheater in which "Rule Britannia" was first sung in 1739. There is a convenient restaurant for lunch. *Grounds—admission: £2.80 adults, £1.40 children, house £1 extra. Open Mar.–Dec., 11–6. House open Apr.–Oct., Thurs. and Sun. only 3–6. Restaurant in the Orangery open Apr.–Oct., Wed.–Sun. 11–5.*

To the east of Cookham you will find an abundance of scenic, wooded areas. **Burnham Beeches,** a 600-acre tract of beeches, great oaks, birches, and other majestic trees, is a beautiful spot for walks throughout the year. In the spring the rhododendrons are in full bloom, while in the fall the beeches turn a vivid russet red. Sadly, the 600-year-old beech under which Mendelssohn composed part of his music for *A Midsummer Night's Dream* was shattered in a storm in January 1990. East again **❺** about 4 miles lies the village of **Stoke Poges.** In 1742, while staying with his uncle, the poet Thomas Gray visited the village church here and was inspired to write his famous *Elegy in a Country Churchyard.* Visitors can explore the church and grounds and stay in the house where this classic poem was composed (*see* Dining and Lodging, below).

Tour 2: From Henley to Wallingford—
"Wind in the Willows" Country

6 Mention **Henley** to Britons, and even those who have scarcely seen a boat will conjure up idyllic scenes of summer rowing. Indeed, Henley Royal Regatta, held in early July each year on a long, straight stretch of the river Thames, has made the charming little riverside town famous throughout the world.

Henley, set in a broad valley between gentle hillsides just off A423, about 8 miles from Reading and 36 miles from central London, has been an important river crossing since the 12th century. The handsome Henley bridge, its keystones carved with personifications of the Thames and Isis rivers, is more than 200 years old. Now, unfortunately, the bridge is a serious traffic bottleneck, especially on weekends.

Henley's many historic buildings, including one of Britain's oldest theaters, are all within a few minutes' walk. Half-timbered Georgian cottages and inns abound. Many have courtyards that once witnessed the brutal sport of bear-baiting, where tethered bears were tormented to death by hungry dogs. There is also an interesting selection of small antiques and gift shops, and several historic pubs.

Just beside the bridge you will see the **Red Lion Hotel,** built in mellow terracotta brick (*see* Dining and Lodging, below). This inn has been the town's focal point for nearly 500 years. Kings, dukes, and authors have stayed here, including Charles I in 1632 and 1642, and the duke of Marlborough, who used the hotel as a base during the building of Blenheim Palace in the early 18th century. He even arranged to have a room in the hotel furnished to his own specifications.

Overlooking the bridge is the 16th-century "checkerboard" tower of **St. Mary's Church** on Hart Street. The building is made of alternating squares of local flint and white stone. If the church's rector (minister) is about, you will be able to climb to the top and enjoy the superb views up and down the river and around the countryside.

The **Chantry House,** connected to the church by a gallery, was built as a school for poor boys in 1420. It is an unspoiled example of the rare timber-frame design, with upper floors jutting out. *Hart St., tel. 0491/577340. Admission free. Open Thurs. and Sat. 10–noon.*

Townspeople launched the Henley Regatta in 1839, initiating the Grand Challenge Cup, the most famous of its many trophies. After 1851, when Prince Albert, Queen Victoria's consort, became its patron, it was known as the Royal Regatta. Oarsmen compete in crews of eight, four, or two, or as single scullers. For many of the spectators, however, the social side of the event is far more important. Elderly oarsmen wear brightly colored blazers and tiny caps, businesspeople entertain wealthy clients, and everyone admires the range of ladies' fashions on parade.

Another traditional event in the third week of July is Swan-Upping. This activity dates back 800 years. Most of the swans on the Thames are owned by the Queen, though a few belong to two City of London livery companies, the Dyers and the Vintners, descendants of the medieval crafts guilds. Swan markers in Thames skiffs start from Sunbury-on-Thames, catching the new cygnets and marking their beaks in order to establish ownership. The Queen's swan keeper, dressed in scarlet livery, presides over this colorful ceremony, complete with festive banners.

Time Out You are never far from a pub in Henley, a town where beer has been brewed for over 200 years. One of the most popular inns is the **Three Tuns** (5 Market Place), which has a buttery with massive beams and a small summer terrace. The bar food is reasonable and filling—hot salt beef, vegetarian lasagne, mixed seafood—all washed down with good local beer.

Across the river, on the eastern side, follow the towpath north along the pleasant, shady banks to **Temple Island,** a tiny, privately owned island with trailing willows and a solitary house. This is where the Regatta races start. On the south side of the town bridge, a riverside promenade passes **Mill Meadows,** where there are gardens and a pleasant picnic area. Along both stretches, the river is alive with boats of every shape and size, from luxury "gin palace" cabin cruisers to tiny rowboats.

Edged by the gently sloping Chiltern Hills and in a wide horseshoe-shaped valley, the Thames meanders eastward from Henley through a cluster of small country towns and villages. Main roads follow the river on both sides, but it is along the narrow lanes that the villages and wooded countryside—generally prettiest north of the river—are best explored. Plan to enjoy the area at a leisurely pace, stopping for morning coffee, a pub lunch, or a cream tea at one of the ancient inns overlooking the river, and then visit shops or stroll along the river towpath to visit a lock. For more serious sightseers, the region offers a wide range of earthworks, churches, and stately homes.

7 About 5 miles southwest of Henley, via Sonning Common, is **Mapledurham House,** a redbrick Elizabethan mansion with tall chimneys, mullioned windows, and battlements. Its 15th-century water mill is the last working grain mill on the Thames. The house is still the home of the Eyston family, and so has kept a warm, friendly atmosphere along with pictures, family portraits, magnificent oak staircases, and Tudor plasterwork ceilings. Mapledurham can also be reached by boat from Caversham Promenade in Reading. (The boat leaves at 2 PM, and travel time is about 40 minutes.) *Mapledurham, near Reading, tel. 0734/723350. Admission: combined house and mill £4 adults; house only £3; grounds and mill £2.50; children half price. Open Easter–Sept., weekends only 2:30–5.*

This section of the river, from Caversham to Mapledurham, inspired Kenneth Grahame's classic children's book, *Wind in the Willows,* which began as a bedtime story for Grahame's son Alastair while the Grahames were living at Pangbourne. E. F. Shepherd's intriguing illustrations for the book were based on specific sites along it.

8 Following A4074 southeast from Mapledurham will take you to **Reading,** the county seat of Berkshire and now a busy industrial town with abundant stores and a major rail interchange. The **Reading Museum,** which has a major collection of finds from the excavated Roman settlement of Silchester nearby, will be closed for rebuilding until at least 1993.

9 Leaving Reading, travel about 4 miles northeast to **Sonning,** another lovely riverside village, its quiet riverbanks overhung with weeping willows. Sonning has a graceful, arched brick bridge, a lock, and a water mill, mentioned in the Domesday Book. The mill has been converted into a dinner theater.

10 Continuing northeast along A4/A404 to Marlow, it is easy to miss the turnoff to **Hurley.** This is probably why the village, with its 12th-century flintstone church and cedar-lined green, feels so peaceful and remote. Though there is no through road, Hurley's lock is one of the busiest of the 44 along the river. On summer weekends, about 400 boats pass through it each day.

11 As you enter **Marlow,** about 4 miles farther on, take particular note of its unusual suspension bridge, which William Tierney Clark built in 1831. (His better-known creation is the bridge over the Danube linking Buda with Pest.) Marlow has a number of striking old buildings, particularly the stylish, privately owned Georgian houses along Peter and West streets. In 1817, the Romantic poet Percy Bysshe Shelley stayed with friends at 67 West Street and then bought **Albion House** on the same street. His second wife, Mary, completed her Gothic novel *Frankenstein* here. Marlow Place, in Station Road, dates from 1721, and has been lived in by several princes of Wales.

Time Out One of the town's fine old hostelries is the 400-year-old **Ship Inn** (on West St.), whose beams were once ship timbers. There's a courtyard for summer drinking.

---

12 About 6 miles northwest of Marlow, lost in the network of leafy country lanes, is **Stonor Park,** the home of the Catholic Stonor family for more than 800 years. A medieval mansion with a Georgian facade, it stands in a wooded deer park. Mass has been celebrated in its tiny chapel since the Middle Ages, and there is an exhibition of the life and work of the Jesuit Edmund Campion, who took shelter here in 1581 before his martyrdom. *Stonor, tel. 049163/587. Admission: £3 adults, children under 14 free, £2.40 senior citizens. Open Apr.–Sept., Sun.; May–Sept., Wed.; July and Aug., Thurs.; Aug., Sat. 2–5:30.*

13 West again, just beyond the towns of Pishill and Cookley Green, lies **Ewelme,** one of England's prettiest and most unspoiled villages. Its picture-book almshouses, church, and school—one of the oldest in Britain—huddle close together, all built more than 500 years ago. The church shelters the carved alabaster tomb of Alice, duchess of Suffolk, the granddaughter of England's greatest medieval poet, Geoffrey Chaucer. Jerome K. Jerome, author of the humorous book *Three Men in a Boat,* describing a Thameside vacation, is also buried here. He came to live in the village in 1887.

14 Two miles west of Ewelme is **Wallingford,** a typical riverside market town. Its busy marketplace is bordered by a town hall, built in 1670, and an Italianate corn exchange (grain market building), now a theater and cinema. Market day is Friday.

Thirteen miles northwest on A329/423 will bring you into Oxford.

Tour 3: Oxford and Area

⑮ The most picturesque approach to **Oxford** is from the east, over Magdalen Bridge. Among the ancient honey-colored buildings and elegant spires, you will see the 15th-century tower of Magdalen (pronounced "Maudlin") College, famous for its May Day carol service. Magdalen Bridge leads you directly into the broad, gently curving High Street, flanked by ancient colleges.

In Oxford the rarefied air of academia and the bustle of modern life compete with one another. For in addition to its historic university, Oxford is home to two major industrial complexes: the Rover car factory and the Pressed Steel works. In the city center, "town and gown" merge as modern stores sit side by side with centuries-old colleges and their peaceful quadrangles. With its tremendous historical and architectural wealth—no fewer than 653 buildings are designated as being of "architectural or historical merit"—Oxford deserves a lengthy visit. Keep in mind, however, that congested sidewalks jammed with students, townspeople, tourist groups, and legions of foreign schoolchildren, can be hell to negotiate.

Newcomers are surprised to learn that the University of Oxford is not one unified campus, but a collection of many colleges and buildings, new as well as old, scattered across the city. Altogether there are 40 different colleges where undergraduates live and study. Most of their grounds are open to tourists, including the magnificent dining halls and chapels, though the opening times (displayed at the entrance lodges) vary greatly. Some colleges are open only in the afternoons during university semesters, when the undergraduates are in residence.

Numbers in the margin correspond to points of interest on the Oxford map.

⑯ Let's begin with **Magdalen College,** one of the largest and most impressive of Oxford's colleges, founded in 1458. Its ancient vaulted cloisters, overhung with wisteria, enclose a serene quadrangle. Beyond this, a narrow stone passage leads through to a large, open park with grazing deer and a cluster of imposing classical buildings. Beyond this lies the sleepy Cherwell River. At the foot of Magdalen Bridge you can rent (for £5 an hour) a punt, a shallow-bottomed boat that is poled slowly up the river. Students punting on summer afternoons sprawl on cushions, dangling champagne bottles in the water to cool them.

⑰ Farther along the High Street is **St. Edmund Hall,** one of the smallest and oldest colleges (founded c. 1220). Its tiny quadrangle, entered through a narrow archway off Queen's Lane, has an ancient well in the center. Farther up Queen's Lane you will
⑱ see the far grander **New College** (founded in 1379), with its extensive gardens overlooking part of the medieval city wall. This was the home of the celebrated Dr. Spooner, known for his tongue- twisting "spoonerisms." He is reputed to have told a dilettante student, "You have hissed your mystery lectures and tasted a whole worm."

⑲ The 14th-century tower of the **University Church** (St. Mary's), a few yards farther on, provides a splendid panoramic view of the city's famous skyline—the pinnacles, towers, domes, and

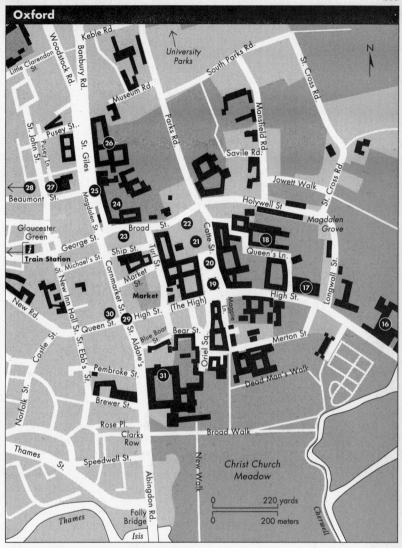

Oxford

Ashmolean, **27**
Balliol College, **24**
Bodleian Library, **21**
Carfax, **29**
Christ Church College, **31**
Magdalen College, **16**
Martyrs' Memorial, **25**
New College, **18**
Oxford Story Exhibition, **23**
Radcliffe Camera, **20**
St. Edmund Hall, **17**
St. John's, **26**
St. Martin's Church, **30**
Sheldonian Theatre, **22**
University Church, **19**
Worcester College, **28**

spires spanning every architectural style since the 11th century. *Admission: 75p adults, 40p children. Tower open daily 9:15–7, 9:15–4:30 in winter.*

Immediately opposite the church is the third-largest dome in Britain, that of the **Radcliffe Camera.** This building contains part of the **Bodleian Library,** an important collection begun 300 years ago. It holds more than two million volumes.

㉒ The university's ornate **Sheldonian Theatre** is where the impressive graduation ceremonies (conducted entirely in Latin) are held. Built in 1663, it was the first building designed by Sir Christopher Wren. Semicircular like a Roman amphitheater, it has pillars, balconies, and an elaborately painted ceiling. There is an impressive view from the top. Outside, beige stone pillars are topped by the massive stone heads of 18 Roman emperors, sculpted in the 1970s to replace the originals that had been rendered faceless by air pollution. *Tel. 0865/241023. Admission: 50p adults, 25p children. Open Mon.–Sat. 10–12:45 and 2–4:45; Dec.–Feb., closes 3:45.*

Broad Street, known to undergraduates as "the Broad," is a wide, straight thoroughfare lined with colleges and bow-fronted, half-timbered shops. Among them is **Blackwell's,** a family-run bookstore offering one of the largest selections of books in the world. It has been in business since 1879.

㉓ While you are in Broad Street, stop in at the **Oxford Story Exhibition,** situated in a converted warehouse. The imaginative presentation makes 800 years of Oxford life come alive with models, sounds, and smells. Visitors ride through the exhibition in small cars shaped like medieval students' desks. *Tel. 0865/728822. Admission: £3.50 adults, £2 children, £3 senior citizens, £10 family ticket. Open daily 9:30–5.*

㉔ Broad Street leads westward to **St. Giles,** reputed to be the widest street in Europe. At the corner is prestigious **Balliol College** (1263). The wooden doors between Balliol's inner and outer quadrangles still bear scorch marks from 1555 and 1556, during the reign of Mary I ("Bloody Mary"), when Bishops Latimer and Ridley and Archbishop Cranmer were burned on huge pyres in Broad Street for their Protestant beliefs. A small cross on the roadway marks the actual spot. The three men are also **㉕** commemorated by the tall **Martyrs' Memorial** in St. Giles. A lit- **㉖** tle farther up St. Giles, step inside **St. John's College** (1555), whose huge gardens are among the city's loveliest.

Time Out If you are in St. Giles at the right time, stop in for lunch at the **Eagle and Child** pub, with its narrow interior leading to a conservatory and small terrace. This was the meeting place of J. R. R. Tolkien and his friends, the "Inklings." It gets crowded on the weekend.

㉗ **Beaumont Street,** running west from St. Giles, is the site of the **Ashmolean,** Britain's oldest public museum. Among its priceless collections (all university-owned) are a large number of Egyptian, Greek, and Roman artifacts, most uncovered during archaeological expeditions conducted by the university. Michelangelo drawings, antique silver, and a wealth of important paintings are also on display. *Beaumont St., tel. 0865/278000. Admission free. Open Tues.–Sat. 10–4, Sun. 2–4.*

(28) Beaumont Street leads on to **Worcester College** (1714), noted for its wide lawns, colorful cottage garden, and large lake. It was built on the site of a former college, founded in 1283 by the Benedictines.

A side trip into the southern part of town should begin in **Cornmarket,** Oxford's main shopping street. As you pass through (29) (30) **Carfax,** where four roads meet, you will see the tower of **St. Martin's Church,** where Shakespeare once stood as godfather for William Davenant, who himself became a playwright. Con(31) tinue south on St. Aldate's to reach **Christ Church College** (1546), referred to by its members as "The House." Christ Church boasts Oxford's largest quadrangle, "Tom Quad," named after the huge bell (6¼ tons) that hangs in the gate tower. Its clock is stubbornly set to its own time, calculated by its distance from the Greenwich Meridian. The vaulted, 800-year-old chapel in one corner has been Oxford's cathedral since the time of Henry VIII. The college's medieval dining hall contains portraits of many famous alumni, including John Wesley, William Penn, and 14 of Britain's prime ministers. The **Canterbury Quadrangle** offers a fine picture gallery exhibiting works by Leonardo, Michelangelo, Rubens, Dürer, and other old masters. *Deanery Gardens, tel. 0865/276172. Admission: 50p adults, 25p children. Open Mon.–Sat. 10:30–1 and 2–4:30 (5:30 in summer), Sun. 2–4:30 (5:30 in summer).*

Beyond the quadrangle lies the extensive **Christ Church Meadow,** where the wide, tree-lined paths are as quiet and green as the depths of the countryside. On its journey through here, the Thames takes on a new name—the Isis. During university terms it is always busy as college "eights" (teams of oarsmen) practice their rowing.

Time Out The **Perch** at Binsey and the **Trout** at Godstow are two excellent Thameside pubs on the northern edge of Oxford. Connoisseurs go to the thatched Perch at lunchtime to enjoy its wide lawn, unusual sandwiches, and cooing doves. In the evening they go to the creeper-covered Trout for a meal or a drink and to watch its peacocks strutting back and forth beside the weir.

Numbers in the margin correspond to points of interest on the Thames Valley map.

Leaving Oxford, follow A34 north about 8 miles to the village of (32) **Woodstock**—site of **Blenheim Palace**, Britain's largest stately home and the birthplace of Winston Churchill. During the summer you can catch an open-top bus to the palace from the Oxford train station.

A classical-style mansion built by Sir John Vanbrugh in the early 1700s, Blenheim Palace stands in 2,000 acres of parkland and gardens landscaped by Capability Brown. Queen Anne gave the palace to General John Churchill, first duke of Marlborough, after his victory over Louis XIV's armies in 1704 at the Battle of Blenheim. It is now the home of the 11th duke. Winston Churchill, who was born at the palace in 1874 (his father was the younger brother of the then-duke), wrote that the unique beauty of the Blenheim estate lay in its perfect adaptation of an English parkland to an Italian palace. In addition to paintings, tapestries, and furniture, it houses an exhibition devoted to Winston Churchill, including some of his own paintings. There are both a restaurant and a cafeteria at the palace. *Woodstock, tel. 0993/811325. Palace—admission: £5.50 adults, £2.80 children, £4.20 senior citizens. Open mid-Mar.– Oct., daily 10:30–5:30. Park—admission free. Open daily 9–5.*

33 Sir Winston Churchill is buried in the village of **Bladon**, about 2 miles south on A4095. His grave in the small, tree-lined churchyard—on the southeast edge of the palace park—is all the more impressive for its total simplicity.

Eight miles south of Oxford along A34 is the market town of **34** **Abingdon**. The town's origins can be traced to AD 675, when its abbey was founded. St. Ethelwold, the 10th-century abbot, carried out an ambitious project to divert water from the Thames and create a millstream here. Today the Upper Reaches Hotel (*see* Dining and Lodging, below) stands on the tiny island that Ethelwold's millstream formed. *Abbey Buildings, Thames St., tel. 0235/25339. Admission: small charge. Open daily 2–6.*

Continuing 7 miles southeast from Abingdon you come to the **35** town of **Dorchester-on-Thames**, where you'll find another ancient abbey. In addition to secluded cloisters and gardens, this abbey has a spacious church, built in 1170, with interesting medieval windows. The east window was restored in 1966 by the American Friends of the Abbey in memory of Sir Winston Churchill. One of the abbey's corbels (projecting stone supports) shows the sculpted head of Mrs. Edith Stedman of Cambridge, Massachusetts, who founded the association to raise money for the abbey's restoration. She also sponsored the construction of the museum in the abbey's old guest house. *Tel. 0865/340056. Admission free. Open May–Sept., Tues.–Sat. 10:30–12:30 and 2–6, Sun. 2–6.*

Dorchester itself, founded by the Romans, is a charming village with timbered houses, thatched cottages, and ancient inns. Crossing the Thames at Day's Lock and turning left at Little Wittenham takes you on a pleasant walk past the intriguing remains of the village's Iron Age settlements. At the top, at **Sinodun Hillfort**, you can catch a spectacular view across the broad, flat valley of the Thames to the Chiltern Hills.

Southwest of Oxford, beginning in the valley of the river Och and stretching up into the foothills of the Berkshire Downs, is a wide, fertile plain known as the **Vale of the White Horse**. To reach it, follow A420, then B4508 south from Oxford to arrive in **36** the village of **Uffington**. Here, cut into the chalk hillside, is the huge figure of a white horse. No one really knows when it was done. Some historians suggest that it may have been carved to commemorate King Alfred's victory over the Danes in 871, while others think it dates back to the Iron Age, around 750 BC. **Dragon Hill**, below, is equally mysterious. An unlikely legend suggests that St. George slew his dragon there. Uffington was the home of Tom Brown, fictional hero of the Victorian classic *Tom Brown's Schooldays*. It was from here that he set off to study at Rugby School. The novel's author, Thomas Hughes, was born in Uffington in 1822.

Oxford has been a major focus for Britain's writers and artists for centuries, so the area's estates and country villages are alive with literary associations. About 7 miles north of Uffing- **37** ton, in Kelmscott, is **Kelmscott Manor**, home of the Victorian artist, writer, and socialist William Morris, who is buried in the local churchyard. The handsome, 400-year-old gabled house is built of Cotswold stone, and contains many examples of Morris's work. *Tel. 0367/52486. Admission: £3.50. Open Apr.– Sept., Wed. only 11–1 and 2–5.*

Back in the direction of Oxford—about 12 miles east, through twisting lanes—lies **Stanton Harcourt Manor**. Nestled among streams, small lakes, and woods, the house boasts an interesting medieval tower. It was here, in 1718, that Alexander Pope worked on his translation of Homer's *Iliad*. But the manor is worth a visit apart from this association; it has 12 acres of gardens, and inside, a fine collection of silver, pictures, and antique furniture. There's a splendid view from the top of the tower. *Stanton Harcourt, tel. 0865/881928. Admission: £2 adults, £1 children. Open Apr.–Sept., certain Sun. and Thurs. 2–6. Check locally.*

What to See and Do with Children

Windsor Safari Park, set in 150 acres of Windsor Great Park, has seven drive-through enclosures in which, with appropriate segregation, tigers, lions, elephants, giraffes, zebras, and baboons roam freely. Daily aquarium shows (Easter–Oct.) include whales, dolphins, and sea lions. There is also an adventure playground and several fast-food restaurants and bars. *Winkfield Rd., tel. 0753/869841. Admission (peak season): £8.95 adults, £6.95 children over 4, £4.95 senior citizens. Open daily 10–dusk.*

Queen Mary's Doll's House at Windsor Castle (*see* Tour 1).

Boat trips provide an excellent way to see the Thames and the towns along it. The stretch from Caversham to Mapledurham inspired Kenneth Grahame's *The Wind in the Willows*. Children will enjoy exploring the extensive grounds of Mapledurham House (*see* Tour 2).

Punting on the river Cherwell, a favorite pastime among Oxford undergraduates, will also appeal to most children (*see* Tour 3).

At the **Shire Horse Center,** on A4 just 2½ miles west of Maidenhead, children will enjoy watching the world's largest draft horses being groomed and harnessed. They can also watch blacksmiths at work. *Littlewick Green, tel. 0628/824848. Admission: £2 adults, £1.50 children, children under 4 free. Open Mar.–Oct., daily 11–5.*

Off the Beaten Track

The Thames area abounds with tiny villages hidden from the major highways. While you are driving along the main roads, it's worth turning off from time to time to see if that tiny hamlet, deep in the trees, is as attractive as its name sounds.

Basildon Park, a huge, 18th-century house near **Pangbourne,** 7 miles northwest of Reading on A329, boasts some exceptionally fine plasterwork, and the windows of its unusual **Octagon Room** provide magnificent views over the Thames Valley. The gardens are handsomely laid out, and the surrounding woods are ideal for relaxed walks. *Tel. 0734/843040. Admission:*

House and Grounds, £2.80 adults, £1.40 children; grounds only, £1.80 adults, 90p children. Open Apr.–Oct., Wed.–Sat. 2–6, Sun. noon–6.

In the tiny village of **Nuffield,** half a mile south of A423 between Wallingford and Henley, a simple lettered slab beside the 13th-century flint church marks the **grave of William Morris**—not the writer who lived at Kelmscott, but the man who built an automobile factory at Cowley, on the edge of Oxford, having begun his career repairing undergraduates' bicycles. His immense success—he was England's version of Henry Ford—led to his being granted the title 1st Viscount of Nuffield. He later founded Oxford's Nuffield College, and he is still celebrated in the name of a classic auto, the MG, initials which stand for "Morris Garages."

Great Milton, just south of M40 about 7 miles east of Oxford, has attractive thatched cottages built of local stone, and a single street around a mile long with wide grass verges. This is another stop on the literary pilgrim's route, for the poet John Milton, author of *Paradise Lost* (1667), was married in the church here. The church also has an unusual collection of old musical instruments.

On the edge of **Witney,** 14 miles west of Oxford by A40, is the **Cogges Farm Museum,** a working farm which operates just as it did some 80 years ago. The animals are descendants of those which were bred then, the interior is furnished as it would have been in Edwardian days, and you can watch demonstrations of early 19th-century farming methods. *Tel. 0993/72602 in the summer, 0993/811456 in winter. Admission free. Open May–Oct., Tues.–Sun. 10:30–5:30.*

Shopping

The towns and villages of the Thames Valley offer a wide selection of small specialty stores, branches of chain stores, and markets. As the whole area is relatively prosperous, you can expect to find a range of quality British goods, from antiques to clothing. Generally the stores are geared to serve local people, but shops specializing in gifts may be found in popular stops such as Windsor and Henley. Antiques are worth looking for in most towns—particularly Eton, Windsor, and Dorchester-on-Thames—but will be pricey.

Dorchester At 16 Dorchester High Street, **Halliday's,** in a splendid Georgian building, is one of the largest antiques showrooms in England. It specializes in 18th-century pieces.

Eton Eton has a reputation for excellent antiques shops, most of them along the High Street. **Turk's Head Antiques** (at No. 98) has jewelry, silver, and lace; **Mostly Boxes** (at No. 92) stocks antique boxes from the 16th century onward, but sells larger items as well; **Eton Antique Bookshop** (at No. 88) carries rare and antiquarian books.

Henley Henley's small shopping area includes some very individual boutiques, as well as antiques dealers and fine art galleries. The **Thames Gallery** in Thameside specializes in Georgian and Victorian silver, while the **Century Galleries** next door has a range of 19th-century oil paintings and watercolors.

Oxford As a major shopping location, Oxford has improved recently with the arrival of several malls within easy walking distance of Carfax, at the city center. Cornmarket and Queen Street are lined with small stores, while the Clarendon and Westgate centers which lead off them have branches of several nationally known stores. Stores along High Street include traditional tailors like **Shepherd & Woodward** (No. 109) and specialists in Scottish woolens and tweeds. The **Oxford Gallery** (No. 23) carries prints in limited editions, as well as a wide stock of crafts. It holds monthly art exhibitions.

A particularly good selection of specialty stores is gathered around Golden Cross, a cobbled courtyard with pretty window boxes, between Cornmarket and the excellent covered food market. They include **Chico and Pilot** for ladies' fashions and accessories; **Rafaels** for leather items; the **Oxford Collection,** which has a stylish selection of gifts such as glassware and table mats; and the **Tea House,** specializing in teapots and tea. Broad Street, parallel to High Street, is famous for its bookstores, including **Blackwell's,** whose Norrington Room boasts the largest selection on sale in one room anywhere in the world. **Culpepers** (7 New Inn Hall St.) is an herbalist specializing in natural toiletries and soaps. **The Antiquary** (50 St. Giles), as its name suggests, is a good place to visit for antique glass, jewelry, porcelain, and silver.

Windsor Windsor has a busy shopping district with a range of shops and stores. Unusually, many are open on Sunday, particularly those specializing in antiques. Peascod Street is the main shopping road, but High Street and King Edward Court, a new precinct, are also worth a look.

The **Edinburgh Woollen Mill** (10 Castle Hill) has a large range of Scottish knitwear and classic styles in tartans and tweeds, particularly for women. **Best of British** (44 King Edward Court) has handmade items by British craftsmen, so it is a useful store for gifts.

Sports and Fitness

Bicycling Bikes can be rented at: **Oxford: Dentons,** 294 Banbury Rd., tel. 0865/53859 (£5 a day, £8 a week); and **Pennyfarthing,** 5 George St., tel. 0865/249368 (£5 a day, £9 a week).

Golf The fine courses in this area include **Southfield** (tel. 0865/242158), a parkland 18-hole course close to Oxford; visiting players welcome on weekdays. **Huntercombe,** Nuffield (tel. 0491/641207), is a wooded, heathland 18-hole course, and rather formal, with jacket and tie required in the clubhouse. At **Badgemore Park,** Henley-on Thames (tel. 0491/572206), a parkland, 18-hole course, visitors are welcome on weekdays, weekends by arrangement.

Hiking For long-distance walkers, the **Oxfordshire Way** runs 60 miles from Henley-on-Thames to Bourton-on-the-Water, on the eastern edge of the Cotswolds (*see* Chapter 9). A 13-mile ramble starts in Henley, runs north through the **Hambleden Valley,** takes in Stonor Park, and returns to Henley via the Assendons, Lower and Middle. For a less arduous walk, try the trails through the beechwoods at **Burnham Beeches,** north of Burnham (*see* Tour 1).

Spectator Sports **Henley Royal Regatta,** one of the highlights of Britain's sporting and social calendar, takes place over four days at the beginning of July each year. A vast community of large tents goes up, especially along both sides of the unique stretch of straight river here (1 mile, 550 yards), and every surrounding field becomes a parking lot. The most prestigious place for spectators is the stewards' enclosure, but admission is by invitation only and, however hot, men must wear jackets and ties—and ladies in trousers are refused entry. Fortunately, there is plenty of space on the public towpath to see the early stages of the races.

Oxford's Eights Week at the end of May is much more informal. From mid-afternoon to early evening, Wednesday to Saturday, men and women from the university's colleges compete to be "Head of the River." Because the river is too narrow and twisting for eights to race side-by-side, they set off, 13 at a time, one behind another. Each boat tries to catch and "bump" (touch) the one in front. Spectators can watch all the way.

Oxford University Cricket Club competes against leading county teams and also has a game each summer against the major foreign team visiting Britain. The massive trees surrounding the club's grounds in the University Parks make it one of the loveliest in England.

Dining and Lodging

Dining Simple pub food, as well as classic French cuisine, can be enjoyed in waterside settings at the many restaurants which capitalize on their locations beside the Thames. Even in towns away from the river, well-heeled commuters support top-flight establishments. At weekends it is advisable to make reservations.

Highly recommended restaurants are indicated by a star ★.

Category	Cost*
Very Expensive	over £35
Expensive	£25–£35
Moderate	£12–£25
Inexpensive	under £12

per person, including first course, main course, dessert, and VAT; excluding drinks

Lodging Many hotels in the area started out centuries ago as coaching inns. Others have been converted more recently from country mansions. Both types of hotel usually have plenty of character, with antiques and attractive decor—and often with lovely, well-kept gardens. This is an area that tends to the manicured, helped by the wealth of the local population.

Highly recommended hotels are indicated by a star ★.

Category	Cost*
Very Expensive	over £130
Expensive	£80–£130

Moderate	£45–£80
Inexpensive	under £45

All prices are for two people sharing a double room, including service, breakfast, and VAT.

Abingdon
Lodging

The Upper Reaches. This Trusthouse Forte hotel has a spectacular setting overlooking the Thames. Surrounded by a millstream, it was once a grain mill and has been cleverly converted. *Thames St., OX14 3JA, tel. 0235/22311. 26 rooms with bath, 6 in annex. Facilities: restaurant, terrace garden, river mooring. AE, DC, MC, V. Expensive.*

Burnham
Lodging

Burnham Beeches Hotel. In 1742, Thomas Gray wrote the famous elegy inspired by Stoke Poges churchyard while staying in this secluded country house with large grounds. Its room capacity has been greatly increased by a modern extension. *Grove Rd., SL1 8DP, tel. 0628/603333. 75 rooms with bath. Facilities: restaurant, indoor swimming pool, sauna, games room, in-house movies, tennis, croquet lawn. AE, DC, MC, V. Expensive.*

Cumnor
Dining

The Bear and Ragged Staff. This excellent spot, close to Oxford (4½ miles southwest via A420), is a 17th-century inn—the name comes from the sign, which is the medieval insignia of the Warwick family—and has long been a popular out-of-town stop for Oxford town and gown. The food is traditional British, with dishes such as roast duck or venison with a wine sauce. *19 Appleton Rd., tel. 0865/862329. Reservations advised. Jacket and tie required. AE, DC, MC, V. Moderate.*

Dorchester-on-Thames
Lodging

George Hotel. Overlooking Dorchester Abbey, this 500-year-old hotel was built as a coaching inn—there's still an old coach parked outside—and it retains whitewashed walls, exposed beams, and log fires. Each room has an individual style and some have four-poster beds. *High St., OX9 8HH, tel. 0865/ 340404. 17 rooms with bath. Facilities: restaurant, garden. AE, DC, MC, V. Moderate.*

Eton
Dining

The Cockpit. Cockfighting once took place in the courtyard of this 500-year-old inn with oak beams, in Eton's quiet High Street. Specialties include guinea fowl, and bacon casserole in mushroom sauce. *47–49 High St., tel. 0753/860944. Reservations advised. Jacket and tie required. AE, DC, MC, V. Closed Mon. Expensive.*

Great Milton
Dining and Lodging

Le Manoir aux Quat' Saisons. Although this 15th/16th-century manor house is also a hotel—with sumptuously luxurious rooms—it has held its position as one of Britain's leading restaurants for years. The owner/chef, Raymond Blanc, exercises his award-winning French culinary skills in a captivating English setting. Aux Quat ' Saisons is both very popular and *very* expensive (well above our normal range) though the set menus can make it almost reasonable—the *Menu Gourmand* will give you a chance to taste a selection of the house specialties. There is a new conservatory extension to the restaurant. *Church Rd., OX9 7PD, tel. 0844/278881. Reservations essential. Jacket and tie required. Restaurant closed 4 weeks at Christmas. 19 rooms with bath. Facilities: heated pool, tennis, gardens. AE, DC, MC, V. Very expensive.*

Henley
Dining

Little Angel Inn. Housed in a quaint building over 500 years old, this is an associate of the French Routier chain of restaurants,

which are known for their good value and no-nonsense food.
Specialties include fish and duck. Less expensive meals are
served in the bar, which is open even when the restaurant is
closed. *Remenham (¼ mi from Henley on A423), tel. 0491/
574165. Reservations advised. Dress: informal. AE, DC, MC,
V. Closed Sun. eve., Mon. Expensive.*

Stonor Arms. Four miles north of Henley lies this 18th-century
restaurant, once a pub. There is a simple brasserie in an old
conservatory and two dining rooms—one formal, the other
bright and summery. The food is as good to eat as it is to look
at—local game, poached turbot, fried mussels and scallops,—
and there's a comprehensive wine list. *Stonor, tel. 049163/345.
Reservations advised. Dress: informal. Dinner only Mon.-
Sat. AE, MC, V. Expensive.*

Dining and Lodging **Flohr's.** This small, elegant Georgian hotel is only a short walk
from the town center. Its *cordon bleu* restaurant is personally
supervised by the owner, Gerd Flohr. *15 Northfield End, RG9
2JG, tel. 0491/573412. 9 rooms, 3 with bath. AE, DC, MC, V.
Moderate.*

The Red Lion. This historic hotel overlooks the river and the
town bridge. During its 400-year history, guests have included
King Charles I and Dr. Samuel Johnson, the 18th-century critic, poet, and lexicographer. The hotel has recently been refurbished. *Hart St., RG9 2AR, tel. 0491/572161. 26 rooms, 21 with
bath. Facilities: restaurant, four-poster beds, garage. AE,
MC, V. Moderate.*

Hurley **Ye Olde Bell.** This is reputed to be the oldest inn in England,
Lodging having been built in 1135 as a Benedictine guest house for the
monastery nearby. Some rooms are attractively modern,
others are elegantly furnished in traditional style, a few overlook the pretty courtyard gardens. *High St., SL6 5LX, tel.
062882/5881. 24 rooms with bath. Facilities: restaurant, four-
poster beds, garden, garage. AE, DC, MC, V. Expensive.*

Oxford **Elizabeth's.** These small, elegant dining rooms in a 16th-cen-
Dining tury bishop's palace have the best views of any restaurant in
Oxford, overlooking Christ Church College. Salmon rolls,
roast lamb, and crème brûlée are among the Spanish chef's
specialties. *85 St. Aldates, tel. 0865/242230. Reservations
advised. Dress: informal. AE, DC, MC, V. Closed Mon. Expensive.*

Fifteen North Parade. Just outside the city center, this intimate restaurant is decorated with attractive cane furniture
and plants. Dishes such as medallions of lamb with garlic, Mediterranean fish soup, and venison with madeira and celeriac
sauce are all light and tasty. *15 North Parade, tel. 0865/513773.
Reservations advised. Dress: informal. MC, V. Closed Sun.
dinner. Moderate.*

La Sorbonne. La Sorbonne serves classic French cuisine in
surroundings that are archetypically English—the building
dates from the 1630s and the decor is of the beams-and-plaster
variety. For 25 years the Chavagnon family has been prepar-
ing serious dishes like Mediterranean fish soup or coq au
vin, and backing them up with excellent—though a touch
pricey—wines. *130A High St., tel. 0865/242883. Reservations
advised. Dress: informal. AE, DC, MC, V. Open daily. Moderate.*

Browns. So popular is this restaurant with both undergraduates and local people that you may have to wait for a table. The

wide choice of informal dishes includes steak, mushroom and Guinness (sweet ale) pie, and hot chicken salad. Potted palms and mirrors give the otherwise plain rooms a cheery atmosphere. *5–9 Woodstock Rd., tel. 0865/511995. No reservations. Dress: informal. No credit cards. Inexpensive.*

Munchy Munchy. In spite of the dreadful name, this is a fine place, offering spicy Malaysian dishes that change every day, as well as a good selection of fish and fresh vegetables. The surroundings are unpretentious and the prices very reasonable, as in the owners' home city of Singapore. *6 Park End St., tel. 0865/ 245710. Reservations not required. Dress: informal. No credit cards. Closed Sun. and Mon. Inexpensive.*

Lodging **The Eastgate Hotel.** Retaining the style of a traditional inn, this hotel is conveniently situated on High Street and flanked by ancient university buildings and colleges. Its bar is a favorite with undergraduates, so this is a good place to get an insight into university life. *The High, OX1 4BE, tel. 0865/248244. 42 rooms with bath. Facilities: carvery restaurant, four-poster beds, no smoking in public rooms. AE, DC, MC, V. Expensive.*

The Randolph. This is Oxford's only large, central hotel and is just across from the Ashmolean. In neo-Gothic style, and elegantly traditional, its grand Victorian interior has recently been extensively restored. There is a spaciously handsome restaurant, **Spires.** *Beaumont St., OX1 2LN, tel. 0865/247481. 109 rooms with bath. Facilities: coffeeshop, garage. AE, DC, MC, V. Expensive.*

Cotswold Lodge. Located on the main road to Banbury, about half a mile from downtown Oxford, the hotel is privately owned, and attracts both visitors and conference delegates. The bedrooms have been refurbished and the decor is mainly modern throughout. *66A Banbury Rd., OX2 6JP, tel. 0865/ 512121. 52 rooms with bath. Facilities: restaurant, garden. AE, DC, MC, V. Moderate.*

Shinfield **L'Ortolan.** This elegant country restaurant lies just over 4
Dining miles south of Reading, on A327. It's an attractive spot, with an airy, light feel to the dining room. The nouvelle dishes are the imaginative work of the owner/chef, John Burton-Race, and are every bit as interesting as the setting. Try the *mousseline loup de mer et de homard* (seafood and lobster mousse). The fixed-price menus allow for a serious tasting session. *The Old Vicarage, Church Lane, tel. 0734/883783. Reservations required. Jacket and tie required. AE, MC, V. Closed Sun. dinner, Mon. Expensive.*

Sonning-on-Thames **The French Horn.** This establishment has had its French chef,
Dining René Emin, for 15 years. He uses local produce for his blend of traditional French and English dishes. Dinner is served by candlelight in a dining room overlooking floodlit gardens leading to the river. *Tel. 0734/692204. Reservations advised. Jacket and tie required. AE, DC, MC, V. Expensive.*

Lodging **The Great House.** A former 16th-century inn, this hotel commands superb views over the river and has extensive gardens— the roses are lovely—leading to a half-mile of moorings. There is a choice of period or modern rooms, some in cottage annexes. *Thames St., RG4 0UT, tel. 0734/692277. 34 rooms with bath. Facilities: restaurant, gardens, moorings. AE, DC, MC, V. Expensive.*

Weston-on-the-Green
Lodging

Weston Manor Hotel. Eight miles from Oxford northeast on A43, this hotel is one for the history buffs. Once a monastery, it's set in 11 acres of grounds. The oak-paneled restaurant has a minstrels' gallery, and one of the bedrooms even boasts a ghost. It is part of the reliable Best Western chain. *OX6 8QL, tel. 0869/ 50621. 37 rooms, 36 with bath. Facilities: outdoor heated swimming pool, squash, fishing, croquet. AE, DC, MC, V. Expensive.*

Windsor
Dining and Lodging

Oakley Court. This ornate hotel stands in large grounds beside the river just outside Windsor, 3 miles by the A308. It was originally a Victorian mansion, but half the rooms are in a modern annex. There is an excellent restaurant, the **Oak Leaf Room,** which serves essentially English fare such as fillet of beef with Stilton mousse, and has a good wine list. *Windsor Rd., Water Oakley, SL4 5UR, tel. 0628/74141. 91 rooms with bath. Facilities: gardens, croquet, fishing, putting green, pocket billiards, helipad. AE, DC, MC, V. Expensive.*

Sir Christopher Wren's House Hotel. This was a private mansion built by the famous architect in 1676, but modern additions have converted it into a hotel. Restoration of antique features complements the fine design, and its restaurant overlooks the river. It is renowned, too, for its cream teas on the terrace. *Thames St., SL4 1PX, tel. 0753/861354. 41 rooms with bath. Facilities: four-poster beds, air conditioning, terrace garden. AE, DC, MC, V. Expensive.*

Ye Harte and Garter. Originally two Tudor taverns, the hotel was rebuilt in Victorian times. It is in a busy spot just opposite Windsor Castle. *21 High St., SL4 1PH, tel. 0753/863426. 50 rooms, 43 with bath. Facilities: steak house, 4 bars. No parking, but there's a British Rail parking lot nearby. AE, DC, MC, V. Moderate.*

Woodstock
Dining and Lodging

The Feathers. The hotel here, is small, but, very comfortable, and expertly staffed. It's a 17th-century building which has recently been thoughtfully refurbished by the new owners. In the restaurant's luxurious, wood-paneled rooms, you can enjoy a set-price, five-course gourmet menu. Among the specialties are tartlet of quails' eggs and leeks, wild salmon, roast duck with orange and cointreau sauce, and a selection of rich desserts. *Market Square, Woodstock, tel. 0993/812291. Reservations required. Jacket and tie required. AE, DC, MC, V. Expensive.*

The Arts

Festivals and Music

Henley Festival takes place during the week following the regatta each year. All kinds of open-air concerts and events are staged, making a popular summer occasion for both local people and tourists. *Henley Festival, Festival Yard, 42 Bell St., Henley, tel. 0491/410414.*

Oxford Pro Musica, the city orchestra, performs concerts throughout the year in the Oxford area and abroad. In July and August, the orchestra gives concerts twice a week, in a "Beautiful Music in Beautiful Places" series, in some of the city's most historic buildings, and "Music in the Meadows" in Christchurch meadows. *The Old Rectory, Paradise Sq., OX1 1TW, tel. 0865/252365.*

Music at Oxford is a highly acclaimed series of weekend chamber concerts performed from late June to mid-September in such illustrious surroundings as Christ Church Cathedral and Sir Christopher Wren's Sheldonian Theatre, or outdoors on the grounds of stately homes in the area. The music is mainly early Baroque and is performed by chamber ensembles and choirs from all over the world, as well as from both Oxford and Cambridge. Information and tickets are available from *Music at Oxford, 6A Cumnor Hill, Oxford OX2 9HA, tel. 0865/864056.*

The **Windsor Festival** is usually held in early fall, September or October, with occasional events taking place in the castle itself. A concert in the Waterloo Room is quite an event to attend.

Theaters Windsor's **Theatre Royal** (Thames St., tel. 0753/853888), where productions have been staged for nearly 200 years, is one of Britain's leading provincial theaters. It stages a range of plays and musicals throughout the year, frequently starring leading actors and actresses. A traditional pantomime is staged for six weeks after Christmas.

The Apollo (George St., tel. 0865/244544) is Oxford's main theater. It stages a varied program of plays, opera, ballet, pantomime, and concerts, and is the recognized second home of both the Welsh National Opera and the Glyndbourne Touring Opera.

During university terms, many undergraduate productions are staged in the colleges or local halls. In the summer, there are usually some outdoor performances in ancient quadrangles or college gardens. Posters, with details of how to obtain tickets, appear in store windows or on college bulletin boards.

9 The Heart of England

Introduction

The Heart of England is a name we have borrowed from the tourist powers-that-be—and by which they mean the heart of *tourist* England, so immensely popular are its attractions. Here it means the three counties of west-central England, Warwickshire (pronounced Worrick . . .), Gloucestershire (pronounced Gloster . . .), and Avon. Together they make up a sweep of land stretching from Shakespeare country in the north down through Bath to the Bristol Channel in the south.

The Forest of Arden, immortalized in Shakespeare's *As You Like It*, once overspread the county of Warwickshire; only a few small pockets of actual forest are left now, but the whole area is still shaded by ancient trees, scattered through rich farmlands. Timber was always readily available here for building, and the Tudor houses of Stratford-upon-Avon and its surrounding villages are typically half-timbered, with wattle-and-daub sections (plaster over woven sticks) between the beams. The grandest houses here were built of brick, mellowed now to a rich, velvety red.

Stratford is the key town for the visitor. It is a small market town, like dozens of others across the land, but set apart from them by being the birthplace of Shakespeare. It is that rare thing, a living shrine—living because it contains, apart from the houses connected with Shakespeare, a theater which performs his works, and, for the most part, performs them to the highest international standard. The town can be vulgar—it is full to overflowing with souvenir shops—but it also has a lot of quiet charm. To wander along the riverbank from the theater to the parish church on a spring day can be a gently fulfilling experience. Only a few miles away, Warwick, with its magnificent castle and picturesque houses, provides yet another "Heart of England" thrill.

Gloucestershire is dominated by the Cotswolds, high, treeless hills crisscrossed by dry-stone (unmortared) walls to control the sheep which have grazed here for centuries. This is another area of England to which sheep brought great prosperity in the Middle Ages, and the legacy of those times can be seen in the substantial buildings of the idyllic little towns and villages nestling in the valleys. Local stone was easy to quarry, and the houses built from it have now seasoned to a glorious golden-gray. The churches, manor houses, and cottages still stand as solidly as the day they were built, anything up to five centuries ago. This is an area for walking, for getting to know the countryside intimately. Here you will see hovering kestrels; wildflowers from February to late fall; newborn lambs and "boxing" hares in March; and tiny, wild blueberries in August. All the year round the remnants of ancient woods, and the long rolling vistas over the hills, will delight.

To the south of this region is the city of Bath—like Stratford, one of the tourist meccas of Britain. Although it was originally founded by the Romans when they discovered here the only true hot springs in England, it was its popularity during the 17th and 18th centuries which ensured Bath's immortality. Bath's fashionable fame luckily coincided with one of Britain's most elegant architectural eras, producing quite a remarkable urban phenomenon—money available to create virtually a whole town of stylish buildings. Today's city fathers have been wise enough to make sure that Bath is kept spruce and welcoming, with the streets overflowing with flowers in the summer, and its present prosperity has been channeled into cleaning and painting the city center, making it a joy to explore.

Essential Information

Important Addresses and Numbers

Tourist Information
The Heart of England Tourist Board, 2–4 Trinity St., Worcester, Hereford & Worcs WR1 2PW, tel. 0905/29512. Information on the whole region apart from Bath. Open. Mon.–Thurs. 9–5:30 and Fri. 9–5.

The West Country Tourist Board, Trinity Court, 37 Southernhay E., Exeter, Devon EX1 1QS, tel. 0392/76351. Information on Bath/Avon. Open weekdays 9:30–5.

Local tourist information centers are normally open Mon.–Sat. 9:30–5:30, but times vary according to season. Centers include: **Bath:** 8 Abbey Church Yard, tel. 0225/462831.
Bristol: 14 Narrow Quay, tel. 0272/260767.
Cheltenham: Municipal Offices, Promenade, tel. 0242/522878.
Gloucester: St. Michael's Tower, The Cross, tel. 0452/421188.
Stow-on-the-Wold: Talbot Court, tel. 0451/31082.
Stratford-upon-Avon: 1 High St., tel. 0789/293127.

Travel Agencies
American Express, 5 Bridge St., Bath, tel. 0225/66186.
Thomas Cook, 20 New Bond St., Bath, tel. 0225/63191; 6 Ironmonger Row, Coventry, tel. 0203/229233; and 24 Eastgate St., Gloucester, tel. 0452/29511.

Car Rental Agencies
Bath: Budget Rent a Car, Kingsmead Motor Co., James St. West, tel. 0225/60518.
Cheltenham: Budget Rent a Car, Haines & Strange Ltd., 53 Albion St., tel. 0242/35222; **Hertz,** Pike House Service Station, Tewkesbury Rd., 0242/242547.
Gloucester: Avis, Gloster Service Station, Hucclecote Rd., Hucclecote, tel. 0452/64214; **Budget Rent a Car,** Herts Rent Ltd., 26 Worcester St., 0452/506026.
Stratford-upon-Avon: Ford Rent a Car, Arden Garages Ltd., Arden St., tel. 0789/67446.

Getting Around

By Car
M4 is the principal route from London to Gloucestershire and Avon. From exit 18, take A46 for Bath. From exit 20, take M5 north to Gloucester (109 miles), Cheltenham, and Tewkesbury; or south to Weston-super-Mare (136 miles). From M4 exit 15 you can take A361 to the Cotswolds, or you can take M40 exit 7 to A40 to Bourton-on-the-Water and Cheltenham. For Stratford-upon-Avon (97 miles) take A40/A34. For Coventry and Warwick, take M1 to exit 17, then A45 for Coventry, A46 for Warwick (you can travel south from there to Stratford-upon-Avon).

By Train
British Rail serves the western part of the region from London Paddington Station (tel. 071/262–6767). Some average travel times are: an hour and 55 minutes to Bath (though there are trains which take just over an hour); an hour and 50 minutes to Moreton-in-Marsh; and two hours 25 minutes to Stratford-upon-Avon. Visitors should be warned that a trip to Stratford

involves changes at Oxford and Leamington Spa, and that the Stratford station is closed on Sundays during the winter. Service to Coventry is from London Euston Station (071/387–7070), from where there are connections to Stratford.

A seven-day "Heart of England Rover" ticket is valid for unlimited travel within the region.

By Bus **National Express** (tel. 071/730–0202) serves the region from London's Victoria Coach Station. Average travel times include: three hours to Bath, Stratford, and Warwick; two hours and 40 minutes to Cheltenham; and three hours and 10 minutes to Gloucester.

Flights Coach Travel Ltd. (tel. 021/554–5232) operates "Flightlink" services from London's Heathrow and Gatwick airports to Coventry and Warwick.

Cheltenham & Gloucester Omnibus Co. Ltd. (tel. 0452/27516) provides service in Gloucestershire, with ticket offices in Cheltenham, Gloucester, and Stroud. Day "Explorer" tickets for unlimited travel within the network are available.

Midland Red (South) Ltd. (tel. 0785/535555) serves the Stratford-upon-Avon and Coventry areas, including Nuneaton and Leamington Spa. An "Explorer" ticket is valid for a day's unlimited travel within the region.

Guided Tours **The Heart of England Tourist Board** (tel. 0905/29512) and the **West Country Tourist Board** (tel. 0392/76351) have details of numerous guided tours within their regions, and can book you with registered guides for outings ranging from short walks to luxury tours that include accommodations in stately homes.

Historic Gloucester Guided Walks (tel. 0452/301903) organizes regular tours of the city and docks during the summer.

Guide Friday (based in Stratford-upon-Avon) does guided tours of the Shakespeare Country and Bath. Stratford: £4.25 adults, £2 children; Bath: £4 adults, £2 children. Tel. 0789/294466 (Stratford), 0225/444102 (Bath).

Wallace Arnold (tel. 0532/636456, head office; 081/202–5577, London reservations) offers five-day guided tours by bus from London to the Cotswolds and Shakespeare country.

Exploring the Heart of England

Orientation

The four tours in this chapter have been organized around the region's three major points of interest for the visitor—Stratford-upon-Avon, the Cotswold Hills, and Bath.

Stratford, one of Britain's most important tourist centers, is well suited as an exploring base, though for a limited area only. It is a locality of tiny villages, several with legends connected with Shakespeare (dubious for the most part), some beautiful architecture dating from his time, and one magnificent castle, Warwick.

The Cotswolds are peppered with pretty villages, set in woods and hills. Our circular swing around this area, using Bourton-on-the-Water as a base, goes to: Chipping Campden; the oversold village of Broadway, which has many rivals for beauty hereabout; Winchcombe and Sudeley Castle; Northleach; Burford; and back to Bourton. This is definitely a region where it pays to wander off the beaten track to take a look at that village hidden in the trees.

To the west of this tour lie Gloucester and Cheltenham, almost twin towns, and beyond them the mysterious Forest of Dean. The road from Gloucester to Bath takes you through Roman territory at Cirencester, and by the evocative castle at Berkeley.

Bath, which can also be easily visited as a day out from London, serves as an elegant center from which to travel westward to Bristol, the Severn Estuary, and prehistoric sites, this time in the Chew Valley.

Highlights for First-time Visitors

Bath: Tour 4
Berkeley Castle: Tour 3
Chedworth Roman Villa: Tour 2
Corinium Museum, Cirencester: Tour 3
Forest of Dean: Tour 3
Gloucester Cathedral: Tour 3
Hidcote Manor Garden: Tour 2
Stratford-upon-Avon Shakespeare Trust Properties: Tour 1
Sudeley Castle: Tour 2
Warwick Castle: Tour 1

Tour 1: Stratford-upon-Avon and the Shakespeare Zone

Numbers in the margin correspond to points of interest on the Shakespeare Zone and the Cotswolds and the Stratford-upon-Avon maps.

❶ Its connections with Shakespeare have made **Stratford-upon-Avon** a mecca for tourists from all over the world. But it is conceivable that the town would have attracted a fair number of tourists even without its famous son. By Elizabethan times (16th century), this was a prosperous market town with thriving guilds and industries. Its characteristic, half-timbered houses date from this era, and have been preserved over the centuries, set off by the charm of later architecture, such as the elegant Georgian storefronts on Bridge Street, which display the porticoes and arched doorways favored by 18th-century tastes.

Yet Stratford is far from being a museum piece. It has adapted itself well to the rising tide of visitors, and though the town is full of souvenir shops—every back lane seems to have been converted into a shopping mall, with boutiques selling everything from sweaters to china models of Anne Hathaway's Cottage— Stratford isn't particularly strident in its search for the quick buck. If you prefer to seek out traces of its history in peace, try to hit the place out of season, or at a time of day before the bus tours arrive, or after they leave.

❷ Start your tour at the **Shakespeare Centre** on Henley Street, home of the Shakespeare Birthplace Trust. This modern building was erected in 1964 as a 400th-anniversary tribute to the playwright; it contains a small BBC Television **Shakespeare**

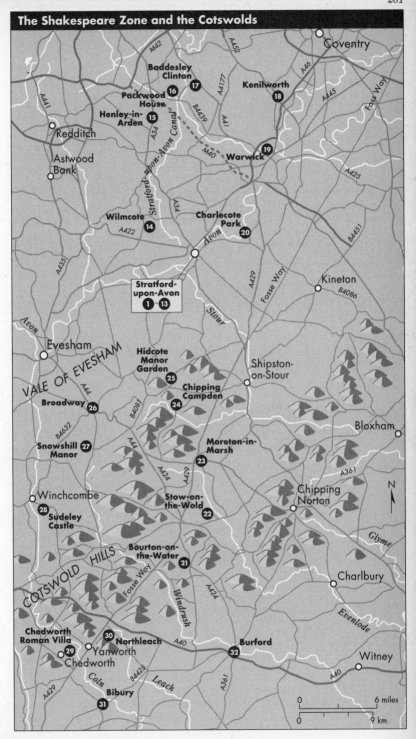

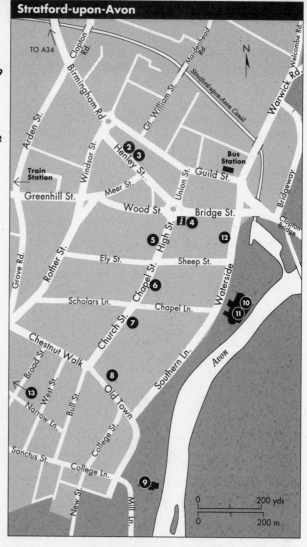

Costume Exhibition. Next door, and reached from the Centre, is **Shakespeare's Birthplace,** a half-timbered house typical of its time, although much altered and restored since Shakespeare lived here. Half the house has been furnished to reflect Elizabethan domestic life, the other half contains an exhibition illustrating Shakespeare's professional life and work. *Henley St., tel. 0789/204016. Admission: Shakespeare's Birthplace only, £2.20 adults, £1.90 children. Joint tickets for all five Shakespeare Trust properties, £6 adults, £2.50 children. (All Shakespeare Trust properties have the same opening times, unless otherwise noted.) Open Mar.–Oct., Mon.–Sat. 9–6, Sun. 10–6. Nov.–Feb., Mon.–Sat. 9–4:30, Sun. 1:30–4:30. Closed Good Friday and Jan. 1, and Dec. 24–26.*

The Birthplace is one of five Shakespeare Trust properties in the area. **Guide Friday** tours to all the properties are available. *Every 15 minutes from any of the Shakespearian properties. Open-top bus plus guide costs £4.25 adults, £2 children.*

Time Out **Mistress Quickly** (named after Falstaff's long-suffering hostess in Shakespeare's *Henry IV Parts 1* and *2*) on Henley Street serves meals and snacks throughout the day. Look for its jigsaw tree sculpture as you climb the stairs.

④ At the end of Henley Street, turn right into High Street, where the Stratford tourist information center is housed in **Judith Shakespeare's House.** This was once the home of Shakespeare's younger daughter. From here you can take a guided walking tour of the town. *1 High St., tel. 0789/69890 or 0789/68340.*

⑤ Farther along High Street, next to the Garrick Inn, is **Harvard House,** the half-timbered, 16th-century home of Catherine Rogers, mother of the John Harvard who founded Harvard University in 1636. *Opening times have been irregular, and the 1992 times will not be decided until the spring. Contact the Shakespeare Centre for information.*

⑥ Across the street is **Nash's House,** home of Thomas Nash, who married Shakespeare's granddaughter, Elizabeth Hall. Heavily restored, the house has been furnished in 17th-century style, and it also contains a local museum. In the house's gardens, which include a reproduction of an Elizabethan "knot" (i.e., intricately laid out) garden, are the foundations of New Place, the house in which Shakespeare died in 1616, aged 52. New Place, built in 1483 for a Lord Mayor of London, was Stratford's grandest piece of real estate when Shakespeare bought it in 1597 for £60. Unfortunately, New Place was torn down in 1759. *Chapel St., tel. 0789/293455. Admission: £1.50 adults, 60p children. Shakespeare Trust opening times.*

⑦ Continue into Church Street. On your left are poorhouses built by the Guild of the Holy Cross in the early 15th century. On the second floor of the adjoining **Guildhall** is the **Grammar School,** which Shakespeare probably attended as a boy and which is still used as a school. *Open Easter and summer school vacations, daily 10–6.*

⑧ Turning left at the end of Church Street into Old Town (a street), you will see **Hall's Croft,** one of the finest surviving Tudor town houses, with a walled garden behind. This was the home of Shakespeare's elder daughter Susanna and her husband Dr. John Hall, whose dispensary is on view along with the other rooms, all containing heavy oak Jacobean (early 17th-century) furniture. *Tel. 0789/292107. Admission: £1.50 adults, 60p children. Shakespeare Trust opening times but closed Nov.–Mar., Sun.*

⑨ At the end of Old Town is the 13th-century **Holy Trinity Church,** in which are buried William Shakespeare, his wife Anne, his daughter Susanna, his son-in-law John Hall, and his granddaughter's husband, Thomas Nash. The bust of Shakespeare in the church is thought to be an authentic likeness, executed a few years after his death.

⑩ From the church, walk either along Southern Lane or through the gardens along the river Avon to the **Royal Shakespeare The-**

atre, where the Royal Shakespeare Company (RSC) stages plays from late March to late January (*see* The Arts, below). At
(11) the rear is the new **Swan Theatre,** created in the only part of the Victorian theater to survive a fire in the 1930s. It was built with the financial backing of an anglophile American philanthropist, Frederick Koch. The theater follows the lines of Shakespeare's original Globe and is one of the most exciting acting spaces in Britain. Beside the Swan is an art gallery where you can see the RSC's exhibition of costumes and props, and book tours of the theater, preferably well in advance. *Southern Lane, tel. 0789/296655, ext. 421. Cost (tours): £3.50 (Swan only £2.50). Exhibition open daily 9:15–6. Tours weekdays except Thurs. and Sat. (matinee days) at 1:30, 5:30, and after evening performances; Sun. 12:30, 2:15, 3:15, 4:15.*

Time Out The **Black Swan,** locally called the Dirty Duck, has a little veranda overlooking the river. It serves draft beer and bar meals on Southern Lane.

Across the small park in front of the theater is the Heritage
(12) Theatre's **World of Shakespeare,** a glorified waxworks show, using recorded dialogue and dramatic lighting to recreate the "royal progress" of Queen Elizabeth I from London to Kenilworth, where she was lavishly entertained by her favorite, the Earl of Leicester, in 1575. Some will consider it a mite pricey for just under half an hour's show. *13 Waterside, tel. 0789/ 269190. Admission: £2.50 adults, £2 children, senior citizens, and students; family ticket £7. Open daily 9:30–5.; performances every half-hour. Closed Dec. 25.*

The most picturesque of the Shakespeare Trust properties is
(13) **Anne Hathaway's Cottage,** family home of the woman Shakespeare married in 1582, in what was evidently a shotgun wedding. The Hathaway "cottage," actually a beautiful and substantial farmhouse, with a thatched roof and large garden, is in the village of Shottery, now a western suburb of Stratford. The best way to get there is to walk, especially in late spring when the hawthorns and apple trees are in blossom. *Tel. 0789/ 292100. Admission: £1.80 adults, 80p children. Shakespeare Trust opening times.*

Numbers in the margin correspond to points of interest on the Shakespeare Zone and the Cotswolds map.

(14) Three miles northwest of Stratford, at the village of **Wilmcote,** off A34, is the fifth Shakespeare Birthplace Trust Property, **Mary Arden's House,** another authentic Tudor farmhouse. It was the family home of Shakespeare's mother. The farmhouse has been combined with the adjoining glebe (church-owned farm) to form the **Shakespeare Countryside Museum,** offering exhibitions of rural crafts and, among other things, a remarkable 16th-century dovecote (pigeon house). *Tel. 0789/293455. Admission: £2.50 adults, £1 children, family ticket £6. Shakespeare Trust opening times.*

Return to A34 and continue north, passing under the Stratford-upon-Avon Canal aqueduct and through the village of
(15) **Henley-in-Arden,** whose wide main street is an architectural pageant, presenting attractive buildings of various periods. You are now in the area of what was once the Forest of Arden, where Shakespeare set one of his greatest comedies, *As You Like It.*

After following A34 north another four or five miles, turn
right, just before Hockley Heath, onto B4439, and follow the
16 signs to **Packwood House,** which is two miles farther on a back
road. This house combines red brick and half-timbering, while
its tall chimneys are another distinctive Tudor characteristic.
The grounds include a formal 17th-century garden, as well as a
remarkable topiary garden of that period, in which yew trees
have been trained and clipped so as to form a living representa-
tion of Christ's Sermon on the Mount. *Near Hockley Heath, tel.
05643/2024. Admission: £2.50, family ticket £6.90. Open Apr.–
Sept., Wed.–Sun. and national holiday Mon. 2–6; Oct., Wed.–
Sun. 12:30–4. Closed Good Friday.*

Just two miles from Packwood House, on a winding back road
17 off A41, is **Baddesley Clinton,** a moated, medieval manor house
which still has its great fireplaces, 17th-century paneling, and
"priest-holes" (secret chambers for Roman Catholic priests,
who were persecuted at various times throughout the 16th and
17th centuries). *Near Chadwick End, 6 mi north of Warwick,
tel. 05643/3294. Admission: £3.10, family ticket £8.50. Open
Apr.–Sept., Wed.–Sun. and national holiday Mon. 2–6; Oct.,
Wed.–Sun 12:30–4. Closed Good Friday. Restaurant, National Trust store, and grounds open at 12:30, and are also open
Nov.–Dec., 12:30–4.*

In Baddesley Clinton village, turn right onto A41; then left,
northeast, onto A4177; and finally right again, onto A452, to-
18 ward **Kenilworth.** Soon the great, red ruins of **Kenilworth Castle** loom ahead. Founded in 1120, this castle remained one of the
most formidable fortresses in England until it was finally dis-
mantled by Oliver Cromwell after the Civil War in the mid-17th
century. Its keep (central tower), with 20-foot-thick walls; its
great hall; and its "curtain" walls (low outer walls forming the
castle's first line of defense) are largely intact. Here the Earl of
Leicester (pronounced Lester), one of Queen Elizabeth I's favorites, entertained her four times, most notably in 1575 with
19 days of sumptuous feasting and revelry. *Kenilworth, tel.
0926/52078. Admission: £1.30 adults, 65p children, 95p senior
citizens. Open Easter–Sept., daily 10–6, Oct.–Easter Tues.–
Sun. 10–4;. also Apr.–Oct., Sun. morning. Closed Dec. 24–26.*

Time Out Have a substantial bar meal in the village atmosphere of the
Clarendon Arms (Castle Green, Kenilworth), a cozy, flagstone-
floored pub.

---

19 Four miles south on A46 is **Warwick,** the county seat of Warwickshire, an interesting architectural mixture of Georgian
red brick and Elizabethan half-timbering. Much of the town
center has been spoiled by unattractive postwar development,
but find the 15th-century **Lord Leycester Hospital,** which has
been a home for old soldiers since the Earl of Leicester dedicated it to that purpose in 1571. *High St., tel. 0926/492797. Admission: £2 adults, 50p children, £1 senior citizens. Open
Apr.–Sept., Mon.–Sat. 10–5:30; Oct.–Mar., Mon.–Sat. 10–4.
Closed Good Friday and Dec. 25.*

Well worth visiting, too, is the **Collegiate Church of St. Mary,**
on Church Street, especially for the florid Beauchamp Chapel,
burial chapel of the earls of Warwick. Its gilded, carved, and
painted tombs are the very essence of late medieval and Tudor
chivalry.

The city's chief attraction is **Warwick Castle,** the finest medieval castle in England, which is built on a cliff overlooking the Avon. Its most powerful commander was the 15th-century earl of Warwick, known during the Wars of the Roses as "the Kingmaker." He was killed in battle near London in 1471 by Edward IV, whom he had just deposed in favor of Henry VI. Warwick Castle's monumental walls now enclose one of the best collections of medieval armor and weapons in Europe, as well as paintings by Rubens, Van Dyck, and other old masters, and historic furnishings. Twelve rooms are devoted to an imaginative Madame Tussaud's wax exhibition, "A Royal Weekend Party—1898." Below the castle, along the Avon, strutting peacocks patrol 60 acres of grounds landscaped by Capability Brown in the 18th century. There is a restaurant in the cellars, for lunch during your visit. *Tel. 0926/495421. Admission: £5.50 adults, £3.50 children, £4 senior citizens; family tickets £16 or £18. Open Mar.–Oct., daily 10–5:30; Nov.–Feb., daily 10–4:30. Closed Dec. 25.*

㉒ To continue the circular tour back to Stratford, go on to **Charlecote Park** by taking A429 south from Warwick four or five miles, and then turning right (west) onto B4088. Queen Elizabeth I is known to have stayed at Charlecote Park, the Tudor manor house of the Lucy family, which was extensively renovated in neo-Elizabethan style in the 19th century. According to tradition, soon after his marriage Shakespeare was caught poaching deer here and forced to flee to London. Years later he is supposed to have retaliated by portraying Charlecote's owner, Sir Thomas Lucy, as the foolish Justice Shallow in *Henry IV Part 2. Charlecote, tel. 0789/470277. Admission: £3.20; family ticket £8.80. Open Apr.–Oct., Fri.–Sun., Tues., Wed., 11–6 (house closed 1–2). Closed Good Friday.*

To return to Stratford, find B4056 at the southern end of B4088 (less than half a mile below the village of Charlecote), and follow it into Stratford.

Tour 2: The Cotswold Hills

Occupying the eastern end—and the largest part—of Gloucestershire, the Cotswolds offer small towns and villages, built of the golden Cotswold stone, which nestle comfortably in valleys and on wooded hillsides.

㉑ **Bourton-on-the-Water,** off A429 on the eastern edge of the Cotswold Hills, is deservedly famous as a classic Cotswold village. The little river Windrush runs through Bourton, crossed by low stone bridges. This village makes a good touring base because of its facilities as well as its central location in Gloucestershire. Be warned, however, that in summer Bourton, like Stratford and Broadway, is overcrowded with tourists, and at that time you will find a quieter, more typical Cotswold atmosphere in nearby villages with such evocative names as Upper Slaughter, Lower Slaughter, Upper Swell, and Lower Swell, all of which lie to the north.

A stroll through Bourton takes you past Cotswold cottages, many now converted to little stores and coffee shops. Follow the rushing stream and its ducks to the end of the village and the old mill, now the **Cotswold Motor Museum and Exhibition of Village Life.** In addition to 30 vintage motor vehicles and the largest collection of old advertising signs in Britain, this museum offers an Edwardian store, a blacksmith's forge, a wheelwright's shop, a country kitchen, and a huge collection of children's toys. *The Old Mill, tel. 0451/21255. Admission: £1.20 adults, 60p children, £3.60 family ticket. Open Feb.–Nov., daily 10–6.*

22 **Stow-on-the-Wold,** 3 miles north of Bourton on A429, is another exemplary Cotswold town, its imposing golden stone houses built around a wide square. Many of these have now been discreetly converted into quality antiques stores. Look for the Kings Arms Old Posting House, its wide entrance still seeming to wait for the stagecoaches that once stopped here on their way to Cheltenham. At 800 feet elevation, Stow is the highest, as well as the largest, town in the Cotswolds. It's also an antique-hunter's paradise, and, like Bourton, a convenient touring base.

Time Out The **Queen's Head** (The Square) is an excellent stopping–off spot for a pub lunch. In summer, the courtyard out back or the bench in front, under a climbing rose, make for relaxed outdoor drinking.

23 From Stow, take A429 5 miles north to **Moreton-in-Marsh** for the fine views across the hills. In Moreton the houses have been built not around a central square but along a street wide enough to accommodate a market every Tuesday.

24 West of Moreton-in-Marsh, off A44, B4081 swings north to **Chipping Campden,** a lovely Cotswold market town, its broad High Street lined with houses in an attractive variety of styles, many the product of medieval wealth from the wool trade. In the center is the **Market Hall,** a gabled, Jacobean structure built later by Sir Baptiste Hycks in 1627 "for the sale of local produce." *High St. Admission free. Always open.*

One of the oldest buildings in Chipping Campden, built in the 14th century, is **Woolstaplers Hall.** As well as housing the local tourist information center, it houses the local museum, a 1920s movie theater, and collections of medical equipment. *High St., tel. 0386/840289. Admission: £1 adults, 50p children. Open Apr.–Oct., daily 11–6.*

Time Out **Greenstocks** (Cotswold House Hotel, The Square) is just the place for a delicious lunch or a coffee break.

25 Three miles north of Chipping Campden—the route is clearly marked—is **Hidcote Manor Garden,** a 20th-century garden laid out around a Cotswold manor house (the house is not open to the public). The horticulturalist Major Lawrence Johnson designed the garden as a series of "rooms" divided from one another by walls and hedges, each "room" featuring a different style of garden. Shakespeare plays are performed each summer on the Theater Lawn. *Hidcote Bartrim, tel. 038677/333. Admission: £3.80 adults, £1.90 children, £10.40 family ticket. Open Apr.–Oct., Mon., Wed., Thurs., and weekends 11–7. Closed Tues. and Fri.*

26 Take B4081 and then A44 southwest to **Broadway;** on the way you can glimpse the distant Malvern Hills to the west in Worcestershire. Named for its wide main street, Broadway offers many shops and one of the most renowned hotels in the

Cotswolds, the **Lygon Arms** (*see* Dining and Lodging, below). This hotel's striking facade dates from 1620, but the building has been restored and has several modern extensions. Sophisticated travelers tend to avoid Broadway in the summer, when it is clogged with tourists' cars and buses.

On the outskirts of Broadway, off A44, is **Broadway Tower Country Park.** From the top of the tower, an 18th-century "folly" (architectural extravaganza) built by the sixth earl of Coventry, you can see over 12 counties. Nature trails, picnic grounds with barbecue grills, an adventure playground, and rare animals and birds can all be enjoyed in a peaceful countryside setting. *Tel. 0386/852390. Admission: £2 adults, £1.25 children and senior citizens; family ticket, £6. Open Apr.–Oct., daily 10–6.*

27 Two miles farther south is **Snowshill Manor,** whose 17th-century facade hides the house's Tudor origins. It contains a delightful clutter of musical instruments, clocks, toys, bicycles, weavers' and spinners' tools, and much more. Children love it. *Snowshill, tel. 0386/852410. Admission: £3.50 adults, £1.75 children, £9.60 family ticket. Open May–Sept., Wed.–Sun. and national holiday Mon. 11–1 and 2–6; Apr. and Oct., weekends and national holiday Mon. 11–1 and 2–6. (National holidays and summer Sun. overcrowded.)*

Follow B4632 southwest from Broadway for 7 miles to Winch-
28 combe and **Sudeley Castle,** the home and burial place of Catherine Parr (1512–48), Henry VIII's sixth and last wife, who outlived him by one year. The castle was once at the center of great affairs of state; today its peaceful air belies its turbulent history. Its magnificent grounds are the setting for outdoor theater, concerts, and other events in the summer. *Winchcombe, tel. 0242/602308. Admission: £4.20 adults, £2.20 children, £10 family ticket. Grounds open Apr.–Oct., daily 11–5:30; castle open noon–5.*

Just west of Winchcombe, turn left (south) and follow the back roads, passing through Brockhampton and across A40 to Compton Abdale and on to Yanworth and Chedworth, to pick
29 up the signs to **Chedworth Roman Villa,** the best-preserved Roman villa in England. Surrounded by woodland, the site overlooks the Cotswold Hills. Thirty-two rooms, including two complete bath suites, have been identified. The visitor center and museum give a picture of Roman life in Britain. *Yanworth, tel. 024289/256. Admission: £2.20 adults, £1.10 children, £6 family ticket. Open Mar.–Oct., Tues.–Sun. and national holiday Mon. 10–5:30; Nov.–mid-Dec., Wed.–Sun. 11–4. Closed Good Friday.*

30 From the Roman Villa follow the signs east to **Northleach.** After a look at the magnificent church, follow the signs south to
31 B4425 and **Bibury,** in its idyllic setting beside the little river Coln. Bibury's huge, 17th-century water mill, on a site recorded in the Domesday Book (William the Conqueror's census of all English real estate in 1086), has been restored and is now open to the public as **Arlington Mill Museum.** Its 16 rooms contain examples of the work of William Morris (1834–96) and the late-19th-century Arts and Crafts Movement, as well as many agricultural and country exhibits. Morris, a writer and artist, devoted much of his time to encouraging traditional English arts and crafts. *Tel. 028574/368. Admission: £1.80 adults, £1*

*children, £1.50 senior citizens. Open Mar.–Oct., daily
10:30–7; Nov.–Feb., weekends only 10:30–7.*

32 From Bibury, B4425 takes you east to A40 and on to **Burford,**
whose broad main street leads steeply down to a narrow bridge
across the river Windrush. Burford can boast more historic
inns than any other Cotswold town, having been a stagecoach
stop for centuries.

Time Out   At **The Golden Pheasant Hotel** (High St., Burford), have afternoon tea in the lounge while relaxing in a deep, velvet arm-
chair, and warmed by a log fire in winter.

West from Burford follow signs north from A40 onto back
roads, through the villages of **Great Rissington** and **Little Rissington** back to Bourton-on-the-Water.

Tour 3: Cheltenham, Gloucester, and the Forest of Dean

*Numbers in the margin correspond to points of interest on the
Forest of Dean and Bath Environs map.*

West of the Cotswolds there are two main sections to Gloucestershire—the rather urbanized axis connecting Gloucester,
the county seat, with the resort town of Cheltenham; and westward, the low-lying Forest of Dean, bordered by the Wye and
Severn rivers.

33 We begin our tour with **Cheltenham** in the north. If you visit
this historic health resort in the spring or summer, you may
find it difficult to decide which is more attractive, its profusion
of flower gardens or its architecture. The flowers cover even
traffic circles, while the town's elegantly laid out avenues, crescents, and terraces, with their characteristic row houses, balconies, and iron railings, make Cheltenham an outstanding
example of the Regency style of architecture and town planning.

Although it can't compare either in fame, history, or scale with
Bath, Cheltenham has been a popular health resort since the
visit of George III and his consort Queen Charlotte in 1788.
During the Regency period Cheltenham's status was assured
by the visits of the Duke of Wellington, the national hero who
defeated Napoleon at Waterloo in 1815. A stroll around the
town will reveal many of its most interesting Regency features.
The **Rotunda** building on Montpellier (street)—now a bank—
contains the spa's original "pump room," i.e., the room in which
the mineral waters were on draft; such rooms, as in Bath, often
evolved into public drawing rooms of polite society. Wander
past **Imperial Square,** with its intricate ironwork balconies;
past the ornate Neptune's Fountain and along the elegant
Promenade; and continue through Lansdown toward Pittville.

The mineral waters can still be tasted at the **Pittville Pump
Room,** built in the late 1820s. Surrounded by parkland, the
pump room now houses the **Gallery of Fashion,** which tells the
history of the town through displays drawn from an extensive
costume collection. *Pittville, tel. 0242/512740. Admission: 50p
adults, 25p children. Open Nov.–Mar., Tues.–Sat. 10:30–5;
Apr.–Oct., Tues.–Sun. 10:30–5.*

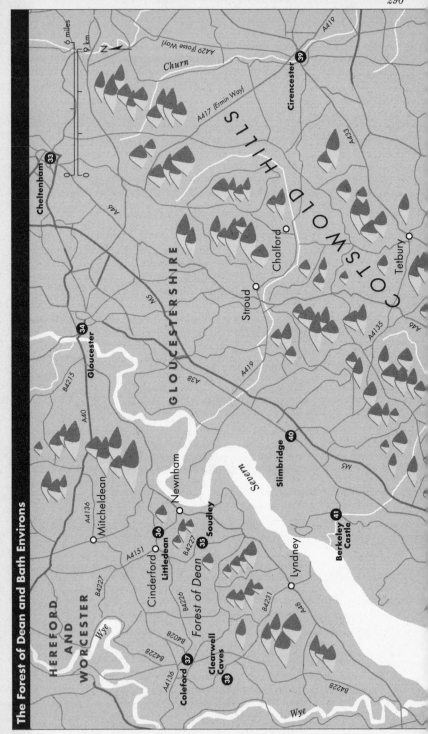

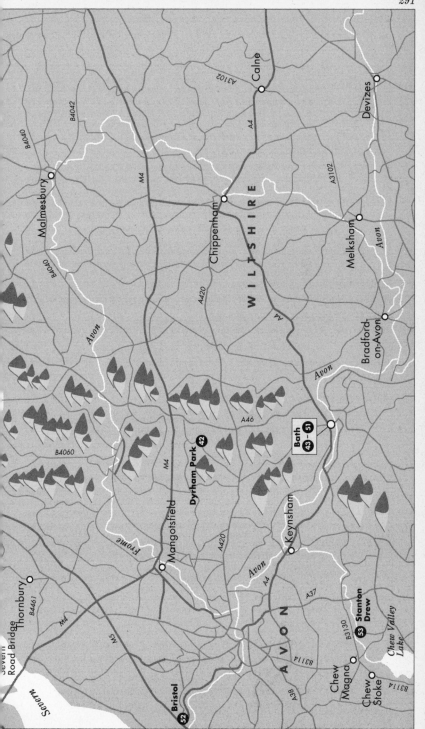

Time Out The **Old Swan** (37 High Street) is a large, comfortable old pub, serving homemade lunchtime food, with tea and coffee on tap all day.

㉞ Just 8 miles west of Cheltenham, along A40, is **Gloucester.** Much of this city's ancient heritage has been lost to nondescript modern stores and offices, but look for the **Gloucester Folk Museum,** housed in a row of fine Tudor and Jacobean half-timbered houses, with displays of the social history, folklore, crafts, and industries of the county. *99–103 Westgate St., tel. 0452/26467. Admission free. Open Oct.–June, Mon–Sat. 10–5; July–Sept., Mon.–Sat. 10–5, Sun. 10–4.*

Across Westgate Street is **Gloucester Cathedral,** originally a Norman abbey church, consecrated in 1100. The exterior soars in elegant lines, while the interior of this magnificent building has largely been spared the sterilizing attentions of modern architects who like to strip cathedrals down to their original bare bones. The place is a mishmash of periods, and the clutter of centuries mirrors perfectly the slow growth of ecclesiastical taste, good, bad, and indifferent. The interior is an almost complete Norman carcass, with the massive pillars of the nave left untouched since their completion. The fan-vaulted roof of the cloisters is the finest in Europe. The cloisters enclose a peaceful garden, where one can easily imagine medieval monks pacing thoughtfully around. Look, too, for the tomb of Edward II—to your left as you stand in the choir facing the high altar—who was imprisoned and murdered in Berkeley Castle in 1327 (*see* below). *Westgate St., tel. 0452/28095. Admission free, but a donation of at least £1 per adult requested. Open daily 8–6, except during services and special events.*

Time Out The **Dick Whittington** (100 Westgate St.), a large, wooden-floored pub serving beer and wine from the barrel, commemorates one of Gloucestershire's most famous sons, who was three times Lord Mayor of London during the Middle Ages. Its lunches and snacks are excellent, and in summer there are garden barbecues.

At the end of Westgate Street, along the canal, are the historic **Gloucester Docks.** The docks still function, though now on a much reduced scale; the vast Victorian warehouses have fallen into disrepair, but are being restored. Tours, starting at the **Mariner's Chapel** by the Southgate Street entrance to the docks, are conducted every Friday in July and August at 2:30.

One of the already restored warehouses holds **The National Waterways Museum.** Outside are examples of canal houseboats and barges; inside is the national canal and waterway exhibition. *Llanthony Warehouse, Gloucester Docks, tel. 0452/25524. Admission: £3.25 adults, £2.25 children and senior citizens; family ticket, £8. Open Apr.–Sept., daily 10–6; Oct.–Mar., daily 10–5.*

Take A40 and A4136 west past Mitcheldean, and continue on to the **Forest of Dean.** This mysterious, prehistoric forest covers much of western Gloucestershire in the valley between the rivers Severn and Wye. Although the primordial forest has long since been cut down and replanted, the landscape here remains one of strange beauty, hiding in its folds and under its hills deposits of iron, silver, and coal that have been mined for thousands of years.

When you see A4151, take it south to Cinderford and then on to **35** **Soudley**, where you'll find the **Dean Heritage Centre.** Based in a restored mill building in a wooded valley, the center tells the history of the forest, including reconstructions of a mine and a miner's cottage, a water wheel, and a "beam engine" (a primitive steam engine used to pump water from flooded coal mines). Outside the center is a tiny farm with a pig and poultry, as well as natural history exhibitions. Watch craftsmen at work in the outbuildings. *On B4227, tel. 0594/822170. Admission: £2.25 adults, £1.25 children, £1.75 senior citizens. Open Apr.–Oct., daily 10–6; Nov.–Mar., daily 10–5.*

A short distance north on B4227, turn east on A4151, to **36** **Littledean.** From here "Scenic Drive" signs direct you through the best of the forest. Of the original royal forest established in 1016 by King Canute, 27,000 acres are preserved by the Forestry Commission. It's still an important source of timber, but parking lots and picnic grounds have been created and eight nature trails marked. One trail links sculptures, commissioned by the Forestry Commission, around **Speech House,** the medieval verderer's court in the forest's center. The verderer was the royal officer responsible for the enforcement of the forest laws. It was usually a capital offense to kill game or cut wood without royal authorization.

Drive west on A4151, and then west again on B4226 and B4028 **37** to reach **Coleford.** The tourist information center (tel. 0594/ 36307) there has details of picnic grounds and nature trails in the forest.

The area is a maze of weathered and moss-covered rocks, huge ferns, and ancient yew trees—a shady haven on a summer's day. Underground iron mines, worked continuously from Ro- **38** man times to 1945, can be visited at **Clearwell Caves.** *Off B4228 southwest of Coleford, tel. 0594/32535. Admission: £2.50 adults, £1.50 children, £2 senior citizens. Open Mar.–Oct. and Dec., Christmas workshops, daily 10–5.*

B4231 heads back southeast through the forest toward the river Severn. At the junction with A48 (at Lydney), turn left (north) and continue on through Newnham.

From Gloucester head southeast toward Cirencester on A417, which follows the Roman Ermin Way for 11 miles, and should get you in the mood for the Roman experience you are about to **39** have. **Cirencester** (usually pronounced "Sirensester") has been the hub of the Cotswolds since Roman times. Then called Corinium, this town lay at the intersection of two strategic Roman roads, the Fosse Way and the Ermin Way. Cirencester is a lovely old market town, full of mellow stone buildings—take a stroll down Dollar Street to see the bow-fronted stores—and with a magnificent parish church, St. John the Baptist. The whole town is built on ancient Roman remains, and the **Corinium Museum** offers an excellent collection of Roman artifacts, as well as full-scale reconstructions of local Roman interiors—kitchen, dining room, and workshop. Their motto is "Roman Britain comes alive." *Park St., tel. 0285/655611. Admission: 80p adults, 40p children, 60p senior citizens and students. Open Apr.–Oct., Mon.–Sat. 10–5:30, Sun. 2–5:30; Nov.–Mar., Tues.–Sat. 10–5, Sun. 2–5. Closed Dec. 25–26.*

Travel now southwest along A433. After 2 miles you will pass the source of the River Thames off to your left. At Tetbury turn west onto A4135 for 12 miles through an arm of the Cotswolds toward the fertile, flat Severn valley. Cross the M5 motorway

40 to reach **Slimbridge.** Head west from Slimbridge and across the little swing bridge over the Sharpness Canal to the **Wildfowl Trust** on the banks of the Severn. Its 73 acres of river bank and marshland harbor Britain's largest collection of wildfowl. Thousands of swans, ducks, and geese come to winter here; in spring and early summer, you will be delighted by the cygnets, ducklings, and goslings thriving in this rich marshland. *Near Slimbridge, tel. 0453/890333. Admission: £3.50 adults, £1.90 children, £2.50 senior citizens. Open daily 9:30–5 or dusk if earlier. Closed Dec. 24–25.*

41 **Berkeley Castle** in the sleepy little village of **Berkeley** (pronounced "Barkley"), 4 miles south of Slimbridge between A38 and the River Severn, is a perfectly preserved building, everyone's ideal castle. It was the setting for the gruesome murder of King Edward II in 1327—the cell can still be seen. He was deposed by his French consort, Queen Isabella, and her paramour, the Earl of Mortimer. They then connived at his imprisonment and subsequent death. The castle was begun in 1153 by Roger De Berkeley, a Norman knight, and has remained in the family ever since. It vies with Windsor as the oldest inhabited castle in the country. The state apartments here are furnished with magnificent pieces, and with tapestries and pictures. The surrounding meadows, now the setting for pleasant Elizabethan gardens, were once flooded to make a formidable moat. *Berkeley, tel. 0453/810332. Admission: £2.90 adults, £1.45 children, £2.60 senior citizens and students. Open May–Sept., Tues.–Sat. and national holiday Mon. 11–5, Sun. 2–5; Apr., Tues.–Sun. 2–5; Oct., Sun. only 2–4:30.*

From Berkeley you can take A38 down to Bristol, or cross back over the M5 and head southeast toward Bath (30 miles via **42** A4135 and A46). Eight miles north of Bath lies **Dyrham Park,** a late-17th-century country house with paneled interiors and a deer park which is the setting for occasional open-air concerts in the summer. *Dyrham, tel. 027582/2501. Admission: £4 adults, £2 children; park only: £1.20 adults, 60p children. House and garden open Apr.–Oct., Sat.–Wed. 2–3:30; Park open daily all year noon–6 or dusk if earlier.*

Tour 4: Bath and Beyond

Numbers in the margin correspond to points of interest on the Bath map.

43 One of the delights of staying in **Bath** is the chance to experience firsthand the magnificent 18th-century architecture, a lasting reminder of the elegant world described by Jane Austen. Bath suffered slightly from World War II bombing and even more from unattractive postwar urban renewal, but the damage was halted before it could ruin the center of the city.

Bath is not a museum. It is a lively and interesting place, offering dining and entertainment, excellent art galleries, and a thriving cultural center, with theater, music, and other performances throughout the year. It is also a city with plenty of civic pride, and the streets are filled with lavish flower displays in summer.

It was the Romans who first put Bath on the map when they built a temple here in honor of the goddess Minerva, and a sophisticated network of baths to make full use of the curative springs which gush from the earth at a constant temperature of 116°F. Much later, 18th-century socialites took the city to their hearts, and Bath became the most fashionable spa in Britain. The architect John Wood (1704–54) created a harmonious city from the same local stone used by the Romans, with beautifully executed terraces, crescents, and Palladian (i.e., 16th-century Italian style) villas.

44 The **Pump Room,** described by Jane Austen, is Bath's primary "watering hole." People still gather here to drink the mineral waters—which taste revolting—and to socialize. The baths as such are no longer in use, and this magnificent Georgian building now houses the tourist information center, a souvenir store, and a restaurant. Almost the entire Roman bath complex has been excavated, and you can see the remains of swimming pools, saunas, and Turkish baths, as well as part of the temple of Minerva itself, with the bronze head of the goddess and votive offerings left by worshippers nearly 2,000 years ago. *Abbey Churchyard, tel. 0225/461111, ext. 327. Admission: £3.50 adults, £1.70 children, combined ticket with Roman Baths and Costume Museum, £4.20 adults, £2.20 children. Pump Room only free. Open daily 10–5.*

Time Out | The **Pump Room** serves morning coffee and afternoon tea, perhaps accompanied by a string trio. Nearby **Sally Lunn's** (North Parade Passage), the oldest house in Bath, still serves the famous Sally Lunn bun invented here.

45 Next to the Pump Room is the **Abbey,** dating from the 15th century. It was built in the Perpendicular (English Gothic) style on the site of a Saxon abbey, and has superb, fan-vaulted ceilings in the nave. *Abbey Churchyard. Admission: £1 donation requested. Open most times, though visitors asked not to enter during services.*

Off Abbey Churchyard, where a rich variety of buskers (strolling musicians) perform, are tiny alleys leading to little squares of stores, galleries, and eating places. Walk up the main shopping streets of Stall and Union Streets toward Milsom Street, and you'll find numerous alleyways with fascinating small stores (*see* Shopping, below). Work your way east toward **46** Bridge Street and **Pulteney Bridge,** an 18th-century bridge over the river Avon, lined with little shops. Head back along **47** Upper Borough Walls to find the **Theatre Royal,** one of the finest Georgian theaters remaining in England (*see* The Arts, below). Next door is the former home of the dandy, Richard "Beau" Nash—the dictator of fashion for mid-18th-century society in Bath—and his mistress Juliana Popjoy. This is now a restaurant called Popjoy's (*see* Dining and Lodging, below).

Turning north will take you to the Georgian houses of Queen **48** Square, Gay Street, and **The Circus,** its three perfectly proportioned Georgian terraces outlining the round garden in the center. As in London's Piccadilly Circus, "circus" means a circular interchange of streets, an arrangement popular with Georgian **49** town planners. Turn east from The Circus to the **Assembly Rooms,** which figure in Jane Austen's novel *Persuasion.* This classical-style building, once a social center like the Pump

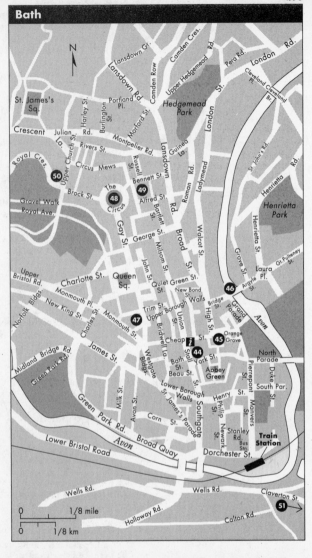

Room, now houses the **Museum of Costume,** which has been
completely redesigned. It displays costumes from Beau Nash's
day up to the present, in lavish settings. *Bennett St., tel. 0225/
61111. Admission: £2.30 adults, £1.30 children. Open Mar.–
Oct., Mon.–Sat. 9:30–6, Sun. 10–6; Nov.–Feb., Mon.–Sat.
10–5, Sun. 11–5.*

Turn west from The Circus and you'll arrive at Royal Crescent,
the crowning glory of architecture in Bath, and much used as a
location for period films. At the center is Bath's most elegant
hotel, the Royal Crescent (*see* Dining and Lodging, below). On
the corner, **Number 1, Royal Crescent** has been turned into a
museum and furnished as it might have been when Beau Nash
and his circle strutted around the crescents of Bath. The muse-

um crystallizes a view of the English class system in its 18th-century setting: "Upstairs" is all gentility and elegance; "downstairs" is the servants' world, with a fascinating kitchen museum. *Tel. 0225/428126. Admission: £2.50 adults, £1.50 children, senior citizens, and students. Open Mar.–Oct., Tues.–Sun. 11–5; Nov.–mid-Dec., weekends 2–5.*

51 High above the city—2½ miles southeast on the Warminster road, A36—is **Claverton Manor,** a Greek revival (19th-century) mansion housing the first museum of Americana to be established outside the United States, quietly sponsored by an American millionaire, Dallas Pratt. A series of furnished rooms portrays American domestic life from the 17th to the 19th century. The fine parkland includes a replica of George Washington's garden and an arboretum. You can even have tea with American cookies. *Claverton Down, tel. 0225/460503. Admission: £4 adults, £2.50 children, £3.25 senior citizens. Open Easter–Oct., Tues.–Sun. 2–5, national holidays and preceding Sun. 11–5. Closed Mon.*

Numbers in the margin correspond to points of interest on the Forest of Dean and Bath Environs map.

52 Leave Bath by A4 to travel the 13 miles to **Bristol** on the river Avon, which has been a major city since medieval times. In the 17th and 18th centuries, Bristol was an important port for the North American trade, but now that the city's industries no longer rely on the docks, the historic harbor has been largely given over to pleasure craft. The quayside offers an arts center, movie theaters, museums, stores, pubs, and restaurants; carnivals, speedboat races, and regattas are held regularly.

On view in the harbor is the **S.S.** *Great Britain,* the first iron ship to cross the Atlantic. Built by the great English engineer Isambard Kingdom Brunel in 1845, it remained in service until the end of the century, first on the North American route and then on the Australian. *Great Western Dock, off Cumberland Rd., tel. 0272/260680. Admission: £2.50 adults, £1.70 children and senior citizens. Open Apr.–Sept., daily 10–6; Oct.–Mar., 10–5. Closed Dec. 24–25.*

Bristol is also the home of the **Church of St. Mary Redcliffe,** called "the fairest in England" by Queen Elizabeth I. It features rib-vaulting and dates from the 1300s, when it was built by Bristol merchants who wanted a place in which to pray for the safe (and profitable) voyages of their ships. *Redcliffe Way, a 5-minute walk from the train station toward the docks.*

Those who dissented from the Church of England also found a home in Bristol; John Wesley built the first Methodist church in England here in 1739. Its austerity contrasts sharply with the ornate Anglican churches. *Broadmead. Open Thurs.–Tues. 10–4. Closed Wed.*

Time Out | The Scottish mailboat **Lochiel** is now a floating pub and restaurant moored on St. Augustin's Reach, behind the Watershed Exhibition Centre.

If you cross the Avon Gorge via Clifton Suspension Bridge, built in 1828 (also by Brunel), you will reach the **Bristol Zoo,** where more than 1,000 species of animals live in 12 acres of landscaped gardens. *Clifton, tel. 0272/738951. Admission: £4*

*adults, £2 children and senior citizens. Open Mon.–Sat. 9–
dusk, Sun. 10–dusk. Closed Dec. 25.*

From Bristol, take B3114 south to the villages of Chew Magna
and Chew Stoke, and on to Chew Valley Lake. At Chew Magna
turn east on B3130 to Stanton Drew. Beyond **Stanton Drew** are
the neolithic (New Stone Age) **Stanton Drew Circles,** where
three stone circles, two avenues of standing stones, and a burial chamber make up one of the grandest and most mysterious
monuments of its kind in the country. The site lies in a field
reached through a farmyard—you'll need suitable shoes to visit
it. *Stanton Drew. The stones stand on private land, but are supervised by English Heritage. The landowner charges a small
admission fee. Open any reasonable time (not Sun.).*

What to See and Do with Children

One of the best hands-on experiences for children in the region
can be had at the Memorial Theatre in Stratford-upon-Avon,
where they can play with the props in the gallery attached to
the theater.

The **Cotswold Motor Museum,** with its huge collection of toys
(see Tour 2), in Bourton-on-the-Water, is well worth a family
visit. So is the **Model Railway Exhibition,** also in Bourton-on-
the-Water, which is in itself interesting for kids. It has some
toys on sale. *Box Bush, High St., tel. 0451/20686. Admission:
£1 adults, 80p children. Open daily in summer 11–5:30, weekends only in winter 11–5:30.*

Two other places we have already covered which will appeal to
children are the **Dean Heritage Centre** at Soudley (Tour 3), and
the **Broadway Tower Country Park,** Broadway (Tour 2).

Just south of Newent (8 miles northwest of Gloucester on
B4215, then south on B4221 at Cliffords Mesne) is a **Falconry
Centre,** which holds daily flying demonstrations with falcons,
eagles, and hawks. It shelters the largest collection of birds of
prey in Europe. *Tel. 0531/820286. Admission: £3.50 adults,
£1.95 children. Mon–Sat. 10:30–6 (5 in winter), Sun. 10:30–6
(5 in winter).*

Weston-super-Mare, 20 miles west on A370 or M5 from Bristol,
is a brash and lively town, its wide, sandy beach making it popular with children, though at low tide the sea retreats to the
horizon. In the summer, children are entertained here by
Punch and Judy puppet shows and donkey rides on the sands,
and by a miniature railroad along the seafront. Beyond Worl-
bury Hill to the north is Sand Bay, whose sandy beach ends
with a long spit reaching into the sea, ideal for a gentle coastal
walk.

Off the Beaten Track

After visiting Stratford, drive north on A46 for about 20 miles
to **Coventry** to visit the **cathedral.** As a testament to history, the
original 1,000-year-old cathedral, destroyed by air raids in 1940
and 1941, has been left as a bombed-out shell next to the magnificent new cathedral. The new building contains the best of
modern religious art in Britain at the time (1954–62), including
an engraved glass screen by John Hutton, a tapestry by Graham Sutherland, who painted Churchill's 80th birthday por-

trait; stained-glass windows by John Piper; and various pieces by Sir Jacob Epstein, the New York–born sculptor. The visitors' center beneath the cathedral uses audiovisual aids and holograms to show the history of Coventry and its old and new cathedrals. About the rest of Coventry, which contains some of the worst postwar rebuilding to be seen in Britain, the less said the better. *Priory Row, tel. 0203/227597. Admission free; tower, £1 adults, 50p children; visitors center, £1.25 adults, 75p children and senior citizens, family ticket, £3. Open Apr.–Sept., daily 9–7:30; Oct.–Mar., 9–5:30. Closed during services.*

From Gloucester, take A38 north 10 miles to **Tewkesbury,** an ancient town of black-and-white, half-timbered buildings on the river Avon, from which you can enjoy a cruise up the river in the *Avon Belle*. The stonework in the Norman **Tewkesbury Abbey** bears the same mason's marks as that of Gloucester Cathedral, but the abbey has been built in the Romanesque (12th-century) and Decorated Gothic (14th-century) styles. It is a beautifully kept church, often with massive flower displays ranged along the nave. *Church St., tel. 0684/292896 or 0684/293333. Open daily.*

Shopping

This is an excellent region for shopping, with both Bath and Stratford full of interesting stores to explore. Both, too, have good branches of the popular national chains, and abound in souvenir shops, not all of which are tacky. All the Cotswold villages have craft shops, and you may well find excellent pottery hidden away in a most unexpected spot, but perhaps the chief reason for shopping here is the hundreds of small antiques shops which line every high street—and most back streets, too. Marketing antiques has reached the level of a major industry in the Cotswolds, so don't expect to find many bargains.

Bath Bath's excellent shopping district centers on Stall and Union streets (modern stores) and Milsom Street (traditional stores). In both areas you'll find many famous names. Leading off these main streets are fascinating alleyways and passages lined with galleries and a wealth of antiques shops. Unfortunately, like many other British cities, Bath is suffering badly from the financial climate. Even long-standing stores are being forced to close.

The **Lantern Gallery** (9 George St.) stocks antiquarian prints and maps.
Western Antiques Center (Bartlett St.) is an antique-lover's mecca, with over 100 stalls selling every kind of antique you can imagine, including clothing, linens, and furniture.
Two craft shops worth visiting in Bath are: **Glass Designs** (17 Barton St.), a specialist gallery with an excellent stock of studio glass from many of Britain's leading artists; and **Beaux Arts Ceramics** (York St.), which carries the work of prominent potters, and holds six solo exhibitions a year.

Bourton-on-Water The **Cotswold Perfumery** (Victoria St.) has a wide range of perfumes which are manufactured here. While deciding what to buy, visit the **Exhibition of Perfumery** and the **Perfumed Garden** (admission to exhibition: £1 adults, 80p children and senior citizens). Perfume bottles, jewelry, and porcelain dolls are also on sale.

Chestnut Gallery (High St.) sells an exciting range of British crafts, including batik prints, carved and turned wood, ceramics, and jewelry. Another place to visit for handthrown pots is the **Bourton Pottery** (Clayton Row).

Cheltenham Cheltenham has one of the most elegant shopping streets in England, Montpellier. A walk along this street, where the storefronts are supported by caryatids, and then along the flower-bedecked Promenade, will take you past boutiques like **Jaeger** and **Hoopers.** Both **Martin** and **Scott Cooper** on the Promenade are worth visiting for jewelry and silver. Behind the Promenade is the Regent Arcade, a modern shopping area with a wide variety of stores.

Hatton **Hatton Craft Center** (3 miles north of Warwick off A41), houses 32 workshops in converted cattle pens and stables. Here, you can watch craftspeople making jewelry, dried and silk flower arrangements, applique cushions and clothing, candles, ceramics, model locomotives, corn dolls, Windsor chairs, and a host of other items, and buy the finished products. There is also a café (open daily), a farm store, and an adventure playground (open Mar.–Dec., 1st weekend each month).

Newent A trip to Newent (8 mi northwest of Gloucester) takes you to a good selection of English wines, glassware, and jewelry. **Newent Silver** (13E Church St.) sells handcrafted gold and silver jewelry. At **Cowdy Glass Workshop** (Culver St.), you can watch handblown and colored glass being made, and buy from the seconds store.

At **Three Choirs Vineyard** (Rhyle House, Welsh House Lane, 3 mi on B4215 northwest of Newent), you can wander around the vineyard before buying the award-winning wines and ciders. Open daily; sometimes closed weekends—check in advance (tel. 0531/85223 or 0531/85555). You may be able to take a guided tour of the winery. Cost: £2.50; includes tasting. There is also a ploughman's lunch for £3.

Stow-on-the-Wold The highest concentration of antiques shops in Stow-on-the-Wold is around the town square, but a wander through nearby streets will take you by many more. One among many is **Preston Antiques** (The Square), which has some interesting clocks among the varied stock.

Stratford-upon-Avon Stratford-upon-Avon's bustling shopping district has many famous-name chain stores, such as **Jaeger,** for excellent clothes, and **Waterstone** for books, as well as antiques and specialty shops.

Centre Arts (Studio 1, Henley St.) has a varied collection of ceramics, glassware, woodwork, and jewelry, all handmade by local artists.

Antique Arcade (Sheep St.) offers antiques from 14 dealers, located on two floors—china, jewelry, and art deco.

At the **Antique Market** (Ely St.), you will find 50 stalls selling jewelry, silver, linen, porcelain, and memorabilia.

Jean A. Bateman (Sheep St.) specializes in antique jewelry.

Robert Vaughan (20 Chapel St.) is the best of Stratford's many secondhand bookshops, with a large stock, especially good on books about Shakespeare and the theater, as you would expect.

Markets In **Stratford-upon-Avon,** there is an open market every Friday in the Market Square. In **Cheltenham** there is a market every

Sunday at the race course, a produce market every Thursday morning on Market Street, and undercover stalls Tuesday through Saturday on Winchcombe Street.

Two markets held in Cotswold villages are: **Moreton-in-Marsh** on Tuesday; and **Chipping Norton** on Wednesday.

Sports and Fitness

Bicycling The Gloucestershire Tourist office (tel. 0452/425673) has a full range of "go as you please" cycle touring route packs (£1).

Hiking This part of England offers glorious yet gentle countryside to ramble over. **Offa's Dyke,** demarcating the old Welsh border, and the **Cotswold Way** are both long-distance hiking routes that cross the region. Among the firms that provide guided walking tours is **Walkways** (23 Southfield Rd., Westbury on Trym, Bristol BS9 3BG, tel. 0272/623586), which runs 7-day walks along the Cotswold Way. Contact local tourist centers for details and maps; most local bookstores sell a range of books concentrating on countryside walks in specific regions.

Horse Racing England's most important steeplechase races take place at the **Cheltenham** race track; the National Hunt Festival is staged in mid-March, crowned by the Gold Cup awards on the last day. *For information, tel. 0242/513014.*

Show Jumping The Whitbread Horse Championships, held annually in late April at the Duke of Beaufort's estate in **Badminton,** feature show jumping and other equestrian competitions. Princess Anne and Captain Mark Phillips are regular participants. *For information, tel. 045421/272.*

Dining and Lodging

Dining The steady flow of tourism to this area has created the need for good restaurants–a need that has largely been met, although the distribution is patchy. One thing that chefs have no problem with here is a supply of excellent produce for their kitchens. Apart from easy access to fresh vegetables, there are salmon from the rivers Severn and Wye, local lamb, and venison from the Forest of Dean. Game, including pheasant, partridge, quail, and grouse, is also in seasonal abundance.

Highly recommended restaurants are indicated by a star ★.

Category	Cost*
Very Expensive	over £35
Expensive	£25–£35
Moderate	£12–£25
Inexpensive	under £12

per person, including first course, main course, dessert, and VAT; excluding drinks

Lodging This is touring country, and every kind of accommodation exists, from comfortable, friendly bed-and-breakfasts in village homes and farmhouses, to ultimate luxury in country-house hotels—formerly private mansions that have been converted for paying guests. Most hotels offer two- and three-day packages.

Highly recommended lodgings are indicated by a star ★.

Category	Cost*
Very Expensive	over £130
Expensive	£80–£130
Moderate	£45–£80
Inexpensive	under £45

All prices are for two people sharing a double room, including service, breakfast, and VAT.

Bath
Dining
★

Popjoy's Restaurant. The home of the mistress of 18th-century socialite Beau Nash provides an elegant setting for a fine, English-style, after-theater dinner. Coffee and *petits fours* are served upstairs in a lovely Georgian drawing room. *Beau Nash House, Sawclose, tel. 0225/460494. Reservations advised, required after theater and weekends. Dress: informal. AE, MC, V. Closed Sat. lunch, Sun. dinner, and Mon. Moderate.*

Tarts. This is a good spot, close to the Abbey, for a meal on a sightseeing day. In a network of small and snug cellar rooms, you can choose from either the set menu or the daily specials. As the dishes change regularly, it's difficult to recommend specialties, but all are attractively presented, and the desserts are rich and delicious. There's a very good wine list. *8 Pierrepont Pl., tel. 0225/330280. Reservations advised. Dress: informal, MC, V. Closed Sun. Moderate.*

Number Five. A great spot for summer dining, though good all year. This winebar/restaurant has a courtyard with a fountain and serves delicious buffet food—try the pigeon breast or monkfish. *5 Argyle St., tel. 0225/444499. Reservations not needed. No credit cards. Inexpensive.*

Lodging
★

Royal Crescent Hotel. This lavishly converted house is part of the Regency sweep of the Royal Crescent, an architectural treasure. The decor has been carefully designed to preserve the building's period elegance, and if some of the bedrooms are on the small side, there are ample luxuries to compensate. The Palladian villa in the garden provides extra rooms. *16 Royal Crescent, BA1 2LS, tel. 0225/319090. 45 rooms with bath, including 13 suites. Facilities: restaurant. AE, DC, MC, V. Very expensive.*

Bath Hotel. Just a couple of minutes from the station, this very attractive modern hotel is delightfully sited beside the confluence of the river Avon and the Kennett and Avon Canal. The recently refurbished interior is light and cheerful with lots of plants, cane furniture, cool colors, and big windows looking out on the waterscape. *Widcombe Basin, BA2 4JP, tel. 0225/338855. 94 rooms with bath. Facilities: restaurant, garden, fishing. AE, DC, MC, V. Expensive.*

Francis Hotel. Another successful conversion, this one from six Georgian houses, fronts a leafy square. You have a choice of period furnishings in the old part of the hotel, or more functional ones in the newer part. All the bedrooms are quite large. *Queen Sq., BA1 2HH, tel. 0225/24257. 94 rooms with bath. Facilities: restaurant. AE, DC, MC, V. Expensive.*

Priory Hotel. Out beyond the Royal Crescent, the Priory is an early 19th-century Gothic-styled building, standing in attractive grounds. Guest rooms are roomy and comfortable, the public areas elegant with fine old furniture and big windows looking out on the two acres of gardens. Three dining rooms serve solid old-fashioned English fare. *Weston Rd., BA1 2XT, tel. 0225/331922. 21 rooms with bath. Facilities: restaurant, garden, outdoor pool. AE, MC, V. Expensive.*

Tasburgh Hotel. This refurbished Victorian mansion in two acres of lovely gardens boasts views over the valley and a canal at the bottom of the grounds. Attentive service is given by the owner/managers, Mr. and Mrs. Archer. *Warminster Rd., tel. 0225/425096. 14 rooms, 10 with bath. AE, DC, MC, V. Moderate.*

Bourton-on-the-Water
Dining

Rose Tree Restaurant. English and French food is served with old-world style here, overlooking the river Windrush and the village. The chef has an especially light touch with fish and such specialties as sautéed pheasant breast with orange. *Riverside, tel. 0451/20635. Reservations advised. Dress: informal. AE, DC, MC, V. Closed Sun. evening and Mon. Moderate.*

Lodging

The Old Manse. A manse is a minister's house, and this one was built of Cotswold stone on the river Windrush in the village center. It has bedrooms in the old, 18th-century building and in a modern wing, all impressively furnished and decorated. *Victoria St., GL54 2BX, tel. 0451/20642 or 0451/20082. 10 rooms with bath. Facilities: restaurant. MC, V. Moderate.*

Breadstone
Lodging

Greenacres Farm. Inglenook (chimney corner) fireplaces and pretty bedrooms with sweeping views are some of the features of this 300-year-old farmhouse; it is located on a horse-raising and beef farm. *A38 north from Bristol, then B4509. Near Berkeley, GL13 9HF, tel. 0453/810348. 4 rooms, 2 with bath. No credit cards. Closed Dec. Inexpensive.*

Bristol
Dining

L' Hermitage. Yet another restaurant in a converted building, this time a library. It's been elegantly redone with chandeliers and polished stairs, and the food matches the suave surroundings. The regularly changing menu features the finest local fish and meat in its French cuisine. *30 King St., tel. 0272/29111. Reservations required. Dress: jacket and tie. AE, DC, MC, V. Closed Sat. lunch, Sun. Expensive.*

Marwick's This restaurant is located in a busy part of downtown Bristol, in a basement which was once a safety deposit. Black-and-white marble floors and iron grille doors retain the vault-like atmosphere, but the food is excellent. Try the fish soup, or the local turbot and sea bass. *43 Corn St., tel. 0272/262658. Reservations advised. Dress: informal. MC. Closed Sat. and Sun. Expensive.*

Lodging

Redwood Lodge Hotel. This is a handy stopover for anyone touring by car as it is located just off A4 close to the Clifton Suspension Bridge. Modern and attractively furnished, it has a number of amenities including pleasant woodland surroundings. *Beggar Bush Lane, Failand, BS8 3TG, tel. 0272/393901. 112 rooms with bath. Facilities: restaurant, coffee shop, tennis, gym, squash, indoor and outdoor pools, in-house movies. AE, DC, MC, V. Moderate–Expensive.*

Broadway
Dining and Lodging

The Lygon Arms. Here you'll find luxury combined with old-world charm (at least in the older sections)—the Lygon has been in business since 1532. Although on the main street, it has three acres of formal gardens for guests to enjoy. But be warned that it is *very* popular, and can be crowded and correspondingly noisy. *The Green, WR12 7DU, tel. 0386/852255. 62 rooms with bath. Facilities: restaurant, garden, tennis, helipad. AE, DC, MC, V. Very expensive.*

★ **Dormy House Hotel.** Guest rooms here overlook the Vale of Evesham from high on the Cotswold ridge. This luxurious country-house hotel has been converted from a 17th-century Cotswold farmhouse. Bedrooms are individually and beautifully furnished, some with four-poster beds. *Willersey Hill (2 mi on A46 north from Broadway), WR12 7LF, tel. 0386/852711. 50 rooms with bath. Facilities: restaurant, garden. AE, DC, MC, V. Closed Christmas period. Expensive.*

Buckland
Dining and Lodging
★
Buckland Manor. As an alternative to the razzmatazz of Broadway, try this exceptional hotel just 2 miles away. Parts of the building date back to Jacobean times and there are gracious old pictures and fine antiques everywhere. The garden is lovely, the restaurant outstanding, and the place is so peaceful you can hear a swan's feather drop. *Near Broadway, WR12 7LY, tel. 0386/852626. 11 rooms with bath. Facilities: garden, outdoor pool, tennis, riding, croquet. MC, V. Closed mid-Jan.–early Feb. Expensive.*

Burford
Dining and Lodging
Bay Tree. Quietly located away from Burford's bustle, the atmospheric Bay Tree is in a 16th-century stone house. It recently had a facelift and has emerged more comfortable than ever. Try for a room in the main house. The restaurant, looking out into the garden, serves a 3-course set menu of mainly English dishes. *Sheep St. OX8 4LW, tel. 099382/2791. 24 rooms with bath. Facilities: restaurant, garden. AE, DC, MC, V. Expensive.*

Charlecote
Lodging
The Charlecote Pheasant. Farm buildings have been converted into a pleasant, country-house hotel across from Charlecote Park (follow B4086 northeast out of Stratford). The fine, 17th-century red brick has been matched in the new wing, and the bedrooms—some with 4-poster beds—in both the old and the new buildings are prettily decorated and have ceiling beams. *CV35 9EN, tel. 0789/470333. 60 rooms with bath. Facilities: restaurant, two bars, swimming pool, tennis court, solarium, Turkish baths, sauna, exercise room, pool tables. AE, DC, MC, V. Moderate.*

Cheltenham
Dining
Le Champignon Sauvage. Everything is made on the premises here, including bread and vinegar! Relaxing music—classical at lunch, soft jazz in the evening—accompanies French-style dishes like wild rabbit stuffed with coriander in light shrimp and Madeira sauce. *24 Suffolk Rd., tel. 0242/573449. Reservations advised. Dress: informal. AE, MC, V. Closed Sat. lunch and Sun. Expensive.*

Malvern View Hotel Restaurant. Views of the Malvern Hills from Cleeve Hill outside Cheltenham enhance the atmosphere of this Continental-style restaurant. The tables are decked with fine linen, crystal, and silver, and specialties include fresh salmon and sweetbreads. *On A46, 4 miles north of Cheltenham, Cleeve Hill, tel. 0242/672017. Reservations advised. Jacket and tie required. MC, V. Closed Sun. dinner. Expensive.*

Lodging
Queens Hotel. Overlooking Imperial Gardens from the center of The Promenade, this classic Regency building has welcomed visitors to Cheltenham since 1838, when the town was a major

resort. The hotel's decor is very British, and every bedroom is individually designed. It has a garden. *The Promenade, GL50 1NN, tel. 0242/514724. 77 rooms with bath. Facilities: restaurant. AE, DC, MC, V. Very expensive.*

Stretton Lodge Guest House. Bedrooms here are decorated with color-coordinated curtains and quilt covers, and comfortably furnished. Although set in a quiet Regency street, the Lodge is only 10 minutes' walk from Cheltenham's busy center. *Western Rd., GL50 3RN, tel. 0242/528724. 9 rooms with bath. MC, V. Moderate.*

★ **Lypiatt House.** This splendid Victorian house is an award-winning B&B—only a short walk from central Cheltenham. The bedrooms are a comfortable size, with modern bathrooms. There's a small dining room and attentive service from the two young owners, the Malloys. *Lypiatt Rd., GL50 2QW, tel. 0242/224994. 10 rooms with bath. MC, V. Moderate.*

Chipping Campden
Dining and Lodging

Cotswold House Hotel. Though it is in the center of a small country town, the Cotswold House has an acre of stone-walled garden at the back and a flair for dramatic design inside. The bedrooms here are small masterpieces of theme decor. There's an Indian room, a French room, and, for homesick travelers, a Colonial Room. The restaurant is also striking, with windows onto the garden. The game and fish dishes are always interestingly presented. *The Square, GL55 6AN, tel. 0386/840330. 15 rooms with bath. Dress in restaurant: jacket and tie. Lunch Sun. only. Facilities: restaurant, garden, coffee shop. AE, DC, MC, V. Expensive.*

Lodging

Noel Arms Hotel. In the heart of Chipping Campden, this inn was built for foreign wool traders in the 14th century and is the oldest inn in the town. It retains its period atmosphere with exposed beams and stonework, even though it has been recently enlarged. Its individually decorated bedrooms—some with four-posters—offer every modern comfort. *High St., GL55 6AT, tel. 0386/840317. 26 rooms with bath. Facilities: restaurant, garden. AE, MC, V. Moderate.*

Cinderford
Dining

The Rock House. Here, in the Forest of Dean, you may feel you are dining in a well-heeled friend's home, but with waiter service. The bar is in the corner of a comfortable lounge, and the dining area has been created out of two smaller rooms. English specialties are the main fare. *89 St. Whites Rd., tel. 0594/822252. Reservations advised. Dress: informal. AE, DC, MC, V. Closed Sun. dinner and Mon. Moderate.*

Clearwell
Dining
★

Wyndham Arms. This may be a modest, old-world village inn, but its restaurant offers sophisticated cuisine. Try the local salmon or one of the excellent steaks, followed by *zuppa inglese*—a mouth-watering chocolate, rum, and meringue concoction. *Near Coleford, tel. 0594/33666. Reservations required. Dress: informal. AE, MC, V. Expensive.*

Lodging

Clearwell Castle. Peacocks strut around this recently refurbished neo-Gothic castle built in 1727. Lounges are large and imposing; the gatehouse bedrooms are decorated like country cottages, while those in the castle have four-poster beds and are individually furnished. There are plenty of antiques scattered about. *GL16 8LG, tel. 0594/32320. 15 rooms with bath. Facilities: restaurant, gardens. AE, DC, MC, V. Very expensive.*

Easton Grey
Dining and Lodging

Whatley Manor. This was once a manor/farmhouse, built of warm Cotswold stone thickly covered with creeping vines. Guest rooms are large, furnished in appropriate period style, with great views over the River Avon. The restaurant serves interesting set menus with local produce well to the fore. *Near Malmesbury SN16 0RB, tel. 0666/822888. 26 rooms with bath. Facilities: garden, outdoor pool, tennis, sauna, croquet. AE, DC, MC, V. Expensive.*

Gloucester
Dining

College Green. With a keen notion of the right meal in the right place, this upstairs restaurant, with views out over the cathedral, serves classic English cooking—beef casserole, duck with apricot sauce—accompanied by a respectable wine list. *9 College St., tel. 0452/20739. Reservations advised. Dress: informal. AE, MC, V. Closed Sun. and dinner Mon.–Tues. Moderate.*

Lodging

Hatherley Manor. Hatherley Manor stands on about 37 acres of grounds and therefore, is fairly quiet when it is not hosting a conference. It is a 17th-century house, recently renovated, and lies 2 miles north of Gloucester off A38. *Down Hatherley La., GL2 9QA, tel. 0451/730217. 55 rooms with bath. Facilities: restaurant, garden, croquet, helipad. AE, DC, MC, V. Expensive.*

Hunstrete
Lodging
★

Hunstrete House Hotel. Located in 90 acres of parkland, with its own deer park, this hotel seems more like a friendly, though luxurious, country house. Fresh flowers and log fires mark the passing seasons, and discreet, efficient service adds to the cossetting effect. *A368 west from Bath, 8½ miles; Hunstrete is north of A368 just past Marksbury. Near Chelwood, BS18 4NS, tel. 07618/578. 24 rooms with bath, 2 cottage suites. Facilities: restaurant, outdoor swimming pool, tennis court, croquet lawn. AE, DC, MC, V. Very expensive.*

Kenilworth
Dining

Restaurant Bosquet. This attractive, small restaurant serves set menus cooked by the French patron, with regularly changing à la carte selections. Try the boned ox-tail wrapped in cabbage, or breast of duck with fig sauce. The desserts are mouthwatering. It is mainly a dinner spot, though lunch is available on request. *97A Warwick Rd., tel. 0926/52463. Dress: informal. AE, MC, V. Closed Sat. lunch and Sun. Moderate.*

Stow-on-the-Wold
Lodging

Fosse Manor. This lovely manor house hotel, just out of town (1¼ miles south on A429), has a long-standing reputation for solid comfort and service. It has recently been refurbished. There are golf, hunting, and riding available nearby. *Fosse Way, GL54 1JX, tel. 0451/30354. 20 rooms, 18 with bath. Facilities: restaurant, garden. AE, DC, MC, V. Moderate.*

Stow Lodge Hotel. Set well back from the main square of Stow-on-the-Wold in its own quiet gardens, the Lodge is a typical Cotswold manor house; its large, open fireplaces provide added warmth in the winter. *The Square, GL54 1AB, tel. 0451/30485. 20 rooms with bath. Facilities: restaurant. AE, DC. Closed Dec. 25–Jan. 31. Moderate.*

Stratford-upon-Avon
Dining
★

Box Tree Restaurant. This elegant dining spot in the Royal Shakespeare Theatre overlooks the river Avon, and has some of the very best food in town. It's worth eating here, even if you're not taking in a play. Specialties include *noisettes* of lamb, and poached fillet of Scottish beef. *Waterside, tel. 0789/293226. Reservations required. Jacket and tie required. AE, MC, V. Closed when theater closed. Expensive.*

River Terrace. For informal cafeteria dining right at the theater, the meals and snacks here are crowd-pleasers. They include lasagna, shepherd's pie (minced beef and potato), salads, sandwiches, and cakes, with wine or beer available. *Royal Shakespeare Theatre, Waterside, tel. 0789/293226. No reservations. Dress: informal. No credit cards. Closed when theater closed. Inexpensive.*

Shepherd's. Located within the Stratford House Hotel, in a big conservatory at the back with a small garden round about, this restaurant has a properly summery feel. The food is generally light and tasty and the service friendly. *Sheep St., tel. 0789/268233. Reservations required. Dress: informal. AE, DC, MC, V. Closed Sun. and Mon. Moderate.*

Lodging **Alveston Manor.** Across the river from the Royal Shakespeare Theatre, this red brick, Elizabethan manor house has a modern extension. In the old manor house, rooms have individual, old-world style. Decor is modern in the extension, but all rooms have modern facilities. *Clopton Bridge, CV37 7HP, tel. 0789/204581. 108 rooms with bath. Facilities: restaurant, recreation center. AE, DC, MC, V. Very expensive.*

★ **Ettington Park Hotel.** This marvelously restored, huge Victorian house makes an ideal spot to stay if you want to visit the plays at Stratford but don't want to cope with the crowds. It stands in its own grounds—which feature a ruined church—and looks across tranquil river meadows haunted by herons. The bedrooms are furnished with Victorian Gothic pieces, and complementary decor. The restaurant has extremely good food, imaginatively cooked. *6 mi from Stratford southeast on A34. Alderminster, CV37 8BS, tel. 0789/740740. 49 rooms with bath. Facilities: health club with pool; tennis; fishing. AE, DC, MC, V. Very expensive.*

Shakespeare Hotel. Minutes from the theater and right in the heart of Stratford, this half-timbered Elizabethan town house is also close to most of the Shakespeare Trust properties. Inside, it has been comfortably modernized. *Chapel St., CV37 6ER, tel. 0789/294771. 70 rooms with bath. Facilities: restaurant. AE, DC, MC, V. Very expensive.*

Falcon Hotel. Founded as a tavern in 1640, the hotel still has the atmosphere of a friendly inn. The heavily beamed rooms in the oldest part of the building are small and quaint; the modern extension has international-standard bedrooms. *Chapel St., CV37 6HA, tel. 0789/205777. 73 rooms with bath. Facilities: restaurant. AE, DC, MC, V. Expensive.*

Caterham House. Built in 1830, this landmark building is in the center of town, close to the theater: You may spot an actor or two among the guests. Its bedrooms are individually decorated in early 19th-century style, featuring brass beds and antique furniture. *58 Rother St., CV37 6LT, tel. 0789/267309. 14 rooms, 2 with bath. No credit cards. Closed Christmas week. Inexpensive.*

Thornbury **Thornbury Castle.** These are the kind of baronial surroundings
Dining and Lodging where Douglas Fairbanks might come sliding down a velvet
★ drape. Thornbury has everything a genuine 16th-century castle should have: huge fireplaces, antiques, paintings, and mullioned windows, to say nothing of a lovely garden. The standards of comfort and luxury are legendary, and people come from all over to eat in the restaurant. *Castle St., BS12 1HH, tel. 0454/418511. 18 rooms with bath. Reservations re-*

quired for the restaurant. *AE*, *DC*, *MC*, *V*. *Closed 2 weeks Jan. Very Expensive.*

Upper Slaughter
Dining and Lodging

Lords of the Manor Hotel. A characteristic 16th-century Cotswold manor house, "the Lords" also has its own fishing stream. It offers comfort and a warm welcome, and its location, Upper Slaughter, is a quintessential Cotswold village. (The name has nothing to do with mass murder. It comes from the Saxon word *sloh* which means a marshy place.) Extensive refurbishment has meant additional bedrooms available in converted outbuildings, now more modern than those in the main house. *GL54 2JD, tel. 0451/20243. 29 rooms, all with bath. Facilities: fishing, restaurant. AE, DC, MC, V. Very Expensive.*

Warwick
Dining

Randolph's. As often happens in this part of the world, a row of tiny, timbered cottages has been turned into an attractive single building—a low-beamed, intimate restaurant. Unfortunately, if you are visiting Warwick during the day, you're out of luck, because Randolph's is open for dinner only. The cuisine is French, verging on nouvelle cuisine, with special attention paid to delicious sauces. *19–21 Coten End, tel. 0926/491292. Reservations required. Dress: informal. MC, V. Closed Sun. Moderate–Expensive.*

The Arts

Festivals

The **Bath International Festival** celebrates its 43rd anniversary in 1992 (May 22–June 7). Concerts, dance, and exhibitions will be held in Bath itself and nearby locations. *Bath Festival Office, Linley House, Pierrepont Pl., Bath BA1 1JY, tel. 0225/462231.*

Cheltenham's annual **International Festival of Music** (July) highlights new compositions, often conducted by the composer, together with classical repertory pieces. The town's **Festival of Literature** (October) brings together world-renowned authors, actors, and critics. *For details of both events contact Festival Office, Town Hall, Imperial Sq., Cheltenham GL50 1QA, tel. 0242/521621.*

The **Stratford-upon-Avon Shakespeare Birthday Celebrations** take place on the weekend nearest to April 23, when ambassadors and diplomats join townspeople and tourists in colorful receptions, processions, a special performance of one of the plays, lectures, and a church service, as well as fringe events such as morris (folk) dancing. *Details from Shakespeare Center, Henley St., Stratford-upon-Avon CV37 6QW, tel. 0789/204016.*

Theater

The **Royal Shakespeare Theatre,** Stratford-upon-Avon CV37 6BB (tel. 0789/205301), home of the Royal Shakespeare Company, usually features five of Shakespeare's plays in a season lasting from March to January each year. In the excitingly designed **Swan Theatre** at the rear, plays by Shakespeare contemporaries such as Christopher Marlowe and Ben Jonson are staged. Reserve seats well in advance, although "day of performance" tickets are often available, and it is always worth asking if there are any returned tickets.

The **Theatre Royal** in Bath, opened in 1805 and restored to its former glory in 1982, is now one of the finest Georgian theaters in England. Its year-round program often includes pre- or post-London tours. You have to reserve the best seats well in advance, but you can line up for same-day standby seats or standing room. Check the location of your seats at the box office—the theater dates from the days when the public went to be seen, rather than to see the performance, and sightlines can be poor. *Box Office, Sawclose, Bath BA1 1XX, tel. 0225/ 448844.*

10 The Welsh Borders

Introduction

England's border with the principality of Wales stretches from the town of Chepstow on the Severn estuary in the south to the city of Chester in the north. Along this border, in the counties of Herefordshire, Shropshire, and southern Cheshire, lies some of England's loveliest countryside, with a special air of remoteness and tranquillity. But today's rural peace belies a turbulent past. Relations between the English and the Welsh have seldom been easy, and from the earliest times the English have felt it necessary to keep the "troublesome" Welsh firmly on the other side of the border. A string of medieval castles bears witness to this history. Many are romantic ruins; some are dark and brooding fortresses. Built to control the countryside and repel invaders, they still radiate a sense of mystery and menace.

For the last 500 years or so, the people of this border country have enjoyed more peaceful lives, with little to disturb the traditional patterns of country life. In the 18th century, however, one small corner of Shropshire heralded the birth of the Industrial Revolution, for it was here, in a pretty, wooded stretch of the Severn Gorge, that the first coke blast furnace was invented and the first iron bridge was erected (1774).

Herefordshire, in the south, is a county of rich, rolling countryside and river valleys, gradually opening out in the high hills and plateaus of Shropshire. North of the Shropshire hills, the gentler Cheshire plain stretches towards the great industrial cities of Liverpool and Manchester. This is dairy country, dotted with small villages and market towns, many rich in the 13th- and 14th-century black-and-white, half-timbered buildings so typical of northwestern England. These are the legacy of a forested countryside, where wood was easier to come by than stone. In the market towns of Chester and Shrewsbury, the more elaborately decorated half-timbered buildings are monuments to wealth, dating mostly from the early Jacobean period at the beginning of the 17th century.

The Welsh borders are for unwinding, and for making your own quiet discoveries. The region offers few large hotels and major attractions; the towns and countryside help you get the feel of an older, more traditional Britain.

Essential Information

Important Addresses and Numbers

Tourist Information The two major tourist information centers for the region are: **The Heart of England Tourist Board,** 2–4 Trinity St., **Worcester,** Hereford & Worcester WR1 2PW, tel. 0905/29512, open Mon.–Thurs. 9–5:30, Fri. 9–5; and **The North West Tourist Board,** The Last Drop Village, Bromley Cross, Bolton, Greater Manchester BL7 9PZ, tel. 0204/591511, open weekdays 9–5. Local tourist information centers, normally open Mon.–Sat. 9:30–5:30, but varying according to the season, include: **Chester:** Town Hall, Northgate St., tel. 0244/324324. **Hereford:** Town Hall Annexe, St. Owen St., tel. 0432/268430. **Ludlow:** Castle St., tel. 0584/875053.

Manchester: Town Hall Extension, Lloyd St., tel. 061/234–3157.
Ross-on-Wye: 20 Broad St., tel. 0989/62768.
Shrewsbury: The Square, tel. 0743/50761.
Worcester: The Guildhall, High St., tel. 0905/726311.

Travel Agencies   **Thomas Cook:** 10 Bridge St., Chester, tel. 0244/23045; 4 St. Peter's St., Hereford, tel. 0432/35641; 23 Market St., Manchester, tel. 061/833–1110 (and two branches); 22 High St., Shrewsbury, tel. 0743/231144; and 26 High St., Worcester, tel. 0905/28228.
American Express: 20 Graham Rd., Malvern, tel. 06845/63221; 10–12 St. Mary's Gate, Manchester, tel. 061/833–0121; 27 Claremont St., Shrewsbury, tel. 0743/236387.

Car Rental   **Chester: Avis,** 128 Brook St., tel. 0244/311463; **Hertz,** Auto
Agencies   Travel Agency, Stadium Autopoint, Sealand Rd., tel. 0244/374705.
Hereford: Europcar Ltd., Hartford Motors Ltd., Commercial Rd., tel. 0432/276494.
Manchester: Avis, Gateway Garage, Piccadilly Station Approach, tel. 061/236–6716; **Budget Rent a Car,** Quick Ltd., 660 Chester Rd., tel. 061/872–8386; **Hertz,** 31 Aytoun St., tel. 061/236–2747.
Worcester: Europcar Ltd., Peter Cooper Ltd., Redhill Filling Station, London Rd., tel. 0905/354096.

Arriving and Departing

By Car   M4/M5 from London takes you to Worcester in just under three hours. The more direct route (120 miles) on M40 via Oxford to A40 across the Cotswolds, is prettier, but, because it is only partly motorway, slower. To get to Ross-on-Wye, follow M5 to exit 8, then join M50. For Shrewsbury (150 miles) and Chester (180 miles), take M1/M6.

By Train   British Rail serves the region from **London Paddington** (tel. 071/262-6767) and **London Euston** (tel. 071/387-7070) stations. Average travel times include: From Paddington to Hereford, three hours; to Worcester, 2½ hours; from Euston to Shrewsbury and Chester, three hours. A direct local service links Hereford, Shrewsbury, and Chester.

By Bus   National Express (tel. 071/730–0202) serves the region from London's Victoria Coach Station. Average travel time to Chester is 4¼ hours; to Hereford, four hours; to Shrewsbury, three hours; and to Worcester, three hours.

Getting Around

By Car   Driving becomes more difficult in the western reaches of this region—especially in the hills and valleys west of Hereford in the shadow of the Black Mountains—where steep, twisting roads often narrow into mere trackways. Winter travel here can be particularly grueling.

By Train   **Midland Day Ranger** tickets and seven-day **Heart of England Regional Rover** tickets allow unlimited travel within the region.

By Bus   For information about local services and unlimited, day-long Rover tickets, contact **Crosville Bus Station** in Chester (tel. 0244/381461); **W. H. Smith Travel** in Hereford (tel. 0432/

278737); and **Midland Red (West) Travel** in Worcester (tel. 0905/ 359393). For information on **Greater Manchester** buses call 061/ 273-5341; for **city buses,** 061/205-2835.

Guided Tours   All local tourist offices carry leaflets of firms which offer day or half-day visits around the region, and most will have the names of registered Blue Badge guides, who can be hired for personalized tours.

Tours of the Wye Valley can be taken with **Yeomans Travel** (Coach Station, Commercial Rd., Hereford, tel. 0432/56201). Guided walking tours of Ludlow leave The Cannon, outside the castle entrance, every Saturday and Sunday from Easter to the end of September, with extra tours on Wednesday and Thursday from late July to August, at 2:30 PM; cost £1. The tours take place every day during the Ludlow Festival. Information tel. 0584/875079.

Exploring the Welsh Borders

Orientation

We begin our tour of the border region in the ancient Severn Valley city of Worcester, renowned for its proud cathedral and fine bone china. From there we work our way south and west, along the lovely Malvern Hills, taking in the peaceful Victorian spa town of Great Malvern before stopping in the prosperous agricultural city of Hereford, on the banks of the river Wye. Leaving Hereford, we head north to the town of Bewdley, terminus of the Severn Valley Railway, and continue into the West Midlands—England's notorious "Black Country"—birthplace of modern British industry.

Tour 2 begins in the handsome medieval city of Shrewsbury, and then moves on to the wooded banks of the river Severn to visit the cluster of Ironbridge museums, memorials to an area which was responsible for much of Britain's industrial preeminence during the 18th and 19th centuries. After crossing Wenlock Edge, with its panoramic views, the tour ends in Ludlow, an architectural jewel of a town.

Tour 3 runs from Chester to Manchester, taking in along the way Nantwich, the Jodrell Bank Observatory, Knutsford— another attractive old town—and the stately home at Tatton Park.

Highlights for First-time Visitors

The Black Country Museum—Dudley: Tour 1
The Rows—Chester: Tour 3
Hereford Cathedral: Tour 1
Ironbridge Gorge Museum: Tour 2
Jodrell Bank Science Centre: Tour 3
Knutsford: Tour 3
Ludlow: Tour 2
Worcester Cathedral: Tour 1

Tour 1: From Worcester to Shrewsbury

Numbers in the margin correspond to points of interest on the Welsh Borders map.

❶ Worcester (pronounced as in Wooster, Ohio), is situated on the Severn River in the center of Worcestershire, 118 miles northwest of London. It is an ancient city proud of its history, and in particular, its nickname, "The Faithful City," bestowed on it for its steadfast allegiance to the crown during the English Civil War. Worcester played an important role in this conflict between king and Parliament, and two major battles were waged here. The second one, the decisive Battle of Worcester in 1651, resulted in the exile of Charles II. More recently the town's name has become synonymous with the fine bone china produced here.

The city suffered considerable "modernization" during the 1960s, but happily some of medieval Worcester remains. This ancient section forms a convenient and pleasant walking route around the great cathedral.

There are few more quintessentially English sights than that of **Worcester Cathedral**, its towers overlooking the green expanse of the county cricket ground, its majestic image reflected in the swift-flowing—and frequently flooding—waters of the River Severn. The cathedral stands on one of the most ancient sites of English Christianity; there has been a cathedral here since the year 680. Later centuries saw considerable rebuilding, and much of what remains dates from the 13th and 14th centuries. Notable exceptions are the Norman crypt (built in the 1080s), the largest in England, and the ambulatory, a cloister built around the east end. The most important tomb in the cathedral is that of King John (1167–1216), one of the country's least admired monarchs, who so alienated his barons and subjects through bad administration and heavy taxation that he was eventually forced to sign the Magna Carta, the great charter of liberty, in 1215. The cathedral's most beautiful decoration is in the vaulted **chantry chapel of Prince Arthur**, Henry VII's elder son, whose body was brought to Worcester after his death at Ludlow in Shropshire in 1502. (Chantry chapels were endowed by wealthy families to enable priests to sing masses there for the souls of the deceased). *Tel. 0905/28854. Open daily 8:30–6.*

South of the cathedral (follow Severn Street) is the **Royal Worcester Porcelain Factory**. Here you can browse in the showrooms or rummage in the "seconds" stores; especially good bargains can be had in the January and July sales. Tours of the factory take you through the processes of porcelain-making, from raw materials to finished pieces, but reserve in advance to be sure of getting on a tour. Another part of the factory is the **Dyson Perrins Museum**, which houses one of the finest and most comprehensive collections of rare Worcester porcelain, from the start of manufacturing in 1751 to the present day. *Severn St., tel. 0905/23221. Admission free; tours (book in advance), £2.25 adults, £1.25 children; Connoisseur Tours (2 hours) £7. Open weekdays 9:30–5, Sat. 10–5.*

Across the road from the porcelain factory is **The Commandery**, a cluster of 15th-century half-timbered buildings, originally built as a poorhouse. Later it served as the headquarters of the royalist troops during the Battle of Worcester. Now a museum,

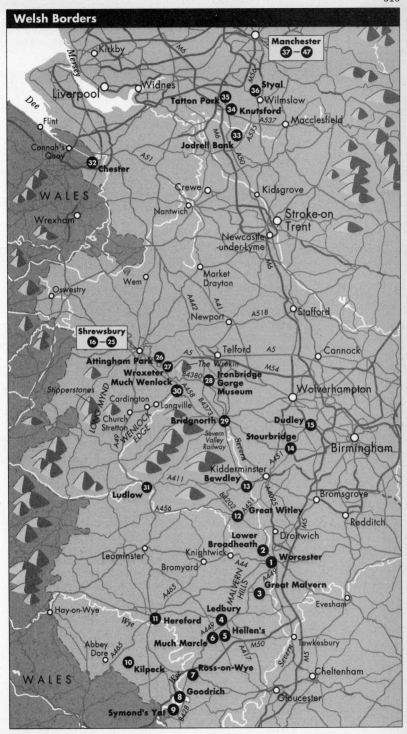

Welsh Borders

Manchester
37 — 47

Kirkby

M6

Styal
36

Widnes

Tatton Park
35

Wilmslow

Liverpool

34 Knutsford

Macclesfield

A537

Mersey

Dee

Flint

33 Jodrell Bank

A535

A50

32 Chester

Connah's
Quay

A51

Crewe

Kidsgrove

WALES

Nantwich

Wrexham

Stoke-on-
Trent

Newcastle
-under-Lyme

M6

Oswestry

Wem

Market
Drayton

Stafford

A442

A41

Newport

A518

Cannock

Shrewsbury
16 — 25

A5

Telford

A5

M54

Attingham Park
26
27

The Wrekin

Wolverhampton

Wroxeter
Much Wenlock

B4380

28 Ironbridge
Gorge
Museum

Stipperstones

30

A458

A5

LONG MYND

Cardington

Longville

Dudley
15

Church
Stretton

WENLOCK EDGE

Bridgnorth
29

Stourbridge
14

A49

B4373

Severn
Valley
Railway

Birmingham

Ludlow
31

A411

Kidderminster

Bewdley
13

A451

A4025

Bromsgrove

A456

B4202

A451

Redditch

12 Great Witley

M5

Leominster

Lower
Broadheath
2

Droitwich

Knightwick

1 Worcester

Bromyard

A44

Hay-on-Wye

Wye

A465

Ledbury

3 Great Malvern

Evesham

MALVERN HILLS

A449

11 Hereford

4

Abbey
Dore

A465

Much Marcle
6 5 Hellen's

M50

Tewkesbury

10 Kilpeck

Wye

7

Ross-on-Wye

A417

M5

Severn

WALES

8 Goodrich

Cheltenham

9 Symond's Yat

B4228

Gloucester

it presents a colorful, audiovisual presentation about the Civil War in the magnificent, oak-beamed **great hall**. *Sidbury, tel. 0905/355071. Admission: £2 adults, £1 children. Open Mon.–Sat. 10:30–5, Sun. 2–5.*

Time Out | **The Commandery** has a small tea room, and if the weather is clear, you can eat on the terrace and watch the houseboats bobbing on the canal.

Between The Commandery and the cathedral lies **Friar Street,** one of Worcester's most notable medieval streets. As you walk toward the Cornmarket, there are three buildings of particular interest: **Tudor House,** a museum of domestic and social history; **Greyfriars,** a late-15th-century half-timbered house with tapestried, paneled rooms; and **King Charles's House,** where the beleaguered Charles II hid before his escape from the city. The last is now a restaurant (*see* Dining and Lodging, below). *Tudor House, tel. 0905/725371. Admission free. Open Mon.–Wed., Fri. and Sat. 10:30–5. Greyfriars, tel. 0905/23571. Admission: £1.30 adults, 65p children, £3.50 family ticket. Open Apr.–Oct., Wed., Thurs. and national holidays 2–5:30.*

Follow High Street, closed to traffic and pleasant for walking, back toward the cathedral. Here you will see the **Guildhall** set back on the right behind ornate iron railings. The hall's 18th-century facade features gilded statues of Queen Anne, Charles I, and Charles II, as well as a smaller carving of Cromwell's head pinned up by the ears, a savage addition by the royalist citizens of Worcester.

At the end of High Street stands a **statue of Sir Edward Elgar** (1857–1934), who spent his early childhood in his parents' music store just a few yards from the cathedral. Elgar was one of Britain's best-known composers of choral and orchestral works, noted particularly for his *Enigma Variations*, his oratorio *The Dream of Gerontius*, and the *Pomp and Circumstance* marches.

If you walk down Deansway, you can turn left into the riverside gardens and work your way back along the river below the cathedral and porcelain factory.

Traveling southwest on A449 from Worcester, you will soon see the **Malvern Hills,** their long, low purple profile rising starkly from the surrounding plain. These were the hills that inspired much of Elgar's so-very-English music, as well as his remark that "there is music in the air, music all around us." Stop in and ② visit the **Elgar Birthplace Museum** at **Lower Broadheath** (follow B4204) before exploring the hills. Set in a peaceful little garden, the tiny brick cottage in which the composer was born now exhibits photographs, musical scores, letters, and other memorabilia, notably the manuscript score of his *Second Symphony*. *Crown East La. Lower Broadheath, tel. 0905/66224. Admission: £2 adults, 50p children. Open Feb.–Apr. and Oct.–mid-Jan., Thurs.–Tues. 1:30–4:30; May–Sept., Thurs.–Tues. 10:30–6.*

The Malverns shelter a string of communities stretching from the village of North Malvern to Little Malvern at the south-③ western end of the range. The main town is **Great Malvern,** off A449 about 7 miles south of Worcester. A Victorian spa town, its architecture has changed little since the mid-1800s. Exceptionally pure spring water is still bottled here and exported all over the world—the queen never travels without a supply. Many of the large hotels built in the spa days remain hotels, while others have been converted into "public" (i.e., private) schools. Great Malvern is known today both as an educational center and as a great place for old folks' homes. The town also has a **Winter Gardens complex** with a theater, movie theater, and gardens, but it is the **Priory** that dominates the steep streets downtown. This is an early Norman Benedictine abbey in Perpendicular style, decorated throughout with vertical lines of airy tracery. The Priory is also interesting for its large quantity of fine 15th-century glass and some local tiles of the same period. *Entrance opposite the church. Admission free. Open 8AM–dusk.*

The most striking feature of Great Malvern are the gentle hills that rise above it. Ideal for leisurely hiking, the hilltops provide magnificent views of the Welsh Black Mountains to the west, and the contrasting patchwork of the Severn plain as it stretches away eastward toward the Cotswold Hills in Gloucestershire.

4   Leaving Great Malvern, follow A449 southwest about ten miles through Malvern Wells and Little Malvern to the market town of **Ledbury.** Here you will see some exceptional black-and-white half-timbered buildings. Take special note of the **Feathers Hotel,** the **Talbot Inn** (both late 16th century), and the 17th-century **market hall** perched on 16 chestnut columns. On Saturdays you can still buy a variety of produce from the market stalls there. Look for the cheesemaker, and be sure to sample his very rare single Gloucester, which is tasty and far less rich and oily than the traditional orange-red Double Gloucester.

Time Out   Right beside the market house stands a small restaurant called **The Market Place,** which is open all day for vegetarian lunches and teas (light afternoon meals).

Almost hidden behind the market house is a cobbled lane leading to the church, with medieval, half-timbered buildings jostling each other and leaning into the narrow lane from either side. One of them is the **Old Grammar School,** now a Heritage Center tracing the town's development from Anglo-Saxon times. It is well worth stopping in. *Admission free. Open June–Sept., daily 11–5; Oct.–May, weekends 11–5.*

5   From Ledbury, rejoin A449 and continue southwest about four miles to **Hellen's** in Much Marcle. This is a beautiful mansion (part of it from the 13th century) in singularly authentic and pristine condition. The gloom and dust are part of the atmosphere—the house is still lit by candles, and central heating has been scorned. *Tel. 0531/6147. Admission: £2.50 adults, £1 children. Open Easter–Sept., Wed. and weekends 2–6.*

6   **Much Marcle** is one of the English villages that still holds an ancient annual ceremony. On Twelfth Night, January 6, the villagers go "wassailing," beating the apple trees to make them fruitful in the coming year.

If you have a good sense of direction, a detailed map, and plenty of time to spare, this is an area to wander around and discover tiny villages down sleepy lanes overhung by high hedges and, in the right season, rich with fruit-heavy trees.

7 Six miles southwest of Much Marcle by A449 lies **Ross-on-Wye,** a small market town with steep streets, perched high above the river Wye. It comes alive on Thursdays and Saturdays—market days—but is always a happy hunting ground for antiques.

8 From here take B4228 for three miles to **Goodrich.** The ruins of **Goodrich Castle,** the English equivalent of a Rhine castle, loom dramatically over the Wye river crossing at Kerne Bridge. From the south it looks picturesque in its setting of green fields, but standing on its battlements on the north side, you quickly see its grimmer face. Dating from the late 12th century, the castle is surrounded by a deep moat carved out of solid rock, from which its walls appear to soar upward. Once inside, walk to the north battlements overlooking the river and savor the imposing heights. Built to repel Welsh raiders, Goodrich was destroyed in the 17th century by Cromwell's troops during the Civil War. *Tel. 0600/890538. Admission: £1.30 adults, 65p children, 95p senior citizens. Open Apr.–Sept., Tues.–Sun. 10–6; Oct.–Mar., Tues.–Sun. 10–4.*

9 Continue south out of Goodrich on B4432 to the village of **Symond's Yat,** where the 473-foot-high Yat Rock ("Yat" means gate) commands superb views of the river Wye as it winds its way through a narrow gorge and swings around in a great five-mile loop.

10 Turning toward Hereford, drive 11 miles northwest on small side roads to **Kilpeck,** a tiny hamlet blessed with one of the best-preserved Norman churches in Britain. It is lavishly decorated inside and out, with exceptional carving for a country church. The carvings depict all manner of subjects, from rabbits to scenes so lewd that they were removed by high-minded Victorians. (One or two ribald ones remain, however, so look carefully.) Don't miss the gargoyles (rainwater spouts), either. From Kilpeck, A465 will lead you the seven miles into Hereford.

11 **Hereford** is a busy country town, the center of a wealthy agricultural area known for its cider, fruit, and cattle—the white-faced Hereford breed has spread across the world. It is also an important cathedral city, its massive Norman cathedral towering proudly over the river Wye. Before 1066, Hereford was the capital of the Anglo-Saxon kingdom of Mercia and, earlier still, the site of Roman, Celtic, and Iron Age settlements. Today, tourists come primarily to see the cathedral, but quickly discover the charms of a town that has changed slowly but fairly unobtrusively with the passing centuries.

The town center is small. Attractive old buildings of various periods remain, but the stores are generally unremarkable, many of them chain stores you could find anywhere. However, **Buttermarket,** in High Town, is a good place for local produce, while the **cattle market** provides an unmistakable glimpse of English country life. Livestock auctions are held every Wednesday, but there are special auctions and market stalls here virtually every day.

Hereford Cathedral, built of local red sandstone with a massive central tower, has some fine 11th-century Norman carvings but like many of England's early churches, suffered considerable "restoration" in the 19th century, which spoiled the naive but skillful work of earlier craftsmen. Inside, the greatest glories include the 14th-century **bishop's throne;** some fine **misericords**

(the elaborately carved undersides of choristers' seats); and the extraordinary **Mappa Mundi,** Hereford's own picture of the medieval world. This great map shows the Earth as flat, with Jerusalem at its center. It is now thought that the Mappa Mundi was the center section of an altarpiece, dating from 1290. The dean of the cathedral caused a furor in 1988 when he began negotiations with Sotheby's to put the piece on the market, to raise funds to help pay the costs of the cathedral's upkeep and restoration. Britain suddenly realized that the rich heritage of art treasures held by the Church, mostly in cathedrals, might be under threat. The map was withdrawn from sale and is now on view in the crypt until a gallery can be prepared for it.

Best of all the cathedral's attractions is the library, containing some 1,500 chained books. Among the most valuable volumes is an 8th-century copy of the four gospels. Chained libraries are extremely rare: There are only six of them in the country, dating from medieval times when books were as precious as gold. *Tel. 0432/59880. Cathedral admission free. Open Mon.–Sat. 8:30–5:30, Sun. 12:30–3:30. Chained library admission: 40p adults. Open Apr.–Oct., Mon.–Sat. 10:30–12:30 and 2–4; Nov.–Mar., weekdays 11–11:30, Sat. 11–11:30 and 3–3:30.*

Leaving the cathedral by the north door, walk down Church Street to find the town's more unusual stores: jewelers, bookstores, and crafts and antiques shops, all stocking unique, high-quality products.

Time Out **Nutter** (2 Capucin Yard, Church St.) serves homemade soup, hot meat pies, and a variety of baked goodies.

From Church Street, cross East Street and follow the passageway into **High Town,** a large pedestrian square, in the corner of which stands a fine example of domestic Jacobean architecture. Called simply **The Old House,** it is furnished on three floors in 17th-century style and is the only building remaining from the original Butchers' Row. *Tel. 0432/268121, ext. 207. Admission: 60p adults, 30p children. Open Apr.–Sept., Mon.–Sat. 10–1 and 2–5:30; Oct.–Mar., Mon.–Sat. 10–1.*

On the west side of High Town is the 13th-century **All Saints Church,** which contains another 300 chained books, as well as canopied stalls and fine misericords.

From All Saints, walk down the pedestrian Eign Gate, go under the ring road using the pedestrian underpass, and proceed down Eign Street, which continues as Whitecross Road. At the traffic lights turn left into Grimmer Road and bear right for the **Cider Museum,** which traces the story of cider-making through the ages. A farm cider-house and a cooper's (cask maker's) workshop have been re-created here, and you can tour ancient cider cellars, complete with huge oak vats. The cellars date back to Napoleonic times. Apple brandy (applejack) has recently been made here for the first time in hundreds of years, and the museum has its own brand for sale. *Pomona Pl., off Whitecross Rd., tel. 0432/354207. Admission: £1.50 adults, £1 children. Open Apr.–Oct., daily 10–5:30; Nov.–Dec., weekdays 1–5.*

We now suggest a northeast leap from Hereford. Take A465 toward Bromyard (14 miles), turn right onto A44 to Knightwick,

⑫ where you turn north on B4197 as far as **Great Witley.** Pause to see the shell of **Witley Court,** burned down in 1937. What remains will conjure up a haunting vision of its Edwardian heyday, when shooting parties met around the fantastic fountains. The tiny Baroque parish church, once the family chapel, escaped the fire, and you can get an idea of the house's former elegance from the chapel's decorations: a balustraded parapet, a small golden dome over its cupola, and, inside, a painted ceiling by Bellucci, 10 colored windows, and the ornate case of an organ once used by Handel.

Two possible routes north of here, A451/B4194/A456 or B4202/
⑬ A456, will bring you to **Bewdley,** an exceptionally attractive Severn Valley town, with many tall, narrow-fronted Georgian buildings clustered around the river bridge. In what was the 18th-century butchers' market, the **Shambles,** there is now an imaginative museum of local crafts. Workshops occupy either side of the old cobbled yard, and there are exhibitions and practical demonstrations of rope-making, charcoal-burning, clay-pipe-making, and glass-blowing; there is also a working brass foundry. *Load St., tel. 0299/403573. Admission: 50p adults, 20p children. Open Mar.–Nov., Mon.–Sat. 10–5:30, Sun. 2–5:30.*

Bewdley is the southern terminus of the **Severn Valley Railway,** a restored steam railroad running 16 miles north along the river to Bridgnorth (*see* Tour 2). It stops at a handful of sleepy stations where time has apparently stood still since the age of steam. You can get off at any of these little stations, enjoy a picnic by the river, and walk to the next station to get a train back. *Severn Valley Railway Co., Railway Station, Bewdley, Worcestershire DY12 1BG, tel. 0299/403816. May–Sept., trains run daily; mid-Mar.–mid-Oct., weekends only.*

⑭ Eight miles northeast of Bewdley via A451 lies **Stourbridge,** home of Britain's crystal glass industry; all the major manufacturers are based in this area. Their sparkling bowls, glasses, and decanters are exported throughout the world, but you can find bargains at their "factory seconds" stores. You can tour the factories, too, and see the glowing lumps of molten glass being skillfully gathered, blown, and molded. ***Stuart Crystal,*** *Redhouse Glassworks, Vine St., Wordsley, tel. 0384/71161. Admission free. Tours weekdays 10–3.* ***Royal Brierley Crystal,*** *North St., Brierley Hill, tel. 0384/70161. Admission free. Tours Mon.–Thurs. 11, noon, and 1; Fri. 11.* ***Thomas Webb Crystal,*** *Dennis Hall, Amblecote, tel. 0384/395281. Admission free. Tours weekdays 10–3.*

Northeast of Stourbridge, on the edge of Birmingham, is
⑮ **Dudley,** in Black Country, an area traditionally associated with heavy industry. Although much of its industrial activity is a thing of the past now, **The Black Country Museum** was established to ensure that the heritage is not forgotten. It occupies a 26-acre site on the edge of Dudley, where an entire industrial village has sprung up as disused buildings have been moved here from other parts of the region. There is a chain-maker's house and workshop, with demonstrations of chain-making; a druggist and general store, where costumed women describe life in a poor industrial community in the last century; a Methodist chapel; the Bottle & Glass pub, serving local ales and the traditional fagots (a fried pork liver dish) and peas; and a coal mine and wharf. All of these reconstructions huddle around a

canal that would have once been the community's lifeblood. You can also ride on a canal houseboat through a tunnel, where an audiovisual show portrays canal travel of yesteryear. *Tipton Rd., tel. 021/557–9643. Admission: £4.50 adults, £3 children, £4 senior citizens. Open daily 10–5.*

Tour 2: Skirting the "Black Country"— Shrewsbury to the Cheshire Plain

Numbers in the margin correspond to points of interest on the Shrewsbury map.

16 **Shrewsbury** (pronounced "Shrose-bury"), the county seat of Shropshire, is strategically located within a great horseshoe loop of the Severn, with only one landward entrance. One of England's most important medieval towns, Shrewsbury has a wealth of well-preserved, 16th-century half-timbered buildings as well as many elegant ones from later periods. The market square forms the natural center of the town; leading off it are narrow alleys overhung with timbered gables. These alleys, called "shuts," were designed to be closed off at night to afford their residents greater protection. The town is especially proud of its flower displays, for which it has won many national awards. In the summer, window boxes and hanging baskets are a riot of color, providing a vivid contrast to the stark black-and-white buildings.

Shrewsbury is an ideal town to see on foot, since its narrow, traffic-congested streets are not pleasant to drive in. Indeed, some of the most historic streets have been pedestrianized. A good starting point for a walking tour is the small square between **Fish Street** and **Butchers Row.** These streets are little changed since medieval times, when they took their names

17 from the principal trades carried on there. Nearby are **St. Alkmund's** (the only church in England to be named after a Saxon

18 saint) and **St. Mary's churches,** both worth a visit for their iron-framed stained glass (an indication of the proximity of the Ironbridge Gorge). Below is **Bear Steps,** a cluster of restored half-timbered buildings which link Fish Street with Grope Alley

19 and Market Square. Here the most notable building is **Ireland's Mansion,** a massive merchant's house. An outstanding example of elaborate Jacobean architecture, this house boasts heavy timbering, richly decorated with quatrefoils (openings carved in the timbers in the shape of four-leafed moldings or foils).

Princess Street, good for bookstores and antiques, leads from

20 the square to College Hill and **Clive House,** the home of Sir Robert Clive when he was Shrewsbury's member of Parliament in the mid-18th century. Better known as "Clive of India," this soldier-statesman was especially famous for winning the Battle of Plassey in 1757, thereby avenging the atrocity of the Black Hole of Calcutta, in which 146 Britons were imprisoned overnight in a stifling Indian dungeon, with only 23 surviving until morning. The house contains rooms furnished in Clive's period, and displays of Staffordshire pottery, particularly pieces from the Caughley and Coalport factories. *College Hill, tel. 0743/54811. Admission: 60p adults, 30p children. Open Mon.–Sat. 10–5.*

Time Out **Poppies** (Princess St.) serves home-baked snacks—or try the **Golden Cross,** next door, for something stronger.

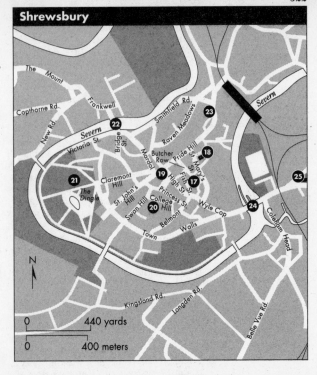

Shrewsbury

Below Swan Hill (turn left out of Clive House, then left again)
㉑ you will see the manicured lawn of **Quarry Park** sloping down to
the river. In a sheltered corner is the Dingle, a colorful garden
offering changing floral displays through the year. St. John's
Hill in the Mardol, another of Shrewsbury's strangely named
㉒ streets, will take you back into town, or you can head for **Welsh
Bridge** and stroll along the river bank. As the river loops away,
the **castle** rises up on the right. Originally Norman, it was dis-
mantled during the Civil War and later rebuilt by Thomas
Telford, the distinguished Scottish engineer who designed a
host of notable buildings and bridges at the beginning of the
19th century. The castle now houses the **Shropshire Regimental
㉓ Museum**, providing an interesting reflection on 200 years of the
county's past. You need not be a military history buff to appreciate it. It was this regiment that was responsible for burning
down the White House in Washington in 1814. *Tel. 0743/58516.
Admission: 70p adults, 35p children and senior citizens. Open
Easter–Sept., daily 10–5; Oct.–Easter, Mon.–Sat. 10–5.*

㉔ ㉕ If you cross the river by the **English Bridge** you'll reach **Shrewsbury Abbey Church**, almost all that remains of the monastery
that stood here from 1083. The abbey figures in a series of popular medieval whodunits by Ellis Peters, which feature the de-
tective Brother Cadfael and provide an excellent idea of life in
this area during the Middle Ages. The Abbey Restoration Project has developed an intriguing series of medieval walking
tours. (Details from Restoration Project Office, 1 Holy Cross
Houses, Abbey Foregate, Shrewsbury SY2 6BS, tel. 0743/
232723.)

Numbers in the margin correspond with points of interest on the Welsh Borders map.

The rural scenery around Shrewsbury is among England's loveliest, with small towns, stately homes, and evocative museums scattered across the wide, open landscape. Four miles southeast of Shrewsbury, just off A5, is **Attingham Park**, a mansion built in 1785 by George Steuart, who designed the round church of St. Chad's in Shrewsbury. It has an impressive three-story portico, with a pediment carried on four tall columns. Inside are painted ceilings, delicate plasterwork, and a collection of 19th-century Neapolitan furniture. *Tel. 074377/203. Admission: £2.70 adults, £1.35 children, £6.75 family ticket. Open Apr.–Sept., Sat.–Wed. 1:30–5, Sun. 11–5; Oct., weekends 1:30–5.*

A mile farther east is **Wroxeter**, originally the Roman city of Viroconium, which flourished around AD 150 and was the fourth-largest city in Roman Britain. Excavations beginning in 1863 revealed the foundations of the shattered pillars of the forum and fragments of the town walls. A complex of buildings around the forum has now been unearthed, providing a clear impression of the original town plan. The museum houses the Roman artifacts found in the last 100 years. *Tel. 074375/330. Admission: £1.30 adults, 65p children, 95p senior citizens. Open Apr.–Sept., daily 10–6, Oct.–Mar., Tues.–Sun. 10–4.*

Continuing southeast on B4380, you will see, rising on the left, the **Wrekin**, a strange, conical-shaped extinct volcano. A few miles farther on you enter the wooded gorge of the Severn river. Here you can see the world's earliest iron bridge (1774), a monument to the discovery of how to smelt iron ore using coke, rather than charcoal, a technological breakthrough which led Britain to glory as the leading industrial nation and workshop of the world. **The Ironbridge Gorge Museum** has been established around a unique series of industrial sites and monuments spread over six square miles. The Museum has six component sections: Museum Visitors Center, Museum of Iron, The Iron Bridge, Jackfield Tile Museum, Blists Hill Open-Air Museum, and the Coalport China Museum. Enthusiasts could spend a couple of days here but a good half-day will let you take in the major sites. You can also spend a pleasant half-hour strolling around the famous bridge, perhaps hunting for Coalport china in the stores clustering around it. To place this seemingly sleepy little place into its proper 18th-century perspective, the best place to start is the **Severn Warehouse**, which has a good selection of literature and an audiovisual show on the gorge's history.

From here you can drive (or in summer, take the museum's "park and ride" service) to Coalbrookdale and the **Museum of Iron**. Iron has been produced on this site since the 17th century, and you can see the original blast furnace built by Abraham Darby, who developed the coke process in 1709. The museum in the adjoining Great Warehouse explains the production of iron and steel through a series of displays, models, and exhibits.

Retrace your steps along the river until the graceful arches of the **Iron Bridge** come into view. Although it is now closed to traffic, you can still walk onto the bridge to enjoy the sight of the river snaking through the gorge. The tollhouse on the far side houses an exhibition on the bridge's history and restoration.

Just one mile farther along the river is the **Coalport China Museum.** Production of Coalport china was transferred many years ago to Stoke-on-Trent 50 miles to the north, but the 19th-century factory buildings and the bottle-shaped kilns remain here. Inside are exhibits of some of the factory's most beautiful wares, and craftsmen give demonstrations of their skills.

Above Coalport is **Blists Hill Open-Air Museum,** where you can see old mines, the remains of two enormous furnaces built into the hillside, and the only surviving wrought-iron works in the western world. But this 42-acre site is particularly fascinating for its re-creation of a Victorian town: There's the doctor's office, the gruesome dentist's chair, the sweet-smelling bakery, the candlemaker's, the saw mill, the printing shop, and the candy store—exactly as they would have appeared in an industrial town in the 19th century.

Although these are the major sites in Ironbridge, there are several more, including **Jackfield Tile Museum,** once the home of Maw & Co., the largest maker of ceramic wall tiles in the world; the **Tar Tunnel,** still oozing natural bitumen; **Rosehill House,** home of the Darby family of ironmasters; and **Rose Cottages.**

For details of all these museums, contact Ironbridge Gorge Museum Trust, Ironbridge, Telford, Shropshire TF8 7AW, tel. 0952/433522. Admission ticket to all sites: £6.95 adults, £4.50 children, £5.95 senior citizens, family ticket £20, valid until all sites have been visited once. Open Mar.–Oct, daily 10–6; Nov.–Feb., daily 10–5.

Time Out | **The New Inn** at Blists Hill has traditional ales on draft and ploughman's lunches (rolls with cheese and pickles), or try a pork pie from the butcher's store next door. The building was moved here from Walsall 22 miles away, as part of the open-air museum.

㉙ From Ironbridge the Severn turns south to **Bridgnorth** (take B4373), a pretty market town perching perilously close to the river. Built on a high sandstone ridge, Bridgnorth has two distinct parts, High Town and Low Town, connected by a winding road, flights of steep steps, and—best of all—a cliff railroad. Even the tower of the Norman castle seems to suffer from vertigo, having a 17-degree list (three times the angle of the Leaning Tower of Pisa). The Severn Valley Railway terminates here.

㉚ Return northwest on A458 for just over seven miles to reach the intriguingly named **Much Wenlock,** a town full of half-timbered buildings, including a 16th-century guildhall and the romantic ruins of the Norman **Wenlock Priory.** *High St., tel. 0952/ 727466. Admission: £1.30 adults, 65p children, 95p senior citizens. Open Apr.–Sept., Tues.–Sun. 10–6; Oct.–Mar., Tues.–Sun. 10–4.*

Running southwest from Much Wenlock toward Ludlow is the high scarp of **Wenlock Edge,** from which you can get a splendid view across the valley to the Shropshire hills linking the English plains and the Welsh mountains. The horizon is dominated by Caer Caradoc, the site of an ancient hill fort; the great whaleback of the ridge called Long Mynd; and the jagged outlines of the Stiperstones beyond. This is hiking country, and if a healthy walk sounds inviting, turn off the Edge down through the villages of Longville and Cardington, and drive through Church Stretton into Cardingmill Valley, or up the Burway to the wide, heather uplands on top of the Mynd. In one of these inviting places, leave your car and set off on foot.

31 Back on A49, drive a few miles south to **Ludlow,** which has often been described as the most beautiful small town in England. With its mix of medieval, Georgian, and Victorian buildings, it is an architectural gem. Cross the river and climb **Whitcliff** for the most spectacular view. The town centers around the cathedral-like bulk of the **Church of St. Lawrence,** and is dwarfed by the massive, red sandstone **castle.** The latter dates from 1085 and was a vital stronghold in this part of the border country. It was the seat of the Marcher Lords who ruled this area, and whose name derived from the local name for the border region, "the Marches." It is still privately owned by the Earl of Powys. Follow the terraced walk around the castle for a lovely view. *Tel. 0584/873947. Admission: £1.50 adults, 75p children. Open Feb.–Apr. and Oct.–Dec., daily 1:30–4; May–Sept., daily 10:30–6.*

If you take the time to wander around the town, look for the **Feathers Hotel,** to admire its extravagantly decorated half-timbered facade.

Tour 3: Chester to Manchester

32 **Chester,** some 35 miles due north of Shrewsbury, is in some ways quite similar to it, though it has many more "magpie" (black-and-white) half-timbered buildings, and its medieval walls are still standing. While Shrewsbury's history has been inextricably linked with English-Welsh feuding since medieval times, Chester has been a prominent city since the latter part of the 1st century AD, when the Roman empire expanded northward and a fortress called Deva was established here, on the banks of the River Dee. The original Roman town plan is still evident in the layout of modern Chester: The principal streets, Eastgate, Northgate, Watergate, and Bridge Street, lead out from the Cross—the site of the central area of the Roman fortress—to each of the four city gates.

Since Roman times, sea-going vessels have sailed up the estuary of the Dee and anchored under the walls of Chester. The port enjoyed its most prosperous period during the 12th and 13th centuries. This was also the time when Chester's unique **Rows** originated. Essentially, they are two rows of stores, one at street level (or sometimes sunken just below), and the other on the second floor with galleries overlooking the street. The Rows line the junction of Watergate, Eastgate, Northgate, and Bridge Streets, in the heart of the old town. They have medieval crypts below them, and some can show Roman foundations.

History seems more tangible in Chester than in many other ancient cities. So much medieval architecture remains that the town center is quite compact, and modern buildings have not been allowed to intrude. A negative result of this perfection is that Chester has become a favorite bus-tour destination, with gift shops and casual restaurants inevitably cropping up as a consequence. It can be noisy, and the streets can be very crowded.

Better to take to the **walls,** which are accessible from various points and provide splendid views of the city and its surroundings. The whole circuit is two miles, but if your time is short, climb the steps at Newgate and walk along toward Eastgate, where a great ornamental clock, erected to commemorate Queen Victoria's diamond jubilee in 1897, marks where the walls cross Eastgate Street below. Here you will get a good aerial view of the street and a much better impression of the architectural detail than would be possible at ground level. There are lots of small shops by this part of the walls, selling old books, old postcards, antiques, and jewelry. Walking on, you'll see the cathedral on the left, and on the right, the canal running along below the wall. Where the **Bridge of Sighs**—named after the enclosed pedestrian bridge in Venice it closely resembles—crosses the canal, descend to street level and walk up Northgate Street into Market Square. The **cathedral** is on St. Werburgh Street just off the Square.

Tradition has it that a church of some sort stood on this site in Roman times, but the earliest records indicate construction around AD 900. However, the earliest building work traceable today is that of the 11th-century Benedictine abbey, mainly in the north transept. Only a little later in date are the undercroft, the nave, and the chapter house. After Henry VIII dissolved the monasteries in the 16th century, the abbey-church became the cathedral-church of the new diocese of Chester. It was extensively restored in the 19th century by the Victorian architect Sir Gilbert Scott.

In Eastgate Street you will see the impressive frontage of the five-star Grosvenor Hotel (*see* Dining and Lodging, below) surrounded by the best of the city's boutiques. Over the Cross in Watergate Street, the stores specialize in antiques and arts and crafts.

Time Out The **Falcon** (Lower Bridge Street) is a typical old pub that serves a wide range of lunch food. The **Witches Kitchen** (19 Frodsham Street), near the cathedral, is in a supposedly haunted building. Good for pizzas and teas.

Bridge Street continues down toward the **castle** and the river. The former is disappointing for those who like keeps (towers), moats, and battlements, for these were largely done away with at the end of the 18th century to make way for the classical-style civil and criminal courts, jail, and barracks. The castle now houses the **Cheshire Military Museum,** exhibiting uniforms and other military memorabilia, as well as some fine silver. *Tel. 0244/347023 (cavalry), 0244/347617 (infantry). Admission: 20p adults, 10p children. Open daily 9–noon and 1–5.*

From here you can follow the riverbank past the old bridge to the site of the **Roman amphitheater** beside Newgate.

It is now a simple, grassy spot, but an information board provides an insight into the part the amphitheater played in the social life of Roman Chester.

The plain surrounding Chester is rich dairy land, famous for Cheshire cheese. To the west lies the coast road to northern Wales. Don't be deceived by the sight of **Flint Castle,** rising up and overlooking the Dee estuary on the Irish Sea; though its position is superb, it is surrounded on all sides by suburban sprawl. To the southeast the countryside is gentle and wooded, dotted with the black-and-white "magpie" villages so characteristic of this region.

From Chester, continue due east on A54 for 23 miles to Holmes Chapel, then turn northeast on A535 for about five miles. Here **(33)** you will see the giant radio telescope of **Jodrell Bank.** Its 250-foot-wide reflector, weighing 2,000 tons, receives radio impulses from a host of distant stars. The planetarium here offers a three-dimensional voyage into outer space; you can also see an exhibition of radio astronomy, watch closed-circuit television demonstrations, and operate a model radio telescope. *Jodrell Bank Science Centre and Tree Park, Lower Withington, Macclesfield, tel. 0477/71339. Admission: £2.75 adults, £1.50 children, £2 senior citizens, £8 family ticket. Open Easter–Oct., daily 10:30–5:30; Nov.–Easter, weekends 2–5.*

(34) **Knutsford,** 6 miles northwest on A50 or A535 and A537, retains a distinctive air of 19th-century gentility. Knutsford was the model for *Cranford,* by Victorian novelist Elizabeth Gaskell, who took the people of Knutsford and its strong sense of local community as the inspiration for her best-known novel. The town seems little changed. There is a pleasant, unhurried atmosphere here, and the narrow streets are lined with fine stores. Walk along Princess Street, down the little cobbled lane beside the church, and onto King Street, noting the Art Nouveau decoration of the early years of this century—the elaborate Belle Époque restaurant is a good example (*see* Dining and Lodging, below).

(35) Just north of Knutsford, 3½ miles off M6 via exit 19, is **Tatton Park,** a fine stately home offering a wide variety of attractions. The mansion, built in the early 19th century for the Egerton family, is sumptuously decorated and furnished. In contrast, the family's previous home, the 15th-century Old Hall also on the site, is austerely furnished in the style of its time. But the park and gardens at Tatton are the prize-winning features: 1,000 acres of parkland in which deer graze and rhododendrons and azaleas flourish. The grand vistas planned 200 years ago are best seen from the south terrace, across the formal gardens to the distances beyond. Tatton's home farm has also been preserved and is now run as it would have been half a century ago. There are marked trails throughout the park, as well as two boating lakes. *Tel. 0565/54882. Admission (inclusive ticket for mansion, gardens, Old Hall, and farm): £5 adults, £2.50 children; there are smaller admission fees for individual sights. Opening times vary for the house, garden, and Old Hall, though all are open daily year-round. Check locally for exact times.*

Time Out There is a cafeteria-style restaurant in the stableblock of Tatton Park. If you want to book a table in advance, call 0565/2914.

A few miles east of the grandeur of Tatton is **Quarry Bank Mill** **(36)** at **Styal,** an evocation of the very different lives of mid-18th-century millworkers. This is one of the country's major industrial museums, centered on one of the few surviving water-powered cotton mills. The massive mill buildings, dating from 1784, have been restored as a living museum of the pioneering days of the cotton industry. Fibers and fabrics, as well as spinning and weaving, are illustrated, and there are frequent live demonstrations. The old village re-creates the Quarry Bank community of the 19th century, contrasting the hardships endured by the millworkers with the affluent lives of their masters, the Greg family, who owned this factory right up until 1959, when it finally ceased production. The whole estate comprises some 250 acres of woodland and riverside, now a country park open throughout the year. *Styal, Wilmslow, tel. 0625/ 527468. Admission: Mill: £3 adults, £2 children and senior citizens, £8 family ticket. Apprentice House and Garden: £2 adults, £1.50 children and senior citizens, £6 family ticket; combined tickets £4 adults, £3 children and senior citizens, £10 family ticket. Open: Mill, Oct.–Mar., Tues.–Sun. 11–4; Apr.– Sept., daily 11–5; Apprentice House times change seasonally from the Mill ones, so check locally.*

From Styal, which is close to Manchester Airport, you have a choice of routes into town, but the easiest may well be via M56, exit 6.

The mechanization of the cotton industry—the first cotton mill powered by steam opened in 1783—caused the rapid growth of
③⑦ Manchester; then, in 1894, the opening of the Manchester Ship Canal turned the world's cotton capital into a major inland port. Until only a few years ago, Manchester was a blackened, forbidding city, unlovely and unloved. But now it has been spruced up, and the once-begrimed buildings in the center of town, masterpieces of sturdy Victorian architecture, have been cleaned. Severe damage caused by World War II bombing has been remedied by modern development, not all of it attractive, and the visitor now sees an expansive center city, which has managed to keep at least some of its architectural heritage safe.

Numbers in the margin correspond to points of interest on the Manchester map.

Within just a few blocks you can visit most of the important
③⑧ sights. Start at the **City Art Gallery,** a strikingly neoclassical building housing a fine collection. Many Manchester industrial barons of the 19th century spent some of their vast wealth on buying paintings, and their interests are reflected in the art on display here. Apart from a large collection of Pre-Raphaelites, there are works by Gainsborough, Samuel Palmer, Turner, Claude Lorrain, and Bellotto. A re-creation of the living room and studio of L. S. Lowry—the popular Manchester artist who died in 1976—adds a touch of local interest. *Mosley St., tel. 061/ 236-5244. Admission free. Open Mon.–Sat. 10–5:45, Sun. 2– 5:45.*

Next door is the **Atheneum Gallery,** a gallery for changing contemporary shows. *Princess St., tel. 061/236-9422. Details same as City Art Gallery.*

③⑨ Two blocks northwest of the Art Gallery is the **Town Hall,** a magnificent Victorian Gothic building (1867–76), with extensions added just before World War II. The Great Hall, with its soaring hammerbeam roof, is decorated with proud murals of the city's history, painted by the Pre-Raphaelites' contemporary, Ford Madox Brown, between 1852 and 1865. As the Town Hall is used for meetings a great deal, the murals are sometimes covered up for their own protection. *Free guided tours*

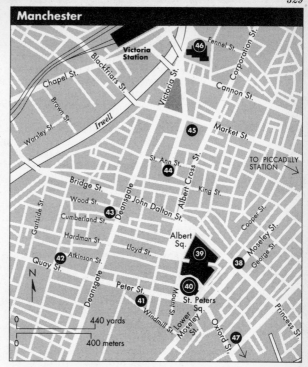

Manchester

Mon., Wed., and Thurs. 10AM; Wed. 2:30 if there are no meetings in progress.

40 To one side of the Town Hall is the **Central Library,** with the Library Theatre as part of the complex (*see* The Arts, below). Turn right at the library onto Peter Street and two blocks down

41 you will find the **Free Trade Hall,** restored after World War II damage; it has been the home of the Hallé Orchestra for more than a century.

42 The **Opera House** lies across Deansgate, on Quay Street, an ornate refurbished building that hosts leading companies, among them major dance and opera groups (*see* The Arts, below). Four

43 blocks north on Deansgate is the **John Rylands Library,** named after a rich weaver whose widow spent his money founding the library. It became part of the University of Manchester in 1972. Built in a late-Gothic style in the 1890s, the library houses one of Britain's most important collections—priceless historical documents and charters, bibles in over 300 languages, manuscripts dating from the dawn of Christianity, and fine bindings. There are always exhibitions from the library's treasures, including one of the possible accurate likenesses of Shakespeare, the Grafton portrait. *Tel. 061/834–5343. Admission free. Open weekdays 10–5:15, Sat. 10–1.*

44 Up Deansgate toward the river Irwell and on the right, down St. Ann's Street, you will come upon **St. Ann's Church,** a handsome 1712 building, with a painting by Annibale Carracci (1561–1609) inside, *The Descent from the Cross.* Outside, to the

45 right side of the square, is the **Royal Exchange,** once the cotton market, and built with impressive panache. In its echoing bulk, it now houses one of the most imaginative theaters in Britain (*see* The Arts, below).

To complete this stroll around downtown Manchester, continue
46 north up Victoria Street to the **cathedral,** beside the river. It was originally the medieval parish church of the city, but gradually went up in the world to finally become a cathedral in 1847. It's a strange shape, very broad for its length, and contains a few attractive items: early 16th-century choir stalls, with intriguing misericord seats; paintings of the Beatitudes by Carel Weight (1908–1989); and a sculpture by Eric Gill (1882–1919), famed for the typeface that he designed and which bears his name; a fine tomb brass of Warden Huntingdon, who died in 1458; and an octagonal chapter house from 1485.

One of the most interesting places to visit outside the center of
47 Manchester is the university-run **Whitworth Gallery,** southeast of town in an area called Moss Side. At the Piccadilly bus depot ask for a bus to the Manchester Royal Infirmary, which is just across the road from the Whitworth. The collections in the gallery are especially strong in British watercolors, Old Master drawings, and Postimpressionism. And its captivating rooms full of textiles—Coptic and Peruvian cloths, Spanish and Italian vestments, tribal rugs, and contemporary fabrics—are just what you might expect in a city built on textile manufacture. There's a gallery bistro for light meals, and a good gallery shop. *Oxford Rd., tel. 061/273–4865. Admission free. Open Mon.–Sat. 10–5, Thurs. 10–9.*

What to See and Do with Children

The revitalized steam trains of Britain make wonderful trips for children, unveiling magnificent countryside via a means of travel that evokes the stories of Sherlock Holmes and the Victorian era in general. The **Severn Valley Railway** is an excellent example (*see* Tour 1).

There's plenty of hands-on participation in the **Black Country Museum** in Dudley (*see* Tour 1), and at the **Ironbridge museum complex** (*see* Tour 2).

For the kids who are into space exploration, nothing can beat the **Jodrell Bank Science Centre** (*see* Tour 3) where, among much else to see and do, there is a model radio telescope to operate.

The **Granada Studios' Tour** has a lot to offer imaginative children, who can see firsthand the work that goes on behind TV programs (*see* Off the Beaten Track).

Off the Beaten Track

The tour of the **Granada Studios** in the center of Manchester is a very British version of the popular Hollywood studio tours. This is a TV set-up, and it is from here that Britain's most popular and longest-running soap opera, *Coronation Street*, is broadcast. *Water St., tel. 061/833–0880. Admission: £6.95 adults, £4.75 children, £21 family ticket. Phone for latest tour times.*

The area traditionally known as **the Potteries,** less than an hour's drive from Shrewsbury northwest on A53, is the center of Britain's ceramic industry, immortalized in Arnold Bennett's novels, particularly *The Old Wives' Tale* and *Anna of the Five Towns*. There are, in fact, six towns—all now administered as "the City of **Stoke-on-Trent**." The area has three award-winning museums (*see* below), which evocatively portray the industrial and social history of this area; combined with some factory visits showing the making of various crafts, the museums make a fascinating day out.

The Gladstone Pottery Museum, a preserved Victorian potbank—a local term for a pottery factory—has two of the few remaining bottle-ovens originally used for firing the wares in an area where there were once hundreds. These kilns stand in a cobbled yard around which cluster the old workshops, now used for exhibitions—including a gallery of chamberpots and a wonderful collection of colorful tiles. There are also displays on the past way of life of Staffordshire's potters, and demonstrations by local craftsmen. *Uttoxeter Rd., Longton, tel. 0782/319232. Admission: £2.50 adults, £1.25 children and senior citizens. Open Mon.–Sat. 10:30–5:30, Sun. 2–6.*

The Stoke-on-Trent City Museum and Art Gallery has a ceramic gallery of international standing, a particularly well-designed modern museum. Its extensive collection of Staffordshire porcelain is unique; there are also excellent galleries devoted to the fine arts. *Bethesda St., Hanley, tel. 0782/202173. Admission free. Open Mon.–Sat. 10–5, Sun. 2–5.*

Stop in at **Wedgwood's Visitor Centre and Museum** which will provide a good insight into the pottery industry. You don't actually go into the factory itself, but in the craft area you will be able to see every stage of production, as well as chat with the craftspeople. There is also an attractively laid-out museum, an art gallery, and, of course, "firsts" and "seconds" stores. *Barlaston, tel. 0782/204218. Admission: £2 adults, £1.25 children and senior citizens. Open weekdays 9–5, Sat. 10–4, Sun. (Easter–Oct.) 10–4.*

To the south of the Potteries is **Shugborough,** an 18th-century mansion that is the ancestral home of Lord Lichfield, the queen's cousin and a well-known photographer. The **Staffordshire County Museum,** housed in what was formerly the servants' quarters, features re-creations of 19th-century life and beautifully restored kitchens, laundry, and brewhouse. There is also a farm with rare breeds of livestock, and extensive parkland with formal gardens. *Milford, on A513, west of Stafford, tel. 0889/881388. Admission (to each site): £2.50 adults, £1.50 children; all-inclusive ticket: £6 adults, £3 children, family £12. Open Easter–Sept., daily 11–5; Oct.–Dec. 24, daily 11–4.*

Not far from Shugborough (17 miles southeast on A51), **Lichfield Cathedral** is worth a detour. The only English cathedral with three spires, the present building dates mainly from the 12th and 13th centuries, and has some fine 16th-century stained glass from the Cistercian Abbey of Herkenrode, near Liège, in Belgium. It stands in peaceful grounds surrounded by half-timbered houses. *Open daily 7:30–6:15.*

On the Wirral Peninsula, lying west of Chester, the **Boat Museum** at Ellesmere port traces the history of Britain's inland waterways, which played a vital role in transporting manufactured goods from the industrial cities to the seaports. Over 50 boats are on display, many still under restoration. You can board a 19th-century canal houseboat to find out how people managed to live and raise families on boats no wider than a modern hallway. *Dockyard Rd., tel. 051355/5017. Admission: £3.60 adults, £2.30 children, £2.50 senior citizens, £10 family ticket. Open Apr.–Oct., daily 10–5; Nov.–Mar., daily 11–4, closed Fri. Boat trips: £1.30 adults, 85p children.*

Shopping

The rural counties of the borderlands have few specialized shopping areas. Most towns, however, are good for antiques hunting—and roadside advertising signs are usually worth following up.

Chester In an old Georgian building, 16 dealers fill two floors of the **Melodies Galleries** (32 City Road) with a wide mix of fine furniture, porcelain, brass and copper, linen, books, and bric-a-brac—there's even a section selling old radios, called "On the Air." Export can be arranged.

Bookland (12 Bridge St.) is in one of Chester's ancient buildings, with a converted 14th-century crypt below street level housing a wealth of travel and general-interest books. Also stocked are technical maps, sheet music, and plenty of tourist information.

You can watch the whole process of candlemaking, from wicks being dipped in hot wax to the final carving into ribbon patterns, at the **Cheshire Candle Workshops,** at Burwardsley, 11 miles southeast of Chester by A41 and A534.

Hereford **The Hereford Book Shop** on Church Street has new and second-hand books. There is also a large selection of local guidebooks, maps, and unusual greeting cards.

The **Hereford Society of Craftsmen** is based in Capuchin Yard, off Church Street. In this small, cobbled yard, you can see a violin-maker at work, as well as a potter. Aside from the usual crafts, knitwear, posters, and watercolors are also for sale.

Manchester The **Royal Exchange Crafts Centre** (St. Ann's Square) is an unusual glass structure, in the foyer of the Royal Exchange theater, and specializes in jewelry, ceramics, glassware, and textiles produced throughout the country. Next door, the **Royal Exchange Shopping Centre** houses on its first floor **The Design Centre,** a series of stores featuring the creations of young fashion designers. **Red or Dead** is probably the most famous of these stores, and sells imaginative shoes and clothing; other stores specialize in hats and other accessories as well as innovative fashion design. **Sarah O'Hana,** which sells contemporary jewelry, most of it worked in silver, is located just outside the shopping center.

The **Manchester Crafts Centre** (17 Oak St.) is made up of 18 workshops-cum-retail outlets where you can see potters, jewelers, hatters, theatrical costumers, and metal enamelers at work, and where you can buy the fruits of their labors.

The **Whitworth Art Gallery** (Oxford Rd.) has a fine shop that specializes in handmade cards, postcards, and prints. They also sell stationery, art books, jewelry, and ceramics; from time to time there is a potter on the premises. Along the same lines, the **Manchester University Museum** shop, also on Oxford Rd., offers a similar selection, but specializes in books and imaginative toys for children.

Haigh and Hochland Ltd., situated near the University on Oxford Rd., are booksellers specializing in academic texts. Manchester also has branches of **Hatchards, Waterstones,** and **Dillons** chain booksellers, their selection and quality as fine here as they are all over England.

For antiques you should visit **Koopman and Son** (4 John Dalton St.), which has a fine stock of silver and old jewelry. It is within three blocks of the Town Hall.

Shrewsbury   **Manser & Son** (53–54 Wyle Cop) displays quality antiques, and has stores within stores of furniture, silver, lighting, pictures, and jewelry of the 17th to 20th centuries—items may cost as little as £2, or as much as £10,000.

James II (15–16 Mardol) is a gift store with a difference: It offers to supply a present at any price for any age or sex, and gift-wrap it, too. Housed in a 16th-century building in the Mardol, it specializes in glassware and traditional English china.

Worcester   **Framed** (46 Friar St.), a contemporary art gallery housed in one of the street's half-timbered buildings, displays an extensive collection of original paintings, pastels, drawings, sculptures, and prints. Both owners of the gallery exhibit their own work, much of which reflects the local townscape.

Bygones has two stores in Worcester, one at 32 College Street, right beside the cathedral, and the other a few hundred yards away at 55 Sidbury, near the Commandery. Both have antiques and items of fine craftsmanship of various periods; they specialize in Worcester porcelain, and always have a selection of small silver, glass, and porcelain items suitable for gifts.

Markets   Chester has a market every day except Wednesday. Hereford has a different type of market each day—food, clothing, livestock—located on New Market Street. In Shrewsbury, there is a market on Tuesday, Wednesday, Friday, and Saturday; and Worcester holds a market every Friday and Saturday at the Corn Market.

Sports and Fitness

Bicycling   Bikes can be rented from **Little and Hall** (48 Broad St., Ross-on-Wye, tel. 0989/62639) and from the Foregate Street station in **Worcester** (tel. 0905/613501).

Boating   This is an area crisscrossed with rivers and canals. **Severn Bank Centre** (Minsterworth, tel. 045275/357) organizes weekly courses on canoeing.

Golf   The lush tranquillity of much of this region makes it ideal for golf courses. Visitors are welcome at **Belmont** (tel. 0432/277445), two miles south of Hereford at an 18-hole course set amid rolling meadowland. The 18-hole course at **Cirencester** (tel. 0285/2465) is run by a club almost 100 years old. The **Tewkesbury Park Hotel** (*see* Dining and Lodging, below) has an 18-hole course, and visitors are welcome with a handicap certificate. Greens fees are £18 weekdays, £22 weekends.

Hiking   The **Malvern Hills** make for climbs and walks of varying lengths and difficulty. The best places to start are Great Malvern and Ledbury. The route has been designated the "Elgar Way," running for 45 miles, but you don't need to do the whole thing.

The area around **Ross-on-Wye** offers ideal walks with unfolding river views as you go. Check with the local tourist center (*see* Important Addresses and Numbers, above).

One of Britain's major long-distance hikes lies mostly within this area: the **Offa's Dyke Path,** so called after the earthwork built by an 8th-century king to mark the boundary between England and Wales. The whole route runs 168 miles, starting at Sedbury Cliffs south of Chepstow, and finishing at the seafront of Prestatyn, on the north coast of Wales, but only about 60 miles of this walk is along the actual dike. For details contact local tourist centers or the Ramblers Association (*see* Sports and Outdoor Activities in Chapter 1).

Dining and Lodging

Dining   Highly recommended hotels and restaurants are indicated by a star ★.

Formal restaurants are few and far between in this rural area, and those that exist are mostly small. In many the owners do the cooking, concentrating on English country fare and using local produce whenever possible.

Category	Cost*
Very Expensive	over £35
Expensive	£25–£35
Moderate	£12–£25
Inexpensive	under £12

**per person, including first course, main course, dessert, and VAT; excluding drinks*

Lodging   You won't find many large, international-style hotels in the Welsh borders. Our selection aims to present a mix of larger hotels, often with considerable local historical significance, and smaller, family-owned establishments that form the bulk of the accommodations available. The latter are homier, friendlier, and invariably cheaper.

Category	Cost*
Very Expensive	over £130
Expensive	£80–£130
Moderate	£45–£80
Inexpensive	under £45

**All prices are for two people sharing a double room, including service, breakfast, and VAT.*

Abberley   **The Elms Hotel.** This traditional country-house hotel, in an ivy-
Dining and Lodging   clad Queen Anne building surrounded by formal gardens, is 16

miles northeast of Worcester and near Great Witley. All the rooms are individually and comfortably decorated in this former mansion. The restaurant, with its imaginative cooking and pleasant, family-dining-room ambience, is worth a visit on its own. *Abberley, WR6 6AT, tel. 0299/896666. 25 rooms with bath. Facilities: restaurant, garden, tennis. Restaurant reservations required. Jacket and tie required. AE, DC, MC, V. Expensive.*

Bridgnorth
Lodging

Old Vicarage Hotel. This Victorian vicarage lies on the edge of a preserved 17th- and 18th century village, a particularly quiet base only 4 miles northeast of Bridgnorth on A454. Rooms are furnished with Victorian pieces to complement the hotel's architecture. A pretty conservatory restaurant includes deliciously fresh local produce and unpretentious cooking. *Worfield WV15 5JZ, tel. 07464/497. 10 rooms with bath. Restaurant reservations required. Dress: informal. AE, DC, MC, V. Moderate.*

Chester
Dining

Abbey Green. In a Georgian building in downtown Chester, award-winning vegetarian cuisine is served. Specialties include parmigiana, a dish composed of cashew and cream cheese balls on a bed of red-wine ratatouille; and a Szechwan dish of eggplant and tofu parcels, with stir-fried vegetables in wheatflour pancake on a bed of couscous. *2 Abbey Green, off Northgate St., tel. 0244/313251. Weekend reservations advised. Dress: informal. MC. Closed Sun. Moderate.*

Dining and Lodging

Chester Grosvenor Hotel. This is a traditional deluxe hotel in a Tudor-style, downtown building, and it's remarkable to find such quiet luxury and sumptuous comfort in a small country town. The **Arkle Restaurant** is just as splendid as the rest of the hotel, with marble and stone walls, solid mahogany tables, candlelight, and gleaming silver. The style here is *cuisine légère,* using little cream or butter, only natural ingredients, and sauces made by reduction rather than thickening. *Eastgate St., CH1 1LT, tel. 0244/324024. 87 rooms with bath. Facilities: brasserie, sauna, solarium, gym. Restaurant reservations required. Jacket and tie required. AE, DC, MC, V. Closed Christmas. Very Expensive.*

★ **Crabwall Manor.** This dramatic, castellated, part-Tudor, part-neo-Gothic mansion is set on 11 acres of farm and parkland (2¼ miles northwest on A540). It has elegant, subtle furnishings in floral chintzes, and extremely comfortable bedrooms. The spacious restaurant boasts *cordon bleu* cooking and is worth visiting all by itself—say, for lunch while exploring the neighborhood. *Parkgate, Mollington CH1 6NE, tel. 0244/851666. 48 rooms with bath. Restaurant reservations required. Dress: informal. AE, DC, MC, V. Expensive.*

Green Bough Hotel. The Green Bough is in a large, converted Victorian house, with a variety of Victorian furnishings. One of the comfortable bedrooms has a four-poster. There's a handy dining room with a sensible, home-cooked menu. *60 Hoole Rd., CH2 3NL, tel. 0244/326241. 11 rooms with bath. MC, V. Moderate.*

Fownhope
Lodging

Green Man Inn. A friendly 15th-century half-timbered inn, located in a quiet village midway between Hereford (6 mi on B4224) and Ross-on-Wye, the rooms here offer a mix of modern and traditional furnishings. *Near Hereford, HR1 4PE, tel. 0432/860243. 15 rooms with bath. MC, V. Moderate.*

Hereford
Dining
★

Fat Tulip. This is an unusually upmarket brasserie to find in Hereford. Situated in a tall old house beside the Wye bridge, the restaurant serves imaginative and always tasty food—smoked fish from Wales, crab pancake with tomato sauce, excellent best end of local lamb. *2 St. Martin's St., tel. 0432/275808. Reservations advised. Dress: informal. AE, MC, V. Closed Sun., national holidays, 10 days at Christmas. Moderate.*

Effy's. This pretty, modern restaurant has a friendly atmosphere and quietly attentive service. Specialties include pigeon breasts with brandy, figs, and honey; and rack of lamb with oranges. *96 East St., tel. 0432/59754. Weekend reservations advised. Dress: informal. MC, V. Closed Sat. lunch, Sun. and Mon. Inexpensive.*

Lodging

Green Dragon Hotel. An old, traditionally furnished coaching hotel, with most bedrooms recently refurbished, it's a member of the Trusthouse Forte chain and is just beside the cathedral. *Broad St., HR4 9BG, tel. 0432/272506. 88 rooms with bath. Facilities: restaurant. AE, DC, MC, V. Expensive.*

Ferncroft Hotel. This small, family-run hotel is decorated in Victorian style, with some antique furniture. The restaurant serves local produce, thoughtfully prepared. *144 Ledbury Rd., HR1 2TB, tel. 0432/265538. 12 rooms, 4 with bath. MC, V. Closed 2 weeks at Christmas. Inexpensive.*

Ironbridge
Lodging

The Library House. Nestled into the hillside in a central location for the Ironbridge museums, this small hotel is decorated in a dark but attractive Victorian style with comfortable furnishings. *11 Severn Bank, TF8 7AN, tel. 0952/432299. 3 rooms, 2 with bath. No credit cards. Inexpensive.*

Kingston
Dining
★

Penrhos Court. This fascinating restaurant is virtually on the Welsh border. It is housed in an old barn that is part of a jumble of buildings round an Elizabethan manor house; there are tables outside for summer eating. The food is the work of chef/proprietor Daphne Lambert, and is very inventive. Specialties change regularly, but might include breast of chicken with langoustine sauce, or a splendid fish ragout. *Kingston (15 mi west of Leominster on A44), tel 0544/230720. Reservations required. Dress: neat but casual. No credit cards. Closed Mon., Tues., Sun. dinner, and lunches except Sun. Moderate.*

Knutsford
Dining

La Belle Époque. The restaurant contrasts its unusual, somewhat theatrical art nouveau decor with a lighter style of French cooking, typified in such dishes as boned local quail with chicken-liver and pine-nut filling; and saddle of venison with three-fruit sauce. *60 King St., tel. 0565/3060. Reservations advised; required weekends. Dress: informal. AE, DC, MC, V. Dinner only Mon.–Sat. Closed Sun. and national holidays. Expensive.*

Lodging

Royal George Hotel. A coaching inn dating back in part to the 14th century, it is located in the center of this quiet town. Comfortable rooms are furnished in traditional style. *King St., WA16 6EE, tel. 0565/4151. 31 rooms, all with bath. AE, DC, MC, V. Moderate.*

Ledbury
Dining and Lodging
★

Hope End Country House Hotel. An 18th-century house (2 mi north on B4214), with Oriental embellishments and period decorations, it is set in 40 acres of wooded parkland. The house was the poet Elizabeth Barrett Browning's childhood home. Much of it was burned down in 1910, but what's left is architecturally significant. The restaurant, which uses vegetables and herbs from its own kitchen garden, has won awards. *Hope End, HR8 1JQ, tel. 0531/3613. 9 rooms with bath. Facilities: garden. MC, V. Closed Mon., Tues., and Dec.–Feb. Expensive.*

Leominster
Dining and Lodging

The Marsh. This is a new country-house hotel at Eyton, 2½ miles northwest of Leominster off B4361. It is a partly 14th-century house, with a timbered medieval hall, in an idyllic setting teeming with wildlife. The cooking is mainly French provincial, using fresh herbs from the garden. *Eyton, HR6 0AG, tel. 0568/3952. 5 rooms with bath. Facilities: restaurant, garden. AE, MC, V. Expensive.*

Ludlow
Dining and Lodging

Dinham Hall. Dinham Hall is a newly converted merchant's 1792 town house near Ludlow castle. The owners have managed to combine the original historic elements in the house with modern comforts. The dining room serves imaginative dishes such as salmon with wild mushrooms and venison with noodles. This is a good base for exploring the region. *Ludlow SY8 1EJ, tel. 0584/876464. 14 rooms with bath. Facilities: restaurant, garden. Restaurant dress: jacket and tie. AE, DC, MC, V. Restaurant Moderate; hotel Expensive.*

Malvern
Dining and Lodging

The Cottage in the Wood. This hotel sits in its shady grounds on the side of the Malvern Hills. The furnishings are country-house comfortable, with chintz and flower prints everywhere. The restaurant has the best of the panorama through its tall windows. Food is English, with enough international influences to make the menu interesting. *Holywell Rd., WR14 4LG, tel. 0684/573487. 20 rooms with bath. Facilities: restaurant, garden. Reservations required for restaurant. Jacket and tie required. MC, V. Expensive.*

Malvern Wells
Dining
★

Croque en Bouche. In this traditional French restaurant, the food is the very best bourgeois cuisine, with superb handling of excellent local ingredients. The chef/proprietor, Marion Jones, has won herself a considerable reputation. Specialties include local lamb stuffed with mushrooms and sweetbreads, wild rabbit with basil and lemon, and poached brill with watercress sauce. *221 Wells Rd., tel. 06845/565612. Reservations required. Jacket and tie required. MC, V. Dinner only. Closed Mon. and Tues. Expensive.*

Manchester
Dining

Yang Sing. There's a sizable Chinese population in Manchester, so you'd expect to find some good Chinese restaurants here and this is one. It's popular with Chinese families, always a good sign, but *so* popular that you must reserve ahead. The cooking is Cantonese and there's a huge range to choose from; the *dim sum* is always a good bet. *34 Princess St., tel. 061/236–2200. Reservations required. Dress: informal. AE, MC, V. Moderate.*

Dining and Lodging

Hotel Piccadilly. A thoroughly modern, very fancy establishment in a rather shabby shopping mall, of all places. The bedrooms are equipped with most gadgets to make your stay comfortable, and the public rooms are decorated with marble. The executive suites are even equipped with Jacuzzis. The restaurant serves interesting dishes—though not too extreme—and the service is professional but friendly. *Piccadilly Plaza, M60 1QR, tel. 061/236–8414. 271 rooms with bath. Facilities: indoor pool, coffee shop, in-house movies. Restaurant reservations required. Jacket and tie required. AE, DC, MC, V. Expensive.*

Lodging **Britannia Hotel.** This isn't the poshest hotel in the world, but it does rank among the more fascinating ones. It has been imaginatively converted from a 19th-century cotton warehouse, with a soaring gilt staircase rising from the lobby. Some bedrooms are split-level, with an intriguing use of loft space. The wallpaper is garish, the clientele can get noisy, and the maintenance is not all it might be, but the place *is* interesting. *Portland St., M1 3LA, tel. 061/228–2288. 364 rooms with bath. Facilities: restaurant, coffee shop, indoor pool, sauna, solarium, gym, satellite TV. AE, DC, MC, V. Moderate–Expensive.*

Nantwich **Rookery Hall Hotel.** This large, elegant restaurant boasts ma-
Dining and hogany- and walnut-paneled walls and an ornate plasterwork
Lodging ceiling. Cheshire sausages on a bed of leeks, and rack of Welsh lamb with a sauce made from home-grown mustard seed, are typical old English dishes. It is also an excellent place to sample English cheeses, and there's a first rate international wine list. The hotel in which this excellent restaurant is located is a lovely old house, surrounded by wide grounds with lakes. A large extension is being built. The service is friendly and personal, the bedrooms luxurious with old furniture and modern plumbing. *Worleston CW5 6DQ, tel. 0270/626866. 11 rooms with bath. Facilities: restaurant, gardens, helipad. Restaurant reservations required. Jacket and tie required. AE, DC, MC, V. Expensive*

Ross-on-Wye **The Chase Hotel.** This recently renovated Georgian-style coun-
Lodging try house hotel is set in 11 acres. Rooms are simply and comfortably furnished in the main house, and more modern in the newer wing. Bowls of fresh fruit and decanters of sherry welcome you into this hotel. *Gloucester Rd., HR9 5LH, tel. 0989/763161. 40 rooms with bath. Facilities: restaurant. AE, DC, MC, V. Expensive.*

Shrewsbury **Country Friends.** An attractive, black-and-white building, six
Dining miles south of Shrewsbury by the A49, houses this light and airy restaurant overlooking a garden and pool. There are log fires in winter. Specialties include venison with black currant sauce, and lamb noisettes roasted in mustard crust with mint hollandaise. There are also three bedrooms available. *Dorrington, tel. 074373/707. Reservations required. Dress: informal. AE, DC, MC, V. Closed Sun.–Mon., 2 weeks end July, and last week Oct. Moderate.*

Lodging **Albrighton Hall.** This hotel near Shrewsbury (2½ miles north on A528) is housed in a large, elegant building surrounded by 14 acres of formal gardens and lawns. Rooms are decorated with traditional flowered chintzes. *Albrighton SY4 3AG, tel. 0939/291000. 33 rooms with bath. Facilities: restaurant, tennis. AE, DC, MC, V. Moderate–Expensive.*

The Lion. Originally a 16th-century coaching inn, this hotel now has modern additions. Its furnishings are traditional in style and very comfortable; among its attractive features are a tapestry lounge and a beautiful Georgian staircase. One suite is named after Dickens, who stayed here. Located downtown, the hotel makes a good touring base, although it can be noisy. *Wyle Cop, SY1 1UY, tel. 0743/53107. 59 rooms with bath. Facilities: restaurant. AE, DC, MC, V. Moderate–Expensive.*

Prince Rupert Hotel. This black-and-white, half-timbered inn in the historic city center was the headquarters of Prince Rupert, the most famous royalist general (he was also the nephew of Charles I) during the Civil War. It is now furnished in modern style, although four rooms have four-poster beds. *Butcher Row, SY1 1UQ, tel. 0743/236000. 66 rooms with bath. Facilities: restaurant, recreation room, in-house movies. AE, DC, MC, V. Moderate.*

Tewkesbury
Lodging

Tewkesbury Park Hotel, Golf and Country Club. Just outside town (1¼ miles south on A38), this former 18th-century mansion is the ideal stopover point for the athletically inclined. There's almost every sports facility anyone could want, plus the wonderful countryside. *Lincoln Green Lane, GL20 7DN, tel. 0684/295405. 78 rooms with bath. Facilities: restaurant, coffee shop, garden, indoor pool, sauna, gym, tennis, squash, golf course, in-house movies. AE, DC, MC, V. Expensive.*

Worcester
Dining
★

Brown's. A former grain mill houses this light and airy riverside restaurant. The fixed-price menu and daily specialties include warm salad with breast of duck and croutons, and crayfish-and-bacon kebabs. *24 Quay St., tel. 0905/26263. Reservations advised. Dress: informal. AE, DC, MC, V. Closed Sat. lunch and Sun. dinner. Moderate–Expensive.*

King Charles II Restaurant. Here you can enjoy dining in the black-and-white, half-timbered house in which Charles II hid after the Battle of Worcester. It is now an oak-paneled, silver-service restaurant with a very friendly atmosphere. Cuisine is mainly French and Italian, but there are also traditional English selections, such as beef Wellington, and such fresh fish dishes as Dover sole meunière. *29 New St., tel. 0905/22449. Reservations advised. Dress: informal. AE, DC, MC, V. Closed Sun. Inexpensive–Moderate.*

Lodging

Ye Old Talbot Hotel. The Old Talbot was originally a courtroom belonging to the cathedral, which stands close by. The hotel has recently been refurbished, and there are modern extensions to the 16th-century core of the building. *Friar St., WR1 2NA, tel. 0905/23573. 29 rooms with bath. Facilities: restaurant. AE, DC, MC, V. Moderate.*

49 Britannia Square. This guest house in a quiet, elegant, Georgian square is half a mile from downtown. *49 Britannia Square, WR1 3HP, tel. 0905/22756. 3 rooms, 1 with bath. No credit cards. Closed Dec. 25–Jan. 1. Inexpensive.*

The Arts

Festivals

The **Three Choirs' Festival** has been held on a three-year rotation between the cathedral cities of Gloucester, Worcester, and Hereford since about 1717. In 1992 it will be held in Gloucester (August 22–29). The festival celebrates the English choral tradition, often with specially commissioned works. The program appears in March. *Details from The Gloucester Three Choirs Festival, Community House, College Green, Gloucester GL1 2LX, tel. 0452/29819.*

Malvern has historical connections with George Bernard Shaw, who premiered many of his plays there, as well as with Sir Edward Elgar. The **Malvern Festival** was originally devoted to their works, although now it also offers a wide variety of new music and new drama. The **Malvern Fringe Festival** has an exceptional program of alternative events. Both festivals run for two or three weeks from the end of May to early June. *Details from: Malvern Tourist Information Centre, Winter Garden*

Complex, Grange Rd., Hereford & Worcs WR14 3HB, tel. 0684/ 892289.

In Shropshire, the **Ludlow Festival,** starting at the end of June, sums up all that is English: Shakespeare is performed in the open air against the romantic backdrop of the ruined castle to an audience armed with cushions, raincoats, lap robes, and picnic baskets, as well as hip flasks. Reservations are accepted starting in early May. *Details from: The Festival Box Office, Castle Square, Ludlow, Shropshire SY8 1AY, tel. 0584/872150.*

During the **Shrewsbury International Music Festival,** the town vibrates to traditional and not-so-traditional music by groups of performers from America, western Europe, and sometimes eastern Europe. It is held in early July. *Details from: The Music Hall, The Square, Shrewsbury, Shropshire SY1 1LH, tel. 0743/50761.*

Theater   Manchester has an enviable reputation in the arts, especially in the performing arts. There are three main theaters in town: the **Opera House** (tel. 061/831–7766), which hosts touring companies, both British and international, as well as a wide spectrum of entertainment; the **Library Theatre** (tel. 061/236–9422), which stages mostly classic and serious drama; and the **Royal Exchange Theatre** (tel. 061/833–9333), an extremely inventive acting space with a sky-high reputation for daring productions. It is a very modern, airy, tubular steel-and-glass structure, set down in the middle of the vast echoing spaces of this Victorian building, like a space ship delicately parked in a great cathedral.

11 Wales

Introduction

Wales, apart from being called the Land of Song, is also a land of mountain and flood, where wild peaks challenge the sky and waterfalls thunder down steep, tree-clad chasms. It is a land of grim castles, ruined abbeys, little steam trains chugging through dramatic scenery, male-voice choirs, and crowded cities. The south and northeast have been heavily industrialized—largely with mining and steelmaking—since the 19th century, but long stretches of the coast and the mountainous interior remain areas of unmarred beauty. Fewer than 5 percent of American visitors to Britain go to Wales, and many of those are heading for the Irish ferries. To miss out on Wales is to miss one of Britain's great scenic experiences.

Wales was finally united with England in 1536, under the Tudor king Henry VIII (the Tudors came originally from the isle of Anglesey off the Welsh coast), but it has nonetheless retained an identity and character quite separate from that of the rest of Britain; the Welsh will not thank you if you confuse their country with England.

The Welsh are a Celtic race. Although the Romans made sporadic attempts to subdue Wales, the people were never Romanized as, later, they were never Anglicized. When, toward the middle of the first millennium AD, the Anglo-Saxons spread through Britain, they pushed the indigenous Celts farther back into their Welsh mountain holds. (In fact, "Wales" comes from the Saxon word "Weallas," which means "strangers," the impertinent name given by the new arrivals to the natives. The Welsh, however, have always called themselves "Y Cymry," "the companions.") The Normans made attempts to extend their influence over Wales in the 11th century, but it was not until the fearsome English king, Edward I (1272–1307), waged a brutal and determined campaign to conquer Wales that English supremacy was established. Welsh hopes were finally crushed with the death in battle of Llywelyn ap Gruffud, the last native Prince of Wales, in 1282. Dreams of nationhood were revived under the brilliant and popular leadership of Owain Glyndwr between 1400 and 1410. He ruled virtually the whole of Wales at one point, but English might prevailed again.

In the 15th and 16th centuries, the Tudor kings Henry VII and Henry VIII continued England's ruthless domination of the Welsh, principally by attempting to abolish their language. Ironically it was another Tudor monarch, Elizabeth I, who ensured its survival by authorizing a Welsh translation of the Bible in 1588. Today, many people still say they owe their knowledge of Welsh to the Bible. The language is spoken by only a fifth of the population, but it still flourishes. Signs are bilingual, but don't worry; everyone speaks English, too.

Just for the fun of it, here is a short introduction to speaking Welsh. Place-names may look a bit daunting, especially those which seem to have no vowels, but give it a try: Welsh is not as hard to pronounce as it looks at first, for it is almost entirely phonetic.

Each of the consonants has only one sound. **B, d, h, l, m, n, p, t** are all as in English; **c** is always hard, as in *cat;* **ch** as in Scottish *loch;* **dd** the same as *th* in *this;* **f** same as *v;* **ff** same as English *f;* **g** always hard, as in *gate.* **ll** is the classic Welsh problem, pronounced something like *hl;* **r** is trilled as in *merry;* **s** is hard as in *essay.*

The diphthongs are **ng** either as in *long* or *longer,* e.g. Bangor; **ph** as in *phone;* **rh** a trilled r followed by the aspirate; **th** as in *thin.*

The vowels in Welsh are **a, e, i, o, u, w, y,** and they have two values, short and long. **A** is sounded as in English *ah,* or as in French *à;* **e** with an *ay* sound, or as in *pen;* **i** as in *machine,* or as in *pin;* **o** as in *gore,* or as in *not.* **U** depends on where you are in Wales: In the north it can be like a French *u,* in the south like both of the i sounds above. **W** can be like oo in *pool,* or the oo in *good;* long **y** can be like the Welsh i, short like the u in *gun.* The vowels are short when followed by two or more consonants, or by c, ng, m, p, t; they are long when followed by b, ch, d, ff, g, s, th.

As a rule, the stress is on the penultimate syllable. In some place-names, however, it is placed on the last syllable, e.g. Caer**dydd,** Ponty**pridd,** Llan**rwst.**

Essential Information

Important Addresses and Numbers

Tourist Information

The Wales Bureau, The British Travel Centre, 12 Regent St., London SW1 4PQ, tel. 071/409–0969. Open weekdays 9–6:30, weekends 10–4.

The Wales Tourist Board, Brunel House, 12th Floor, 2 Fitzalan Rd., Cardiff, S. Glamorgan CF2 1UY, tel. 0222/499909. Open weekdays 9–5.

Cadw: Welsh Historic Monuments, Brunel House, 2 Fitzalan Rd., Cardiff CF1 2UY, tel. 0222/465511.

Tourist information centers, normally open Mon.–Sat. 9:30–5:30, but varying according to the season, include:

Aberystwyth: Terrace Rd., tel. 0970/612125 or 611955.

Caernarfon: Oriel Pendeitsh (opposite castle entrance), tel. 0286/672232.

Cardiff: 8–14 Bridge St., tel. 0222/227281.

Dolgellau: The Bridge, tel. 0341/422888.

Llandrindod Wells: Town Hall, tel. 0597/822600.

Llandudno: Chapel St., tel. 0492/76413.

Llanfair P.G.: Station Site, Isle of Anglesey, tel. 0248/713177.

Llangollen: Town Hall, tel. 0978/860828.

Swansea: Singleton St., tel. 0792/468321.

Welshpool: Vicarage Gardens Car Park, tel. 0938/552043.

Travel Agencies

American Express: 2 High St., Abergavenny, tel. 0873/5810; and 1–5 Bellevue Way, Swansea, tel. 0792/650321.

Thomas Cook: 16 Queen St., Cardiff, tel. 0222/224886; and 3 Union St., Swansea, tel. 0792/464311.

Car Rental Agencies

Cardiff: Avis, 4 Saunders Rd., Station Approach, tel. 0222/42111; **Hertz,** 9 Central Sq., tel. 0222/24548.

Arriving and Departing

By Car

From London, A5 is the most direct route to north Wales. A55, the coast road from Chester on the English side of the north Wales border, goes through Bangor. For Cardiff (157 miles),

Swansea (196 miles), and south Wales, take M4. Aberystwyth (211 miles) and Llandrindod in mid-Wales are well-served by major roads. The A40 is also an important route through central and south Wales.

By Train **British Rail** serves Wales from London Euston (tel. 071/387–7070) and London Paddington (tel. 071/262–6767) stations. Average travel times include: from Euston, 2¾ hours to Llandudno in north Wales (changing at Chester) and Aberystwyth in mid-Wales (changing at Shrewsbury). From Paddington, it is less than two hours to Cardiff and under three hours to Swansea in south Wales. Local services operate from Llandudno, Dovey Junction, and Swansea.

Scenic options include: **Cumbrian Coast Railway,** running 70 miles between Aberystwyth and Pwllheli; the **Heart of Wales** line, linking Swansea and Craven Arms, near Shrewsbury, 95 miles away; and the private lines (Little Trains), *see* Getting Around, below.

By Bus **National Express** (tel. 071/730–0202) serves Wales from London's Victoria Coach Station. Average travel times include 3½ hours to Cardiff; four hours to Swansea; 5½ hours to Aberystwyth; and 4½ hours to Llandudno.

Getting Around

By Car Distances in miles may not be great in Wales, but getting from place to place takes time because there are few major highways. The mountains mean that there is no single fast route from north to south, although A487 does run along or near most of the coastline. The mountains also mean that many of the smaller roads are winding and difficult to maneuver, but they do reveal magnificent views of the surrounding landscape.

By Train Wales is undoubtedly the best place in Britain for narrow-gauge steam railways. The *Great Little Trains of Wales*—narrow gauge—operate during the summer months through the mountains of Snowdonia and central Wales. Many of these lines wind through landscapes of extraordinary grandeur; for example, the **Ffestiniog Railway,** which now joins two British Rail lines at Bleaunau Ffestiniog and Porthmadog, climbs the mountainside around an ascending loop more reminiscent of the Andes than rural Britain. Tiny, copper-knobbed engines, panting fiercely, haul narrow carriages packed with tourists through deep cuttings and along rocky shelves above ancient oak woods through the heart of Snowdonia National Park to the little harbor of Porthmadog. Other lines include: the **Talyllyn,** following a deep valley from the coastal resort of Tywyn; the **Vale of Rheidol Railway,** from Aberystwyth to Devil's Bridge; the **Welshpool and Llanfair Light Railway,** between Welshpool and Llanfair Caereinion; the **Welsh Highland Railway** from Porthmadog; the **Brecon Mountain Railway;** and the **Llanberis Lake Railway.** You can buy a weekly **Wanderer Ticket,** valid on all eight lines for eight consecutive days, for £22 adults, £11 children. Full details, including summary timetables, are available from **Narrow Gauge Railways of Wales** (c/o Wharf Station, Tywyn, Gwynedd, LL36 9EY, tel. 0654/710472).

Snowdonia also has Britain's only Alpine-style steam rack railway, the **Snowdon Mountain Railway,** where little sloping boilered engines on rack-and-pinion track push their trains

3,000 feet up from Llanberis to the summit of Snowdon, Wales's highest mountain. Details of services from **Snowdon Mountain Railway** (Llanberis, Caernarfon, Gwynedd, tel. 0286/870223).

By Bus **Brown's** (tel. 0597/824537) runs a daily service between Llandrindod Wells and Brecon; and from April to October, a three-times-weekly service between Llandrindod Wells and Aberystwyth.
Crosville Wales (tel. 0492/592111) of Llandudno offers daily, weekly, and monthly "Rover" tickets for unlimited travel throughout its network.

Guided Tours

If you are interested in having a personal guide, contact the **Wales Official Tourist Guide Association,** The Hill College (Booking Agency), Pen-y-Pound, Abergavenny, Gwent, tel. 0873/5221.

Many bus operators run tours, both locally and nationally. Among them are the following three large companies.

Crossgate Motors (tel. 059787/226) runs day excursions by bus from Llandrindod Wells.
Crossville Garages (tel. 0970/617951) of Aberystwyth has extensive tour and day-trip programs to local beauty spots and places of interest.
Ellis Coaches (tel. 0248/750304), Llangefni, on the isle of Anglesey, runs day trips by bus into Snowdonia, to Llandudno, and across to Llangollen near the English border.

Exploring Wales

Orientation

We have chosen to concentrate our five tours of Wales along its coasts and among its soaring mountains. Tour 1 begins off the northwest coast, on the island of Anglesey at Beaumaris, where you'll visit the first of many castles. From there the tour goes via Caernarfon and Llanberis into the mountains of Snowdonia, crossing to Betws-y-Coed and up to the seaside resort of Llandudno and Conwy Castle, taking in the glorious garden at Bodnant en route. The road then turns southeast from the coast, visiting Denbigh and Ruthin, crossing the spectacular Horseshoe Pass to reach Llangollen, and Wales's "Little Switzerland," the Ceiriog Valley.

Our second tour heads westward, through the magnificent mountain scenery around Lakes Vyrnwy and Bala, to visit the slate caverns at Blaenau Ffestiniog, and proceeds from there to the coast and then south along A496 to Aberystwyth.

From Aberystwyth, Tour 3 hugs the coastline southward on route A487, with some magnificent sea views, toward the spiritual heart of Wales, St. David's. There the road turns west within the Pembrokeshire National Coast Park to end at Amroth, just beyond the resort town of Tenby.

The fourth tour explores the capital city of Cardiff, in south Wales. For the fifth tour, we start in Llandrindod Wells, and then circle down to the Black Mountains, just west of Hereford (*see* Chapter 10) to visit the bookselling center of Hay-on-Wye.

From here the route heads north once more, past a former volcano, Sugar Loaf Mountain, and the medieval manor house of Tretower Court, to Welshpool and the striking castle at Powis.

Highlights for First-time Visitors

Beaumaris Castle: Tour 1
Bodnant Gardens: Tour 1
Bwlch y Groes (Pass of the Cross): Tour 2
Caernarfon Castle: Tour 1
Cardigan Wildlife Park: Tour 3
Ceiriog Valley: Tour 1
Harlech Castle: Tour 2
Llechwedd Slate Caverns: Tour 2
Powis Castle: Tour 4
Tretower Court: Tour 4

Tour 1: Beaumaris to Llangollen—Castles and Waterfalls

Numbers in the margin correspond to points of interest on the Wales map.

❶ Beaumaris, which means "beautiful marsh," is on Anglesey, the largest island off the shore of either Wales or England. It is linked to the mainland by the Britannia road and rail bridge and by Thomas Telford's remarkable chain suspension bridge built in 1826 over the dividing Menai Strait. Bangor, 10 minutes away on the mainland, has the nearest mainline train station; a regular bus service operates between it and Beaumaris.

An elegant town of simple cottages, Georgian terraces, and bright shops, Beaumaris looks across the strait to the magnificence of Snowdonia, the dramatic range of north Wales mountains. The town dates from 1295, when Edward I, the English invader, commenced work on the **castle** that guards the entrance to the Menai Strait, the last and largest link in a chain of fortifications around north Wales. Standing at the far end of the town, the castle is solid and symmetrical, with arrow slits and a moat; it is acknowledged as one of the finest examples of medieval defensive planning in Britain. Look for the mooring rings on the southern side, a reminder that the sea once slapped against the castle walls. *Tel. 0248/810361. Admission: £1.25 adults, 75p children and senior citizens. Open mid-Mar.–mid-Oct., Mon.–Sat. 9:30–6:30, Sun. 2–6:30; mid-Oct.–mid-Mar., Mon.–Sat. 9:30–4, Sun. 2–4.*

Opposite the castle is the **courthouse,** built in 1614, which houses the oldest court in Britain still hearing cases. A plaque depicts one view of the legal profession: Two farmers pull a cow, one by the horns, one by the tail, while a lawyer sits in the middle milking. Many people were transported from here to convict colonies in Australia—one woman, in 1773, for stealing goods worth less than a shilling. *Tel. 0248/810921. Admission: 90p adults, 60p children and senior citizens. Open Easter, late May–late Sept., daily 11–5:30, except when court is in session.*

Just beyond is the **Museum of Childhood,** an Aladdin's cave of music boxes, magic lanterns, trains, cars, toy soldiers, rocking horses, and mechanical savings banks. *1 Castle St., tel. 0248/712498. Admission: £2 adults, £1 children, £1.50 senior citizens, £5 families. Open Mon.–Sat. 10–5:30, Sun. noon–5.*

Nearby, in Castle Street, is **The Tudor Rose,** a house dating
back to 1400, and an excellent example of Tudor timberwork.

Time Out   At the other end of Castle Street from the castle, the **Liverpool
Arms** pub, with its nautical bar, specializes in inexpensive seafood—try the crab sandwiches.

Turning right up Steeple Lane brings you to the old **gaol** (jail),
built in 1829 by Joseph Hansom, who was also the designer of
the hansom cab. It was considered a model prison, the best in
Britain at the time, but an exhibition shows what life there was
really like. You can wander the corridors, be locked in the
soundproof punishment cell or the condemned cell, and see the
country's only working treadwheel, where prisoners trudged
hopelessly around like hamsters in a cage. The mood lightens
during the Beaumaris Festival (*see* The Arts, below) when the
jail doubles, improbably, as a wine bar. *Tel. 0248/810921. Admission: £1.35 adults, 85p children and senior citizens; joint
ticket jail and courthouse £1.60 and £1.10, family ticket £4.50.
Open May–Sept., daily 11–6.*

Opposite the jail is the 14th-century **parish church.** In 1862 an
innocent man was hanged on the gibbet outside the prison
wall—to give the crowd a good view—and he cursed the clock
on the church tower. Locals say that to this day the clock has
not kept good time.

Beaumaris is an excellent base from which to explore not only
the isle of Anglesey itself but also Snowdonia, the Llyn peninsula, and the coast of northern Wales.

❷   The town of **Caernarfon** is across the Menai Strait, 13 miles to
the southwest. Dominating it is **Caernarfon Castle,** begun in
1283. Its towers, unlike those of Edward I's other castles, are
polygonal and patterned with bands of different colored stone.
It was here, in 1301, that the first English Prince of Wales was
presented to the Welsh people. Their conqueror, Edward I,
had promised them a prince who did not speak English—and
duly offered his baby son, later Edward II. The tradition that
the first-born son of the monarch shall become Prince of Wales
continues, and in July 1969, Caernarfon glowed with pageantry
when Elizabeth II presented her eldest son, Prince Charles, to
the people of Wales as their prince. This was the first time the
ceremony had been held for 58 years—since 1911, in fact, when
Prince Edward, the late duke of Windsor, was presented by his
father, George V. In the Queen's Tower, an intriguing museum
charts the history of the local regiment, The Royal Welsh Fusil-
iers. *Tel. 0286/77617. Admission to castle: £2.50 adults, £1.25
children and senior citizens, £7 family ticket. museum free.
Open mid-Mar.–mid-Oct., daily 9:30–6:30; mid-Oct.–mid-
Mar., Mon.–Sat. 9:30–4, Sun. 2–4.*

A wander through Caernarfon takes you back centuries. Even
the new administrative complex is built in a moderately convincing medieval style. Don't miss the garrison church of **St.
Mary,** built into the city walls. Outside the town is the extensive excavation site of the **Roman fortress of Segontium** and the
Museum of the Legions, a branch of the National Museum of
Wales. It contains material found on the site, one of Britain's
most famous Roman forts. *Tel. 0286/5625. Admission: a voluntary contribution. Open May–Sept., Mon.–Sat. 9:30–6, Sun.*

Wales

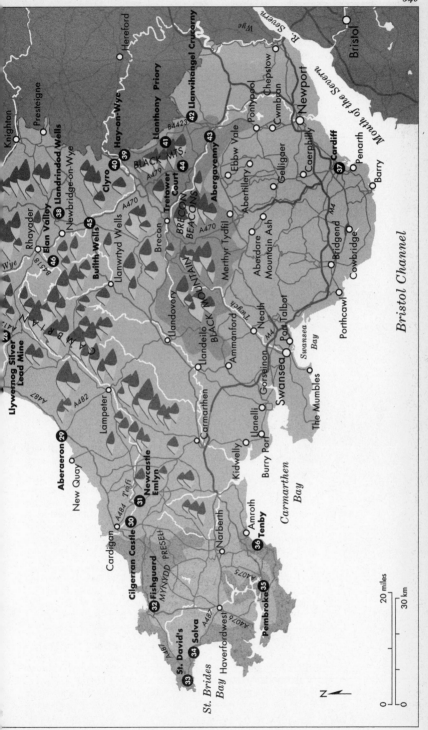

Bristol

Hereford

R. Severn
Wye
Chepstow
Pontypool
Cwmbran
Newport
Mouth of the Severn
Caerphilly
Cardiff
Penarth
Barry

Knighton
Presteigne
Hay-on-Wye
Llanthony Priory
Llanvihangel Crucorny
B4423
Llandrindod Wells
Clyro
39
40
41
42
43
BLACK MTS.
Tretower Court
44
Abergavenny
A479
Ebbw Vale
Aberillery
Gelligaer
Newbridge-on-Wye
38
Rhayader
Elan Valley
46
45
Builth Wells
A470
Brecon
BRECON
BEACONS
Merthyr Tydfil
Aberdare
Mountain Ash
Bridgend
Cowbridge
B4518
Llanwrtyd Wells
A470
Wye
CAMBRIAN
Llandovery
BLACK MOUNTAIN
Neath
Port Talbot
Porthcawl
Llywernog Silver
Lead Mine
A41
Llandeilo
Ammanford
Gorseinon
Swansea
Swansea
Bay
Bristol Channel
A482
Lampeter
Twrch
Llanelli
Burry Port
The Mumbles
Aberaeron
29
New Quay
A484
Teifi
Newcastle
Emlyn
31
Carmarthen
Kidwelly
Carmarthen
Bay
Cilgerran Castle
30
Cardigan
Narberth
Amroth
Tenby
36
Fishguard
32
MYNYDD PRESELI
A40?5
St. David's
Solva
34
A487
A40?0
Haverfordwest
Pembroke
35
33
St. Brides
Bay

20 miles
30 km
N
0
0

2–6; Mar., Apr., and Oct., Mon.–Sat. 9:30–5:30, Sun. 2–5;
Nov.–Feb., Mon.–Sat. 9:30–4, Sun. 2–4.

Time Out **Bakestone,** on Hole in the Wall Street, near the castle entrance,
has been voted the best bistro in Britain, and the food here really is delicious. Try the crêpes.

Caernarfon Airport (at the end of Dinas Dinlle beach road) operates **Pleasure Flights** in light aircraft (including a vintage
Rapide) over Snowdon, Anglesey, and Caernarfon. *Tel. 0286/
830800. From £13.50 per seat. Flights Easter–end Sept., daily
10–5:30.*

❸ The village of **Llanberis,** seven miles east on A4086, is the starting point for the steep **Snowdon Mountain Railway**—some of its
track at a gradient of 1 in 5—which terminates within 70 feet of
the 3,560-foot summit. **Snowdon,** Yr Wyddfa in Welsh, is the
highest peak south of Scotland and is set in more than 800
square miles of national park. From the summit on a clear day
you can see as far as the Irish Wicklow Mountains, about 90
miles away. *Tel. 0286/870223. Maximum round-trip fare,
£10.50 adults, £8.50 children. Open (weather permitting) mid-
Mar.–Oct., weekdays and most weekends 9–5; June–Sept.,
daily.*

Also in Llanberis is the new **Museum of the North,** another
branch of the National Museum of Wales, which sets out to in-
terpret the historical, geological, and social history of the
Snowdonia area. *Tel. 0286/870636. Admission: £3 adults, £1.50
children, £2.25 senior citizens. Open June–Sept., Mon.–Sat.
10–5, Sun. 1:30–5.*

Across the lake, the workshops of the old Dinorwic slate quarry now host the **Welsh Slate Museum.** *Dinorwic Quarry,
Llanberis, tel. 0286/870630. Admission: £1 adults, 50p children and senior citizens. Open Easter–Sept., Mon.–Sat. 9:30–
6:30, Sun. 2–6:30.*

Try a lakeside ride on the **Llanberis Lake Railway,** which once
transported the slate (tel. 0286/870549).

A4086 will carry you across the northern flanks of Snowdon,
through the **Pass of Llanberis,** nearly 1,200 feet up. There are
hiking tracks up from this point, but the going can be rough for
the inexperienced; heed local advice before starting on even the
briefest ramble. At the **Pen-y-Gwryd Hotel,** to the left of the
road, Lord Hunt and his team planned their successful ascent
of Everest in 1953.

Turn off A4086 onto A5 at Capel Curig. From here it is six miles
into Betws-y-Coed, past the **Swallow Falls** (small admission
charge), which tumble down through a wooded chasm.
❹ **Betws-y-Coed** lies among tree-clad cliffs, where the rivers
Llugwy and Conwy meet. This is a striking village, with an ornate iron bridge (1815) over the Conwy, designed by Telford.

Turn due north from here and follow A470 to Conwy, on the river Conwy's east bank. (B5106, on the west bank from Llanrwst,
will take longer, but leads through some lovely scenery.) Beau-
❺ tiful **Bodnant Gardens,** off A470, features terraces, lawns,
thickets of magnolias, and Himalayan rhododendrons, while
the mountains of Snowdonia form a complementary backdrop.

Tal-y-Cafn, tel. 0492/650460. Admission: £2.20 adults, £1.10 children. Open daily mid-Mar.–Oct., 10–5.

6 **Conwy** is the site of another of Edward I's castles, approached by a dramatic suspension bridge, and on the Quay, what is said to be the smallest house in Britain, furnished in mid-Victorian Welsh style—it can hold only a few people at a time. Two miles **7** north of Conwy is **Llandudno,** a charmingly old-fashioned north Wales seaside resort.

8 Head southeast 20 miles for **Denbigh,** served by A55 and A525 and accessible by bus from Llandudno. This market town (Wednesdays) was much admired by Dr. Samuel Johnson, who stayed on Pentrefoelas Road at Gwaenynog Hall, where he designed two rooms. A walk along the river bank at nearby Lawnt, a spot he loved, brings you to a monumental urn placed in his honor. Not that it pleased him: "It looks like an intention to bury me alive," thundered the great lexicographer.

Denbigh Castle is known as "the hollow crown" because it is not much more than a shell set on high ground, dominating the town. A tiny museum inside is devoted to Denbigh native son H. M. Stanley, the 19th-century journalist and explorer who found Dr. Livingstone in Africa. *Tel. 074571/3979. Admission: £1 adults, 60p children and senior citizens. Open mid-Mar.–mid-Oct., daily 9:30–6:30; mid-Oct.–mid-Mar., Mon.–Sat. 9:30–4, Sun. 2–4.*

Below the castle are the ruins of "Leicester's Folly," a church begun but never finished by Elizabeth I's favorite, Dudley, earl of Leicester.

9 From Denbigh it is just 8 miles (A525) southeast to **Ruthin,** the capital of Glyndwr country, where the 15th-century Welsh hero Owain Glyndwr lived and ruled. Its well-preserved buildings date from the 16th to the 19th centuries. Ruthin also has elegant shops, good inns, and, every Wednesday in summer, a medieval market at which townspeople dress in more-or-less convincing period costume. Since the 11th century, they have been ringing the curfew here each evening at 8.

The spectacular **Horseshoe Pass** (on A525, then A542) is 14 miles southeast of Ruthin and leads past the substantial ruins **10** of the Cistercian **Abbey of Valle Crucis** to **Llangollen,** birthplace of the International Musical Eisteddfod. Originally a gathering of bards, the current eisteddfod is more of a competition or festival; it was started as a gesture of friendship after World War II by a newspaperman who wanted, in effect, to have a concert and invite the whole world to join in. Amazingly, it worked, and now choirs from all over the world and poets declaiming their verse make for an unusual arts festival.

While you are in Llangollen, visit **Plas Newydd,** home from 1778 to 1828 of the eccentric "Ladies of Llangollen," who collected curios and magnificent wood carvings and entertained celebrated guests, among them William Wordsworth, Sir Walter Scott, and the Duke of Wellington. The Ladies had a servant with the delightful name of "Mollie the Basher." *Hill St., tel. 08242/2201. Admission: £1 adults, 50p children and senior citizens. Open Easter–Sept., Mon.–Sat. 10–7, Sun. 11–4.*

From the **Canal Museum** on the wharf, you can take a boat trip a short distance along the Shropshire Union Canal, drawn by a horse plodding along the tow path. *Tel. 0978/860702. Museum*

*admission: 75p adults, 45p children. Open daily Easter–Sept.
10:30–5:30; 45-min boat trip: £1.60 adults, 90p children.*

A steam railway with its locomotive is on display at the little
station museum by the bridge. The nearby woolen mill of
Llangollen Weavers offers a view of the production of modern
tweeds as well as demonstrations of hand weaving; the finished
products are sold at the mill shop. The bridge itself, a 14th-cen-
tury stone structure, is named in a traditional Welsh folk song
as one of the "seven wonders" of Wales.

There are easy walks along the banks of the River Dee or along
part of **Offa's Dyke path.** The 167-mile-long dyke, a defensive
wall whose earthen foundations still stand, was built along the
border with England in the 8th century by King Offa of Mercia
to keep out Welsh raiders.

Time Out   By the old Dee bridge, **Bishop Trevor Tearooms** are cheerful
and traditional.

⓫ For a scenic loop drive, head via **Chirk** (8 mi east on A5), site of
an imposing 13th-century castle, just across the border to England and the **Ceiriog Valley,** nicknamed Little Switzerland.
Take B4500 west six miles through the picturesque valley back
⓬ into Wales and the town of **Glyn Ceiriog,** where the **Chwarel
Wynne** slate mine gives another fascinating glimpse into Britain's industrial past. Ask the guide about the ghost and the
Women's Institute outing. *Tel. 069172/343. Admission: £2.30
adults, £1 children, £1.50 senior citizens. Open Easter–Oct.,
daily 10–5.*

Tour 2: Llangollen to Aberystwyth—
Through Mountain and Mine

Take B4500 southwest from Glyn Ceiriog, and then its unnum-
⓭ bered continuation, to reach **Llanrhaeadr ym Mochnant,** in the
peaceful Tanat Valley. Here, in 1588, the Bible was translated
into Welsh, thus ensuring the survival of the language. Turn
northwest and go four miles up the road to **Pistyll Rhaeadr,** the
highest waterfall in Wales, with its peat-brown water thunder-
ing down a 290-foot double cascade.

Time Out   **Tanypistyll,** at the foot of the waterfall, specializes in steak
pies, scones, and *bara brith* (Welsh currant bread).

Return to Llanrhaeadr ym Mochnant and turn right to take
B4396 five miles west to the little village of Penybontfawr.
From here another five miles on B4396 will bring you to **Lake
Vyrnwy** (in Welsh "Efyrnwy"—neither easy to pronounce!)
Lake Vyrnwy, mysterious and romantic, was man-made to
supply the water needs of the English city of Liverpool, 75
miles (as the aqueduct flows) to the north. The damming of the
small river Vyrnwy and the creation of the lake between 1880
and 1890 drowned the little village of Llanwddyn, whose story
is told in the visitor center. *Tel. 069173/246. Admission free.
Open Easter–May, weekends 11–6; June–Sept., weekdays
noon–6, weekends 11–6.*

This is an area of dense woods and sweeping hillsides, with the
waters of the lake still and dark. From Vyrnwy, there is a vertiginous mountain road to the eastern end of Lake Bala, or one

to the north end that is for the less intrepid. The views along both are magnificent, but much better on the western one which clings in places to only a ledge. **Bwlch y Groes** (Pass of the Cross), not quite halfway along, has a sweeping panorama that is literally breathtaking.

Bala, the largest natural lake in Wales, four miles long, has a narrow-gauge railway (tel. 06784/666), one of The Great Little Trains of Wales, running along its southern shore. The town of **14 Bala** is at the northern end of the lake.

From Lake Bala take A4212 to its junction with B4391, passing the **Llyn Celyn** reservoir, only 20 years old, but already an integral part of this dramatic landscape. B4391 will bring you to **15 Ffestiniog**, and **Blaenau Ffestiniog.** At Blaenau, the **Llechwedd Slate Caverns** offer two trips: a tram ride through floodlit tunnels where Victorian working conditions are re-created, or a ride on Britain's deepest underground railway to a mine where you can walk by an eerie underground lake. Above ground are exhibitions and audiovisual shows, house names carved to order in slate, and a restaurant/Victorian-style pub, The Miner's Arms. *Tel. 0766/830306. Admission: surface free; guided tours underground, £4.55 adults, £3.20 children, £3.65 senior citizens. Open Mar.–Sept., daily 10–5:15; Oct.–Feb., daily 10–4:15.*

A mile farther up the road is **Gloddfa Ganol Slate Mine,** the world's largest. Tour the tunnels, try your hand at splitting slate, enjoy the museum, restaurant, and shop. Visit both the caverns and the mine and there won't be much you don't know about Welsh slate. *Tel. 0766/830664. Admission: £2.75 adults, £1.25 children and senior citizens. Open Easter–Sept., weekdays 10–5:30.*

It is now time to turn toward the coast. From Ffestiniog, take A496 and then A487 toward Porthmadog. Just before you reach it you'll come on **Tremadog,** birthplace of T. E. Lawrence, better known as Lawrence of Arabia.

16 The little town of **Porthmadog** is the gateway to the Lleyn, an unspoiled peninsula of beaches, wildflowers, and country lanes. The **Ffestiniog Railway,** oldest of the Welsh narrow-gauge railways, was built in the mid-19th century to bring slate from the Blaenau Ffestiniog quarries down to the harbor at Porthmadog. *Tel. 0766/512340. Open Mar.–Nov., also Christmas (see timetable for details).*

Beyond the embankment (east of A487) across the river mouth known as the "cob" (the small toll charge goes to charity) is **17 Portmeirion,** a tiny fantasy Italianate village built in 1926 by architect Clough Williams-Ellis, complete with hotel, restaurant, and town hall. He called it his "light opera approach to architecture" and the result is pretty, though distinctly un-Welsh. The cult '60s TV series "The Prisoner" was filmed here (*see* Dining and Lodging, below). *Tel. 0766/770228. Admission: £2.50 adults, £1 children, £2 senior citizens. Open Mar.–Nov., daily 9:30–5:30.*

18 South on A496 or B4573 for six miles lies **Harlech.** Dominating the town from a craggy hilltop are the ruins of 13th-century **Harlech Castle.** Its ominous presence, visible for miles and commanding wide views, is as dramatic as its history. It withstood several sieges—at the beginning of the 15th century

Owain Glyndwr held out for five years against the English, and later in the same century the Lancastrians survived an eight-year siege during the Wars of the Roses. It was the last Welsh stronghold to fall in the 17th-century Civil War. *Tel. 0766/ 780552. Admission: £1.50 adults, 90p children and senior citizens. Open mid-Mar.–mid-Oct., daily 9:30–6:30; mid-Oct.– mid-Mar., Mon.–Sat. 9:30–4, Sun. 2–4.*

Time Out   **Plas Café** on High Street, with a crafts shop and a summer terrace overlooking the golf course, serves excellent snacks.

From Harlech, start the long journey following the coast, which will finally end at Amroth, near Tenby. Along this stretch, the shore is lined with sandy beaches. A496 will lead ⑲ you 11 miles to the seaside resort of **Barmouth** (**Abermaw** in Welsh). There are not many full-fledged seaside resorts in Wales, in the English sense of the term, but Barmouth is one of them. Ideally situated on the northern side of the picturesque estuary of the Mawddach, it boasts a two-mile-long promenade, wide expanses of golden beach, and facilities for sea, river, and mountain lake fishing. Even 100 years ago Barmouth was one of the most popular holiday resorts in Britain. Tennyson wrote part of his *In Memoriam* while staying there, and was inspired to write *Crossing the Bar* by the spectacle of the Mawddach rushing to meet the sea. Percy Bysshe and Mary Shelley stayed there in 1812; Darwin worked on *The Origin of Species* and *The Descent of Man* in a house by the shore. Essayist and art critic John Ruskin was a constant visitor and was trustee of the St. George's cottages built there by the Guild of St. George in 1871.

From Barmouth, you can strike inland along the Mawddach estuary to **Dolgellau** (pronounced Dolgethlee), a solidly Welsh ⑳ town with attractive dark buildings and handsome old coaching inns. To the south rises the menacing bulk of Cadair Idris (2,927 feet); the name means "the Chair of Idris," though no one is completely sure just who Idris was—probably a warrior bard. It is said that anyone sleeping for a night in a certain part of the mountain will awaken either a poet or a madman. The Talyllyn narrow-gauge railway (tel. 0654/71071) runs from Tywyn on the coast to the foothills of Cadair Idris. There are several routes up Cadair Idris. Be sure to check at the Dolgellau tourist centre for the best one for you. For those strong of foot and head there is the famous Precipice Walk above the winding Mawddach estuary.

Return west on the south side of the estuary, along A493. Twenty-four miles south you will have to make another inland ㉑ detour, via **Machynlleth,** to negotiate the estuary of the river Dovey. From here A487 will bring you 18 miles southeast to Aberystwyth.

Tour 3: Aberystwyth to Tenby— A Spectacular Coast

Numbers in the margin correspond to points of interest on the Aberystwyth map.

㉒ The seaside resort of **Aberystwyth** on hill-sheltered Cardigan Bay is an ideal vacation center for exploring mid-Wales and the Pembrokeshire coast. Being a resort, it has plenty of hotels and guest houses, good bus and rail service, a once-elegant sea-front promenade with a bandstand, a pier, and the King's Hall for summer shows. Aberystwyth, which can be a fairly brash place at the height of the season, is also a university town and a major shopping center. A fine, curving beach edges the bay, with the university at the southern end and Constitution Hill

❷❸ on the northern. The **university campus,** the oldest in Wales, includes the National Library of Wales, an arts center with galleries, a theater, concert hall, and crafts shop—all open to visitors. *The Library, tel. 0970/623816. Admission free. Open weekdays 9:30–6, Sat. 9:30–5.*

❷❹ The **castle,** at the southern end of the bay, was built in 1277 and rebuilt in 1282 by Edward I. It was one of several strongholds to fall, in 1404, to the Welsh leader Owain Glyndwr. Recaptured by the English, it became a mint in the 17th century, using silver from the Welsh hills. Today it is a romantic ruin on a headland separating the north shore from the harbor shore.

Long before its resort days, Aberystwyth was a major fishing port and ship-building center. The names of many small inns, such as **Ship and Anchor,** reflect its origins.

❷❺ At the end of the promenade, **Constitution Hill** offers the energetic a zigzag cliff path/nature trail to the view from the top. But it's more fun to travel up by the **Aberystwyth Electric Cliff Railway.** Opened in 1896, to great excitement—520 passengers used the new attraction on its first day—it has recently been refurbished without diminishing its Victorian look. It takes you up 430 feet to the **Great Aberystwyth Camera Obscura,** a modern version of a Victorian amusement: Its massive 14-inch lens gives a bird's-eye view of more than 1,000 square miles of sea and scenery, including the whole of Cardigan Bay and 26 Welsh mountain peaks, Snowdon among them. *Tel. 0970/617642. Admission to Camera Obscura free; railway £1.95 adults, £1.25 children, £1.50 senior citizens. Open Easter–Oct., daily 10–6.*

❷❻ Back in town, the excellent **Ceredigion Museum** in an old theater on Terrace Road displays coins minted at the castle, and its fascinating Aberystwyth Yesterday collection shows 19th-century fashions, furniture, toys, and photographs. *Terrace Rd., tel. 0970/617911. Admission free. Open Apr.–Oct., Mon.–Sat. 10–5.*

❷❼ At Aberystwyth Station you can hop on British Rail's last steam-operated line, the **Vale of Rheidol Railway** (tel. 0685/4854), once used to carry lead ore. The terminus, an hour's ride away, is **Devil's Bridge,** where the Rivers Rheidol and Mynach meet in a series of spectacular falls. The walk down to the lowest bridge, "the devil's," is magnificent but strictly for the sure-footed!

Numbers in the margin correspond to points of interest on the Wales map.

❷❽ Three miles north of Devil's Bridge on A4120, the award-winning **Llywernog Silver Lead Mine** lies near Ponterwyd, 13 miles east of the town on A44. Silver and lead were produced here from 1740 to 1910; restoration work and an imaginative exhibition, "The California of Wales," have turned the clock back to the mining boom of the 1870s. *Tel. 097/085620. Admission:*

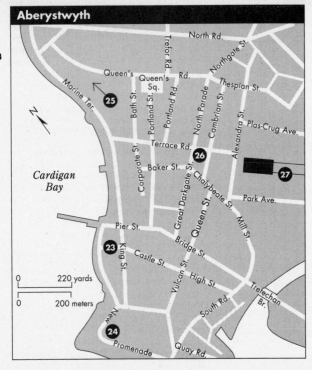

Aberystwyth

£2.50 adults, £1 children, £1.95 senior citizens, family ticket, £6.50. Open Easter–Aug., daily 10–6; Sept., daily 10–5; Oct., daily 11–4.

A scenic drive leads along the coast, from the village of Borth, five miles north of Aberystwyth, down to Cardigan, and then circles around the Pembrokeshire Coast National Park farther south to Tenby. This is one of the most spectacular coastal stretches in Britain—150 miles or so, allowing for the broken coastline. As far as Cardigan the ruggedness of the north is still apparent, but the county of Pembrokeshire, now part of Dyfed, manifests a gentler mood, with tiny coves and sheltered beaches.

㉙ Sixteen miles south of Aberystwyth on A487, **Aberaeron** was nearly all built in Georgian style in the early 19th century, giving the town a pleasing sense of harmony and coherence. The **Aerial Ferry,** a form of cable car, can carry you across the harbor in a gondola. Like Aberystwyth's Camera Obscura, it is a Victorian replica. *Tel. 0970/617642. Admission: 70p round trip, 40p one way. Open June–Sept., daily 10–6.*

㉚ Just past Cardigan, 22 miles from Aberaeron by A487, the dramatic ruins of 13th-century **Cilgerran Castle** stand above a deep wooded gorge through which flows the river Teifi. *Tel. 0239/ 615136 (summer only). Admission: £1 adults, 60p children and senior citizens. Open Apr.–Sept., Mon.–Sat. 9:20–6:30, Sun. 2–4; Oct.–Mar. (when key must be picked up from the village general store at The Old Post House on the High Street), Mon.–Sat. 8–7, Sun. 9–6.*

Every August the village of Cilgerran holds a festival week culminating in coracle races. A coracle is a tiny, light, one-man
boat, built on a frame of hazel and willow laths in a style which
has scarcely changed since the Iron Age—and it's extremely
tricky to handle. To appreciate this sport's original context,
visit **Cardigan Wildlife Park,** a sanctuary for some of the animals that were once indigenous to the area—wolves and bison,
wild boar, and ferret-like polecats. A nature trail winds
through at least four different habitats, and fishermen on the
Teifi River expertly maneuver their coracles in pursuit of salmon, as their ancestors did for thousands of years. *Tel. 0239/
614449. Admission: £2 adults, £1 children, £1.50 senior citizens. Open 10–sunset all year. Café and shop open Easter–
Oct.*

❸❶ For still another glimpse of the past, travel inland on A484, past
the Cenarth Falls, to visit **Felin Geri Mill** at **Newcastle Emlyn**
(11 mi). Here flour is ground, as it has been for 350 years, by the
only water-powered mill in Wales still in use. A bakery, using
the mill's fresh-ground flour, supplies a restaurant serving traditional farmhouse lunches and cream teas. A rare waterwheel-
powered sawmill, craft workshops, a fishing museum, and a falconry complete the picture. *Tel. 0239/710810. Admission: £2.50
adults, £1.50 children, £2 senior citizens. Open Easter–Oct.,
daily 10–6.*

From Cardigan A487 skirts the **Preseli Hills,** from which the
bluestone used for the monoliths at Stonehenge was mined. In
❸❷ **Fishguard,** 17 miles down the coast from Cardigan, the harbor
at Lowertown was the film location for Dylan Thomas's *Under
Milk Wood*, starring Richard Burton. Historically it is famous
as the place where the last invading foreign army landed in
Britain: a French force, in 1797, commanded by an American,
Colonel Tate. Legend holds that the invaders surrendered after being frightened by a group of women in red shawls and tall
black hats whom they mistook for Guardsmen. The surrender
was signed at the **Royal Oak Inn.**

❸❸ Half an hour's drive away (16 miles west on A487) is the smallest city in Britain, **St. David's,** where the patron saint of Wales
established a monastery in the 6th century; Christian tradition
has continued unbroken here ever since. St. David's is actually
not much more than a large, friendly village, but is legally a
city because it has a cathedral. The **cathedral,** unlike other
British cathedrals, nestles in a valley, and indeed was probably
built there to hide it from Viking raiders. The exterior is simple, but inside treasures include the fragile fan vaulting in
Bishop Vaughan's Chapel, the intricate carving on the choir
stalls, and the substantial oaken roof over the nave. Across the
brook are the ruins of the 14th-century Bishop's Palace.

A spectacular cliff walk of about an hour takes you to **St. Non's
Bay.** St. Non was St. David's mother, and the path leads between tall hydrangea bushes to her well, reputed to have the
power to heal eye diseases. Beyond is her ruined chapel, possibly the oldest religious building still standing in Wales, where
St. David is said to have been born in 530 AD.

❸❹ **Solva** lies three miles eastward along the coast on A487 to
Haverfordwest. It is a village of white, typically Welsh cottages clustering at the foot of the hillside. For an extraordinary
experience, visit the **Nectarium** housed in a group of attractive

old buildings. Wander through the rain-forest vegetation of the humid Tropical House while brilliantly colored butterflies from the Amazon, India, and Malaysia—some as large as bats—flutter around you. If they settle on you, you must not brush them off or otherwise injure them! The Insect Gallery crawls with pupating caterpillars, locusts, and tarantulas—mercifully all behind glass. There are two shops selling locally designed clothing, leather goods, and ceramics, as well as exotic preserves and toiletries. *Tel. 0437/721323. Admission: £2 adults, £1 children, £1.50 senior citizens. Open Easter–Sept., Mon.–Sat. 10–6, Sun. 2–6, last admission 5.*

35 Thirteen miles southeast on A487 to Haverfordwest, then another 9 on A4076, the town of **Pembroke** has a magnificent **castle** dating from 1190, although the foundation is 100 years older. Its walls remain stout, its gatehouse mighty, and the enormous cylindrical keep proved so impregnable to cannon fire in the Civil War that Cromwell's men had to starve out its royalist defenders. It was the birthplace, in 1457, of Henry VII, the Tudor king who seized the throne of Britain in 1485, and whose son Henry VIII united Wales and England. *Tel. 0646/681510. Admission: £1.50 adults, 80p children and senior citizens. Open Apr.–Sept., daily 9:30–6; Mar. and Oct., daily 10–5; Nov.–Feb., Mon.–Sat. 10–4.*

36 The Pembrokeshire Coast National Park ends some 15 miles northeast, at **Amroth** just beyond the resort of **Tenby.** A coast path with spectacular views runs almost its entire length (*see* Sports, below).

Tour 4: Cardiff

37 To visit **Cardiff,** from Tenby follow A478, A47, and A48 eastward through Carmarthen (43 miles). Join the M4 at its end (exit 49), and take it to Cardiff (45 miles). Cardiff has been the Welsh capital since 1956. Although the city's history is long—it was settled by the Romans and used by the Normans as a strategic fortress—it wasn't until the Industrial Revolution and the arrival of the railroad in the 19th century that the city suddenly began to expand. A period of decline in this century has given way to a massive redevelopment scheme designed to restore Cardiff and its once-bustling waterfront to its former glory.

Begin your exploration at Cardiff's **castle,** easily the city's oldest central building. Located in Bute Park—one section of Cardiff's hundreds of acres of parkland—the castle is a mishmash of periods: Parts of the walls are Roman, the solid keep is Norman, and the whole complex was restored a hundred years ago by the 3rd Marquess of Bute. Bute employed William Burges (1827–81), an architect obsessed by the Gothic period, to carry out the work, and Burges transformed the castle inside and out into an extravaganza of medieval color and detailed craftsmanship. It's well worth a visit. *Tel. 0222/822083. Admission: Guided tour of the castle, £3 adults, £1.50 children and senior citizens; grounds only, £1.65 adults, 85p children and senior citizens. Open May–Sept., daily 10–6, Mar., Apr., Oct., daily 10–5; Nov.–Feb., daily 10–4:30.*

Two blocks east of the castle is Cardiff's **Civic Centre,** a well-designed complex of civic buildings boasting impressive Portland stone facades. City Hall, the National Museum of Wales, the Law Courts, the Welsh Office (seat of government), and the University campus are all located here. The city tourist office (8–14 Bridge St., tel. 0222/227281), organizes walking tours of the Civic Centre throughout the summer.

The **National Museum** could take several hours to explore properly. It sets out to tell the story of Wales through its plants, rocks, archaeology, art, and industry. It also has a fine collection of modern European art, especially Postimpressionist works—don't miss *La Parisienne* by Renoir. The museum has a convenient cafeteria on the top floor. *Main Building, Cathay's Park, tel. 0222/397951. Admission: £1 adults, 50p children, 75p senior citizens. Open Tues.–Sat. 10–5, Sun. 2:30–5.*

Surrounding the Civic Centre, with its tree-lined avenues, are the shopping and business areas of Cardiff. Here you will find a large, modern shopping mall that includes **St. David's Hall.** One of Europe's best new concert halls, with outstanding acoustics, St. David's hosts performances in classical music, jazz, rock, ballet—even snooker championships. This popular spot also includes a coffee bar and a restaurant.

Time Out At the bottom of Queen's Street is the Capital shopping mall, with the large **Box Office** cafeteria, an ideal spot for morning coffee or a light lunch.

Cross the River Taff and follow Cathedral Road for about three miles, to reach the village of Llandaff and Llandaff Cathedral, which was completely renovated after serious bomb damage in World War II. Inside you will immediately be drawn to the overwhelming statue by Jacob Epstein (1880–1959) of *Christ in Majesty*, a massive figure on a great cylinder, supported high over the center of the nave on a free-standing arch. The cathedral also has some pre-Raphaelite works.

Four miles west of Llandaff is the open-air **Welsh Folk Museum** at St. Fagan's. In 100 acres of parkland and gardens lie farmhouses, cottages, and terraced houses that show the evolution of Welsh building styles. Visitors here can also view an Elizabethan mansion, built within the walls of a Norman castle. There are craft workshops, a saddler, cooper, blacksmith, and woodturner; demonstrations of these country skills are given during the summer. Special events are held during the year to highlight ancient rural festivals—May Day, Harvest, and Christmas among them. There is a cafeteria, a coffee tavern, restaurants, and a museum shop. *Tel. 0222/569441. Admission: £3 adults, £1.50 children, £2.25 senior citizens. Open Easter–Oct., daily 10–5; Nov.–Easter, Mon.–Sat. 10–5.*

North of Cardiff, four miles via A470, beside the village of Tongwynlais, is the 13th-century **Castell Coch,** the Red Castle. It was restored in the 1870s around the time that Ludwig of Bavaria was creating his fantastic dream castles, and it might almost be one of them. Instead, the castle was another collaboration of the 3rd Marquess of Bute and William Burges, whose work you will already have seen in Cardiff castle. Here Burges recreated everything—architecture, furnishings, carvings, murals—in a remarkable exercise in Victorian-Gothic whimsy. *Tel. 0222/810101. Admission: £1.50 adults, 90p children and senior citizens. Open mid-Mar–mid-Oct., Mon.–Sat.*

9:30–6:30, Sun. 2–6:30; mid-Oct.–mid-Mar., Mon.–Sat. 9:30–4, Sun. 2–4.

Tour 5: Llandrindod Wells to Powis

③⑧ **Llandrindod Wells,** known locally as Llandod, is a Victorian spa town, elegant and stylish. It is architecturally magnificent, with an array of fussy turrets, cupolas, loggias, and balustrades, and greenery and flowers everywhere. The climate—it is 700 feet above sea level—is said to be exceptionally healthy, making it a very comfortable base for exploring the region. On a main line rail route, it also enjoys good bus service.

Llandrindod emerged as a spa in 1670 but did not reach its heyday until the second half of the 19th century when the railway came and most of the town was built. The **Museum,** in Memorial Gardens, details the development of the spa from Roman times and explains some of the Victorian "cures" in gruesome detail. *Tel. 0597/824513. Admission free. Open all year Mon.–Sat. 10–1 and 2–5; closed Sat. 2–5 Oct.–Apr.*

Llandrindod is easily explored on foot. Cross over to South Crescent, passing the Glen Usk Hotel with its wrought-iron balustrade and the Victorian bandstand in the gardens opposite, and you soon reach Middleton Street, another Victorian gem with some tony specialty shops. From there head to Rock Park and the path that leads down through wooded glades to the handsomely restored Pump Room.

The **Pump Room,** tiled and airy, offers three types of water— "saline for the bowels, sulphur for the blood, and magnesium to line the stomach," as custodian Mary Price says. Sufferers from gout, rheumatism, bronchial ailments, and anemia were also said to benefit from the water. In the late 19th century, at the height of its popularity, the spa had 80,000 visitors a season. There is a spa museum, and the Pump Room is a fitting center for the town's Victorian Festival (*see* Arts, below). *Tel. 0597/4307. Admission free. Open Apr.–Oct., daily 10–6.*

On the other side of town, the lake with its boathouse, café, and gift shop is in a lovely setting: wooded hills on one side, a broad common on the other, flooded in spring by golden daffodils. Interesting species of waterfowl, including grebe, live on the lake, and in early spring thousands of toads arrive from up to half a mile away to spawn, giving Llandrindod the unappetizing nickname of "Toad Town."

Time Out Drop in at **Spencer's Bar,** Hotel Metropole (Temple St.), where inexpensive snacks are served in the height of Victorian luxury.

The countryside around Llandrindod Wells varies considerably. The land that lies along the border with England is soft and rich, with rolling green hills and lush valleys, but in the Black Mountains to the southeast and the Elan Valley in the northwest the scenery is more dramatic.

③⑨ **Hay-on-Wye,** about 28 miles southeast of Llandrindod, is a border town nestling in a hilly landscape and dominated by its mostly ruined castle. In 1961 expatriate American Richard Booth established a small secondhand and antiquarian bookshop here; it now fills several houses, a movie theater, and a pub, and has attracted dozens of other bookstores, making the town the largest secondhand bookselling center in the world. In the 1970s Booth gained additional notoriety by styling himself "King of Hay" and proposing customs barriers, a zany idea that got short shrift from inhabitants and visitors alike. Among the million-plus books, you will find priceless 14th-century manuscripts rubbing spines with "job lots" selling for a few pounds.

40 One mile westward across the river Wye is **Clyro,** the village made famous by the Rev. Francis Kilvert, whose 1870–72 diary gives a charming and evocative picture of his simple world and the people in it. As you enter the village, don't miss Adam Dworski's **Wye Pottery,** with its powerful, swirling sculptures and gentle Madonnas.

Southeast from Hay you can take a narrow road (unnumbered) ten miles over the Black Mountains through the high Gospel
41 Pass and Capel-y-ffin to **Llanthony Priory,** founded in 1108 and now a romantic ruin in the breathtakingly beautiful **Vale of Ewyas.** Keep going another five miles as the narrow road be-
42 comes B4423 to **Llanvihangel Crucorny,** where you'll discover the Skirrid Inn, mentioned in 1110 and possibly the oldest inn in Britain, certainly in Wales. In 1685 it was used as one of the courts of the so-called "Bloody Assize" by the notorious Judge Jeffreys. Some of the accused, who supported the duke of Monmouth's rebellion against the monarchy, are said to have been hanged from a beam in the inn, which, as you'd expect, has the reputation of being haunted.

43 Six miles south, the market town of **Abergavenny** has a **castle** founded early in the 11th century. At Christmas in 1176 the Norman knight William de Braose invited the neighboring Welsh chieftains to a feast—and, in a crude attempt to gain control of the area, had them all slaughtered as they sat, unarmed, at dinner. Afterward the Welsh attacked and virtually demolished the castle. Little remains of the building now, but you can visit the **museum,** with exhibits ranging from the Iron Age to the early part of this century. The Welsh kitchen is particularly appealing, with its old utensils, pans, and butter molds. *Castle St. Tel. 0873/4282. Admission: 70p adults, 35p children and senior citizens. Open Mar.–Oct., Mon.–Sat. 11–1 and 2–5; Nov.–Feb., Mon.–Sat. 2–4.*

Taking the Crickhowell road (A40) northwest out of Abergavenny, you pass the **Sugar Loaf** mountain, an extinct
44 volcano. Two miles farther (by A479) is **Tretower Court,** a splendid example of a fortified medieval manor house, with gatehouse, galleried courtyard, and banquet hall, furnished in appropriate period style by local craftsmen. Nearby is a ruined Norman castle. *Tel. 0874/730279. Admission: £1.25 adults, 75p children and senior citizens. Open mid-Mar.–mid-Oct., weekdays 9:30–6:30, Sun. 2–6:30; mid-Oct.–mid-Mar., weekdays 9:30–4, Sun. 2–4.*

From Tretower take A479 and then A470 25 miles north to
45 **Builth Wells,** home of Wales's premier agricultural show, the Royal Welsh, usually held in July. From Builth continue another 14 miles on A470 via Newbridge-on-Wye to Rhayader,
46 where a southwest turn on B4518 brings you to the **Elan Valley,** Wales's Lake District. This four-mile chain of lakes, winding between green-gray hills, was created in the 1890s by a system of dams to supply water to the city of Birmingham, 73 miles to

the east. The giant dam in **Claerwen reservoir** to the west was built in 1952 to supplement supplies. The area is one of Britain's foremost ornithological sites, still home to red kite, peregrine, merlin, and buzzard. You can see and hear all about it at the **Elan Valley Visitor Centre** by Caban Coch reservoir. *Admission free. Open Easter–Oct., daily 10–6.*

Return to Rhayader and take A470 again, northwest about 9 miles to Llangurig.

Time Out The **Glansevern Arms,** Pant Mawr, 4½ miles northwest of Llangurig, is a snug inn with tasty lunches—cold salmon in season—in its reliable restaurant. There's no food on Sundays.

47 Five miles northeast (still on A470) is **Llanidloes,** remarkable for its half-timbered market house, standing on sturdy timber legs, the only one of its kind left in Wales; it now contains the Museum of Local History and Industry. *Market Hall. Admission free. Open Easter–Sept., Mon.–Sat. 11–1 and 2–5.*

Hamer's, the butcher shop on the main street, bears the Royal Arms, having served eight royal families. The lamb sold here, from nearby Plynlimon mountain, is exceptionally sweet and succulent.

Follow A470 east 14 miles to Newtown and then 14 miles northeast by A483 to Welshpool. Just before you reach Welshpool ("Trallwng" in Welsh) you will see one of mid-Wales's greatest **48** treasures, **Powis Castle.**

In continuous occupation, with various adaptations, since the 13th century, and now a National Trust property, Powis is one of the most desirable residential castles in Britain. Its battlements rearing high on a hilltop, the castle is surrounded by terraced gardens, bounded by gigantic yew hedges, which fall steeply down to wide lawns and neat Elizabethan gardens. Inside are many treasures: Greek vases; magnificent paintings by Gainsborough, Reynolds, and Romney among others; superb furniture, including a 16th-century Italian table inlaid with marble; and, since 1987, the **Clive of India Museum,** containing the best British collection of Indian art outside London. The tearoom here is an excellent spot for a break, serving homemade cakes. *Tel. 0938/554336. Admission: £5 adults, £2.50 children, £13.50 family ticket; museum and gardens only: £3 adults, £1.50 children, £7.50 family ticket. Open Apr.–June, Sept. and Oct., Wed.–Sun. noon–5; July and Aug., Tues.–Sun. 11–6.*

What to See and Do with Children

The **Museum of Childhood** in Beaumaris (*see* Tour 1) is an excellent attraction for children.

Twelve miles southwest along the Menai Strait at Brynsiencyn is another kid's fun spot, **The Anglesey Sea Zoo.** Here is almost every form of marine life found in the surrounding waters, including a 9-foot conger eel. There's a mysterious wreck, a "touch tank" where you can pick up lobster and crab, and a "tide tank" which simulates conditions on the nearby beach. The tearoom sells ice cream with fishy names, gifts in the shop have fishy motifs. Radio-controlled motor boats, also undercover, are popular. *The Oyster Hatchery, Brynsiencyn, tel. 0248/*

430411. Admission: £3 adults, £1.50 for children, $2.50 senior citizens. Open Feb.–Nov., daily 10–5; July and Aug., daily 9:30–5:30.

The **Welsh Mountain Zoo** at Colwyn Bay is in a beautiful setting, just right for the free-flying displays of hawks, falcons, and eagles that take place daily. The **Jungle Adventure Trail** is also fun. *Colwyn Bay, tel. 0492/532938. Admission: £2.60 adults, £1.35 children. Open daily 9:30–dusk.*

Rhyl Sun Centre is an enclosed "tropical island" on the northern coast with surfing, splash pool, and roof-top monorail. *East Parade, Rhyl, tel. 0745/344433. Admission: £2.45 adults, £1.40 children and senior citizens. Evenings, £1.40 adults, 95p children and senior citizens. Open Apr.–Sept., daily 10–11; Oct.–early Nov., weekends only.*

The **Nectarium** at Solva (*see* Tour 3) is also fascinating for children.

Off the Beaten Track

Plas Newydd is an 18th-century mansion on the Menai Strait close to the Menai Bridge. (Note this is the second Plas Newydd we mention; the other is in Tour 1, at Llangollen.) In 1936–40 the society artist Rex Whistler painted the mural in the dining room here, his largest work. A military museum commemorates the Battle of Waterloo, where the first marquess of Anglesey, Wellington's cavalry commander, lost his leg. The interior has some fine 18th-century Gothic-revival decorations, and the gardens have been restored to their original design. There are magnificent views across the strait from here. *Llanfairpwll, Anglesey, tel. 0248/714798. Admission: £2.40 adults, £6 family ticket. Gardens only: £1.10 adults, 50p children. Open Easter–Sept., Sun.–Fri. noon–5; Oct., Fri. and Sun. noon–5.*

Bodelwyddan Castle (off A55, between Abergele and St. Asaph), is a restored Victorian castle in spacious formal gardens and surrounded by lovely countryside. It now houses an offshoot of the National Portrait Gallery in London, exhibiting noteworthy examples of Regency and Victorian portraiture by such famous names as John Singer Sargent, Lawrence, G. F. Watts, and Sir Edwin Landseer. This magnificent house and collection won the National Heritage's Museum of the Year award in 1989. *Tel. 0745/584060. Admission: £3 adults, £1.75 children, £8 family ticket; grounds only: £1.80 adults, 80p children, £4.50 family ticket. Open Easter–Oct., Sat.–Thurs. 10–5; Oct.–Easter, Sat.–Tues. 11–5.*

Dolaucothi Gold Mines (8 mi southeast of Lampeter), a source of gold for almost 2,000 years, has a museum of working machinery and a visitor center, but the best part is the guided tour underground—helmet with lamp provided. *Pumsaint, near Lampeter, tel. 05585/359. Surface admission: £1.75 adults, £1 children; underground tour (mid-June–mid-Sept. only): £2.75 adults, £1.75 children. Open Apr.–Oct., daily 1–5.*

Shopping

Wales is particularly noted for its crafts—tweeds woven at local mills, pottery, slate sculpture, knitwear, carved wooden lovespoons—and you'll find crafts stores throughout the principality. Look for the Daffodil label of the Wales Crafts Council, which is a guarantee of quality.

Beaumaris: Rainbows (5 Market Sq.) is a glass workshop, with an imaginative and wide range of items.

Betws-y-Coed: This is one of several towns with a branch of the **Craftcentre Cymru,** a chain that markets craft goods (you can get information about it from Waleslink, in New York, tel. 212/683–5384). At this branch, **Penmacho Woollen Mill,** just outside Betws-y-Coed on B4406, fabric is woven for exclusively designed clothing.

Cardiff: Cardiff is one of Wales's major shopping centers, with branches of all Britain's major store chains. Among the unusual places is the **Craft Centre Shop** in the Old Library (The Hayes), close to the St. David's Hall. It has exhibits of Markers Guild crafts, all for sale.

Corwen: Ten miles northeast of Bala by A494 lies Corwen, where **Cynwyd Pottery** (Waterfalls Rd.) offers lovely handmade pottery. The town itself affords great views of the area.

Harlech: At **John Rainbow's** craft shop (Hen Clogwyn, Pentre'r Efail), you'll discover attractive hand-enameled jewelry with a wide range of prices.

Hay-on-Wye: Book lovers are unlikely to do better anywhere in Britain—or, arguably, the world—than here. Bookshops jostle each other on the main street, and on many side streets. Give yourself several happy hours of exploring.

Llanfairpwllgwyngyllgogerychwyrndrobwllllantysiligogogoch: This (the complex is in The Station) really is the name of a place on Anglesey. The **James Pringle Woollen Mill** here markets good, if expensive, clothing. By the way, unless you can get the name down pat, just say "Llanfair P. G.," like everyone else.

Portmeirion: Portmeirion pottery, with its distinctive design, is almost as famous as the hotel there. You can buy firsts in nearby Porthmadog at 9 High Street, while the Seconds Shop in Portmeirion village sells pottery with tiny and often invisible flaws.

Ruthin: Antiques enthusiasts should stop in at **Castle Antiques** (Castle St.), where the stock ranges from 17th-century oak tables to dainty Victorian plates. For china, clocks, and lace, try **Old Tyme Antiques,** also on Castle Street. **The Craft Centre** (Park Rd.), on the traffic circle, has craft workshops, a gallery, restaurant, and tourist information center. It's a good all-around place for Welsh crafts. **The Bookshop** (Upper Clwyd St.) is a bookworm's haven.

Tenby: The **Pembrokeshire Craftsmen's Shop** (Brychan Yard, Upper Frog St.) is a co-operative run by the craftsmen, selling goods made of wood and leather, silver jewelry, wooden toys, pottery, and Celtic artwork.

Sports and Fitness

Golf Welsh golf courses tend to the spectacular. **Llandrindod Wells,** at 1,000 feet above sea level, is one of the highest in Britain (tel. 0597/2010); at **Llangollen,** the ninth, with its dog-leg left and two-tier green, is said to be the most challenging in north Wales (tel. 0978/860040); **Llanymynech,** near Oswestry, has fifteen holes in Wales and three across the border in England (tel. 0691/830542). **Royal Porthcawl** in south Wales (tel. 065671/ 2251) hosted the Sixteenth European Amateur Golf Team Championships in 1989; **Royal St. David's** at Harlech (tel. 0766/ 780361) is also a championship links.

Hiking The **Ramblers Association** (Pantwood, Pant Lane, Morford, Wrexham, Clwyd LL12 8SG, tel. 097883/5148) can supply you with information on walking in Wales. Local tourist information centers have information on guided walks; those in Snowdonia National Park are among the most spectacular, although among the most dangerous. One of the longest (and hardest) official trails in Wales is Glyndwr's Way, 121 miles from Knighton to Welshpool, with some spectacular panoramic views along the route. The **Pembrokeshire Coast Path** starts 2 miles northwest of St. Dogmael's and stretches 180 miles around the coast of Pembrokeshire to Amroth, which is near Saundersfoot, right back in Carmarthen Bay. You can join or leave the path at several points, mostly where inns are available for overnight stops; and there is also a special bus service linking the particularly interesting stretches. *Information from any Wales Tourist Board office.* Rolling hills and open moorlands await hikers in the **Brecon Beacons National Park,** a 519-square-mile area containing some of the most beautiful scenery in southeast Wales. Contact the **Brecon Beacons Mountain Centre** (tel. 0874/3366) for suggested routes and further information.

For the Rugged The truly intrepid should contact **Plas Menai National Outdoor Pursuits Centre** (Llanfairisgaer, Caernarfon, Gwynedd LL55 1UE, tel. 0248/670964), which runs day, weekend, or week-long courses in canoeing, rock climbing, mountaineering, and sailing.

Horseback Riding Even beginners can go pony trekking on amiable Welsh cobs; the more experienced can try trail riding and even show jumping. The **Pony Trekking and Riding Society of Wales** (c/o 32 North Parade, Aberystwyth, Dyfed SY23 2NF, tel. 0970/ 617849) will supply a full list of approved centers, many of which offer accommodation as well.

Some riding centers near our tours are: **Gromlech Riding Centre,** Tyn-y-Gongl, Anglesey, tel. 0248/853489; **Lion Royal Hotel Pony Trekking Centre,** Weir St., Rhayader, tel. 0597/810202; **Pinewood Riding Stables,** Sychnant Pass Rd., Conwy, tel. 049263/2256; and at Clynderwen, near Haverfordwest, **Tregach Manor Pony Trekking Centre,** Mynachlog Ddu, tel. 09912/457.

Water Sports Aberaeron, Aberdovey, Aberystwyth, and Barmouth are sailing centers, and Aberdovey and Barmouth are particularly good for waterskiing. However, there are water sports facilities and sailing clubs around most of the Welsh coast. Check at tourist centers for the local possibilities.

The **Brenig reservoir** on B4501 lies southwest of Denbigh and east of Betws-y-Coed. This 919-acre lake, surrounded by wooded peaks, is excellent for water sports enthusiasts, anglers, and walkers. There are well-marked footpaths, an interesting **archaeological trail,** and an exhibition and information center (tel. 049082/463) where you can pick up leaflets on the area and its facilities.

Dining and Lodging

Dining In recent years there has been a revolution in dining out in Wales. Many restaurants now are of an extremely high standard and, generally speaking, not as expensive as those across the border in England. Salmon from local rivers, seafood, and Welsh lamb are all cooked in the traditional way, and there is often an emphasis on fresh, home-produced food. Imaginative appetizers and an amazing range of desserts also are served. Look for the sign "Blas Ar Cymru" ("A Taste of Wales"), which means that the establishment produces traditional Welsh specialties.

Highly recommended restaurants are indicated by a star ★.

Category	Cost*
Expensive	£25–£30
Moderate	£12–£25
Inexpensive	under £12

per person, including first course, main course, dessert, and VAT; excluding drinks

Lodging A 19th-century dictum, "I sleeps where I dines" still holds true in Wales. Good hotels and good restaurants mostly go together, and since conversion is the rage, that means castles, country mansions, farmhouses, smithies, even workhouses and small railroad stations are being transformed into hotels and restaurants. Traditional inns, many with four-poster beds, remain the country's pride.

Highly recommended lodgings are indicated by a star ★.

Category	Cost*
Very Expensive	over £110
Expensive	£80–£110
Moderate	£40–£80
Inexpensive	under £40

All prices are for two people sharing a double room, including service, breakfast, and VAT.

Aberystwyth **Connexion.** This is a simple bistro, decorated with the work of
Dining local artists. Traditional bistro fare includes Portuguese chicken and apple tart. Other dishes include paella, locally caught lobster, and a variety of pastas. *19 Bridge St., tel. 0970/615350. Reservations advised. Dress: informal. MC, V. Inexpensive.*
Gannets. Another simple bistro, Gannets specializes in locally supplied meat, fish, and game, which are transformed into

hearty roasts and pies. Organically grown vegetables and a good Italian house wine are further draws for a university crowd. *7 St. James' Sq., tel. 0970/617164. Reservations advised. Dress: informal. MC, V. Closed Sun. Moderate.*

Lodging **The Four Seasons.** Located in Aberystwyth's town center, this family-run hotel/restaurant has a relaxed atmosphere and friendly staff. The spacious rooms are simply and attractively decorated, and the restaurant serves excellent meals at reasonable prices. *50–54 Portland St., SY23 2DX, tel. 0970/612120. 15 rooms, 7 with bath. MC, V. Moderate.*

The Groves Hotel. Family-owned and in the heart of town, the hotel has comfortable bedrooms with tea- and coffee-making facilities; a paneled lounge bar; and Welsh, English, and French dishes on the menu in the **Tapestry Restaurant.** *44–46 North Parade, SY23 2NF, tel. 0970/617623. 12 rooms with bath. Facilities: sea fishing and pony trekking arranged. AE, DC, MC, V. Moderate.*

Bala **Palé Hall.** This sumptuous country mansion hotel, with fabu-
Dining and Lodging lous Snowdonia views, was built in 1870 and has been painstak-
★ ingly restored by its new owners. There's a library/bar, a Great Hall with a magnificent oak staircase, and spacious bedrooms, some with open fireplaces. The restaurant is magnificently ornate and the food and service live up to their surroundings. *Llandderfel, near Bala, Gwynedd LL23 7PS, tel. 06783/285. 17 rooms with bath. Facilities: garden, horseback riding, golf, fishing. Restaurant reservations advised. Jacket and tie required. AE, DC, MC, V. Expensive.*

Beaumaris **Ye Olde Bull's Head.** Originally a coaching inn built in 1472, the
Dining and Lodging place is small and charming. The oak-beamed dining room, dating from 1617, serves French specialties including warm salad of pigeon breast with hazelnut oil, as well as local widgeon (wild duck). *Castle St., Anglesey LL58 8AP, tel. 0248/810329. 11 rooms with bath. Restaurant reservations advised. Jacket and tie required. Restaurant closed Sun. dinner. MC, V. Moderate.*

Lodging **The Bulkeley Arms.** This is an elegant, early Victorian hotel, with spacious rooms and superb views over the Menai Strait. *19 Castle St., Anglesey LL58 8AW, tel. 0248/810415. 40 rooms, 37 with bath. Facilities: restaurant, gameroom, garden. AE, DC, MC, V. Moderate.*

Henllys Hall. This romantic country manor house built in 1852 is set in 40 acres of woodland. A mile from town, it looks across the strait to Snowdonia. *Anglesey LL58 8HU, tel. 0248/810412. 36 rooms with bath. Facilities: health and fitness studio, pool, tennis, gameroom. AE, MC, V. Moderate.*

Betws-y-Coed **The Ty Gwyn.** After a browse through the antiques shop next
Dining door, stop for a bite at the restaurant, which is under the same management. Inside the 17th-century building it's all prints and chintz, old beams and copper pans, and affords a nice view of the nearby Waterloo bridge. Homemade pâté is a specialty. *Gwynedd LL24 0SG, tel. 0690/710383. Reservations advised. Dress: informal. MC, V. Moderate.*

Cardiff **Armless Dragon.** (Out beyond the Cathays stadium.) A window-
Dining front full of plants enlivens this bright, friendly restaurant, popular with the university crowd. Seafood dishes are always a good bet here; much of the fish comes from local waters. For even more uniquely Welsh flavor, try a laverburger, made out of seaweed. *97 Wyeverne Rd., Cathays, tel. 0222/382357. Res-*

ervations advised. Dress: informal. Closed Sat. lunch and Sun. AE, DC, MC, V. Moderate.

Le Cassoulet. A genuinely French restaurant, decorated with touches of red and black, in the maze of Victorian streets west of Cathedral Road. Try the namesake cassoulet for a filling meal. The patron/chef also creates a very tasty fish soup. *5 Romilly Cres., tel. 0222/221905. Reservations advised. Dress: informal. Closed Sat. lunch, Sun., and Mon. MC, V. Moderate.*

La Chaumière. Located behind the Maltsters pub near Llandaff cathedral, La Chaumière is a bit difficult to find but you'll be rewarded for your efforts. Green-and-white decor and a French ambience are backdrops to the interesting food created by husband and wife Cliff and Kay Morgan. Try the braised rabbit in an apricot sauce or roast duck with lentils. Specialties change regularly. *44 Cardiff Rd., Llandaff, tel. 0222/555319. Reservations advised. Dress: informal. Closed Sat. lunch, Sun. dinner, and Mon. AE, MC. Moderate.*

Lodging **Holiday Inn.** The highrise Holiday Inn is a fair representative of Cardiff's new breed of hotels. It is central—close to St. David's Hall and the shopping center—practical, and with plenty of facilities. The Executive rooms have been refurbished. *Mill Lane, CF1 1E2, tel. 0222/399944. 182 rooms with bath. Facilities: restaurant, coffee shop, indoor pool, sauna, squash. AE, DC, MC, V. Expensive.*

Angel. Built around the turn of the century, the Angel hotel has recently been restored and is once again one of Cardiff's leading hotels. An attractive brick building with stone detailing, it's located on a corner site close to the castle and just minutes from the shopping and business districts. Inside, renovations have managed to preserve the original plasterwork, and pastel colors help create a quietly elegant atmosphere. The bedrooms are capacious, decorated in a turquoise-and-peach combination. Service is friendly and adept. *Castle St., CF1 2QZ, tel. 0222/232633. 91 rooms with bath. Facilities: restaurant, sauna, solarium. AE, DC, MC, V. Moderate–Expensive.*

Ceiriog Valley **The Golden Pheasant.** Jenny Gibourg searched the country to
Dining and Lodging furnish the 200-year-old hotel with antiques and Victorian-
★ style fabrics, and the result is chinoiserie in the bar, horse prints and aspidistras in the lounge, draped curtains and parlor palms in the dining room, and no two bedrooms alike. Specialties include Ceiriog trout and game pie. *Glyn Ceiriog, near Chirk, Clwyd LL20 7BB, tel. 069172/281. 18 rooms with bath. Facilities: shooting, riding center. Restaurant reservations advised. Jacket and tie required. AE, DC, MC, V. Moderate.*

The Hand and **The West Arms** are two 16th-century inns in the same village square under the same ownership. You can stay in one and dine in the other, or just sample the excellent menus of both. Specialties include lobster croquettes and West Arms Kebabs. Both modern and more traditional rooms are available. *Llanarmon Dyffryn Ceiriog, near Llangollen, Clwyd LL20 7LD, tel. 069176/666 (Hand), 069176/665 (West Arms). 14 rooms with bath (Hand); 13 rooms, 8 with bath (West Arms). Facilities: tennis, private fishing. Restaurant reservations advised. Dress: informal. AE, DC, MC, V. Moderate.*

Harlech **The Cemlyn.** Located in peaceful green surroundings, the
Dining small intimate restaurant is evocatively decorated with modern
★ art (and lots of model frogs!). Local lobster and other seafood

are specialties, as is the Welsh lamb. There are two attractive bedrooms available as well, cozily crammed with easy chairs and books and each with a large and luxurious bath. *High St., tel. 0766/780425. Reservations essential. Dress: informal. MC, V. Closed Nov.–Mar. Moderate.*

Lodging **Hotel Maes-y-Neuadd.** Set in 8 acres of its own glorious gardens
★ and parkland (3½ miles northeast of Harlech by B4573), this hotel dates from the 14th century. Purportedly favored once by Jackie Onassis, it has walls of Welsh granite, oak-beamed ceilings, an inglenook fireplace, and a menu that features Welsh, English and French specialties. *Talsarnau, near Harlech, Gwynedd LL47 6YA, tel. 0766/780200. 14 rooms with bath. AE, DC, MC, V. Closed mid-Jan.–early Feb. Expensive.*

Hay-on-Wye **Old Black Lion.** This 13th-century inn is right in the middle of
Dining and Lodging Hay, ideal for lunch while ransacking the bookshops, or for an overnight stay. The low-beamed, atmospheric bar serves home-made food—tables outside in summer—and the breakfasts are especially good. *Lion St., HR3 5AD, tel. 0497/820841. 10 rooms, 8 with bath. AE, DC, MC, V. Inexpensive.*

Lodging **Llangoed Hall.** Since it opened in May 1990, this hotel has al-
★ ready made a name for itself. An early guest was Arthur Miller. It is the brainchild of Sir Bernard Ashley, widower of Laura Ashley. The Hall is set in the spectacular valley of the Wye, with views over the Black Hills. Inside there are Laura Ashley fabrics everywhere, of course, complementing the antiques and paintings. The restaurant serves a six-course, set-price menu using mostly local produce. *Llyswen (8 miles from Hay on B4350), LD3 0YP, tel. 0874/754525. 23 rooms, all with bath. Facilities: restaurant, garden, tennis, helipad. AE, DC, MC, V. Very Expensive.*

Lake Vyrnwy **Lake Vyrnwy Hotel.** This country mansion on 27 acres of lake-
Lodging side grounds overlooking superb scenery offers the ultimate sporting holiday: Guests can fish, shoot, bird-watch, play tennis, or take long walks around the estate. Bicycles and sailboats are also available. Rooms are quite comfortable and the restaurant is excellent. The menu centers around trout, pheasant, and duck from the estate and vegetables and fruit from the garden. *Llanwddyn, via Oswestry, Shropshire SY10 0LY, tel. 069173/692. 30 rooms with bath. Facilities: fly fishing, shooting over 16,000 acres, tennis, bicycling, clay shooting, sailing, nature trails, and in-house movies. AE, DC, MC, V. Expensive.*

Llandrindod Wells **The Metropole.** The hotel is grand and gracious, the rooms styl-
Dining and Lodging ish and comfortable, the food magnificent. *Temple St., Powys*
★ *LD1 5DY, tel. 0597/822881. 121 rooms with bath. Facilities: restaurant, fitness center with pool, solarium, and steam room. AE, DC, MC, V. Moderate–Expensive.*

★ **The Llanerch.** Comfortable rooms, fine home cooking, and a grand lounge complete with inglenook fireplace grace this 16th-century coaching inn. The style is simple; the restaurant offers a wide range of bar snacks as well as fuller meals. *Waterloo Rd., Powys LD1 5BG, tel. 0597/822086. 11 rooms, 5 with bath. V. Inexpensive.*

Llandudno **Bodysgallen Hall.** Set in wide, walled gardens two miles out of
Dining and Lodging town, the Hall is part 17th-, part 18th-century, full of antiques,
★ comfortable chairs by cheery fires, pictures, and polished wood. The bedrooms (a few suites are available) combine elegance and practicality, and from some of them you'll catch

views of the not-so-distant mountains. The restaurant serves fine traditional meals, with an emphasis on local produce such as lamb and locally smoked salmon; its prices are surprisingly low for the standard it offers. *Gwynedd LL30 1RS, tel. 0492/ 584466. 28 rooms with bath. Facilities: croquet, tennis. Restaurant reservations advised. Dress: neat but informal. AE, DC, MC, V. Expensive.*

Llangammarch Wells
Lodging

The Lake Hotel. This is the place to go for total Victorian country elegance. Its 50 acres of sloping lawns and lush rhododendrons contain a trout-filled lake which attracts keen anglers. The Lake Hotel is also very popular with golfers—the Builth Wells course is only seven miles away. The rooms are large and tastefully furnished; some boast four-poster beds. *Powys LD4 4BS, tel. 05912/202. 18 rooms with bath. Facilities: fishing, shooting, golf. AE, MC, V. Closed first 2 weeks in Jan. Moderate.*

Llangollen
Dining

Gales. This wine bar/bistro (with accommodations) dates from 1775. Its infectiously cheerful atmosphere makes specialties such as whisky-smoked salmon and homemade ice cream even more enjoyable. There's a huge selection of wines besides. *18 Bridge St., tel. 0978/860089. No reservations. Dress: informal. No credit cards. Inexpensive.*

Llanrhaedr ym Mochnant
Dining and Lodging

The Hand. Yet another 16th-century inn with enormous inglenook fireplaces, it's special nevertheless: small and secluded, with only four charming rooms and a cozy restaurant where steaks are a specialty. *Near Oswestry, Shropshire SY10 0JJ, tel. 069181/451. 4 rooms with bath. No credit cards. Inexpensive.*

★ **Bron Heulog.** This guest house with lovely antique furniture and paintings also offers magnificent dinners for less than £10. *Waterfall Rd., near Oswestry, Shropshire SY10 0JX, tel. 069189/521. 3 rooms, guest bath. No credit cards. Inexpensive.*

Pontfaen
Dining and Lodging

Tregynon Country Farm Hotel. This 16th-century farmhouse, overlooking the Gwaun valley, is ideal for a quiet, reasonably priced stay in the country. The cooking concentrates on wholefood dishes and vegetarian fare. Try the bacon, apple, and cider Fidget Pie. *Near Fishguard, Dyfed SA65 9TU, tel. 0239/ 820531. 8 rooms with bath. No credit cards. Inexpensive.*

Porthgain
Dining

Harbour Lights. Tucked away on an attractive stretch of coast about seven miles northeast of St. David's, this family-run shore restaurant prides itself on serving everything homemade, right down to the cheese and biscuits. The walls are hung with pictures by local artists, all for sale. *Croesgoch, Dyfed SA62 5DW, tel. 0348/831549. Reservations advised. Dress: informal. MC. Closed Jan. and Feb. Inexpensive.*

Portmeirion
Lodging
★

Hotel Portmeirion. This is one of the most elegant—and unusual—places to stay in Wales. The mansion house that is now its main building was already here when Clough Williams-Ellis began to build his Italianate fantasy-village around it; he restored its original Victorian splendor, preserved the library and the Mirror Room, and created the curved, colonnaded dining room. Accommodation has been increased by 20 fully serviced rooms in cottages around the village, none further than a few minutes' walk from the main building. *Gwynedd LL48 6ER, tel. 0766/ 770228. 14 rooms with bath in main hotel, 20 rooms with bath in village. Facilities: pool, tennis, free golf at Porthmadog Golf Club. AE, DC, MC, V. Moderate.*

Rhayader
Dining and Lodging

Brynafon Country House. This hotel is in a former Victorian workhouse, now converted and with all modern comforts, although its exterior might be still a bit forbidding. Apart from its attractions as a hotel, it also has a notable restaurant—**The Workhouse,** once the workhouse kitchen, with white-painted stone walls and a flagstone floor. Here you can put visions of *Oliver Twist* behind you and enjoy such delicacies as Welsh cheeses and bread-and-butter pudding. Food, glorious food! *South St., Rhayader, Powys LD6 5BL, tel. 0597/810735 (hotel), 0597/810111 (restaurant). 8 suites with bath. Facilities: pool, table tennis, bowls. Reservations advised. Dress: informal. No credit cards. Restaurant closed Sun. evening, Mon. and Tues. Hotel: Inexpensive. Restaurant: Moderate.*

Dining

Hunters. The decor here is on the ritzy side—pink and green, with tassels and velour—but the food is affordably down-to-earth. Young Robert Hunter is a Ruthin native who trained at Miller Howe in the Lake District. Some of his specialties are boned quail with pâté, Welsh lamb cutlets, and fresh salmon with salmon roe sauce. *57 Well St., tel. 08242/2619. Reservations advised for weekends. Dress: informal. MC, V. Closed Sun. Moderate.*

Ruthin
Dining and Lodging
★

Ruthin Castle. This luxury hotel is a 19th-century Gothic-style construction on the site of a 13th-century fortress, set in 38 acres of grounds through which the River Conwy flows. The regular Welsh medieval banquets are phony but fun. Specialties include Welsh lamb with spices and mead. *Corwen Rd., Clwyd LL15 2NU, tel. 08242/2664. 60 rooms with bath. Facilities: fishing, gardens. Dress in restaurant: informal. Restaurant reservations required. AE, DC, MC, V. Hotel: Moderate–Expensive. Restaurant: Moderate.*

Lodging
★

Eyarth Old Railway Station. This Victorian railway station was closed for 17 years before being converted in 1981 to an award-winning bed-and-breakfast establishment. (In 1988 it won merit awards from both the Welsh and British tourist boards and was voted "Best Bed-and-Breakfast Establishment in the World" by the Worldwide Bed-and-Breakfast Association.) The bedrooms are spacious, with large windows looking out onto breathtaking rural scenery. The cafe, located on the old station platform, serves country snacks all day. *Llanfair District of Clwyd, Ruthin, Clwyd LL15 2EE, tel. 08242/3643. 6 rooms, 5 with bath. Facilities: pool. No credit cards. Inexpensive–Moderate.*

St. David's
Lodging

Warpool Court Hotel. Built in the mid-19th century as St. David's Cathedral Choir School, this hotel stands in lovely Italianate gardens, with panoramic sea views. Both the public rooms, cozy with books and tiled walls, and the bedrooms are spacious and comfortably furnished. Ask for a room overlooking the sea. *Dyfed SA62 6BN, tel. 0437/720300. 25 rooms with bath. Facilities: restaurant, pool, tennis, gymnasium, sauna, game room. AE, DC, MC, V. Moderate.*

St. Non's Hotel. There's nothing too fancy about this comfortable old house, enlarged with a modern wing, but it is near the cathedral, and has a relaxed atmosphere. The staff is friendly and helpful. If you don't want to eat in—there's usually succulent crab or lobster on the menu—they'll provide a packed lunch. *Dyfed SA62 6RJ, tel. 0437/720239. 24 rooms with bath. Facilities: restaurant, free golf, large garden. AE, DC, MC, V. Inexpensive.*

The Arts

Festivals The leading national event of 1992 will be **Garden Festival Wales (Gwyl Gerddi Cymru)** held in Ebbw Vale, 45 minutes north of Cardiff by car. It will open on May 1 and run until October. The site was once one of Wales's leading mining areas and a major eyesore, littered with slag heaps and industrial debris. After shifting 1½ million cubic meters of slag and shale, the landscaping began. 1½ million trees, shrubs, and bedding flowers have been planted, pavillions and restaurants built, a lake formed. Two million visitors are expected to visit Ebbw Vale during the festival.

The **Beaumaris Festival** is held annually in late May. The whole town is used as a site, from the 14th-century parish church, to the concert hall, to the jail (which becomes a wine bar). The festival offers an eclectic mix of concerts, recitals, jazz, madrigals, art, sculpture, poetry, folk singing and dancing, a regatta on the strait, and medieval and Civil War battles in the castle. Details from *Beaumaris Festival, 44a Castle St., Beaumaris, Gwynedd LL58 8BB, tel. 0248/810930.*

The **North Wales Music Festival** (tel. 0745/584508) takes place at the end of September at the cathedral of St. Asaph in Clwyd (noted for its almost perfect acoustics) and nearby Bodelwyddan Castle, where jazz is performed. The **Llangollen International Musical Eisteddfod** in 1992 will be held July 7–12 (tel. 0978/860236). It attracts singers and dancers to Llangollen from all over the world. Just wandering around the field is fun. The evening concerts are of international standard. Aberystwyth holds a **Summer Festival** (tel. 0970/4897) every year in July and August with cultural and holiday entertainment lasting from mid-morning to late evening.

The **Bach Festival** (tel. 03483/311) in St. David's Cathedral in May/June features international artists.

Llandrindod Wells has its **Victorian Festival** in September. Naturally, everyone is encouraged to wear costume and most do, including shop assistants, hotel staff, and postmen. *Festival Office, Old Town Hall, Llandrindod Wells, Powys, LD1 5DL, tel. 0597/823441.*

In 1992, Wales's greatest festival, the **Royal National Eisteddfod** (tel. 0222/398399), is being held at Mold in Clwyd, August 1–8. It is a totally Welsh festival of music, theater, dance, art, and crafts. The pseudo-historical ceremonies are fascinating.

Opera Wales, as might be expected in a country where singing is a way of life, has one of Britain's four major opera companies, the **Welsh National.** Its home base is at the **New Theatre** in Cardiff, but it spends most of its time touring Wales and England. Its performances, even in a small Welsh town, are of an international standard, and its productions often among the most exciting in Britain. For details of performances contact *Welsh National Opera, John St., Cardiff CF1 4SP, tel. 0222/464666.*

Theater **Theatr Clwyd** in Mold has two theaters within the same arts complex. It has its own professional company, with an international reputation. *Tel. 0352/55114.*

12 The Lake District

Introduction

The Lake District is one of the most concentrated areas of alpine and lake scenery in the world. Lying in England's northwest corner, in the county of Cumbria, it measures roughly 35 miles square and can be crossed by car in less than an hour. Yet within this compact area is a landscape of extraordinary beauty and variety, changing with every valley, lake, and mountain. Rugged peaks and cliffs give way to deep blue lakes, rolling green pastures, isolated farms and villages, and beyond these to the south, the waters of Solway Firth, Morecambe Bay, and the Irish Sea.

The mountains here are not high by international standards—Scafell Pike, England's highest peak, is only 3,210 feet above sea level—but they can be as steep and craggy as the Alps. In the spring, many of the higher summits remain snowcapped long after the weather below has turned mild. The valleys between them cradle famous lakes, more than 100 altogether, ranging in size from tiny mountain pools to 11-mile-long Windermere, the largest lake in England.

As with many regions of England, the Lake District has its own language variations. For instance a lake is a mere as in Buttermere, or water as in Ullswater; a smaller lake is a tarn; mountains are frequently referred to as fells; a waterfall is a force; a small stream is a beck; and the addition of "thwaite," of Scandinavian origin, to place names implies a clearing.

The deep, tranquil lakes bring an extra dimension to the landscape, clearly reflecting the skies, mountain summits, and the rich, ever-changing colors of the surrounding hillside vegetation. For centuries, the region has attracted painters eager to capture the delicate greens of the woods and pastures, the grays and browns of the mountaintops, the white of winter snow, and the brilliant blaze of red, gold, and copper in the fall. October, or even early November, is probably the best time to visit: Colors are at their best and the swamping tide of summer visitors has subsided.

The Lake District is probably best known for its associations with the English Romantic poets, especially William Wordsworth, whose vivid descriptions brought the first tourists here in the early 19th century. Wordsworth was born in the area, and lived in Grasmere, on the banks of Rydal Water. Other literary figures who made their homes in the region include Samuel Taylor Coleridge, Thomas de Quincey, Robert Southey, John Ruskin, Matthew Arnold, and later, Hugh Walpole, children's writer Beatrix Potter, and the poet Norman Nicholson.

The whole area of the Lake District is a national park, the largest and most popular in Britain. Many thousands of acres of land here—about one quarter of the entire park—have been given to or purchased by the National Trust, and the area observes rigid controls on growth and pays strict attention to conservation. But that doesn't mean visitors are not welcome; indeed, the Lake District is one of Britain's most popular vacation spots.

Essential Information

Important Addresses and Numbers

Tourist Information
The main tourist information center for the region is **The Cumbria Tourist Board**, Ashleigh, Holly Rd., Windermere, Cumbria LA23 2AQ, tel. 09662/4444. It is open Mon.–Thurs. 9:30–5:30, Fri. 9:30–5.

Local tourist information centers, normally open Mon.–Sat. 9:30–5:30, but varying according to the season, include:

Kendal: Town Hall, Highgate, tel. 0539/725758.
Keswick: Moot Hall, Market Sq., tel. 07687/72645.
Windermere: The Gateway Centre, Victoria St., tel. 09662/6499.

Travel Agencies
Thomas Cook: 49 Stricklandgate, Kendal, tel. 0539/24258.

Car Rental Agencies
Kendal: Ford Rent a Car, Lakeland Ford, Mintsfeet Rd. S, Mintsfeet Industrial Estate, tel. 0539/23534.
Windermere: Mallison's Motor Tours Ltd., Ellerthwaite Sq., tel. 09662/3215.

Arriving and Departing

By Car
To get to the Lake District from London, take M1 north to M6, getting off either at exit 36 and joining A591 west (around the Kendal bypass to Windermere) or at exit 40, joining A66 direct to Keswick and the northern lakes region. Travel time to Kendal is about four hours; to Keswick, allow about five hours.

By Train
British Rail serves the region from London's Euston Station (tel. 071/387–7070). Take an InterCity train bound for Carlisle, Edinburgh, or Glasgow and change at Oxenholme Lake District Station for the branch line service to Kendal and Windermere. Average travel time to Windermere (including the change) is 4½ hours.

By Bus
National Express (tel. 071/730–0202) serves the region from London's Victoria Coach Station. Average travel time to Kendal is just over seven hours; to Windermere, 7½ hours; and to Keswick, 8¼ hours.
Mountain Goat (tel. 09662/5161) runs a bus service between York and Keswick (Apr.–Oct.).

Getting Around

By Car
Roads within the region are generally very good, although many of the minor routes and mountain passes can be both steep and narrow. Warning signs are normally posted if snow has made a road impassable. In July and August and during the long public holiday weekends, expect heavy traffic congestion. The area has plenty of parking lots, which should be used to avoid blocking narrow lanes or gateways.

By Train
If you're heading for Keswick, it is best to take the train to Windermere and continue from there by **Ribble Motor's** hourly bus service or by taxi. Penrith Station is nearer Keswick, but is awkward to get to by road. Train connections are good around the edges of the Lake District, especially on the Oxeholme–Kendal–Windermere line and the Furness and West Cumbria

branch lines from Lancaster to Grange-over-Sands, Ulverston, Barrow, and Ravenglass.

Seven-day regional **North East Rover** tickets are good for unlimited travel within the area (including trips on the scenic Carlisle–Settle line running just east of the Lake District).

The **Lakeside & Haverthwaite Railway Co.** (tel. 05395/31504) runs vintage steam trains on the branch line between Lakeside and Haverthwaite along Lake Windermere's southern tip.

Ravenglass & Eskdale Railway (tel. 09403/221) offers a steam train service covering the seven miles of glorious countryside between Ravenglass and Dalegarth.

By Bus **Mountain Goat** (tel. 09662/5161) runs a local Lake District minibus service linking Windermere, Ambleside, Glenridding, Ullswater, Keswick, and Buttermere.

The **Cumberland Motor Services** cover the area. Information from tel. 0539/733221.

By Boat An assortment of boats and ferries travel up and down the larger lakes, and offer a fast and fun way to see the region.

Bowness Bay Boating Co. (tel. 09662/3360) runs small vessels around Lake Windermere and to Brockhole National Park Centre.

Keswick-on-Derwentwater Launch Co. (tel. 07687/72263) conducts cruises on vintage motor launches around Derwentwater, leaving from Keswick.

Steam Yacht Gondola (tel. 05394/41288) runs the National Trust's luxurious Victorian steam yacht *Gondola* between Coniston and Park-a-Moor at the south end of Coniston Water, daily from late March through October.

Ullswater Navigation & Transit Co. (tel. 0539/721626) sends its oil-burning 19th-century steamers the length of Lake Ullswater between Glenridding and Pooley Bridge.

Windermere Iron Steamboat Co. (tel. 05395/31539) employs its handsome fleet of vintage cruisers in a regular service between Ambleside, Bowness, and Lakeside on Lake Windermere.

Guided Tours

Guides The **National Park Authority** (tel. 09662/6601) has an advisory service that puts you in touch with members of the Blue Badge Guides, who are experts on the area. They will take you on half-day or full-day walks, and introduce you to the history and natural beauties of the Lake District. The Authority has nine information offices throughout the district.

Special Interest Tours **Mountain Goat Holidays** (tel. 09662/5161) provides special minibus sightseeing tours with skilled local guides.

Tracks North (1 Railway Terr., Lowgill, Kendal, LA8 0BN, tel. 053984/666) conducts escorted railroad tours on vintage steam trains. These run mainly on the Settle and Carlisle line, but also use other scenic rail routes. The package includes hotel accommodations.

Exploring the Lake District

Orientation

Our first tour begins at Windermere, on the wooded shores of the region's largest lake. From here we begin to explore the southern lakes, stopping in Grasmere, a town closely associated with the poet William Wordsworth, then swinging south to the lakeland fells. From here we head south again to Barrow-in-Furness and the bayside resort of Grange-over-Sands before turning north to Kendal.

Our second tour takes us north from Kendal through the wondrously desolate countryside at the foot of Shap Fells to the attractive market town of Penrith. Next we make a sharp detour to Helvellyn, one of the Lake District's most celebrated mountains. On the way west to Keswick and Cockermouth, Wordsworth's birthplace, we pass under the imposing shadow of Blencathra and Skiddaw. Finally we swing east again to Windermere, our starting point.

Highlights for First-time Visitors

Aira Force Waterfalls: Tour 2
Boat Trip on Windermere: Tour 1
Brantwood—Ruskin's Home: Tour 1
Cartmel Priory: Tour 1
Derwentwater: Tour 2
Dove Cottage—Wordsworth's Home: Tour 1
Helvellyn: Tour 2
Holker Hall: Tour 1
Levens Hall Garden: Tour 1
Lodore Falls: Tour 2

Tour 1: From Windermere to Kendal— The Southern Lakes

Numbers in the margin correspond to points of interest on the Lake District map.

Windermere is a natural touring base for the southern half of the Lake District, with its wealth of tourist facilities and good transportation links. The name "Windermere" applies both to the lake and to the main town nearby. The town of **Windermere** was a hamlet originally called Birthwaite, but when the railroad was extended here from Kendal in 1847, local officials named the new station Windermere in order to cash in on the lake's reputation, already well-established thanks to Wordsworth and the Romantic poets. Later, another village by the lake, **Bowness-on-Windermere,** was swallowed by the new town. Today the part of town around the station is known as Windermere, while the lakeside area is still called Bowness. A minibus links the two.

Bowness is definitely more attractive than Windermere. Of special interest is the **New Hall Inn**—best known as the **Hole in t'Wall**—just behind the village center. Its most famous landlord was Thomas Lagmire, a 19th-century Cumbrian wrestler who won no fewer than 174 championship belts (*see* Sports and

The Lake District

CUMBRIA

18 Penrith
Beacon Pike
Pooley Bridge
20 Aira Force
Ullswater
19 Glenridding
Patterdale
Helvellyn
Shap Fells
A6
M6
Lake District National Park Visitor Center
Windermere
3
4 Ambleside
5 Rydal Mount
6 Rydal Water
7 Grasmere
Dove Cottage
A591
Thirlmere
Castlerigg Stone Circle
Keswick
Blencathra
Skiddaw
Latrigg
Derwentwater
21
30 Portinscale
23 Watendlath
22 Borrowdale
24 Lodore
25 Grange
26 Seatoller
27 Borrowdale Fells
Scafell Pike
Bassenthwaite Lake
Newlands Pass
28 Buttermere
Buttermere Fell
Rosthwaite
Crummock Water
B5289
Ennerdale Water
West Water
29 Cockermouth
A66
Bannock
A592
A5091
A591
B5289

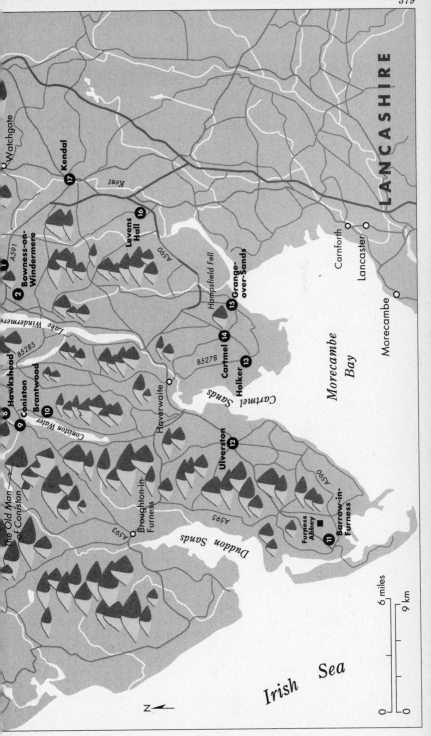

Fitness, below). Charles Dickens once stayed at the inn and described Lagmire as a "quiet-looking giant."

Time Out   At the **Hole in t'Wall** (Fallbarrow Rd.), sample traditional Cumbrian ales and pub lunches of meat pies or Cumbrian sausage in authentic 19th-century surroundings, with slate floors and a flagstoned courtyard.

In Bowness, also visit the 15th-century parish church of **St. Martins,** which has an Anglo-Saxon font, chained Bibles, original stained-glass windows, and an unusual wooden sculpture of St. Martin. One of the stained-glass windows shows the striped coat-of-arms of John Washington, ancestor of George; the design is said to have been the original source of the stripes in the American flag.

Although Windermere's marinas and piers have some charm, you can bypass the busier stretches of shoreline (and in summer they can be packed solid) by walking beyond the boat houses. Here, from among the pine trees, is a fine view across the lake. The car ferry (which also carries pedestrians) crosses the water at this point to reach Far Sawrey and the road to Hawkshead; ferries depart frequently throughout the day and into the evening.

On the other side of the promenade, beyond the main cluster of hotels in Bowness, is the **Windermere Steamboat Museum,** which exhibits a remarkable collection of steam- and motor-powered yachts and launches. The *Dolly,* built around 1850, is one of the two oldest mechanically powered boats in the world. She was raised from the bottom of Ullswater in 1962, having lain there for 70 years. *Rayrigg Rd., tel. 09662/5565. Admission: £2.20 adults, £1.40 children, £5.80 families. Open Easter–Oct., daily 10–5.*

The lake itself, which is 11 miles long, 1½ miles wide, and 200 feet deep, fills a rocky gorge between steep, thickly wooded hills. Its waters make for superb fishing, especially for char, a rare kind of reddish lake trout prized by gourmets.

During the summer, Lake Windermere is alive with all kinds of boats. Waterskiing is a favorite pastime here, and the area can become extremely noisy, so if you're seeking peace and tranquillity, you might be happier on any other of the dozens of lakes in the region (waterskiing is not permitted anywhere else). Nevertheless, a boat trip on Windermere, particularly the round trip from Bowness to Ambleside and down Lakeside (*see* Getting Around, above), remains a wonderful way of spending a few summer hours.

For a memorable view of Lake Windermere—at the cost of a rigorous climb—follow signs near the Windermere Hotel (across from the station) to **Orrest Head.** These will guide you to a rough, uphill track (*see* What to See and Do with Children, below). Eventually you will see a stile on your right; climb over it and continue up the path to a rocky little summit where you can sit on a bench and enjoy a breathtaking panorama of the mountains and lake. The walk back is only a mile, but takes most people at least an hour.

From Windermere, it's easy to reach most of the Lake District's attractions, especially the southern part of the national park and the Furness area. **Brockhole National Park Centre,** three miles northwest from Windermere station on A591, makes a good starting point; it's easily accessible by bus and boat. A magnificent lakeside mansion with terraced gardens sloping down to the water houses the official **Lake District National Park Center.** In addition to tourist information, the center offers a fine range of exhibitions about the Lake District, including geological, agricultural, industrial, wildlife, and literary displays. The gardens are at their best in the spring, when floods of daffodils cover the lawns and the azaleas are bursting into bloom. Park activities include lectures, guided walks, and demonstrations of such lakeland crafts as dry-stone-wall building. There's also a bookstore. *Ambleside Rd., near Windermere, tel. 09662/6601. Admission: £1.90 adults, 90p children, £4.40 family ticket. Open Easter–late Oct., daily 10–4.*

Time Out The **Terrace Cafeteria Restaurant** at Brockhole specializes in local delicacies such as Cumbrian courting cake, "millom yo yos" (chocolate cookies), Helvellyn tarts, rum butter, and tempting salads. It's an ideal place for morning coffee, lunch, or afternoon tea.

Four miles north of Brockhole along A591 at the head of the lake is the town of **Ambleside,** a popular center for Lake District excursions. It lies in the green valley of River Rothay, which empties into Windermere. One of the town's most unusual features is **Bridge House,** a tiny 17th-century cottage perched on an arched stone bridge spanning Stock Beck. Beck is the local word for stream. The building now houses a National Trust shop and information center, open daily from Easter through November.

North of Ambleside the road winds around the lakeside edges of Rydal Water and Grasmere, through a delicate landscape of birch and oak woods, carpeted with wild daffodils in the spring. Here, the craggy mountain summits form a dramatic backdrop.

Continuing north along A591 from Ambleside toward Grasmere (a journey of around 3 mi), you'll pass two places closely associated with William Wordsworth. First you'll come to **Rydal Mount,** where he lived from 1813 until his death 37 years later. Wordsworth and his family moved to these grand surroundings when he was nearing the height of his career, and his descendants still live here, surrounded by his furniture, portraits, and the 4½-acre garden laid out by the poet himself. *Rydal, Ambleside, tel. 05394/33002. Admission: £2 adults, 80p children. Open Mar.–Oct., daily 9:30–5; Nov.–Feb., Wed.–Mon., 10–4.*

You will reach Wordsworth's earlier home, **Dove Cottage,** just before coming to Grasmere. A much humbler place than Rydal Mount, it was the poet's home from 1799 (he moved here when he was 19) until 1808. This tiny house, formerly an inn, still contains much of his furniture and many personal belongings. There's also a coffee shop and restaurant. *Grasmere, tel. 09665/544 or 547. Admission: £3.50 adults, £1.60 children. Open mid-Feb.–mid-Jan., daily 9:30–5. Closed mid-Jan.–mid-Feb.*

Dove Cottage is also the headquarters of the **Centre for British Romanticism,** which documents the contributions Wordsworth and his remarkable associates (sometimes called the Lake Poets) made to world literature. Among these were his sister

Dorothy, Samuel Taylor Coleridge, Thomas De Quincey, and Robert Southey, the last of whom Wordsworth succeeded as poet laureate in 1843. The museum places this outburst of creative genius in its historical, social, and regional context, exhibiting portraits, watercolors, letters, and memorabilia. Poems can be heard on headphone sets in front of display cases of the poets' original manuscripts. The center holds residential summer study conferences on Wordsworth and the Romantics, as well as winter study schools. *The Wordsworth Trust, Dove Cottage, Grasmere LA22 9SH, tel. 09665/544 or 547.*

7 Although Wordsworth was born in Cockermouth, northwest of Keswick, it is the town of **Grasmere,** with its tiny, wood-fringed lake, that is most closely associated with him. Among his American guests here were the American authors Ralph Waldo Emerson and Nathaniel Hawthorne. Grasmere is sometimes overwhelmed in summer by tourists and cars, but it is worth braving the crowds to explore the interesting shops, cafés, and galleries (*see* Shopping, below). Wordsworth, his wife Mary, his sister Dorothy, and his daughter Dora are buried in Grasmere churchyard.

8 Take the minor road out of Grasmere, skirting Rydal Water, and follow the signs south about eight miles to **Hawkshead.** Just outside of town, on B5286, you'll see the **Hawkshead Courthouse,** built by the monks of nearby Furness Abbey in the 15th century. If you're driving, you'll have to leave your car outside the village; it's closed to traffic. Walk in and enjoy its narrow, cobbled streets and little bow-fronted stores. You can see Wordsworth's name carved on a desk at the **Hawkshead Grammar School,** where the poet was a pupil from 1779 to 1787. He later boarded at Ann Tyson's cottage, half a mile north of the village on B5286. *The Courthouse, tel. 05394/33883. Admission free. Open Apr.–Nov., daily 10–5. If you find it locked, ask for the key at the Hawkshead information center.*

9 From Hawkshead, continue south along B5285 for about three miles until you come to **Coniston.** Formerly a copper-mining village, Coniston is now a small lake resort and boating center. Its lake, **Coniston Water,** is also called Goat Tarn. Tracks lead up from the village past an old mine to the **Old Man of Coniston;** you can reach its peak (2,635 feet) in about two hours. Many world speedboat records have been set on the lake at Coniston. Sadly, one attempt ended in tragedy; a stone seat in the village commemorates Sir Donald Campbell's death here in 1967. His body was never recovered after his boat crashed.

10 Just outside Coniston is **Brantwood,** the home of Victorian art critic and social reformer John Ruskin (1819–1900). Drive along the eastern lake shore from Coniston (about 2½ miles), or take the steam yacht gondola from Coniston Pier (*see* Getting Around, above). Brantwood is a rambling white 18th-century house (with Victorian alterations) set in a 250-acre estate. Here you'll find a collection of Ruskin's own paintings, drawings, and books, as well as much of the art he collected in his long life, not least a superb group of drawings by Turner. Ruskin's coach and private boat are still here, too. The extensive grounds, complete with woodland walks, were laid out by Ruskin himself. *Tel. 05394/41396. Admission: £2.40 adults, £1.20 children, £6.25 family ticket. Open mid-Mar.–mid-Nov., daily 11–5:30; mid-Nov.–mid-Mar., Wed.–Sun. 11–4.*

Time Out Brantwood's **Jumping Jenny's** restaurant and tea room offers Pre-Raphaelite decor, an open log fire, and mountain views as the setting for morning coffee, lunch, or afternoon tea.

Leaving Coniston, continue southwest on A593 to A595, passing through **Broughton-in-Furness,** a peaceful little town that seems to have been built with hardly a level space anywhere, until you come to **Barrow-in-Furness,** a trip of about 27 miles. Although Barrow itself is a rather gloomy iron- and steel-producing town, you can visit the ruins of **Furness Abbey,** once one of the wealthiest monasteries in Britain, in the darkly named Vale of Deadly Nightshade, 1½ miles north of town. Founded in 1124, this abbey once owned large tracts of land all over the Lake District. The red sandstone ruins are extensive; what's left intact is a series of graceful arches overlooking the cloisters, and some magnificent canopied seats in the presbytery (the part of the church reserved for the officiating priest). A small visitors center and museum outline the abbey's history. *Tel. 0229/823420. Admission: £1.60 adults, 80p children, £1.20 senior citizens. Open Apr.–Sept., daily 10–6; Oct.–Mar., Tues.–Sun. 10–4.*

About nine miles northeast of Furness Abbey by A590 is the typically Cumbrian market town of **Ulverston,** whose claim to fame is that it is the birthplace of the comedian Stan Laurel (1890–1965). The **Laurel and Hardy Museum** here exhibits films, tapes, props, and personal items of the famous comedy team. *4C Upper Brook St., tel. 0229/52292. Admission: £1 adults, 50p children, £2 family ticket. Open Mon.–Sat. 10–5.*

From Ulverston, follow A590 to Haverthwaite, then turn right onto B5278 for the village of **Holker,** and watch for signs to **Holker Hall.** This mainly 17th-century country house (not to be confused with Holkham Hall in East Anglia), surrounded by a splendid 122-acre deer park, is still owned by the Cavendish family, relatives of the duke of Devonshire. The gardens are not to be missed. There are 25 acres of magnificent displays and an impressive array of fountains, waterfalls, and ponds. A Victorian wing is filled with richly carved woodwork, fine furniture, porcelain, and paintings. There's also a museum of vintage cars, a Victorian and Edwardian kitchen exhibition, an exhibition of patchwork and quilting, an adventure playground, and a cafeteria—enough to occupy the entire family for hours. *Cark-in-Cartmel, tel. 05395/58328. Admission to gardens, grounds, and exhibition: £2.50 adults, £1.40 children; Hall and motor museum extra. Open Easter–Oct., Sun.–Fri. 10:30–4:30 (park until 6).*

When you are at Holker Hall, look for signs to the nearby village of **Cartmel.** This is a charming town with a particularly pretty market square, and its noble **church,** the surviving portion of an Augustinian priory dating from the 14th century, is built on the scale of a cathedral. It has some fine carved choir stalls, impressive memorials, and an unusual, "skewed" central tower. In the churchyard are the graves of local citizens who drowned crossing the sands of the nearby Kent and Leven estuaries. Until the coming of the railroad, these treacherous sand bars provided the only practical route across the area.

From Cartmel, continue east along the minor roads to **Grange-Over-Sands,** an unspoiled 19th-century seaside resort about three miles away. Its sheltered cove overlooks the broad sands of Morecambe Bay. The gardens, quiet promenades, hotels, and shops here offer an atmosphere very different from that of the central lakeland. You can enjoy magnificent views of the lakeland mountains to the north from the top of **Hampsfield Fell** (727 ft.) behind the town.

16 Leaving Grange-Over-Sands, pick up A590 toward Kendal, stopping off after eight miles at **Levens Hall.** This 16th-century house is famous for its rare topiary garden laid out in 1692, with yew and box hedges cut into curious and elaborate shapes. The hall is also notable for its ornate plasterwork, oak paneling, and leather-covered walls. It has a spacious deer park, a fascinating steam engine collection, a store, and a cafeteria. (Buses from Kendal stop here.) *Levens Park, Levens, tel. 05395/60321. Admission: £3.25 adults, £1.65 children, £2.65 senior citizens; gardens only £1.90 adults, 95p children, £1.70 senior citizens. Open Easter–Sept., Sun.–Thurs. 11–5.*

17 Next, continue north 5 miles to the ancient town of **Kendal,** one of the most important textile centers in northern England before the Industrial Revolution. Once you're away from the busy main road, you'll discover quiet, narrow, winding streets and charming courtyards, many dating from medieval times. Take a pleasant stroll along the River Kent where you can visit **Abbott Hall.** Here the **Museum of Lakeland Life and Industry,** housed in the former stable block, offers interesting exhibits on blacksmithing, wheelwrighting, farming, weaving, printing, local architecture and interiors, and regional customs. In the 18th-century main building is the **Art Gallery,** featuring works by Ruskin and 18th-century portrait painter George Romney. *Abbott Hall Park, tel. 0539/722464. Admission: £1.50 adults, 75p children. Open summer, Mon.–Sat. 10:30–5, Sun. 2–5; winter, weekdays 11–4, weekends 2–5.*

Another attraction in Kendal is the multi-faceted **Brewery Arts Centre** (*see* The Arts, below). The town also offers a wide selection of restaurants and pubs.

Tour 2: From Kendal to Keswick

The journey north from Kendal is the longest and bleakest leg of our Lake District tour. This 32-mile drive on A6 will take you through the wild and desolate **Shap Fells,** which rise to a height of 1,304 feet. Even in the summer it's a lonely place to be, and in the snows of winter, the road can be dangerous. As you draw closer to Penrith, the busy M6 expressway, carrying traffic to Scotland, will appear on your right.

18 The town of **Penrith** was the capital of the semi-independent kingdom of Cumbria in the 9th and 10th centuries. Later, Cumbria was part of the Scottish kingdom of Strathclyde; in the year 1070, it was incorporated into England. Even at this time, Penrith was a thriving market town and an important staging post on the road to Scotland. The warning beacon on the hill above the town (**Beacon Pike,** where a stone tower still stands) was lit to alert townsfolk of approaching enemies, usually Scots. The last invasion from Scotland was that of the Jacobites in 1745, who followed Bonnie Prince Charlie in his romantic but ill-fated attempt to restore the Stuart dynasty to the British throne. Charlie and his aides stayed in part of the present **George Hotel** before their retreat.

To find out more about Penrith's history, stop in at the **Penrith Museum** on Middlegate. Built in the 16th century, the building served as a school from 1670 to the 1970s; it now contains a fascinating exhibit of local historical artifacts. Ask at the museum about the historic "town trail" route. It takes you through narrow byways to the **plague stone** on King Street, where food was left for the plague-stricken; to a churchyard with 1,000-year-old "hog-back" tombstones (i.e., stones carved as stylized "houses of the dead"); and finally to the ruins of the 15th-century red sandstone **castle**. *Robinson's School, Middlegate, tel. 0768/64671. Admission free. Opening hours are complicated and liable to change, so check locally.*

Also in Penrith is **Dalemain,** a country house with a 12th-century peel (tower) built to protect the occupants from raiding Scots. A medieval hall was added, as well as a number of extensions from the 16th to the 18th century, culminating in an imposing Georgian facade of local pink sandstone. The result is a delightful hodgepodge of architectural styles. Inside you can see a magnificent oak staircase, furniture dating from the mid-17th century (including Cumbrian "courting" chairs), a Chinese drawing room adorned with hand-painted wallpaper, a 16th-century "fretwork room" with intricate plasterwork, a nursery complete with an elaborate 18th-century dollhouse, and many fine paintings, including masterpieces by Van Dyck. The tower houses a small military museum with mementos from local army regiments. There's also a coffee shop, a picnic area, and sweeping gardens, which include an intriguing Tudor grotto. *Penrith, tel. 07684/86450. Admission to house, garden, and museum: £3 adults, £2 children, £8 family ticket. Open Easter–mid-Oct., Sun.–Thurs. 11:15–5.*

Time Out Five miles northeast of Penrith by A686, in Melmerby, is **The Village Bakery.** It's well worth the detour as the baking is done in a wood-fired brick oven, and the result is cakes and sponges that are sensational. Try the Celebration Fruit Cake. The Calthwaite Jersey cream that accompanies the scones and home-made jam is a weight-watcher's idea of hell.

Leaving Penrith, follow A592 south about six miles along the River Eamont to Ullswater, the region's second-largest lake. Hemmed in by towering hills, it is certainly spectacular. Follow the main road around to **Glenridding** and **Patterdale** at the southern end of the lake and you'll reach the foot of **Helvellyn** (3,118 feet). It is an arduous climb to the top, and shouldn't be attempted in poor weather or by inexperienced hikers. For those who'd rather see Ullswater from a less exalted level, steamers leave Glenridding's pier for Pooley Bridge, offering a pleasant tour along the lake.

Next, backtrack a bit along A592 and make a five-mile detour north on A5091 to **Aira Force,** a spectacular series of waterfalls pounding through a wooded ravine to feed into Ullswater. Just above Aira Force in the woods of Gowbarrow Park, William Wordsworth and his sister Dorothy were walking on April 15, 1802. Dorothy remarked that she had never seen "daffodils so beautiful . . . they tossed and reeled and danced and seemed as if they verily laughed with the wind that blew upon them." Two years later Wordsworth transformed his sister's words into one of the best-known lyric poems in English, "I Wandered Lonely as a Cloud."

21 Leaving Aira Force, continue to follow A5091 north through the tiny villages of Dockray and Matterdale End. When you hit A66, five miles farther on, follow the signs west to **Keswick,** a distance of about 12 miles. Before you enter the town, you might stop off at **Castlerigg Stone Circle.** A clearly marked route leads to a 200-foot-long path running through a pasture; beyond this, set in a great natural hollow called St. John's Vale, stands an intriguing circle of Neolithic or Bronze Age stones, none of them tall, but nonetheless impressive in this awesome setting ringed with mountains. The circle can be visited during daylight hours, and there is no admission charge. The great lakeland mountains of Skiddaw and Blencathra brood over the gray slate houses of Keswick (pronounced "Kezzick"), on the scenic shores of Derwentwater. An old market and mining center, Keswick was transformed by the arrival of the railroad. Since many of the best hiking routes radiate from here, it is more of a touring base than a tourist destination. People stroll the congested, narrow streets in boots and corduroy hiking trousers, and there are plenty of mountaineering shops in addition to hotels, guest houses, pubs, and restaurants.

With a population of only 5,000, Keswick is a compact town, and all the interesting sights lie within easy walking distance of the central streets: Market Place, Main Street, and Lake Road. The town received its market charter in the 13th century, and its Saturday market is still going strong. Later centuries brought a wealth of industries, especially textile manufacturing, which was dependent on power from the area's fast-flowing streams. The introduction of lead and copper mining in the 16th century brought scores of skilled German laborers here.

Time Out   **Bryson's Tearoom** (38–42 Main Street) is a comfortable eatery over a family bakery, with home-cooked lunches and freshly made cakes. You can have a Lakeland tea here with rum butter.

The handsome 19th-century **Moot Hall** (assembly hall) on Market Place has served as both the Keswick town hall and the local prison. Now it houses the **Lake District National Park Information Centre,** as well as the main **tourist information center** for the region.

Keswick offers a number of outdoor attractions, among them **Hope Park,** just beside the lake, with a putting green and an aviary. **Fitz Park,** a garden area bordering the River Greta (just behind the town center), is pleasant for picnics and leisurely strolls. Here you will also find the **Keswick Museum and Art Gallery.** Exhibits include manuscripts by Wordsworth and other lakeland writers, a diorama of the Lake District, a local geological and natural history collection, some unusual "musical" stones, and an assortment of watercolor paintings. *Tel. 07687/73263. Admission: 50p adults, 25p children. Open Mon.–Sat. 10–12:30 and 2–5:30.*

Another aspect of Keswick's history comes into sharp focus at the **Cumberland Pencil Museum.** Keswick was the first place in the world to manufacture pencils, as graphite (the material from which pencil lead is made) was discovered in neighboring Borrowdale in the 16th century. Pencils are still produced here. The museum, housed in the factory just off Main Street, outlines the history of pencils from early times to the present. *Southey Works, tel. 07687/72116. Admission: £1 adults, 50p* *children and senior citizens. Open weekdays 9:30–4:30, weekends 2–5.*

Hill walks originating in Keswick include routes across the **Latrigg** and **Skiddaw** mountains, and the great ridge of **Blencathra.** You can reach Latrigg (1,203 feet), the nearest of the three, from Station Road: Pass the Keswick Hotel, then follow the road under the old railroad bridge, keeping left, toward Briar Rigg. After about 100 yards, a sign on the right indicates the trail to Latrigg—a two-hour round trip from Keswick.

To understand why **Derwentwater** is considered one of England's finest lakes, take a short walk from Keswick's town center to the lake shore, and follow the **Friar's Crag** path—about 15 minutes' level walk from the center. This pine-tree-fringed peninsula is a favorite vantage point, with its view over the lake, the surrounding ring of mountains, and many tiny wooded islands. Ahead you will see the crags that line the **Jaws of Borrowdale** and overhang a dramatic mountain ravine—the perfect setting for a Romantic painting or poem.

Another essential excursion is a wooden-launch cruise around Derwentwater. Between late March and November, cruises set off every hour in each direction from a wooden dock at the lake shore. You can also rent a rowboat here. Landing stages around the lake provide access to some spectacular hiking trails in the nearby hills.

Walking is perhaps the best way to discover the delights of this area. Don't worry if you don't have all the equipment; you can rent a pair of approved hiking boots in Keswick. You may want to leave your car behind, as parking is difficult in the higher valleys, and both the Derwentwater launches and the Borrowdale bus service between Keswick and Seatoller run frequently. A number of pleasant country hotels, guest houses, and bed-and-breakfasts, both on the lake and in the interior valley, can provide a base for your walking excursions.

㉒ If you do decide to explore the area by car, follow B5289 from Keswick along the eastern edge of Derwentwater and turn left when you see the sign for **Watendlath.** Follow either the country lane or the adjacent National Trust path past an old, humpbacked bridge at **Ashness.** Here you are rewarded with a panoramic view of the lake. Next you will come to an isolated · farm beside a small mountain tarn (lake) where one-day fishing licenses are available.

Time Out Daily from April to November, **Watendlath Farm** serves old-fashioned farmhouse teas in its parlors or, in warm weather, on scrubbed tables outside.

㉓ Next rejoin B5289 and turn left. **Lodore's** spectacular waterfall, behind the Lodore Hotel (*see* Dining and Lodging, below), is well worth another slight detour from the main road. Follow **㉔** B5289 about a mile south to the village of **Grange,** at the head of Borrowdale. This is a popular center for walkers, particularly in the summer. An assortment of cafés allows you to fuel up before beginning your vigorous walk across the fells.

㉕ From Grange, drive south about two miles to **Rosthwaite,** a tranquil farming village with an ample supply of bed-and-**㉖** breakfasts and guest houses. **Borrowdale,** the next village along the road, offers a beautiful and varied landscape. The scale is smaller, but the grandeur of these mountains and high meadows recalls the dramatic heights of the Swiss and Austrian Alps. Not all walks in Borrowdale have to be full-fledged hikes or climbs; you can confine yourself to relatively easy lakeshore walks or valley and woodland routes.

㉗ Seatoller, near Borrowdale, is the southernmost village in the Borrowdale valley, lying at 1,176 feet; it's the starting and terminus point for buses to and from Keswick. It is also the location of a Lake District National Park information center (Dalehead Base, Seatoller Barn, tel. 059684/294). Behind Seatoller, the vaultingly steep **Borrowdale Fells** rise up dramatically. Get out and walk wherever inspiration strikes, and in the spring, keep an eye open and your camera ready for newborn lambs roaming the hillsides. From here, to the south, you can also see England's highest mountain, **Scafell Pike** (3,210 feet).

Beyond Seatoller, B5289 turns westward through Honister Pass and Buttermere Fell to the appealing lakeland town of **㉘ Buttermere,** sandwiched between two lakes—the small, narrow **Buttermere** and the much larger **Crummock Water**—at the foot of high, craggy fells. From here, you can return to Keswick by a scenic minor road through **Newlands Pass** (once a silver mining center). The first Lake District guidebook, published in 1778, described the area as having "Alpine views and pastoral scenes in a sublime style."

If you wish to explore further, continue north along B5289 about 13 miles, skirting the east shore of **Crummock Water,** to **㉙ Cockermouth,** the birthplace of William Wordsworth. His childhood home, **Wordsworth House,** is a typical 18th-century north-country gentleman's home, now owned by the National Trust. Some of the poet's furniture and personal items are on display here, and you can explore the garden he played in as a child. *Main St., tel. 0900/824805. Admission: adults £2, children £1. Open Apr.–Oct., Mon.–Wed. and Fri.–Sat. 11–5, Sun. 2–5.*

Wordsworth's father is buried in the churchyard nearby, and in the church itself is a stained-glass window in memory of the poet. Outside is the site of the old grammar school Wordsworth attended, now covered with other buildings. Another pupil here was Fletcher Christian, ringleader of the notorious mutiny on HMS *Bounty;* he was born in 1764 at **Moorland Close,** a farmhouse in the village of Eaglesfield, about two miles outside of town. It is not open to the public. If you wander around Cockermouth you will find a maze of narrow streets, a ruined Norman castle (public access is not permitted), and a traditional outdoor market, held each Monday. An old bell is still rung at the start of trading.

Leaving Cockermouth, start making your way back to Keswick along A66, which hugs the western shore of pretty Bassenthwaite Lake. Stop off at **Lingholm Gardens** in **Portinscale,** just **㉚** outside of Keswick; it's best in the spring or fall, when the rhododendrons, azaleas, gentias, and begonias are in bloom. *Tel. 07687/72003. Admission: £1.95 adults, children free if accompanied. Open Apr.–Oct., daily 10–5; tearoom open Mon.–Sat. 11–5, Sun 1–5.*

If you want to return to Windermere, where Tour 1 began, rejoin A591 just outside Keswick and follow it due south for 26 miles, along the shores of Thirlmere, in the imposing shadow of Helvellyn.

What to See and Do with Children

The Lake District has a lot to offer lively, energetic children, with all those walking trails, lake trips, and scenic steam train rides. The Lake District is an ideal place to introduce children to hiking, providing you start with a modest itinerary. The scenery is wonderful, and you can often plan a walk to an easily reached summit such as **Orrest Head** or **Cat Bells.** The latter was the imaginary home of Beatrix Potter's Mrs. Tiggy-Winkle (*see* Off the Beaten Track, below). **Loughrigg,** near Grasmere, provides another good, gentle climb for young hikers, ending on a dramatic mountaintop.

Boat trips embarking at **Windermere, Coniston, Ullswater,** or **Derwentwater** are popular with children of all ages (*see* Getting Around, above).

A trip on the **Lakeside & Haverthwaite** steam train from Lakeside, Windermere, can be easily combined with a Windermere boat trip. One train journey will provide almost a full day of entertainment. "Little Ratty," the 7½-mile narrow-gauge **Ravenglass & Eskdale Railway,** has small steam locomotives made precisely to scale, hauling a string of miniature cars through glorious scenery. Either drive to Ravenglass or drive to Grange-over-Sands and then catch the **Furness Line** train from Grange to Ravenglass. This line, too, offers a spectacular trip across an undulating landscape of mountains and estuaries. Train schedules are available at tourist information centers.

Several of the larger country houses in Cumbria, including **Dalemain, Levens Hall,** and **Holker Hall,** offer fun-filled adventure parks (*see* Tour 1).

Abundant wildlife and livestock populations in the Lake District can provide an extra treat for children, at special unexpected moments. Watch for hares leaping across your path, pheasants starting out of the woods, or newborn lambs wobbling around in search of their mothers.

Off the Beaten Track

Superb areas of scenic desolation are never far away in the Lake District. One such area lies to the east, toward the hills of the North Pennines. To get there, take A591 from Windermere directly to Kendal, then follow the signs on A684 to **Sedbergh,** nine miles east. This quiet, small town sits on the edge of the **Howgill Fells,** a cluster of dome-like, green hills offering marvelous hiking territory.

It was in this quiet setting that the Friends (Quaker) sect was founded. In 1642, on a hillside here called **Firbank Knots** (about 4 mi from Sedbergh), George Fox preached to a thousand "seekers," who were later to become the founding members of the international Quaker movement. At **Brigflatts,** just off A683, a mile west of Sedbergh, you can visit one of the world's first Quaker meeting-houses, virtually unchanged since it was built in the 1670s.

To complete a circular tour of the Howgills, follow scenic A683
north about 12 miles to the little-known town of **Kirkby Stephen,** with its ancient church and attractive old marketplace.
From here you can return to Kendal (via Tenby) along A685. On
the way you'll pass the dramatic scenery of **Lune Gorge** where
highway, expressway, and railroad squeeze through a narrow
pass between the mountains. From Windermere, the round-
trip to the Howgills is about 60 miles.

There is some lovely, tranquil countryside north and east of
Keswick. **Silloth,** for example, is an old seaside resort on the
Solway Firth (the body of water tucked between north
Cumbria and southwest Scotland), famous for its beautiful sunsets. To get there, follow A591 north past Lake Bassenthwaite
to Bothel, turn southwest onto A595, and then travel 3 miles
before picking up B5301 to Silloth, via Aspatria. You can return
by taking the coastal road B3500 to Maryport, then A594 to
Cockermouth. In Cockermouth, pick up A66 south to Keswick.

It is difficult to escape literary associations in the Lake District, as so many writers have been inspired by its landscape or
have sought a quiet refuge here. If you travel to the village of
Hawkshead via the Windermere ferry, you'll pass **Hill Top,**
home of children's author and illustrator Beatrix Potter, most
famous for her *Peter Rabbit* stories. Now run by the National
Trust, Hill Top is a popular—and often crowded—spot, even
though it is definitely off the beaten track. The house is so tiny
that admission has to be strictly controlled. Try to avoid visiting on summer weekends and during school vacations. You can
also get to Hill Top by car. It's two miles south of Hawkshead on
B5285. *Near Sawrey, Ambleside, tel. 09666/269. Admission:
£2.90 adults, £1.50 children. Open Apr.–Oct., Sat.–Wed. 11–5.*

Another popular National Trust reserve in this area is **Tarn
Hows.** Here you can take an easy walk through ancient pines
and around a magnificent, man-made lake (about 45 minutes).
Follow signs on B5285 between Hawkshead and Coniston;
parking is available at the reserve.

Shopping

The huge influx of visitors to the Lake District has proved a
spur to shopkeepers in general, and craft workshops in particular. Jewelry and knitted wear are particularly well served here,
while items made from horn and wood, together with pottery
and glassware, are featured all over the area.

Grasmere **Craglands, The Weaving Mill Shop,** and **Jumpers** (all on Stock
La.) sell high-quality woolens, including cashmeres, mohairs,
and Arran sweaters.
For something a little different try **The English Lakes Perfumery** (College St.), which offers locally produced perfumes, floral scents, lotions, soaps, and creams; you can sample the
perfumes at a test bar before buying.
Heaton Cooper Studio (opposite the village green) has a large
selection of reproductions of watercolors of the Lake District,
as well as changing exhibits of originals.

Kendal An excellent place for serious shopping, Kendall has its more
interesting stores tucked away in the quiet lanes and courtyards around Market Place, Finkle Street, and Stramongate.
Henry Roberts Bookshop (Stramongate), in Kendal's oldest

house (a 16th-century cottage), has a superb selection of lakeland books.

Seasons (Market Pl.), within a cluster of medieval courtyards, sells stylish ladies' clothing and jewelry.

The main road through town, although busy, has some good antiques shops and galleries, but for high-quality Lake District crafts, you might want to concentrate your efforts on the store in the **museum** at the bottom of Highgate, where you can buy woven goods, tiles, ceramics, and glass, all of exceptional quality.

At Sedburgh, you'll find the Farfield Mill, where **Pennine Tweeds** (Hawes Rd.) produce and sell all kinds of scarves, ties, and hats.

Keswick Thanks to its size, Keswick is probably the most sophisticated shopping area in the Lake District. Around Lake Road you'll find such stores as **Maysons** (Lake Rd.), which sells Celtic Art Nouveau and jewelry, as well as leather and glass goods.

Fine Designs (John St.) sells pottery, baskets, small chests, and silver jewelry.

Look, too, for **Derwent Jewellers,** which specializes in semiprecious stone mounting, including blue agates, garnets, cairngorms (a type of quartz), rose quartz, and turquoises.

George Fisher (Borrowdale Rd.) is famous for outdoor clothing: parkas, boots, skiwear, and many other kinds of sportswear.

You will also find a good choice of bookstores, crafts shops, and wool clothing stores in Keswick. There are a few boutiques, too, such as **Laura Hardy** (Bank St.), which sells classic tweeds, knitwear, gloves, and hats; this store also has a mailing service for sending purchases anywhere in the world.

Millom Across the channel from Barrow-in-Furness, in Millom, is **Schone Leder Mode** (Newton St.), which makes leather clothing to measure.

Windermere You'll find the best range at the Bowness end of town on Lake Road and around Queen's Square: clothing stores, craft shops, and souvenir stores of all kinds.

Titus Wilson (Queen's Sq.) has an outstanding range of English cut glass and fine bone china, including Royal Brierly, Wedgwood, Royal Doulton, and Crown Derby.

Abbey Horn of Kendal (Crag Brow) is one of the last British firms to practice the craft of horn-carving; its craftsmen make a remarkable variety of goods, including jewelry, utensils, mugs, and walking sticks with elaborately carved handles.

Glasform (Quarry Rigg), in a newer shopping area higher up Lake Road, sells blown glassware shot through with color, after designs by the local artist John Ditchfield.

Lakeland Jewellers (Crag Brow) has the local experts setting semiprecious stones in necklaces, pendants, rings, bracelets, earrings, and brooches.

Hawthorns (Crag Brow) specializes in quality English and Scottish clothing and designer knitwear in lambs' wool and cashmeres; some of the brands sold are Ballantyne, Pringle, and Burberry.

The Lakeland Sheepskin Centre (Lake Rd.), which also has branches in Bowness, Ambleside, and Keswick, offers moderately priced leather and sheepskin goods, as well as woolens and knitting wool.

If you'd like to take a piece of lakeland slate back home, **Brian**

Johnson (Oak St.) will, given a day's notice, etch your address on a slate shingle; it also sells slate-mounted clocks and ther-mometers.

Markets The town center in Kendal holds a market on Mondays, Wednesdays, and Saturdays. Keswick's market is on Wednesdays and Saturdays.

Sports and Fitness

Fishing If you are tempted by the thought of landing the elusive char, or even the common perch, pike, and eel, you can buy a one-day fishing license for Windermere, Derwentwater, or the River Greta, at the **Windermere Tourist Information Center** or at **Temple's Sports** (9 Station St., Keswick).

Golf Visitors are welcome at the **Windermere** (tel. 09662/3123) and **Grange-over-Sands** (tel. 05395/33180) golf courses. **The Derwentwater Hotel** near Keswick (*see* Dining and Lodging, below) will arrange special golf vacations.

Hiking Walking and mountaineering are, inevitably, the primary sports in the Lake District. Rock climbing, except for the experienced, should be undertaken only with a guide. **Mountain Adventure Guides** (Eel Crag, Melbecks, Braithwaite, west of Keswick, CA12 5TL, tel. 059682/517), and **Summitreks** (14 Yewdale Rd., Coniston, LA21 7DU, tel. 05394/41212) coordinate climbing trips for either individuals or groups on a daily or weekly basis, and accommodations are arranged where needed.

Water Sports Water sports thrive on the lakes, especially Windermere. The **Lakeside Hotel** (Newby Bridge, Ulverston, LA12 8AT, tel. 05395/31207) on Windermere arranges full programs for guests, including sailing, fishing, and waterskiing, at package prices.

At **Windermere Lake Holidays Afloat** (Shepherds Boatyard, Bowness Bay, Windermere, LA23 3HE, tel. 09662/4315) you can rent every kind of boat, from small sailboats to large cabin cruisers.

Wrestling and Fell Running Folk sports in the Lake District include Cumberland and Westmorland wrestling, a variety of traditional English wrestling in which the opponents must maintain a grip around each others' body. Fell (cross-country) running is also popular in these parts. Not surprisingly, local shepherds dominate the latter sport. These sports are often the highlights at local shows and meets like the Grasmere sports event in August. A calendar of events is available at tourist information centers.

Dining and Lodging

Dining Cumbria is noted for its good country food. Dishes center on the abundant local supply of lamb, beef, game, and fish, especially salmon and river and lake trout hooked from the district's network of freshwater streams and lakes. Cumberland sausage, a thick, meaty pork sausage which is a meal in itself, is another regional specialty. You may also enjoy the baked goodies here: bread, cake, pastries, gingerbread, and scones.

Apart from local traditional fare, Cumbria offers health food and vegetarian restaurants as well as some excellent Continental ones. Standards vary, so it's worth doing a little research. Pubs often give the best value at lunchtime, offering appetizing bar lunches at prices beginning as low as £1.50.

Highly recommended restaurants are indicated by a star ★.

Category	Cost*
Expensive	£25–£30
Moderate	£12–£25
Inexpensive	under £12

per person, including first course, main course, dessert, and VAT; excluding drinks

Lodging The Lake District has been attracting tourists for over 200 years, and has built up a reputation for taking good care of them. You'll find everything from small country inns to grand lakeside hotels, most with a charm befitting their rich past. There are more modern hotels and motels as well, but these tend to lack the rural ambience most visitors expect from the Lake District. Medium-size, family-run hotels can offer the best value and plenty of comfort and hospitality. Don't overlook the bed-and-breakfasts (B&Bs), however: They provide the cheapest, simplest accommodations, and come in every shape and size, from the house on Main Street renting out one room to farmhouses with an entire wing to spare.

Most hotels gladly cater to keen hikers and climbers, and can provide you with on-the-spot information and advice for these pursuits. Their lounges and bars are filled with photographs, route maps, and newspaper clippings recording the derring-do of Lake District climbers past and present.

Summer is the busiest season here—and that means *very* busy indeed; at other times of the year you can travel easily without advance reservations, choosing your accommodations once you're actually in the region.

Highly recommended lodgings indicated by a star ★.

Category	Cost*
Very Expensive	over £130
Expensive	£80–£130
Moderate	£45–£80
Inexpensive	under £45

All prices are for two people sharing a double room, including service, breakfast, and VAT.

Askham
Lodging

Queen's Head Inn. The Queen's Head is a very friendly 17th-century inn. Big open fires, plenty of shining copper and brass, pleasant old furniture, and simple, comfortable bedrooms, all make this a good selection. *Near Penrith, CA10 2PF, tel. 09312/225. 6 rooms, none with bath or shower. Facilities: restaurant. No credit cards. Inexpensive.*

Braithwaite
Lodging

Coledale Inn. This early 19th-century inn and adjacent guest house in the quiet village of Braithwaite (about 3 mi west of Keswick on A66) offers good food, real ale, and comfortable rooms with great views. Superb mountain hiking, guided walks, and mini-tours can be arranged here. *Braithwaite, CA12 5TN, tel. 059682/272. 8 rooms with bath. Facilities: restaurant. MC. Inexpensive.*

Kendal
Dining
★

The Moon. A bistro ambience prevails in this small, centrally located restaurant. Its good reputation has been won with quality homemade foods, including chicken dishes. Caribbean seafood chowder, beef and mango casserole, and cheesecake and homemade ice cream are among the selections. Good house wines are available, too. *129 Highgate, tel. 0539/729254. Reservations advised. Dress: informal. MC, V. Inexpensive.*

Keswick
Dining

La Primavera. The River Greta runs below this stylish restaurant at the north end of town. Here you have a choice of English or Italian dishes—the grilled steaks are particularly good—and a good wine list. *Greta Bridge, High Hill, tel. 07687/74621. Reservations advised. Dress: informal. MC, V. Moderate.*

★ **The Four in Hand.** This is a typical Cumbrian pub, with a 19th-century paneled bar decorated with horse brasses and banknotes. The imaginative touches in its lunch menu include hot asparagus rolled in ham, and pâté with red currant jelly; the traditional dishes are steaks, meat pies, and Cumberland sausage. *Lake Rd., tel. 07687/72744. Reservations not required. Dress: informal. No credit cards. Inexpensive.*

The Oasis. This is a pleasant and unpretentious restaurant in the center of Keswick. Fresh trout, savory pancakes, and fine desserts are among the specialties. *13 Main St., tel. 07687/ 72722. Reservations not required. Dress: informal. No credit cards. Closed Wed. Inexpensive.*

Lodging

Keswick Hotel. Turrets and balconies are the most noticeable architectural characteristics of this Victorian hotel. Built to serve railroad travelers in the 19th century, it has all the grandeur and style of that age, although it has been modernized and incorporated into the Trusthouse Forte hotel chain. It sits in 4½ acres of private gardens in the center of Keswick. There is a large conservatory where tea is served. *Station Rd., CA12 4NQ, tel. 07687/72020. 66 rooms with bath. Facilities: restaurant, putting green, croquet lawn. AE, DC, MC, V. Expensive.*

★ **Lyzzick Hall Country House Hotel.** Set in two acres on the lower slopes of Skiddaw (2 mi northwest of Keswick on A591), this converted country house boasts superb views across Derwentwater. *Underskiddaw, near Keswick, CA12 4PY, tel. 07687/72277. 20 rooms with bath. Facilities: heated pool, restaurant. AE, DC, MC, V. Closed Feb. Moderate.*

Skiddaw Hotel. Recently renovated, this is a modern hotel at the edge of Market Square, with a fine interior decor and good facilities. *Market Sq., CA12 5BN, tel. 07687/72071. 40 rooms with bath. Facilities: restaurant, gym, sauna, solarium, free golf (weekdays). AE, DC, MC, V. Moderate.*

Highfield Hotel. Overlooking the lawns of Hope Park between Keswick and Derwentwater, this small hotel is comfortable and serves good, home-cooked food. *The Heads, CA12 5ER, tel. 07687/72508. 19 rooms, 15 with bath. Facilities: restaurant, bar. No credit cards. Closed Nov.–Easter. Inexpensive.*

Lodore
Dining and Lodging
★

Lodore Swiss Hotel. Opened by a Swiss family, this famous hotel is now run by a Greek hotelier. Near the great waterfall at Lodore on Derwentwater, this large, comfortable, world-class country lodge, with its plethora of facilities, is about two miles south of Keswick on B5289 (served by motor launch) in the Borrowdale Valley. The restaurant offers superb Anglo-Swiss cuisine in elegant surroundings. *Lodore, CA12 5UX, tel. 059684/285. 70 rooms with bath. Facilities: bar, swimming pool, squash, tennis, solarium, sun terrace, gym. Restaurant reservations advised. Jacket and tie required. AE, DC, MC, V. Closed Nov.–Feb. Expensive.*

Penrith
Dining

Passepartout. Continental, Italian, and unusually good English cuisines are offered here, with the emphasis on local specialties like wild boar, venison, Dumfries (Scottish) salmon, and lobster. There is also an international wine list. *51 Castlegate, tel. 0768/65852. Reservations advised. Jacket and tie required. MC, V. Dinner only Mon.–Sat. Moderate.*

Pooley Bridge
Dining and Lodging
★

Sharrow Bay. Set between the lush green fields near Pooley Bridge and the increasingly rugged crags around Howtown, the hotel commands a view of exceptional and varied beauty. Its luxurious appointments complement its stunning surroundings; the bedrooms are extremely comfortable and the cuisine renowned for many years. If the hotel has one fault it is that the decoration, both of the rooms and of the food, could be a little more restrained. The rooms in the two annexes are somewhat more simple, especially those in Bank House, about 1½ miles away. *Pooley Bridge, Ullswater, CA10 2LZ, tel. 07684/86301. 30 rooms, 26 with bath. Room charges include dinner. Restaurant reservations necessary. Jacket and tie required. AE, DC, MC, V. Closed Nov.–early Mar. Very expensive.*

Portinscale
Lodging

Derwentwater Hotel. Named after the lake it is set on, this handsome hotel has 16 acres of gardens, and specializes in activity vacations for those interested in wind surfing, fishing, hiking, mountaineering, and golf. Equipment loans and instruction are offered at the hotel. *West of Keswick, Portinscale, CA12 5RE, tel. 07687/72538. 57 rooms with bath. Facilities: 9-hole putting green, tennis, lawn bowling, restaurant, bar, coffee shop. AE, DC, MC, V. Moderate.*

Seatoller
Dining
★

Yew Tree Restaurant. The atmosphere here is intimate and gracious, and the inventive menu is based largely on local produce. Specialties include pan-fried trout and, as an appetizer, avocado with Stilton sauce and port. Other English country dishes, including venison, hare, eel, and salmon, are seasonally available. The low-beamed ceiling, long open fireplace, and excellent bar add to the pleasure of eating here. *Borrowdale, tel. 07687/77634. Reservations advised. Dress: informal. Closed Mon., Sat. lunch and Nov.–Mar. MC. Moderate.*

Ulverston
Dining

Bay Horse Inn. This restaurant, 1¼ miles east of Ulverston, is a pub and bistro combined, with the bistro situated in a veranda over the water. The cooking here is thoroughly imaginative and unexpected. There may be cheese and fennel soup, pork cutlet with sage and apple purée, moules marinière, or sweetbreads with tongue and mushrooms in marsala listed on one of the ever-changing menus. There's a great view over the Morecambe estuary to enjoy while you eat. *Canal Foot, tel. 0229/53972. Reservations necessary. Dress: informal. MC, V. Closed Sun. evening and Mon. Moderate.*

Windermere
Dining

Jackson's Bistro. Classic dishes such as seafood mornay, barbecued chicken, duck liver pâté, and veal *cordon bleu* are served with panache in this stylish Victorian cellar restaurant. *West End Buildings, Bowness-on-Windermere, tel. 09662/6264. Reservations advised. Dress: informal. AE, MC, V. Moderate.*

★ **Porthole Eating House.** Located in an 18th-century house in the center of Bowness, the restaurant has a French and Italian menu featuring homemade pasta and excellent fish dishes, including fresh salmon and (when available) Windermere char; the cellars contain some excellent German wines. *3 Ash St., Bowness-on-Windermere, tel. 09662/2793. Reservations advised. Dress: informal. Closed Tues. AE, DC, MC, V. Moderate.*

Roger's. This is a central restaurant, small and darkly decorated, but with a menu that contains the best French food in the region. There may be suckling pig with apricot sauce or fillet of salmon with sorrel sauce offered. There's a good selection of cheeses, some very rich desserts, and a short but interesting wine list. *4 High St., tel. 09662/4954. Reservations essential. Dress: informal. AE, DC, MC, V. Dinner only Mon.–Sat. Moderate.*

Dining and Lodging **Miller Howe.** A small hotel with an international reputation for ★ comfort and cuisine, it is beautifully situated, with views across Windermere to the Langdale Pikes. Every attention has been given to the decor, which includes fine antiques and paintings in the lounges. The bedrooms, too, have exceptional style, and fresh flowers are everywhere. The outstanding restaurant serves an imaginative set menu that has been masterminded by John Trovey, renowned for his experimental cuisine. This award-winning restaurant also has an excellent wine list. *Rayrigg Rd., Bowness-on-Windermere LA23 1EY, tel. 09662/ 2536. 13 rooms with bath. Half-board only. Restaurant reservations required. Jacket and tie required. AE, DC, MC, V. Closed Dec.–mid-Mar. Hotel: Very Expensive. Restaurant: Expensive.*

Holbeck Ghyll. Holbeck Ghyll lies a little to the north of Windermere town, beyond the Brockhole Visitor Centre. It is a sturdy stone country house, with sweeping views over lake and fells. Open fires, four-poster beds, and magnificent food in the paneled dining room contribute to the uniqueness of this inn. *Holbeck Lane, LA23 1LU, tel. 05394/32375. 14 rooms with bath or shower. Facilities: restaurant, garden. MC, V. Moderate.*

Lodging **The Langdale Chase.** This hotel's four acres of gardens overlook Windermere, and it has its own dock. Built in the 19th century and tastefully refurbished, its atmosphere of grandeur is evoked by the baronial entrance hall and oak-paneled lounge. The hotel is just off A591, halfway between Windermere and Ambleside. *Ambleside LA23 1LW, tel. 05394/32201. 35 rooms, some in separate lodges, 33 with bath or shower. Facilities: restaurant, lake swimming, boating, tennis, miniature golf. AE, DC, MC, V. Expensive.*

Craig Foot Country House. A stone villa built in 1848 for a retired admiral has been converted into a charming small hotel with its own garden. Several bedrooms overlook the lake. *Lake Rd., Bowness-on-Windermere, LA23 3AR, tel. 09662/3902. 10 rooms with bath. Call for restrictions. Facilities: restaurant, cocktail lounge. Closed Nov.–Mar. V. Moderate.*

Hideaway Hotel. Ivy-covered lakeland-stone walls and a large garden surround this hotel, a tranquil setting for its comfortable rooms and good service. There are fireplaces in the bar and lounge, and the restaurant's Swiss-trained chef prepares English and Continental dishes. *Phoenix Way, LA23 1DB, tel. 09662/3070. 16 rooms with bath. No credit cards. Moderate.*

The Mortal Man. This converted 17th-century lakeland inn is in a valley about three miles north of Windermere, well away from the bustle of the town; there are magnificent views all around. *Troutbeck LA23 1PL, tel. 05394/33193. 12 rooms with bath. Call for restrictions. Facilities: restaurant, bar. No credit cards. Closed mid-Nov.–mid-Feb. Moderate.*

★ **Archway.** This is a centrally located guest house on a quiet street, but with some terrific mountain views. It's a stone Victorian building, with some solid Victorian furnishings and comfortable bedrooms. The home cooking is notably good. *13 College Rd., LA23 1BY, tel. 09662/5613. 6 rooms, 4 with bath. No credit cards. Inexpensive.*

The Arts

Theaters The **Brewery Arts Centre** in Kendal is a converted brewery that now holds an **art gallery,** a **theater,** a **theater workshop,** and a **cinema.** One of the most active centers of creative performance in the southern part of the Lake District, it offers special events, festivals, and art exhibitions throughout the year. It also has an excellent coffee bar, a real-ale bar, and a health food café open for lunch. *Highgate, tel. 0539/725133. Open Mon.–Sat. 9 AM–11 PM. Free parking.*

The Lake District has a history of little theaters that come and go, providing excellent entertainment during the summer season. **Theatre-in-the-Forest** in Grizedale offers daytime exhibitions and evening plays, folk concerts, special events, and guest appearances. *Near Hawkshead, tel. 0229/860291. Open Tues.–Sat. 10–5.*

Another little theater that has had its ups and downs, but if still running in 1992 would provide an exciting summer evening's entertainment, is Keswick's **Century Theater,** *tel. 07687/74411.*

13 East Anglia

Introduction

Occupying an area of southeastern England which juts out, knoblike, into the North Sea, East Anglia comprises the counties of Essex, Norfolk, Suffolk, and Cambridgeshire.

Despite its easy access from London, East Anglia (with the notable exception of Cambridge) is relatively unfamiliar to tourists. Although it was a region of major importance in ancient and medieval times, East Anglia was bypassed by the Industrial Revolution and has remained somewhat of a backwater ever since. The deflection of industrialization preserved much of the special cultural character and the stunning landscape—which inspired two of the greatest English painters in that genre, Thomas Gainsborough, who was born in Sudbury, Suffolk; and John Constable, also born and bred in Suffolk.

The fens in Norfolk are unforgettable, the water in the marshes and dikes reflect the arching sky that stretches to seemingly infinite horizons, a sky deeply blue and with ever-changing cloudscapes. The sunsets here are to be treasured. The fens resemble areas of Holland directly across the North Sea and, indeed, much of the drainage work here was carried out by Dutch engineers.

To the south, in both Norfolk and Suffolk, the reed-bordered Broads make a gentler landscape of canals and lakes that are ideal for boating and alive with birds and animals. Along the coast, stretches of sand dunes alternate with low cliffs and with areas—in some cases whole communities—lost to the encroaching sea.

The cities and villages of East Anglia have kept intact their ancient architecture, much of it financed with the wealth from medieval wool, once prized across Europe. Few parts of Britain can boast so many stately churches and half-timbered houses. The area encourages one to savor the past, as generations of local families have done in this inspiring landscape.

Essential Information

Important Addresses and Numbers

Tourist Information
East Anglia Tourist Board. Toppesfield Hall, Hadleigh, Suffolk IP7 7DN, tel. 0473/822922. Open weekdays 9–5:15; May–Sept., also Sat. 10–4.

Tourist information centers, normally open Mon.–Sat. 9:30–5:30 but varying according to the season, include:

Bury St. Edmunds: 6 Angel Hill, tel. 0284/764667.
Cambridge: Wheeler St., tel. 0223/322640.
Colchester: 1 Queen St., tel. 0206/712233.
Ipswich: Town Hall, Princes St., tel. 0473/258070.
Lincoln: 9 Castle Hill, tel. 0522/529828.
Norwich: Guildhall, Gaol Hill, tel. 0603/666071.

Travel Agencies
American Express, 25 Sidney St., Cambridge, tel. 0223/351636.
Thomas Cook, 5 Market Hill, Cambridge, tel. 0223/312996; 15 St. Stephens St., Norwich, tel. 0603/621547; and 4 Cornhill Pavement, Lincoln, tel. 0522/26789.

Car-Rental Agencies	**Cambridge. Avis,** 243 Mill Rd., tel. 0223/212551; **Budget Rent a Car,** Cecil & Larter, 303–305 Newmarket Rd., tel. 0223/323838; **Hertz,** Willhire Ltd., 41 High St., Chesterton, tel. 0223/63443.

Colchester. Godfrey Davis Europcar Ltd., Crescent Garage, Pownall Cres., tel. 0206/45676; **Hertz,** Willhire Ltd., Rota House, Cowdray Ave., tel. 0206/866559.

Lincoln. Godfrey Davis Europcar Ltd., Hartford Motors, Wragby Rd., tel. 0522/30101.

Norwich. Budget Rent a Car, Paxstar Ltd., Clarence Garage, Thorpe Rd., tel. 0603/666986/7.

Arriving and Departing

By Car From London, Cambridge (54 miles) is just off M11. At exit 9, M11 connects with A11 to Norwich (114 miles), A45, off A11, goes to Bury St. Edmunds. A12 from London goes through east Suffolk via Colchester, Ipswich, and Great Yarmouth. For Lincoln (131 miles), take A1 via Huntingdon, Peterborough, and Grantham to A46 at Newark-on-Trent. A more scenic alternative is to leave A11 at Grantham and take A607 to Lincoln.

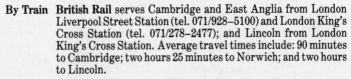

The new London orbital freeway, M25, has opened alternative routes into East Anglia. From the west of London, take M11 to the M25 intersection and then head east on M25, taking the first exit (A12). From south London, take A2 to Dartford/Swanley, join M25 heading through the Dartford Tunnel (toll 70p); 10 miles after the tunnel, take A12 heading east.

By Train **British Rail** serves Cambridge and East Anglia from London Liverpool Street Station (tel. 071/928–5100) and London King's Cross Station (tel. 071/278–2477); and Lincoln from London King's Cross Station. Average travel times include: 90 minutes to Cambridge; two hours 25 minutes to Norwich; and two hours to Lincoln.

By Bus **National Express** (tel. 071/730–0202) serves the region from London's Victoria Coach Station. Average travel times: 2½ hours to Bury St. Edmunds; two hours to Cambridge; two hours five minutes to Colchester; four hours to Lincoln; and three hours to Norwich.

Getting Around

By Car East Anglia has few fast main roads. Within Norfolk, for example, there are only a couple of short stretches of dual-carriageways (four-lane highways) and no motorways at all. Traveling within the region often means taking country lanes with many twists and turns. These are also used by slow-moving farm vehicles but as the countryside is mainly flat, open land, visibility is excellent.

By Train You can get a one-day, round-trip ticket for the East Suffolk line from Ipswich to Lowestoft (50 miles) which lets you disembark to explore any of the little towns en route. A seven-day "Regional Rover" ticket for unlimited travel in East Anglia is also available.

By Bus **Eastern Counties** (tel. 0603/760076) provides local bus services for East Anglia.

Guided Tours

Qualified guides for walking tours of the five touring bases—Bury St. Edmunds, Cambridge, Colchester, Lincoln, and Norwich—may be booked through the respective tourist information centers.

Scudamores Boatyards (tel. 0223/359750) offer a 40-minute chauffeur punt tour through the Backs of the Cambridge colleges.

The Colchester Carriage Company (tel. 0206/46498) runs tours for up to 11 people in its unique, 1930s-style minibus.

Mrs. Harvey (tel. 072876/226) offers a tour of rural Suffolk by horse and carriage followed by lunch or dinner.

Byways Bicycles (tel. 072877/764) has a choice of bicycles for hire, with planned routes to choose from in Suffolk.

Exploring East Anglia

Orientation

We have divided East Anglia into four tours. The first starts in the ancient university city of Cambridge, then moves to the cathedral town Ely to the north. South of Cambridge lie the attractive small towns whose prosperity was built on the medieval wool trade. They have lovely buildings and disproportionally large churches to see. The second tour starts in Norwich, a town with atmosphere to spare, which lies beside the lake-strewn Broads and near to the beaches and salt marshes of the North Sea coast. The third tour begins in Colchester, in the south of East Anglia, and takes in the sweep of the Suffolk Heritage Coast, which runs northeast toward Aldeburgh. A final jump takes you away to Lincoln in the north of the region, with its tall, fluted cathedral towers rising above the rolling hills of the Lincolnshire Wolds; and then to Boston, from where the Pilgrims tried, without success, to sail to the New World.

Highlights for First-time Visitors

Audley End House: Tour 1
Blickling Hall: Tour 2
Cambridge—Queen's College and King's College Chapel: Tour 1
Ely Cathedral: Tour 1
Flatford: Tour 3
Holkham Hall: Tour 2
Lavenham Church: Tour 1
Lincoln Cathedral: Tour 4
Norwich Cathedral: Tour 2
Suffolk Heritage Coast: Tour 3

Tour 1: Cambridge and the Suffolk Wool Churches

Numbers in the margin correspond to points of interest on the East Anglia and Cambridge maps.

With the spires of its university buildings framed by towering trees and expansive meadows, its medieval streets and passages enhanced by gardens and the riverbanks, the city of
❶ **Cambridge** is among the loveliest in England. Situated on a

East Anglia

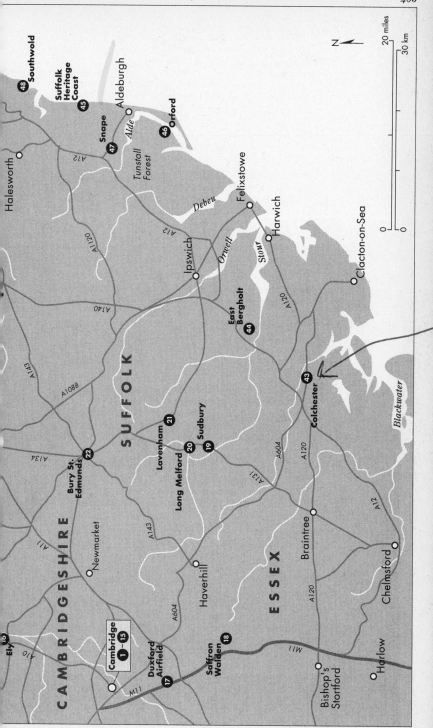

bend of the River Cam, on the edge of the once uninhabited and inhospitable Great Fen, the city has been settled since prehistoric times. It was a Roman town, and later the Cam helped to protect it from Danish raiders. During the Middle Ages, Cambridge gained its real importance with the founding of the university which is still the heart of the city. Several college buildings survive from the medieval period, and most generations since have added more buildings. These were often designed by the best architects of their respective periods and financed by royal or aristocratic foundations, with the result that today the city and university provide an illustrated history of the best of English architecture.

For centuries the University of Cambridge has been among the very greatest universities, rivaled in Britain only by Oxford; and, since the time of its most famous scientific alumnus, Sir Isaac Newton, it has outshone Oxford in the natural sciences. During the past 10 years, the university has taken advantage of its scientific prestige, pooling its research facilities with various "high-tech" industries. The city is now surrounded by space-age factories, and a new prosperity has enlivened the city center.

The colleges are built around a series of courts, or quadrangles, whose velvety lawns are the envy of many an amateur gardener. As students and fellows (faculty) live and work in these courts, access for tourists is restricted, especially in term time (when the university is in session). Tourists are not normally allowed into college buildings other than chapels and dining halls. The peace of the college courts is quite remarkable, and just to stroll through them gives an immediate sense of over 700 years of scholastic calm.

2 The oldest college is **Peterhouse,** on Trumpington Street, founded in 1280 by a monk from Merton College, Oxford. Parts of the dining hall date from 1286; the chapel, in late Gothic style, dates from 1632. On the river side of the buildings is a large and tranquil deer park—without any deer, but with some good apple trees!

3 Across the road stands **Pembroke College,** whose first court has some of the oldest buildings in Cambridge, dating from the 14th century. On the south side Christopher Wren's chapel, completed in 1665, looks like a distinctly modern intrusion. You can walk through the college, around a delightful garden, and past the fellows' bowling green.

Down Pembroke Street and Downing Street, on St. Andrew's
4 Street, is **Emmanuel College,** whose chapel and colonnade are again by Christopher Wren. Among the portraits of famous members of the college hanging in Emmanuel Hall is one of John Harvard, founder of Harvard University. Indeed, a number of the Pilgrim Fathers were Emmanuel alumni, and they remembered their alma mater in naming Cambridge, Massa-
5 chusetts. The gateway of **Christ's College,** also on St. Andrew's Street, bears the enormous coat of arms of its patroness, Lady
6 Margaret Beaufort, mother of Henry VII. **Sidney Sussex College,** located where St. Andrew's Street becomes Sidney Street, is a smaller foundation with many 17th-century buildings. Oliver Cromwell was a student here in 1616, and his head has been buried here since 1961.

Cambridge

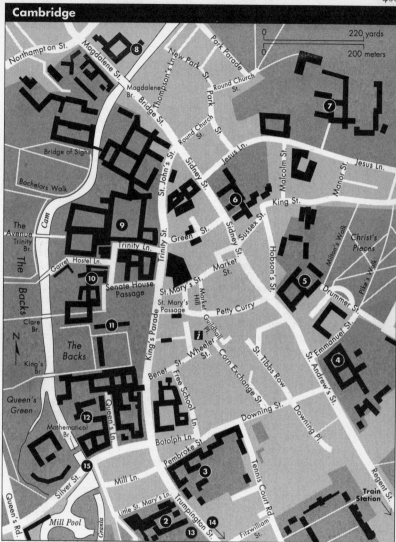

Christ's College, **5**
Emmanuel College, **4**
Fitzwilliam Museum, **13**
Jesus College, **7**
King's College Chapel, **11**
Magdalene College, **8**

Pembroke College, **3**
Peterhouse, **2**
Queens' College, **12**
Sidney Sussex College, **6**
Silver Street Bridge, **15**
Trinity College, **9**
Trinity Hall, **10**
University Botanic Garden, **14**

Time Out Walk across Jesus Green to the **Fort St. George,** a riverside pub overlooking the college boathouses, with plenty of outdoor space for summer drinking.

---

7 In contrast to the compact Sidney Sussex College is its spacious neighbor, **Jesus College.** Parts of the chapel here were built in the Middle Ages for the nunnery of St. Radegund, which existed on the site before the college. Victorian restoration of the building includes some Pre-Raphaelite stained-glass windows. Uniquely in Cambridge, this college incorporates cloisters, also a remnant of the nunnery.

8 Across Magdalene (pronounced "maudlin") Bridge, a cast-iron 1820 structure, is **Magdalene College,** distinguished by pretty redbrick courts. It was originally a 15th-century hostel for Benedictine monks. The college's Pepysian Library contains the books and desk of the 17th-century diarist, Samuel Pepys. *Admission free. Open Apr.–Sept., daily 11:30–12:30 and 2:30–3:30.*

9 **Trinity College,** the largest of the colleges, with over 800 students, straddles the river, and can sometimes be approached by a bridge that joins it with neighboring St. John's College. This approach gives a fine view of Christopher Wren's magnificent library, colonnaded and seemingly constructed as much of light as of stone. Many of Trinity's features match its size, not least its 17th-century "great court," and the massive and detailed gatehouse that houses Great Tom, a giant clock that strikes each hour with high and low notes. Prince Charles was an undergraduate at the college at the end of the 1960s.

10 Cambridge's celebrated **"Backs"** are gardens and meadows running down to the river Cam's banks; some colleges back onto them. A good vantage point from which to appreciate the Backs is Trinity's neighbor, **Trinity Hall,** where you can sit on a wall by the river and watch students in punts manipulate their poles under the ancient bridges of Clare and King's. Between the bridges is one of the few strictly university buildings (i.e., not part of a particular college), the **Senate House,** a classical structure of the 1720s which is used for commencement ceremonies.

Time Out **The Copper Kettle** is a strategically placed coffee shop, on King's Parade, and a traditional students' hangout, with a view of King's College.

---

11 **King's College Chapel** is for most people the high point of their visit to Cambridge. It is one of the most beautiful buildings in England. Begun in the mid-15th century by Henry VI, it was not completed for 100 years, mainly through lack of funds. Built in the late-Gothic, English style known as Perpendicular, its great fan-vaulted roof is supported only by a tracery of soaring side columns, and it seems to float over a huge space, lit by ever-changing light from the vast and ancient stained-glass windows. Rubens's *Adoration of the Magi* hangs behind the altar. Every Christmas Eve, a festival of carols is broadcast from the chapel to the world.

12 Tucked away on Queens Lane, next to the wide lawns that lead down from King's to the Backs, is **Queens' College,** named after the respective consorts of Henry VI and Edward IV. The secluded "cloister court" looks untouched since its completion in the 1540s. Queens' boasts a very different kind of masterpiece from King's College Chapel in the **Mathematical Bridge** (best seen from the Silver Street road bridge), an arched wooden structure across the river that was originally held together without fastenings. The present bridge, dating from 1902, is securely bolted.

⑬ Trumpington Street, where a stream runs beside the road, has elegant 18th-century houses and the **Fitzwilliam Museum,** a classical building with an outstanding collection of art (including paintings by John Constable) and antiquities, with a particularly good display from ancient Egypt. The museum has a coffee bar and restaurant. *Tel. 0223/332900. Admission free. Open Tues.–Sat., lower galleries 10–2; upper galleries 2:15–5; Sun. all galleries 2–5.*

⑭ A little beyond central Cambridge, in Bateman Street off Trumpington Road, is the **University Botanic Garden** which was laid out in 1846 and contains, among its rare specimens, a limestone rock garden. *Cory Lodge, Bateman St., tel. 0223/ 336265. Admission free Mon.–Sat., Sun. £1 adults, 50p children. Open May–Sept., Mon.–Sat. 8–6, Sun. 2:30–6:30; Nov.– Jan., Mon.–Sat. 8–4; Feb.–Apr. and Oct., daily 8–5.*

⑮ The **Silver Street Bridge** and **Mill Lane** are good places to rent punts on the river. You can either punt along the Backs to Magdalene Bridge and beyond, or punt upstream to **Grantchester,** a village celebrated by Rupert Brooke, one of a generation of poets lost in World War I. Grantchester is a long way for the inexperienced punter, so you may prefer to make the scenic two-mile trip on foot. The path roughly follows the river, going through college playing fields and the Grantchester Meadows.

Time Out   Walkers (or punters) to Grantchester can reward themselves with a pint and lunchtime food at the **Red Lion,** the **Rupert Brooke,** or the **Green Man** pubs. All three are centrally located by the river.

Numbers in the margin correspond to points of interest on the East Anglia map.

About four miles west of Cambridge (by A1303 and A45), you can visit the **American Military Cemetery** at Madingley, now more or less a suburb of Cambridge. It contains the graves of 3,811 U.S. servicemen who lost their lives during World War II. There is also a memorial wall for more than 5,000 American servicemen who have no known graves.

⑯ From Cambridge, make a single foray north to **Ely,** 15 miles on A10. Ely is the fenland's "capital," the center of what used to be a separate county called, appropriately, the Isle of Ely. It is a small, dense town dominated by its cathedral. The shopping area and little market square lie to the north and lead down to the attractive riverside, while the well-preserved medieval buildings of the cathedral grounds and the King's School (which trains cathedral choristers) spread out to the south and west.

Ely Cathedral, on one of the few ridges in the whole of the fens, can be seen for miles. Known affectionately as "the Ship of the Fens," the cathedral was begun by the Normans in 1081, on the site of a Benedictine monastery founded by the Anglo-Saxon Queen Etheldreda in the year 673. In the center can be seen one of the marvels of medieval architecture, the octagonal lantern—a sort of stained-glass skylight of vast proportions. Much of the decorative carving of the Lady Chapel was defaced during the Reformation (mostly by knocking off the heads of the statuary), but enough of the delicate tracery-work remains to show its original beauty. The fan-vaulted, carved ceiling remains intact, as it was too high for the iconoclasts to reach.

A major program of restoration is being undertaken on the cathedral's main fabric. The diocese of Ely was one of the first to charge admission to a cathedral, not only to help with the restoration, but to cover the enormous maintenance costs of a building this size. The cathedral also includes a stained-glass museum. *Chapter Office, The College, tel. 0353/667735. Admission to cathedral: £2.40 adults. Up to 2 school-age children admitted free if accompanied by an adult. Admission free on Sun. Open summer, daily 7–7; winter, weekdays 7:30–6, Sun. 7:30–5. Admission to Stained-Glass Museum: £1 adults, 50p children. Open Mar.–Oct., daily 10:30–4.*

Time Out **The Steeplegate Café and Gallery** (Steeplegate Street), on the 16th-century street that originally led to the churchyard of St. Cross but now connects the cathedral grounds with High Street, offers light food as well as high-quality local crafts, especially wood carvings.

Return to Cambridge to begin a swing round the wool churches southeast of the city.

Eleven miles south of Cambridge, at junction 10 of M11, is **Duxford Airfield.** This former Royal Air Force base, used in the Battle of Britain and assigned to the U.S. Air Force in the latter years of World War II, is now the Imperial War Museum's aviation branch, set up in the 1970s to house an extensive collection of fighters, bombers, and ancillary equipment. By skillful use of the original hangars, control tower, and other structures, the whole place powerfully evokes a World War II air base in action. In addition, there are historic examples of civil aircraft, including a prototype Concorde, and occasional demonstration flights. *Duxford, tel. 0223/833963 or 0223/835000 (recorded information). Admission: £4.50 adults, £2.25 children under 16 and senior citizens, £12 family ticket. Open Mar.–Oct., daily 10–6; Nov.–Mar., daily 10–4 (limited viewing only). Closed Christmas Eve, Christmas Day, day after Christmas, New Year's Day.*

Time Out It is a short drive from Duxford to the **Chequers** (High St.) at Fowlmere (off A505), an elegant old pub visited by Samuel Pepys in 1660.

A few miles south on M11 (junction 9) is the town of **Saffron Walden,** which owes its name to its saffron fields. It has many typical East Anglian, timber-frame buildings, some with elaborate pargeting (decorative plasterwork), especially on the walls of the former Sun Inn. The old **Grammar School** here was the World War II headquarters of the U.S. Air Force's 65th Fighter Wing.

On the edge of Saffron Walden is palatial **Audley End House,** a famous example of Jacobean (early 17th-century) architecture. Remodeled in the 18th and 19th centuries, it shows the architectural skill of Sir John Vanbrugh, Robert Adam, and Biagio Rebecca; as well as original Jacobean work in the magnificent Great Hall. You can also enjoy a leisurely walk around the park, which was landscaped by Capability Brown in the 18th century. *Tel. 0799/22399. Admission: £4 adults, £2 children under 16, £3 senior citizens. Open Apr.–Sept., park, daily noon–5, house, 1–5. Closed Mon. except national holidays.*

⑲ Sudbury, 15 miles east of Saffron Walden (B1053/B1054/A1092/B1064), is the fictionally famed "Eatanswill" of Dickens's *Pickwick Papers.* In real life, Thomas Gainsborough, one of the greatest English portrait and landscape painters, was born here in 1727; a statue of the artist holding his palette stands on Market Hill. His family's home is now a museum, containing paintings by the artist and his contemporaries, as well as an arts center. Although the **Gainsborough House** presents an elegant Georgian facade, with touches of the 18th-century neo-Gothic style, the building is essentially Tudor. In the walled garden behind the house, a mulberry tree planted in 1620 is still growing. *46 Gainsborough St., tel. 0787/72958. Admission: £1.50 adults, 75p children. Open Apr.–Oct., Tues.–Sat. 10–5, Sun. and national holidays 2–5; Nov.–Mar., Tues.–Sat. 10–4, Sun. 2–4.*

⑳ Long Melford, one of the great wool towns of the area, lies just two miles north of Sudbury on A134. By approaching it from this direction, you will appreciate the effect of the two-mile-long main street as it broadens to include green squares and trees, and finally opens out into the large triangular green on the hill. The buildings of the town are an attractive mixture—mostly 15th-century half-timbered or Georgian—and many house antiques shops. Telegraph poles are banned from both Long Melford and Lavenham, to preserve the towns' ancient look. On the hill, the **Church** is unfortunately obscured by **Trinity Hospital,** thoughtlessly built there in 1573. But close up, the delicate, flint flushwork and huge, 16th-century Perpendicular windows that take up most of the church's walls have great impact, especially as the nave is 150 feet long. Much of the original stained glass remains, notably the Lily Crucifix window. The Lady Chapel has an unusual interior cloister.

Now a National Trust property, **Melford Hall,** distinguished from the outside by its turrets and topiaries (trees trimmed into decorative shapes), is an early 16th-century house with a fair number of 18th-century additions. Much of the porcelain and other fine pieces in the house come from the *Santissima Trinidad,* a ship captured by one of the house's owners in the 18th century, when she was sailing back to Spain full of gifts from the emperor of China. The hall is set in parkland leading down to a walk by Chad Brook. *Tel. 0787/880286. Admission: £2.40 adults, £1.20 children. Open May–Sept., Wed.–Sun. 2–5:30; Oct., weekends 2–5:30; closed Nov.–Apr. Tours May–Sept., Wed. and Thurs. cost £2 adults, £1 children.*

Time Out **The Bull,** a black-and-white, timber-framed, medieval inn with antique furniture and an open fire, serves good bar lunches and real ale in Long Melford.

To the north of Long Melford Green is **Kentwell Hall.** This redbrick Tudor manor house, surrounded by a wide moat, has remained untouched for centuries. A restoration program is now well under way, and the original gardens are being re-created. Two or three weekends a year, a reenactment of Tudor life is performed here by costumed "servants" and "farmworkers," with great panache and detail. Other theatrical and craft events also take place here. *Long Melford, tel. 0787/310207. Admission: £2.75 adults, £1.60 children, £2.40 senior citizens. Open Apr.–June, Sun. 2–6; July–Sept., Wed.–Sun. 2–6.*

㉑ Continue north from Kentwell Hall up A134 for a mile and a half, then turn right onto a side road which will lead you to **Lavenham,** a town virtually unchanged since the height of its wealth in the 15th and 16th centuries. The weavers' and wool merchants' houses occupy not just one show street, but most of the town. These are timber-framed in black oak, the main posts looking as if they could last for another 400 years. The grandest building of them all, the **Guildhall,** is owned by the National Trust and open to visitors. *Market Place, tel. 0787/247646. Admission: £1.80 adults, 60p children. Open Apr.–early Nov., daily 11–5.*

The **Wool Hall** was torn down in 1913, but it was reassembled immediately at the request of Princess Louise, sister of the then-reigning king, George V. In 1962, it was joined to the neighboring **Swan Hotel** (*see* Dining and Lodging, below), a splendid Elizabethan building in its own right. The Swan Inn had a long history as a coaching inn, and in World War II served as the special pub for the U.S. Air Force's 48th Bomber Group.

Lavenham Church is set apart from the village. Around the year 1500, it was rebuilt (except for the chancel) with wool money; the height of its tower (141 feet) was meant to surpass those of the neighboring churches and succeeded. Inside, all is spaciousness, light, and perfect proportion.

Time Out Have lunch or tea at **The Priory,** a timber-framed building on Water Street with a garden growing over 100 varieties of herbs, or at the **Great House** (Market Sq.), where you can have tea in the garden.

㉒ From Lavenham take A1141 and A134 north for 12 miles to **Bury St. Edmunds,** which rises from the pleasant valley of the rivers Lark and Linnet. The town owes its unusual name and its initial prosperity to the martyrdom of Edmund, last king of the Anglo-Saxon kingdom of East Anglia, who was hacked to death by the pagan Danes in 896. He was subsequently canonized and his shrine attracted pilgrims, settlement, and commerce. In the 11th century the building of a great Norman abbey confirmed the town's importance as a religious center. Today only the Norman Gate Tower, the fortified Abbot's Bridge over the Lark, and a few picturesque ruins remain, for the abbey was yet another that fell during Henry VIII's dissolution of the monasteries. You can get some idea of the abbey's enormous scale, however, from the surviving gate tower. The ruins are now the site of the **Abbey Botanical Gardens,** with rare trees including a Chinese tree of heaven originally planted in the 1830s. The abbey walls enclose separate, specialized gardens. One of these, the yew-hedged **Appleby Rose Garden,** was founded with the royalties from *Suffolk Summer*, a best-selling novel by a U.S. serviceman, John Appleby, who had been stationed at nearby Rougham during World War II. *Tel. 0284/*

757490. Admission free. Open weekdays 7:30 AM–½ hour before dusk, weekends 9 AM–dusk.

Originally there were three churches within the abbey walls, which gives some idea of the extent of the grounds, but only two have survived. **St. Mary's,** built in the 15th century, is the finer, with a blue-and-gold embossed "wagon" (i.e., barrel-shaped) roof over the choir. Mary Tudor, Henry VIII's sister and queen of France, is buried here. **St. James's** also dates from the 15th century; the brilliant paintwork of its ceiling and the stained glass windows gleaming like jewels are the result of restoration in the 19th century by the architect Sir Gilbert Scott. Don't miss the memorial (by the altar) to an event in 1214, when the barons of England gathered here to take a solemn oath to force King John to grant the Magna Carta. The cathedral's original **Abbey Gate** was destroyed in a riot, and it was rebuilt in the 15th century on clearly defensive lines—you can see the arrow slits.

A walk along **Angel Hill** is a journey through the history of Bury St. Edmunds. Along one side, the Abbey Gate, cathedral, Norman Gate Tower, and St. Mary's Church make up a continuous display of medieval architecture. On the other side, the elegant Georgian houses include the **Athenaeum,** an 18th-century social and cultural meeting place and still the site of concerts and recitals, and the splendid **Angel** hotel, the scene of Sam Weller's meeting with Job Trotter in Dickens's *Pickwick Papers*. Dickens stayed in Room 15 while he was giving readings at the Athenaeum. A pretty Queen Anne–style house known as **Angel Corner** houses a collection of "time-measuring instruments"— the word *clock* does not do justice to their range, ingenuity, and decorativeness. *Gershom-Parkington Memorial Collection of Clocks and Watches, 8 Angel Hill, tel. 0284/757072. Admission free, but donations welcome. Open Mon.–Sat. 10–5, Sun. 2–5.*

Time Out Opposite the **Greene King** brewery, farther along Angel Hill, try Greene King draft ale and local sausages in the lofty back room of the **Dog and Partridge,** where the rough brick walls are hung with dray horse mementos.

Continuing south along Angel Hill and on to the end of Crown Street, turn right into Westgate Street to one of the National Trust's most unusual properties, the **Theatre Royal** (*see* The Arts, below).

The shopping streets of Bury St. Edmunds follow an ancient grid pattern from Abbey Gate to Cornhill, with Abbeygate Street in the center. The public buildings within this area have a varied grandeur; there is, first, the medieval **Guildhall;** next, 18th-century classicism as interpreted by Robert Adam in the **Art Gallery;** and then Victorian classicism in the **Corn Exchange.**

The Art Gallery has no permanent collections; instead there are changing exhibits of paintings, sculpture, and crafts, as well as frequent concerts. *Market Cross, Cornhill, tel. 0284/762081. Admission: 30p adults, 15p children. Open Tues.–Sat. 10:30–4:30, Sun. by appointment.*

Also in Cornhill is the 12th-century **Moyse's Hall,** probably the oldest building in East Anglia, which houses in the original tiny rooms the local archaeological collections. It also has a macabre display relating to the Red Barn murder, a Victorian case that gained notoriety in a contemporary blood-and-thunder play, *Maria Marten*, or the *Murder in the Red Barn*. *Tel. 0284/ 757072. Admission free. Open Mon.–Sat. 10–5, Sun. 2–5.*

To travel from Bury St. Edmunds to Norwich, first take A134/ A11 north and east for 30 miles to Wymondham (pronounced Windham). The road passes through **Thetford Forest,** the largest forest in the country, covering almost 150 square miles. The principal landowners now are the Ministry of Defense and the Forestry Commission. Much of the northern part is reserved for military exercises and is clearly marked "Battle Area." In King's Forest and West Stow, however, it is possible to wander freely along paths among oak, beech, and mature pine. If you are lucky you will see wild deer. Look for the reconstructed Saxon village in a forest clearing. *West Stow Country Park. Admission free. Open daily 9 AM–1 hour before sunset.*

㉓ **Wymondham** is an ancient market town with timber-framed houses overhanging the sidewalks, steep streets lined with a variety of fascinating architecture, and a magnificent abbey church that seems far too grand not to be a cathedral. The soaring roof has great hammerbeams decorated with flying angels, while the altar screen gleams with golden figures. The remaining structure is only a part of the original building, but it gives a good idea of just how huge Wymondham abbey must have been.

Another nine miles along A11 will bring you to Norwich.

Tour 2: Norwich and the Broads

Numbers in the margin correspond to points of interest on the Norwich map.

㉔ Established by the Saxons because of its fine trading position on the rivers Yare and Wensum, **Norwich,** now a modern county town, still has its heart in the triangle between the two waterways, dominated by the castle and cathedral. The inner beltway follows the line of the old city wall, much of which is still visible; and it is worth driving around after dark to see the older buildings uncluttered by their much newer neighbors, thanks to skillful floodlighting.

㉕ The spire of Norwich **Cathedral** is visible everywhere at 315 feet, but you cannot see the building itself until you go through St. Ethelbert's Gate. The cathedral was begun in 1096 by Herbert de Losinga, who had come from Normandy in 1091 to be its first bishop. His splendid tomb is by the high altar. The plain west front and dramatic crossing tower, with its austere, geometrical decoration, are distinctively Norman. The remarkable length of the nave is immediately impressive; unfortunately, the similarly striking height of the vaulted ceiling makes it a strain to study the delightful colored bosses (ornamental knobs at junction points), where Bible stories are illustrated with great vigor and detail—look for the Pharaoh and his cohorts drowning in a vivid Red Sea. Note also the woodcarving on the choir-stall misericords (semi-seats), a wonderful revelation of medieval skill and religious beliefs. The stalls were originally intended for the Benedictine monks who ran the cathedral, and the beautifully preserved cloister is part of what remains of their great priory.

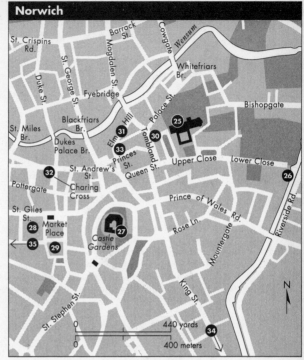

26 Past the buildings of various periods on the cathedral grounds, a path leads down to the ancient water gate, **Pulls Ferry.** The grave of Norfolk-born nurse Edith Cavell, the British World War I heroine shot by the Germans, is outside the cathedral. *62 The Close, tel. 0603/626290. Admission free but donation requested. Open daily, summer 7:30–7, winter 7:30–6.*

27 From Pulls Ferry retrace your steps to St. Ethelbert's Gate and proceed to the traffic lights where you will turn left and see the **castle** on the hill to your right. The castle is also Norman, but the wooden bailey (wall) on the castle mound was later replaced with a stone keep (tower). The thick walls and other defense works attest to the castle's military function, but the unique, decorated stone facing of the walls makes the castle seem like a child's illustration. For most of its history the castle has been a prison, and executions took place here well into the 19th century. An excellent museum here features displays of different facets of Norfolk's history, including a gallery devoted to the Norwich School of painters who, like the Suffolk artist John Constable, devoted their work to the everyday Norfolk landscape and seascape as revealed in the East Anglian light. *Norwich Castle, tel. 0603/222222, ext. 71224. Admission: 70p adults, 10p children, 30p senior citizens. Open Mon.–Sat. 10–5, Sun. 2–5.*

At the castle, turn right at the traffic lights on the right, cross over, and go down the steps to the market. Behind the market,
28 **City Hall** has one of the best views in Norwich from its steps, between the bronze Norwich lions. On your right rises the
29 elaborate church tower of **St. Peter Mancroft,** below are the

brightly colored awnings of the market stalls, and opposite looms the castle. Narrow lanes that used to be the main streets of medieval Norwich lead away from the market, and end at

30 **Tombland** by the cathedral. Neither a graveyard nor a plague pit, Tombland was the site of the Anglo-Saxon trading place, now a busy thoroughfare. In Tombland turn left and take the

31 second turning on the left which is **Elm Hill,** a cobbled and pleasing mixture of Tudor and Georgian houses that culminate in the thatched Briton's Arms Café.

32 At the top of Elm Hill, turn right and walk down to **Strangers Hall,** a good example of a medieval merchant's house. Built originally in 1320, it went on growing until the mid-18th century, and is now a museum of domestic life, each room appropriately furnished. *Charing Cross, tel. 0603/667229. Admission: Easter–Oct., 50p adults, 40p students and children; Nov.–Easter, 25p adults, 20p students and children.*

The river Yare was once a busy commercial waterway; now most of the traffic is for pleasure. During the summer months, a boat trip starting from Roaches Court at Elm Hill will give you an alternative perspective on Norwich, and longer trips are available down the rivers Wensum and Yare to the nearer Broads. There is also a marked riverside walk which follows the Wensum from St. George's Bridge to the city wall at Carrow Bridge.

Time Out **The Adam and Eve** is said to be Norwich's oldest pub, convenient from both the river and the cathedral on Bishopsgate.

33 **St. Peter Hungate** on Princes Street displays church art and furnishings, and you can try your hand at brass rubbing. *Princes St., tel. 0603/667231. Admission free; brass-rubbing charge 50p–£5. Open Mon.–Sat. 10–5.*

In complete contrast to Norwich's historical composition, the

34 **University of East Anglia** is a modern construction, built during the great expansion of higher education in the 1960s. Its site on the slopes of the river Yare was used by the architect to give a dramatic, stepped-pyramid effect. The campus is linked by walkways that open out at different levels and center on a fountain courtyard.

35 The award-winning **Sainsbury Centre for the Visual Arts,** which was opened in 1972, holds the remarkable private art collection of the Sainsbury family, owners of a huge supermarket chain. The collection includes a remarkable quantity of tribal art and 20th-century works, especially Art Nouveau. *Earlham Rd., tel. 0603/56060. Admission: 75p adults, 40p children and senior citizens. Open Tues.–Sun. noon–5.*

To the east of Norwich, the **Norfolk Broads** stretch all the way to the coast. This is the popular image of Norfolk: a maze of small lakes, reed beds, and rivers that provides a haven for wildlife and boat lovers.

Numbers in the margin correspond to points of interest on the East Anglia map.

For an excellent example of what the Broads have to offer, take B1140 east out of Norwich, and turn left at Panxworth (about 7 mi) for **Ranworth Broad.** A 450-yard nature trail leads through oak woods, swamp, and reed beds to the center, where the moored floating Broadland Conservation Center has an exhibition on the ecology of the Broads. *Ranworth, tel. 060549/479. Admission: 90p adults, 75p students and senior citizens, 50p children. Open Apr.–Oct., Sun.–Thurs. 10–5, Sat. 2–5. Closed Mon. and Fri.*

36 The view from the church tower at **Ranworth** is well worth the climb. It provides a special perspective on the Broads, the horizons vanishing away to infinity. Inside the church are 12 beautiful screen paintings of saints, all painstakingly restored in the 1960s. Look for St. Michael's dragon with seven heads.

Until recently, rivers were the main routes of trade for the Broads—much more important than roads—with traditional Norfolk sailing barges, known as wherries, plying their trade
37 all over the area from their main port at **Great Yarmouth** (now mainly a seaside resort). In the late 19th and early 20th century, the leisure potential of these fine boats was first realized, and some were built as wherry yachts for luxurious vacations afloat. The *Albion*, based at Ludham, is the only working wherry left, maintained by the Norfolk Trust, while the *Norada* and the *Olive* are historic wherry yachts based at Wroxham. All may be chartered for cruises of up to 12 people. *The* Albion, *Norfolk Wherry Trust, tel. 0603/413720. The* Olive *and the* Norada, *tel. 0603/782470.*

38 Directly north of Norwich (14 miles), A140 leads to **Blickling Hall** (turn left onto B1354, then right, down a little lane). Now a National Trust property, it formerly belonged to a succession of historical figures, including Sir John Fastolf, the model for Shakespeare's Falstaff; Anne Boleyn's family, who owned it until Anne was executed by her husband, Henry VIII; and finally Lord Lothian, an ambassador to the United States. This redbrick Jacobean house is framed by a mighty yew hedge and the grounds include a formal flower garden and parkland whose woods conceal a temple, an orangery, a pyramid, and a secret garden! Blickling Hall houses a National Trust's textile conservation workshop, fine tapestries, and a long gallery with an intricate plasterwork ceiling decorated with Jacobean emblems. *Blickling, tel. 0263/733084. Admission: £4.50 house and garden, £2 garden only, children half-price. Open Apr.–Oct., 1–5; national holiday Mon. 1–5. Closed Mon. and Thurs.*

If you head north on B1354, then B1149 to Holt, then take B1156, a total of around 14 miles, you'll come to the coast and a string of villages along the A149 coast road, with harbors used for small fishing boats and yachts. You can take a boat trip from
39 **Blakeney,** one of the most attractive of the coastal villages, past Blakeney Point, a National Trust nature reserve, to see the seals on the sandbanks and the birds on the dunes.

Time Out **The Lifeboat** at Thornham, west of Brancaster, which has low ceilings and five open fires, serves warming pub lunches throughout the year.

40 At **Holkham,** eight miles farther along A149, is **Holkham Hall,** amidst a huge expanse of sandy beaches, dunes, and salt marsh backed by pine woods. The estate is the seat of the Coke (pronounced "Cook") family, the earls of Leicester. In the late 18th century, Thomas Coke went on the fashionable "grand tour" of the Continent, returning with art treasures and determined to build a house according to the new Italian ideas; the result was this Palladian palace, one of the most splendid in Britain. The magnificence of the Marble Hall pales in comparison to the great hall, which is 60 feet high, and brilliant with gold and alabaster. Twelve stately rooms follow, each filled with Coke's collection of masterpieces, including paintings by Gainsborough, Rubens, Raphael, and other old masters. This transplant from neoclassical Italy is set in extensive parkland landscaped by Capability Brown. *Near Wells-next-the-Sea, tel. 0328/710227. Admission: £2 adults, 75p children, £1.75 senior citizens. Open June–Sept., Sun.–Thurs. 1:30–5. Closed Fri.–Sat.*

Fifteen miles west of Holkham, the coast road turns sharply south at the coastal resort of **Hunstanton.** Nine miles south and just off this road is **Sandringham House,** one of the queen's country residences, used for royal family vacations. This huge, redbrick Victorian mansion was clearly designed for enormous country-house parties, with a ballroom, billiard room, and bowling alley, as well as a shooting lodge on the grounds. House and gardens are closed when the queen is in residence, but the woodlands, nature walks, and museums remain open, as does the church, medieval but in heavy Victorian disguise. *Sandringham, tel. 0553/772675. Admission: house and gardens, £2.20 adults, £1.40 children, £1.70 senior citizens; grounds only, £1.70 adults, £1 children, £1.30 senior citizens. Open Apr.–Sept., Mon.–Thurs. 11–5, Sun. noon–5.*

Time Out Five miles north of Sandringham, at Caley Mill, homemade teas (light meals) are served at **The Old Miller's Cottage** in the middle of Norfolk's lavender fields.

This tour from Norwich can finish in **King's Lynn,** 8 miles south of Sandringham close to the mouth of the Great Ouse on the Wash. Now an important container and fishing port, King's Lynn gained importance in the 15th century, especially for trade with northern Europe. **Trinity Guildhall,** with its striking checkered stone front, is now the Civic Hall of the Borough Council and is not generally open to the public, although you can visit it during the King's Lynn Festival (*see* The Arts, below). However, the **Regalia Rooms,** housed in the Guildhall Undercroft and entered through the Old Gaol (jail) House (now the tourist information center), exhibits charters dating from the time of King John (reigned 1199–1216), as well as the 14th-century chalice known as King John's Cup. *Market Place, tel. 0553/763044. Admission: 40p adults, 20p children. Open May–Sept., Mon.–Sat. 10–4.*

Another early 15th-century guildhall, St. George's, forms part of the **Fermoy Centre,** now a thriving arts and theater complex administered by the National Trust, and the focal point for the annual King's Lynn Festival. There is also an art gallery, and a crafts fair every September. The center's coffee bar serves snacks all day. St. George's Guildhall is the largest surviving English medieval guildhall, and it adjoins a Tudor house and a warehouse used during the Middle Ages. *27 King St., tel. 0553/774725. Admission free. Open weekdays 10:30–5, Sat. 10–12:30.*

Tour 3: Colchester and the Aldeburgh Coast

Less than an hour's journey from London is **Colchester,** England's oldest recorded town. Recent archaeological research indicates a settlement at the head of the Colne estuary at least as early as 1000 BC It was a trading post for the Romans in the 1st century BC, and by AD 40, under the name Camuldonum, the center of the domain of Cunobelin (Shakespeare's Cymbeline), who was king of the Catuvellauni and recognized by the Romans as king of Britain. On Cunobelin's death, the Romans invaded in AD 43 and the Emperor Claudius—who was supposed to have entered Colchester on an elephant—built his first stronghold here and made it the first Roman colony in Britain, appropriately renaming the town *Colonia Victricensis* ("Colony of Victory"). Colchester received its royal charter in 1189 from King Richard the Lionheart; throughout 1989, the 800th-year anniversary, special celebrations were held.

Evidence of Colchester's four centuries of Roman history is visible everywhere. Although the Romans prudently relocated their administrative center to London after the Celtic Queen Boudicca burned the place in AD 60, Colchester was important enough for them to build massive fortifications around the town. The **Roman Walls** can still be seen, especially along Balkerne Hill (to the west of the town center), with its splendid Balkerne Gate, and along Priory and Vineyard Streets, where there is now a Roman drain exposed halfway along. In Maidenburgh Street, near the castle, the remains of a Roman amphitheater have been discovered—the curve of the foundations is outlined in the paving stones of the roadway, and part of the walls and floor have been exposed and preserved in a modern building, where they can be viewed through the window.

Colchester has always had a strategic importance and there is still a military garrison here and a tattoo (military spectacle) is held in even-numbered years. The **Castle** was built by William the Conqueror in about 1076, one of the earliest to be built of stone (largely taken from the Roman ruins) and although all that remains is the keep (main tower), it is the largest in Europe. The castle was actually built over the foundations of the huge Roman Temple of Claudius, and in the vaults you can descend through 1,000 years of history. A museum inside contains an ever-growing collection of Roman and prehistoric remains, mostly from Colchester itself. *Tel. 0206/712939. Admission: £1 adults, 50p children and senior citizens. Open Apr.–Oct., Mon.–Sat. 10–5, Sun 2–5; Nov.–Mar., Mon.–Sat. 10–5. Closed Good Friday and Christmas week.*

Next door to the castle is **Hollytrees,** a pleasing early 18th-century brick house with a collection of costumes, dolls, and toys. *High St., tel. 0206/712940. Admission free. Open Mon.–Sat. 10–1 and 2–5; Oct.–Mar., Sat. 2–4.*

Opposite Hollytrees is a group of graceful 18th-century townhouses, two of which have been turned into an art gallery known as **The Minories.** The gallery has 19th-century works by John Constable and Auguste Rodin. The collection of 20th-century works by modern East Anglian artists John and Paul Nash can be viewed by appointment. There are also temporary exhibitions. The restaurant provides light meals and drinks during the gallery's opening hours. *74 High St., tel. 0206/577301. Admission free. Open Tues.–Sat. 10–5, Sun. 2–6. Closed Mon. and Christmas week.*

Opposite the castle, in High Street, **All Saints Church** has been turned into a county museum of natural history, while **Holy Trinity Church** on Trinity Street, which was begun around AD 1000 and which incorporates visible Roman materials, has been converted into the **Social History Museum.** Opening times are the same as for the Hollytrees, above, and admission to both is free. The church of **St. Mary-at-the-Wall** is now an arts center, offering a varied program throughout the year.

Not far from St. Mary's, and close to Balkerne Gate is Colchester's **Mercury Theatre** (*see* The Arts, below). At the theater turn right and walk down Balkerne Passage which leads to the top of North Hill; there, turn right again into High Street, which follows the line of the main Roman road. Along High Street you will pass the Victorian **Town Hall,** standing on the site of the original Moot (assembly) Hall. The narrow, medieval streets behind the town hall are called the **Dutch Quarter** because weavers from the Low Countries settled here in the 16th century. Across the High Street and beyond the modern Culver Square pedestrian mall, lie the medieval streets of Long Wyre Street, Short Wyre Street, and Sir Isaac's Walk, where there are many small antiques stores, and crafts and gift shops.

Off Culver Street West, on Trinity Street, **Tymperley's Clock Museum** displays a unique collection of Colchester-made clocks in the surviving wing of an Elizabethan house. *Tel. 0206/ 712943. Admission free. Open Apr.–Oct., Mon.–Sat. and national holidays, 10–1 and 2–5.*

Colchester is the traditional base for exploring **Constable Country,** that quintessentially English rural landscape on the borders of Suffolk and Essex made famous by the early-19th-century painter, John Constable. This area runs north and west of Colchester along the valley of the river Stour, and includes his birthplace at **East Bergholt** (5 miles north of Colchester, off A12); **Dedham** (2 miles south), where he went to school and whose church and other town features served as inspiration for his works; and **Flatford,** a mile east, where those familiar with Constable's *The Hay Wain* will recognize the Mill and **The Thatched Bridge Cottage,** the latter open to the public and featuring a display about the artist's life. *Near East Bergholt, tel. 0206/298260. Admission free. Open Apr.–May, Sept.–Oct., Wed.–Sun. 11–5:30; June–Aug., daily 11–5:30.*

From Felixstowe—18 miles northeast of Colchester (A12/A43) —northward to Kessingland, lies the **Suffolk Heritage Coast,** a beautiful 40-mile stretch including many sections designated by an Act of Parliament as "Areas of Special Scientific Interest." Fifteen miles north you will find **Orford** and **Orford Castle,** a splendid keep (tower) built in 1160. *Orford, tel. 03944/ 50472. Admission: £1.30 adults, 95p students, 65p children and senior citizens. Open Easter–Sept., daily 10–6; Oct.–Easter, daily 10–4.*

Heading north on the little road through **Tunstall Forest** you come to **Snape** and its disused Victorian malt works now converted into **the Maltings,** an opera house and general arts center hosting the Aldeburgh Festival, founded by the composer, Lord Benjamin Britten. *Tel. 0728/452935. Admission free. Open daily 10–5.*

Aldeburgh itself, 5 miles east on A1094, is a quiet seaside resort and was Britten's home. **Southwold,** 15 miles north, is a very attractive seaside town of old houses set among seven greens. **Southwold Museum** is housed in a typical, Dutch-gabled cottage. *Victoria St., no phone. Admission free. Open late May–Sept., daily 2:30–4:30.*

Tour 4: Lincoln and Boston

Numbers in the margin correspond to points of interest on the Lincoln Region map.

㊾ Northeast of the area already covered in this section lies **Lincoln,** an old settlement going back to Roman times and beyond; its crowning glory is the great Cathedral of St. Mary (which you should try to see at night, when it is floodlit). Commanding views from the top of the steep limestone escarpment above the river Witham reveal the strategic advantages of the city's site from earliest times. Weapons from the pre-Roman, tribal era have been found in the river; later, the Romans (always quick to see the potential of a site) left their usual permanent underpinning; and a wealth of medieval buildings—quite apart from the cathedral and castle—seem to tumble together down the steep hillside lanes leading to the river.

The **cathedral** is the most obvious starting point for any visitor to Lincoln. For hundreds of years, it was the tallest building in Europe, but this magnificent medieval building is now among the least known of the European cathedrals. It was begun in 1072 by the Norman bishop Remigius; the Romanesque church he built was irremediably damaged, first by fire, then by earthquake (in 1185), but you can still see parts of the ancient structure at the west front. The next great phase of building, initiated by Bishop Hugh of Avalon, is mainly 13th century in character. The west front, topped by the two west towers, is a unique structure, giving tremendous breadth to the entrance. It is best seen from the 14th-century Exchequergate arch in front of the cathedral, or from the castle battlements beyond.

Inside, a breathtaking impression of space and unity belie the many centuries of building and rebuilding. The stained-glass window at the north end of the transept, known as the Dean's Eye, is one of the earliest (13th-century) traceried windows, while its opposite number at the south end shows a 14th-century sophistication in its tracery (i.e., interlaced designs). St. Hugh's Choir in front of the altar and the Angel Choir at the east end behind it have remarkable vaulted ceilings and intricate carvings. Look for the famous Lincoln Imp up on the pillar nearest to St. Hugh's shrine, and even farther up (binoculars or a telephoto lens will help!) to see the 28 angels who are playing musical instruments, and who give this part of the cathedral its name.

Among the many chapels is one commemorating Lincolnshire's connections with North America and Australia. Through a side door on the north side lies the chapter house, a 10-sided building that sometimes housed the medieval Parliament of England. The chapter house is connected to the cloisters, notable for its grotesquely amusing ceiling bosses. The cathedral library, a restrained building by Christopher Wren, was built onto the north side of the cloisters after the original library collapsed. *Lincoln Cathedral, tel. 0522/544544. Admission: (recommended contribution) £1.50 adults, 50p children and senior citizens. Cathedral open: May–Aug., Mon.–Sat. 7:15 AM–8*

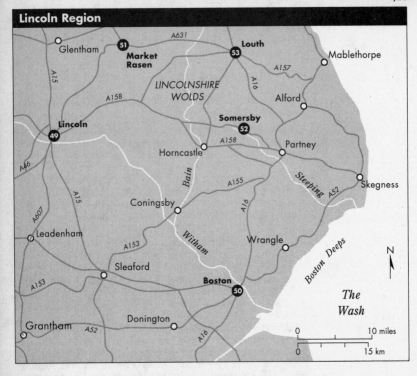

Lincoln Region

PM, Sun. 7:15 AM–6 PM; Sept.–Apr., Mon.–Sat. 7:15 AM–6 PM, Sun. 7:15 AM–5 PM.

In the **Minster Yard,** which surrounds the cathedral on three sides, are buildings of various periods, including graceful examples of Georgian architecture. A statue of Alfred, Lord Tennyson, who was born in Lincolnshire, stands on the green near the chapter house exterior, and the medieval **Bishop's Palace,** on the south side, is open to the public. *Tel. 0522/527468. Admission: 60p adults, 30p children, 45p senior citizens. Open Apr.–Sept., Mon.–Sat. 10–6, Sun. 2–6:30.*

Time Out   There is a pleasant coffee shop serving light meals just off the cathedral cloisters. It can also be reached from the Tennyson statue green.

Lincoln Castle, facing the cathedral across Exchequergate, was originally built on two great mounds by William the Conqueror in 1068, incorporating part of the remains of the Roman garrison walls. The castle was a military base until the 17th century, after which it was used primarily as a prison. In the extraordinary prison chapel you can see the cage-like stalls in which Victorian convicts were compelled to listen to sermons. *Tel. 0522/511068. Admission: 80p adults, 50p children and senior citizens. Open Apr.–Oct., Mon.–Sat. 9:30–5:30, Sun. 11–5:30; Nov.–Mar., Mon.–Sat. 9:30–4, Sun. 11–4.*

The Roman presence in Lincoln is particularly evident near the cathedral. At the end of Bailgate, traffic still passes under the **Newport Arch,** once the north gate of the Roman city, *Lindum*

Colonia. Ermine Street, stretching north from the arch to the river Humber, replaced an important Roman road lying eight feet below the surface. The foundations of the east gate have been excavated and permanently exposed in the forecourt of the Eastgate Post House Hotel, and the columns of a 175-foot Roman colonnade are marked along the roadway in Bailgate.

South of the cathedral the ground slopes away sharply down to the river. Here narrow medieval streets cling to the hillside, with the aptly named **Steep Hill** at their center. Well-preserved domestic buildings such as the early 12th-century Jew's House, and 14th- and 15th-century buildings such as Harding House and the Harlequin and Dernstall House (at the end of High St.) now contain bookstores, antiques shops, boutiques, and restaurants. These hillside streets lead into Lincoln's shopping district (mainly pedestrianized).

Through the busy shopping district, where you can walk under the 16th-century **Stonebow arch** with the **Guildhall** above it, the river Witham flows unobtrusively, crossed by the incongruously named **High Bridge**—a low, vaulted Norman bridge topped by 16th-century, timber-framed houses. West of High Bridge the river opens out into **Brayford Pool,** still busy with river traffic (and, unfortunately, road traffic, as a large, unsightly, multistoried parking lot has been built on one side). Here you can rent various kinds of boats.

Time Out | Have a pub lunch with a view of Brayford Pool at **The Royal William IV** on Brayford Wharf East.

The countryside around Lincoln, especially the Lincolnshire Wolds (chalk hills) to the northeast, consists of rolling hills and copses, with dry-stone (unmortared) walls dividing well-tended fields. The unspoiled rural area of the Wolds, strikingly evoked in Tennyson's poetry, is particularly worth a visit, while the long coastline with its miles of sandy beaches and its North Sea air offers all the usual, if occasionally tacky, seaside facilities for the family.

The river Witham flows right through the Lincolnshire Fens, **50** from Lincoln to the port of **Boston,** whose 14th-century **Church of St. Botolph** has a lantern tower (288 ft.) known affectionately as "Boston Stump." It can be seen for 20 miles from both land and sea and serves as a directional beacon for aircraft as well. The Pilgrims, who were finally to reach Massachusetts in 1620, originally tried to sail from Boston to Holland in their search for religious freedom, but were captured and imprisoned here in 1607. The 15th-century guildhall, now the **Boston Borough Museum,** contains the cells where they were held. *St. Mary's Guildhall, South St., tel. 0205/365954. Admission: 70p adults, 50p senior citizens, accompanied children free. Admission includes a personal audio guided tour. Open Mon.–Sat. 10–5, Sun. (Apr.–Sept. only) 1:30–5.*

There are other reminders of Boston's transatlantic links, especially the 18th-century **Fydell House,** now a school, where a room is set aside for visitors from Boston, Massachusetts. *South St., tel. 0205/351520. Admission free. Open weekdays 9:30–12:30 and 1:30–4:30.*

51 Northeast of Lincoln, **Market Rasen** (on A46 from Lincoln) is one of the major centers of horse racing in England. Between

Market Rasen and Louth lie the **Lincolnshire Wolds,** designated an Area of Outstanding Natural Beauty; Tennyson was born at **Somersby,** toward the south of the area. **Louth,** almost directly east of Market Rasen on A631, is most famous for its splendid parish church of St. James, which boasts the tallest parish church spire in England.

Time Out | Mr. Chips (17–21 Aswell St.) in Louth is a classic English fish-and-chip shop, offering a substantial meal for a bargain price.

What to See and Do with Children

Almost all the seaside resorts have something to offer children in the way of amusement parks, shows, and sports. Clacton-on-Sea (Essex), Lowestoft (Suffolk), Great Yarmouth and Hunstanton (Norfolk), and Mablethorpe and Skegness (Lincolnshire) have some of the best children's attractions.

Inland, **Colchester Zoo** (tel. 0206/330253) offers 40 acres of parkland exhibiting a worldwide collection of mammals, birds, fish, and reptiles, as well as a miniature railroad. The **Banham Zoo and Monkey Park,** (tel. 095387/476) has a children's play area. A more unusual wildlife attraction is the **Otter Trust** (Suffolk, tel. 0986/893470) near Bungay, where otters can be observed in near-natural conditions; there are also attractive river walks.

In Essex, the **Colne Valley Railway** (tel. 0787/61174), runs steam trains through the Colne Valley, from Castle Hedingham Station (near Halstead on A604). There are dining and buffet cars on the train. A permanent display of vintage steam and diesel locomotives is open daily except Monday, and there are "steam days" from Easter to October on most Sundays and national holiday weekends. The narrow-gauge railroad in Suffolk at the **Bressingham Live Steam Museum** (tel. 0379/88386) offers a six-mile ride on a small steam train through internationally famous gardens. In northern Norfolk, the **Wells and Walsingham Light Railway** (contact Wells tourist office, tel. 0328/051981) is the longest 10¼-gauge railroad in Britain—eight miles round trip. It runs daily from Easter to October, the first train leaving Wells at 10 AM.

Off the Beaten Track

Those who enjoy solitary outdoor walks should try the embankments of the Ouse inlets (called "washes") or the fenland drainage canals. For birdwatchers, the **Wildfowl Reserve** (tel. 0353/860711) at Welney, 12 miles north of Ely, has rare Bewick and Whooper swans in winter. Alternatively, drive to **Sutton Gault** off B1381 at Sutton (16 miles north of Cambridge), where the washes are at their narrowest point and the causeway floods so regularly there is a footbridge to the other side.

Southwest of King's Lynn lies **Peterborough** (34 miles on A47). This ancient city was an important Roman settlement on the road north from London, and has been recently largely developed. But the city's heart is the **cathedral,** whose history traces back to its original 7th-century Anglo-Saxon foundation. Originally a monastery church, the building is basically Norman, but one gets a sense of light inside, partly because the original

12th-century Norman windows were replaced by larger ones in the 13th and 15th centuries, and also because Cromwell's troops smashed all the stained glass during the Civil War. The painted wooden nave ceiling, dating from the 13th century, is one of only three surviving in Europe. From the gallery which runs around the inside of the central tower you can see across the fens to Ely. Two queens were buried here: Katherine of Aragon, Henry VIII's first wife, lies under a plain, gray stone in the north choir aisle under the 16th-century standards of England and Spain. Mary, Queen of Scots, was buried in the south aisle after her execution in 1587, although her son James I later had her body moved to Westminster Abbey in London. *Chapter Office, 12 Minster Precincts, tel. 0733/343342. Admission free. Open May–Sept., 8:30–8; Oct.–Apr., 8:30–6:30.*

Near the beautiful town of **Stamford** (15 miles along A1 from Peterborough) is **Burghley House,** the splendid mansion built in 1587 by William Cecil, 1st Baron Burghley, when he was Elizabeth I's High Treasurer. It has 18 staterooms, with carvings by Grinling Gibbons and ceiling paintings by Verrio, as well as a priceless art collection. *Tel. 0780/52451. Admission: £3.80 adults, £2.30 children, £3.50 senior citizens. Open Apr.– Sept., daily 11–5.*

East Anglia has many connections with America. From **Hingham,** west of Wymondham on B1108, nearly 200 inhabitants left between 1633 and 1638 to start a new life in America, including, in 1637, a young apprentice named Samuel Lincoln, paternal ancestor of Abraham Lincoln. A monument to the great president stands in the **church,** which is amazingly large, with a 120-foot tower. It is not particularly beautiful as Norfolk churches go, but impressive all the same.

Shopping

Basically agricultural, East Anglia is not particularly known for any manufactured products, apart from woolens. However, its many old towns and farming communities ensure that antiques dealers and craftspeople thrive in the area.

Bury St. Edmunds The area around Abbeygate Street contains the best stores in town. The **Parsley Pot** (Abbeygate St.) has a good selection of local crafts, and **Thurlow Champnes** (14 Abbeygate St.) has above-average silver, jewelry, and Copenhagen porcelain. The **Silk House** (Hatter St.) concentrates on Macclesfield silk goods and men's neckties (Macclesfield has been the center of England's silk production for centuries).

Cambridge Cambridge is a main shopping area for a wide region, and it has all the usual chain stores, many situated in the **Grafton Centre Shopping Precinct.** More interesting are the small specialty stores found among the colleges in the center of Cambridge, especially in and around Trinity Street, King's Parade, Rose Crescent, and Market Hill.
Heffer's is one of the world's biggest bookstores, with an enormous stock of books, many rare or imported. The main bookstore (20 Trinity St.) is spacious, with a galleried upper floor. There is also a charming children's branch (30 Trinity St.). Cambridge is also known for its second-hand bookshops. Antiquarian books can be found at **G. David** (16 St. Edward's Passage), which is tucked away near the Arts Theatre. Three

doors away, **The Haunted Bookshop** (9 St. Edward's Passage) offers a great selection of old, illustrated books. Across the bridge at 24 Magdalene Street, **The Bookshop** is the best of Cambridge's second-hand bookshops, with a wide variety of books on offer. Hand-crafted jewelry and leather goods, much of it made on the premises, can be found at **Workshop Designs** (31 Magdalene St.). Brian Jordan, at **Music Books** (10–12 Green St.), specializes in all types of books on music, scores, and sheet music, including facsimiles of antiquarian scores and books. **Primavera** (10 King's Parade) is an excellent gallery, where top-class craftspeople exhibit and demonstrate in a small but lively ground floor and basement; all the works are for sale at reasonable prices, often less than £50. Also on King's Parade is the **Benet Gallery** (no. 19), which specializes in antique prints and lithographs. **Midsummer Glassmakers** (Auckland Rd.) specializes in designing glassware, with glass sculpture and enamel work.

Colchester Colchester's most interesting stores are in the medieval streets between High Street and St. John's Street, some of which are pedestrianized or have restricted traffic. **Gunton's Food Shop** (81 Crouch St.) is an old family business, considered a local version of London's Harrods' food shop. **Cants of Colchester** (Nayland Rd., Mile End) are rose specialists who cultivate new varieties, with rose fields on view from July to September, and **Berrimans** (68 Culver St. East) sells china, glass, porcelain, novelties, and collectibles. Among the many antiques stores in the town, the **Trinity Antiques Centre** has the widest selection of portables such as china, glass, linen, military items, and silver.

Ely Ely has handmade wooden crafts at the **Steeplegate Tearoom and Gallery** (16 High St.), and affordable paintings and prints by local fenland artists at **The Old Fire Engine House Restaurant** (*see* Dining and Lodging, below). The real treasure trove, however, is the **Waterside Antiques Warehouse,** where a wealth of antiques at very competitive prices are sold in an authentic river warehouse (The Wharf, tel. 0353/667066). The **Herbary,** a mile past Prickwillow (2 mi northeast of Ely) on B1382, has three acres of herbs and a large formal herb garden.

Kersey Kersey, a hidden village of exquisite medieval buildings, is the location of the **Kersey Pottery,** where Dorothy Gorst and Fred Bramham make a wide variety of stoneware pots. Their pottery is by the watersplash across the village's main street.

King's Lynn In addition to its well-established open markets, King's Lynn is home to the **Caithness** factory, producers of fine crystal, which welcomes visitors on weekdays throughout the year (9:30–3:30; Shop weekdays 9–5, Sat. 9–4; apply to the Tours Organizer, Oldmeadow Rd., Hardwick Industrial Estate, tel. 0553/765111).

Lincoln Lincoln's main shopping area, mostly pedestrianized, is at the bottom of the hill below the cathedral, around the Stonebow gateway and Guildhall, and along High Street. However, the best stores are on Bailgate, Steep Hill, and the medieval streets leading directly down from the cathedral and castle. Steep Hill has several good bookstores, antiques shops, and crafts and art galleries, such as **Harding House, Steep Hill Galleries,** and **The Long Gallery** (the top of High St.). **David**

Hansord (32 Steep Hill) specializes in antiques, especially antique scientific instruments.

Long Melford This little town is packed with good antiques shops, many very specialized, such as the **Enchanted Aviary** (stuffed birds and beasts), **Seabrook Antiques** (decorated 18th- and 19th-century furniture), and **Fires and Things** (grates, ornaments, mantels, etc.).

Norwich The medieval lanes of Norwich, around Elm Hill and Tombland, contain the best stores. Antiquarian books can be found at **Peter Crowe** (75 Upper St. Giles St.). The **Crome Gallery** (34 Elm Hill) and **Frames Gallery** (25 Timberhill) feature art by contemporary painters and old masters. Antiques shops abound in this area: **As Time Goes By** (5 Wrights Court, Elm Hill) specializes in clocks, and **St. Michael-at-Plea** is a church converted into an antiques market.

The **Elm Hill Craft Shop** has interesting stationery and dollhouses, while **Hovell's** (Bedford St.) is a basketware specialist, among other things.

Sports and Fitness

Hiking **Peddar's Way,** the most walkable Roman road in England, runs for 50 miles from Knettishall on the Norfolk/Suffolk border due northwest to Holme-next-the-Sea, close to Hunstanton. Although you can do the whole distance, perhaps the best part is from Castle Acre, just north of Swaffam, to Holme, around 20 miles.

Horse Racing The center of British horse racing lies at Newmarket, where there are meets on weekdays and Saturdays (no Sunday racing in Britain), depending on the season. There are also race tracks at **Huntingdon** (near Cambridge) and **Market Rasen** (near Lincoln).

Water Sports River or sea fishing is available almost everywhere. Many rivers have *no-public-fishing* areas usually clearly marked, but fishing licenses are often available on a daily basis for a small fee. Local tourist information centers will be able to advise you on this. There are plenty of facilities for other water sports, especially on the Broads, along the north Norfolk coast, and on the estuaries around Colchester. The University of Cambridge is, of course, well-known for rowing, and in June the college "eights" (i.e., boats rowed by eight men) compete on the Cam in "bumps" (a kind of boat tag race) for the coveted position of "Head of the River."

Other Sports There are many tennis courts and golf courses in East Anglia, especially near coastal resorts such as Great Yarmouth (Norfolk), Lowestoft (Suffolk), and Clacton-on-Sea (Essex). Peterborough has a particularly well-equipped leisure center with year-round facilities for many sports. Bury St. Edmunds is the home of the national roller-skating center, **Rollerbury.**

Dining and Lodging

Dining East Anglia is a rich agricultural region with excellent produce. Traditional favorites like Norfolk Black turkeys and a variety of game are frequently available. The long coastline also provides a wide selection of fish year-round—Cromer crabs and Yarmouth bloaters (a kind of smoked herring) are notable—and the Essex coast near Colchester has been producing oysters since Roman times.

Among the touring bases, Lincoln is particularly well-served with downtown restaurants. Cambridge, which was once a gastronomic desert, has seen a renaissance, probably as a result of its economic upturn.

Highly recommended restaurants are indicated by a star ★.

Category	Cost*
Very Expensive	over £35
Expensive	£25–£35
Moderate	£10–£25
Inexpensive	under £10

per person, including first course, main course, dessert, and VAT; excluding alcohol

Lodging   The intimate nature of even East Anglia's larger towns has meant that there are few hotels with more than 100 rooms. As a result, even the biggest have a friendly atmosphere and offer personal service. Cambridge has relatively few hotels downtown, and these tend to be rather over-priced: There simply isn't room for hotels among the historic buildings crowded together, although there are many guest houses in the suburbs. The town fills up in the summer months, and you may have to look farther afield for accommodation.

Highly recommended hotels are indicated by a star ★.

Category	Cost*
Very Expensive	over £110
Expensive	£75–£110
Moderate	£40–£75
Inexpensive	under £40

All prices are for two people sharing a double room, including service, breakfast, and VAT.

Bury St. Edmunds
Dining

The Vaults. This restaurant below the Angel Hotel occupies a genuinely medieval cellar, appropriately lit and decorated, with tapestried walls and antique furniture. Don't let the fact that it was once the town morgue put you off! Traditional English cuisine is served (the elegant and more formal Regency Restaurant is upstairs). *Angel Hill, tel. 0284/753926. Reservations advised, especially weekends. Dress: informal. AE, DC, MC, V. Expensive.*

Mortimer's Seafood Restaurant. Mortimer's gets its name from the original watercolors by a Victorian artist, Thomas Mortimer, which are displayed on the green-and-white walls of the dining room. The seafood menu varies with the season's catch. *31 Churchgate St., tel. 0284/760623. Weekend reservations (at least a week in advance) required. Dress: informal. AE, DC, MC, V. Closed Sat. lunch, Sun., national holiday Mon., and Tues. Moderate.*

Lodging   **Angel Hotel.** This is the quintessential ivy-clad, historic, market-town hotel. A former coaching inn, its rooms are spacious and well-furnished, with the best ones overlooking the Abbey ruins. *Angel Hill, IP33 1LT, tel. 0284/753926. 38 rooms with bath. Facilities: 2 restaurants, bar. AE, DC, MC, V. Expensive.*

Suffolk Hotel. This reliable Georgian hotel has nicely proportioned and pleasantly furnished rooms overlooking the busy and historic downtown area. *38 Buttermarket, IP33 1DC, tel. 0284/753995. 33 rooms with bath. Facilities: restaurant, bar. AE, DC, MC, V. Expensive.*

Chantry Hotel. The older part of this pretty, 18th-century town house is traditionally furnished, but modern in its new extension. *8 Sparhawk St., IP33 1RY, tel. 0284/767427. 17 rooms with bath. Facilities: restaurant, bar. MC, V. Moderate.*

Cambridge   **Midsummer House.** This is an isolated restaurant, beside the
Dining   river across Midsummer Common. The cuisine is fundamental-
★   ly classic French, but it includes gastronomic influences from other places in which chef Hans Schweitzer has cooked: Louisiana, Iran, the Caribbean, and Germany. There is a stunning array of pastries and other sweets to end the meal. *Midsummer Common, tel. 0223/69299. Reservations necessary. Dress: informal. AE, DC, MC, V. Closed Sat. lunch, Sun. dinner, Mon. Expensive*

Twenty-Two. An intimate dining room in a modest, semidetached house half a mile from the center of Cambridge, the restaurant offers an extremely good-value fixed-price dinner cooked by the owner/proprietor. The modern English specialties include fish and game. *22 Chesterton Rd., tel. 0223/351880. Reservations advised. Dress: informal. MC, V. Closed Sun., Mon., and Christmas week. Moderate.*

Brown's. This huge, airy, French-American-style diner was converted from the outpatient department of the old Addenbrooke's Hospital, directly opposite the Fitzwilliam Museum. The large menu ranges from tuna sandwiches to fillet of pork stuffed with hazelnuts and salmon trout. *23 Trumpington St., tel. 0223/461655. No reservations. Dress: informal. No credit cards. Closed Dec. 25–26. Inexpensive.*

Three Horseshoes. This is an early 19th-century thatched cottage which includes a recently added conservatory. A pub restaurant serves beautifully prepared grilled fish, and the conservatory menu offers traditional English fare and seafood, also beautifully presented. There are homemade sorbets and ice creams for dessert. *Madingley (3 mi outside Cambridge, 10-minute taxi ride), tel. 0954/210221. Dress: informal. AE, DC, MC, V. Moderate*

Lodging   **Cambridgeshire Moat House.** This modern hotel is 5½ miles from Cambridge, off the A604 Huntingdon road. The rooms have a bit more character than those of the average modern hotel; they are light and airy, but not chintzy and all contain a double and a single bed. *Bar Hill, CB3 8EU, tel. 0954/80555. 100 rooms with bath. Facilities: restaurant, 2 bars; 18-hole golf course, 3 squash courts, 2 tennis courts, putting green, indoor heated swimming pool, paddling pool, and fitness center with spa bath, steam room, solarium. AE, DC, MC, V. Expensive.*

Garden House Hotel. Famous and quite luxurious, the hotel is set among the colleges, with a large new extension and gardens beside the river Granta. *Granta Place, CB2 1RT, tel. 0223/*

63421. 118 rooms with bath. Facilities: restaurant, bar, garden. AE, DC, MC, V. Expensive.

Arundel House Hotel. This is an elegantly proportioned Victorian row hotel that overlooks the river Cam, with Jesus Green in the background. Bedrooms have been redecorated and all are furnished very comfortably with locally made mahogany furniture. *53 Chesterton Rd., CB4 3AN, tel. 0223/67701. 90 rooms, 73 with bath. Facilities: restaurant, bar, TV with video of guided tour of Cambridge. AE, DC, MC, V. Closed Dec. 25–26. Moderate.*

University Arms Hotel. There has been an impressive refurbishment of the public areas and bedrooms in this city-center De Vere hotel. The central lounge provides a cozy, comfortable place for afternoon tea, where you can sit by the fire enjoying a pot of Darjeeling and smoked salmon sandwiches. *Regent St., CB2 1AD, tel. 0223/351241. 117 rooms with bath. Facilities: restaurant, bar, TV, 24-hr room service. AE, DC, MC, V. Expensive.*

Colchester   **Pasquale.** This cheerful and friendly Italian restaurant serves
Dining   well-cooked pastas and other classic Italian dishes in a light, simple, Italian-style dining room near the Roman Balkerne gate and the Mercury Theatre. *1 Balkerne Passage, tel. 0206/549080. Weekend reservations advised. Dress: informal. Closed Sun. MC, V. Moderate.*

Lodging   **King's Ford Park Hotel.** This large, 18th-century country-house hotel about two miles from the center of Colchester boasts individually decorated rooms and antique furniture; some rooms have four-poster or oval beds. *Layer Rd., CO2 0HS, tel. 0206/34301. 13 rooms with bath. Facilities: restaurant, bar, 18 acres of gardens and woodlands. AE, DC, MC, V. Expensive.*

George Hotel. In downtown Colchester, this 500-year-old hotel has been renovated to incorporate a modern extension. The rooms are furnished in English style, and the Vaults Bar has a section of Roman pavement. *116 High St., CO1 1TD, tel. 0206/578494. 47 rooms with bath. Facilities: Carver's Room restaurant and grill, sauna, mini-gym, solarium; AE, DC, MC, V. Expensive.*

The Maltings. This very friendly bed-and-breakfast establishment is about four miles from the center of Colchester. Rooms are homey and cottage-style, and guests have their own dining room and lounge with an open fire. *Mersea Rd., Abberton, CO5 7NR, tel. 020635/780. 3 rooms, 1 family room with bath. Facilities: light suppers on request, open-air swimming pool in garden. No credit cards. Closed Christmas week. Inexpensive.*

Dedham   **Le Talbooth.** In a Tudor house idyllically situated beside the
Dining   river Stour, with a floodlit terrace where drinks are served in the summer, the restaurant offers a four-course, gourmet fixed-price menu, including such dishes as tournedos of hare or lobster compote. *Gun Hill, tel. 0206/323150. Reservations advised, especially weekends. Jacket and tie required. AE, MC, V. Expensive.*

Dining and Lodging   **The Dedham Vale Hotel.** This small, friendly hotel in a converted Victorian house offers prettily decorated bedrooms, a restful, sea-green lounge, and a fine bar and restaurant famous in its own right for its large rôtisserie selection. *Stratford Rd., CO7 6HW, tel. 0206/322273. 6 rooms with bath. Facilities: live music in restaurant. MC, V. Expensive.*

Duxford
Lodging

The Duxford Lodge Hotel. This Georgian country house, set in its own grounds in Duxford village, was the operations headquarters for Duxford Airfield during World War II. Extensively renovated, the rooms are comfortably furnished and individually decorated in traditional style, although those in the modern annex are more basic. *Ickleton Rd., CB2 4RU, tel. 0223/836444. 16 rooms with bath. Facilities: restaurant, bar. AE, DC, MC, V. Closed 2 days between Christmas and New Year's. Expensive.*

Ely
Dining

The Old Fire Engine House. This restaurant near the cathedral has two dining rooms: The main one, with scrubbed pine tables, opens into the garden; the other, with an open fireplace and a polished wood floor, is also an art gallery. Among the English dishes are traditional Fenland recipes, including eel pie and game in season. Local artists exhibit here, and all their work is for sale. *25 St. Mary's St., tel. 0353/662582. Reservations required at least 24 hours in advance. Dress: informal. MC, V. Closed Sun. dinner and 2 weeks at Christmas. Moderate.*

Lodging
★

The Black Hostelry. A bed-and-breakfast establishment with a difference, the Black Hostelry has enormous rooms situated right in the cathedral grounds, in one of the finest medieval domestic buildings still in use. Extremely comfortable, with antiques and old-fashioned English furnishings, this medieval hostel offers a high degree of privacy. *Cathedral Close, The College, CB7 4DL, tel. 0353/662612. 1 room with bath, 1 suite. Facilities: full English breakfast in the Undercroft. No credit cards. Closed Dec. 24–26. Inexpensive.*

Ipswich
Dining and Lodging
★

Hintlesham Hall. This is a luxurious Georgian-style manor house hiding a basically Tudor building. There are grand rooms with antique furniture, but the house has been completely renovated and features an excellent restaurant with a *menu gastronomique* which is an excellent way of sampling a good cross-section of the chef's talented offerings. *Hintlesham, IP8 3NS, tel. 047387/334. 33 rooms with bath. Facilities: tennis, billiards, trout fishing, an 18-hole championship golf course, clay pigeon shooting, croquet, 9 acres of gardens and parkland; special rates for overseas bookings. AE, DC, MC, V. Very Expensive.*

Ixworth
Dining
★

Theobalds. This is a small, well-established restaurant with a good, varied menu. Try the crab and sweetcorn soup, a fillet steak with brandy and green peppercorns, or the lemon tart. There are excellent cheeses and reasonable wines. *68 High St., tel. 0359/31707. Reservations required. Dress: informal. MC, V. Closed Mon. dinner. Moderate.*

King's Lynn
Dining

Riverside Rooms. Part of the Fermoy Centre, the building housing this restaurant reflects the style of the original 15th-century warehouse. There are some tables outside. The English cuisine emphasizes locally caught fish and Cromer crabs. There is also an inexpensive coffee shop in the historic undercroft that serves homemade snacks and pastries. *27 King St., tel. 0553/773134. Reservations not necessary. Dress: informal. MC, V. Closed Sun. Moderate.*

Lavenham
Lodging
★

The Swan. A gloriously atmospheric 14th–15th-century lodging, this inn has oak beams, rambling public rooms, and antique furniture. The bedrooms are all individual, and some have four-poster beds. *High St., near Bury St. Edmunds, CO10 9QA, tel.*

0787/247477. 47 rooms with bath and 3 suites. Facilities: restaurant, 2 bars, 5 lounges, garden, baby-sitting. AE, DC, MC, V. Very Expensive.

Lincoln
Dining
★

Jew's House Restaurant. Situated in the 12th-century Jew's House, one of Lincoln's oldest buildings, the intimate atmosphere is enhanced by antique tables and oil paintings on the walls. The cosmopolitan menu, featuring Continental specialties, changes daily, and the restaurant is renowned for its rich desserts, all homemade. *The Jew's House, 15 The Straight, tel. 0522/24851. Reservations advised. MC, V. Closed Sun. and Mon. lunch. Closed 2–4 weeks in Feb. each year for redecoration. Moderate.*

Harvey's Cathedral Restaurant. This attractive establishment in a 250-year-old building between the cathedral and the castle has a Victorian feel, with lots of old photographs and lace tablecloths. Traditional English dishes such as crisp roast Bailgate duck, and Lincolnshire rabbit-and-pigeon pie are featured. There is now a bistro, **Troffs,** upstairs. *1 Exchequergate Castle Sq., tel. 0522/510333. Reservations advised. Dress: informal. MC, V. Closed Sat. lunch and Sun. dinner. Moderate.*

Lodging
★

The White Hart. Lincoln's most elegant hotel is luxuriously furnished with a wealth of antiques, including some fine clocks and china. The service is personal and extremely friendly. The hotel abuts the cathedral grounds, although cathedral views are somewhat obscured by the surrounding buildings. *Bailgate, LN1 3AR, tel. 0522/526222. 50 rooms with bath, 13 full suites. Facilities: King Richard restaurant, Orangery coffee shop, lounge bar, AE, DC, MC, V. Very expensive.*

Hillcrest Hotel. A small, unpretentious hotel, formerly a Victorian rectory, Hillcrest is in a very quiet area about 5 minutes' walk from the cathedral. The interior was completely redone in 1987 with simple but pleasing modern furnishings. Rooms at the back look out over the garden and arboretum. *15 Lindum Ter., LN2 5RT, tel. 0522/510182. 17 rooms with bath. Facilities: restaurant, bar. AE, MC, V. Closed 2 weeks at Christmas. Moderate.*

Norwich
Dining
★

Adlard's. This is a very comfortable restaurant, mainly decorated in green, that offers highly accomplished cooking. The specialties change regularly, but you might be lucky and find lamb with Jerusalem artichokes, or Dover sole with all kinds of fish sauces. The cheese board has lots of English and French cheeses, and the wine list has delicious selections from all over the world. *79 Upper St. Giles, tel. 0603/633522. Reservations necessary. MC, V. Closed Sun. and Mon., no lunch weekends. Expensive.*

Brasted's. Tucked away down one of Norwich's medieval lanes, this restaurant has a plain outside which gives nothing away. Inside, excellent, carefully prepared meals are served in elegant, rust-and-cream-draped Regency rooms. The specialties include *soupe de poisson* (fish soup) and steak, kidney, and oyster pie. *8–10 St. Andrews Hill, tel. 0603/625949. Reservations advised. Dress: informal. AE, DC, MC, V. Closed Sat. lunch and Sun. Expensive.*

★ **Marco's.** The Georgian architecture of this building is complemented inside by paneled walls, open fires, and pictures, all contributing to a warm, friendly, private atmosphere. Specialties of the Italian cuisine include *salmone al cartoccio* and *gnocchi alla Marco. 17 Pottergate, tel. 0603/624044. Reservations advised. Dress: informal. AE, DC, MC, V. Closed Sun., Mon., and 2nd week Aug.–1st week Sept. Expensive.*

Green's Seafood Restaurant. Seafood cuisine is served here, where fresh linen and live piano music contribute to the pleasant ambience. Specialties include turbot with prawns and herb butter, and poached salmon. There is a new oyster bar serving seafood in a less formal atmosphere. *82 Upper St. Giles St., tel. 0603/623733. Reservations required. Dress: informal. MC, V. Closed Sat. lunch, Sun., Mon., national holidays. Moderate.*

Lodging **The Hotel Nelson.** This new hotel by the river is brightly decorated, with good modern furniture, especially in the Executive wing. Ask for a room with a balcony overlooking the water. *Prince of Wales Rd., NR1 1DX, tel. 0603/760260. 122 rooms with bath. Facilities: 2 restaurants, 2 bars, riverside lounge, gardens. AE, DC, MC, V. Expensive.*

The Georgian House Hotel. This central hotel offers comfortable, traditional accommodations in an elegant, 18th-century house. *32–34 Unthank Rd., NR2 2RB, tel. 0603/615655. 27 rooms with bath or shower. Facilities: restaurant, bar. AE, DC, MC, V. Closed Christmas. Moderate.*

Sprowston Manor. This inviting Victorian country house is set in 8 acres of gardens next to a golf course. *Wroxham Rd., NR7 8RP, tel. 0603/410871. 111 rooms with bath. Facilities: restaurant, lounge bar serving food, sauna, solarium, fitness center, gardens. AE, DC, MC, V. Expensive.*

Orford **Butley-Orford Oysterage.** What started as a little café that sold
Dining oysters and cups of tea has become a large, bustling, no-nonsense restaurant. It still specializes in oysters and smoked salmon, as well as other seafood in season. *Market Hill, tel. 0394/450277. Reservations advised, especially weekends. Dress: informal. No credit cards. Closed evenings in winter except Fri. and Sat. Moderate.*

Lodging **The Crown and Castle.** Near Orford Castle is this small, well-established hotel in an 18th-century building thought to have had smuggling connections. The rooms are small, cozy, and very quiet. *Market Hill, IP12 2LJ, tel. 0394/450205. 19 rooms, 11 with bath. Facilities: restaurant, secluded garden, bar, lounge, baby-listening service. AE, DC, MC, V. Moderate.*

Saffron Walden **Saffron Hotel.** This conversion of three houses into one has re-
Dining and Lodging sulted in a comfortable, modern hotel inside a 16th-century building. The restaurant has straightforward food, with plenty of local specialties, such as a delicious lamb dish. *10–18 High St., CB10 1AY, tel. 0799/22676. 21 rooms, 16 with bath. Restaurant closed lunch Sat., dinner Sun. Dress in restaurant: informal. MC, V. Moderate.*

Shipdam **Shipdam Place.** This former rectory maintains the air of a pri-
Dining and Lodging vate country house in its beautifully furnished rooms. The excellent restaurant serves English dishes, accompanied by a good wine list. *Church Close, IP25 7LX, tel. 0362/820303. 8 rooms with bath. Facilities: 2 lounges, gardens. MC, V. Expensive.*

Southwold **Crown Hotel.** Since Adnams Brewery took it over, this restau-
Dining rant has been vastly improved. It specializes in locally caught
★ fish and has one of the best wine lists in England. The set dinner, served in the simple, but tastefully decorated yellow-and-green dining room by friendly and informed staff, is an amaz-

ingly good value. The cuisine is modern English. *90 High St.,
0502/722275. Reservations required. Dress: informal. AE,
MC, V. Moderate.*

Lodging   **The Swan Hotel.** The lovely, 17th-century inn near the beach
★   (scenes from *David Copperfield* were filmed here) features spa-
          cious public rooms and decent-size bedrooms decorated in tra-
          ditional English country style. There are 18 secluded and quiet
          garden rooms. The hotel staff prides itself on personal service.
          *Market Place, IP18 6EG, tel. 0502/722186. 45 rooms, 42 with
          bath. Facilities: restaurant, bar. AE, MC, V. Expensive.*

Sudbury   **Mabey's Brasserie.** The former chef of Hintlesham Hall has
Dining   opened this simple brasserie, bringing with him the excite-
★   ment of his cooking. This isn't pretentious food but excellently
              prepared local produce, with the specialties always changing
              depending on the market. This is haute cuisine at middling
              prices. *47 Gainsborough St., tel. 0787/74298. Reservations nec-
              essary. Dress: informal. MC, V. Closed Mon. Moderate.*

Lodging   **The Bull and Trivets.** This 16th-century inn is furnished with
          leather chairs and antiques. Some bedrooms have beams and
          galleries and one room has a four-poster bed. The excellent
          informal restaurant serves French dishes. *Church St.,
          Ballingdon, CO10 6BL, tel. 0787/74120. 8 rooms with bath or
          shower. Facilities: lounge, patio garden. AE, DC, MC, V.
          Moderate.*

The Arts

Festivals   The most important arts festival in East Anglia, and one of the
            best known in Great Britain, is the **Aldeburgh Festival,** held for
            two weeks in June every year. Founded by the composer Benja-
            min Britten, it naturally concentrates on music, but there are
            also related exhibitions, poetry readings, and even walks. *Pro-
            gram published in March by Aldeburgh Foundation, High St.,
            Aldeburgh, IP15 5AX, tel. 0728/452935.*

            The **Maltings Concert Hall** at Snape (tel. 0728/453543) has a
            year-round program of events, apart from the Aldeburgh Fes-
            tival.

            Only slightly less notable than Aldeburgh are the festivals in
            Cambridge (last 2 weeks of July) and King's Lynn (roughly the
            same time as Cambridge's, although for a slightly shorter peri-
            od). The **Cambridge Festival** is mainly music, performed by in-
            ternational orchestras and artists in some of the most beautiful
            venues in England, including King's College Chapel and Ely
            Cathedral. *Program, published in May, is obtainable from the
            Festival Administrator, Mandela House, 4 Regent St., Cam-
            bridge, CB2 1BY, tel. 0223/358977, ext. 3836.*

            Much of the **King's Lynn Festival** is based at the Fermoy Centre
            and is wide-ranging, encompassing concerts, exhibitions, thea-
            ter, dance, films, literary events, and children's programs.
            *King's Lynn Festival Office, 27 King St., King's Lynn, PE30
            1HA, tel. 0553/773578.*

            Smaller festivals are held in **Lincoln, Bury St. Edmunds,** and
            Ely during the summer. Check with these tourist information
            centers for details.

Theaters In Cambridge, **The Arts Theatre** (Peas Hill, tel. 0223/352000) puts on major touring productions, a Christmas pantomime every year, and one of the classical Greek dramas every three years. It also hosts the annual Cambridge Footlights Review, training ground for much comic talent in the past 30 years. The **Arts Cinema** (tel. 0223/352001) is an important venue for art films and the annual Cambridge Animated Film Festival.

Cambridge's other theater, the **ADC Theatre** (Park St., tel. 0223/352001), is the headquarters of the University Amateur Dramatics Club. Anything but amateur, the club stages productions comparable with those of the best professional theater.

Bury St. Edmunds's splendid **Theatre Royal** is run by the National Trust. A working theater offering a wide variety of touring shows, it was built in 1819, and is a perfect example of Regency theater design, a delightfully intimate place to watch a performance. It may be closed altogether during parts of the summer, so telephone first to avoid disappointment. *Westgate St., tel. 0284/755127. Open Mon.–Sat. 9:15–8, and for performances. Closed Good Friday and national holiday Mon.*

In Norwich, the **Maddermarket Theatre** (Maddermarket, tel. 0603/620917), patterned after Elizabethan theater design, was founded in 1911 by an amateur repertory company and now performs all sorts of plays, including Shakespeare, to a high standard. The theater is closed for performances in August; but there are guided tours all year. Norwich has a small **Puppet Theatre** (White Friars, tel. 0603/629921), housed in a former church. Not just for children, this theater has a national reputation in its field.

Colchester's **Mercury Theatre** (Balkerne Gate, tel. 0206/573948) stages a wide variety of plays, including tour productions, pre–West End runs, and local productions. It's in a modern building not far from the **Colchester Arts Centre** (St. Mary-at-the-Walls, Church St., tel. 0206/577301) hosts theater, exhibitions, and workshop events. Jazz is featured every other Thursday, with top names from Britain, the Continent, and America.

The **Theatre Royal** in Lincoln (Clasketgate, tel. 0522/525555) is a fine Victorian theater previewing shows before their London runs and offering tour productions. There are also occasionally concerts on Sundays.

Music Both Cambridge and Lincoln support symphony orchestras, and regular musical events are held in many of the colleges, especially those with large chapels like King's College. Concerts are also held in the recently revamped Corn Exchange in Cambridge (tel. 0223/357851). You can listen to music in **St. Andrews Hall** in Norwich (tel. 0603/628477), and hear organ recitals in **St. Peter Mancroft.** The cathedrals of Ely, Norwich, Peterborough, and Lincoln serve as uplifting settings for orchestral and choral performances.

In a country-house setting, Wingfield College (Wingfield, near Diss, tel. 0379/384505) has an annual season of concerts, talks, and recitals by artists of international standing.

14 The Peaks and Yorkshire Moors

Introduction

If you imagine England as a small, cozy country of cottages and gently flowing streams, the Peak District of Derbyshire (pronounced "Darbyshire") and the Yorkshire Moors might come as a bit of a surprise. For this is a wilder, grander part of England, a region of open spaces, wide horizons, and hills that seem to rear violently out of the plain. On a stormy day on the Moors, it's not hard to imagine Charlotte Brontë's Mr. Rochester from *Jane Eyre* galloping on horseback over their cloud-swept ridges.

The Pennines, a line of hills that begins in the Peak District and runs as far north as Scotland, is sometimes called the "backbone of England," and it's a fitting description. This is a landscape of rocky outcrops and vaulting meadowland, where you'll see nothing for miles but sheep, dry-stone (unmortared) walls, and farms, interrupted only occasionally by villages made of the local dark gray stone.

To the east, the bleak areas of moorland that characterize Yorkshire are linked by lush, green valleys. Here, the high rainfall produces luxuriant vegetation, swift rivers, sparkling streams, and waterfalls that contrast with the dark, heather-covered Moors. Its villages are among the most utterly peaceful in England. Three of Britain's 10 national parks are in this region: the Peak District itself; the Yorkshire Dales; and across the fertile Vale of York, the great, flat hills and spectacular coastline of the North York moors.

In the center of the fertile plain that separates the Pennines from the Moors lies York, dominated by the towers of its great minster. Once England's second-most important city, this ancient town has survived the ravages of time, war, and industrialization; its medieval walled city is one of the best preserved in Europe (and an eager-beaver tourist office makes the most of it).

Buxton, Haworth, and Scarborough on the east coast are three very different, rather provincial, towns, yet each provides a peaceful place to stay or use as a base for forays into the deeper countryside.

Essential Information

Important Addresses and Numbers

Tourist Information The Yorkshire and Humberside Tourist Board, 312 Tadcaster Rd., York, N. Yorks YO2 2HF, tel. 0904/707961. Open Mon.–Thurs. 9–5:30, Fri. 9–5.
East Midlands Tourist Board, Exchequergate, Lincoln LN2 1PZ, tel. 0522/531521. Open weekdays 9–5:30.
Tourist information centers, normally open Mon.–Sat. 9:30–5:30, but varying according to season, include the following:
Buxton: The Crescent, Derbyshire SK17 6BQ, tel. 0298/25106.
Scarborough: St. Nicholas Cliff, North Yorkshire YO11 2EP, tel. 0723/373333.
York: De Grey Rooms, Lendel Bridge, Exhibition Sq., North Yorkshire YO1 2HB, tel. 0904/621756.

Travel Agencies **Thomas Cook:** Ivebridge House, 67 Market St., Bradford, tel. 0274/732411; 51 Boar La., Leeds, tel. 0532/432922; 47 Westborough, Scarborough, tel. 0723/364444; and 4 Nessgate, York, tel. 0904/653626.

Car Rental Agencies **York: Budget Rent a Car,** Station House, Foss Island Goods Yard, Foss Islands Rd., tel. 0904/644919 and **Viking Motors,** 32 Lawrence St., tel. 0904/414969.

Arriving and Departing

By Car M1, the principal route north from London, gets you to the region in about two hours, with longer travel times up into north Yorkshire. For the Peak District, leave M1 at exit 29, then head via A219/A6020/A6 to Buxton.

For York (193 miles) and Scarborough areas, and then the north York moors, stay on M1 to Leeds (189 miles), then take A64. For the Yorkshire dales, take M1 to Leeds, the A660 to A65 north and west to Skipton.

By Train **British Rail** serves the region from London King's Cross (tel. 071/278–2477) and London Euston (tel. 071/387–7070) stations. Average travel times from King's Cross, 2½ hours to Leeds and two hours to York.

By Bus **National Express** (tel. 071/730–0202) serves the region from London's Victoria Coach Station. Average travel times include four hours to York and 6½ hours to Scarborough. To reach Buxton, change to the **Trans-Peak** bus service at Derby.

Getting Around

By Car The trans-Pennine route, M62, between Liverpool and Hull, crosses the region. (From Buxton, the A515 south is a former Roman road and a good route through the dales.)

Some of the steep, narrow roads in the countryside off the main routes are difficult drives and can be particularly perilous in winter, but the landscape is simply beautiful.

By Train There are local services from Leeds to Skipton, from York to Scarborough (which has connections on to the seaside towns of Filey and Bridlington), and from Manchester to Buxton. To reach Buxton from London take the Manchester train and switch at Stockport.

Two **Regional Rover** tickets for seven days' unlimited travel are available: **North East** and **Coast and Peaks.**

By Bus There are local buses from Leeds and Bradford into the more remote parts of the Yorkshire Dales on the weekends. An all-day Derbyshire Wayfarer ticket is available for unlimited travel on local buses and trains serving the Peak District.

Guided Tours

The **Yorkshire Guild of Guide Lecturers** (tel. 0904/641952) can arrange fully qualified Blue Badge guides for customized tours according to your interests. A number of operators offer "ghost walks" of York, and other inexpensive sightseeing tours. Contact the tourist office for a list.

The **York Association of Voluntary Guides** (tel. 0904/640780, Mon.–Sat. 9:30 AM–11:30 AM) runs short walking tours daily around the city of York, leaving from Exhibition Square, April to the end of October, at 10:15 and 2:15; and, June to August, also at 7 PM. There is no charge, but tips are normally given. **Yorktour** (tel. 0904/641737) offers open-top bus, riverboat, and walking tours of the city of York, as well as bus trips to such area attractions as Castle Howard, Fountains Abbey, the dales, the moors, and the coast.

Exploring the Peaks and Yorkshire Moors

Orientation

Our exploration of the Peak District and Yorkshire is broken into four distinct areas. The first tour starts in Buxton, a gracious spa town, and then swings through the Peak District, calling at Bakewell, Matlock, the stately home of Chatsworth House, the Peak Cavern, and, finally, Edale.

Tour 2 explores the Yorkshire dales: Wharfedale; the Yorkshire Dales National Park; Haworth, the home of the Brontës; Bolton Abbey, the ruins of a great monastery; Wensleydale and Swarfedale, stomping grounds of James Herriot, the celebrated vet; and, finally, the lovely little town of Richmond.

Tour 3 starts in the city of York, whose medieval attractions alone merit a visit. From York we go to Marston Moor, site of a fierce battle; to Harrogate, another of the area's fine spa towns; the magnificent Fountains Abbey; and, finally, Newby Hall.

The last tour explores the coast around Scarborough, then strikes inland to the North Moors National Park, and visits Rievaulx Abbey and splendidly elegant Castle Howard.

Highlights for First-time Visitors

Bolton Abbey: Tour 2
Brontë Parsonage Museum: Tour 2
Castle Howard: Tour 4
Chatsworth House: Tour 1
Fountains Abbey: Tour 3
North Moors National Park: Tour 4
Rievaulx Abbey: Tour 4
York: Tour 3

Tour 1: Buxton and the Peak District

Numbers in the margin correspond to points of interest on the Buxton and Peak District map.

❶ If you approach **Buxton** from the north, south, or west, you'll traverse wild, mountainous roads over the last great contortions of the Pennine Hills before they level out into the gentler country of the English Midlands. From the east, however, it's a gradual ascent through a series of limestone valleys. Buxton's sheltered position in a great, natural bowl of hills gives it a surprisingly mild climate, considering its altitude: at over 1,000 feet, it's the second-highest town in England.

Buxton and the Peak District

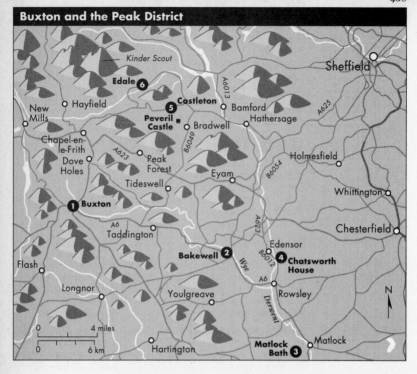

The Romans named Buxton *Aquae Arnemetiae*—loosely translated as "The Waters of the Goddess of the Grove"—suggesting they considered this Derbyshire hill town to be special. The mineral springs, which emerge from 3,500 to 5,000 feet below ground at a constant 82°F, were believed to cure a variety of ailments, and in the 18th century established the town as a popular spa, a minor rival to Bath. You can still drink water from the ancient St. Anne's Well (across from The Crescent), and it's also bottled and sold throughout Britain; it's excellent with a good malt whiskey.

Buxton's spa days have left a legacy of 18th- and 19th-century buildings, parks, and open spaces that now give the town an air of faded grandeur. A good place to start exploring is **The Crescent** on the northwest side of The Slopes park (the town hall is on the opposite side); almost all out-of-town roads lead toward this central green. The three former hotels that comprise the Georgian-era Crescent, with its arches, Doric colonnades, and 378 windows, were built in 1780 by the fifth duke of Devonshire (of nearby Chatsworth House). The splendid ceiling of the former assembly room now looks down on the town's public library, and the thermal baths at the end of The Crescent house look out on a shopping center.

The Devonshire Royal Hospital, behind The Crescent, was originally a stable with room for 110 of the hotel guests' horses; it was converted into a hospital in 1859. The circular area for exercising horses was covered with a massive 156-feet-wide slate-colored dome and incorporated into the hospital.

The Buxton Museum, on the eastern side of The Slopes, has a collection of Blue John stone, a semiprecious mineral found only in the Peak District (*see* Shopping, below), while in The Crescent itself, **The Buxton Micrarium,** an unusual natural-history museum, features microscopic displays of insects, plants, and other specimens. *The Buxton Museum: Terrace Rd., tel. 0298/24658. Admission free. Open Tues.–Fri. 9:30–5:30; Sat. 9:30–5. The Buxton Micrarium: The Crescent, tel. 0298/78662. Admission: £2 adults, £1 children, £1.50 senior citizens. Open late Mar.–early Nov., daily 10–5.*

Just adjacent to The Crescent and The Slopes on the west, the **Octagon**—part of the Pavilion—with its ornate iron-and-glass roof, was originally a concert hall and ballroom. Erected in the 1870s, it is still a lively place, with a conservatory, several bars, a restaurant, and a cafeteria. The surrounding 25 acres of well-kept Pavilion gardens are pleasant to stroll in on a summer's day.

Bordering the Pavilion gardens on the north, **The Parish Church of St. John the Baptist** on St. John's Road is in a handsome, Regency-Tuscan-style building dating from 1811, with some extremely fine mosaic and stained glass. A good deal more architecturally exuberant is the **Opera House** on the same road (Water St. end); built in 1903, it's a massive marble structure bedecked with carved cupids and is the center for Buxton's annual Festival (*see* The Arts, below).

If you follow the Broad Walk through the Pavilion gardens and continue southwest along Temple Road for about half an hour, you'll come to **Poole's Cavern,** a large limestone cave far beneath the 100 wooded acres of County Park. Named after a legendary 15th-century robber's lair, the cave was inhabited in prehistoric times and contains, in addition to the standard stalactites and stalagmites, the source of the River Wye, which flows through Buxton. Poole's Cavern was also known to the Romans, who built baths nearby; a display of Roman archaeology as well as a nature trail and visitors center are outside. *Green La., tel. 0298/26978. Admission (including tour): £2.40 adults, £1.40 children, £2 senior citizens. County Park and visitors center free. Open Easter–Nov., daily 10–5. Closed Wed. in Apr., May, and Oct.*

If you're still feeling energetic, walk southeast from Poole's Cavern up to Grin Low. Here **Solomon's Temple,** a Victorian folly—the technical name for a fanciful building, a popular way of dramatizing the landscape—offers panoramic views. (There's a trail, too, from the south side of town, but it's much steeper.) Access to the temple is unrestricted.

Buxton is a convenient base for exploring the Peak District, Britain's oldest national park, internationally recognized for its conservation activities. "Peak" is perhaps misleading here; although this is a hilly area, it contains only long, flat-topped rises that don't reach much higher than 2,000 feet. Yet the views are enchanting, and the inclines can be fairly steep. You will become much better acquainted with the area if you explore it on foot rather than by car. The national park centers at Castleton, Edale, and Bakewell offer maps and guides covering everything from short strolls to day-long hikes. You can also join a guided hike led by an experienced ranger with detailed knowledge of the region's local and natural history (*see* Sports, below).

② Make the quiet market town of **Bakewell,** 12 miles southeast of Buxton on A6, your first stop. On the way, you'll pass through the spectacular valleys of Ashwood Dale, Wyedale, and Monsal Dale. Bakewell, set on the winding river Wye, is appealing with its narrow streets and houses built out of the local gray-brown stone. Market day (Monday), attended by local farmers, is an event not to be missed. Bakewell is also the source of the renowned Bakewell Tart, said to have been created by accident when, sometime last century, a cook at the town's Rutland Arms Hotel spilled a rich cake mixture over some jam tarts.

As in other parts of the Peak District, the inhabitants of Bakewell still practice the early-summer custom of "well-dressing," during which certain wells or springs are elaborately decorated or "dressed" with flowers. Although the floral designs usually incorporate biblical themes, they are just a Christian veneer over an ancient pagan celebration of the water's life-giving powers. In Bakewell, the lively ceremony is the focus of several days of festivities in June.

③ **Matlock** and its neighbor **Matlock Bath,** both about seven miles southeast of Bakewell on A6, are former spa towns compressed into a narrow gorge on the River Derwent. The **Matlock River Illuminations,** a flotilla of beautifully lit boats shimmering after dark along the still waters of the river, take place on weekends from mid-August through mid-October.

From Matlock Bath, one of the British Isles' rare cable cars takes visitors to **The Heights of Abraham,** a cave with a visitor center on the crags above.

Back on A6, head north for five miles and turn off at Rowsley onto B6012, which will take you another four miles through glo-**④** rious parkland to **Chatsworth House,** ancestral home of the dukes of Devonshire and one of England's greatest country houses. As you approach, the great expanse of parkland, grazed by deer and sheep, opens before you to set off the Palladian-style elegance of "the Palace of the Peak." Built by various dukes over several generations starting in 1686, Chatsworth was conceived on a grand, even monumental, scale. It is surrounded by woods, elaborate colorful gardens, greenhouses, rock gardens, cascading water, and terraces—all designed by two great landscape artists, Capability Brown and, later, Joseph Paxton, an engineer as well as a brilliant gardener. He was responsible for most of the eye-catching waterworks. Plan on at least half a day to explore the grounds properly, and avoid going on Sunday, when the place is very crowded.

Inside, the 175 rooms are filled with treasures: intricate carvings, Van Dyck portraits, Rembrandt's *Portrait of an Oriental,* sculptures, tapestries, superb furniture, and china. The magnificent condition of much of the furnishings and decorations is largely due to the dowager duchess, who supervises an ongoing program of in-house repair and restoration. *Bakewell, tel. 0246/582204. Admission: £4.25 adults, £2 children, £3.50 senior citizens, £11 family ticket; Garden only: £2.25 adults, £1.10 children; £6.25 family ticket. Open late Mar.—early Nov., daily house 11–4:30; garden 11–5.*

⑤ Castleton (take A623, then B6049 north from Chatsworth), a town in the Hope Valley, which also tends to be crowded in the peak season, is somewhat commercialized, but is worth a visit to see the ruins of **Peveril Castle** behind the town. Also interesting is the massive **Peak Cavern,** where rope has been made on a great ropewalk for over 400 years: a prehistoric village has been excavated here as well. *Tel. 0433/20285. Admission: £2 adults, £1 children and senior citizens. Open Apr.–Oct., daily 10–5; Nov.–Mar., Tues.–Sun. 10–5.*

Castleton has a number of other caves and mines open to the public, including some former lead mines and Blue John mines. (Blue John is amethystine spar; the unusual name is a local corruption of the French *bleu-jaune.*) Try to visit the **Speedwell Cavern** at the bottom of Winnats Pass, the only mine in England you can tour by boat, traveling 840 feet below ground through great illuminated caverns to reach the "Bottomless Pit." There is also an exhibition and a store selling Blue John jewelry. *Tel. 0433/20512. Admission: £3.75 adults, £2.50 children under 14. Open daily 9:30–5:30 (Nov.–Mar. to 4:30. Closed Christmas, Dec. 26, and New Year's Day.*

If you're interested in hiking, take the sign-posted road to **⑥ Edale,** a sleepy village in the shadow of Mam Tor and Lose Hill, and the moorlands of Kinder Scout. This extremely popular walking center is the starting point of the 250-mile Pennine Way. The Edale information center has maps, guides, and information on walks in the area. *Tel. 0433/70207. Open Easter–Oct., daily 9–5:30; Nov.–Mar., daily 9–5.*

Tour 2: Brontë Country and the Yorkshire Dales

Numbers in the margin correspond to points of interest on the Yorkshire and the Dales map.

This tour begins in Haworth, 43 miles as the crow flies north of Buxton through the hills and valleys of the Peak District (by A624, A6016, or any of the more picturesque minor roads), and—skirting Manchester (via A6052, A640, A6033)—into the heart of Brontë country and the Yorkshire Dales.

Many are drawn to this part of Yorkshire by the tragic story of the Brontë sisters, who wrote at least two immortal novels, *Jane Eyre* and *Wuthering Heights*, here. They lived in **⑦ Haworth,** a straggling stone village on the edge of the Yorkshire Moors.

Haworth's steep, cobbled Main Street has changed little since the days of the famous sisters, and it is now largely free of traffic. At the end is the **Black Bull** pub, where Branwell, only brother of the Brontë sisters, drank himself into an early grave. Here also are the post office from which Charlotte, Emily, and Anne sent their manuscripts to their London publishers; an information center with guides and maps; the church, with its gloomy graveyard (Charlotte and Emily are buried inside the church); and the **Brontë Parsonage Museum,** which has some enchanting mementos, including their spidery, youthful graffiti on the nursery wall. *Tel. 0535/42323. Admission: £2.50 adults, 50p children 16 and under, £1 senior citizens. Open Apr.–Sept., daily 11–5:30; Oct.–Mar., 11–4:30. Closed Jan. 21–Feb 8 and Dec. 24–26.*

Yorkshire and the Dales

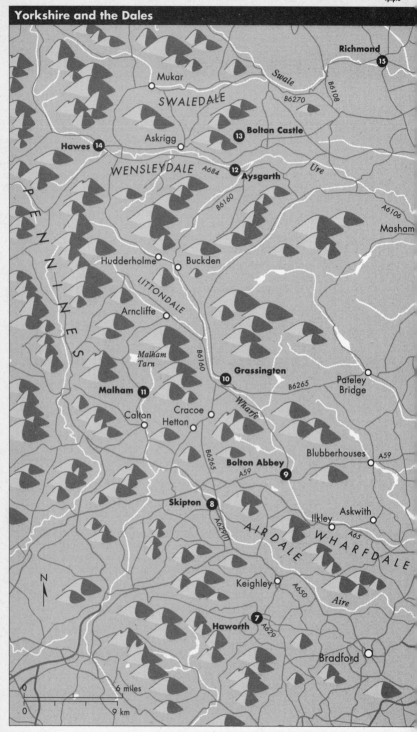

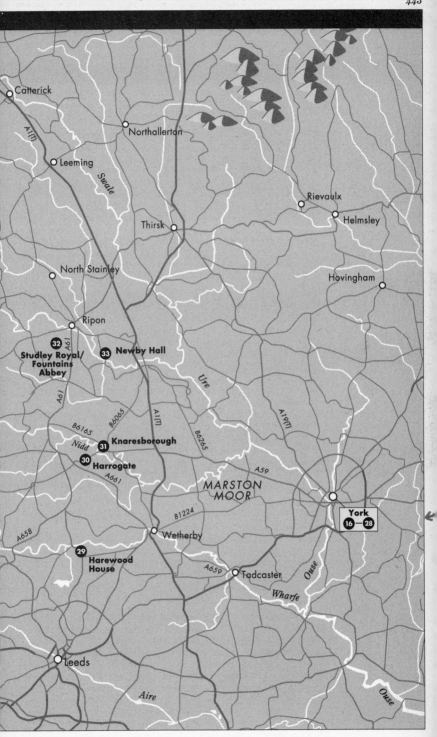

If you know and love the Brontës' works, you'll also probably want to walk (an hour or so along a field path, a lane, and a moorland track) to the **Brontë Waterfall,** described in Emily's and Charlotte's poems and letters. Farther into the austere moor is **Top Withins,** the remains of a bleak hilltop farm, which was probably the main inspiration of Heathcliff's gloomy mansion, Wuthering Heights. Wear sturdy shoes and protective clothing: If you've read *Wuthering Heights,* you'll have a fairly good idea of what weather can be like on the Yorkshire moors!

It's only 12 miles north from Haworth through Airedale on **8** A629 to **Skipton,** a typical Dales market town (markets every day except Tuesday and Sunday), with as many farmers as tourists milling in the streets. At the top of busy High Street is **Skipton Castle,** built by the Normans and unaltered since the Civil War (17th century). In the central courtyard, a yew tree, planted 300 years ago by feminist and philanthropist Lady Anne Clifford, still flourishes. Lady Anne was the last of the Cliffords, one of England's most famous baronial families; you can see the striking heraldry on the tombs of her ancestors, the earls of Cumberland, inside Skipton Church. *Skipton Castle, tel. 0756/792442. Admission: £2.20 adults, £1.10 children under 18. Open Mon.–Sat. 10–6, Sun. 2–6.*

From Skipton, strike east into **Wharfedale,** one of the longest of the Yorkshire dales; most, but not all, take their names from the rivers that run through them. About five miles along A59, **9** **Bolton Abbey,** the ruins of an Augustinian priory, sits on a grassy embankment inside a great curve of the river Wharfe. You can wander through the 13th-century ruins or visit the priory church, which is still the local parish church; it's open daily, with free access during daylight hours. Among the famous visitors enchanted by Bolton Abbey were William Wordsworth (who described "Bolton's mouldering Priory" in his poem "The White Doe of Rylstone"); J. M. W. Turner, the 19th-century painter; and John Ruskin, the Victorian art critic. The abbey is surrounded by some of the most romantic woodland scenery in England, and nearby the river plunges between a narrow chasm in the rocks before reaching a medieval hunting lodge, **Barden Tower.** Barden Tower is now a ruin and can be visited just as easily as Bolton Abbey, in whose grounds it stands.

From Bolton, follow the river north through Wharfedale (via **10** B6160) for seven miles until you get to **Grassington.** A stone village, built around an ancient cobbled marketplace, it's a good place to begin exploring Upper Wharfedale. The National Park Centre (near the bus station) has information on a wide choice of village and country tours. In Grassington itself, you'll find a small museum and a surprisingly good range of stores, pubs, and cafés. *National Park Centre, tel. 0756/752748. Open Apr.–Oct., daily 10–5; Nov.–Mar., weekends 10–5.*

From Grassington take B6265 south two miles through Cracoe, then branch west onto the minor road past Hetton and Calton **11** to reach **Malham,** a village surrounded by some of Britain's most remarkable limestone formations. **Malham Cove,** a huge natural rock amphitheater, is a short walk from the National Park Centre. Also nearby is **Gordale Scar,** a deep natural chasm between overhanging limestone cliffs, through which the white waters of a moorland stream plunge 300 feet. This is an area of international importance in the fields of natural history and Roman archaeology, and maps at the National Park Centre will give you some idea of what there is to do and see. *Tel. 07293/363. Open Easter–June, Sept.–Oct., daily 9:30–5; July–Aug., daily 9–5:30; Nov.–Easter, daily 10–3:30.*

Continuing this dramatic moorland drive, take the road north (skirting Malham Tarn), to Arncliffe in Littondale. Follow the signs for B6160 and go north to **Buckden**, the last village in Wharfedale. From here you can go directly through Kidstone **⑫** Pass (still on B6160) to **Aysgarth** in Wensleydale (don't forget to sample some of the local cheese). Here you can view the **Aysgarth Force**, a series of waterfalls on the river Ure, and **⑬** **Bolton Castle**, where Mary, Queen of Scots, was imprisoned in the 16th century—the tower in which she was held still stands.

Now continue to Hawes from Aysgarth, by following A684 for ten miles due west.

⑭ The market town of **Hawes** serves the two main northern dales, **Wensleydale** and **Swaledale**. This is where the James Herriot TV series was filmed; if you've seen it, you might recognize the village of Askrigg, east of Hawes, which was dubbed "Darrowby" in the program.

Hawes's National Park Information Centre in the old train station contains the **Dales Countryside Museum,** an excellent collection of domestic and agricultural implements, which helps give a picture of dales life in past centuries; a traditional rope-walk (rope-making shop) here also welcomes visitors. And there's a good range of pubs and cafés in the area. *National Park Centre, The Old Station, tel. 0969/667494. Open Apr.–Oct., daily 10–5. The Dales Countryside Museum, Station Yard, tel. 0969/667494. Admission: £1 adults, 50p children 5–15 and senior citizens. Open Apr.–Oct., daily 10–5; some winter weekends, phone for details.*

Many people regard **Swaledale,** the next dale north, as the finest of all the Yorkshire dales. Awesomely crooked and steep, its narrow valley road twists over the Buttertubs Pass between Hawes and **Muker.**

At the eastern end of Swaledale (B6270 and A6108) is **⑮** **Richmond,** a jewel of an English town, with a network of narrow Georgian streets and terraces opening into a typically English marketplace. The immense keep of a Norman **castle** towers above the river Swale. *Castle, tel. 0748/2493. Admission: £1.30 adults, 70p children, £1 senior citizens. Open Apr–Sept., daily 10–6, Oct.–Mar., Tues.–Sun. 10–4. Closed Dec. 24–26 and Jan. 1.*

On Friars Wynd, in Richmond, you'll discover the tiny 18th-century **Georgian Theatre Royal,** the oldest theater in England still in use, and unchanged since the days of the 18th-century Shakespearean actor, David Garrick. You can watch a period performance here from either gallery boxes or old wooden seats. It's an intimate theater, remarkable for its authentic detail (except that it uses electric lights instead of candles). Try to reserve tickets well in advance. Also open to visitors outside performance times, the theater has a small museum with unique painted scenery dating from 1836. *Tel. 0748/3021. Museum admission: £1 adults, 60p children. Open late March–Oct., Mon.–Sat. 11–4:45, Sun. 2:30–4:45.*

From Richmond take the fast, though largely unattractive, A1 and A59 roads south to York.

Tour 3: York to Harrogate and Fountains Abbey

Numbers in the margin correspond to points of interest on the York map.

⑯ Be prepared to spend several days in **York** if you can, or come more than once; the layers of history within its walls cannot be explored quickly.

Named "Eboracum" in Latin, York was the military capital of Roman Britain, and traces of Roman garrison buildings still survive in the Museum gardens, among other places. The base of the medieval Multangular Tower was also part of the garrison, and the foundations of York Minster (cathedral) itself rise from remains of the *principia*, or garrison headquarters. If you ask the landlord at the Roman Bath Inn (St. Sampson's Sq.), he'll show you part of a Roman hot-air bath below his pub.

Following the fall of the Roman Empire in the 5th century, Anglo-Saxon invaders built a town in the ruins of the Roman fort. On Christmas Eve, AD 627, the Northumbrian King Edwin introduced Christianity to the area by being baptized in a little wooden church in York. The city grew in importance in the 9th century, after the Viking conquerors of northern and eastern England made York—which they called "Jorvik"— their English capital.

One memorable way to see the city is from atop the city walls. Originally earth ramparts erected by York's Viking kings to repel raiders, the present stone structure (probably replacing a stockade) dates from the 13th century and has been extensively restored. A narrow paved walk runs along the top of the walls (originally 3 mi in circumference), passing over fortified gates or "bars."

Because of its strategic position on the River Ouse, York developed throughout Norman and Plantagenet times (11th–14th century) into a trade center and inland port, particularly for the export of wool to the Continent. Wealthy guilds of craftsmen and merchants flourished, and kings and queens frequently visited the city: Edward III held a parliament here in 1332 and Richard II gave the city its first Sword of State. The great York Minster, officially the Cathedral of St. Peter, was founded in Norman times, and its size and beauty reflect medieval York's wealth and importance. The archbishop of York is second only to the archbishop of Canterbury in the hierarchy of the Church of England.

The old city center of York is a compact, dense web of narrow streets and tiny alleys—"snickleways"—and not a good place for driving. Congestion has gotten so bad that traffic has been banned around the minster: The exhaust fumes and vibration can cause too much damage. It's easy to lose your sense of direction in the crooked streets, so have a street map handy. Bus tours of the city leave from outside the train station, but you'll probably get a better sense of York by walking through it. It's a popular place; try to avoid July and August when crowds choke the narrow streets and cause long lines at the popular museums. April, May, and October are far better; April is also the time to see the embankments beneath the city walls filled with the pale gold ripple of daffodils.

(17) Start your tour in the north of the city, at the largest Gothic church in England, **York Minster:** It is 534 feet long, 249 feet across its transepts, and 90 feet from floor to roof; the central towers are 184 feet high. Mere statistics, however, cannot convey the scale and beauty of the building. Its soaring columns; the ornamentation of its 14th-century nave; the great east window; the enormous choir screen portraying every king of England from William the Conqueror (reigned 1066–1087) to Henry VI (reigned 1422–1461); the Rose Window commemorating the marriage of Henry VII and Elizabeth of York in 1486 (the event that ended the Wars of the Roses and began the Tudor dynasty)—all contribute to its magnificence. The minster also contains a rich array of chapels, monuments, and tombs, and don't miss the exquisite 13th-century **Chapter House.** The **Undercroft Museum and Treasury,** with Saxon and Roman remains, houses among other treasures the ancient Horn of Ulf given to the minster by a relative of the Danish king Canute, who ruled England from 1016 to 1035.

After exploring the interior, you might take the 275 winding steps to the roof of the great **central tower** (strictly for those with a head for heights), not only for the close-up view of the cathedral's detailed carving but also for a magnificent panorama of York and the surrounding Pennines and Yorkshire moors. *York Minster Undercroft Museum and Treasury, Chapter House, and Central Tower, tel. 0904/624426. Admission to undercroft: £1.30 adults, 60p children; Chapter House: 50p adults, 20p children; Central Tower: £1 adults, 50p children; Crypt 50p adults, 20p children. Open Mon.–Sat. 10–6, Sun. 1–6 (summer till 7).*

(18) After leaving the minster, walk down Low Petergate to Colliergate. The town center's mixed architectural heritage ranges over many periods, although in some places nondescript modern development has taken its toll. **The Shambles** (right off Colliergate), however, is a perfectly preserved medieval street with half-timbered stores and houses whose overhangs are so massive you could almost reach across the street from one second-floor window to another.

(19) Walk the length of the Shambles, taking time to browse in the crafts and souvenir shops along the way, and into The Pavement. From here turn right into Fossgate where you'll find the **Merchant Adventurers' Hall** on the right. This former guildhall, dating from the mid-14th century, is the largest half-timbered hall in York, with a pretty garden in the back. *Tel. 0904/654818. Admission: £2. Open May–Sept., daily 9:30–5.*

(20) From the Merchant Adventurers' Hall you can walk along the river a little way before turning right into an area containing two interesting museums: the Jorvik Viking Centre and the Heritage Centre in St. Mary's church. In the **Jorvik Viking Centre,** on an authentic Viking site, archaeologists have re-created a Viking street with astonishing attention to detail. Its "time-cars" take visitors through the streets to experience the sights, sounds, and smells(!) of Viking England. *Coppergate, tel. 0904/643211. Admission: £3 adults, £1.50 children, £2.25 senior citizens. Open Apr.–Oct., daily 9–7; Nov.–Mar., daily 9–5:30.*

York's 20 or so surviving medieval churches—almost any of which could stand alone as an architectural showpiece—tend to

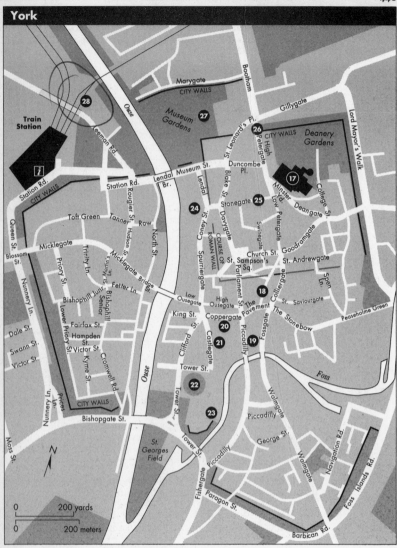

York

be largely ignored by tourists and are therefore good places to
㉑ explore without the crowds. **St. Mary's** now houses **The York Story,** an exhibit devoted to the history of the city. *Castlegate, tel. 0904/628632. Admission: £1.20 adults, 60p children and senior citizens. Open Mon.–Sat. 10–5, Sun. 1–5.*

Continue down Castlegate and turn right into Tower Street. On
㉒ your left you'll see **Clifford's Tower,** which dates from the early 14th century. It stands on the mound originally erected for the keep of York Castle, long since gone (the site now occupied by the Assize Courts and the Castle Museum). In 1190 this was the scene of one of the worst outbreaks of anti-semitism in medieval Europe, when 150 Jews who had sought sanctuary in the castle were massacred. There was a poignant commemoration of the 800th anniversary in 1990.

㉓ The **Castle Museum,** a former 18th-century prison, offers a number of detailed exhibitions and re-creations, including a cobblestoned Victorian street complete with crafts shops; a working water mill; domestic and military displays; and, most important, the Coppergate Helmet, a 1,200-year-old Anglo-Saxon helmet (one of only three ever found) discovered during recent excavations of the city. You can also visit the cell where Dick Turpin, the 18th-century highwayman and folk hero who once rode nonstop from London to York on his horse, Black Bess, spent the night before his execution. *Clifford St., tel. 0904/653611. Admission: £3 adults, £1.50 children. Open Apr.–Oct., Mon.–Sat. 9:30–5:30, Sun. 10–5:30; Nov.–Mar., Mon.–Sat. 9:30–4, Sun. 10–4.*

A walk up Castlegate to Spurriergate into Coney Street brings
㉔ you to the **Mansion House** and the **Guildhall.** Although damaged by World War II bombing, the Guildhall has been faithfully restored to its mid-15th-century glory. *St. Helen's Sq., tel. 0904/613161. Admission free. Open May–Oct., Mon.–Thurs. 9–5, Fri. 9–4, Sat. 10–5, Sun. 2–5; Nov.–Apr., Mon.–Thurs. 9–5, Fri. 9–4.*

㉕ From the Guildhall, make your way across into **Stonegate,** a narrow street of Tudor and 18th-century storefronts and court-yards with considerable charm. A passage just off Stonegate, at 52A, leads to a 12th-century Norman stone house, one of the very few to have survived in England.

Back on Stonegate, continue northward to the minster and turn left onto High Petergate. Walk out of the walled city
㉖ through **Bootham Bar,** one of its old gates. To your left are the gardens and ruins of St. Mary's Abbey, founded in 1089, which
㉗ now houses the **Yorkshire Museum.** In these gardens the city's cycle of mystery plays is performed every four years (*see* The Arts, below); the next performance is in 1992. The museum itself covers the natural and archaeological history of the whole county, including a great deal of material on the Roman, Anglo-Saxon, and Viking aspects of York. *Museum Gardens, tel. 0904/629745. Admission: £1.80 adults, £1 children, family ticket, £4.50. Open Mon.–Sat. 10–5, Sun. 1–5.*

Enjoy a stroll through the gardens and then make your way to Lendal Bridge and cross the river onto Station Road. Take a
㉘ right onto Leeman Road and follow the signs to the **National Railway Museum,** which houses Britain's national collection of locomotives and is perhaps the world's best train museum. Among the exhibits are gleaming giants of the steam era, in-

cluding *Mallard*, holder of the world speed record for a steam engine (126 mph). You can clamber aboard some of the trains. Passenger cars used by Queen Victoria are also on display. *Tel. 0904/621261. Admission: £3 adults, £1.50 children, £2 senior citizens, family ticket, £8. Open Mon.–Sat. 10–6, Sun. 11–6.*

Numbers in the margin correspond to points of interest on the Yorkshire and the Dales map.

From York make your way west along B1224 across Marston Moor where in 1644 Oliver Cromwell won a decisive victory over the royalists during the Civil War. At Wetherby, ten miles away, continue another six miles westward along A659 to **Harewood House** (pronounced "Harwood"), home of the earl of Harewood, a cousin of the queen. This neoclassical-style mansion, built in 1759 by John Carr of York, is known for its Robert Adam interiors, important painting and ceramics collections, and Chippendale furniture (Chippendale himself was born in nearby Otley). Within the grounds are gardens, woods, a lake, a bird garden, and a butterfly house. *Harewood, tel. 0532/886225. Admission: £4.50 adults, £2 children. Open Apr.–Oct., daily 11–5.*

From Harewood, follow the signs northward (9 mi) to **Harrogate**, an elegant town which flourished during Regency and early Victorian periods, when its mineral springs began to attract the noble and wealthy. You can still drink the evil-smelling (and -tasting) spa waters at the newly restored **Royal Pump Room Museum,** which charts the story of Harrogate from its modest 17th-century beginnings. *Opposite Valley Gardens. Tel. 0423/503340. Admission: £1.10 adults, 55p children and senior citizens, family ticket, £2.75. Open Mon.–Sat. 10–5, Sun. 2–5.*

Numerous coffee shops and wine bars line the town's gracious esplanades, and tea and toasted teacakes are served in the pump room in the **Royal Baths.** You can still take a Turkish bath or a sauna in its exotic, tiled rooms.

When the spas no longer drew crowds, Harrogate shed its old image to become a modern business center, and built a huge complex that attracts international conventions. However, it has been tactfully located so as not to spoil the town's landscape of poised Regency row houses, pleasant walkways, and sweeping green spaces (the one in the town center is known as "The Stray").

Just two miles northeast of Harrogate on A6055, the photogenic old town of **Knaresborough** is built in a steep, rocky gorge along the river Nidd. Its attractions include a boat-filled river, a little marketplace, a medieval castle, a house carved out of the cliff face, and a "petrifying well" which will cover anything placed in it with a thin layer of limestone in a matter of weeks.

From Knaresborough take B6165 west five miles, then A61 north another four miles until you reach the back road leading to Fountains Abbey and Studley Royal. The 18th-century water garden and deer park, **Studley Royal,** together with the ruins of **Fountains Abbey,** blends the glories of English Gothic architecture with a neoclassical vision of an ordered universe. The gardens include lakes, ponds, and even a diverted river, while waterfalls splash around classical temples, statues, and a grotto; the surrounding woods offer long vistas toward the great tower of Ripon Cathedral, some three miles north. Next to the Studley Royal grounds the majestic ruins of Fountains Abbey, with its own high tower and soaring 13th-century arches, make a striking picture on the banks of the river Skell. Founded in 1132, but not completed until the early 1500s, the abbey still possesses many of its original buildings, and it's one of the best places in England to learn how medieval monastic life was organized. The whole of this complex is now owned by the National Trust, which manages a small restaurant (lunch only) at the eastern entrance, as well as stores at both the east and west entrances, and an exhibition and video display in the 17th-century **Fountains Hall**, one of the earliest neoclassical buildings in northern England. *Tel. 0765/86333. Admission: £2.70 adults, £1.20 children, family ticket £6.60 (reduced rates in winter). Open daily Oct.–Mar., 10–dusk; Apr.–June and Sept., 10–7, July–Aug., 10–8.*

㉝ Not far from Fountains Abbey (via back roads heading east across A61) is **Newby Hall,** an early-18th-century house which was redecorated later in the same century by Robert Adam for his patron William Weddell; it contains some of the finest interior decorative art of its period in western Europe. One room has been designed around a set of priceless Gobelin tapestries, and another was created to show off Roman sculpture. The gardens, which extend down to the river Ure, are among the most famous in northern England, with their collection of old species roses, rare shrubs, and delightful sunken gardens. The children's adventure playground, narrow-gauge steam railroad, river steamers, and garden restaurant make a visit to Newby a full day's outing. *Tel. 0423/322583. Admission: £4.50 adults, £2.50 children, £3.60 senior citizens. Open Easter–Oct., Tues.–Sun. 11–5.*

The return to York, 21 miles due southeast, can be along B6265/A59, part of which is the old Roman Dere Street.

Tour 4: Scarborough and the North York Moors

Numbers in the margin correspond to points of interest on the Scarborough and North York Moors map.

㉞ A great sweep of cliffs above its sandy bay, a rocky promontory capped by a ruined castle, and a harbor with a lighthouse make **Scarborough** on the northeast Yorkshire coast the classic picture of an English seaside resort. In fact, the city claims to be the earliest seaside resort in Britain, dating from the chance discovery in the early 17th century of a mineral spring on the foreshore. Not unexpectedly, this led to the establishment of a spa, whose users were encouraged not merely to soak themselves in sea water but even to drink it. By the late 18th century, when sea bathing was firmly in vogue, no beaches were busier than Scarborough's with "bathing machines," cumbersome wheeled cabins drawn by donkeys or horses into the surf and anchored there. These contraptions afforded swimmers, especially modest ladies, relative privacy, as the cabin door faced seaward.

Scarborough's initial prosperity dates from this period, as evidenced in the handsome Regency and early Victorian residences and hotels in the city. The advent of train travel further popularized seaside vacations in Britain, and the extension of the railroad from York to Scarborough in the mid-19th century

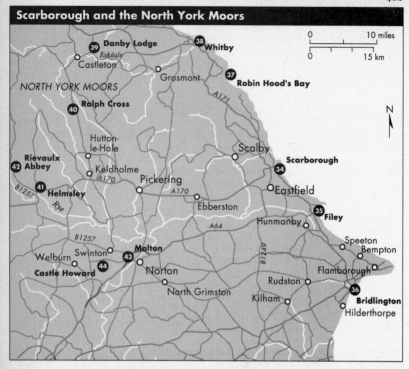

made it accessible for larger numbers of people. Smaller hotels and boardinghouses sprang up to accommodate less wealthy vacationers, and an atmosphere of cheerful vulgarity soon became as characteristic of Scarborough as of the other British seaside resorts.

Yet Scarborough has kept its two distinct faces. Its older, more genteel side in the southern half of town consists of carefully laid out crescents and squares, and clifftop walks and gardens with spectacular views across Cayton Bay. The northern side is a riot of ice cream stands, cafés, stores selling "rock" (no British seaside vacation is complete without this hard candy), crab hawkers, bingo halls, and cotton candy. The contrast between the two makes Scarborough all the more appealing. Enough also survives of the tight huddle of streets, alleyways, and red-roofed cottages around the harbor to give one an idea of what the city was like before the resort days. One revealing relic is a tall, 15th-century stone house, now a restaurant, which is said to have been owned by Richard III.

Scarborough harbor is busy with coastal fishing and shipping, as well as pleasure cruises. Stop in at the old harbor lighthouse, which doubles as a deep-sea fishing museum.

Paths link the harbor with the ruins of **Scarborough Castle** on the promontory; dating from Norman times, it is built on the site of a Roman signal station and near a former Viking settlement. From the castle there are spectacular views across the North Bay, the beaches, and the shore gardens. *Tel. 0723/ 72451. Admission: £1.30 adults, 65p children, 95p students* *and senior citizens. Open Apr.–Sept., Tues.–Sun. 10–6; Oct.–Mar. Tues.–Sun. 10–4.*

At the little medieval church of **St. Mary**, near the castle on the way into town, you'll find the grave of Anne, the youngest of the Brontë sisters; she was taken to Scarborough from Haworth in a final desperate effort to save her life in the sea air.

Happier literary associations in Scarborough are to be found at **Wood End** on the Crescent, vacation home of 20th-century writers Edith, Osbert, and Sacheverell Sitwell, a sister and two brothers. Wood End, an early Victorian house with delightful grounds, is now the **Woodend Museum of Natural History**; the adjoining house is the **Art Gallery**. *Museum and art gallery tel. 0723/367326. Admission free. Open May–Sept., Tues.–Sat. 10–1 and 2–5, Sun. 2–5; Oct.–Apr., Tues.–Sat. 10–1 and 2–5.*

A short walk below Wood End leads to the **Rotunda Museum,** an extraordinary circular building housing important archaeological and local history collections. Constructed in 1829 for the Scarborough Philosophical Society, it was one of the first public buildings in the country to be erected as a museum. *Vernon Rd., tel. 0723/374839. Admission and opening times same as Woodend Museum.*

Except for the hottest summers, England's northeastern seaboard isn't the warmest place for a beach vacation, but there are some good sandy beaches in the area, such as those at **Filey** and **Bridlington** to the south. Scarborough's own beaches are a mixture of sand and rock. However, not the least of Scarborough's attractions as a touring base is its proximity to outstanding countryside. The 55-mile stretch of coast from **Saltburn-by-the-Sea** north of Scarborough down to Bridlington has some of the sheerest seacliffs in the British Isles. Inland, unspoiled country towns and villages provide a pleasant contrast to the sometimes garish esplanades of resorts and the overcrowded trailer parks.

Begin by making your way north, either on A171 or by the more interesting minor roads, and take time to stop off at **Robin Hood's Bay** (20 miles), a tiny fishing village squeezed into a narrow ravine near where a stream courses over the cliffs. Space is so tight here you are not allowed to drive into the village center. The tiny beach was once a notorious smugglers' landing; contraband was passed up the streambed beneath the cottages, often with customs officers in hot pursuit.

North another 5 miles brings you to **Whitby**. Now a small resort, Whitby was once a great whaling port, and it was here that Captain James Cook (1728–79), explorer, navigator, and discoverer of Australia, served his apprenticeship. Visit the **Captain Cook Memorial Museum** in the 18th-century house where Cook lived, and see mementos of his epic expeditions, including maps, diaries, and drawings. *Grape La., tel. 0947/601900. Admission: £1 adults, 60p children and senior citizens. Open Easter–Oct., daily 9:45–5.*

Climb the 199 steps from Whitby harbor and you are at the romantic ruins of **Whitby Abbey,** set high on the cliffs. St. Hilda founded the abbey in AD 657, and Caedmon (died c. 670), the first identifiable poet of the English language, was a monk

here. The nearby Mariners' Church of **St. Mary** is designed in
the style of an 18th-century ship's deck. It was in this churchyard that Bram Stoker's Dracula claimed Lucy as his victim.
*Tel. 0947/603568. Admission: 95p adults, 45p children. Open
Apr.–Sept., Tues.–Sun. 10–6, Oct.–Mar., Tues.–Sun. 10–4.*

From Whitby, follow the minor roads west through sleepy
moorland villages across the top of the dramatic north York
moors. The area set off by the **North Moors National Park** is
dominated by rolling heather-covered hills which, in late summer and early fall, are a rich blaze of crimson and purple. Other
parts of the park are densely wooded, and between the woods
and moorland lie the grassy valleys that shelter Yorkshire's
charming older villages and hamlets. Unlike the Pennine dales
to the west, where everything is built in gray stone, the natural
building material here is a mellower brown stone.

39 Take time if you can to visit the National Park's **Moor's Centre**
at **Danby Lodge,** Eskdale (about 15 miles from Whitby and not
far from Danby Station). Here, in a converted country house,
exhibitions, displays, and a wide range of pamphlets and books
about the area are available, as well as a varied program of lectures, guided walks, and national park events. *Danby, tel.
0287/60654. Admission free. Open Mar.–Oct., daily 10–5.*

From Danby take the road due west 1½ miles to Castleton, then
south over the top of the moors—where it is called Blakely
Ridge Road—to Hutton-le-Hole (14 miles; there's also a visitors' information center here) and Keldholme (16 miles). The
road offers magnificent views over the park, especially at
40 **Ralph Cross,** the highest point.

For more domestic-style pleasures after these vast, romantic
landscapes, head six miles west from Keldhome on A170 to
41 **Helmsley,** a town with a castle and a traditional country marketplace surrounded by fine old inns, cafés, and stores. It's just
over two miles from here by road (B1257) or hiking path to the
42 ruins of **Rievaulx Abbey,** once a great Cistercian center of learning, whose graceful Gothic arches are superbly set off by its
dramatic setting on the river Rye. The best view of the ruins is
from **Rievaulx Terrace,** a long, grassy walkway on the hillside
above flanked by Tuscan- and Ionic-style temples. Now a National Trust property, the terraces can be reached via B1257
from Helmsley. *Rievaulx Abbey, tel. 04396/228. Admission:
£1.60 adults, 80p children. Open Apr.–Sept., daily 10–6; Oct.–
Mar., Tues.–Sun. 10–4. Rievaulx Terrace, admission: £1.70
adults, 80p children. Open Apr.–Oct., 10:30–6.*

Continuing southeast on B1257 for 16 miles, you come to
43 **Malton,** a pleasant market town and once an important Roman
44 post. One of Yorkshire's most famous houses, **Castle Howard,**
lies in the Howardian Hills to the west of Malton. Perhaps best
known these days as the setting for the TV series *Brideshead
Revisited*, it was designed by Sir John Vanbrugh, who also designed Blenheim, Winston Churchill's birthplace. Castle Howard took 60 years to build (1699–1759), and the baroque
grandeur of its conception inside and out is without equal in
northern England. A magnificent central hallway spanned by a
handpainted ceiling leads to a series of staterooms and galleries packed with furniture and works of fine art; there is also a
costume gallery in the stables. A neoclassical landscape was
created for the house: Carefully arranged woods, lakes,

bridges, obelisks, temples, pyramids, and a mausoleum compose a scene far more like a painting than a natural English landscape. *Coneysthorpe, tel. 065384/333. Admission: £5 adults, £2 children, £4 senior citizens. Open late Mar.–Oct., daily, grounds 10–4:30, house 11–4:30.*

What to See and Do with Children

Scarborough has a children's activity center in North Bay known as **Kinderland,** designed to keep children (and their parents) entertained whatever the weather. *Burniston Rd. (North Bay) tel. 0723/35455. Admission: £2.50. Open Easter, then weekends until May Day Monday, then May–mid-Sept., daily 10–8.*

Flamingo Land, between Malton and Pickering, combines a traditional zoo with an amusement park complete with white-knuckle rides and dolphin shows. *Flamingo Land Zoo and Family Fun Park, Kirkby Misperton, tel. 0653/86287. Admission: £6 (all rides included). Open Easter–Oct., daily 10–6.*

Farther inland, **Lightwater Valley Theme Park** features buggy rides, a miniature Wild West railroad, waterslides, an old-time fair, and pony rides. *North Stainley, near Ripon, tel. 0765/ 85321. Admission: £7.50 (all rides included). Open Apr.– Sept., phone to check opening times.*

Older children will enjoy a ride behind a real steam locomotive, an experience you can have either at the **North York Moors Railway** (tel. 0751/73535) between Pickering and Grosmont or on the **Keighley and Worth Valley Railway** (Keighley Station, eight miles north of Haworth on A629; tel. 0535/45214). The **National Railway Museum** at York (*see* Tour 3) and the **National Museum of Photography, Film, and Television** (tel. 0274/ 727488) at Bradford are additional attractions.

Off the Beaten Track

Outside the main towns and sites, there are dozens of quiet roads and isolated villages which time has little disturbed. A trip into the **Yorkshire wolds**—a range of low chalk hills and valleys east of York—is an ideal change from crowded cities. Such tranquil hamlets as **Bishop Burton, Fridaythorpe,** and **Londesborough** have appealing narrow lanes, old churches, and country pubs. Take A66 from York to Fridaythorpe and then the scenic B1251 route from Pocklington along the crest of the wolds (via Sledmere House and Rudston with its prehistoric megaliths) toward Bridlington, a little fishing port and resort with an ancient harbor. Continue northward to **Flamborough** and **Flamborough Head,** where a huge bank of chalk cliffs juts out into the North Sea; from there, a coastal path over the clifftops ends at **Bempton Cliffs,** one of the finest sea bird sanctuaries on the east coast.

Scarborough is just as convenient for a trip into the wolds. Take A64 as far as Staxton, where B1249 will take you along the wolds escarpment; once there, you have your choice of back roads and trails to follow.

If you drive from Ilkley (9 miles east of Skipton on A65) across the river Wharfe, then along back roads to Askwith, you can pick up a moorland road that climbs the Washburn Valley to

Blubberhouses. Many quiet routes lead north from here to **Pateley Bridge, Grewelthorpe, Masham,** and the gentle, unchanging, eastern dales country.

From Buxton it's a little harder to find the quiet spots, particularly on weekends, but the smaller roads from the western edge of the national park down into the **Goyt Valley** and through **Macclesfield Forest** provide a restful, scenic drive.

Shopping

Shops naturally congregate where the trade is busiest, and the vast influx of tourists to York means that not only that city, but several of the surrounding ones, have a high concentration of stores. Like our next region, the Northeast, the area is full of crafts outlets, with woolen cloth and garments especially good buys.

Buxton   You'll find a wide variety of stores in Buxton, especially around Spring Gardens, the main shopping street. Near the Old Court House complex there is a pleasant arcade of small stores, while on The Crescent, try the new Cavendish Arcade built on the site of the old thermal baths. The **Old Court** and the **Cavendish Arcade** offer a pleasing range of fashion, cosmetic, and leather stores in stylish surroundings.

Buxton is also well-stocked with antiques shops and jewelers. **Radcliffe's** (Cavendish Circus) specializes, among other things, in items made out of the rare Blue John stone, mined in the Peak District and nowhere else in the world.

Haworth   Yorkshire is synonymous with wool production, and the region has a large number of "mill shops" where high-quality knitting wool, sweaters, and woven wool for skirts or suits can be bought at factory prices; the tourist information center will supply a full list of mill shops in the area.

In Haworth, at the **Brontë Weaving Shed and Edinburgh Woollen Mill** (Townend Mill), you can see handloom weavers making tweed the traditional way; an attached store sells the finished product, and is happy to accept U.S. dollars or traveler's checks.

Scarborough   Scarborough's most fashionable stores are on or near Bar Street (off Newborough), the main shopping street. On this quiet, pedestrian street near the sea, you'll find **Premier Engraving,** for jewelry; **Henry Dowells,** which sells high-quality dishes and glassware; and the **Potter's Wheel,** offering local, handcrafted pottery. Newborough and Eastborough comprise the rest of the main shopping area, with department stores like **Debenham's.** There is also a large, indoor market near the harbor, selling fresh produce and locally caught fish.

Whitby   For something special from the Yorkshire coast, when in Whitby select some jet jewelry, which was very popular in Victorian times as mourning decoration. You can choose from earrings, brooches, signet rings, and handsome strings of beads. For new jet jewelry try the **Abbey Gift Shop** (156 Church St.); for second-hand goods, **Jowsey and Row** (7 Sandgate).

York   You are not likely to find any bargains in York, but the new and secondhand bookstores around Petergate, Stonegate, and the Shambles are excellent. **Godfrey's,** on Stonegate, is nationally known for both new and secondhand books, and the **Penguin Bookshop** on Coppergate has just about every Penguin paperback in print.

If you are interested in silver, you should drop by **Henry Hardcastle** (51 Stonegate).

For something high in quality and typically English, **Mulberry Hall** on Stonegate, a large, half-timbered house dating from the 15th century, is a sales center for all the famous names in fine bone china: Wedgwood, Royal Worcester, Spode, Minton, Royal Doulton, Coalport, and Royal Crown Derby. You'll also find outstanding cut glass and crystal, like Waterford, Stuart, Webbs, and Edinburgh. Mulberry Hall offers a reliable mailing service for its glass and china to any part of the world, and the staff can advise you on customs duties and sales tax rebates.

Markets Colorful local markets are held on the following days—Bakewell, Monday; Buxton, Tuesday and Saturday; Hawes, Tuesday; York, street markets on Newgate every weekday.

Sports and Fitness

Bicycling Strenuous or gentle routes are equally accessible, and it's easy and inexpensive to rent bikes; try **C. S. Russell**, 1 Clifford St., York, tel. 0904/622744. National parks information centers have information on rentals, roads, and traffic-free routes (such as the High Peak and Tissington Trails).

Caving Caving (or "potholing"), which entails underground exploration, is popular here, especially as a family activity. Contact national park information centers.

Fishing Yorkshire is famous for its fishing, whether salt or fresh water, and the dales rivers are excellent for trout fishing. For a license, inquire at your hotel or at an information center. Sea angling is a busy trade in Scarborough; scheduled fishing trips are much cheaper than individually chartered ones—look for ads in the town, or, again, check at the information center.

Hiking Hiking is a natural sport in this area, and no equipment should be necessary except for all-weather clothing and waterproof shoes. One of the major trails is the High Peak trail, which runs for 17 miles from Cromford to Dowlow, following the route of an old railway. It has some fine scenery along the way. The national parks offices all have guidebooks, guide services, and maps.

Horse Racing Horse racing is quite popular in Yorkshire. The main race track is Knavesmire near York (tel. 0904/620911), but there are also tracks at Wetherby (tel. 0937/62035), Thirsk (tel. 0845/22276), and Doncaster (tel. 0302/20066).

Dining and Lodging

Dining This part of the country, with its fresh air and exhilarating hilltop walks, positively encourages hearty appetites. Locally produced meat and vegetables are excellent. One not-to-be-missed specialty is Yorkshire pudding, a popover-like pastry cooked in meat juices and served with gravy. In the days when meat was a real luxury, it was offered as a first course in hopes of filling you up so you wouldn't want much to eat for the main course.

Now it usually comes with meat and vegetables, although some places still serve it in the traditional way.

Fresh fish from Whitby or Scarborough is a real treat with freshly fried chips (thick french fries); don't bother asking for a fish and chip shop—just follow your nose! The cheese from Wensleydale has a subtle, delicate flavor with a slightly honeyed aftertaste. Bakewell Tart, made from the traditional recipe and sold in many local Bakewell bakeries, is a good, sticky snack. Wherever you are, go for the freshly baked bread and homemade cakes.

Highly recommended restaurants are indicated by a star ★ .

Category	Cost*
Very Expensive	over £35
Expensive	£25–£35
Moderate	£10–£25
Inexpensive	under £10

per person, including first course, main course, dessert, and VAT; excluding drinks

Lodging Accommodations to suit all tastes and pocketbooks are available, from plush top-class hotels to modest but welcoming bed-and-breakfasts; these in particular are usually an excellent value, offering simple but comfortable rooms and traditional home-cooking. Look for farmhouse bed-and-breakfasts as you're traveling around the countryside. If you want to be more in the center of things, town inns and hotels will usually have more in the way of creature comforts and sophisticated facilities. Combine hotel stays with a couple of nights in countryside bed-and-breakfasts to get a real flavor of northern hospitality and cuisine.

Highly recommended lodgings are indicated by a star ★ .

Category	Cost*
Very Expensive	over £110
Expensive	£75–£110
Moderate	£40–£75
Inexpensive	under £40

All prices are for two people sharing a double room, including service, breakfast, and VAT.

Baslow **Fischer's.** The menu at this award-winning restaurant, run by
Dining the friendly Fischer family, represents a range of Continental cuisines, with some fine local produce. Try the venison with pepper sauce or one of the especially good fish dishes. *Baslow Hall, Calver Road, Baslow (5 mi outside Bakewell), tel. 0246/ 583259. Reservations advised. Dress: informal. AE, MC, V. Closed Mon. lunch, Sun. dinner. Expensive.*

Bolton Abbey **Devonshire Arms.** Originally a coaching inn belonging to the
Lodging dukes of Devonshire, this hotel is in a superb setting on the ri-
★ ver Wharfe. It's within easy walking distance of Bolton Abbey. Portraits of various dukes hang on the walls, and bedrooms in

the original building have four-poster beds. *Bolton Abbey, Skipton, N. Yorks, BD23 6AJ, tel. 075671/441. 40 rooms with bath. Facilities: restaurant, fishing. AE, DC, MC, V. Expensive.*

Buxton
Dining

Nathaniels. Decorated with Victoriana, Nathaniels offers a choice of English and French cuisine. *35 High St., tel. 0298/78388. Reservations advised. Dress: informal. AE, DC, MC, V. Closed Sun. dinner and Mon. Moderate.*

Dining and Lodging
★

The Palace. A hotel on a grand scale from the halcyon days of the spa, it's set on five acres overlooking the town center and surrounding hills. All rooms have been totally refurbished, with modern conveniences added. At the well-equipped Aquarius sports and fitness complex, you can work off the excellent English and French meals of the restaurant. *Palace Rd., SK17 6AG, tel. 0298/22001. 122 rooms with bath. Facilities: heated pool, sauna, gym. Jacket and tie suggested. AE, DC, MC, V. Hotel: Expensive. Restaurant: Moderate.*

Lodging

The Old Hall. Mary, Queen of Scots, stayed here between 1567 and 1568. Refurbished since then and still offering quality accommodation, this centrally located hotel has a restaurant, wine bar, and in some rooms, four-poster beds. *The Square, SK17 6BD, tel. 0298/22841. 38 rooms, 33 with bath. AE, MC, V. Moderate.*

★

Lakenham Guest House. This large Edwardian house with a sweeping garden has been converted into a comfortable guest house. Bedrooms have been totally refurbished and redecorated, and all enjoy excellent views. The house has a number of attractive pieces of antique furniture; and there's ample parking for guests. *11 Burlington Rd., SK17 9AL, tel. 0298/79209. 6 rooms, 5 with bath. MC, V. Inexpensive.*

Matlock
Dining and Lodging
★

Riber Hall Restaurant. This Elizabethan manor house restaurant—also a hotel—is worth a visit to see the building as well as to sample the cooking. Chef Jeremy Brazelle prepares imaginative dishes with superbly fresh ingredients, many locally produced. The 14th-century manor house is decorated with antiques, flowers, oak beams, and four-poster beds, in keeping with the style of the inn. *Riber Hall, Riber, tel. 0629/582795. 11 rooms with bath. Reservations required in the restaurant. Jacket and tie required. AE, DC, MC, V. Expensive–Very Expensive.*

Pool-in-Wharfedale
Dining

Pool Court. Located on the northern edge of Leeds, Pool Court is very popular with the local food fanciers and is a distinctly elegant, professional place, with a highly experienced chef, David Watson, at the helm. Try the seafood sausage with dill butter, monkfish done with beanshoots, ginger, and water chestnuts, or a delicious saddle of local lamb. There's a widely priced wine list. *Pool, near Otley, tel. 0532/842288. Reservations necessary. Jacket and tie required. AE, DC, MC, V. Closed Sun. and Mon; lunch by appointment only for parties of 10 or more. Expensive.*

Scarborough
Dining
★

Laterna Restaurant. An intimate atmosphere and a high standard of international cuisine, particularly Continental and Italian specialties, make this restaurant a good choice. It's also noted for the quality of its service and its wine cellar. *33 Queen St., tel. 0723/363616. Reservations advised. Dress: informal. MC, V. Closed Sun, Mon., and lunch. Moderate.*

Lodging **The Crown.** The centerpiece of Scarborough's Regency Esplanade, this period hotel overlooks South Bay and the castle headland. Originally built to accommodate fashionable 19th-century visitors to Scarborough Spa, it has been considerably refurbished. *The Esplanade, YO11 2AG, tel. 0723/373491. 83 rooms with bath. Facilities: restaurant, cocktail bar, pocket billiards, table tennis, baby-listening service. AE, DC, MC, V. Expensive.*

★ **Gridley's Crescent Hotel.** This small, family-run hotel, in a gracious historic building on one of Scarborough's Regency streets, has an excellent carvery and restaurant. *Belvoir Terr., YO11 2PP, tel. 0723/360929. 20 rooms with bath. Facilities: lounge. MC, V. Moderate.*

Whitby **Magpie Café.** This restaurant, situated in a one-time whaling
Dining port, is a real bargain! With the fishing quay within a stone's throw, everything is ultra-fresh. Go for the set lunch, with Whitby crab if you're lucky, and sole, haddock, plaice, or even lobster to follow. The Mackenzie family has been running the Magpie for upwards of 40 years, and what they don't know about fish isn't worth knowing. *14 Pier Rd., tel. 0947/602058. Reservations not necessary. Dress: informal. Open daily 11:30–6:30 (last orders). Closed end-Nov.–early Mar. MC, V. Inexpensive–Moderate.*

York **19 Grape Lane.** This two-story restaurant in the heart of town is
Dining an ideal spot to people-watch or to come to relax after a day of shopping. The set menus are especially good values, and the food is contemporary English cooking. A light-lunch menu is also available. *19 Grape Lane, tel. 0904/636366. Reservations advised. Dress: informal. MC, V. Closed Sun. and Mon. Expensive.*

Judge's Lodging. In one of York's finest 18th-century buildings, this small hotel's restaurant is a place to enjoy bar lunches, as well as French *haute cuisine* dinners in superb surroundings. The wine cellar is well-stocked. *9 Lendal, tel. 0904/638733. Reservations required. Jacket and tie suggested. AE, DC, MC, V. Moderate–Expensive.*

★ **Hudson's Below Stairs.** Roast beef and Yorkshire pudding as well as a few French dishes are available in this Victorian-style hotel restaurant. Morning coffee, lunch, afternoon tea, and dinner are all served. *60 Bootham, tel. 0904/621267. Reservations advised. Dress: informal. AE, DC, MC, V. Moderate.*

St. William's Restaurant. Here is a pleasant way of combining a heritage visit with lunch or afternoon tea. This restaurant, part of the St. William College complex (dating from 1461), offers excellent homemade lunches, including soup, quiche, and salad. *3 College St., tel. 0904/634830. Reservations not required. Dress: informal. No credit cards. Closed dinner. Inexpensive.*

Dining and Lodging **Middlethorpe Hall.** This handsome, supremely elegant mansion
★ on the city's outskirts was built in 1699. It has been magnificently restored and features antique furniture and paintings, and bedrooms of period charm connected to practical bathrooms. The grounds include a lake, a dovecote, and a "ha-ha"—a drop in the garden level to create a cunning view—as well as a large kitchen garden that produces fresh vegetables for the hotel's award-winning French restaurant. *Bishopthorpe Rd., YO12 1QP, tel. 0904/641241. 30 rooms with bath. Reservation essential for restaurant. Jacket and tie required*

for dinner. Facilities: large gardens, croquet. AE, DC, MC, V. Very Expensive.

Lodging **Dean Court.** Close to York Minster in the heart of the city, this family-run establishment in a Victorian house has recently been refurbished. The restaurant serves excellent English food. *Duncombe Place, YO1 2EF, tel. 0904/625082. 40 rooms with bath. Facilities: coffee shop, lounge, in-house movies. AE, DC, MC, V. Expensive–Very Expensive.*

Mount Royale Hotel. Dating from the time of William IV (1830s), this hotel comprises two elegant town houses that are comfortably furnished in a quintessentially English style. A paneled bar; several lounges, one with piano; and lovely gardens all make for a restful stopover, as popular with the British as it is with foreigners. It's about 15 minutes' walk from the town center. *The Mount, YO2 2DA, tel. 0904/628856. 23 rooms with bath. AE, DC, MC, V. Closed over Christmas period. Expensive.*

4 South Parade. Anne and Robin McClure run an extremely friendly and comfortable guest house here, just outside the ancient walls, close to Micklegate Bar. The cobbled street is five minutes away from the rail station and 15 from the Minster. The three bedrooms are attractively furnished. Meals are available. *4 South Parade, YO2 2BA, tel. 0904/628229. 3 rooms with bath. Facilities: Jacuzzi. No credit cards. Moderate.*

Savages. A comfortable small hotel on a tree-lined road near the town center, with a reputation for good service; you can get picnic hampers for day trips. *15 St. Peter's Grove, YO3 6AQ, tel. 0904/610818. 18 rooms with bath. Facilities: garden, baby-listening service. AE, DC, MC, V. Moderate.*

Abbey Guest House. As quaint and pretty as it is convenient— just a short walk from the train station and town center—this establishment enjoys a quiet, riverside site. *14 Earlsborough Terr., Marygate, YO3 7BQ, tel. 0904/627782. 7 rooms, with basins. Facilities: lounge. MC, V. Inexpensive.*

The Arts

Festivals The northern cities tend to hold most of their cultural activities in the fall and winter months, while summer is the time for festivals and country exhibitions.

Buxton's Opera House (tel. 0298/72190) is the focal point of the town's renowned **Festival of Music and the Arts** (Hall Bank, tel. 0298/70395), held during the second half of July and the beginning of August each year. It includes opera, drama, classical concerts, jazz, recitals, and lectures. An amateur drama festival also takes place at the opera house during the summer.

Playing on its Viking past, York hosts the annual **Viking Festival,** held in February. The celebrations end with the Jorvik Viking Combat, when ravaging Northmen confront their Anglo-Saxon enemies. *Jorvik Viking Centre, Coppergate, tel. 0904/643211.*

The quadrennial festival performance of the great cycle of the medieval **York Mystery Plays** in the ruins of St. Mary's Abbey held from June 13 to July 5 is one of many musical and theatrical events in York. An **Early Music Festival** is held each summer (except in Mystery Play years). *For details of the York Festival call 0904/613161, ext. 1823.*

Opera   **Opera North,** England's first major provincial opera company, has its home in Leeds at the **Grand Theatre** (tel. 0532/459351 or 0532/440971). The Grand has an opulent, gold-and-plush auditorium, modeled on Milan's La Scala, and it's worth getting a seat to see both the excellent company and its ornate home.

Theater   Scarborough has an internationally known artistic native son in Alan Ayckbourne, a widely popular contemporary playwright. The **Stephen Joseph Theatre in the Round** at Valley Bridge near the train station (tel. 0723/370541) stages many of his plays before they head for London or Broadway. You might be lucky enough to catch an Ayckbourne premiere, directed by the master himself, at this small theater.

York's **Theatre Royal** (St. Leonard's Place, tel. 0904/623568) is a lively professional theater in a lovely old building, with many other events beside plays: string quartets, choral music, poetry reading, and art exhibitions.

The ultra-modern **West Yorkshire Playhouse** in Leeds, costing £13.5 million, was opened in March 1990. It is located on the slope of an old quarry (where a notorious slum once stood), and its interior is designed to be completely adaptable to all kinds of staging. Anyone interested in modern theater design should make the trip to Leeds. *Information and box office tel. 0532/ 442111.*

15 The Northeast

Introduction

England's northeast corner is relatively unexplored by tourists. Although one of its villages (Allendale Town, southwest of Hexham) lays claim to being the geographical center of the British Isles, there is a decided air of remoteness to much of the region. Consequently, visitors are often impressed by the wide-open spaces and empty country roads; they also like the value for money in shopping and accommodation, the unspoiled villages and uncrowded beaches, and the warmth and friendliness of the people.

Mainly composed of the two large counties of Durham and Northumberland (also known as Northumbria), the northeast includes among its attractions the English side of the Scottish Border area, renowned in ballads and romantic literature for feuds, raids, and battles. Hadrian's Wall, much of it still intact, runs through this region, marking the northern limit of the Roman Empire. There was another Roman wall farther north, the Antonine, which was built around AD 145, but it was abandoned as unworkable within about 50 years. Also in this area are Kielder Forest, the largest planted forest in Europe; Kielder Water, the largest man-made lake in northern Europe; and some of the most interesting parts of Northumberland National Park.

The western side of the region is dominated by the range of hills known as the Pennines. The north Pennines, officially designated an Area of Outstanding Natural Beauty, feature some of England's wildest and least populated countryside. Farther north the Pennine hills merge almost imperceptibly with the rolling, sheep-cropped Cheviot (pronounced "Cheeviot") hills, which stretch along the border with Scotland.

On the region's eastern side is a 100-mile line of largely undeveloped coast, including quiet villages, empty beaches with the occasional outcrop of high cliff or offshore rocks, and islands populated by multitudes of sea birds. Several outstanding castles perch on headlands and promontories along here. For 1,000 years, the great cathedral of Durham was the seat of bishops who had their own armies and ruled the turbulent northern diocese as prince bishops with quasi-royal authority.

In more recent times, industrialization left its mark on parts of the area. Steel, coal, railroads, shipbuilding, and chemicals underpinned the prosperity of towns and cities such as Newcastle-upon-Tyne, Darlington, Sunderland, Hartlepool, and Middlesbrough in the 19th and early-20th centuries. Attractions that reflect the area's industrial history are the open-air museum at Beamish (northwest of Durham), voted "Best Museum in Europe"; the Railway Museum at Darlington, on the site of the world's first passenger railroad line; and a tiny cottage at Wylam (west of Newcastle) housing a birthplace museum devoted to George Stephenson, who invented the steam locomotive (*see* Off the Beaten Track, below).

Essential Information

Important Addresses and Numbers

Tourist Information   **Northumbria Regional Tourist Board,** Aykley Heads, Durham DH1 5UX, tel. 091/384–6905. Open weekdays 9–5.

Tourist Information Centers, normally open Mon.–Sat. 9:30–5:30, but varying according to the season, include:

Alnwick: The Shambles, Northumberland NE66 1TN, tel. 0665/510505.
Durham: Market Pl., Co Durham DH1 3NJ, tel. 091/384–3720.
Hexham: Manor Office, Hallgate, Northumberland NE46 1XD, tel. 0434/605225.

Travel Agencies **Thomas Cook:** 24–25 Market Pl., Durham DH1 3NJ, tel. 091/384–8569.

Car Rental Agencies **Alnwick: AMC Ford,** Central Garage, Clay Port, tel. 0665/602294.
Hexham: Adams and Gibbon plc, Parkwell, tel. 0434/602411.

Arriving and Departing

By Car The most direct north-south route is A1, linking London and Edinburgh via Newcastle-upon-Tyne (274 miles from London) and Berwick-upon-Tweed (338 miles from London).

A697, which branches west off A1 north of Morpeth, is a more attractive road north. It leads the motorist right past the 16th-century battlefield of Flodden. A696/A68 northwest out of Newcastle is also a more attractive alternative to A1, but it is an increasingly busy road.

By Train **British Rail** serves the region from London's King's Cross Station (tel. 071/278–2477). Average travel times include 2¾ hours to Darlington; 3 hours to Durham; 3¼ hours to Newcastle; and 3¾ hours to Berwick-upon-Tweed.

By Bus **National Express** (tel. 071/730–0202) serves the region from London's Victoria Coach Station. Average travel times include 4¾ hours to Durham; 5¼ hours to Newcastle; and 8¼ hours to Berwick-upon-Tweed. Connecting services to other parts of the region leave from Newcastle.

Getting Around

By Car A66 and A69 run east–west, providing cross-country access. Many traffic-free country roads provide quiet and scenic, if slower, alternatives to the main routes.

Part of the Cheviot hills, which run along the Northumbrian side of the Scottish border, is now a military firing range. Don't drive here when the warning flags are flying. The military, though, has restored the Roman Road, Dere Street, which crosses this region. Try also B6318, which is a well-maintained road that runs alongside Hadrian's Wall on the south side.

By Train From Newcastle, there is local service north to Alnmouth (for Alnwick) and to Corbridge and Hexham on the east–west line to Carlisle. A seven-day "Northeast Regional Rover" ticket is available for unlimited travel in the area, which includes the scenic Carlisle–Settle line. The one-day "Tees Ranger" ticket covers unlimited travel in the Teesside area, including the "heritage line" from the town of Bishop Auckland, and the handsome Esk Valley.

By Bus **The United Bus Company** (tel. 0325/465252) in Darlington and Northumbria Motor Services (tel. 091/232–4211) in Newcastle offer reasonable one-day "Explorer" tickets for unlimited travel on local services.

Guided Tours **The Northumbria Regional Tourist Board** (tel. 091/384–6905) has a register of professional guides.
Beth Carr PR (tel. 0207/503841) provides a personal guide service in Northumberland and Durham. Tour subjects include Romans, Christian heritage, and castles; also after-dinner talks and guided hikes.
Escorted Tours Ltd. (tel. 091/536–3493) runs day and half-day tours of Northumbria by luxury minibus; itineraries vary.
Holiday with a Knight (tel. 0287/632510) is run by Shirley Knight, a guide specializing in general tours of northern England, as well as theme tours based on history, literature, and ghosts and legends.
Visit Northumbria (tel. 091/374–3454) has specialized in northeast tours for 25 years.

Exploring the Northeast

Orientation

Our exploration of the northeast begins in the cathedral city of Durham, which has dominated the region for centuries. From Durham, Tour 1 continues along Weardale to a lead-mining center and a folk museum, followed by the massive waterfall, High Force. The ruins of Barnard Castle and the riches of the Bowes Museum come next, followed by Raby Castle and the large industrial towns of Darlington and Middlesbrough. The tour ends at the Beamish Open-Air Museum.

Tour 2 opens in Hexham, with its medieval abbey, then explores the fascinating archaeology of Hadrian's Wall. The huge lake at Kielder Water and the vast man-made Forest of Kielder nearby, along with surrounding areas, close this tour.

The coast, from ancient Alnwick north to Berwick-upon-Tweed is explored in Tour 3, which includes a series of impressive castles and offshore islands, especially the Farne Islands and Holy Island, otherwise known as Lindisfarne.

Highlights for First-time Visitors

Alnwick Castle: Tour 3
Beamish Open-Air Museum: Tour 1
Bowes Museum: Tour 1
Darlington Railway Centre: Tour 1
Durham Cathedral: Tour 1
Hexham Abbey: Tour 2
High Force Waterfall: Tour 1
Housesteads Roman Fort: Tour 2
Lindisfarne: Tour 3
Washington Old Hall: Tour 1

Tour 1: Durham to Beamish

Numbers in the margin correspond to points of interest on the Northeast and Durham maps.

❶ The cathedral and castle of the city of **Durham,** county seat of Durham County, stand high on a wooded peninsula almost en-

The Northeast

tirely encircled by the river Wear (pronounced to rhyme with "beer"). For centuries these two ancient buildings have dominated the city—now a thriving university town—and the surrounding countryside. Durham was once the capital of the Anglo-Saxon kingdom of Northumbria (i.e., the land north of the river Humber, the 40-mile-long estuary on the east coast which flows into the North Sea). For 1,000 years, the city was also the seat of powerful "prince bishops" who exercised near-monarchical power within the diocese. The city's glorious past is proudly preserved and protected. Ingenious street plans keep pedestrians and traffic separate, and older buildings have been carefully restored. Recently, the castle and cathedral were jointly designated a World Heritage Site in official recognition of their international importance.

❷ The centrally located **cathedral** on Palace Green is an ideal starting point for a walking tour of Durham. Architectural historians come from all over the world to admire and study the great church's important Norman features such as the relief work on its massive pillars, and the rib vaulting in the roof. But no special expertise is needed to appreciate its exceptional position, impressive size, and wealth of detail.

The origins of the cathedral go back to the 10th century. Monks fleeing a devastating Viking raid in the year 875 on Lindisfarne Abbey (on Holy Island off the northeast coast, 78 miles from Durham) had carried the body of St. Cuthbert from the shrine at Lindisfarne to this site. By 995, the wealth attracted by Cuthbert's shrine paid for the construction of a cathedral. The prestige of the area grew until the bishop of Durham acquired his title of "prince bishop," a title held until the 19th century. This gave the bishop power to rule Durham County in both a political and a religious sense, and even to raise armies, mint coins, and appoint judges. The **prince-bishop's throne** in the cathedral is still the loftiest in all Christendom; his miter is the only one to be encircled by a coronet; and his coat of arms is the only one to be crossed with a sword as well as a crosier.

Many visitors take a snapshot of the 12th-century **bronze knocker,** shaped like the head of a ferocious mythological beast, on the massive north entrance door. By grasping the ring clenched in the animal's mouth, medieval felons could claim sanctuary; cathedral records show that 331 criminals (especially murderers) sought this protection between 1464 and 1524. But the knocker now in place is, in fact, a replica; the original is kept for security in the cathedral **treasury,** along with many other valuables from the church.

The power and the glory of the prince bishop, as manifested in the richly decorated **tomb of Bishop Hatfield** and the lofty episcopal throne described above, are a marked contrast to the simple **tomb and shrine of St. Cuthbert** (behind the high altar), and the tomb (in the Galilee Chapel) of the Venerable Bede, the scholar and saint whose body was brought here in 1020.

Many more ornate features would have survived had not the cathedral been used to imprison 4,000 Scottish soldiers after the Battle of Dunbar in 1650. These fierce Protestants went on a rampage, smashing effigies and burning woodwork, although they spared the cathedral's elaborate **clock** because the thistle emblem of Scotland figures in its design.

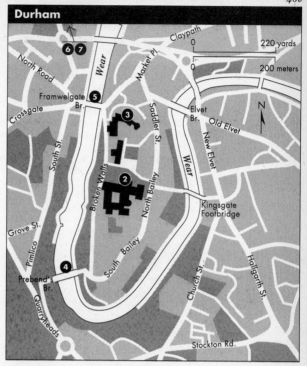

Durham

0 — 220 yards

0 — 200 meters

The **Chapel of the Nine Altars** has soaring, polished pillars made from a local limestone known as Frosterley marble. Polishing this stone was a painstaking and time-consuming task, so perhaps it is not surprising to find that only the visible surfaces were polished (probe behind the pillars and you can feel the rough, unfinished parts). There is also a restaurant in the Undercroft that is open seven days a week. *Tel. 091/386–2367. Admission free to cathedral; treasury: 50p adults, 10p children. Cathedral open May–Sept., daily 7:30 AM–8 PM; Oct.–Apr. 7:30–6; tower open Mon.–Sat. 10–4:30; Choral evensong service weekdays 5:15, Sun. 3:30.*

3 On the opposite side of Palace Green is **Durham Castle,** which commands a strategic position overlooking the river Wear. For over 750 years the castle was the home of successive warlike prince bishops. Today the castle houses University College, one of several colleges of the University of Durham, the oldest university in England after Oxford and Cambridge. You can tour the castle at certain times, and, during college vacations, tourist accommodation is available. The great hall, dating from 1284, is still in use, as are the original kitchens and buttery; the castle crypt serves as a student lounge, while the old servants' hall is now the college library. *Palace Green, tel. 091/374–3800. Admission: £1.20 adults, 50p children. Open July–Sept., daily 10–noon, 2–5; Oct–June, check locally for times.*

Time Out **Almshouse Café** serves lunch and afternoon meals in a historic almshouse on Palace Green, between the cathedral and castle.

❹ From the southern end of Palace Green, a path to **Prebends Footbridge** (which bears an inscription of several lines by Sir Walter Scott) leads across the river and along South Street. Re-
❺ cross the River Wear at **Framwelgate Bridge,** and go into Market Place. From here, Saddler Street and South Bailey lead back to the cathedral by Dun Cow Lane. Many of the elegant town houses on these streets are now departments of the university. At every turn there are glimpses of river, castle, cathedral, and town. Durham Regatta, held on the river every year in mid-June, is the oldest rowing event in Britain, and attracts teams in all classes from the entire country.

Time Out   **Shakespeare Inn** (Saddler St.) is a half-timbered pub serving bar meals in the historic quarter.

---

❻ The **Durham Light Infantry Museum** at Aykley Heads (½ mile northwest of the city center on A691) is devoted to the history of the county regiment, exhibiting uniforms, weapons, and regalia alongside mementos of campaigns in India, Iran, the Crimea, and Africa. On the second floor is an arts center offering a changing program of events throughout the year. Outdoor events such as brass-band concerts and military vehicle rallies take place in the landscaped grounds. *Tel. 091/384–2214. Admission: 70p adults, 30p children and senior citizens. Open Tues.–Sat. 10–5, Sun. 2–5.*

❼ The **Durham University Oriental Museum** is Britain's only museum devoted solely to Oriental art and crafts. Collections cover all parts of the East, showing everything from tiny, meticulously carved jade and ivory ornaments to full-size representations of Buddha, a Chinese portable bedroom, and an Egyptian mummy. *Elvet Hill, off South Rd. (A1050), near Van Mildert and Trevelyan colleges, tel. 091/374–2911. Admission: 50p adults, 30p children, and senior citizens. Open Mon.–Sat. 9:30–1 and 2–5, Sun. 2–5; closed weekends Nov.–Feb.*

The city of Durham is a good base from which to explore Durham County, peppered with coal mines now closed and landscaped.

Numbers in the margin correspond to points of interest on the Northeast map.

Leave the city by A690, continuing about four miles through
❽ the village of **Brancepeth,** which boasts a flamboyantly restored castle (not open to the public), rows of well-preserved cottages, and a church containing tombs of the Nevilles, one of the most powerful northern families in feudal times. Ten miles farther west at Wolsingham, take A689, which follows the river west through Upper Weardale (the valley of the River Wear).
❾ Near the hamlet of **Frosterley,** three miles away, the limestone known as Frosterley marble was once quarried. When polished, this stone becomes glossy, and it can be seen in many local churches, as well as in Durham Cathedral.

❿ Another ten miles west, at the head of the dale, is the **Killhope Wheel Lead Mining Centre,** where a restored 34-foot-high waterwheel looms over the site. The visitor center incorporates working models, push-button audiovisual shows, and displays of minerals in portraying the story of the local lead mines and the harsh lives of the miners and millworkers. You can pan for lead in the stream and operate the primitive machinery once used to separate valuable ore from gravel. A wild, high, remote place, close to the Cumbrian border, the center is a remarkable testimony to a vanished industry. *2 mi northwest of Cowshill on A689, tel. 0388/537505. Admission: £1.50 adults, 75p children and senior citizens. Open Easter–Oct., daily 10:30–5.*

⑪ Retrace your route three miles southeast on A689 to the village of **Ireshopeburn**; the **Weardale Folk Museum** has been established here in a former parsonage close to a chapel where John Wesley, the founder of Methodism, often preached. One room is set out as an 1870 cottage would have looked, and a collection of crystallized minerals is included in a display on local life and landscape. The caretaker can show you around the adjoining chapel, which has a plaque (provided by the Lowville United Church of Ontario) in memory of parishioners who emigrated to Canada in the early 1800s: "They went out in faith as founders and pioneers." *Tel. 0388/537417. Admission: 60p adults, 30p children. Open July–Aug., daily 1–5; Easter, May, June, and Sept., Wed., Thurs., Sat. and national holidays 1–5, Sun. 1–4.*

⑫ From the village of **St. John's Chapel,** about a mile southeast of Ireshopeburn, a moorland road provides an exhilarating drive "over the tops" into the valley of Teesdale, where England's ⑬ highest waterfall (72 feet) can be viewed at **High Force** just south of B6277. This road leads downstream through the dales town of Middleton-in-Teesdale (3½ miles) to the village of ⑭ **Romaldkirk** (7½ miles), whose extravagantly proportioned church is known as "the Cathedral of the Dale," and where the stocks for punishing wrongdoers are still on the village green. Two miles farther on, at Cotherstone, a soft, crumbly cheese is made and sold at the village store.

⑮ Continue 3 more miles on your southeast route to **Barnard Castle,** where the substantial ruins of the fortress which gave this market town its name cling to an aerie on a cliff overlooking the river. In the little town, the unusual butter-market hall, surmounted by a fire alarm bell, marks the junction of the streets Thorngate, Newgate, and Market Place, which are lined with stores, pubs, and cafés. In 1838 Charles Dickens stayed at the **King's Head Inn** here while researching his novel *Nicholas Nickleby*, which dealt with the abuse of children in local boarding schools. The local tourist office has a *Dickens Drive* leaflet of the places he visited in the area.

The town's main attraction is **Bowes Museum,** a vast French-inspired chateau built between 1869 and 1885 to house an international collection of art, including paintings by Canaletto, El Greco, and Boucher; the intricately inlaid Warwick Cabinet; a porcelain-mounted desk; and Meissen figurines. Individually furnished period rooms, French furniture from the 1850s, and Britain's largest collection of Spanish paintings are among the museum's other exhibits. Mechanical objects are also well represented, including a splendid clock in the form of a celestial globe. Most unusual of all, perhaps, is the 18th-century silver swan which Mark Twain described in *Innocents Abroad*. Once every day an attendant ceremoniously activates the mechanism that enables the swan to gracefully catch and swallow a fish to the accompaniment of a haunting tune. (Phone to check the time the swan "performs," as this varies each day.) *Follow signs from Barnard Castle town center, tel. 0833/690606. Admission: £1.60 adults, 80p children and senior citizens. Open*

May–Sept., Mon.–Sat. 10–5:30, Sun. 2–5; Mar., Apr., Oct., Mon.–Sat. 10–5, Sun. 2–5; Nov.–Feb., Mon.–Sat. 10–4, Sun. 2–4. Closed Christmas week and Jan. 1.

Time Out The **Market Place Teashop** (29 Market Pl.) is an old house, dating back to 1710, which serves excellent hot lunches, with steak and kidney pudding or leek au gratin, as well as cakes and scones at teatime.

16 In the village of **Bowes,** 4 miles southwest of Barnard Castle on A67, the house on which Dickens modeled *Nicholas Nickleby*'s Dotheboys Hall can still be seen, although it's not open to the public. A notoriously cruel boarding school once occupied the last building in the main street, west of the village. The courtyard pump described in the novel is still there.

From Barnard Castle, A688 leads 6 miles northeast to **17** Staindrop and **Raby Castle,** home of the 11th baron Barnard. Set in 200 acres of landscaped deer park, this castle displays luxuriously furnished rooms crammed with treasures, well-preserved medieval kitchens, and original Victorian copperware and other domestic equipment. The chapel was built in the 1360s and is still consecrated. Stone arcades display five full-length portraits of Raby personages, including Richard III's mother, who died here. One of the castle estate surveyors was Jeremiah Dixon, who in the 1760s helped survey the Mason-Dixon line marking the boundary between Maryland and Pennsylvania. *1 mi. north of Staindrop, tel. 0833/60202. Admission: £2.50 adults, £1.20 children, £1.90 senior citizens; park, gardens, and carriage collection only: 80p adults, 60p children and senior citizens. Open April–June, Wed. and Sun. 1–5 (castle), 11–5:30 (park and gardens); July–Sept., Sun.–Fri. 1–5 (castle), 11–5:30 (park and gardens).*

From Raby Castle, continue about seven miles northeast on **18** A688 to the town of **Bishop Auckland,** where the prince bishops of Durham had their official residence in **Auckland Castle** for 700 years. This grand episcopal palace dates mainly from the 16th century, though the chapel was built in 1665 from the ruins of a 12th-century banqueting hall. The unusual 18th-century "deerhouse" of adjoining Bishops Park testifies to at least one of the bishops' extracurricular interests. The castle itself offers architectural styles ranging from the medieval to the neo-Gothic. *Off Market Place, tel. 0388/609766. Admission: 80p adults, 30p children, 50p senior citizens. Open mid-May–Sept. Sun. and Wed. 2–5. Chapel only on Thurs. 10–noon.*

To travel southeast from Bishop Auckland on A6072 is to move from the medieval world of the bishops of Durham into the 19th-century world of industrialization. Ten miles away the **19** town of **Darlington** (on A68 east of A1[M]) expanded quickly with the success of the railroads in the 1830s. That expansion brought not only prosperity but fame, for here, on the Stockton–Darlington route, the world's first steam passenger railroad was established by George Stephenson in 1825. The **Darlington Railway Centre and Museum** is housed in one of his original railroad stations, built in 1842. You can inspect historic engines, including Stephenson's *Locomotion I*, as well as photographs, documents, and models. *North Road Station, north of town center, tel. 0325/460532. Admission: £1.20 adults, 60p* children, 80p senior citizens. Open daily 9:30–5; closed Christmas and New Year's.

About 12 miles farther east, toward the mouth of the river Tees, lies the industrial town of **Middlesbrough.** In 1802, a mere dozen people lived here, but the local discovery of iron ore spawned a boom town based on steel mills; later, development focused on chemical industries. The town's unusual claim to fame is its iron transporter bridge built in 1911 to replace a ferry crossing. The largest of its kind in the world, this vast structure looms up like a giant's erector-set model. A gantry system still takes 12 cable cars, holding 200 passengers each, across the river every 20 minutes. A special viewing platform stands on the south bank. Upstream you'll find Newport Bridge, the world's largest lift span bridge. For travelers willing to forsake the usual tourist routes, these structures present a remarkable sight. *Tel. 0642/247563. Crossing time, 2 minutes. Fare: 15p pedestrians, 50p cars. Open Mon.–Sat. 5 AM–11 PM, Sun. 2 PM–11 PM.*

Middlesbrough's more conventional attraction is the **Captain Cook Birthplace Museum** in the leafy suburb of Marton. Here the life and times of the 18th-century circumnavigator and explorer are vividly depicted, including his remarkable voyages to Australia, New Zealand, Canada, Antarctica, and Hawaii, where he was murdered. A conservatory near the museum houses many of the exotic plants Cook discovered during his travels. *Stewart Park, Marton, off A174, south of city center, tel. 0642/311211. Admission: 60p adults, 30p children and senior citizens. Open Oct.–Apr., Tues.–Sun. 9–4; May–Sept., Tues.–Sun. 10–6.*

From Middlesbrough, it's less than 20 miles on A177 back to Durham. About 12 miles north of the city, near the town of **Washington,** careful navigation will take you to **Washington Old Hall,** the ancestral home of the family of the first U.S. president. His direct ancestors lived here between 1183 and 1288; other members of the family continued to live in the house until 1613, when the present property was rebuilt. Now owned by the National Trust, the mansion retains a decidedly Jacobean (17th-century) appearance. There are special celebrations on the Fourth of July. *From A1(M), 5 mi west of Sunderland, follow signs to Washington New Town, District 4, and then on to Washington Village; hall is clearly marked. Tel. 091/416–6879. Admission: £1.50 adults, 75p children. Open Apr.–Oct., Sat.–Thurs. and Good Friday 11–5 (last admission 4:30).*

A few miles southwest of Washington in the town of **Beamish,** the **Beamish Open-Air Museum** won the European Museum of the Year Award in 1987. Set aside at least half a day to fully enjoy all the facilities on the 260-acre site. A streetcar will take you across a reconstructed 1920s Main Street, including a dentist's operating room, a saloon, and a grocery. In the coal miner's cottage, you will be offered "stotty cake" (unleavened bread) hot from the oven and thickly buttered. A stableman will talk to you about the Clydesdale workhorses in his care, once used to draw brewery wagons. On the farm you can see such local breeds as Durham Shorthorn cattle and Cheviot sheep. Other attractions include a railroad station, a coal mine, and a transportation collection. The large gift store specializes in period souvenirs and locally made crafts. *Off A693, between Chester-le-Street and Stanley, tel. 0207/231811. Admission:*

£5–£6 adults, £4 children and senior citizens, reduced charges in winter. Open Nov.–mid-Mar., Tues.–Sun. 10–5; Easter–Oct., daily 10–6.

Time Out At the entrance to the museum a traditional-style inn, **The Shepherd and Shepherdess,** serves hot and cold bar meals and afternoon teas (light meals). Stop at least to admire the inn sign. It's a good idea to grab refreshments here and avoid the lines inside the museum.

Tour 2: Hexham and Hadrian's Wall

㉓ Best-known as the gateway to Hadrian's Wall country, the historic market town of **Hexham,** on A69 about 21 miles west of Newcastle, is well worth a visit for its own sake.

The best day to visit is Tuesday, when the weekly market is held in Market Place; at your leisure you can sample, among other products, the locally renowned Border Tart, a confection of nuts, dried fruit, and icing (*see* Shopping, below). In 1761, the marketplace was the site of a massacre of protesting lead miners by the North Yorkshire Militia, henceforth known as "The Hexham Butchers."

From Market Place, you can enter ancient **Hexham Abbey,** which forms one side of the square. Inside, climb the 35 worn stone "night stairs," which once led from the main part of the abbey to the canon's dormitory, to overlook this tranquil, peaceful place where Christ has been worshiped for over 1,300 years. Most of the present building dates from the 12th century, with much of the stone being taken from the Roman fort at Corstopitum a few miles northeast. Near the foot of the stairs, a Roman tombstone set into the wall records the death of one Flavinus, a 25-year-old standardbearer, shown on horseback above a crouched Briton armed with a dagger. Death is also starkly depicted on the unusual altar screen, which is ornamented with skeletons. Fugitives could claim sanctuary by sitting on the stone throne called both the Frith Stool and St. Wilfred's Chair, after the abbey's founder. *Beaumont St., tel. 0434/602031. Admission free. Open daily May–Sept., 9–7; Oct.–Apr., daily 9–5. No tours during services.*

Upon leaving the abbey, you can either stroll through the gardens and parkland opposite or explore the shops around Market Place. From the bowling green there is a particularly fine view of the abbey. Paths lead to the cheerful-looking bandstand and on to **Queens Hall,** built in the style of a French chateau and now incorporating a library, a 400-seat theater, an arts center, and exhibition galleries. On display is the Tynedale Tapestry (8 by 14 feet), made in the early 1980s by more than 300 people working from a loom on a scaffold. The tapestry illustrates the theme of "theater," with the bright, traditional figures of Harlequin, Columbine, and Pantaloon.

Continuing away from the abbey and past Queens Hall, turn left down Battle Hill to Priestpopple, and turn down Fore Street, a thronged, traffic-free shopping area which leads back into Market Place. On the side of Market Place opposite the abbey an exhibition gallery now occupies the ground floor of the Moot Hall in which the archbishop's court was held. A little way beyond, toward the main parking lot, the Manor Office, built as a jail in 1330, now houses the Information Center.

Manor Office also hosts the **Border History Museum.** Photographs, models, drawings, a reconstructed blacksmith's shop, a Border house interior, armor, and weapons help tell the story of the "Middle March"—the medieval administrative area governed by a warden and centered on Hexham. *The Old Gaol, Hallgate, tel. 0434/604011, ext. 245. Admission: 90p adults, 45p children. Open late Mar.–Oct., daily 10–4.*

Time Out   **Mrs. Miggin's Coffee Shop** (St. Mary's Wynd) serves light refreshments and homemade cakes on pine tables, or at a sofa where you can read magazines and newspapers.

Hexham is the best base from which to explore **Hadrian's Wall,** recently designated a World Heritage Site. Begun after the Roman emperor Hadrian's visit in AD 121 following repeated barbarian invasions from Scotland, the wall spanned 73 miles from Wallsend ("Wall's End") just north of Newcastle, in the east, to Bowness-on-Solway beyond Carlisle, in the west. Each mile was reinforced by a "milecastle," or small fort, and each third of a mile by a turret. In addition, at strategic points, large garrison forts were built behind the wall. This formidable line of fortifications marked the northern border of the Roman Empire, which stretched eastward for 2,500 miles to what is now Iraq.

Although a path can be followed along the entire wall, this is rugged country, unsuited to the inexperienced hiker. Most trekkers here organize their routes around the various excellent visitor centers, which are near the best-preserved sections of the wall or in the area of milecastles, turrets, or excavations.

One of the best ways to approach Hadrian's Wall is to begin with the **Roman Army Museum** at the garrison fort Carvoran, near the village of **Greenhead** (at the junction of A69 and B6318, about 18 miles west of Hexham) and work your way eastward.

Take B6318 from Hexham; it follows much of the length of the wall, with roadside signs indicating paths to reach major sites. At the museum, full-size models and excavations bring to life this remote outpost of empire: You can even inspect authentic Roman graffiti on the walls of an excavated barracks. The gift store stocks, among other unusual items, Roman rulers (1 foot = 11.6 inches) and Roman cookbooks. Opposite the museum, at Walltown Crags on the Pennine Way (a long-distance hiking route), are 400 yards of the best-preserved section of the wall. *Tel. 06977/47485. Admission: £2 adults, £1 children, £1.50 senior citizens. Open Mar.–Oct., daily 10–5; Apr.–Sept., daily 10–5:30.*

From the Roman Army Museum at Greenhead, head back toward Hexham on A69. At Bardon Mill, approximately 8 miles east of Greenhead, a one-lane road (with ample passing places) leads north about two miles to the great garrison fort of **Vindolanda.** Excavations are always going on here, and a section of the wall has been reconstructed. Recorded information interprets the site. *Near Bardon Mill, tel. 0434/344277. Admission: £2.50 adults, £1.25 children, £1.75 senior citizens. Open Jan.–Feb. and Nov.–Dec., daily 10–4; Mar., Oct., daily 10–5; Apr., Sept., daily 10–5:30; May–June, daily 10–6; July–Aug., daily 10–6:30.*

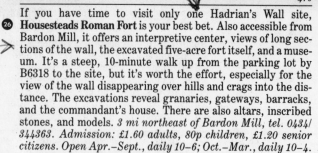

26 If you have time to visit only one Hadrian's Wall site, **Housesteads Roman Fort** is your best bet. Also accessible from Bardon Mill, it offers an interpretive center, views of long sections of the wall, the excavated five-acre fort itself, and a museum. It's a steep, 10-minute walk up from the parking lot by B6318 to the site, but it's worth the effort, especially for the view of the wall disappearing over hills and crags into the distance. The excavations reveal granaries, gateways, barracks, and the commandant's house. There are also altars, inscribed stones, and models. *3 mi northeast of Bardon Mill, tel. 0434/ 344363. Admission: £1.60 adults, 80p children, £1.20 senior citizens. Open Apr.–Sept., daily 10–6; Oct.–Mar., daily 10–4.*

For a garrison fort with equal, if different, appeal, return to Hexham and head north on A6079 for almost four miles. **27** **Chesters Roman Fort,** just southwest of Chollerford (junction B6318), lies in a wooded valley close to the North Tyne river. This fort protected the point where the wall crossed the river; you approach it directly from the parking lot and, while the site cannot compete with Housesteads in terms of setting, there is a fascinating collection here of Roman artifacts, including statues of river and water gods, altars, milestones, iron tools, weapons, and handcuffs. The military bathhouse near the river is the best-preserved example in Britain. Drawings and diagrams provide an idea of what the fort looked like originally; its present, mellowed appearance gives little sense of the Romans' brightly painted pillars, walls, and altars. *½ mi southwest of Chollerford (on B6318), tel. 0434/681379. Admission and opening times same as for Housesteads.*

Take A6079 southeast from Chesters Fort and head seven miles **28** toward Corbridge for the remains of **Corstopitum,** a Roman fort occupied longer than any other on the wall; in fact, it predates the wall by 40 years. Strategically positioned at the junction of the east/west and north/south Roman routes—Stanegate ran west to Carlisle, Dere Street led north to Scotland and south to London—the fort now contains a museum rich in artifacts. The Corbridge Lion sculpture probably decorated an important tomb at one time; it later graced a fountain. A temple frieze depicts Castor and Pollux, the god Jupiter's twin sons, and there is an altar dedicated to their father as well. *On a back road ½ mi northwest of Corbridge, tel. 0434/632349. Admission: £1.60 adults, 80p children, £1.20 senior citizens. Open Apr.–Sept., daily 10–6; Oct.–Mar., Tues.–Sun. 10–4.*

29 **Corbridge** itself is a small town of honey-colored stone houses and riverside walks. In the churchyard of St. Andrew's Church by Market Place is the Vicar's Peel. Nearly 700 years old, this fortified tower was a refuge from Scottish raiders; now it's an information center.

Time Out The **Angel Inn** (Market Pl.) in Corbridge is a traditional pub serving well-priced bar meals, lunch and evening.

After exploring Hadrian's Wall, you can drive into the rugged hills to the north, which the Romans must have scanned anxiously from their watchtowers (from Corbridge, take A68 back to Chollerford; from there, drive ten miles on B6320 to a minor road picked up at Bellingham, and drive another ten miles west). On the western edge of Northumberland National Park, **30** only three miles from the Scottish border, lies **Kielder Water,** northern Europe's largest man-made lake, surrounded by Europe's largest planted forest. This modern reservoir has become an established attraction since it was completed in 1982, and it actually encourages visitors, offering facilities for such aquatic sports as waterskiing. A cruise service (tel. 0434/240436 or 220423) operates from May to September from Tower Knowe Visitor Centre. Fishing is popular, and the upper part of the lake, designated a conservation area, attracts many bird-watchers.

The **Tower Knowe Visitor Centre** (tel. 0434/240398), at the southeast corner of the lake, approaching it from Bellingham, is a springboard from which to enjoy and explore not only the lake area but also the vast **Forest of Kielder.** Exhibitions and films illustrate the region's wildlife and natural history, and guided forest walks are offered in the summer. A 12-mile toll road heads north of the lake through the forest, starting at **③** **Kielder Castle** at the lake's northwest corner, formerly a shooting lodge belonging to the duke of Northumberland and now a Forestry Commission visitor center. After about 10 miles, the toll road rejoins A68 south of Carter Bar close to the Scottish border.

③ **Wallington House,** a striking 17th-century mansion with Victorian decoration, can be visited at Cambo, 15 miles northeast of Hexham. Take A6079 from Hexham past Chollerford, Chollerton, and junction A68, and follow the highway signs marked Wallington. This cross-country approach shows Wallington House, in the midst of an extensive, sparsely populated agricultural region, to its best advantage. The stone heads of beasts glare at passing drivers from the grounds in front of the hall. In addition to the house itself, with its fine plasterwork, furniture, porcelain, and dollhouse collection, the walled, terraced garden is a major attraction. Striking murals depict scenes from Northumbria's history, including the death of the Venerable Bede (AD 673–735), England's scholar-saint; incidents from the life of St. Cuthbert; and the building of Hadrian's Wall. During the summer, open-air events are held in the gardens and grounds (there are 100 acres of woodlands and lakes), including recitals, productions of Shakespeare, and concerts. *Tel. 067074/283. Admission: £3 adults, £1.50 children; walled garden only £1.50 adults, 75p children. Hall open Apr.–Oct., Wed.–Mon. 1–5:30; Oct., Wed. and weekends 1–5:30. Walled garden open Apr.–Sept., daily 10–7; Oct., daily 10–6; Nov.–Mar., daily 10:30–4.*

Tour 3: The Coast from Alnwick to Berwick

③ **Alnwick** (pronounced "Ann-ick"), 30 miles north of Newcastle on route A1 to Berwick, is a good base from which to explore the coast and countryside of northern Northumberland. Once a county seat, the town is dominated by its vast castle, but there is plenty more to see. Start at the cobbled Market Place, where a weekly open-air market (now every Saturday) has been held for over 800 years (*see* Shopping, below); beginning on the last Sunday in June, this site is also host to the annual week-long Alnwick Fair, a festival noteworthy for the enthusiastic participation of a colorfully decked-out local populace. Note the market cross, built on the base of an older cross: The town crier once made his proclamations from here. Along the unusually named Bondgate Within Street, the White Swan Hotel has a unique claim to fame: Its large, paneled lounge on the ground floor was removed intact from the *Olympic,* sister ship of the *Titanic.* Here you can dine in an alcove and imagine you are at sea in a pre–World War I liner (*see* Dining and Lodging, below).

Another town curiosity is the window of **Olde Cross Inn** on Narrowgate Street, at the opposite end of Bondgate Within. The grimy bottles in the window have been left untouched for over 150 years. Why? A 19th-century proprietor fell down dead while arranging the window display, and all subsequent proprietors have refused to touch the bottles, believing them to carry a curse. Not surprisingly, the pub has been nicknamed "The Dirty Bottles."

Alnwick Castle, on the edge of the town center just above the junction of Narrowgate and Bailifgate, is still the home of the dukes of Northumberland, whose family (the Percys) dominated the northeast for centuries. Everything about this castle is on a grand scale, earning it the well-justified epithet, "the Windsor of the North." The entrance, at the side of the barbican (gate tower) doorway, is surmounted by a lion rampant (rearing on hind legs), the heraldic emblem of the dukes of Northumberland; on the dizzy heights of the battlements, remarkably realistic life-size statues stand guard. In contrast with the cold, formidable exterior, the inside of the building has all the opulence of the palatial home it still is: a galleried library; Meissen dinner services; ebony cabinets mounted on gilded wood; tables inlaid with intricate patterns; niches with larger-than-life-size marble statues and Venetian-mosaic floors. The terrace overlooks the river and the parkland laid out by Capability Brown (an 18th-century, Northumberland-born landscape architect). *Tel. 0665/510777. Admission: £2.50 adults, £1 children, £2 senior citizens. Open Apr. 28–Oct. 4, 1– 4:30; closed Sat. in May and Sept.*

To begin your tour of the Northumbrian coast, leave Alnwick by B1340 heading north.

㉞ About 2½ miles on, at Littlehoughton, take a side road to the tiny fishing village of **Craster,** whose harbor smokehouses are known for that great English breakfast delicacy, kippers: herring salted and smoked over smoldering oak shavings. You can visit the tar-blackened smokehouses, eat your fill of fresh and traditionally smoked fish, and even have smoked salmon mailed home to your friends.

Time Out Opposite the smokehouse near the harbor, you can savor Craster kippers for lunch or afternoon tea at **Craster Fish Restaurant,** open Easter–Sept.

㉟ Just north of Craster, the romantic ruins of **Dunstanburgh Castle** stand on a cliff 100 feet above the shore. Built in 1316 by the earl of Lancaster as a defense against the Scots, and later enlarged by John of Gaunt (the powerful duke of Lancaster who virtually ruled England in the late 14th century), the castle is known to many from the popular paintings by 19th-century artist J.M.W. Turner. You can approach it by a bracingly windy, mile-long path along the coast from Craster village. *Tel. 066576/231. Admission: 95p adults, 45p children, 75p senior citizens. Open Apr.–Sept., daily 10–6; Oct.–Mar., Tues.–Sun. 10–4. Closed Christmas and New Year's.*

Farther north are several sandy bays, such as those at **High Newton-by-the-Sea** (3 miles from the castle) and **Beadnell** (4 miles), good for swimming and other water sports. From **36** Seahouses (6 mi), boat trips visit the **Farne Islands** (owned by the National Trust), which host impressive colonies of sea birds and gray seals; you can land on two of them, Inner Farne and Staple Island. Inner Farne, where St. Cuthbert, the great abbot of Lindisfarne, died in AD 687, features a tiny chapel dedicated to his memory. *Boat trips to the islands sail from Seahouses 7 days a week, Apr.–Sept. weather permitting; tel. 0665/720308, 720388, 721144, 720825. Fares: £3.50 adults, £2.50 children. Landing fees vary, and are payable to the wardens. Access is restricted during the seal breeding season (May 15–July 15). Information from tel. 0665/720884 or 0665/721099.*

37 On a great crag north of Seahouses is **Bamburgh Castle,** whose ramparts offer sweeping views of Lindisfarne (Holy Island), the Farne Islands, the stormy coastline, and the Cheviot hills inland. Much of the castle has been restored—although the great Norman keep (central tower) remains intact—and the present Lord Armstrong lives there now. Exhibits include collections of armor, porcelain, jade, furniture, and paintings. *Bamburgh, 3 mi. north of Seahouses, tel. 06684/208. Admission: £2 adults, 90p children. Open Apr.–June and Sept., daily 1–5; July–Aug., daily noon–6; Oct., daily 1–4:30.*

Below the castle, in the village of Bamburgh, the **Grace Darling Museum** commemorates a local heroine as well as the Royal National Lifeboat Institute, an organization of unpaid volunteers who keep watch at the rescue stations on Britain's coasts. Grace Darling became a folk heroine in 1838, when she and her father rowed out to save the lives of nine shipwrecked sailors from the S.S. *Forfarshire.* The museum displays the rowboat (a Northumbrian fishing "coble") she used in the rescue, as well as letters and contemporary accounts of Darling's life. *Radcliffe Rd., opposite church near village center. Admission free. Open Apr.–Sept., daily 11–6.*

38 Continue northward around 8 miles along the coast to **Holy Island** (or **Lindisfarne),** which is linked to the mainland by a long causeway. As the causeway is flooded at high tide, you *must* check locally to find out when crossing is safe. The times change every day. Times are displayed at the causeway, or phone 0289/307283. As traffic can be heavy, allow at least half-an-hour for your return trip.

Seen from a distance, **Lindisfarne Castle** appears to grow out of the rocky pinnacle on which it was built 400 years ago. In 1903, architect Sir Edwin Lutyens sensitively converted the castle into a private home which retains the original's ancient features. Across several fields from the castle is a walled garden, surprisingly sheltered from the storms and winds; its 16th-century plan was discovered in, of all places, California, and the garden has since been replanted, providing again a colorful summer display. *Holy Island, 6 mi. east of A1, north of Bamburgh, tel. 0289/89244. Admission: £2.80 adults, £1.40 children. Open Easter–Sept., Sat.–Thurs. 1–5; Oct., Wed. and weekends 1–5.*

The ruins of **Lindisfarne Priory** are also open. The religious history of the island dates back to the very origins of Christianity in England, for St. Aidan established a monastery here in AD 635. Under its greatest abbot, the sainted Cuthbert, Lindisfarne became one of the foremost centers of learning in Christendom. But in the year 875, Vikings destroyed the Lindisfarne community; only a few monks managed to escape, carrying with them Cuthbert's bones, which they finally reburied in Durham (*see* Tour 1, above). It was refounded in the 11th century by monks from Durham, and today the Norman ruins remain both impressive and beautiful. *Tel. 0289/89200. Admission: £1.60 adults, 80p children, £1.20 senior citizens. Open Apr.– Sept., daily 10–6, Oct.–Mar., Tues.–Sun. 10–4. Closed Christmas and New Year's.*

The island is also notable for Lindisfarne Mead, which is still brewed here and exported to many parts of the world. This sweet—and potent—blend of herbs and fermented honey is prepared from the monks' original recipe.

39 **Berwick-upon-Tweed** lies 10 miles farther up the coast, just within England's border, although historians estimate that it has "changed hands" between the Scots and the English 14 times. The market on Wednesday and Saturday draws plenty of customers from both sides of the border. The town's 16th-century walls are among the best-preserved in Europe (a path follows the ramparts). The parish church, Holy Trinity, was built during Cromwell's Puritan Commonwealth with stone from the castle.

In Berwick's **Military Barracks,** built between 1717 and 1721, three accommodation wings surround a square, with the decorated gatehouse forming the fourth side. An exhibition called "By Beat of Drum" depicts the life of the common soldier from the 1660s to the 1880s. *The Parade, off Church St. in town center, tel. 0289/304493. Admission: £1.60 adults, 80p children, £1.20 senior citizens. Open Apr.–Sept., daily 10–6; Oct.–Mar., Tues.–Sun. 10–4. Closed Christmas and New Year's.*

Time Out **The Town House** (Marygate) serves a delicious variety of fresh quiches, pastries, and other snacks. It's a bit tricky to find: Cross Buttermarket under the Guildhall and go through the old jail. The café's proprietors say, "Please persevere to find your way in—it's easy when you know how!"

What to See and Do with Children

Hadrian's Wall is a good bet for children, and of all the sites and centers, the two most appealing are the **Roman Army Museum** and the line of wall and path at **Housesteads** (*see* Tour 2).

Children may also enjoy a boat trip to the **Farne Islands** (*see* Tour 3) to see the sea-bird colonies and seals.

Near Durham (*see* Tour 1), you and your children can pan for minerals at the **Killhope Wheel Lead Mining Centre.** At **Bowes Museum** you'll find, in addition to the mechanical swan, a collection of 19th-century games, toys, models, dollhouses, etc. Next to the **Captain Cook Birthplace Museum** in Middlesbrough (*see* Tour 1) is a small children's zoo.

At **Washington Waterfowl Park** (091/416-5454), 100 acres of ponds, woods, and riverside are home to ducks, geese, swans, and other birds, including such exotic creatures as the Chilean Flamingo.

Off the Beaten Track

Chillingham Park (16 miles northwest of Alnwick on B6346, with a right turn just before New Berwick) is famous for its wild cattle. Ruled by a bull "king," they are thought to be descendants of the extinct European bison, a herd of which may have been enclosed when the 600-acre Chillingham estate was walled in over 700 years ago. Remember that these creamy-white cattle with curved, black-tipped horns are dangerous; approach them only under the supervision of an experienced guide. *Estate House, tel. 06685/213. Admission: £1.50 adults, 50p children, £1 senior citizens. Open Apr.–Oct., daily 10–noon and 2–5, Sun. 2–5. Closed mornings Tues. and Sun.*

Venerable Bede Monastery Museum and **St. Paul's Church,** in the town of Jarrow, on the River Tyne east of Newcastle, offer substantial monastic ruins, a visitor center-cum-museum, and the church of St. Paul, all reflecting the long tradition of religion and learning that began here in AD 681. A model of the monastery in its days of glory is on display, and the excellent audiovisual program tells its history, quoting an early monk: "Here at Jarrow we are lighting a candle which will spread the light of Christ throughout Northumbria." Still used for regular worship, St. Paul's contains some of the oldest stained glass in Europe and the oldest dedicatory church inscription in Britain (a carved stone inscribed in AD 685). *Church Bank, tel. 091/489-2106. From southern exit traffic circle at South Tyne tunnel, take A185 to South Shields; then follow signs to "St. Paul's Church and Jarrow Hall." Admission: 50p adults, 25p children and senior citizens. Open Apr.–Oct., Tues.–Sat. 10–5:30, Sun. 2–5:30; Nov.–Mar., Tues.–Sat. 11–4:30, Sun. 2:30–5:30. Coffee shop open same times.*

George Stephenson's Birthplace is a tiny, red-roofed stone cottage in Wylam, now a wooded suburb of Newcastle-upon-Tyne. Here, in 1781, the "Father of the Railroads" was born. One room of the house is open to the public—a modest tribute to an engineer whose invention of the steam locomotive touched every corner of the world. The house can be approached only on foot or bicycle, by a path through a country park. You can park your car in the village by the war memorial, 10 minutes' walk away. *Wylam (8 mi west of Newcastle; 1½ mi south of A69), tel. 0661/853457. Admission: 60p adults, 30p children. Open Apr.–Oct., Thurs., Sat., and Sun. 1–5:30; other times by appointment.*

Nine miles southwest of Alnwick (B6341), lies Rothbury, on the edge of Northumberland National Park. One mile north on B6341 is the National Trust's Victorian mansion of **Cragside,** built between 1864 and 1895 by the first Lord Armstrong, an early electrical engineer. The house was the first to be lit by hydroelectricity, generated by the ingenious Lord Armstrong's system of artificial lakes and underground piping. In the library you can see antique vases adapted for use as electric lamps; staircase banisters are topped with specially designed lights. An energy center, with restored mid-Victorian machinery, including a hydraulic pump and a water turbine, is being established on the grounds; this project has won a Ford European Conservation Award. In June, rhododendrons bloom in the 660-acre park surrounding the mansion; 30 rooms of the house, some with Pre-Raphaelite paintings, are open to the public. *Tel. 0669/20333. Admission: £3.50; country park only, £2. Opening times: House: Easter–Oct., Tues.–Sun. 1–5:30; Country Park and Energy Centre: Easter–Oct., daily 10:30–7, Nov.–Mar., weekends 10:30–4.*

Shopping

The Northeast is an area full of hidden valleys, ancient towns, and people still close to their country heritage. Crafts abound. Some of the local craft centers act as co-operatives for groups of craftspeople. One such is the **Northumbria Crafts Centre** (the Chantry, Bridge St., Morbeth, tel. 0670/514351), which also has artists in residence, and the **Gate Gallery** (12 Bondgate Within, Alnwick, tel. 0665/886332), which features the work of up to 70 craftsmen and women. Naturally, pottery, woolens—especially knitwear—and wooden items (treen) lead the field, but all crafts are available. The **Northumberland County Council** issues an excellent booklet of Northumbria Crafts; contact the regional tourist office (*see* Essential Information, above).

Alnwick **Northumbria** (35 Fenkle St.) is chock-full of collectors' items on three floors, including paintings, pottery, ceramics, and figurines. The last-named are a specialty and include a limited edition of a tableau, *Grace Darling to the Rescue*, showing the heroine battling a stormy sea in her tiny rowboat. Paintings of dog breeds are another specialty.

Narrowgate Pottery (22 Back Narrowgate) is a small workshop specializing in domestic stoneware pottery, including the distinctive Alnwick "pierced ware." The proprietors, Andrew and Jacqueline Chilcott, can often be found working at their wheel or decorating and glazing pots.

Lizzy Sharp Knitwear (40 Narrowgate) is stocked with hand-knitted designer garments for children and adults, all characterized by beautifully colored, warm, hard-wearing yarns.

The **House of Hardy,** just outside Alnwick (from downtown, take A1 south to just beyond traffic circle on left, clearly marked), is one of Britain's finest stores for country sports, especially fishing. It has a worldwide reputation for handcrafted tackle. You can even try out their golf clubs on an indoor range.

Barnard Castle Anyone interested in rummaging around second-hand bookstores should visit the **Barnard Castle Book Sale** (M. M. Books, Thorngate Mill), which claims to be the largest book sale in the north. It's open every day from 11–5.

Blanchland Blanchland is an ancient village, 12 miles south of Hexham by B6306, at one end of the Derwent reservoir. In **The Old School Gallery**, a converted schoolhouse on the village green, the eccentric, "social comment" painter Helen C. Houlston paints scenes of village life, often with sardonic insight. You can buy greeting cards with tarot and zodiac designs from this delightfully opinionated and friendly artist.

Cornhill-on-Tweed **Merrylegs** (Oakhall) is a delightful craft workshop that produces hand-carved wooden rocking horses, perky and proud. The craftsman is Michael Lyndon Skeggs, who will also undertake restoration work, if your own rocking horse is the worse for wear.

Craster   **L. Robson and Son** are specialists in curing fish. They and their staff are happy to explain the smoky mysteries of their trade, which hasn't altered for over a century.

Durham   The **University Bookshop** (55 Saddler St.) offers both general and academic books, with over 25,000 volumes in stock, including secondhand and antiquarian books. Here you'll find the largest selection in this university city.

Bramwells Jewellers (Elvet Bridge) sells jewelry, watches, clocks, silverware, crystal, and enamel boxes. The specialty of the store is a pendant replica of the gold-and-silver cross of St. Cuthbert.

New Elvet Gallery (7 New Elvet), sited just across the Elvet Bridge from the cathedral, holds regular exhibitions and carries a selection of crafts in most media.

Hexham   Run by church authorities, the **Abbey Gift Shop** (Beaumont St.) next to the abbey provides a good selection of moderately priced gifts, some unique to the abbey, such as commemorative plates, tapes of on-site choir and music recitals, and various hallmarked items.

In **Bordercraft** (4 Market St.), Brenda Coggins specializes in pure wool fashion knitwear, including mohair and Arrans. Made-to-measure and mail-order services are provided.

The **Northumbrian Country Clothing Design Studio** (Monks House, Woodlands, (tel. 0434/604790) produces designer jackets for men and women from natural Hardwick tweed, as well as hand-printed cotton clothing with Celtic designs by Sorcha. Monday–Saturday visits are by appointment.

Ireshopburn   **Michael and Mary Crompton, Weavers** (Forge Cottage, Ireshopeburn, Weardale), create striking tapestries inspired by the changing seasons of Weardale. Also on sale are smaller handspun and handwoven fabrics, including rugs, shawls, bags, belts, and made-to-order items.

Rothbury   **Ray Brown** (2 Addycombe Cottage, Rothbury, 12 mi southwest of Alnwick, tel. 0669/20906) casts in tin, pewter, and bronze. Trophies and commemorative items can be commissioned. All visits are by appointment only.

South Shields   The **Gambling Man Gallery** (Wapping St.), in a fishing harbor by the Tyne river, is run by Robert Olley, a former coal miner. His cold-cast bronze sculptures reflect life in the Tyne valley. He also portrays characters from the novels of Catherine Cookson, a noted author of historical romances.

Wooler   At the **High Humbleton Pottery** (High Humbleton House, Wooler, 16 mi northwest of Alnwick), Vanessa Taylor has revived the Victorian technique of mocha ware production, creating tree designs in glaze. She also specializes in domestic stoneware and ceramic castles.

Markets   In Alnwick, the open-air market takes place every Saturday on the cobbled main street of this ancient town, which serves a large agricultural area. On Shrove Tuesday (Mardi Gras), a traditionally boisterous game of soccer is played in the streets. Tuesday market in Hexham's Market Place means crowded stalls set out under the long slate roof of the Shambles; other stalls take their chances with the weather, protected only by their bright awnings.

Sports and Fitness

Bicycling This is an area to gladden the heart of any cyclist, offering wide vistas, quiet roads, and magnificently fresh air. Rent bikes from **Weardale Mountain Bikes** (39 Front Street, Frosterley, Weardale, Co. Durham DL13 2QP. tel. 0388/528129).

Boating In Durham, **Brown's Boat House** (Elvet Bridge, tel. 091/386–4292) rents rowboats and offers short cruises from April to early November.

Golf The northeast has a wide range of nine- and 18-hole courses to choose from. One 18-holer is the **Gosforth Park Golf Centre** (Wideopen, Newcastle-upon-Tyne, tel. 091/236–4480), which also boasts a floodlit, 30-bay driving range and a pitch-and-putt course.

Hiking For the experienced hiker, there are long-distance paths following the **Pennine Way** and **Hadrian's Wall;** the **Heritage Way** winds some 69 miles, beginning at Gateshead near Newcastle-upon-Tyne. Information on these hiking routes is available from any tourist information center in the northeast.

Water Sports Many quiet, unspoiled beaches may be found on the coast north of Amble; you can swim there in summer. **Northumbria Waters** offers a wide range of water sports facilities at Kielder Water and 16 other regional reservoirs. *Details from Regent Center, Gosforth, tel. 091/284–3151.*

Dining and Lodging

Dining The northeast is one of the best areas in England for fresh local produce. Keep an eye out for restaurants that serve game from the Kielder Forest, local lamb from the hillsides, and fish both from streams threading through the wild valleys and from the fishing fleets plying their trade from the small harbors along the coast. Two of the more unusual local specialties you might find are venison sausage and Craster kippers—oak smoked herrings.

You might also wish to sample Alnwick Vatted Rum, a blend of Guyanese and Jamaican rum.

Highly recommended restaurants are indicated by a star ★.

Category	Cost*
Expensive	£25–£35
Moderate	£10–25
Inexpensive	under £10

per person, including first course, main course, dessert, and VAT; excluding drinks

Lodging The northeast is not an area where the large hotel chains have much of a presence outside the few large cities. Rather, this is a region where you can expect to find country houses converted into welcoming hotels, old coaching inns that still greet guests after 300 years, and cozy bed-and-breakfasts conveniently located near hiking trails.

Highly recommended lodgings are indicated by a star ★.

Category	Cost*
Expensive	£75–£110
Moderate	£40–£75
Inexpensive	under £40

*All prices are for two people sharing a double room, including service, breakfast and VAT.

Allendale
Lodging

Heatherlea Hotel. This family-run, four-story townhouse overlooks the central square of Allendale, the village that claims to be the geographical center of the British Isles. Guests can play bowls, putt, or simply relax in the hotel's large garden by the river Allen. *The Square, NE47 9BJ, tel. 0434/683236. 15 rooms, 8 with bath. Facilities: table tennis, billiards. No credit cards. Closed Oct.–Dec. 23 and Jan. 2–Mar. Inexpensive.*

Alnwick
Dining and Lodging

White Swan Hotel. Standing on the site of the Old Swan Inn on the stagecoach route between Newcastle and Edinburgh, this building was restored by a Victorian architect, Salvin, who also worked on Alnwick Castle. The main lounge, reconstructed from the paneling and furnishings of an ocean liner, is memorable. One of the hotel's assets is its refurbished **Bondgate Restaurant.** The modern but romantic blue-and-pink decor is a relaxing background for a menu largely drawn from classic Northumbrian cooking. Specialties include Kielder game pie, cooked in rich Guinness sauce, and cranachan, a thick cream dessert made with Alnwick rum, red raspberries, and oatmeal. *Bondgate Within, NE66 1TD, tel. 0665/602109. 43 rooms with bath. Facilities: use of local recreation center and squash club. Restaurant reservations advised, especially in summer. Dress: informal. AE, MC, V. Moderate.*

Lodging

Bondgate House. Bondgate House is a small, family-run hotel, close to the medieval town gateway. It is a good bet for a reasonably priced base for touring the area, having parking space for 8 cars. *20 Bondgate Without, NE66 1PN, tel. 0665/602025. 8 rooms, 3 with bath. Facilities: restaurant. No credit cards. Inexpensive.*

Bamburgh
Dining and Lodging

Lord Crewe Arms. This is a cozy inn, close to Bamburgh Castle, and an ideal spot to have lunch while touring the area. Though a bit remote, the area and the coast offer a wild fascination. The bedrooms are fairly simple, but the food, especially the local seafood, is excellent. *Front St., NE69 7BL, tel. 06684/243. 25 rooms, 21 with bath. MC, V. Moderate.*

Berwick-upon-Tweed
Dining

Funnywayt'Mekalivin. This is an idiosyncratic eatery, and with a name like that who could resist? It's in a cottage which was once a craft shop, and the place is still full of interesting bits and pieces. It is not large, and the chef/owner, Elizabeth Middlemiss, produces imaginative dishes like venison casserole, seafood crumble, or carrot and apple soup. *53 West St., tel. 0289/308827 or 86437. Reservations necessary. Dress: informal. No credit cards. Bring your own wine. Open Thurs.–Sat., dinner only. Moderate.*

Lodging **Turret House.** Turret House, just outside Berwick, is a privately owned guest house, standing in 2 acres of grounds. It would make an excellent stop-over either on the way to or from Scotland. This is a quiet, elegant hotel, with open-plan bar/dining room/lounge, and comfortable bedrooms. *Etal Rd., Tweedmouth TD15 2EG, tel. 0289/330808. 13 rooms, 8 with bath. Facilities: restaurant. AE, DC, MC, V. Moderate.*

Blanchland **Lord Crewe Arms Restaurant.** Part of a historic hotel that once
Dining provided guest accommodations for Blanchland Abbey, this eatery's decor reinforces an atmosphere of cloistered calm. Specialties drawn from traditional cuisine include game in season (venison, grouse, pheasant). *In Lord Crewe Arms Hotel, Blanchland (off B6306, about 8 mi south of Hexham), tel. 0434/675251. Reservations advised. Dress: informal. AE, DC, MC, V. Moderate.*

Chester-le-Street **Lumley Castle Hotel.** This is a real castle, right down to the
Dining and Lodging dungeons, and a hotel experience not to be missed. Attractive bedrooms in all sizes (some with four-poster beds and/or Jacuzzis) are combined with up-to-date facilities. There's plenty of space to wander, and an appealing library-bar for your before-dinner drinks. The **Black Knight Restaurant** features such specialties as *filet de boeuf* (prime roast beef with Stilton cheese, wrapped in bacon), and Landes duck (duck caramelized and served with *pâté de foie gras*, mango, and piquant ginger sauce). *1 mile east of Chester-le-Street by B1284, DH3 4NX, tel. 091/389–1111. 68 rooms with bath. Restaurant reservations advised. Dress: informal, but no jeans. AE, DC, MC, V. Closed Christmas and Jan 1. Expensive.*

Durham **Royal County Hotel.** Recently refurbished, this comfortable
Dining and Lodging Georgian hotel retains many of its historic details. It's the city's top establishment, with a convenient downtown location and spacious rooms, some with four-poster beds. There is also the luxurious **County Restaurant,** with romanesque decor. Specialties include wild boar steaks and seafood paella. *Old Elvet, DH1 3JN, tel. 091/386–6821. 150 rooms with bath. Facilities: coffee shop, satellite TV, leisure center. Restaurant reservations advised. Jacket and tie required. AE, DC, MC, V. Hotel: Expensive. Restaurant: Moderate.*

Greenhead **Holmhead Guest House.** This former farmhouse is not only built
Lodging on Hadrian's Wall but also *of* it. It has stone arches, exposed beams, and antique furnishings; there's open countryside in front and a ruined castle almost in the backyard. In addition to "the longest breakfast menu in the world," a set dinner is served at the farmhouse table, and ingredients for all three courses are likely to have been growing in the kitchen garden only hours before. Specialties include homemade soup, steak pie, and roast lamb with fresh herbs. Local guidebooks are on hand, and Mrs. Pauline Staff is a qualified guide who can give talks and slide shows on Hadrian's Wall and the area. *Near Greenhead (off A69, about 18 mi west of Hexham), CA6 7HY, tel. 06977/47402. 4 double rooms with shower. No smoking in bedrooms or dining rooms. AE, MC, V. Closed Christmas and New Year. Inexpensive.*

Hexham **Harlequin's Restaurant.** Occupying the ground floor of the
Dining Queen's Hall Arts Centre, this light and airy place overlooks the park and abbey. The dining room is decorated with original modern paintings, and the cheerful staff is busy at lunchtime

serving neighborhood workers and shoppers. Local game and fish are the specialties, but there are also vegetarian and pasta dishes. *Beaumont St., tel. 0434/607230. Dinner reservations advised. Dress: informal. AE, DC, MC, V. Closed Sun. and national holidays. Inexpensive.*

Dining and Lodging **County Hotel.** The proprietor here is proud of the old-fashioned, homey feel of his establishment, known to local people simply as "the County." Reminders of his former occupation as a pheasant breeder decorate the walls of the public rooms, which are usually crowded with farmers on auction days. Food is served all day in the paneled dining room and in the more informal lounge. High teas (late afternoon meals) are a specialty (5:30–6:30), and homemade meat pies, pastries, and Northumbrian lamb are often featured on the menu, along with international dishes. *Priestpopple, NE46 1PS, tel. 0434/602030. 10 rooms, 4 with bath. Restaurant reservations advised. Dress: informal. AE, MC, V. Moderate.*

★ **Langley Castle Hotel.** A genuine 14th-century castle, rescued by its American owner and converted into a luxury hotel and restaurant, its seven-foot-thick walls are complete with turrets and battlements. All public rooms are grandly furnished, and the bedrooms have luxurious appointments. The restaurant has an unusual atmosphere—although perhaps not for a castle—with exposed beams, wall tapestries, and a welcoming fire. Specialties include beef Cadwallader and smoked trout fillet. *Langley-on-Tyne (6 mi west of Hexham), NE47 5LU, tel. 0434/688888. 8 rooms with bath. Restaurant reservations required. Dress: informal. AE, DC, MC, V. Moderate–Expensive.*

Longframlington **Embleton Hall.** The 5 acres of beautiful grounds are reason
Dining and Lodging enough to stay in this stone country mansion dating from 1730 and decorated with lovely antiques and original paintings. Another reason to visit is the restaurant, its chintz drapes and cut-glass chandeliers perfect accompaniment to the traditional English dishes, especially game, served here. Entrees include *entrecôte* (rib steak) stuffed with game pâté in red wine sauce, and roast Northumbrian pheasant in rich gravy. *On A697 10 mi southwest of Alnwick, NE65 8DT, tel. 0665/570249. 10 rooms with bath. Restaurant reservations required. Jacket and tie suggested. AE, DC, MC, V. Moderate–Expensive.*

Besom Barn. You can enjoy comfortable lodging in one of the four bedrooms in this converted farmhouse, all on the ground floor and with direct access to a patio where breakfast is served in good weather. There are moorland views from the picture windows. The **Besom Barn Restaurant** features a wood-burning stove in the center of the dining room. Specialties include Besom Pie (pork, venison, and rabbit with Scottish ale). *On A697, ½ mi north of the village, NE65 8EN, tel. 0665/570627. 4 rooms with bath. Restaurant reservations required. Dress: informal. AE, DC, MC, V. Moderate.*

St. John's Chapel **Pennine Lodge.** You will enjoy the comfortable rooms in this
Dining and Lodging converted farmhouse set in the striking scenery of Weardale. Many features of the original longhouse-style building remain; some parts are over 400 years old. The restaurant serves home-style cooking, with fresh produce every day. Country specialties include pheasant casserole with port, and North Country steak pie. In good weather teas are served outside in the spacious grounds. *Weardale (off A689) DL13 1QX, tel. 0388/*

537247. 5 rooms with bath. Restaurant reservations required for dinner. Dress: informal. No credit cards. Closed Nov.– mid-Mar. Hotel: Inexpensive–Moderate.

South Shields
Dining

The Grotto. Built into a cliff from which there are spectacular views of the sea and the Marsden Rock Bird Sanctuary, this unusually sited restaurant is entered from the clifftop promenade via an elevator that descends into the rock. Lobster and steak are the staples here. *Coast Rd., Marsden, tel. 091/455–2043. Reservations required. Dress: informal. AE, MC, V. Moderate.*

Wylam
Dining

Laburnam House. Laburnam House is a friendly restaurant in a 1716 building, with simple decor and a copious blackboard menu. Try the seafood dishes—always a good bet in this area— which come in many guises, all tasty, or the duck or pheasant. There are also four bedrooms available. *Main St., tel. 0661/ 852185. Reservations required. Dress: informal. AE, DC, MC, V. Closed Dec. 25–26, Jan. 1–2, lunch, Sun. and Mon., and 2 weeks in Feb. Expensive.*

The Arts

Northern Arts is the official body which promotes the arts in the northeast. *9–10 Osborne Ter., Jesmond, Newcastle-upon-Tyne NE2 1NZ, tel. 091/281–6334.*

Festivals

The **Alnwick Fair,** held in June/July, features a costumed re-enactment of a medieval fair, processions, a market, and concerts. *Alnwick Fair, Box 2, 19 Lindisfarne Rd., Alnwick NE66 1AU, tel. 0665/602234.*

Billingham International Folklore Festival is held each year in the third week of August. *Festival Office, Municipal Buildings, Town Center, Billingham (north of Middlesbrough), Cleveland TS23 2LW, tel. 0642/558212.*

16 Scotland: Edinburgh and the Borders

Introduction

Although, of course, Edinburgh was not deliberately designed as a top-notch tourist attraction, it might well have been. A variety of factors have combined to make it one of the most interesting city environments anywhere in the world. These include an outstanding geographical position—Edinburgh is built, like Rome, on seven hills—the survival of an Old Town district which retains striking evidence of a colorful history; and a large number of outstanding buildings conceived during the upsurge of Scottish intellectual, scientific, and artistic activity in the second half of the 18th century.

The result for today's visitor is a skyline of sheer drama, and an aura of grandeur. Edinburgh Castle watches over the city, frowning down on Princes Street, the main downtown shopping area, as if disapproving its modern razzmatazz. Its ramparts still echo with gunfire each day when the traditional one o'clock gun booms out over the city, startling unwary shoppers. To the east, the top of Calton Hill is cluttered with sturdy, neoclassical structures, somewhat like the abandoned set for a Greek tragedy.

Also conspicuous from Princes Street is Arthur's Seat, a backdrop of bright green and yellow furze springing up just behind the spires of the Old Town. This child-sized mountain, which juts 800 feet above its surroundings, offers steep slopes and little crags, like a miniature highlands right in the middle of the busy city.

There is no escaping the very literal sense of theater if you visit the city from August to early September. The Edinburgh International Festival has attracted all sorts of international performers since its inception in 1947. Even more obvious to the casual stroller during this time is the refreshingly irreverent Edinburgh Festival Fringe, unruly child of the official festival, which spills out of halls and theaters all over town and onto the streets.

These theatrical elements give a unique identity to downtown, but turn a corner, say, off George Street (parallel to Princes Street), and you will see, not an endless cityscape, but blue sea and a patchwork of fields. This is the county of Fife, beyond the inlet of the North Sea called the Firth of Forth; a reminder, like the highlands to the northwest glimpsed from Edinburgh's highest points, that the rest of Scotland lies within easy reach.

The Borders area comprises the great rolling hills, moors, wooded river valleys, and farmland that stretch south from Lothian, the region crowned by Edinburgh, to England. All the distinctive features of Scotland—paper currency, architecture, opening hours of pubs and stores, food and drink, and accent—start right at the border; you won't find the Borders a dilute form of England.

Essential Information

Important Addresses and Numbers

Tourist Information The **Edinburgh and Scottish Travel Centre** is adjacent to Edinburgh Waverley railway station, above Waverley Market.

Here, visitors arriving in Edinburgh can get expert advice on what to see and do in the city and throughout Scotland. In addition to free information and literature, services include accommodation reservations, route-planning, a Scottish bookshop, and currency exchange. Visitors can also buy National Trust, Historic Scotland, and Great Britain Heritage passes. *3 Princes Street, tel. 031/557–1700. Open May, June, Sept., Mon.–Sat. 8:30–8, Sun. 11–8; July, Aug., Mon–Sat. 8:30 AM–9 PM, Sun. 11–9; Oct.–Apr. Mon.–Fri. 9–6, Sat. 9–1.*

Travel Agencies **American Express:** 139 Princes St., Edinburgh EH2 4BR, tel. 031/225–7881.
Thomas Cook: 79A Princes Street, Edinburgh EH2 2ER, tel. 031/220–4039.

Car Rental Agencies **Edinburgh: Avis,** 100 Dalry Rd., tel. 031/337–6363, also at the airport;
Budget Rent-a-Car, J & D Braid, 116 Polwarth Gdns, tel. 031/228–6088;
Hertz U.K. Ltd., 10 Picardy Pl., tel. 031/556–8311, also at the airport and Edinburgh Waverley railway station.

Emergencies **Lothian and Borders Police Headquarters** (including lost property), Fettes Ave., Edinburgh, tel. 031/311–3131.

Pharmacy **Boots,** 48 Shandwick Pl. (west end of Princes St.), Edinburgh, tel. 031/225–6757. Open Mon.–Sat. 8:45 AM–9 PM, Sun. 11–4:30.

Post Office 2 Waterloo Pl. (east end of Princes St.), tel. 031/550–8232. Open weekdays 9:30–5:30, Sat. 9:30–12:30.

Arriving and Departing by Plane

Edinburgh Airport has air links with all the major airports in Britain and many in Europe. The **Airport Information Centre** (tel. 031/344–3136) answers questions regarding schedules, tickets, and reservations. **Glasgow Airport** is also less than an hour from Edinburgh by car or train. It offers a wide range of links to the south and internationally. Call the **Glasgow Air Information Desk** (tel. 041/887–1111, ext. 4552). Transatlantic passengers flying direct to Scotland may use Glasgow Airport (*see* above) or **Prestwick Airport** on the Clyde coast. For information on international flights, call **Prestwick Information Desk** (tel. 0292/79822, ext. 5090 or 5091).

From the Airport to Downtown Buses run at 30-minute intervals during peak times from the Edinburgh airport main terminal building to Waverley Bridge downtown; they are less frequent after rush hours and on weekends. The roughly 25-minute trip costs £2 for a one-way ticket. Taxis are also available outside the terminal; the 20-minute trip costs roughly £10. By car, the airport is about 7 miles west of Princes Street downtown, and is clearly marked from A8. The usual route to downtown is via Corstorphine.

Glasgow Airport to Edinburgh. Glasgow Airport is 8 miles from Glasgow city center. There are regular bus and train services between them. (Trains leave from Paisley Gilmour Street Station, 2 miles from the airport; take a taxi or bus—service every 10 minutes from the main entrance.) From Queen Street Station you can get a train to Waverley Station in Edinburgh (departures every half hour). Adjacent to Queen Street Station is the Buchanan Street Bus Station, with connections to

Edinburgh and other areas. By car, Glasgow Airport is about an hour from Edinburgh via M8.

Arriving and Departing by Car, Train, and Bus

By Car Downtown Edinburgh usually means Princes Street, which runs east–west. Entering from the east coast, drivers will come in on A1, Meadowbank Stadium serving as a good landmark. The highway bypasses the suburbs of Musselburgh and Tranent; therefore, any bottlenecks will occur close to downtown. From the Borders, the approach to Princes Street is by A7/A68 through Newington, an area offering a wide choice of accommodation. From Newington, the east end of Princes Street is reached by North Bridge and South Bridge streets. Approaching from the southwest, drivers will join the west end of Princes Street, via A701 and A702, while those coming west from Glasgow or Stirling will meet Princes Street from M8 or M9, respectively. Slightly more complicated is the approach via M90—from Forth Bridge/Perth/east coast; the key road for getting downtown is Queensferry Road, which joins Charlotte Square close to the west end of Princes Street.

By Train Edinburgh's main train station, Waverley, is downtown, below Waverley Bridge. The station has recorded summaries of services to King's Cross Station in London—telephone for weekday information (tel. 031/557–3000), Saturday service (tel. 031/557–2737), and Sunday service (tel. 031/557–1616). For information on all other destinations, or other inquiries, telephone 031/556–2451. Kings' Cross Station can be reached on 071/278–2477. Travel time from Edinburgh to London by train is as little as four hours for the fastest services.

By Bus Several companies provide bus service to and from London, including **Scottish Citylink Coaches** (Bus Station, St. Andrew Sq., tel. 031/556–8464. Recorded timetable: tel. 031/556–8414). Edinburgh is approximately eight hours by bus from London.

Getting Around

By Car Edinburgh can be explored easily on foot, so a car is hardly needed. The roads south of the city, in the Borders, are easy and, except close to the city at rush hours, relatively free of heavy traffic.

By Bus **Lothian Region Transport,** operating dark-red-and-white buses, is the main operator within Edinburgh. The **Edinburgh Freedom Ticket,** allowing unlimited one-day travel on the city's buses, can be purchased in advance. More expensive is the **Tourist Card,** available in units of from two to 13 days, which gives unlimited access to buses and includes vouchers for savings on tours. *Waverley Bridge, tel. 031/220–4111. Open Mon.–Sat. 7 AM–8 PM, Sun. 8:30–6:30; also 14 Queen St., tel. 031/554–4494. Open weekdays 9–5.* **Scottish Motor Transport (S.M.T.)** (Bus Station, St. Andrew Sq., tel. 031/556–8464), operating green buses, provides much of the service into Edinburgh, and also offers day tours around and beyond the city.

Guided Tours

Bus Tours **Lothian Region Transport** and **Scottish Motor Transport** both offer tours in and around the city (*see* Getting Around, above).

Chauffeured Tours	**Ghillie Personal Travel** (64 Silverknowes Rd. East, tel. 031/336–3120) offers flexible, customized tours in all sizes of cars and buses, especially suitable for groups.
Walking Tours	**The Cadies** (1 Upper Bow, tel. 031/225–6745) organize historic Old Town walks, Ghost Hunt, pub, and Murder and Mystery tours of Edinburgh throughout the year, featuring costumed guides and other costumed theatrical characters en route.

Exploring Edinburgh and the Borders

Orientation

We have divided our coverage of Edinburgh (Tour 1) into two sections, but only the Old Town and the Royal Mile area is really an organized route. The New Town is ideal for unstructured wandering, drinking in the classical elegance of the squares and terraced houses, exploring the antiques shops, and dropping into pubs and wine bars.

Tour 2 surveys Sir Walter Scott territory south of Edinburgh among the ruined Border abbeys. This tour can be done in one long day, or better still, taken in two bites, returning to Edinburgh overnight.

Highlights for First-time Visitors

Abbotsford: Tour 2
Edinburgh Castle: Tour 1
Holyrood House: Tour 1
Melrose Abbey: Tour 2
National Gallery of Scotland: Tour 1
Royal Museum of Scotland: Tour 1
Traquair House: Tour 2
The view from Calton Hill: Tour 1

Tour 1: Edinburgh

Numbers in the margin correspond to points of interest on the Scottish Borders and Edinburgh maps.

❶ The dark, brooding presence of the castle dominates **Edinburgh,** the very essence of Scotland's martial past. The castle is built on a crag of hard, black volcanic rock formed during the Ice Age when an eastward-moving glacier scoured around this resistant core, forming steep cliffs on three sides. On the fourth side, a "tail" of rock was left, a ramp from the top that gradually runs away eastward. This became the street known as the Royal Mile, the backbone of the Old Town.

Time and redevelopment have swept away some of the narrow "closes" (alleyways) and tall tenements of the Old Town, but enough survives for you to be able to imagine the original shape of Scotland's capital, straggling between the guardian fortress on its crag at one end of the Royal Mile, and the royal residence, the Palace of Holyroodhouse, at the other. It was not until the Scottish Enlightenment, a civilizing time of expansion in the 1700s, that the city fathers decided to break away from the

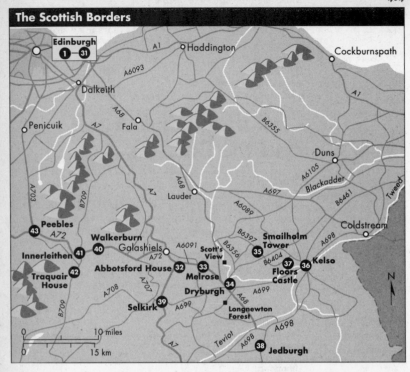

The Scottish Borders

Royal Mile's rocky slope and build another Edinburgh, a little to the north, below the castle. This is the New Town, with elegant squares, classical facades, wide streets, and harmonious proportions. The main street, Princes Street, was conceived as an exclusive residential address with an open vista south and up at the castle. It has since been completely altered by the demands of business, especially of shopping.

Victorian expansion and urban sprawl have hugely increased the city's size, and the Old and New Towns are now separated by Princes Street Gardens (and the railroad), yet their contrasting identities are still the key to understanding Edinburgh.

❷ Probably every visitor to the city tours **Edinburgh Castle**—which is more than can be said for many residents! Its popularity as an attraction is due not only to the castle's symbolic value as the center of Scotland but to the outstanding views offered from its battlements.

Recent archaeological discoveries have established that the rock was inhabited as far back as 1000 BC, in the later part of the Bronze Age. There have been fortifications here since the mysterious people called Picts first used it as a stronghold in the 3rd and 4th centuries AD. They were dislodged by Saxon invaders from northern England in AD 452, and for the next 1,300 years the site saw countless battles and skirmishes.

The castle has been held by Scots and Englishmen, Catholics and Protestants, soldiers and royalty; during the Napoleonic

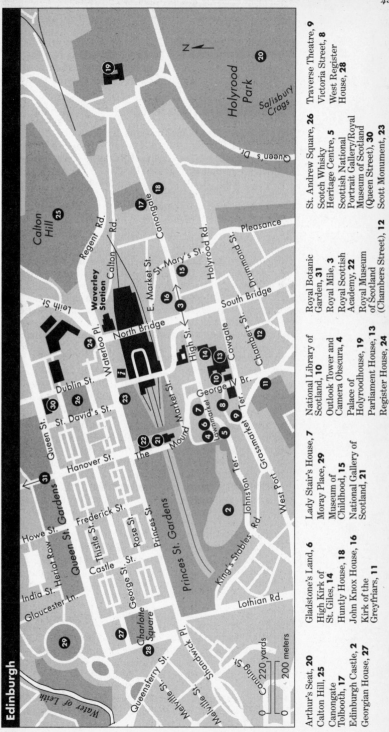

Edinburgh

St. Andrew Square, **26**
Scotch Whisky
Heritage Centre, **5**
Scottish National
Portrait Gallery/Royal
Museum of Scotland
(Queen Street), **30**
Scott Monument, **23**

Traverse Theatre, **9**
Victoria Street, **8**
West Register
House, **28**

Royal Botanic
Garden, **31**
Royal Mile, **3**
Royal Scottish
Academy, **22**
Royal Museum
of Scotland
(Chambers Street), **12**

National Library of
Scotland, **10**
Outlook Tower and
Camera Obscura, **4**
Palace of
Holyroodhouse, **19**
Parliament House, **13**
Register House, **24**

Lady Stair's House, **7**
Moray Place, **29**
Museum of
Childhood, **15**
National Gallery of
Scotland, **21**

Gladstone's Land, **6**
High Kirk of
St. Giles, **14**
Huntly House, **18**
John Knox House, **16**
Kirk of the
Greyfriars, **11**

Arthur's Seat, **20**
Calton Hill, **25**
Canongate
Tolbooth, **17**
Edinburgh Castle, **2**
Georgian House, **27**

Holyrood Park

Salisbury
Crags

Calton
Hill

Waverley
Station

North Bridge

Princes St. Gardens

Charlotte
Square

Water of Leith

0   220 yards
0   200 meters

Wars, it even contained French prisoners of war, whose carvings can still be seen on the vaults under the great hall. In the 16th century Mary, Queen of Scots, chose to give birth there to the future James VI of Scotland, who was also to rule England as James I. In 1573, it was the last fortress to hold out for Mary as rightful Catholic queen of Britain, only to be virtually destroyed by English artillery.

The oldest surviving building in the complex is the tiny 11th-century **St. Margaret's Chapel,** the only building spared when the castle was razed in 1313 by Scots determined not to surrender it to their English foes. Also worth seeing are the **crown room,** which contains the **regalia of Scotland**—the crown, scepter, and sword that once graced the Scottish monarch; the **old parliament hall;** and **Queen Mary's apartments,** where she gave birth to James. The **great hall** features an extensive collection of arms and armor, and has an impressive vaulted, beamed ceiling.

There are several military features of interest, including the **Scottish National War Memorial,** the **Scottish United Services Museum,** and the famous 15th-century cannon *Mons Meg,* which is so huge that 100 men, five carpenters, and a large number of oxen were needed to heave it into position. The **Esplanade,** the huge forecourt of the castle, was built in the 18th century as a parade ground, using earth from the foundation of the Royal Exchange to widen and level the area. Although it now serves as the castle parking lot, it comes alive with color each year when it is used during the Festival for the Tattoo, a magnificent military display and pageant. *Tel. 031/244–3101. Admission: £2.20 adults, £1.10 children and senior citizens, family ticket, £5. Open Apr.–Sept., Mon.–Sat. 9:30–5:05, Sun. 11–5:05; Oct.–Mar., Mon.–Sat. 9:30–4:20, Sun. 12:30–3:35.*

❸ The **Royal Mile** starts immediately below the Esplanade. It runs roughly west to east, from the castle to the Palace of Holyroodhouse *(see below),* and progressively changes its name from Castlehill to Lawnmarket, High Street, and Canongate. On your stroll downhill from the castle, you will need first, imagination, to re-create the former life of the city; and second, sharp eyes, to spot the numerous details such as historic plaques or ornamentation that make the excursion more than simply a parade of buildings. Note on Castlehill, for example, the little fountain recalling the burning of hundreds of witches here between 1479 and 1722. Notice also the cannonball imbedded in the wall of Cannonball House. Legend says it was fired from the castle during the Jacobite rebellion in 1745 led by Bonnie Prince Charlie, the most romantic of the Stuart pretenders to the British throne.

❹ On the left of Castlehill, the **Outlook Tower and Camera Obscura** offer armchair views of the city. The building housing this optical instrument was originally constructed in the 17th century, but was significantly altered in the 1850s with the installation of the camera obscura, which, on a clear day, projects an image of the city onto a white, concave table. *Tel. 031/226–3709. Admission: £2.20 adults, £1.10 children, £1.45 senior citizens and students, £6 family. Open Apr.–Oct., weekdays 9:30–5:30, weekends 10–6; Nov.–Mar., weekdays 9:30–5, weekends 10:30–4:30.*

5 Opposite, the **Scotch Whisky Heritage Centre** reveals the mysterious process that turns malted barley and spring water into one of Scotland's most important exports. *358 Castlehill, tel. 031/220–0441. Admission: £2.50 adults, £2 students, £1.25 children, £1.50 senior citizens, £6.50 family ticket. Open Jun.– Sept., daily 9–6:30, Oct.–May, daily 10–5.*

Farther down on the left, the **Tolbooth Kirk,** built in 1842–44 for the General Assembly of the Church of Scotland ("kirk" means "church"), boasts the tallest spire in the city—240 feet.

From Lawnmarket you can start your discovery of the **Old Town closes,** the alleyways that are like ribs leading off the Royal Mile backbone.

6 The six-story tenement known as **Gladstone's Land,** just beside the Assembly Hall, is a survivor from the 17th century, demonstrating typical architectural features, including an arcaded ground floor and an entrance at second-floor level. It is furnished in the style of a 17th-century merchant's house. *Tel. 031/ 226–5856. Admission: £1.80 adults, 90p children. Open Apr.– Oct., Mon.–Sat. 10–5, Sun. 2–5.*

7 Close by Gladstone's Land, down yet another close, is **Lady Stair's House,** a good example of 17th-century urban architecture. Built in 1622, it evokes Scotland's literary past with exhibits on Sir Walter Scott, Robert Louis Stevenson, and Robert Burns. *Off Lawnmarket, tel. 031/225–2424, ext. 6593. Admission free. Open June–Sept., Mon.–Sat. 10–6, Sun. during festival 2–5; Oct.–May, Mon.–Sat. 10–5.*

8 For a worthwhile shopping diversion, turn down **Victoria Street** to the right, a 19th-century improvement—or intrusion—on the shape of the Old Town. Its shops offer antiques, old prints, and quality giftware. Down in the **Grassmarket,** which for centuries was, as its name suggests, an agricultural market, the **9** shopping continues. The **Traverse Theatre** is here, too (*see* The Arts, below).

To visit another of Edinburgh's historic churches, walk from the Grassmarket back along Victoria Street to George IV **10** Bridge, where you'll see the **National Library of Scotland** straight ahead (free exhibitions; open weekdays 9:30–8:30, Sat. 9:30–1). A little farther down, to the right, is the **Kirk of 11 the Greyfriars,** built on the site of a medieval monastery. Here, in 1638, the National Covenant was signed, declaring the independence of the Presbyterian Church in Scotland from government control. The covenant plunged Scotland into decades of civil war. *Greyfriars Pl., tel. 031/225–1900. Admission free. Open Easter–Sept., weekdays 10–4, Sat. 10–noon.*

Before returning to Lawnmarket, you might detour down Chambers Street, which leads off from George IV Bridge. **12** Here, in a lavish Victorian building, the **Royal Museum of Scotland** displays a wide-ranging collection drawn from natural history, archaeology, scientific and industrial history, and the history of mankind and civilization. The great Main Hall, with its soaring roof, is architecturally interesting in its own right. *Chambers St., tel. 031/225–7534. Admission free. Open Mon.– Sat. 10–5, Sun. 2–5.*

Return to High Street and, near Parliament Square, look on the right for a heart set in the cobbles. This marks the site of the vanished Tolbooth, the center of city life from the 15th century until its demolition in 1817. This ancient civic building, formerly housing the Scottish parliament, then used as a prison from 1640 onward, inspired Scott's novel *The Heart of Midlothian*. Nearly every city and town in Scotland once had a Tolbooth—originally a customs house where tolls were gathered, the name came to mean the town hall and later a prison, since the detention cells were located in the basement of the town

⑬ hall. **Parliament House**—the seat of Scottish government until 1707, when the crowns of Scotland and England were united—is partially hidden by the bulk of St. Giles's Cathedral. *Parliament Sq., 031/225–2595, ext. 223. Admission free. Open Tues.–Fri. 10–4.*

⑭ The **High Kirk of St. Giles,** originally the city's parish church, became a cathedral in 1633, and is now usually called St. Giles's Cathedral. There has been a church on the site since AD 854, although most of the present structure dates from 1829. The spire, however, was completed in 1495, the choir is mostly 15th-century, and four of the interior columns date from the early 12th century. The **Chapel of the Order of the Thistle,** bearing the belligerent national motto "Nemo Me Impune Lacessit" ("No one assails me with impunity"), was added in 1911. *High St., tel. 031/225–4363. Admission free. (Thistle Chapel: 30p adults, 5p children.) Open Mon.–Sat. 9–5 (7 in summer), Sun. 2–5.*

Another landmark in Old Town life can be seen just below St. Giles's. The **Mercat Cross** ("mercat" means "market"), a focus of public attention for centuries, is still the site of royal proclamations.

On the right, two blocks below the North Bridge–South Bridge
⑮ junction, is the **Museum of Childhood,** a celebration of toys that even adults may well enjoy. *42 High St., tel. 031/225–2424. Admission free. Open June–Sept., Mon.–Sat. 10–6, Sun. during festival 2–5; Oct.–May, Mon.–Sat. 10–5.*

⑯ Opposite is the **John Knox House,** a 16th-century dwelling. It is not absolutely certain that Knox, Scotland's severe religious reformer (1514–72), lived here, but mementos of his life are on view inside. *45 High St., tel. 031/556–9579 or 556–2647. Admission: £1 adults, 50p children, 80p senior citizens. Open Mon.–Sat. 10–5.*

Beyond this point, you would once have passed out of the safety of the town walls. A plaque outside the **Netherbow Theatre** depicts the **Netherbow Port (gate),** which once stood at this point. Below is the **Canongate** area, named for the canons who once ran the abbey at Holyrood, now the site of Holyrood Palace. Canongate originally was an independent "burgh," a Scottish term meaning, essentially, a community with trading rights granted by the monarch. This explains the presence of the
⑰ handsome **Canongate Tolbooth,** on the left, where the town council once met. It's now the setting for "The People's Story" exhibition which tells the history of the people of Edinburgh.

Almost next door, in the graveyard of **Canongate Kirk,** are buried some notable Scots, including Adam Smith, author of *The*
⑱ *Wealth of Nations* (1776). Opposite is timber-fronted **Huntly House,** a museum of local history. *142 Canongate, tel. 031/225–2424. Admission free. Open June–Sept., 10–6, Sun. during Festival 2–5; Oct.–May, Mon.–Sat. 10–5.*

Time Out   You can get a good cup of tea and a sweet bun (a quintessentially Scottish indulgence) from **Clarinda's** (69 Canongate) or the **Abbey Strand Tearoom** (The Sanctuary, Abbey Strand) near the palace gates.

---

19 Facing you at the end of Canongate are the elaborate wrought-iron gates of the **Palace of Holyroodhouse,** official residence of the queen when she is in Scotland.

Holyrood Palace came into existence originally as a guest house for the medieval abbey founded in 1128 by Scottish king David I, after a vision of the cross ("rood" means "cross") saved his life on a hunting trip. David gave the land for the abbey to Augustinian friars in gratitude to God, and commanded them to build the Abbey of Holyrood—the Church of the Holy Cross. Since then, the palace has been the setting for high drama, including at least one notorious murder, a spectacular funeral, several major fires, and centuries of the colorful lifestyles of larger-than-life, power-hungry personalities. The murder occurred in 1566 when Mary, Queen of Scots, was dining with her favorite, David Rizzio, who was hated at court for his social-climbing. Mary's second husband, Lord Darnley, burst into the chamber with his henchmen, dragged Rizzio into an antechamber, and stabbed him over 50 times. (Darnley himself was murdered in Edinburgh the next year, to make way for the queen's marriage to her lover, Bothwell.) Only 22 years before these shocking events, the palace had been severely damaged by an invading English army, which set fire to it; only the great tower (on the left as you look at the front facade) survived. In 1650, this time by accident, the palace burned again, and the great tower's massive walls again resisted the flames. Oliver Cromwell, the Protestant Lord Protector of England, who had conquered Scotland, ordered the palace rebuilt after the 1650 fire, but the restorations were poorly carried out, and lasted only until the restoration of the monarchy after Cromwell's death. When Charles II ascended the British throne in 1660, he ordered Holyrood rebuilt in the architectural style of the French "Sun King," Louis XIV, and that is the palace that visitors see today.

In 1661 Holyroodhouse was the scene of what must be one of the most bizarre funerals in history. The Marquis of Montrose, a Scottish royalist general, had been executed by Cromwell for high treason, and his limbs and head displayed around the country. Following the restoration of the Stuart monarchy, Montrose's body was put together for a final farewell ceremony. One of his legs was brought from Aberdeen; his head from a spike in London; his other leg and his arms from, respectively, Glasgow, Stirling, and Perth; and the rest of his remains from the local gallows. The body lay in state in Holyrood for four months, after which the coffin was paraded through the streets, borne aloft by 14 earls, and buried in the Kirk of St. Giles. When the royal family is not in residence, you can walk freely around the palace and go inside for a conducted tour. *Tel. 031/556-7371. Admission: £2 adults, £1 children, £1.50 senior citizens. Open Apr.–Oct., Mon.–Sat. 9:30–5:15, Sun. 10:30–4:30; Nov.–Mar., Mon.–Sat. 9:30–3:45; closed during royal and state visits.*

⑳ Behind the palace lie the open grounds of **Holyrood Park,** which enclose Edinburgh's own mini-mountain, **Arthur's Seat.** The park was the hunting ground of early Scottish kings.

In 1767, a civic competition to design a new district for Edinburgh was won by an unknown young architect, James Craig. His plan was for a grid of three main east–west streets, balanced at either end by two grand squares. These streets survive today, though some of the buildings that line them were altered by later development. Princes Street is the southernmost, with Queen Street to the north and George Street as the axis, punctuated by St. Andrew and Charlotte squares. A look at the map will show you its geometric symmetry, unusual in Britain. Even Princes Street Gardens are balanced by Queen Street Gardens to the north.

Start your walk on **The Mound,** the sloping street that joins Old and New Towns. Two galleries tucked immediately east of this great linking ramp are both the work of W. H. Playfair (1789–1857), an architect whose neoclassical buildings contributed greatly to Edinburgh's earning the title, the "Athens of the
㉑ North." **The National Gallery of Scotland,** at the foot of the Mound, has a wide-ranging selection of paintings, from the Renaissance to Postimpressionism, with works by Velásquez, El Greco, Rembrandt, Turner, Degas, Monet, and Van Gogh, among many others, as well as a fine collection of Scottish art. The rooms of the gallery are attractively decorated, making it a pleasure to browse. *Tel. 031/556–8921. Admission free. Open Mon.–Sat. 10–5 (extended during festival), Sun. 2–5.*

㉒ The other museum, **The Royal Scottish Academy,** with its imposing columned facade overlooking Princes Street, holds an annual exhibition of students' work. *Princes St., tel. 031/225–6671. Admission: £1.40 adults, 70p children. Open late Apr.–July, Mon.–Sat. 10–7, Sun. 2–5, and during the Festival.*

The north side of **Princes Street** is now one long sequence of chain stores whose unappealing modern storefronts can be seen in almost any large British town. Luckily, the other side of the street is occupied by well-kept gardens, which act as a wide green moat to the castle on its rock. Walk east until you reach the unmistakable soaring Gothic spire of the 200-foot-high
㉓ **Scott Monument,** built in 1844 in honor of Scotland's most famous author, Sir Walter Scott (1771–1832), author of *Ivanhoe, Waverley,* and many other novels and poems. Note the marble statue of Scott and his favorite dog. The monument will be under renovation for at least a year.

㉔ **Register House,** on the left opposite the main post office, marks the end of Princes Street. This was Scotland's first custom-built archives depository, and was partly funded by the sale of estates forfeited by Jacobite landowners following their last rebellion in Britain (1745–46). Work on the building, designed by Robert Adam, Scotland's most famous neoclassical architect, started in 1774. The statue in front is of the Duke of Wellington. *Tel. 031/556–6585. Admission free. Open weekdays, legal collection 9:30–4:30, historical collection 9–4:45, general exhibitions 10–4.*

Time Out Immediately west of Register House is the **Café Royal** (17 West Register St.), one of the city's most interesting pubs. It has good beer and lots of character, with ornate tiles and stained glass contributing to the atmosphere.

25 The monuments on **Calton Hill,** growing ever more noticeable ahead as you walk east along Princes Street, can be reached by continuing along Waterloo Place, and either climbing steps to the hilltop or taking the road farther on that loops at a more leisurely pace up the hill. Beyond the photogenic collection of columns and temples, the views from Calton Hill range over the Lomond Hills of Fife in the north, to the Pentland Hills southwest, behind the spire of St. Giles's. Close to the incomplete Parthenon look-alike known as Edinburgh's Disgrace—it was intended as a National War Memorial in 1822 but contributions did not come in—is a monument to Abraham Lincoln and the Scottish-American dead of the Civil War. (An impressive American monument to the Scottish soldiers of World War I stands in West Princes Street Gardens, among various memorials of Scottish and foreign alliances.) The tallest monument on Calton Hill is the 100-foot-high **Nelson Monument,** completed in 1816 in honor of Britain's naval hero. *Tel. 031/225–2424, ext. 6689. Admission: 55p. Open Apr.–Sept., Mon. 1–6, Tues. and Sat. 10–6; Oct.–Mar., Tues. and Sat. 10–3.*

26 Make your way to **St. Andrew Square** by cutting through the **St. James Centre** shopping mall.

On St. Andrew Square, next to the bus station, is the headquarters of the **Royal Bank of Scotland;** take a look inside at the lavish decor of the central banking hall. In the distance, at the other end of George Street, on Charlotte Square, you can see the copper dome of the former St. George's Church. In Craig's symmetrical plan for the New Town, a matching church was intended for the bank's site, but Sir Lawrence Dundas, a wealthy and influential baronet, somehow managed to acquire the space for his town house—string-pulling at city hall is nothing new! The grand mansion was later converted into the bank. The church originally intended for the site, St. Andrew's, is a little way down George Street.

Walk west along George Street, with its variety of shops, to Charlotte Square. Note particularly the palatial facade of the square's north side, designed by Robert Adam—it's considered one of Europe's finest pieces of civic architecture. Here **27** you will find the **Georgian House,** which the National Trust for Scotland has furnished in period style to show the elegant domestic arrangements of an affluent family of the late 18th century. Note, for instance, how the hallway was designed to take sedan chairs, in which 18th-century ladies were carried through the streets. *7 Charlotte Sq., tel. 031/225–2160. Admission: £1.90 adults, 95p children and senior citizens. Open Apr.–Oct., Mon.–Sat. 10–5, Sun. 2–5.*

Also in the square, the former St. George's Church, mentioned above as part of the New Town plan, now fulfills a different role **28** as **West Register House,** an extension of the original Register House. *Tel. 031/556–6585. Admission free. Open weekdays, exhibitions 10–4, research room 9–4:45.*

To explore further in the New Town, choose your own route northward, down to the wide and elegant streets centering on **29** **Moray Place,** a fine example of an 1820s development, with imposing porticoes and a central, secluded garden. The area remains primarily residential, in contrast to the area around Princes Street. The gardens in the center of the square are still for residents only.

③⓪ A neo-Gothic building on Queen Street houses the **Scottish National Portrait Gallery** and the Queen Street premises of **the Royal Museum of Scotland.** The gallery contains a magnificent Gainsborough, and portraits by the Scottish artists Ramsay and Raeburn. In the museum, don't miss the 16th-century Celtic harps and the Lewis chessmen—mysterious, grim-faced chess pieces carved from walrus ivory in the Middle Ages. *Tel. 031/225-7534. Admission free to both. Both open Mon.–Sat. 10–5, Sun. 2–5.*

③① Another attraction within reach of the New Town is the **Royal Botanic Garden.** Walk down Dundas Street, the continuation of Hanover Street, and turn left across the bridge over the Water of Leith, Edinburgh's small-scale river. These 70-acre gardens offer the largest rhododendron and azalea collection in Britain; peat, rock, and woodland gardens; a magnificent herbaceous border; an arboretum; and capacious greenhouses. There is also a convenient cafeteria. *Inverleith Row, tel. 031/552–7171. Admission free. Open Mar.–Oct., Mon.–Sat. 9–one hr. before sunset, Sun. 11–one hr. before sunset; Nov.–Feb.; Mon.–Sat. 9–sunset, Sun. 11–sunset. Greenhouses close daily at 5.*

The **Scottish National Gallery of Modern Art,** also close to the New Town, occupies a former school building on Belford Road, and features paintings and sculpture, including works by Picasso, Braque, Matisse, and Derain. *Belford Rd., tel. 031/556–8921. Admission free. Open Mon.–Sat. 10–5, Sun. 2–5 (extended during the Festival).*

Tour 2: The Scottish Borders— In the Footsteps of Scott

Numbers in the margin correspond to points of interest on the Borders map.

One of the best ways to approach the Borders region is to take as the theme of your tour the life and works of the man who focused world attention on this part of Scotland and is largely responsible for its romantic image—Sir Walter Scott. Route A7, to Galashiels, 27 miles southeast of Edinburgh, then a mile far-

③② ther on A6091, will take you through the Moorfoot Hills to **Abbotsford House,** the small, castellated mansion which Scott built for himself between 1818 and 1823. He took a rather damp farmhouse on the banks of the River Tweed, and transformed it into a pseudo-monastic, pseudo-baronial hall. Ruskin called the result "the most incongruous pile that gentlemanly modernism ever devised." Here Scott entertained such visitors as Wordsworth and Washington Irving. Abbotsford is still owned by Scott's descendants; and Scott's library as well as a large collection of weapons, armor, and Scottish artifacts are on display. *Tel. 0896/2043. Admission: £1.80 adults, 90p children. Open late Mar.–Oct., Mon.–Sat. 10–5, Sun. 2–5.*

③③ In the peaceful little town of **Melrose,** 3 miles east on A6091, you'll find the ruins of a Cistercian abbey that was the most famous of the great Borders abbeys. All the abbeys were burned in the 1540s in a calculated act of barbarism by English invaders acting on the orders of Henry VIII; Scott himself supervised the partial reconstruction of **Melrose Abbey,** one of the most beautiful ruins in Britain. In keeping with the Romantic spirit, he wrote:

> If thou would'st view fair Melrose aright,
> Go visit it by the pale moonlight;
> For the gay beams of lightsome day
> Gild, but to flout, the ruins grey.

Tel. 089682/2562. Admission: £1.20 adults, 60p children and senior citizens. Open Apr.–Sept., Mon.–Sat. 9:30–7, Sun. 2–7; Oct.–Mar., Mon.–Sat. 9:30–4, Sun. 2–4.

㉞ Five miles southeast of Melrose, still on A6091, is Scott's burial place at **Dryburgh,** another of the ruined Borders abbeys, set in a bend of the Tweed among strikingly shaped trees. Combine a visit here with a stop at **Scott's View,** 3 miles north on B6356, which provides a good view of the Tweed valley and the Eildon Hills. It is said that the horses pulling Scott's hearse paused automatically at Scott's View, because their master had so often halted them there. *Dryburgh, near St. Boswells, tel. 089682/ 0835. Admission and opening hours same as Melrose Abbey.*

㉟ Another famous Borders lookout point is **Smailholm Tower,** a 16th-century watchtower that now houses a museum displaying costumed figures and tapestries relating to Scott's collection of Border folk ballads (5 miles east of St. Boswells, off B6404). Scott himself spent his childhood on a nearby farm, where he imbibed his love of Border traditions and romances. *Smailholm, tel. 05736/332. Admission: 60p adults, 30p children and senior citizens. Open Apr.–Sept., Mon.–Sat. 9:30–7, Sun. 2–7.*

㊱ From Smailholm, take B6397 and then A6089 southeast to **Kelso,** where Scott attended the grammar school. Kelso has an unusual Continental air, with stout buildings surrounding a spacious, cobbled marketplace. Its abbey is a magnificent ruin, and the baker next door sells fresh Selkirk "bannocks" (the Scots are very good at baking cakes).

㊲ Rennie's Bridge on the edge of town provides good views of **Floors Castle.** Designed by Adam in 1721 and later altered by Playfair, this is the largest inhabited house in Scotland, an architectural extravagance of pepper-mill turrets and towers. Parts of *Greystoke* were filmed here. *Tel. 0573/23333. Admission: £2.50 adults, £1.50 children over 8, £2 senior citizens, £7 family. Open Easter, and May–Sept., Sun.–Thurs. 10:30– 5:30 (also Fri., July–Aug.); Oct., Sun. and Wed. 10:30–4. Check locally for variations.*

Time Out   Try the 18th-century coaching inn, the **Queen's Head** (Bridge St.), for ample helpings of home-cooked food, and cool, draught Belhaven beer—a widely drunk Scottish brand.

㊳ To round out your tour of the Borders abbeys, take A698 12 miles southwest to **Jedburgh,** a little town just 13 miles north of the border, which lay in the path of marauding armies for centuries. **Jedburgh Abbey** is the most intact of the Borders abbeys and has an informative visitor center that explains the role of the abbeys in the life of the Borders until their destruction around 1545. *High St., tel. 0835/63925. Admission and opening hours same as Melrose Abbey, except closed Thurs.* PM *and* Fri. *in winter.*

From Jedburgh, take A68 7 miles north to the A698 junction, turn right, and follow the A698 seven miles through attractive river-valley scenery to reach the ancient hilltop town of **Selkirk.** Scott was sheriff (county judge) of Selkirkshire from 1800 until his death in 1832, and his statue stands in Market Place, outside the courthouse where he presided. *Sir Walter Scott's Courtroom, tel. 0750/20096. Admission free. Open July–Aug., weekdays 2–4, other times by appointment.*

Take A707 north from Selkirk and turn west onto A72—15 miles in all. At **Walkerburn** is the **Scottish Museum of Woollen Textiles,** with the entrance through a tempting tweeds and woolens store. *Tel. 089687/281. Admission free. Open Mon.– Sat. 10–5:30 all year, and Sun. noon–4:30 Easter–Christmas.*

A few miles west of Walkerburn on A72, turn south on B709, passing through the old spa of **Innerleithen** (setting of Scott's novel *St. Ronan's Well)* to reach **Traquair House.** This is said to be the oldest continually occupied house in Scotland, and is probably the friendliest and most cheerful of the Borders' grand houses. Its laird (or "lord") supported Stuart aspirations to the British throne in the Jacobite uprisings, closing the gates at the end of the driveway after the departing Bonnie Prince Charlie and swearing never to open them until he returned as king. They remain closed to this day and the Traquair family has, with pleasing eccentricity, installed two parallel main driveways. Scott's first novel, *Waverley,* still the best tale about the 1745 rising, owes something of its setting to the atmosphere of Traquair House. Among the romantic items on view is a hidden priest's room, with secret stairs. Traquair House Ale is still brewed in the 18th-century brewhouse. *Near Innerleithen, tel. 0896/830323. Admission: £2.75. Open Easter; May, Sun. and Mon. 1:30–5:30, June and Sept., daily 1:30–5:30; July and Aug., daily 10:30–5:30.*

From Traquair, return to A72 and continue west to the pleasant town of **Peebles,** on the banks of the Tweed. Walk a mile upstream along the river until **Neidpath Castle** comes into view through the tall trees, perched artistically above a bend in the river. The walk can be continued, returning on the opposite riverbank after crossing an old, finely skewed, railroad viaduct. The castle is a medieval structure remodeled in the 17th century, with dungeons hewn from solid rock. *Near Peebles, tel. 08757/201. Admission: £1 adults, 50p children and senior citizens. Open Easter–Sept., Mon.–Sat. 11–5, Sun. 1–5.*

From Peebles, you can either return due north on A703 to Edinburgh (23 miles) or continue west on A72 toward the Clyde valley and Glasgow, 53 miles.

What to See and Do with Children

Edinburgh Butterfly and Insect World is a warm and humid indoor experience of breathtaking color, with butterflies in profusion, along with other insect life. *Melville Nurseries, near Dalkeith, tel. 031/663–4932. Admission: £2.25 adults, £1.25 children, £1.75 senior citizens, £6.50 family ticket. Open Apr.– Oct., daily 10–5:30.*

The **Museum of Childhood** should appeal to both adults and children (*see* Tour 1).

Traditional in design, **Edinburgh Zoo** now offers areas for children to approach or handle animals. Noted for its penguins, the zoo puts them on a delightful parade every day during the summer. *Corstorphine Rd., tel. 031/334–9171. Admission: £3.20 adults, £1.80 children and senior citizens. Open Mon.–Sat. 9–6 or dusk, Sun. 9:30–6.*

Dalkeith Park (7 miles south of Edinburgh on A68) is a rugged woodland adventure playground, offering plenty of anxiety for the nervous parent. More sedate children will enjoy the woodland walks and the 18th-century bridge. Not suitable for toddlers. *Dalkeith Palace (east end, Dalkeith High St.), Dalkeith, tel. 031/663–5684. Admission: £1 for adult-and-child ticket. Open Easter–Oct., daily 11–6, Nov., weekends 11–6.*

Edinburgh Brass Rubbing Centre offers a varied selection of replica brasses and inscribed stones, with full instructions and materials supplied. *Trinity Apse, Chalmers Close, Royal Mile, tel. 031/225–2424, ext. 6638/6678. Admission: free, but a charge (40p–£10.50) is made for every rubbing. Open June–Sept., Mon.–Sat. 10–6; during Festival, Sun. 2–5; Oct.–May, Mon.–Sat. 10–5.*

Off the Beaten Track

Tucked behind Arthur's Seat, **Duddingston** village is a brisk walk from Princes Street via Holyrood Park. This little community—formerly of butchers and weavers—has an interesting church with a Norman doorway and a watchtower in its graveyard to guard against "bodysnatchers," who sold corpses for dissection. The church overlooks **Duddingston Loch,** popular with birdwatchers.

On the coast, less than half an hour from Princes Street by bus (41, 18 on Sundays and evenings), **Cramond** village is a wonderful place to watch summer sunsets over the Firth of Forth, with the nearby **Cramond Inn** offering refreshments. The little river Almond joins the main estuary here. Its banks, once the site of mills and factories, now offer pleasant, leafy walks.

The old-fashioned village of **Swanston** is in sight of, but a world apart from, Edinburgh's southern suburbs and bypass. Whitewashed cottages and walks in the hills are part of the village's appeal. Helpful information boards explain the connection with Robert Louis Stevenson (his family had a summer cottage here). *Bus 4 to Fairmilehead (near Hillend artificial ski slope), about 30 min., then a 15–20 minute walk west across two fields and a golf course.*

Edinburgh's ancient seaport, **Leith,** has been revitalized in recent years, with restoration of the remaining fine commercial buildings which survived an earlier and insensitive redevelopment phase. It is worth exploring the lowest reaches of the Water of Leith and especially the proliferating pubs and restaurants. *Buses 7, 10, 11, 16; 10–15 min. from Princes St.*

Near A701, 7 miles south of Edinburgh, **Rosslyn Chapel** is located on a pleasantly wooded site near the village of Roslin, east of the Pentland Hills. This 15th-century chapel houses some of Scotland's finest examples of stone carving, including the ornate **Prentice Pillar,** said to have been carved by a medieval apprentice while his master was absent. When the master returned, he killed the boy in a fit of jealousy. According to another legend, a red glare over the chapel portends disaster to the Sinclair family, who were buried there in their armor instead of coffins. *Tel. 031/440–2159. Admission: £1.50 adults, 75p children, £1 senior citizens. Open Apr.–Oct., Mon.–Sat. 10–5, Sun. 12–4:45.*

About 10 miles west of Edinburgh, overlooking the Firth of Forth, the great Robert Adam–designed **Hopetoun House** is the most spectacular of a number of stately homes in the area, with an especially grand approach. Inside, you'll find the usual stately home panoply of fine furniture, paintings, tapestries, and carpets. Outside there are gardens, a deer park, and a nature trail. *South Queensferry, off A904, tel. 031/331–2451. Admission: £2.80 adults, £1.40 children. Open May–Sept., daily 10–5.*

Shopping

As a capital city and a very important tourist center, Edinburgh features a cross section of Scottish specialties such as tartans and tweeds, rather than products peculiar to the Edinburgh area. For tartans, tweeds, and knitwear, see the section under Princes Street, below, although a variety of stores on the Royal Mile should also be visited. If you are interested in learning the background of your tartan accessories, try **Scotland's Clan Tartan Centre** (Bangor Rd., Leith), where extensive displays on various aspects of tartanry will keep you informed.

For some ideas on exactly what Scotland has to offer in the way of crafts, use as your yardstick and price guide the **Scottish Craft Centre** (140 Canongate). It carries the work of over 300 Scottish craftspeople and is a major outlet.

Also along the Royal Mile, you will find several shops selling high quality tartans and woollen goods, among them **Cameron of Edinburgh** (361 High Street).

A popular gift selection comes from **Edinburgh Crystal** (Edinburgh Crystal Visitor Centre, Eastfield, Penicuik, tel. 0968/75128). Many department and gift stores in town stock this fine glassware, but you can also visit the firm's premises, which include a visitor center and a restaurant, as well as the largest crystal glassware store in Britain. It's just a few miles from the city.

The antiques business is currently booming in Scotland, and Edinburgh has a reputation for high prices. By the nature of the trade, what may be a good store one week is empty the next. Thus, it is easier to concentrate on visiting areas with a number of stores close together, for instance, **Bruntsfield Place** or **St. Stephen Street.**

Princes Street **Jenners,** opposite the Scott Monument, is not only Edinburgh's last surviving independent department store, but (so it claims) the oldest of its type in the world. It's a wide-ranging store, but it does specialize in upscale tweeds and tartans. The **Scotch House** (no. 60) is another Princes Street store popular with overseas visitors; it also offers top quality. **Gleneagles of Scotland,** nearby in Waverley Market, is not quite so upscale. All three stores can be combined in a short trip.

George Street   Behind Princes Street, George Street features a few London names, such as **Laura Ashley, Liberty,** and **Waterstones** bookstore. Do not confuse the last-mentioned with Edinburgh-based **Waterston's** (no. 35) with its range of Scottish gifts. Farther along, there is a good selection of Scottish titles in the **Edinburgh Bookshop** (no. 57). The **Scottish Gallery** (no. 94), has a wide stock of art/fashion jewelry, studio ceramics, and 20th-century Scottish painting.

Victoria Street/West Bow/Grassmarket   Quite close to the castle end of the Royal Mile, Victoria Street concentrates a number of specialty stores in a small area. There's a wide choice of antique prints, maps, watercolors, and drawings at **John Nelson** (no. 22), while **Robert Cresser's** brush store—featuring, not surprisingly, brushes of all kinds, each one handmade—is a little farther down the hill. **Charles Hay** (no. 18) has a wide range of antiques, furniture, pottery, and porcelain.

At **Mr. Wood's Fossils,** down in the Grassmarket, an unusual item such as a small primitive shark encased in rock may solve your gift-buying problems. Just opposite is **Bill Baber, Sheepish Looks** (no. 68), one of a number of enterprising and original Scottish knitwear designers.

Stockbridge   This is an oddball shopping area of some charm, particularly on St. Stephen Street. Look for **Hand in Hand** (3 North West Circus Place) for beautiful antique textiles. There are also several antiques shops and yet more knitwear.

William Street/Stafford Street   This is a small, upscale shopping area in a Georgian setting. **Studio One** (10–14 Stafford St.), is well-established and wide-ranging in its inventory of gift articles. **June Johnston** (5 William St.) will take care of ladies' shoe and accessory needs, while **Something Simple,** opposite, could complete the new outfit.

Flea Markets   Edinburgh is far too self-conscious to do this sort of thing really well. **Byzantium** (9A Victoria St.), with its antiques, crafts, paintings, books, and jewelry is the nearest, though perhaps too tasteful, clean, and restrained. **Jacksonville Furniture Bazaar** (83 Causewayside) is more authentically downscale, if a wardrobe *c.* 1950 is your idea of a souvenir of Edinburgh.

Kelso   While you are on your tour of the border abbeys, you might like to pick up a craft souvenir in Kelso. **Norman Cherry** (36 Woodmarket) has handmade jewelry, ceramics, and some paintings. You'll find excellent stoneware pottery for the home at the **Kelso Pottery** (The Knowes).

Sports and Fitness

Golf   Edinburgh is well-endowed with **golf courses,** with 20 or so near downtown (even before the nearby East Lothian courses are considered). **Braids United** course, south of the city center, welcomes visitors (tel. 031/447–6666); **Bruntsfield Links** (tel. 031/336–1479) welcomes visitors on weekdays by appointment; **Duddingston** (tel. 031/661768) takes visitors weekdays only.

Courses abound in the Borders, too. Here are three to go with the abbeys we list—**Jedburgh** (tel. 0835/63587) is an old 9-hole course, which welcomes visitors on any day there isn't a competition; **Melrose** (tel. 089682/2855) is an even older 9-hole course, with visitors welcome weekdays, or Sundays by arrangement;

St. Boswells (tel. 0835/22359), welcomes visitors any day except for competition ones.

A quite exceptional destination is **Gullane** (tel. 0620/842255) about 20 miles east of Edinburgh on A198. It has three courses of its own, all 18-hole, and there are several others grouped nearby, **Luffness New** (tel. 0620/843114) among them.

Jogging The most convenient spot in the downtown area for joggers is West Princes Street Gardens, just off Princes Street, but separated from traffic by a 30-foot embankment. Under the shadow of Edinburgh Castle and the High Kirk, you can do a half-mile loop on asphalt paths (stay off the delicate grass). More ambitious and challenging courses are in Holyrood Park, at the eastern end of the city. Stick to the road around the volcanic mountain for a 2.25-mile trip. For a real challenge, charge up to the summit of Arthur's Seat, or to the halfway point, the Cat's Nick. Both provide a fine view of the city—you can even time yourself by the clock of the 19th-century Balmoral Hotel.

Swimming **The Commonwealth Pool** (tel. 031/667–7211) was constructed for the 1970 Commonwealth Games, and is the largest in the city. Admission: £1. Open weekdays 9–9, Sat. and Sun. 10–4.

Dining and Lodging

Dining Edinburgh is a diverse, sophisticated city, which its cuisine reflects with an interesting, diverse mix of traditional and exotic offerings, from Scottish dishes to infinite ethnic variety. Be sure, particularly at festival time, to make reservations well in advance. Be warned also that there is an element of "it'd be fun to open a restaurant" about Edinburgh's eating scene, and some restaurants come and go in a very few months.

Look for the "Taste of Scotland" sign in the windows of Scottish restaurants, indicating that the establishments use the best Scottish ingredients whenever possible, including game, cheese, fruit, vegetables, and seafood. The sign usually attests to high standards of preparation as well. However, one word of warning: The fact that a menu is written in creaking, mock-antique Scots does not guarantee that it is adventurous. For instance, "tassie o' bean bree"—"tassie" being an uncommon word for "cup," and "bree" usually meaning "soup" or "brine"—translates as a plain cup of coffee.

Highly recommended restaurants are indicated by a star ★.

Category	Cost*
Very Expensive	over £40
Expensive	£30–£40
Moderate	£15–£30
Inexpensive	under £15

per person, including first course, main course, dessert, and VAT; excluding drinks

Lodging Edinburgh offers a range of accommodation, quite a lot of it in lovely traditional Georgian properties, some even in the New Town, only a few minutes from downtown. There are also a number of upscale hotels in the downtown area, each with an international flavor. Your choice, however, will be greatly restricted during the festival.

Highly recommended lodgings are indicated by a star ★.

Category	Cost*
Very Expensive	over £110
Expensive	£75–£110
Moderate	£40–£75
Inexpensive	under £40

All prices are for two people sharing a double room, including service, breakfast, and VAT.

Edinburgh
Dining

Indian Cavalry Club. This restaurant is cool and sophisticated; its menu reflects a confident, up-to-date approach—almost an Indian *nouvelle cuisine*. It features steamed specialties. The **Tiffin Room** in the basement serves light meals. *3 Atholl Pl., tel. 031/228–3282. Reservations required. Jacket and tie required. AE, DC, MC, V. Moderate.*

Kweilin. This excellent, very popular Chinese restaurant specializes in Cantonese cuisine made from very fresh ingredients. The water chestnut pudding is recommended. Service is particularly speedy and efficient. *19-21 Dundas St., tel. 031/557–1752. Reservations advised. MC, V. Moderate.*

Mackenzies Restaurant. This elegant French/Scottish restaurant, with its fresh tablecloths and friendly service, offers a varied menu cooked in classic style; steaks and fish dishes are recommended. *2 Bridge Rd., Colinton, tel. 031/441–2587. Reservations advised. Dress: informal. AE, MC, V. Closed Sun. and Mon. Moderate.*

★ **Martins.** Don't be put off by the look of this restaurant on the outside. It's tucked away in a little back street, and has a typically forbidding northern facade. All's well inside, though, and the food is tops. There are three chefs, and David McRae is a name to conjure with. The specialties are all light and extremely tasty, with fish in the lead—langoustine and gurnard (said to grunt when caught!) in phyllo pastry and a ginger sauce, halibut in a nettle and black-pepper sauce, plus gorgeous homemade sorbets. *70 Rose St., North Lane, tel. 031/225–3106. Reservations required. Dress: informal. AE, DC, MC, V. Closed Sat. lunch, Sun. and Mon. Moderate.*

Mr. V's. This friendly downtown restaurant has a slightly rustic decor. Bustling and popular, with a predominantly business clientele (usually a sign of good quality), Vito's specialties include *filleto d'agnello al caffe*, lamb fillet seasoned with crushed coffee beans in a coffee sauce, and tournedos Rossini. *7 Charlotte Lane, tel. 031/220–0176. Reservations required. Dress: informal. AE, DC, MC, V. Closed Sun., Mon. Moderate.*

Ristorante Tinelli. A little removed from downtown, this restaurant offers authentic Italian cuisine in a relaxed atmosphere. *139 Easter Rd., tel. 031/652–1932. Reservations advised. Dress: informal. MC, V. Closed Sun. Moderate.*

★ **The Vintner's Room.** Located in the Leith section of Edinburgh, this is a pleasant escape from the bustle of downtown, only a few minutes' walk away. Tasteful decor, including fine plasterwork, and a relaxed atmosphere combine with dishes such as sautéed scallops and smoked salmon, and grilled oysters with bacon and hollandaise sauce, to make any meal here a treat. *The Vaults, 87 Giles St., Leith, tel. 031/554–6767. Reservations advised. Dress: informal. AE, MC, V. Moderate.*

The Witchery. As its name indicates, a somewhat eerie ambience, complete with flickering candlelight, reigns. There are, in fact, supposed to be three ghosts in the place, one of whom haunts the refrigerator! There's nothing spooky about the food, however, with fine venison Marie Stuart, and Auld Reekie fillet steak among the specialties. *352 Castlehill, Royal Mile, tel. 031/225–5613. Reservations advised. Dress: informal. AE, DC, MC, V. Moderate.*

Henderson's Salad Bowl. This was Edinburgh's original vegetarian restaurant, long before that cuisine became fashionable. Try the vegetarian haggis! *94 Hanover St., tel. 031/225–2131. Reservations not required. Dress: informal. Closed Sun. except Festival. AE, DC, MC, V. Inexpensive.*

★ **Kalpna.** This eatery has a reputation for outstanding value. Indian art adorns the walls, enhancing your enjoyment of the exotic specialties like *shahi sabzi* (spinach and nuts in cream sauce), and mushroom curry. All dishes are vegetarian and are skillfully and deliciously prepared. *2–3 St. Patrick's Sq., tel. 031/667–9890. Reservations advised. Dress: informal. MC, V. Closed Sun. Inexpensive.*

Dining and Lodging **Caledonian Hotel.** "The Caley" recalls the days of the great
★ railroad hotels, although its nearby station has long gone. Recently modernized and refurbished at vast expense, its imposing Victorian decor has been faithfully preserved and has lost none of its original dignity and elegance. Its fine restaurant, **the Pompadour,** is all ornate, Louis XV–gilt-and-red furnishings; the menu balances French-influenced evening meals with hearty Scottish lunches. *Princes St., EH1 2AB, tel. 031/225–2433. 237 rooms with bath. Facilities: restaurant, bar, garden, in-house movies. Restaurant reservations advised. Jacket and tie required. AE, DC, MC, V. Hotel: Very Expensive. Restaurant: Expensive.*

King James Thistle Hotel. Do not judge this hotel by its rather grim architectural exterior: Inside, modernity combines with a high standard of service. Its rooms are softly colored, and filled with reproduction antiques. Its **Brasserie St. Jacques** features dishes such as roast Aberdeen Angus beef with chef's mealie pudding (very Scottish!), and a mélange of seafood with fresh herbs. *107 St. James Centre, 1 Leith St., EH1 3SW, tel. 031/556–0111. 147 rooms with bath. Facilities: brasserie, bar, in-house movies. Restaurant reservations advised. Jacket and tie required. AE, DC, MC, V. Hotel: Moderate–Expensive; restaurant: Expensive.*

Lodging **George Hotel.** This imposing and extensively refurbished 18th-
★ century building in the heart of the New Town retains some elegant Georgian features in its public areas, while the bedrooms are up-to-date and moderately luxurious. Although busy keeping this large hotel running smoothly, the courteous staff will always take the time to be helpful. *19 George St., EH2 2PB, tel. 031/225–1251. 195 rooms with bath. Facilities: restaurant, two bars. AE, DC, MC, V. Very Expensive.*

Howard Hotel. The Howard, close to Drummond Place, is a good example of a New Town building, elegant and superbly proportioned. It is small enough to continue to offer personal attention. All bedrooms and suites are spacious and well-equipped, some looking out onto the garden. *32 Great King St., EH3 6QH, tel. 031/557–3500. 16 rooms with bath. Facilities: restaurant. AE, DC, MC, V. Expensive.*

Mount Royal Hotel. Overlooking Edinburgh Castle and the Princes Street Gardens, the reception and other public areas of this modern building have recently been redecorated to great effect; improvements to the bedrooms have just been completed, making the hotel a pleasure to stay in. *53 Princes St., EH2 2DQ, tel. 031/225–7161. 160 rooms with bath. Facilities: restaurant. AE, DC, MC, V. Expensive.*

Bruntsfield Hotel. This elegant gabled hotel is in a Victorian building removed from the bustle of downtown. Antiques and floral motifs grace the interior; and each room is decorated individually. *74 Bruntsfield Pl., EH10 4HH, tel. 031/229–1393. 53 rooms with bath. Facilities: brasserie restaurant. AE, DC, MC, V. Moderate–Expensive.*

Dorstan Private Hotel. A villa dating from the Victorian era, this hotel is located in a quiet neighborhood a fair way from the city center. Bedrooms have been modernized to offer both the charm of the old and ease of the new. Peaceful pastel colors predominate in the decor, adding to this hotel's restfulness. *7 Priestfield Rd., EH16 5HJ, tel. 031/667–6721. 14 rooms, 9 with bath. No credit cards. Closed Dec. 24–Jan. 2. Moderate.*

Roxburghe Hotel. The Roxburghe couldn't be better located. It's on the corner of Charlotte Square and George Street. The handsome Georgian interiors have recent'.y been refurbished, and the hotel makes an ideal base for exploring. *38 Charlotte Sq., EH2 4HG, tel. 031/225–3921. 75 rooms with bath. Facilities: restaurant, coffee shop. AE, DC, MC, V, Moderate.*

Thrums Private Hotel. There is a pleasing mix of the modern and traditional in this detached Georgian house. It is small, cozy, and quiet, yet surprisingly close to downtown Edinburgh. *14 Minto St., EH9 1RQ, tel. 031/667–5545. 14 rooms, 12 with bath. Facilities: restaurant, bar. No credit cards. Closed Christmas and Jan. 1. Moderate.*

★ **Salisbury Guest House.** This guest house in a Georgian building is located in a peaceful conservation area. It is also convenient for city touring, and offers excellent value for money. *45 Salisbury Rd., EH16 5AA, tel. 031/667–1264. 13 rooms, 8 with bath. No credit cards. Closed Christmas and Jan. 1. Inexpensive.*

Galashiels
Dining and Lodging

Woodlands House Hotel. This wonderful hotel has stunning views over Tweeddale. The restaurant, too, is first-class, and specializes in fresh seafood and hearty Scottish cuisine. *Windyknowe Rd., TD1 1RG, tel. 0896/4722. 9 rooms with bath. Facilities: restaurant, garden, golfing, horseback riding. Open all year. AE, DC, MC, V. Moderate.*

Gullane
Lodging

Greywalls. Gullane is 19 miles northeast of Edinburgh by A198 and totally surrounded by golf links. It is, in fact, the ideal hotel to choose for a golfing vacation, comfortable, with excellent food and attentive service. The house itself is an architectural treasure. Edward VII used to stay here, as have Nicklaus, Trevino, Palmer, and a host of other golfing greats. *Muirfield, Gullane, EH31 2EG, tel. 0620/842144. 23 rooms with bath. Facilities: restaurant, garden, tennis, golf. AE, MC, V. Expensive.*

Innerleithen
Lodging

Traquair Arms. Near Innerleithen, famous for its medicinal springs and for Traquair House, this family-run hotel is a fine traditional inn offering a warm welcome; simple, clean rooms;

and very good food. *Traquair Rd., EH44 6PD, tel. 0896/830229. 10 rooms, 4 with bath. Facilities: restaurant, private fishing, horseback riding. AE, DC, MC, V. Inexpensive.*

Jedburgh
Lodging
★

Spinney Guest House. Made up of unpretentiously converted and modernized farm cottages, this is a bed-and-breakfast offering the very highest standards for the price. *Langlee, TD8 6PB, tel. 0835/63525. 3 rooms, 2 with bath. Closed Nov.–Mar. No credit cards. Inexpensive.*

Kelso
Dining and Lodging

Sunlaws House Hotel. Run by the Duke of Roxburghe, this large restful country house has a library that doubles as the bar, a plant-filled conservatory, spacious bedrooms, and all the other facets of gracious living intact. The restaurant is excellent; the menu changes daily and the chef is outstanding. The food is archetypically Scottish—with local salmon prominent on the menu—and the wine comes from the grand cellars of nearby Floors Castle, where the duke makes his home and where guests can visit free. *Heiton, Kelso, Roxburghshire TD5 8JZ, tel. 05735/331. 22 rooms with bath. Facilities: restaurant, bar, fishing, tennis, helipad. AE, DC, MC, V. Expensive.*

Lodging
★

Ednam House Hotel. This large, attractive hotel is right on the banks of the River Tweed, close to Kelso's grand abbey and the many fine Georgian and early Victorian buildings in the old Market Square. Ninety percent of the guests are return visitors, and the open fire in the hall, sporting paintings, and cozy armchairs give the place a homey feel. *Bridge St., TD5 7HT, tel. 0573/24168. 32 rooms with bath. Facilities: restaurant, garden, fishing, horseback riding. Closed Dec. 24–Jan. 12. V. Moderate.*

Melrose
Dining
★

Marmion's Brasserie. This cozy restaurant features outstanding country-style cuisine. It is a great place to stop for lunch after a visit to nearby Abbotsford or Dryburgh Abbey. *Buccleuch St., tel. 089682/2245. Reservations advised. Dress: informal. No credit cards. Closed Sun. Moderate.*

Dining and Lodging

Burts Hotel. This distinctive black-and-white traditional town hostelry dates from the early 18th century, yet offers every modern comfort. The elegant dining room features dishes such as pheasant terrine, and venison with a whisky-and-cranberry sauce. *Market Sq., TD6 9PN, tel. 089682/2285. 21 rooms, 18 with bath. Facilities: restaurant; fishing and game shooting arranged. Restaurant reservations advised. Dress: informal. AE, DC, MC, V. Moderate.*

Peebles
Dining and Lodging

Park Hotel. This hotel on the banks of the River Tweed at the northern tip of the Ettrick Forest offers comfort and tranquillity. The restaurant serves superior Scottish cuisine, many of the dishes based around local salmon, trout, and other seafood. *Innerleithen Rd., EH45 8BA, tel. 0721/20451. 25 rooms with bath. Facilities: restaurant, golfing, woodlands. Restaurant reservations advised. Dress: informal. AE, DC, MC, V. Moderate.*

Quothquan
Lodging

Shieldhill. This foursquare Norman manor has been standing here since 1199 (though greatly enlarged in 1560). It is in an ideal location for touring the Borders—just 27 miles from Edinburgh and 31 from Glasgow. The rooms are named after great Scottish battles—Culloden, Glencoe, Bannockburn, etc.—and are furnished with great comfort (miles of Laura Ashley fabrics and wallpapers). Shieldhill is one of the very few

British members of the Romantik Hotels association. *Quothquan, near Biggar, ML12 6NA, tel. 0899/20035. 11 rooms with bath. Facilities: restaurant, garden. AE, DC, MC, V. Expensive.*

St. Boswells
Dining and Lodging

Dryburgh Abbey Hotel. Right next to the abbey ruins, this civilized hotel is surrounded by beautiful scenery and features a satisfactory restaurant (dinner only). Specialties include traditional Scottish fare. *St. Boswells TD6 ORQ, tel. 0835/22261. 29 rooms, 21 with bath. Facilities: restaurant, golfing. Restaurant reservations required. Dress: informal. AE, DC, MC, V. Moderate.*

Selkirk
Lodging
★

Philipburn House Hotel. This Georgian-style country house stands on four acres of gardens and woodland. The house has recently been extended and the bedrooms updated; they and the dining room have a Scandinavian feel, all pine and florals. The owners are attentive and helpful. *Linglie Rd., TD7 5LS, tel. 0750/20747. 16 rooms with bath. Facilities: restaurant, outdoor heated swimming pool. AE, DC, MC, V. Moderate.*

The Arts

The flagship of arts events in the city is the **Edinburgh International Festival** (1992 dates: Aug. 16–Sept. 5), which for more than 40 years has attracted performing artists of international caliber in a great celebration of music, dance, and drama. *Advance information, programs, tickets, and reservations during the Festival available from Edinburgh Festival Office, 21 Market St., Edinburgh EH1 1BW, tel. 031/226–4001.*

The **Edinburgh Festival Fringe** offers a huge range of theatrical and musical events, some by amateur groups (you have been warned), and is much more of a grab bag than the official Festival. The Fringe offers a vast choice (a condition of Edinburgh's artistic life found only during the three- or four-week Festival season). During Festival time, it's possible to arrange your own entertainment program from morning to midnight and beyond, if you do not feel overwhelmed by the variety available. *Information, programs, and tickets available from Edinburgh Festival Fringe, 180 High Street, Edinburgh EH1 1QS, tel. 031/226–5257 or 5259.*

The **Edinburgh Film Festival** (held in August) is yet another aspect of this busy summer festival logjam. *Advance information and programs available from the Edinburgh Film Festival, at The Filmhouse, 88 Lothian Rd., Edinburgh EH3 9BZ, tel. 031/228–4051.* (Outside Festival time, the Filmhouse is also Edinburgh's best venue for modern, "highbrow," offbeat, or simply less commercial films.)

The **Edinburgh Military Tattoo** might not be art, but it is certainly entertainment. It is sometimes confused with the Festival itself, partly because the dates overlap. This great celebration of martial music and skills is set on the castle esplanade and the dramatic backdrop augments the spectacle. Dress warmly for the late-evening performances. Even if it rains, the show most definitely goes on. *Tickets and information available from Edinburgh Military Tattoo, 22 Market St., tel. 031/225–1188.*

Away from the August–September festival overkill, the **Edinburgh Folk Festival** usually takes place around Easter each year. This 10-day event blends performances by Scottish and international folk artists of the very highest caliber.

Theater Edinburgh's main theaters are the **Royal Lyceum** (Grindlay St., tel. 031/229–9697), which offers contemporary and traditional drama; the **King's** (Leven St., tel. 031/229–1201), offering both "heavyweight" material, such as ballet, and light entertainment, including Christmas pantomime; and the **Traverse** (West Bow, tel. 031/226–2633), which has toned down its previously avant-garde approach in an attempt to secure sponsorship. (Do not wear your best clothes to the Traverse—the seats are also steps.)

Concert Halls **Usher Hall** (Lothian Rd., tel. 031/228–1155) is Edinburgh's grandest, and the venue for the Scottish National Orchestra in season; the **Queen's Hall** (Clerk St., tel. 031/668–3456) is more intimate in scale and hosts smaller recitals. The **Playhouse** (Greenside Pl., tel. 031/557–2692) leans toward popular artists, although it is also a base for Scottish Opera, the Glasgow-based national opera company.

Nightlife

Edinburgh's nightlife is quite varied, including both discos and Scottish musical evenings or "ceilidhs" (pronounced "kay-lees") for the older set. The Edinburgh and Scottish Travel Centre above Waverley Market (*see* Important Addresses, above) can supply up-to-date information on various categories of nightlife, especially venues offering dinner-dances.

Discos With the most modern light show in Scotland, **Amphitheatre** (Lothian Rd., tel. 031/229–7670) is open Wed.–Sun. from 10 PM.
Live music is offered at **Calton Studios** (26 Calton Rd., tel. 031/556–7066), which is open Fri. and Sat. from 9 PM.
Café St. James (25 St. James Centre, tel. 031/557–2631) is open Fri. and Sat. from 10 PM till 3 AM.
Coasters (3 West Tollcross, tel. 031/228–3252) features reggae music. Guests must be at least 18; open Sat. and Sun. 10:30 PM–3:30 AM.
For over-21s only, **Madison's** (Greenside Pl., tel. 031/557–3807), features a laser light show. Open Thurs.–Sat. from 10 PM; no sneakers allowed.
Red Hot Pepper Club (3 Semple St., tel. 031/229–7733) features "hard-core, non-hip, non-chart night" on Sun., with disco Fri. and Sat.; it's open from 10 PM.

Casinos **Berkeley Casino Club** (2 Rutland Pl., tel. 031/228–4446) is a private club that offers free membership on 48 hours' notice.
Public casinos include **Casino Martell** (7 Newington Rd., tel. 031/667–7763) and **Royal Chimes Casino** (3 Royal Ter., tel. 031/556–1055).
Stakis Regency Casino (14 Picardy Pl., tel. 031/557–3585) makes membership available after a 48-hour waiting period. It also features a restaurant.

Folk Clubs There are always folk performers in various pubs throughout the city. **Edinburgh Folk Club** (Osborne Hotel, York Pl., tel. 031/339–4083) features folk music every Wed. at 8:15 PM.

Scottish Evenings and Ceilidhs Several hotels feature traditional Scottish music evenings, including the **Carlton Highland Hotel** (North Bridge, tel. 031/556–7277); **George Hotel** (George St., tel. 031/225–1251); and **Post House Hotel** (Corstorphine Rd., tel. 031/334–0390). Contact the individual hotel for information.

Other well-established Scottish entertainments include **Gibby's Ceilidh** (Berry Suite, 3 Abbeyhill La., tel. 031/449–5447); and **Jamie's Scottish Evening** (King James Hotel, Leith St., tel. 031/556–0111).

17 Scotland: Southwest and Highlands

Introduction

Glasgow, Scotland's largest city, suffered gravely from the industrial decline of the 1960s and '70s, but recent efforts at commercial and cultural renewal have restored much of the style and grandeur it had in the 19th century at the height of its economic power. Now it is again a vibrant metropolitan center, with a thriving artistic life—so much so that it was selected as Europe's Cultural Capital for 1990. Glasgow is a very convenient touring center, too, in easy reach of the Clyde coast to the south, and with excellent transport links to the rest of Scotland.

The Dumfries and Galloway region to the southwest is a hilly and sparsely populated area, divided from England by the Solway Firth; it's a region of somber forests and radiant gardens, where the palm, in places, is as much at home as the pine. The county seat is Dumfries, associated with Robert Burns (1759–96) in much the same way as the Borders are with Sir Walter Scott. Burns's poems and songs, such as *Auld Lang Syne* and *A Red, Red Rose*, are among the best-loved lyrics the world over. The "Burns Trail" runs from his birthplace near Ayr on the Clyde coast to his mausoleum in St. Michael's Church, Dumfries.

Stirling was one of the most important cities in Scotland's history, with the proud title of "Scenic Gateway to the Highlands." Commanding the strategic route linking north and south Scotland, it preceded Edinburgh as capital, and its castle is second only to Edinburgh's in grandeur. Grouped around Stirling are other ancient towns that have contributed much to Scotland's colorful past, including St. Andrews on its windswept coast, and Perth, former seat of Scottish kings. Not far from Stirling lie the Trossachs with their woodlands and lochs, the Highlands in miniature.

Ben Nevis, Britain's highest peak, rises from magnificent scenery in the west, while, sweeping southward, the long Kintyre peninsula is a wonderland of sea views, spectacular sunsets, and prehistoric monuments.

West and north lie the Highlands—the romance of "Caledonia stern and wild," the glamor of the clans, the shaggy cattle, the red deer, the golden eagles, the Celtic mists and legends, and a mixture of scenic splendor and profound tranquillity found hardly anywhere else in the world. The great surprise to unprepared visitors is the changing scenery and the stunning effects of light and shade, cloud, sunshine, and rainbows. In a couple of hours you may pass from heather, bracken, and springy turf to granite rock and bog, to serrated peak and snow-water lake, to the red Torridon sandstone of Wester Ross, and the flowery banks of Loch Ewe and Loch Maree. Sea inlets are deep and fjord-like. The black shapes of the isles cluster like basking whales on the skyline. Cliffs where quartzite gleams above crescents of hard sand lead around a northern shore which looks from the air as though it had been trimmed by an axe. Westward, the next stop is North America.

Essential Information

Important Addresses and Numbers

Tourist Information

The Greater Glasgow Tourist Board, 35–39 St. Vincent Pl., Glasgow, tel. 041/204–4400. Open weekdays 9–5.

The Loch Lomond, Stirling, and Trossachs Tourist Board, 41 Dumbarton Rd., Stirling, tel. 0786/75019. Open weekdays 9–5.

Local tourist information centers, normally open Mon.–Sat. 9:30–5:30, but varying according to season, include:

Aviemore: Grampian Rd., tel. 0479/810363.
Campbeltown: The Pier, tel. 0586/52056.
Dundee: City Chambers, tel. 0382/27723.
Fort William: Cameron Centre, Cameron Sq., tel. 0397/3781.
Inverness: 23 Church St., tel. 0463/234353.
Oban: Boswell House, Argyll Sq., tel. 0631/63122.
Perth: 45 High Street, tel. 0738/27958.
St. Andrews: 2 Queens Gardens, tel. 0334/72021.
Stirling: 41 Dumbarton Rd., tel. 0786/75019.

Travel Agencies

American Express, 115 Hope St., Glasgow, tel. 041/221–4366. Thomas Cook: 22 City Sq., Dundee, tel. 0382/200201; 15–17 Gordon St., Glasgow, tel. 041/221–6611; 25 High St., Perth, tel. 0738/35279; 11–13 Murray Pl., Stirling, tel. 0786/51466.

Car Rental Agencies

Dundee: Budget Rent-a-Car, Tayford Motor Co. Ltd., Balfield Rd., tel. 0382/644664; **Hertz,** Roseangles Garage, 19 Roseangles, tel. 0382/23711.
Glasgow: Avis Rent-a-Car Ltd., 161 North St., tel. 041/221–2827; **Budget Rent-a-Car,** 101 Waterloo St., tel. 041/226–4141; **Hertz,** 106 Waterloo St., tel. 041/248–7736.
Inverness: Europcar Ltd., The Highlander Service Station, Milburn Rd., tel. 0463/234886; **Hertz,** Mercury Motor Inn, Junction A9/A96, Millburn Rd., tel. 0463/224475.
Stirling: Europcar Ltd., Mogil Motors Ltd., Drip Rd., tel. 0786/72164.

Arriving and Departing by Plane

Glasgow Airport (tel. 041/887–1111) is 8 miles from town, with a motorway link, buses, and trains; while Prestwick (tel. 0292/79822), on the west coast of Ayrshire, has bus and train links (trains to Glasgow every half hour, travel time one hour).

In April 1990, Glasgow began hosting transatlantic flights. Among the carriers flying from the city are British Airways, Northwest, American, Air Canada, and Worldways. Glasgow is also served by major European airlines, including British Airways, Air France, Iberia, KLM, Lufthansa, Swissair, SAS, and TAP among them. Prestwick is now used mainly by charter flight operators.

Aberdeen Airport (tel. 0224/722331), as the central airport for the North Sea oilfields, handles a wide range of international routes. British Airways (tel. 081/897–4000) and Dan-Air (tel. 0224/722331) have direct flights between London and Aberdeen, and from Aberdeen to other Scottish destinations.

Inverness Airport (tel. 0463/232471) is central for a wide range of internal flights covering the Highlands and Islands region.

Dan-Air (tel. 0667/62666) has direct flights to Inverness from London. **British Airways** serves Inverness from Glasgow, Kirkwall, Stornoway, and the Shetlands.

Loganair (tel. 0667/62332) has direct Glasgow–Inverness flights, and includes Kirkwall among its routes.

Arriving and Departing by Car, Train, and Bus

By Car The quickest route from London into southern Scotland and on to Glasgow is M6/A74 (397 miles). A more visually pleasing route is via A68 over Carter Bar, and the quietest is A697 via Coldstream. A1 via Berwick-upon-Tweed to Edinburgh has recently been improved with by-passes.

By Train **British Rail** serves western Scotland from London's Euston Station (tel. 071/387–7070). Average travel time from Euston to Carlisle is 4⅔ hours and to Glasgow, 5½ hours.

By Bus **Scottish Citylink** (tel. 071/637–1921) serves Scotland from London's Victoria Coach Station. Average travel time to Glasgow is 7¼ hours.

Getting Around

By Car Great improvements have been made on Highland roads in recent years. A9 now has some stretches of divided highway, and A835 puts the northwest touring base of Ullapool little more than an hour beyond Inverness. Ballachulish Bridge on the Oban–Fort William road, and Kylesku Bridge north of Lochinver, have replaced ferries and reduced crossing times. If you are coming from eastern Scotland, allow a comfortable three hours from Edinburgh to such Highland destinations as Oban, Fort William, or Inverness.

By Train Two notably scenic branches are the **Kyle Line,** from Inverness west to Kyle of Lochalsh (the ferry port for Skye); and the **Fort William to Mallaig** section of the former West Highland line (a continuation of local services from Glasgow). The attractions of both lines are further enhanced by the option, in summer months, of vintage carriages to Kyle or steam locomotive to Mallaig. "Freedom of Scotland" Rover tickets for seven or 14 days allow unlimited travel over the entire Scot-Rail network; "West Highland" and "North Highland" local Rovers are also available.

By Bus The **Scottish Citylink** office in Glasgow (tel. 041/332–9644) provides full information on Lowland and Highland bus services and sells network "Explorer" tickets.

By Ferry **Caledonian MacBrayne** (tel. 0475/33755) runs a useful ferry service between the Clyde coast and the southwest Highlands: Wemyss Bay–Rothesay (Bute); Gourock–Dunoon; Androssan–Brodick (Arran).

Highland Travelpass The "Highland Travelpass" is a comprehensive pass covering nearly all bus, train, and ferry transport in the Highlands and Islands for either seven or 13 days. It is available at any main bus, train, or ferry station in the region.

Guided Tours

Orientation Tours The following companies run regular bus tours around the region:

Clydeside Scottish Omnibuses, Paisley, tel. 041/889–3191; **Alex Pringle, Scott Guide Coaches,** Glasgow, tel. 041/942–6453; **Scottish Citylink,** Glasgow, tel. 041/332–9644.

Special-Interest Tours **The Scottish Tourist Guides Association** (tel. 041/776–1052) can recommend fully qualified guides who will arrange walking or driving excursions of varying lengths to suit your own interests.

The following also offer car-and-driver tours tailored to your personal interests and needs:

Little's Chauffeur Drive, Glasgow, tel. 041/883–2111; **Man Friday Services,** Greenock, tel. 0475/33151 or 32378.

Exploring Southwest and Highlands

Orientation

These explorations begin in central and southwest Scotland, covering a handful of major cities and a host of scenic lake and coastal areas. Tour 1 starts in Glasgow, then travels north to Loch Lomond and the Clyde coast. From here the route dips south to the isle of Arran, and on to Ayrshire; some gardens farther south are also included.

The second tour starts in Stirling, then moves northwest to the Trossach lochs. An alternative excursion leads east to St. Andrews, then returns west via the portside cities of Dundee and Perth to Stirling.

Tour 3 explores the western Highlands. From a base in Oban, excursions head south to Kintyre, east to Loch Fyne and Loch Awe and on through Inveraray and Glencoe, and north to Fort William, Glenfinnan, and Mallaig.

The final tour takes in the northern Highlands. Two separate journeys based from Inverness travel east to Culloden Moor and then south to Aviemore, and southwest to Loch Ness.

Highlights for First-time Visitors

Cawdor Castle: Tour 4
Culzean Castle and Country Park: Tour 1
Inverary Castle: Tour 3
Loch Lomond: Tour 1
Loch Ness: Tour 4
Pulpit Hill, Oban: Tour 3
Scone Palace, Perth: Tour 2
Stirling Castle: Tour 2
Victorian Glasgow: Tour 1

Tour 1: Glasgow, the Clyde Valley, and the Southwestern Coast

Numbers in the margin correspond to points of interest on the Southwest Scotland and the Western Highlands and the Glasgow maps.

Until fairly recently a depressed city and infamous for its slums, **Glasgow** today is one of the most vibrant, culturally alive cities in Britain. The renewal of the city shows itself in a variety of ways, including trendy downtown stores, a booming and diverse cultural life, stylish restaurants, and above all, a general air of confidence. Glasgow was named 1990 European City of Culture, and the city went so far into overdrive it will take some years to return to normal!

Glasgow's development over the years has been unashamedly commercial, tied up with the wealth of its manufacturers and merchants, who constructed a vast number of civic buildings throughout the 19th century. Many of these have been preserved, and Glasgow claims, with some justification, to be Britain's greatest Victorian city.

George Square, the focal point of Glasgow's business district, is the natural starting point for any walking tour. The magnificent Italian Renaissance-style **City Chambers** on the east side of the square was opened by Queen Victoria in 1888. *Tel. 041/227-4017. Free guided tours weekdays at 10:30 and 2:30.*

Leave the square by Queen Street to the south, and note the fine neoclassical facade of the Royal Exchange of 1827, now **Stirling's Library.** Pass through Royal Exchange Square and under the arch to the pedestrian section of Buchanan Street. Next, turn east into Argyle Street. Like Buchanan Street, Argyle Street is an important shopping district where you can wander without the threat of traffic. Head toward the River Clyde, via Stockwell Street, to discover the new face of Glasgow shopping at the **St. Enoch Centre.**

In the nearby park, Glasgow Green, is the **People's Palace.** Opened in 1898 and recently refurbished, it has extensive exhibits on Glasgow's social history. The rear half of the premises is a Victorian greenhouse called the Winter Gardens. *Tel. 041/554-0223. Admission free. Open Mon.-Wed., Fri., Sat. 10-5, Thurs. 10-10, Sun. noon-6.*

Glasgow's market, **the Barras,** takes place every weekend just north of Glasgow Green ("barras" means "barrows" [pushcarts], but all of the market stalls are covered). You can find just about anything here, in any condition, from very old model railroads to almost new cheese rolls. Antiques hunters might strike pay dirt, but don't be surprised if you come away empty-handed. *Tel. 041/552-7258. Admission free. Open weekends 9-5.*

Make your way next up High Street, which was the center of the downtown area before Glasgow expanded westward in the 18th century. These days, High Street seems unimpressive, but keep a lookout for **Provand's Lordship,** the oldest building in Glasgow. This 15th-century town house, said to have been the lodgings of three Scottish monarchs, overflows with portraits, stained glass, and tapestries. *Castle St., tel. 041/552-8819. Admission free. Open Mon.-Sat. 10-7, Sun. noon-6.*

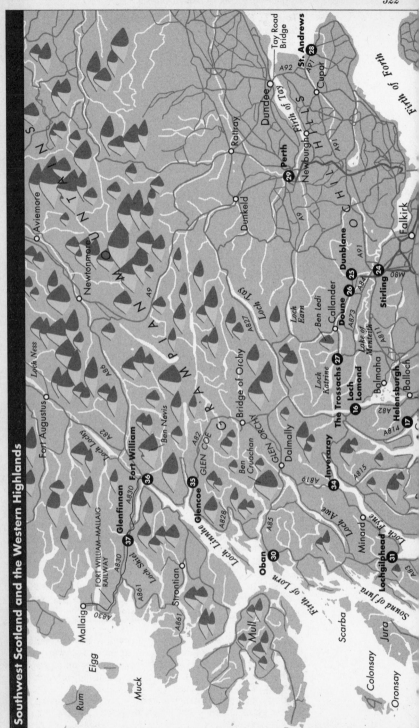

Southwest Scotland and the Western Highlands

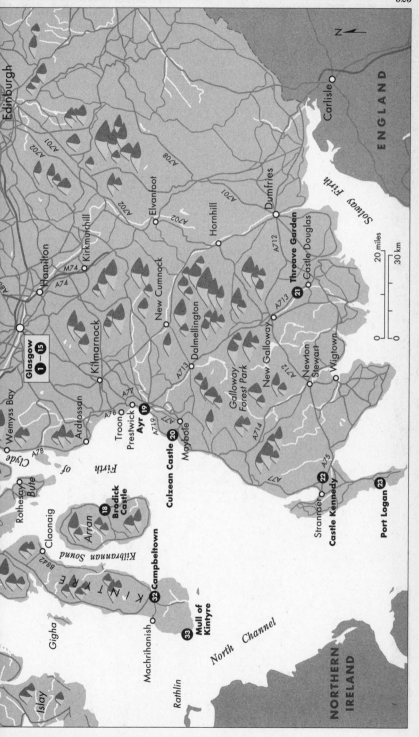

Glasgow

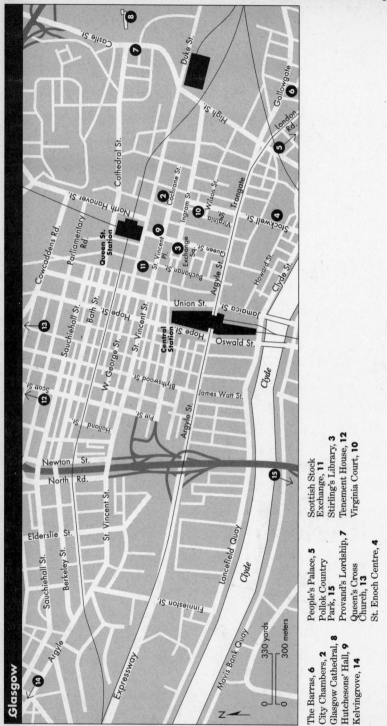

The Barras, **6**
City Chambers, **2**
Glasgow Cathedral, **8**
Hutchesons' Hall, **9**
Kelvingrove, **14**

People's Palace, **5**
Pollok Country
Park, **15**
Provand's Lordship, **7**
Queen's Cross
Church, **13**
St. Enoch Centre, **4**

Scottish Stock
Exchange, **11**
Stirling's Library, **3**
Tenement House, **12**
Virginia Court, **10**

⑧ **Glasgow Cathedral,** on a site sacred since St. Mungo founded a church there in the late 6th century, just north of George Square, is an unusual double church, one above the other. Its 13th-century crypt was built to hold the relics of St. Kentigern. *Cathedral St., tel. 031/244–3101. Admission free. Open Apr.– Sept., Mon.–Sat. 9:30–7, Sun. 2–7; Oct.–Mar., Mon.–Sat. 9:30–4, Sun. 2–4.*

You can enjoy the architecture of this area, known as "Merchant City," on your return to George Square, although you may be diverted by the designer boutiques springing up in this part of town. Just south of George Square, look for **Hutchesons' Hall,** a visitors center, shop, and regional office for the National Trust for Scotland. The elegant, neoclassical building was designed by David Hamilton in 1802. *158 Ingram St., tel. 041/552–8391. Admission free. Open weekdays 9–5. Shop open Mon.–Sat. 10–4.*

⑨ Nearby, just south of Ingram Street, the buildings on Virginia Street recall the days of the rich "tobacco barons" who traded with the Americas. At no. 33, a former tobacco exchange survives. Nearby **Virginia Court,** somewhat faded now, also echoes those far-off days. (Peer through the bars of the gates and note the wagon-wheel ruts still visible in the roadway.) If you ⑪ want to see today's commercial life, visit the **Scottish Stock Exchange** in Buchanan Street, worthwhile for the exterior alone: It was built in 1877 in an ornate "French Venetian" style.

⑩

⑫ Just beyond the downtown area, the **Tenement House,** in the Garnethill area north of Charing Cross Station, is a fascinating time capsule, painstakingly preserved with the everyday furniture and belongings of half a century of occupation by the same owner. The building dates from 1892. *145 Buccleuch St., tel. 041/333–0183. Admission: £1.20 adults, 60p children. Open early Jan.–Mar. and early Nov.–mid-Dec., weekends 2–4, Apr.–Oct., daily noon–5.*

Time Out   The **Willow Tearoom** (217 Sauchiehall St.) is restored to its original archetypal Art Deco design, by Charles Rennie Mackintosh, right down to the decorated tables and chairs. The tree motifs are echoed in the street address, as "sauchie" is an old Scots word for "willow."

To learn more about the Glasgow-born designer Mackintosh, ⑬ head for **Queen's Cross Church,** now the Charles Rennie Mackintosh Society Headquarters. Although one of the leading lights in the turn-of-the-century Art Deco movement, Mackintosh died in 1928 with his name scarcely known, least of all in his native city. Now he is confirmed as a leading innovator. This center provides a further insight into Glasgow's other Mackintosh-designed buildings, which include the Scotland Street School, the Glasgow School of Art, and the reconstructed interiors of the Hunterian Art Gallery. *870 Garscube Rd., tel. 041/946–6600. Admission free. Open Tues., Thurs., Fri. noon–5:30, Sun. 2:30–5.*

⑭ The city's main art gallery and museum, **Kelvingrove**—looking like a combination of cathedral and castle—in Kelvingrove Park, west of the M8 beltway, houses what is claimed to be Britain's finest civic collection of British and Continental paintings, with 17th-century Dutch art, a selection from the French Barbizon school, French Impressionists, Scottish art from the

17th century to the present, silver, ceramics, European armor, even Egyptian archaeological finds. *Tel. 041/357–3929. Admission free. Open weekdays 10–5, Sat. 10–10, Sun. noon–6.*

Across Kelvingrove Park are two more important galleries, both maintained by Glasgow University. They house the collections of William Hunter, an 18th-century Glasgow doctor who assembled a staggering quantity of extremely valuable material. The **Hunterian Museum,** the city's oldest (1807), displays Hunter's hoards of coins, manuscripts, and archeological artifacts in a striking Victorian Gothic building. Even more interesting is the **Hunterian Art Gallery,** which has the doctor's pictures plus other collections bequeathed to the university— works by Reynolds, Rodin, Rembrandt, Tintoretto, Whistler, and a large section devoted to the work of Charles Rennie Mackintosh, including a replica of his town house. *Museum: tel. 041/330–4221. Admission free. Open weekdays 9:30–5, Sat. 9:30–1. Gallery: tel. 041/330–5431. Admission free. Open Mon.–Sat. 9:30–5, Sun. 2–5.*

⑮ **Pollok Country Park** provides a peaceful green oasis off Paisley Road, just 3 miles southwest of the city center. The key attraction here is the **Burrell Collection,** Scotland's finest art collection. A new, custom-built, airy, and elegant building houses treasures of all descriptions, from Chinese ceramics, bronzes, and jade to medieval tapestries, stained glass, and 19th-century French paintings, the magpie collection of an eccentric millionaire. *Tel. 041/649–7151. Admission free. Open Mon., Tues., and Thurs.–Sat. 10–5, Wed. 10–10, Sun. noon–6.*

Also located in Pollok Country Park is **Pollok House,** which dates from the mid-1700s and contains the Stirling Maxwell Collection of paintings, including works by El Greco, Murillo, Goya, Signorelli, and William Blake. Fine 18th-and early-19th-century furniture, silver, glass, and porcelain are also on display. *Tel. 041/632–0274. Admission free. Open Mon., Tues., Thurs.–Sat. 10–5, Wed. 10–10, Sun. noon–6.*

Numbers in the margin correspond to points of interest on the Southwest Scotland and the Western Highlands map.

⑯ Leaving Glasgow, follow A82 northwest toward **Loch Lomond,** at 23 miles long the largest and most famous of Scotland's lochs. The southern end is less than 20 miles (only about 30 minutes) from downtown Glasgow. The town of **Balloch** is the southern gateway to the loch, but it is not especially attractive. The very best view of Loch Lomond is from **Duncryne Hill,** farther east. The loch, dotted with tiny islands, spreads out beyond the fields and lush lowland hedgerows, then narrows and extends northward into the Highlands. Scenic cruises leave from both Balloch and Balmaha, about 6 miles north on the eastern shore.

Time Out The **Inverarnan Inn,** on A82 just above the loch's northern tip, is an authentic drovers' (cattle drivers') inn, full of pleasant wood smoke and popular with climbers and hikers.

The Clyde coast was once the playground for Glasgow's prosperous merchants, who built their splendid Victorian country homes here. These mansions line the shores of Gare Loch (note that this one is spelled differently from the Gairloch that appears later in this chapter) and fill the port town of **Helensburgh** **⑰** (5 miles west of Loch Lomond on B832), where you can embark on a Clyde river cruise. The Mackintosh-designed **Hill House,** complete with his custom-designed furniture, is here, in calm, leafy suburbs on the hill just behind the promenade. It was originally built for Glasgow publisher William Blackie in 1902– 04. *Upper Colquhoun St., tel. 0436/73900. Admission: £1.90 adults, 95p children and senior citizens. Open daily 1–5.*

Three Clyde ferry ports—Gourock, Wemyss Bay, and Ardrossan—all lie within easy touring distance of Glasgow on A78. You can catch a car ferry from Gourock across the Firth of Clyde to **Dunoon,** a traditional coastal resort, or take the ferry from Wemyss Bay (5 miles south of Gourock on A770/A78) to **Rothesay,** a faded but appealing resort on the **Isle of Bute.** The island offers a host of relaxing walks and scenic vistas. Fifteen miles farther down the coast at **Ardrossan,** ferries leave regularly for the island of **Arran,** whose rugged scenery is reminiscent of that of the Scottish Highlands. **Brodick Castle,** dating from the 13th century, and an ancient seat of the dukes of Hamilton, is the island's most famous attraction. It offers lavish interiors and gardens where early rhododendrons enjoy shelter from the frost. The gardens are a country park. *Brodick, tel. 0770/2202. Admission: £2.40 adults, £1.20 children. Open mid-Apr.–Sept., daily 1–5; early Apr. and early Oct., Mon., Wed., Sat. 1–5. Grounds and country park open daily 9:30–sunset.*

⑲ From Ardrossan, follow A78/A77 south about 15 miles to the popular commercial and tourist city of **Ayr,** a good place to begin a tour of the western coast and the County of Ayrshire. The region combines abandoned industries, old mines, and forgotten railroads with vivid green pastures, small seaside ports, and high moors that are home to the celebrated Ayrshire breed of dairy cattle. The county is also known for its associations with Robert Burns, Scotland's national poet, and for its fine coastal golf resorts, such as **Troon,** near Prestwick.

The port of Ayr is Ayrshire's chief town, but if you're on the Burns trail, head for **Alloway** on B7024, in Ayr's southern suburbs. Here, among the many middle-class residences, you'll find the one-room thatched **Burns Cottage,** where the poet was born in 1759. *Admission: £1.50 adults, 75p children and senior citizens. Open Jun.–Aug., Mon.–Sat. 9–7, Sun. 10–7; Apr., May, Sept., Oct., Mon.–Sat. 10–5, Sun. 2–5; Nov.–Mar., Mon.–Sat. 10–4.*

Near the Burns Cottage, opposite Alloway's ruined church, is the **Land o' Burns Centre,** offering exhibitions and audiovisual presentations on the life of Burns. *Admission free (small charge for presentations). Open Sept.–June, daily 10–5:30; July and Aug., daily 10–6.*

Auld (old) **Alloway Kirk** (church), across the road, is where Tam o' Shanter, hero of Burns's well-known poem of the same name, unluckily passed a witches' revel—with Old Nick himself playing the bagpipes—on his way home from a night of drinking. Close by is the **Brig o' Doon** ("brig" is Scots for "bridge") which Tam, in flight from the witches, managed to cross just in time. His gray mare, Meg, lost her tail to the closest witch. (Any resident of Ayr will tell you that witches cannot cross running water.) The **Burns Monument** (entrance fee included in charge for Burns Cottage) overlooks Brig o' Doon.

⑳ For a different perspective on Ayrshire's history, take A719 12 miles southwest from Ayr to **Culzean** (pronounced "Ku*lain*")

Castle and Country Park, the National Trust for Scotland's most popular property. The castle, complete with walled garden, is a superb neoclassical mansion designed by Robert Adam in 1777. The country park welcomes 300,000 visitors a year, yet remains unspoiled. As well as marvelous interiors, the castle contains the National Guest Flat, given by the people of Scotland in appreciation of General Eisenhower's services during World War II. As President he stayed once or twice at Culzean and his relations still do occasionally. Between visits it is used by the N.T.S. for official hospitality. Approach is by way of rooms evoking the atmosphere of World War II: mementoes of Glenn Miller, Winston Churchill, Vera Lynn, and other personalities of the epoch all help create a suitably 1940s mood. *Tel. 06556/269. Castle admission: £2.40 adults, £1.20 children and senior citizens. Country park admission: £4 per car, £6 per minibus or trailer. Castle open Apr.–Oct., daily 10:30–5:30. Country Park open all year, daily 9:30–sunset.*

Time Out　In Maybole, an unpretentious little town between Alloway and Culzean, try a pub lunch at the **Masons Arms** (at the south end of the town on A77). It offers good, honest home cooking and friendly, informal service.

Ayrshire gradually merges with Galloway among the dark, domed hills and forested strips of the southwest. Galloway catches the best of the mild, southwesterly winds and has a south-facing coastline—not very common in Scotland—and as a result, there is a superb range of gardens here as well as the sprawling and impressive **Galloway Forest Park,** 25 miles south of Ayr on A713. The park comprises several separate forests—Glentrool, Carrick, and so on—grouped around a circle of mountains and lakes.

㉑　Among the gardens to look for here are **Threave Garden,** the National Trust for Scotland's School of Gardening near **Castle**
㉒　**Douglas** at the southern end of A713 (tel. 0556/2575); **Castle Kennedy** (tel. 0776/2024), just before **Stranraer** off A75; and the
㉓　**Logan Botanic Garden** (tel. 0776/86231) at **Port Logan** on the Rinns peninsula, 10 miles south of Stranraer. The best time to see these gardens is early in the season when the rhododendrons, azaleas, and magnolias are at their brilliant best, although there's plenty to see all summer and well into the fall. *Admission to Threave: £2.20 adults, £1.10 children; Logan Botanic: 60p adults, 30p children; Castle Kennedy: £1.80 adults, £1 senior citizens, 50p children. Threave is open all year, daily 9–sunset; the other two Easter–Sept., daily, Logan 10–6, Castle Kennedy 10–5.*

The return route to Glasgow can be made via A712 to New Galloway, then A702 and A74 to the southern end of M74. Alternatively, A75 via Dumfries will take you across the border to Carlisle and the English Lake District.

Tour 2: Stirling and the Lowland Lochs to St. Andrews and Perth

㉔　**Stirling,** about 23 miles northeast of Glasgow, is another of Britain's great historic towns. A simple way to enjoy an aerial view of the Highlands is to head for **Stirling Castle;** its esplanade, which is open even when the castle is not, commands superb, sweeping views. The castle, built in the 15th and 16th centuries, was a royal residence of the Stuart kings, who were—in every sense of the word—monarchs of all they surveyed! Take time to inspect this lovely Renaissance citadel of crow-stepped gables, stone carvings, and twisted chimneys. The hammer-beamed Parliament Hall still whispers of dark 14th-century deeds, and across the courtyard, the fine regimental museum of the Argyll & Sutherland Highlanders houses more recent battle memories. Several kings and queens were born or crowned in these buildings. Mary, Queen of Scots, lived there in her infancy before she was sent to France. An embrasure on the battlements with the inscription "MR 1561" is still called Queen Mary's Lookout. *Tel. 031/244–3101. Admission: £1.75 adults, 85p children and senior citizens, family tickets, £4.50. Open Apr.–Sept., Mon.–Sat. 9:30–5:15, Sun. 10:30–4:45; Oct.–Mar., Mon.–Sat. 9:30–4:20, Sun. 12:30–3:35.*

You will have already met the **National Trust for Scotland's Visitor Centre** on the way into the castle. On the esplanade, it houses a shop, tearoom, and exhibition hall with a historical film. *Tel. 0786/62517. 50p adult, 25p child, open same hours as castle.*

On the right as you go down into the town is **Mar's Wark,** the roofless ruin of a mansion that the earl of Mar, premier earl of Scotland, put up in 1570. The building of slightly later date on the left, the **Argyll Ludging** ("ludging" was "lodging," a nobleman's town house), was for many years a military hospital and is now a youth hostel.

Time Out   The building where Lord Darnley (Mary, Queen of Scots' second husband), stayed when she was in residence at Stirling Castle is now the **Darnley Coffee House** (16–18 Bow St.). Try the fresh coffee and homemade cakes.

Before you descend to modern Stirling's shopping streets you pass the old **Town House** (City Hall); the **Mercat Cross,** where proclamations were made; and the parish church of the **Holy Rude** (rood, cross), a fine Gothic building dated 1414. Here King James VI was crowned at the age of one year; the presiding clergyman was John Knox, the Scottish religious reformer.

Close by in Back Walk stands the quaint 17th-century **Cowane's Hospital,** built as a refuge for the old. You can walk from here along the south side of the castle hill to the **Smith Institute,** the local museum and art gallery. As you start, note the square patch of ground beside Dumbarton Road (A811), called the **King's Knot.** It was once a garden of intricately intersecting paths and borders, and dates from around 1628. *Dumbarton Rd., tel. 0786/71917. Admission free. Open Tues.–Sat. 10:30–5, Sun. 2–5.*

Sections of the old town wall survive: Look for it straight ahead as you come out of the Dumbarton Road Tourist Information Centre.

Stirling Castle at one time commanded the only overland route between the Highlands and Lowlands, at the River Forth's lowest bridging point. Many decisive battles were fought near here. The story of the great battle of **Bannockburn** in 1314, which regained 400 years' independence for Scotland, is told at the National Trust for Scotland's **Bannockburn Heritage Centre,** 2 miles south of Stirling on A91. Perhaps the most historically significant location in Scotland, it is today surrounded by sprawling housing developments; but when Robert the Bruce, the Scottish commander, made his stand here against the English army, it was marshy ground, ideal for hampering the heavily armed English knights. *Glasgow Rd., tel. 0786/812664. Admission: £1.10 adults, 55p children. Open Apr.–Oct., daily 10–6.*

㉕ To explore northwestward into the hills, take M9 up to **Dunblane,** 7 miles north of Stirling. In the middle of town, standing in a sleepy square, are the partly restored ruins of a large cathedral. King David built the existing structure in the 13th century on the site of St. Blane's little eighth-century cell. Dunblane Cathedral is contemporary with the Border abbeys (*see* Chapter 16), but more mixed in its architecture—part Early English and part Norman. Dunblane ceased to be a cathedral, as did most others in Scotland, at the time of the Reformation in the mid-16th century. *Tel. 031/244-3101. Admission free. Open Apr.–Sept., Mon.–Sat. 9:30–7, Sun. 2–5; Oct.–Mar., Mon.–Sat. 9:30–4, Sun. 2–4.*

㉖ Just under 4 miles due west of Dunblane on A820 is the little town of **Doune. Doune Castle,** in its impressive setting by the River Teith, is one of the best-preserved of Scotland's medieval fortifications. (Optimum photo vantage point is upstream from the A84 bridge.) *Tel. 031/244-3101. Admission: £1 adults, 50p children. Open Apr.–Sept., Mon.–Sat. 9:30–7, Sun. 2–7; Oct.–Mar., Mon.–Sat. 9:30–4, Sun. 2–4 (closed Fri. and alternate Sats.).*

From Doune, take A84 northwest to **Callander,** where the peak of **Ben Ledi** (2,882 feet) looms menacingly at the end of the main street. The town itself is unashamedly tourist-oriented—an accommodation and refreshment stop on the route west—but worth exploring nonetheless. If you tire of shopping, explore the **Callander Crags** or the less steep **Bracklinn Falls** (both behind the town) for a sample of highland scenery.

Time Out **Dalgair House Hotel** (113 Main St.) is run by a friendly, hardworking family who cater to all tastes. Try them for anything from a real Scottish breakfast to a late supper; nothing seems to ruffle their professional cheeriness.

㉗ From Callander, take A84, then A821, west to **the Trossachs** lochs, beginning at **Loch Venachar.** It is hard to describe the Trossachs or to account for their peculiar charm. They combine the wildness of the Highlands with the prolific vegetation of an old Lowland forest. Their open ground is a dense mat of bracken and heather, their woodland is of silver birch, dwarf oak, and hazel that fasten their roots into every crevice of the rocks and stop short on the very brink of the lochs. The most colorful season is the fall, particularly October when the visitors have departed and the hares, deer, and game birds have taken over. But the district is rich in color from early spring onward, with the variegated greens of the leaves, and the grays and blues of the crags, gradually yielding to the browns and purples of bracken and heather, soft and bright as an old tartan.

Though there is a range of forest tracks and trails, for many people the easiest way to enjoy the Trossachs' splendor is to walk from the main car park along the north bank of **Loch Katrine** (pronounced "*Ka*-trin"). This is on a well-surfaced road owned by Strathclyde Water Board and open only to pedestrians and cyclists.

The steamer *Sir Walter Scott* leaves from a nearby pier on its Loch Katrine cruise. Take the cruise if time permits, as the shores of Katrine remain undeveloped and impressive. This loch is the setting of Scott's narrative poem *The Lady of the Lake,* and Ellen's Isle is named after his heroine. It was Scott's influence that led to the Trossachs becoming a major tourist attraction. *Trossachs Pier, tel. 041/355-5333. Early May–late Sept., weekday cruises at 11, 1:45, 3:15; weekends at 2 and 3:30. Cost: £2.60 (AM) and £2.30 (PM) adults, £1.50 (AM) and £1.30 (PM) children and senior citizens.*

An alternative exploration from Stirling will take you east following A91 along the southern edge of the Ochil Hills, through the communities known as the Hillfoots towns. Here, the streams tumbling off the steep pastures meant water power and grazing for livestock—two factors that combined to create a booming textile industry, second only to that of the Borders. The main road continues, via the market town of Cupar in Fife, all the way to the ancient port town of St. Andrews on the North Sea coast.

㉘ St. Andrews is world-famous as the birthplace of the game of golf, originally played with a piece of driftwood, a shore pebble, and a convenient rabbit hole on the sandy, coastal turf. However, the town also offers a wide range of attractions for nongolfers. The cathedral, its ancient university (founded in 1411), and castle are poignant reminders that the town was once the ecclesiastical capital of Scotland. The now largely ruined cathedral was one of the largest churches ever built in Scotland. Its grounds are always open till sunset , although you must pay an admission charge to visit the small museum and nearby St. Rule's Tower. *Admission to museum and tower: 60p adults, 25p children. Grounds, museum, and tower open Apr.–Sept., Mon.–Sat. 9:30–7, Sun. 2–7; Oct.–Mar., Mon.–Sat. 9:30–4, Sun. 2–4.*

Time Out **Pepita's,** on Crail's Lane (one of the linking lanes at right angles to North St.), is a popular bistro-style restaurant serving students and visitors in happy informality.

From St. Andrews, drive back west to Cupar on A91 and then take A913 northwest to Newburgh on the Firth of Tay. Continue following A913 until it joins A912 and turns up to Perth.

㉙ Perth does not give the impression of being an ancient historical site, yet this old town was the Scottish capital from the 12th century until the King of Scotland, James I, was assassinated here in 1437. His successor, James II, moved the court to the better-fortified castle at Stirling. Today Perth is a bustling place, where the country folk, in from the prosperous hinterland of Lowland farms and Highland estates, mix with strolling tourists on the busy shopping streets.

Perth's main historical interest lies in nearby **Scone Palace** (2 miles northeast by A93, Braemar Rd.). This grandly embellished, castellated mansion stands on the site of earlier royal palaces. While still the home of the earl of Mansfield, it is well-equipped to deal with visitors who flock to view its vast collections of 16th-century needlework, china, furniture, vases, and other objets d'art. Within its grounds is **Moot Hill,** the ancient coronation place of the Scottish kings. To be crowned, they sat upon the Stone of Scone, which was seized in 1296 by Edward I of England, Scotland's greatest enemy, and placed in the coronation chair at Westminster Abbey in London, where it is still on view. Some Scots hint darkly that Edward was fooled by a substitution, and that the real stone is hidden north of the border, waiting for Scotland to regain her independence. *Tel. 0738/ 52300. Admission: £3 adults, £2 children. Open Easter–Oct., Mon.–Sat. 9:30–5, Sun. 1:30–5 (July and Aug. 10–5).*

From Perth, return 30 miles to Stirling on A9 along the north side of the Ochil Hills.

Tour 3: Oban and the Western Highlands

In the mountainous west, the county of Argyll offers some of Scotland's finest scenery. Here, where the west winds bring mild rain, you will find a highly photogenic harmony of hill, loch, and lush woodland.

30 **Oban,** the most lively of the west Highland mainland resorts, faces a bewildering tangle of isles in the Firth of Lorn. It is a great yachting center—for the experienced!—as well as a ferry port for the islands and a collection point for cargoes of shellfish. With its russet-stone, white-painted houses, it has a venerable air, but most buildings were the result of an influx of early 20th-century vacationers. The town is full of bed-and-breakfast signs in summer, with tartans and handicrafts spilling from shopfronts into the busy streets, and evening entertainments of the unashamedly bagpipe-skirling, kilt-waggling variety.

Time Out **MacTavish's Kitchen** (George St.) is the place for a "ceilidh" (Gaelic folk music entertainment) with chips.

Romantic views from this great crossroads of the Highlands are also to be had from **Pulpit Hill** at the south end of Oban; from **MacCaig's Tower,** a Victorian architectural extravagance just behind Pulpit Hill (panorama boards help identify landscape features); and from the high ground beyond **Dunollie Sands**—simply follow the promenade northward until it ends.

One possible trip out of Oban follows A816 onto the long arm of the peninsula that runs due south of town to the Mull of Kintyre, around 70 miles. All the way down this route, intrusive sea lochs cut almost through the peninsula. The 9-mile-wide neck of land at **Lochgilphead** was severed by the picturesque Crinan Canal, surveyed by James Watt around 1793, built by John Rennie and in use by 1801. The Crinan area is famous also for its wealth of prehistoric monuments, cairns, standing stones, medieval carved grave-slabs and, on a high, bare rock overlooking the Crinan levels, **Dunadd Fort,** the ancient capital of Dalriada, an early kingdom from which Celtic Scotland sprang.

The main A83, south from Lochgilphead, is a fast road down the west side of Kintyre, giving superb sea-glittering views of the silhouetted hills of the island of Jura, and also little Gigha, closer to the coast. The east-side road is the narrower and winding

B842, with a summer-only ferry connection to Arran at
32 Claonaig. Either way, you reach **Campbeltown,** a well-stocked
town, complete with palm trees by the harbor, and famed for its
whisky and its local cheeses.

Minor roads from the B842 south of Campbeltown lead down to
33 the **Mull of Kintyre.** Sunsets are spectacular here. Park well
above the lighthouse and stroll on to the moorland nearby.

A second excursion from Oban will lead you into the real heart-
lands of Argyll, around the sea inlet of **Loch Fyne** and **Loch Awe**
slightly to the north. Visit Loch Awe by driving eastward from
Oban along A85, via the Pass of Brander with its tree-strewn
crags. The scale of the lake and mountains, particularly the
spiky dragon-back of **Ben Cruachan** (3,695 feet), can best be
seen by following signs from Dalmally to Monument Hill.

Turn south on A819 just before Dalmally, and drive through
34 Glen Aray 15 miles to **Inveraray.** The duke of Argyll is the chief-
tain of the Campbell clan, and you can visit **Inveraray Castle,**
the duke's seat and headquarters of the clan since the 15th century. The present castle was rebuilt in the 18th century. It's an
elegant place with a self-satisfied air, dominating a well-or-
dered town. Here Dr. Johnson was entertained in 1773 and
here, as Boswell tells, the celebrated lexicographer first tasted
Scotch whisky. At the castle you can inspect items that successive dukes of Argyll have salvaged from the Tobermory galleon, a vessel from the Spanish Armada that sank (legend says it
was blown up by a daring Scot) in the Sound of Mull near
Tobermory. *Tel. 0499/2203. Admission: £2.50 adults, £1.50
children, £2 senior citizens, family ticket, £7. Open Apr.–June
and Sept.–mid-Oct., Mon.–Thurs. and Sat. 10–12:30 and 2–
5:30, Sun. 1–5:30; July–Aug., Mon.–Sat. 10–5:30, Sun.
1–5:30.*

Return north on A819 to Dalmally and turn east for 3 miles to
where narrow B8074 leads off to the left (north). You will now
enter **Glen Orchy,** a scenic glen with particularly fine river-
scapes and waterfalls. It is virtually empty of settlement since
it was ruthlessly cleared of its farming population in the last
century to make way for the sheep of the local landowner, the
marquis of Breadalbane. B8074 joins A82 just before the **Bridge
of Orchy,** the only village for miles around, and a small one at
that. A82 continues north over Rannoch Moor, and then turns
west to enter the portals of **Glencoe,** where great craggy buttresses loom darkly over the road. The National Trust for
35 Scotland's **visitor center** at Glencoe (at the western end of the
glen) offers excellent displays on local geology and history, especially the infamous massacre here in 1692—still remembered
in the Highlands for the treachery with which soldiers of the
Campbell clan treated their hosts, the MacDonalds. According
to Highland code, in his own home a clansman should give shelter even to his sworn enemy. In the face of bitter weather, the
Campbells were accepted as guests by the MacDonalds. Apparently acting on orders from the British government, the
Campbells subsequently turned on their hosts, committing
murder "under trust." *Tel. 08552/307. Admission: 30p adults,
15p children. Open Apr.–May and early Sept.–late Oct., daily
10–5:30; June–early Sept., 9:30–6:30.*

You can return to Oban by way of A828, southward along the
Firth of Lorn (36 miles). Alternatively, you can take A82 north-

ward over the elegant bridge across the Ballachulish narrows to reach **Fort William** (15 miles). As its name suggests, this town originated as a military outpost, first established by Cromwell's General Monk in 1655 and refortified in stone by George I in 1715 to help combat an outbreak by the turbulent Jacobite clans. It remains the southern gateway to the Great Glen—Glen Mor, the 60-mile-long valley (and geological fault) that crosses northern Scotland—and to the far west. Scotland's (and Britain's) highest mountain, the 4,406-foot **Ben Nevis,** looms over Fort William less than 4 miles from the sea. Even non-mountaineers can make the hike to its summit.

From Fort William, A830 runs westward to the port of Mallaig and the southernmost of the ferry connections to the Isle of Skye, the largest of the Inner Hebrides. Each succeeding year detracts from the narrow, winding charm of this modern "Road to the Isles," as bends and dips are sliced off and straightened in the name of progress. The most relaxing way to take in the birch- and bracken-covered wild slopes, with misty views of the Hebridean islands of Rhum, Eigg, and Muck, is on the **Fort William–Mallaig Railway,** especially by the steam locomotive summer services.

This area is strongly associated with the Jacobite hero Prince Charles Edward Stuart ("Bonnie Prince Charlie"). The tale of his doomed struggle to restore the Stuart monarchy is told at the visitor center of the National Trust for Scotland's Glenfinnan Monument at **Glenfinnan,** about 19 miles west of Fort William on A830. Here, at the head of Loch Sheil, Charles raised his standard in 1745 and succeeded in rousing various clans to follow him, especially the Camerons. *Tel. 039783/250. Admission: 90p adults, 45p children. Opening times as for Glencoe visitor center, above.*

Railroad buffs will want to inspect the nearby **Glenfinnan railroad viaduct,** one of the very earliest examples of mass concrete construction. Built at the turn of the century, and 100 feet high, it carries the tracks 1,248 feet across the valley. In summer, you can tell when a steam train is due on this structure by the sudden sprouting of camera tripods on every heathery knoll in the vicinity.

From Glenfinnan you can return to Oban by heading back to Fort William (east on A830) and then traveling 30 miles south with Loch Linnhe on your right, taking A82/A828/A85.

Tour 4: The Inverness Area

Numbers in the margin correspond to points of interest on the Inverness Area map.

The northern Highlands are often described as one of Europe's last wilderness areas. Certainly the landscapes of the northwest have no equal anywhere else in Britain. This stark, uncompromising landscape, glittering with lochans (small lakes), will either cast a lifetime spell on you or make you long for the safe, effete pastures of the south.

Inverness is a logical touring base, with excellent roads radiating out to serve an extensive area. Known for centuries as "the Capital of the Highlands," Inverness is not exclusively Highland in flavor, however. Part of its hinterland includes the farmlands of the Moray Firth coastal strip, as well as of the Black

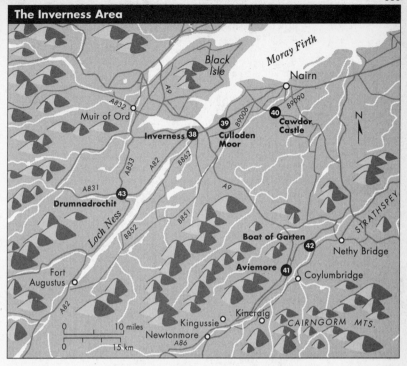

The Inverness Area

Moray Firth

Black Isle

Nairn

A9

A832

Muir of Ord

B9006

B9090

40 Cawdor Castle

39 Culloden Moor

Inverness 38

N

A833

A82

B862

A831

A9

43 Drumnadrochit

B852

B851

STRATHSPEY

Loch Ness

Boat of Garten

42

Nethy Bridge

Aviemore 41

Coylumbridge

Fort Augustus

A82

CAIRNGORM MTS.

Kincraig

Kingussie

Newtonmore A86

0 ___ 10 miles
0 ___ 15 km

Isle. It is open to the sea winds off the Moray Firth, while the high hills, although close at hand, are mainly hidden. Few of Inverness's buildings are of great antiquity—thanks to the Highland clans' careless habit of burning the town to the ground. Even its castle is a Victorian replacement on the site of a fort blown up by Bonnie Prince Charlie. Now bypassed by A9, still the town in summer does not simply bustle, it positively roars. Be careful in its one-way traffic system, whether walking or driving.

The cemetery here is something of a tourist attraction. Spreading over the wooded slopes of Tomnahurich (Hill of the Fairies) about a mile west of the town, it overlooks a panorama of firth, river, canal, and loch. At about the same distance from the town center, following the Ness river upstream toward its loch, you come to the Ness Islands. Footbridges neatly connect them to each other and to either side of the river. Among them are bandstands and an open-air theater with regular programs of summer entertainment—nothing very sophisticated, but convincing demonstrations of the Highland capital's love and respect for the old piping and dancing traditions.

Rather than suggest one single round trip through the country about Inverness, we are suggesting here two separate excursions.

39 The first sallies out 5 miles east on B9006 to visit **Culloden Moor,** scene of the last battle fought on British soil. Here, on a cold April day in 1746, the outnumbered Jacobite forces of Bonnie Prince Charlie, exhausted by a night march, ill-fed and badly led, were decimated by the superior firepower of George II's army, which included the Campbells among other Highlanders, as well as Lowland Scottish regiments. (This was not, in any sense, a Scotland-versus-England confrontation.) The victorious commander, the duke of Cumberland (George II's son), earned the name of "Butcher" Cumberland for the bloody reprisals carried out by his men on Highland families, Jacobite or not, who were caught in the vicinity. The National Trust for Scotland has, slightly eerily, re-created the battlefield as it looked in 1746. The uneasy silence of the open moor almost drowns out the merry clatter from the visitor center's coffee shop and the tinkle of the cash registers. *Tel. 0463/790607. Admission (visitor center and audiovisual display): £1.40 adults, 70p children. Open Apr.–May and mid-Sept.–Oct., daily 9:30–5:30; June–mid-Sept., daily 9–6:30.*

40 From Culloden Moor, continue on B9006, then turn off right on to B9090 (around 10 miles) to reach **Cawdor Castle,** near Nairn. This cheerfully idiosyncratic, mellowed, and mossy family seat has a 15th-century central tower. The castle is associated with Shakespeare's *Macbeth* as the home of the thanes (clan chiefs) of Cawdor. *Tel. 06677/615. Admission: £2.90 adults, £1.50 children. Open May–Sept., daily 10–5.*

If you continue eastward along the Moray Firth from Nairn, just north of Cawdor, you'll pass miles of inviting sandy beaches and a string of fishing communities. From Nairn to Fraserburgh at the extreme eastern end of the coast is around 70 miles. Alternatively, from Cawdor you can take the smaller roads B9090, B9006, and B851 southwest to reach A9, which will lead you for 25 miles across the empty moors on the northern edge of the Grampian mountains to the valley of Strathspey (in Gaelic, "strath" means "broad valley"), where the river Spey links a number of communities. These include **41** **Aviemore**—a 1960s attempt to create a classy St. Moritz-type of Highland playground and ski resort—as well as the more appealing villages of Newtonmore, Kingussie, Kincraig, Coylumbridge, Boat of Garten, and Nethybridge. For a fine view of the great **Cairngorm massif,** increasingly nibbled at and disfigured by resort developers, the **Strathspey Railway** will take you **42** round-trip from Aviemore to **Boat of Garten,** through fine scenery of moor and birch, with the Cairngorm Mountains as a backdrop to the east. You can board the train at Aviemore or Boat of Garten. *Tel. 0479/810725. Round-trip fares (2nd class): £3.20 adults, £1.60 children (1st class add £5 adult), family ticket, £8. Operates May–Sept. daily; Mar.–May, Sun. and Wed. Timetable changes according to season. Call ahead for details.*

Time Out If you enjoy restored steam locomotives, try a pub lunch at the **Boat Hotel** (Boat of Garten), a former station hotel, where whistles and clanking are suitable accompaniments to simple home cooking.

Inverness is also the northern gateway to the Great Glen, the result of an ancient earth movement that dislocated the entire top half of Scotland. The main road south from Inverness is the busy A82 route along the west bank of **Loch Ness,** though leisurely drivers may prefer the east bank road, B862 and B852, to Fort Augustus, at the lake's southern end (32 miles). Monster watchers should visit the "official" **Loch Ness Monster Ex-**

❹ hibition at **Drumnadrochit** on A82, midway on the west bank.
Loch Ness's huge volume of water has a locally warming effect
on the weather, making the lake conducive to mirages in still,
warm conditions. These are often the circumstances in which
the "monster" appears, and you may draw your own conclu-
sions. *Drumnadrochit, tel. 04562/573. Admission: £2.75 adults,
£1.50 children, £2 senior citizens and students, £7.25 family
ticket. Open daily: July–mid-Sept. 9–9:30. Off-season opening
times vary; please phone to check.*

What to See and Do with Children

Haggs Castle in Glasgow is a museum with exhibits aimed exclusively at younger children. Workshops and children's activities abound: there's everything from face-painting to doll-
making. *100 St. Andrew's Dr., tel. 041/427–2725. Admission
free. Open Mon.–Sat. 10–5, Sun. 1–6.*

Blair Drummond Safari Park, near Stirling, offers performing
seals and amusement-park attractions; it's somewhat tame, but
suitable for uncritical children and adults. *Blair Drummond,
near Stirling, tel. 0786/841456. Phone for opening times and
admission charges.*

With plenty of beaches on the west, north, and east coasts—
Dornoch, Gairloch, and Nairn among them—you'll have no
problem arranging a traditional sun-and-sandcastle vacation.
All along the coasts, children's fair-weather entertainment is of
the outdoor variety: fishing, hiking, seal watching, boat trips,
cross-country pony-riding, and so on.

The **Aviemore Centre,** eager to cater to all the family, offers a
wide range of children's activities, including go-karting, ice-
skating, indoor swimming, and visiting Santa Claus (yes, in
summer, too!). *Full information from Stakis PLC, tel. 03552/
47177 or 0479/810624.*

Other outstanding places for children are the **Sea-Life Centres**
at **Barcaldine** (Barcaldine, Connel, Argyll, tel. 0631/72386) and
St. Andrews (St. Andrews, Fife, tel. 0334/74786). Barcaldine is
midway between Fort William and Oban on the west coast, and
easy to reach from either town. St. Andrews is on the east
coast, within day-trip distance of Edinburgh. Both offer a fascinating display of marine life; the restaurant at Barcaldine is
particularly recommended.

Off the Beaten Track

Five miles east of Dumfries by B724 is the **Ruthwell Cross,** one
of the most important monuments surviving from the Dark
Ages. Carved in the 8th century, it stands 18 feet high in an
apse of the Ruthwell Church. *Admission: free.*

The villages of **Leadhills** and **Wanlockhead,** perched more than
1,300 feet above sea level in the Lowther hills of Galloway, are
the highest in Scotland. Once lead was mined from the domed,
heather-covered uplands nearby. The **Museum of the Scottish
Lead Mining Industry** tells the story and offers subterranean
tours. *Goldscaur Rd., Wanlockhead, on B797, northeast of
Sanquhar, 27 miles northwest of Dumfries, tel. 0659/74387.
Admission: £1.80 adults, 90p children, includes visit to mine.
Open Easter–Oct., daily 11–4.*

Nine miles northeast of Moffat, itself about 35 miles southeast of Glasgow, the spectacular waterfall known as the **Grey Mare's Tail** can be seen from A708. Now in the care of the National Trust for Scotland, the waterfall is in an area that offers plenty of hiking routes for the adventurous. There are also interesting botanical specimens on the hills above, especially on White Coomb mountain (2,695 feet).

The little Wester Ross village of **Shieldaig,** curved around a sheltered bay, offers breathtaking views of the Torridon hills—if you can find the lookout point! The main road from Torridon, A896, enters the village and swings south and left along the seafront. From the point where the main road reaches the shore, another dead-end road goes right and uphill. Walk up the latter road. At its end, a path heads north over the heathery headland. Walk as far as you like—the view gets better with every step!

Balquhidder Glen is about 1½ hours' drive from Glasgow via A81 and A84 north. Green hills and silver water, the scent of new birch leaves in spring: This is a breath of the highlands just minutes from A84, between Callander and Lochearnhead.

Loch Lomond may be serenely beautiful, but try one of its islands for real tranquillity. You can reach **Inchcailloch** from the boatyard at Balmaha where a little boat will take you over. This small island has ancient oak woods ringing with birdsong, blankets of bluebells underfoot, and a gentle stroll along a nature trail.

In a sense, all of the Highlands lies off the beaten track, which explains why much of the landscape remains comparatively unspoiled. North of Lochinver, off A837, in Sutherland, B869 runs in a spectacular loop to the Kylesku bridge and some breathtaking views in the area. Beyond the village of **Stoer,** a narrow road heads west to the outlying houses and the lighthouse (Cluas Deas). Park at the lighthouse and stroll northward over the moorland. Away from the cliff edge, rising ground gives a spectacular, arm's-length view of the northwest mountains rising starkly on the horizon. Only the energetic will reach the rock stack called the **Old Man of Stoer.**

Cape Wrath is the tip of northwest Scotland. "Wrath" has nothing to do with anger: The headland got its name from a Norse word meaning "turning-point." You can reach the tip only by minibus along the lighthouse road, after a short ferry crossing of the Kyle of Durness.

On the shore of **Bo'ness,** 15 miles southeast of Stirling by A905, on the Firth of Forth, a typical branch-line railroad station has been reconstructed by the **Scottish Railway Preservation Society.** Its line will eventually join the main Glasgow–Edinburgh line at Linlithgow. Steam trains usually run on weekends and in the summer. Distance, frequency, and fares are subject to change as the line is extended (for full details tel. 0506/822298).

Shopping

Glasgow is rapidly challenging Edinburgh as a shopping center, as it does in many other fields, and is a lot more fun than its staid rival. Elsewhere in the region you will find excellent woolens and tweeds. Keep an eye out for unusual designs in Scottish jewelry, especially when they employ local stones. Scotland has always been a very bookish country, priding itself on the high rate of literacy, and you will often find a surprisingly well-stocked secondhand bookshop in a fairly remote town.

Ayr   **Armstrong's** (234–236 High St.) offers a large range of knitwear manufactured by Scotland's leading companies, such as Pringle and Lyle & Scott. Men's and women's kilts can be made to order in over 1,000 tartans. They also sell plenty of well-crafted souvenirs and tartan accessories.

Galston   Fifteen miles northeast of Ayr on A77/A71, halfway back to Glasgow, is the **Balmoral Knitwear Mill Shop** (Church La., Galston). A wide selection of traditional Scottish knitwear—silk embroidery, lambswool and mohair sweaters, scarves, jackets—is sold here.

Glasgow   Glasgow's main shopping districts occupy the southeastern part of town, in a square grid that runs south to Clyde Street on the banks of the river, north to St. Vincent's Street, and east-west from City Hall to the Central Station. From George Square to Argyle Street the area is called Merchant City—and you'll see why, as you pass the many designer boutiques and great shopping "precincts" (malls), complete with fountains and glass-walled elevators, on Buchanan and Glassford streets. **Ichi Ni San** (123 Candleriggs) is a glitzy fashion shrine, all beaten metal and distressed plaster. **Princes Square,** between Argyle and Buchanan streets, is the most chic and modern of the malls, with specialty shops on three levels and a café complex above, all under a glittering dome. You'll find **Katharine Hamnett** here. **Lady V** (70 Buchanan St.) offers exclusive designer fashion as good as any you'd find elsewhere in Europe. **Daniel de Ruelle** (41 Glassford St.) and **Stockwell China Bazaar** (67–77 Glassford St.) specialize respectively in jewelry, crystal, brassware; also fine china and giftware. **The Warehouse** (61–65 Glassford St.) has designer clothes (Rifat Ozbek, Jean Paul Gaultier, and Jasper Conran) and shoes—floor after floor of them.

Just off Buchanan Street you'll find **William Porteous & Co. Ltd.** (9 Royal Exchange Pl.), which features maps, souvenir books and prints, and Scottish-made crafts and gifts to take home with you. One block north on St. Vincent's Street, the **Scottish Design Centre Shop** (no. 72) has housewares and curios ranging in style from simple and elegant to casual and fun.

At the southern end of this area you'll find the **St. Enoch Centre,** the latest of Glasgow's new generation of shopping malls. Bargain hunters should also visit the adjacent **"Paddy's Market."** The name dates back to the 1850s when impoverished Irish immigrants would sell even the clothes off their backs, and the expression came to mean any jumble of odds and ends. Glasgow's weekend market, the **Barras,** is also here, just north of Glasgow Green, offering a dizzying array of items, from antique toys to fresh vegetables. Two blocks north is Howard Street, another row of shopping outlets including **Slater Mens-**

wear, where you'll find high-quality tweeds, woolens and sportswear for men.

Sauchiehall Street, on Glasgow's west side, has two superior shopping arcades. The **John B. Wylie & Co. Ltd. Bookshop** (406 Sauchiehall St.) is the place for fine books on all subjects.

Uptown Glasgow, in the Kelvingrove/University section, has shopping areas centering on Hillhead and Kelvinbridge, including a selection of small commercial art galleries. **De-Courcy's Arcade,** off Byre's Road, features a number of lovely little antiques shops.

Inverness   As you would expect, Inverness features a number of shops with a distinct Highland flavor. At **Pringle's Woollen Mill** (Dores Rd.) you can take a free guided tour of the mill; a fine shop on the premises sells lovely tweeds, tartans, and, of course, wool clothing. **The Kilt Maker** (4–9 Huntly St.) has a huge selection of kilts, or will run one up for you made to measure. **Duncan Chisholm & Sons** (47–51 Castle St.) is another fine shop specializing in Highland tartans, woolens, and crafts. A variety of both specialty shops and larger department stores can be found at the **Eastgate Shopping Centre** (11 Eastgate).
In addition to these traditional stores, more unusual crafts shops are nearby. **Highland Aromatics Ltd.** (Drumchardine, 7 miles west on A862) sells perfumed toilet soap made with Scottish ingredients, and all manner of perfumes, colognes, bath salts, and toiletries. **Highland Wineries Ltd.** (2 miles farther on B9164, in Kirkhill) makes wine from local products, including birch bark.

Lochinver   About 3 miles south of Lochinver (in the far northwest), the back road to the town (B869) drops steeply downhill, crosses the little river Kirkaig, and turns toward the shore. Immediately beyond the bridge, beside a parking lot, a sign points to a path that goes far into the loch-mirrored interior, toward the rocky flanks of Suilven hill. But much closer, in fact, about two minutes from the parking lot, is **Achins** (Inverkirkaig), one of the best bookstores in Scotland, in one of its least populated regions. You should easily be able to stock up on all your vacation reading and gift-book shopping here.

Luss   In this town, 34 miles west of Stirling and 40 miles north of Glasgow, the **Thistle Bagpipe Works** (tel. 04386/250) will let you commission your own made-to-order bagpipe.

Oban   Oban is the home of one of Scotland's best glassworks. **Oban Glassworks** (Lochavullin Estate, tel. 0631/63386) make Caithness Glass, and here you can see the manufacturing process and buy a memento of Scotland to treasure. Especially lovely are the paperweights with swirling colored patterns.

Perth   Perth has upscale shopping aspirations. Native freshwater pearls feature in the superb gold designs of **Cairncross Ltd., Goldsmiths** (18 St. John's St.). **Timothy Hardie** (25 St. John's St.) sells fine jewelry and antique silver. At the **Perth Craft Centre** (38 South St.), you can choose from a wide variety of Scottish handicraft work. **William Watson & Sons** (163–167 High St.) specializes in quality china and glassware.

Stirling   Stirling offers a range of shops, from down-to-earth to positively eccentric. **R. R. Henderson Ltd.** (6–10 Friars St.) calls itself "Highland outfitters," selling tartans, woolens, and accessories. **Ezhe Hirsh** (The Arcade) specializes in jewelry design.

Whinwell Crafts (22 Broad St.) weave their own unique designs on silk, woolens, and fine knits.

Sports and Fitness

Golfing   It has been argued that golf came to Scotland from Holland, but the historical evidence points to Scotland being the cradle, if not the birthplace, of the game. Citizens of St. Andrews were playing golf on the town links (public land) as far back as the 15th century. In 1754 the first association of players, the Gentlemen Golfers of Edinburgh, moved to the breezy links of St. Andrews, which in due course (1834) became the Royal & Ancient Golf Club. Maximizing the available space, golfers played nine holes out and the same nine holes back. Thus the number of holes on a golf course was fixed for all time.

Scotland is now a land-mass entirely packed with golf courses. The Gleneagles Hotel boasts four 18-hole courses of its own. Every town and village has its course and its club. Celebrated courses—Carnoustie, Muirfield, Royal Troon, Turnberry, and others—attract international championships in their turn.

Golf in Scotland is quite a plebeian game, whereas in England it is a distinctly middle-class pastime. A round on a Scottish municipal course costs very little, and the Scottish clubs, apart from a few pretentious places modeled on the English fashion, demand only modest entrance fees.

Here are the names and descriptions of a few Scottish courses that welcome visitors:

Gleneagles Hotel (Auchterarder, near Perth, tel. 07646/3453) has four 18-hole courses on undulating moorland. (Only three currently open.) Visitors must write in advance. The club was founded in 1908; two of the four courses were designed by James Braid (1870–1950), professional golfer and Scotland's most famous golf-course designer.

St. Andrews Balgrove Course (St. Andrews, tel. 0334/73393). One of a group of five seaside courses, this has 9 holes (the other four are 18-hole courses).

Royal Troon (Troon, Ayrshire, tel. 0292/31155). Two 18-hole courses (Old, 6,649 yards; and Portland, 6,274 yards) make up this club, founded in 1878.

Turnberry Hotel (Turnberry, Ayrshire, tel. 0655/3202). There are two 18-hole seaside courses here, and visitors are welcome with prior reservations.

The Highland Games   Caber-tossing (the "caber" is a long, heavy pole) and other traditional events figure in the **Highland Games,** staged throughout the Highlands during summer. All Scottish tourist information centers have full details. It is said that these games, a unique combination of music, dancing, and athletic prowess, grew out of the contests held by clan chiefs to find the strongest men for bodyguards, the fastest runners for messengers, and the best musicians and dancers to entertain guests and increase the chief's prestige.

Skiing   Scotland entered the winter-sports arena late, although within a couple of decades Aviemore has blossomed into a major winter-sports center, along with other villages at the foot of the Cairngorms. Other popular ski centers have arisen at Glenshee and Glencoe, but accommodations are limited and likely to remain so. Up-and-coming winter-sports developments include the Lecht, near Aviemore, and Aonach Mor, near Fort William.

Compared with the well-known Swiss and Austrian centers, the ski resorts of Scotland suffer from cloudy weather, high winds, and difficulty in keeping access roads snow-free; but when conditions are right the skiing in Scotland can be first-class. The season varies in length because the climate is unpredictable. It can begin as early as November, but the experts prefer February and March.

Walking The Scottish Tourist Board publishes a pamphlet called *Walks and Trails in Scotland* to guide you through hundreds of walks all over the country. Here is a sampling of what's in store:

Cawdor Castle Nature Trails provides a choice of four hikes through some of the most beautiful and varied woodlands in Britain. You will pass ancient oaks and beeches, magnificent waterfalls, and deep river gorges. *Cawdor Castle (Tourism) Ltd., Cawdor Castle, Nairn, near Inverness IV12 5RD, tel. 06677/615.*

Highland Edge Walk runs along the Highland boundary fault edge, offering superb views of both the Highlands and Lowlands, 6 miles south of the Trossachs on A821. *Forestry Commission, Aberfoyle, Stirlingshire FK8 3UX, tel. 08772/383.*

Inchree Waterfall starts from a point 9 miles south of Fort William on A82, and crosses fields and moorland to reach the stunning Inchree waterfall, which descends 120 feet in seven stages. The return journey is along a forest trail with breathtaking views across to Ardgour. *Forestry Commission, Lochaber Forest District Office, Torlundy, Fort William PH33 6SW, tel. 0397/2184.*

Rozelle Nature Trails are two walks centering around Rozelle Mansion House, 2 miles south of Ayr on A719. The first is a pond walk and nature trail taking in a variety of trees, bushes, and plants, with waterfowl, other birds, and small mammals. The second proceeds into the surrounding woodland to observe the extensive flora and fauna. *Director of Parks and Recreation, 30 Miller Rd., Ayr KA7 2AY, tel. 0292/281511, ext. 249.*

Dining and Lodging

Dining Never assume that because a restaurant is a little off the beaten track its cuisine lacks sophistication. In the Highlands, the reverse is often true. Local game and seafood are often presented with great flair; while oatmeal, local cheeses, and even malt whisky (turning up in any course) amplify the Scottish dimension.

As for fish, many restaurants deal directly with local boats, so freshness is guaranteed. The quality and range of fish is such that local residents can afford curious prejudices; mackerel, for instance, no matter how tasty, is considered second-class fare. With rich pastures supporting the famous Aberdeen Angus beef cattle, good meat is also guaranteed.

Highly recommended restaurants are indicated by a star ★.

Category	Cost*
Very Expensive	over £40
Expensive	£30–£40
Moderate	£15–£30
Inexpensive	under £15

per person, including first course, main course, dessert, and VAT; excluding drinks

Lodging In large cities, many hotels are as efficiently faceless and blandly international as you will find anywhere; in general, you must get out of the major population centers if you're looking for real Scottish hospitality. Try Galloway or Argyll, for example, as just two areas with a good choice of smaller, family-run hotels.

Since the removal of much of its indigenous population by forced emigration, many parts of the Highlands have been playgrounds for estate owners or Lowland industrialists, who built themselves shooting lodges, grand mansions, and country estates. Many of these are now fine hotels. Do not, however, expect your hosts always to be Scots—many experienced hoteliers from the wealthy south of England fulfill their ambitions by opening a Highland hotel, where real estate is cheaper, the scenery beautiful, and the pace of life relaxed.

Highly recommended lodgings are indicated by a star ★.

Category	Cost*
Very Expensive	over £110
Expensive	£75–£110
Moderate	£40–£75
Inexpensive	under £40

All prices are for two people sharing a double room, including service, breakfast, and VAT.

Arisaig **Arisaig House Hotel.** This secluded and grand Victorian man-
Dining and Lodging sion offers tranquillity and some marvelous scenery, including views of the Inner Hebrides. The bedrooms are plush and restful, with soft pastel colors, original moldings, and antique furniture. The cuisine at the restaurant is quietly celebrated, with an emphasis on fresh local produce. *Beasdale (6 miles south of Mallaig on A830), Arisaig PH39 4NR, tel. 06875/622. 13 rooms with bath. Facilities: croquet, sailing, fishing, island trips, library, billiards. No children under 10. AE, MC, V. Closed Nov.–Easter. Dinner included in cost of lodging. Expensive.*

Auchterarder **Auchterarder House Hotel.** Secluded and superbly atmospher-
Dining and Lodging ic, here is a wood-paneled, richly furnished, Victorian country
★ mansion. The staff is particularly friendly, and guests will enjoy the personal attention in this family home. The plush, exuberantly styled dining room, filled with glittering glassware, is an appropriate setting for an unusual and creative use of many locally produced foods: Typical dishes include lamb with a Dubonnet and red wine sauce, or poached langoustines with rhubarb. *On B8062, 15 mi southwest of Perth, PH3 1DZ, tel. 0764/63646. 15 rooms with bath. Facilities: restaurant, golf,*

swimming, tennis, squash, croquet. Restaurant reservations required. Jacket and tie required. AE, DC, MC, V. Expensive.
Gleneagles Hotel. One of Britain's most famous hotels, Gleneagles is the very image of modern grandeur. Like a vast, secret palace, it stands hidden in breathtaking coutryside amid three world-famous golf courses. Recreation facilities are nearly endless, and there are also five restaurants: the **Conservatory** for intimate haute cuisine, the **Strathearn** for table d'hôte, and three other more informal restaurants. All this plus a shopping arcade, Champneys Health Spa, the Gleneagles Mark Phillips Equestrian Centre, and Gleneagles Jackie Stewart Shooting School, make a stay here a luxurious and unforgettable experience. *PH3 1NF, tel. 0764/62231. 236 rooms with bath. Facilities: tennis, swimming, saunas, gym. Restaurant reservations advised. Jacket and tie required in formal areas of the hotel after 7 PM; dress informal otherwise. AE, DC, MC, V. Very Expensive.*

Auchterless
Dining

Towie Tavern. On the main Aberdeen-Turriff road, with Fyvie Castle nearby as a good reason for exploring the rural hinterland of Aberdeenshire, the Towie Tavern is a friendly and informal traditional eating place. Food is straightforward local fare; check the blackboard for the "Towie Treats" that feature changing selections of (for example) fresh seafood. The good nature of the staff and the air of coziness more than make up for unsophisticated trimmings. *Auchterless, Nr Turriff AB5 8EP, tel. 08884/201. Reservations advised. Dress: casual. MC, V. Moderate.*

Aviemore
Dining

The Winking Owl. Cozy green-and-red tartan carpets increase the appeal of this "après-ski" resort restaurant. The cuisine includes both English and Scottish dishes. *Grampian Rd., tel. 0479/810646. Reservations advised. Dress: informal. AE, DC, MC, V. Closed Sun. and mid-Nov.–mid-Dec. Inexpensive–Moderate.*

Balloch
Dining and Lodging

Cameron House. This luxury hotel offers a mix of top-quality hotel and country club facilities (swimming pools, gymnasium, squash courts, etc.), set on the shores of Loch Lomond. Award-winning chef Jef Bland (ex-Caledonian Hotel, Edinburgh) oversees cusine of the highest order with a Scottish-French slant in rich Victorian surroundings. Bedrooms are decorated in modern pastel shades with high-quality reproduction antique furniture. The keynote throughout is lavish. *Loch Lomond, Alexandriaa, Dunbartonshire G83 8QZ, tel. 0389/55565. 68 rooms with bath. Dress: smart. Reservations essential. AE, DC, MC, V. Open all year. Expensive–Very Expensive.*

Callander
Lodging

Roman Camp. This former hunting lodge, dating from 1625, has 20 acres of gardens with river frontage, yet is within easy walking distance of Callander town center. Private fishing on the River Teith is another attraction, as are the sitting rooms and library with their numerous antiques. The restaurant is of a high standard, with the menu in imaginative modern French style. *Callander, Perthshire, FK17 8BG, tel. 0877/30003. 14 rooms with bath. Dress: smart casual. AE, DC, MC, V. Reservations strongly advised. Open all year. Moderate–Expensive.*

Crinan
Dining and Lodging
★

Crinan Hotel. This turn-of-the-century property overlooking the picturesque Crinan Canal and the Sound of Jura has been extensively refurbished. Friendly and helpful, the present owner is an interior decorator on the side, hence the very high standard of the decor in each room. Two restaurants offer both Scottish cuisine and the freshest local seafood: **The Telford Room** serves dinner in a luxurious, country-mansion setting, where you are surrounded by antiques and floral arrangements; the rooftop **Lock 16** has a nautical theme, and superb sunsets accompany the award-winning fresh seafood. *Near Lochgilphead (20 mi south of Oban on A816) PA31 8SR, tel. 054683/261. 22 rooms with bath. Facilities: coffee shop, sea fishing. Restaurant reservations advised. Jacket and tie required in Lock 16. MC, V. Lock 16 closed Mon. and Tues. Hotel closed mid-Oct.–mid-Mar. Hotel: Moderate–Expensive. Restaurants: Expensive.*

Drumnadrochit
Dining and Lodging

Polmaily House Hotel. This country house is located on the northern edge of Loch Ness in the middle of some lovely parkland. The restaurant is noted for its international cuisine, which takes full advantage of fresh Highland produce. Specialties include wild salmon with sorrel cream, and peppered venison. *Milton (near A82, 12 mi southwest of Inverness) IV3 6XT, tel. 04562/343. 9 rooms, 7 with bath. Facilities: outdoor swimming pool, tennis. Restaurant reservations advised. Dress: informal. MC, V. Closed mid-Oct.–Easter. Moderate.*

Drybridge
Dining
★

Old Monastery. Sitting high on a hillside, with fabulous views, this restaurant is in a building that was formerly a priory. It boasts pine ceilings and walls stenciled by monks 100 years ago. The chef's imaginative recipes make use of very fresh seafood (some of Scotland's largest fishing ports are nearby) and local game. The puddings are also especially good. *Near Buckie (35 mi east of Inverness off A98), tel. 0542/32660. Reservations advised. Dress: informal. AE, MC, V. Closed Sun., Mon., 2 weeks in Nov., 3 weeks in Jan. Moderate.*

Dunblane
Dining and Lodging

Cromlix House Hotel. This Victorian hunting lodge has remained in the same family since 1874. The period atmosphere is enhanced by cherished furniture and paintings, the original conservatory, and the library. The restaurant offers country-house decor and a choice of three elegant dining rooms. Specialties include game and lamb from the hotel estate, and seasonal fruits with kirsch ice cream. *Kinbuck (on B8033, 3 mi northeast of Dunblane) FK15 9JT, tel. 0786/822125. 14 rooms with bath. Facilities: tennis, trout fishing, grouse and pheasant shooting. Restaurant reservations advised. Jacket and tie required. AE, DC, MC, V. Closed first 2 weeks of Feb. Expensive.*

Dunoon
Lodging
★

Ardfillayne Hotel. Seven acres of wooded garden surround this 150-year-old mansion. The decor is modern, and the owners clearly enjoy looking after their guests. *West Bay (3 mi west of Gourock across the Firth of Clyde) PA23 7QJ, tel. 0369/2267. 8 rooms with bath. Facilities: restaurant. AE, DC, V. Moderate.*

Elgin
Dining and Lodging

Mansion House Hotel. This Scots-baronial mansion complete with tower, 38 miles east of Inverness on A96, is set on the River Lossie. The rooms are individually decorated; all provide comfort and pleasant surroundings. The restaurant serves elaborately presented, above-average meals. *The Haugh, IV30 1AW, tel. 0343/548811. 18 rooms with bath. Facilities: gardens, bistro bar, indoor pool, sauna, gymnasium, solarium, in-house movies. AE, DC, MC, V. Moderate.*

Fort William
Dining and Lodging

Inverlochy Castle. A red-granite Victorian castle, Inverlochy stands in 50 acres of woodlands in the shadow of Ben Nevis, with striking Highland landscape on every side. Queen Victoria stayed here and wrote, "I never saw a lovelier or more romantic spot." Dating from 1863, the hotel retains all the splendor of its period, with a fine frescoed ceiling, crystal chandeliers, handsome staircase in the Great Hall, paintings and hunting trophies everywhere, and plush, comfortable bedrooms. The restaurant is exceptional—a lovely room with wonderful cuisine. Many of the specialties use local produce, such as roast saddle of roedeer or woodpigeon consommé, with orange soufflé as the final touch. *Torlundy (3 mi northeast of Fort William on A82) PH33 6SN, tel. 0397/702177. 16 rooms with bath. Facilities: restaurant, billiards, tennis, fishing. AE, MC, V. Closed mid-Nov.–mid-Mar. Very Expensive.*

Gigha
Dining and Lodging

Gigha Hotel. An old inn that overlooks the Sound of Gigha to Kintyre, the hotel has lovely bedrooms and a stonework-and-pine dining room. The cuisine is Scottish, using local produce from the island's farms and the surrounding sea. *Gigha PA41 7AD, tel. 05835/254. 11 rooms with bath. Restaurant reservations required. Dress: informal. MC. V. Moderate.*

Glasgow
Dining
★

Rogano. The striking art deco design of this restaurant is enough to recommend it—the bonus is that the food, at the lively downstairs diner, at the main restaurant on the ground floor, and at the oyster bar near the entrance, is excellent. Specialties include venison liver pâté, and fresh seafood superbly prepared. Vegetarians are also catered for. A great favorite with Glaswegians, so be sure to book ahead. *11 Exchange Square, tel. 041/248–4055. Reservations required. Jacket and tie required. AE, DC, MC, V. Closed Sun. and national holidays. Very Expensive.*

★ **Buttery.** Located in a former Masonic temple, the Buttery is close to the Ring Street expressway tangle. The food here is down-to-earth, with excellent lamb and seafood to the fore. The service is friendly and the ambience relaxed. *652 Argyle St., tel. 041/221–8188. Reservation required. Dress: informal. AE, DC, MC, V. Closed Sat. lunch and Sun. Expensive.*

Colonial. In a traditional dining room you will find a wide range of Indian cuisine, especially dishes from the south (i.e., hotter and spicier). Goanese fish and prawns, *Sali Boti* (a selection of dishes using sun-dried fruits, spices, and cream), and dishes using wine and cognacs are specialties. *25 High Street, tel. 041/ 552–1923. Reservations advised. Jacket and tie preferred. AE, DC, MC, V. Moderate–Expensive.*

★ **The Ubiquitous Chip.** Much loved locally, this restaurant has a glass-covered courtyard with lush greenery, and a dining room with exposed ceiling beams. Specialties depend on what is available fresh at top quality, but will usually include fish and seafood, roedeer steaks, and lamb. The wine list is outstanding. *12 Ashton La., tel. 041/334–5007. Reservations advised. Dress: informal. AE, DC, MC, V. Moderate.*

Change at Jamaica. This restaurant, just south of the river and under a railway bridge, has a clean modern decor. The menu is long and varied, offering a little of everything. A late-night haven, it usually doesn't close 'til around 5 AM. *Clyde Pl., tel. 041/ 429–4422. Reservations not required. Dress: informal. AE, DC, MC, V. Inexpensive.*

Dining and Lodging
★

One Devonshire Gardens. This fine town mansion offers luxury accommodations. Elegance is the theme, from the sophisticated drawing room to the sumptuous bedrooms with their rich drapery and traditional furnishings, including (in three) four-poster beds. The restaurant is equally stylish, with a new menu for each meal. Specialties include salmon with orange and ginger sauce, chicken livers with almonds, and magnificent fillet steaks. *1 Devonshire Gardens, G12 0UX, tel. 041/339–2001. 8 apartments with bath. Restaurant reservations advised. Dress in restaurant: Jacket and tie required. AE, DC, MC, V. Very Expensive.*

Central Hotel. A typical Victorian railroad hotel, with thick carpets, mobcapped chambermaids, and ample rooms from another era. Public areas feature brass chandeliers and plenty of greenery. The **Entresol** restaurant serves breakfast, lunch, and dinner. *Gordon St., G1 3SF, tel. 041/221–9680. 221 rooms with bath. Facilities: bar, in-house movies. AE, DC, MC, V. Moderate.*

Lodging **Kirklee Hotel.** Located in a quiet district of Glasgow near the
★ university, this hotel is small and cozy. Its owners take pride in being friendly and helpful and in keeping the hotel spotless and comfortable. *11 Kensington Gate, G12 9LG, tel. 041/334-5555. 11 rooms with bath. No credit cards. Moderate.*

Tinto Firs. This modern hotel on the park-like south side of Glasgow is more country-house than city style. The lounge/cocktail bar has dark wood paneling and rattan chairs; the bedrooms have stunning wall coverings and matching fabric furnishings. *470 Kilmarnock Rd., G43 2BB, tel. 041/637–2353. 27 rooms with bath. Facilities: garden, in-house movies. AE, DC, MC, V. Moderate.*

Marie Stuart. Well-equipped rooms and excellent service highlight this hotel. The bar is lively and popular; the staff friendly. *46 Queen Mary Ave., G42 8DT, tel. 041/424–3939. 31 rooms, 9 with bath. No credit cards. Inexpensive.*

Queen's Park Hotel. There's a good all-around standard of comfort and service here. Meal hours are flexible, a plus for late-nighters or late sleepers. *10 Balvicar Dr., G42 8QT, tel. 041/ 423–1123. 35 rooms, 30 with bath. No credit cards. Inexpensive.*

Inverness **Culloden House.** Although this is a hotel, and was Bonnie
Dining Prince Charlie's headquarters during the Battle of Culloden, we have chosen it for its restaurant. The food here, under the eye of the chef, Michael Simpson, is magnificent. Try the wild salmon in a lobster sauce, or venison in madeira, for a taste of the region's delicious produce. *Near Culloden, 6 mi east of Inverness by A9 and B9006, tel. 0463/790461. Reservations essential. Dress: jacket and tie. AE, DC, MC, V. Expensive.*

Dickens. This friendly restaurant offers international fare in a pleasant atmosphere. *77–79 Church St., tel. 0463/713111. Reservations advised. Dress: informal. AE, DC, MC, V. Inexpensive.*

Lodging **Daviot Mains Farm.** A 19th-century farmhouse five miles south of Inverness on A9 provides the perfect setting for home comforts and traditional Scottish cooking; lucky guests may find wild salmon on the menu. *Daviot Mains, tel. 0463/85215. 4 rooms (no private facilities). No credit cards. Inexpensive*

Dining and Lodging **Dunain Park Hotel.** Guests receive individual attention in a
★ "private house" atmosphere in this 18th-century mansion 2½ miles southwest on A82. A log fire awaits you in the living room, where you can sip a drink and browse through books and magazines. Antiques and traditional decor make the bedrooms

equally cozy and attractive. You can enjoy Scottish and French dishes in the restaurant, where candlelight gleams off bone china and crystal. Saddle of venison in port sauce and boned quail stuffed with pistachios are two of the specialties. *Dunain IV3 6JN, tel. 0463/230512. 12 rooms with bath. Facilities: indoor heated swimming pool, sauna. Restaurant reservations advised. Jacket and tie required. AE, DC, MC, V. Closed first week Feb., first week Nov. Hotel: Moderate–Expensive. Restaurant: Moderate.*

Ballifeary House Hotel. A Victorian property redecorated and well maintained, offering especially high standards of comfort and service, this is within easy reach of downtown Inverness. *10 Ballifeary Rd., IV3 5PJ, tel. 0463/235572. 8 rooms with bath. No credit cards. No smoking in hotel. Closed Nov.–Feb. Inexpensive.*

Firs Guest House. The cheerful, dependable owners of this sturdy mansion overlooking the River Ness have put much thought into room decoration; there are interesting antiques as well. *Dores Rd., IV2 4QU, tel. 0463/225197. 5 rooms, 2 with bath. No credit cards. Inexpensive.*

Kentallen
Dining and Lodging

Holly Tree Restaurant. Housed in a former railway station, this restaurant offers views of Loch Linnhe and superb sunsets. The emphasis is on fresh local produce—pigeon, venison, lamb, halibut, and salmon—in modern British cuisine. *On A828, 17 mi south of Fort William, tel. 063174/292. 12 rooms with bath or shower. Facilities: restaurant. Reservations required. Dress: informal. MC, V. Closed Nov.–mid-Mar. Moderate.*

Kilmore
Lodging

Glenfeochan House. This family-run Victorian mansion, 5 miles south of Oban on A816, stands in 350-acre grounds and offers tastefully decorated rooms with original plasterwork. *Kilmore PA34 4QR, tel. 063177/273. 3 rooms with bath. Facilities: garden, fishing. No credit cards. Closed Nov.–Mar. Expensive.*

Langbank
Dining and Lodging

Gleddoch House Hotel. Originally the home of a shipbuilding magnate who constructed this white-painted hotel in the 1920s, the Gleddoch House Hotel's spacious, attractive bedrooms are decorated in floral motifs and either period furnishings or more modern style. Restaurant specialties such as venison on creamed celeriac, and scallops with artichokes in pink pepper sauce with pâté de foie gras, are served in the traditional dining room. *Langbank, Renfrew PA14 6YE (17 miles northwest of Glasgow city center), tel. 047554/711. 33 rooms with bath. Facilities: garden, sauna, squash, golf, horseback riding. Restaurant reservations advised. Jacket and tie required. AE, DC, MC, V. Expensive.*

Mull
Lodging
★

Tiroran House Hotel. Family silver and glassware attest to the fact that this enchanting country house is more a family home than a hotel. Its tranquil island setting adds to the peace and homeyness of the place. Candlelit dinners are served in the intimate dining room. *Tiroran PA69 6ES, tel. 06815/232. 9 rooms with bath. Facilities: recreation room, croquet lawn. No credit cards. Closed Oct.–Apr. Moderate.*

Tobermory Hotel. This 18th-century building by the quay on the northeastern tip of the island commands superb views. The ambience is crisp and bright; fresh flowers dot every windowsill, and the rooms are spacious and sunny (weather permitting, of course!). *Tobermory PA75 6NT, tel. 0688/2091. 15 rooms with bath or shower. AE, DC, MC, V. Moderate.*

Nairn
Dining and Lodging

Clifton Hotel. The Clifton is a very attractive, creeper-clad Victorian villa, full of antiques, flower arrangements, fires, and offering great views over the Moray Firth. You may just want to drop by for a meal while touring eastward; there are two excellent dining rooms to choose from. The seafood is especially good. Nairn lies 16 miles northeast of Inverness via A96. *Viewfield St., IV12 4HW, tel. 0667/53119. 16 rooms with bath. Facilities: garden. AE, DC, MC, V. Closed Nov.–Mar. Moderate.*

Oban
Lodging

Columba Hotel. Situated between the quayside and the town, this lovely hotel offers modern, elegant public areas and attractive bedrooms. There are two bars, one with a cheerful nautical theme; and a cozy coffee shop open from 10 AM to 6 PM. *North Pier, Corran Esplanade, PA34 5QD, tel. 0631/62183. 49 rooms with bath. Facilities: in-house movies. AE, DC, MC, V. Moderate.*

Perth
Dining
★

Timothy's. This restaurant is more Scandinavian than Scottish, as the menu is built on a kind of smørrebrød system, with all kinds of surprising elements making up the small dishes. There are some major offerings, though, such as fondue bourguignonne. *24 St. John St., tel. 0738/26641. Reservations advised. Dress: informal. MC, V. Closed Sun. and Mon. Moderate.*

Lodging

Sunbank House Hotel. This early-Victorian graystone mansion is in a fine residential area near Perth's Branklyn Gardens. Recently redecorated in traditional style, it offers solid, unpretentious comforts along with great views over the River Tay and the city. *50 Dundee Rd., PH2 7BA, tel. 0738/24882. 8 rooms with bath. Facilities: golf. No credit cards. Inexpensive.*

Port Appin
Dining and Lodging
★

Airds Hotel. This hotel may just have the finest views in Scotland. Located in a peaceful little village 24 miles north of Oban via A85 and A828, this former ferry inn, dating back to the 17th century, is a long white building backed by trees. It is furnished in a friendly, homey way, with touches of family history, right down to the quilted bedspreads. The restaurant serves fine Scottish cuisine with the help of prime local produce. *Port Appin, Argyll PA38 4DF, tel. 063173/236. 14 rooms with bath. Facilities: small-game hunting and fishing. Restaurant reservations advised. Jacket and tie required. No credit cards. Closed Jan.–Feb. Moderate.*

St. Andrews
Dining

Grange Inn. This old farmhouse-type building houses a simple, traditional restaurant where excellent bar lunches are individually prepared. Dinner is a candlelit affair, with fine food—try the baked halibut with lobster and brandy sauce—and a good selection of malt whiskies. *Grange Rd., tel. 0334/72670. Reservations advised. Dress: informal. AE, DC, MC, V. Restaurant closed Mon. Inexpensive.*

Lodging

Rusack's Hotel. Right beside the Old Course, this is clearly a hotel for the well-heeled golfer. It has plenty of opulent Victorian elements to the decor—fake marble and crystal chandeliers. Some of the bedrooms have stunning views. *Pilmour Links KY16 9JQ, tel. 0334/74321. 50 rooms with bath. Facilities: restaurant, golf shop. AE, DC, MC, V. Expensive.*

Skye
Lodging

Kinloch Lodge. Elegant comfort on the edge of the world. Kinloch Lodge is run by Lord and Lady MacDonald, with flair and considerable professionalism. It is a supremely comfortable country house, with very snug bedrooms and imaginative cuisine in the handsome dining room. *Sleat IV43 8QY, tel. 04713/333. 10 rooms with bath. Facilities: shooting and fishing, garden. MC, V. Closed Dec.—mid-Mar. Very expensive.*

Stewarton
Lodging
★

Chapeltoun House Hotel. Real log fires and oak paneling are just two of the lovely features of this turn-of-the-century mansion. A feeling of timelessness is enhanced by the seclusion offered on its 20 acres of surrounding private grounds. The rooms are spacious; the restaurant cuisine superb. *On A735 (15 mi southeast of Glasgow), KA3 3ED, tel. 0560/82696. 8 rooms with bath. Facilities: gardens. AE, MC, V. Expensive.*

Stirling
Dining

Heritage. This elegant 18th-century establishment is run by a French family. The decor is all fanlights and candles; the menu features French and Scottish classics. *16 Allan Park, tel. 0786/73660. Reservations advised. Dress: informal. MC, V. Closed Christmas and Jan. 1. Moderate.*

Cross Keys Inn. A quaint, stone-walled dining room adds atmosphere to this restaurant's varied, traditionally Scottish menu. *Main St., Kippen (A811, west of Stirling), tel. 078687/293. Reservations advised. Dress: informal. MC, V. Inexpensive.*

Lodging

Golden Lion Hotel. This large and venerable hotel enjoys a prime position in the center of town, with the resulting hustle and bustle. You can easily escape to the peace and comfort of your room, however, and the service is very good. The restaurant offers first-class cuisine. *8 King St., FK8 1BD, tel. 0786/75351. 69 rooms with bath. Facilities: golf. AE, DC, MC, V. Moderate.*

Terraces Hotel. This is a centrally located hotel, useful for exploring Stirling, and as there is plenty of parking space, it makes a good base for touring the region, too. It's a Georgian town house that has been comfortably converted, and, since it's comparatively small, the service is attentive. *4 Melville Terr. FK8 2ND, tel. 0786/72268. 15 rooms with bath or shower. Facilities: restaurant. AE, DC, MC, V. Moderate.*

Troon
Dining and Lodging

Piersland House Hotel. This is located in a late-Victorian mansion, formerly the home of a whisky magnate. Oak paneling and log fires are the backdrop for specialties such as beef medallions in pickled walnut sauce. *15 Craigend Rd., tel. 0292/314747. 19 rooms with bath. Facilities: restaurant, garden. Reservations required. Jacket and tie required. AE, DC, MC, V. Moderate.*

Ullapool
Dining
★

Altnaharrie Inn. Be prepared for a real treat. Follow A9/A832 to A835 for 60 miles from Inverness to Ullapool, where a private launch takes you to Dundonnell, some 5 miles south, on the banks of Loch Broom. A set menu of local specialties is skillfully prepared, including scallops in white burgundy and bitter cress sauce, or medallions of roedeer with leek, grape juniper, and dill sauce, with wild raspberry ice cream and a good selection of cheeses to finish. As the name implies, this is also an inn—7 rooms are available, but you must book far in advance. *Tel. 085483/230. Reservations required. Jacket and tie required. Lunch is for residents only. No credit cards. Closed late Oct.–Easter. Expensive.*

Whitebridge
Lodging

Knockie Lodge Hotel. Part 18th-century hunting lodge, with traditional and antique furniture, this hotel offers very peaceful surroundings, though with easy access to Inverness. *Whitebridge, IV1 2UP (20 mi southwest of Inverness), tel.*

04563/276. 10 rooms with bath. Facilities: fishing, deer hunting, sailing. AE, MC, V. Closed Nov.–Apr. Moderate–Expensive.

The Arts

Festivals The second largest arts festival in Scotland is now Glasgow's **Mayfest,** held in the city during virtually all of May.

Theaters Glasgow is better endowed with functioning theaters than Edinburgh. One of the most exciting in Britain is the **Citizen's Theatre** (119 Gorbals St., tel. 041/429–0022) where productions of often hair-raising originality are the order of the day. The **King's Theatre** (Bath St., tel. 041/227–5511) stages light entertainment and musicals. The **Theatre Royal** (Hope St., tel. 041/332–9000) is the enchanting home of the Scottish Opera.

A thinly scattered population makes life difficult for theater operations, but there are repertory companies at Perth (**Perth Theatre,** High St., tel. 0738/21031) and Dundee (**Dundee Repertory,** Lochree Rd., tel. 0382/23530).

Inverness's theater, the **Eden Court** (tel. 0463/221718), is a reminder that just because a town is in northern Scotland, it need not be an artistic wasteland. This multi-purpose 800-seat theater and its art gallery offer a varied program throughout the year.

Both Stirling and St. Andrews universities have dynamic arts centers, while the smallest theater in Britain is on the island of Mull. Its small size—just 36 seats—has earned the **Mull Little Theatre** (Dervaig, tel. 06884/267) a place in *The Guinness Book of Records.*

Index

Personal Itinerary

Departure *Date*

Time

Transportation

Arrival *Date* *Time*

Departure *Date* *Time*

Transportation

Accommodations

Arrival *Date* *Time*

Departure *Date* *Time*

Transportation

Accommodations

Arrival *Date* *Time*

Departure *Date* *Time*

Transportation

Accommodations

Personal Itinerary

Arrival *Date*   *Time*

Departure *Date*   *Time*

Transportation

Accommodations

Arrival *Date*   *Time*

Departure *Date*   *Time*

Transportation

Accommodations

Arrival *Date*   *Time*

Departure *Date*   *Time*

Transportation

Accommodations

Arrival *Date*   *Time*

Departure *Date*   *Time*

Transportation

Accommodations

Addresses

Name

Address

Telephone

Name

Address

Telephone

Name

Address

Telephone

Name

Address

Telephone

Name

Address

Telephone

Name

Address

Telephone

Name

Address

Telephone

Name

Address

Telephone

Name

Address

Telephone

Name

Address

Telephone

Name

Address

Telephone

Name

Address

Telephone

Name

Address

Telephone

Name

Address

Telephone

Name

Address

Telephone

Name

Address

Telephone

Fodor's Travel Guides

U.S. Guides

Alaska
Arizona
Boston
California
Cape Cod, Martha's
 Vineyard, Nantucket
The Carolinas & the
 Georgia Coast
The Chesapeake
 Region
Chicago
Colorado
Disney World & the
 Orlando Area
Florida
Hawaii

Las Vegas, Reno,
 Tahoe
Los Angeles
Maine,Vermont,
 New Hampshire
Maui
Miami & the
 Keys
National Parks
 of the West
New England
New Mexico
New Orleans
New York City
New York City
 (Pocket Guide)

Pacific North Coast
Philadelphia & the
 Pennsylvania
 Dutch Country
Puerto Rico
 (Pocket Guide)
The Rockies
San Diego
San Francisco
San Francisco
 (Pocket Guide)
The South
Santa Fe, Taos,
 Albuquerque
Seattle &
 Vancouver

Texas
USA
The U. S. & British
 Virgin Islands
The Upper Great
 Lakes Region
Vacations in
 New York State
Vacations on the
 Jersey Shore
Virginia & Maryland
Waikiki
Washington, D.C.
Washington, D.C.
 (Pocket Guide)

Foreign Guides

Acapulco
Amsterdam
Australia
Austria
The Bahamas
The Bahamas
 (Pocket Guide)
Baja & Mexico's Pacific
 Coast Resorts
Barbados
Barcelona, Madrid,
 Seville
Belgium &
 Luxembourg
Berlin
Bermuda
Brazil
Budapest
Budget Europe
Canada
Canada's Atlantic
 Provinces

Cancun, Cozumel,
 Yucatan Peninsula
Caribbean
Central America
China
Czechoslovakia
Eastern Europe
Egypt
Europe
Europe's Great Cities
France
Germany
Great Britain
Greece
The Himalayan
 Countries
Holland
Hong Kong
India
Ireland
Israel
Italy

Italy 's Great Cities
Jamaica
Japan
Kenya, Tanzania,
 Seychelles
Korea
London
London
 (Pocket Guide)
London Companion
Mexico
Mexico City
Montreal &
 Quebec City
Morocco
New Zealand
Norway
Nova Scotia,
 New Brunswick,
 Prince Edward
 Island
Paris

Paris (Pocket Guide)
Portugal
Rome
Scandinavia
Scandinavian Cities
Scotland
Singapore
South America
South Pacific
Southeast Asia
Soviet Union
Spain
Sweden
Switzerland
Sydney
Thailand
Tokyo
Toronto
Turkey
Vienna & the Danube
 Valley
Yugoslavia

Wall Street Journal Guides to Business Travel

Europe

International Cities

Pacific Rim

USA & Canada

Special-Interest Guides

Bed & Breakfast and
 Country Inn Guides:
 Mid-Atlantic Region
New England
The South
The West

Cruises and Ports
 of Call
Healthy Escapes
Fodor's Flashmaps
 New York

Fodor's Flashmaps
 Washington, D.C.
Shopping in Europe
Skiing in the USA &
 Canada

Smart Shopper's
 Guide to London
Sunday in New York
Touring Europe
Touring USA